T0277133

THE LIFE AND TIMES *of*
GEORGE FERNANDES

THE LIFE AND TIMES *of*
GEORGE
FERNANDES

RAHUL
RAMAGUNDAM

SUPPORTED BY

THE **NewIndia**
FOUNDATION

PENGUIN
ALLEN
LANE

An imprint of Penguin Random House

ALLEN LANE

USA | Canada | UK | Ireland | Australia
New Zealand | India | South Africa | China

Allen Lane is part of the Penguin Random House group of companies
whose addresses can be found at global.penguinrandomhouse.com

Published by Penguin Random House India Pvt. Ltd
4th Floor, Capital Tower 1, MG Road,
Gurugram 122 002, Haryana, India

Penguin
Random House
India

First published in Allen Lane by Penguin Random House India 2022

Copyright © Rahul Ramagundam 2022

ISBN 9780670092888

Typeset in Adobe Garamond Pro by Manipal Technologies Limited, Manipal
Printed at Thomson Press India Ltd, New Delhi

www.penguin.co.in

For my parents,

Mithlesh and Nitya Nand

Contents

Abbreviations

AIADMK	All India Anna Dravida Munnetra Kazhagam
AICC	All India Congress Committee
AILRSA	All India Loco-Running Staff Association
AIRF	All India Railwaymen's Federation
AITUC	All India Trade Union Congress
BEST	Bombay Electricity Supply and Transport
BJP	Bhartiya Janata Party
BMC	Bombay Municipal Corporation
BMS	Bhartiya Mazdoor Sangh
BMSS	Bambai Mazdoor Sangharsha Samiti
BTU	Bombay Taximen's Union
CASC	Catholic Association of South Canara
CBI	Central Board of Investigation
CDC	Citizen's Defence Committee
CDS	Compulsory Deposit Scheme
CGK	C. Gopala Krishnamoorthy
CM	Chief Minister
COD	Corps of Detectives
CPI	Communist Party of India
CSP	Congress Socialist Party
CTBT	Comprehensive Test Ban Treaty
CWC	Congress Working Committee

DA	Dearness Allowance
DIC	District Industrial Centre
DIR	Defence of India Act and Rules
DMK	Dravida Munnetra Kazhagam
HMKP	Hind Mazdoor Kisan Panchayat
HMP	Hind Mazdoor Panchayat
HMS	Hind Mazdoor Sangh
IAS	Indian Administrative Service
IFWJ	Indian Federation of Working Journalists
INTUC	Indian National Trade Union Congress
IPKF	Indian Peace Keeping Force
ITI	Indian Telephone Industry
JD(U)	Janata Dal (United)
JNU	Jawaharlal Nehru University
JP	Jayaprakash Narayan
JS	Jan Sangh
KVIC	The Khadi and Village Industries Commission
LTTE	Liberation Tigers of Tamil Eelam
MLA	Member of Legislative Assembly
MMU	Municipal Mazdoor Union
MP	Member of Parliament
MRA	Moral Re-Armament
NCCRS	National Campaign Committee of Railwaymen's Struggle
NDA	National Democratic Alliance
NEFA	North East Frontier Area, now Arunachal Pradesh
NMML	Nehru Memorial Museum and Library
OBC	Other Backward Classes
PM	Prime Minister
PMO	Prime Minister's Office
PSP	Praja Socialist Party
PSU	Public Sector Unit
RJD	Rashtriya Janata Dal
RMU	Rail Mazdoor Union
RSS	Rashtriya Swayamsevak Sangh
SC/ST	Scheduled Caste/Scheduled Tribe

SCRMU	South-Central Railway Mazdoor Union
SMS	Samyukta Maharashtra Samiti
SP	Socialist Party
SRC	State Reorganization Commission
SRMU	South Railway Mazdoor Union
SSP	Samyukta Socialist Party
TOI	Times of India
UPA	United People's Alliance
VHP	Viswa Hindu Parishad
VP	Vishwanath Pratap Singh
WREU	Western Railway Employees Union

Chronology of Events

13 July 1960	Arrested for protest action inside Dadar Railway Station
26 March 1961	Elected corporator of the Bombay Municipal Corporation
5 May 1961	Jailed for two months at Visapur Jail
5 April 1963	Arrested under Defence of India Rules
12 December 1963	Released from Nagpur Central Jail after eight months of jail-term
1964	Formation of Samyukta Socialist Party (SSP)
23 February 1967	Elected for the first time to the Lok Sabha from Bombay (South) by defeating S.K. Patil
January 1968	Established Bombay Labour Bank
1969	Elected SSP general secretary
24 March 1970	Arrested / beaten by the police at Sardar Patel Chowk, New Delhi
1971	Elected Socialist Party president
21 July 1971	Marries Leila Kabir
October 1973	Elected the AIRF president at railway workers' convention at Hyderabad,
27 February 1974	Formation of National Campaign Committee of Railwaymen's Struggle (NCCRS)
8-28 May 1974	Led all-India railway strike as the AIRF president
25 June 1975	National Emergency declared; goes underground
1 May 1976	Police pick up Lawrence Fernandes from home in Bangalore
10 June 1976	Arrested at Calcutta (now, Kolkata) by the CBI
March 1977	Elected for the second time to the Lok Sabha from Muzaffarpur
March 1977	Appointed Central Minister of Post and Communication
July 1977	Appointed Central Minister of Industries
15 July 1979	Resigns from the Morarji Desai government

9 January 1980	Elected for the third time to the Lok Sabha from Muzaffarpur
December 1984	Tasted defeat at Bangalore (South) in the general elections
1986	Contested the by-election at Banka, but was defeated
30 November 1989	Elected for the fourth time to the Lok Sabha from Muzaffarpur
5 December 1989	Appointed Central Minister for Railways
June 1991	Elected for the fifth time to the Lok Sabha from Muzaffarpur
July 1994	Launched Samata Party by splitting from the Janata Dal
May 1996	Elected for the sixth time to the Lok Sabha from Nalanda
March 1998	Elected for the seventh time to the Lok Sabha from Nalanda
19 March 1998	Appointed Central Minister of Defence
May 1998	Pokhran-II
May–July 1999	Kargil War
March 2001	*Tehelka* Sting broke out leading to his resignation from the government
September 2001	Reinducted into the Vajpayee government as Minister of Defence
May 2004	Elected for the eighth time to the Lok Sabha from Muzaffarpur
May 2009	Contested as independent from Muzaffarpur but lost his deposit
July 2009	Elected for the first time to the Rajya Sabha for a short tenure of one year
January 2010	Leila Fernandes takes control of George's Alzheimer's disease-stricken body
29 January 2019	Died after a prolonged bedridden illness

Dramatis Personae

All his Prime Ministers: George Fernandes had a knack of being in the good books of his prime ministers, a colleague recalled. His governmental sojourn began in 1977 under the leadership of Morarji Desai (1896–1995), who made him at first minister of post and communication and then the minister of industry. In Vishwanath Pratap Singh's (1931–2008) short-lived Janata Dal government during 1989–1990, George was a minister in his cabinet and a trusted colleague. Atal Bihari Vajpayee (1924–2018) gave him a trusted position in the ruling alliance as well in his government, in which he served as the defence minister. Charan Singh (1902–87) and Chandrasekhar (1927–2007), both short-lived prime ministers from those opposed to Congress, didn't have George in their cabinets.

Fernandes Family: Leila Kabir Fernandes (b. 1937) and Sushanto [Sean] Fernandes (b. 1974), as wife and son, were part of George's failed family. As for Fernandes brothers, they were six—George, the eldest, and Richard (b. 1952), the youngest and a doctoral degree holder in Physics from Raman Institute, Bangalore. Brother no. 2 was Lawrence (1932–2005). He was close to George and supported his political activities. He himself delved in the local politics of Bangalore and was once elected city mayor. Other three are Michael (b. 1934), Paul (b. 1936) and Aloysius (b. 1939). While Michael worked in the public sector ITI and remained in Bangalore for much of his life, Paul migrated to Canada in the mid-1960s and Aloysius stalled himself to domestic bliss in Bombay.

Political Comrades and Colleagues: The friendship between Madhu Limaye (1922–95) and George is a legend in the contemporary political history of India. Jaya Jaitly (b. 1942), a 'close personal friend and confidante' of his was married to IAS Officer Ashok Jaitly (1942–2015), who in the period 1977–1979 was a secretary to him. While G.G. Parikh (b. 1923) was a Mumbai-based colleague, Fredrick D'Sa (b. 1948) was a trusted back room boy who looked after his affairs. Karpoori Thakur (1924–1988), Nitish Kumar (b. 1951) and Laloo Prasad Yadav (b. 1948) were the Bihari comrade, protégé and opponent respectively to him. Among the trade union colleagues, there were Venkatram (1924–81) and Bal Dandavate (1929–81), who were personally valuable to him.

Mentors and Influencers: In Mangalore, George found, at first, Ammembal Balappa (1922–2014) and then Placid D'Mello (1919–58). Both introduced him to the Socialist Party, whose leader Ram Manohar Lohia (1910–1967) would prove his ideological mentor along with the first two. Krishna Menon (1896–1974), a Nehruvian loyalist, contested the 1967 general elections from Bombay as an independent candidate as he was denied the Congress Party nomination. While he himself was defeated, Menon played a facilitating role in George's victory in the 1967 election. S.M. Joshi (1904–89), Jagjivan Ram (1908–86) and Jayaprakash Narayan (1902–79) were the other three influences on George, whom he approached in times of crisis. Frank Buchman (1876–1961) was also one of the people who left some ideological imprint on him.

Brotherhood in the Underground: Journalist K. Vikram Rao (b. 1938); newspaper manager C.G.K. Reddy (1921–94); Gujarat-based politician Prabhudass Patwari (1909–85); Vijay Narayan from Varanasi; Bombay Taximen's Union's Fredrick D'Sa (b. 1948); medical graduate Girija Huilgol (b. 1951); socialist and scholar Kamlesh Shukla (1937–2015), the founder-editor of George's *Pratipaksh;* Padmanav Shetty (b. 1954), the run-away boy who became the youngest member of those 23 accused of conspiring against the state; were some of George's comrades in the underground movement against the National Emergency (1975–77). The actress Snehalata Reddy (1932–77) and her husband Pattabhi Rama Reddy (1919–2006) were Lohia acolytes whose friendship George inherited and they later became part of his underground resistance.

Prologue

George Fernandes
Always for the people *and never with the establishment*

The Life and Times of George Fernandes tells the story of India's tortuous post-Independence making and the role of George Fernandes in it. In some ways, at least the way I felt while writing it, the book presents a contemporary history of India through the lens of George's life and his political work. The story has George's political emergence at its centre but does not emanate merely from his perspective.

This book is not a narrative of events however defining they might have been. A biography is a chronicle of an evolutionary process and not a conglomeration of self-standing events in the subject's life. Events shall feature here, as they are bound to in a book dealing with a political personality. But more than the events, the book is a delineation of processes that define Indian politics. It delves deep into the evolution of India that George lived in and worked for. It also attempts to enter the political mind and probe the political choices George made. I have tried to present an insider's account though I have not had any fleeting proximity to those processes. My effort has been to construct those processes with documentary evidence and oral testimonies that I was fortunate as a researcher to gain access to. I have tried in a somewhat old-fashioned way to be true to my sources.

I am not just tracing the growth and development of a political personality in this book; that is an obvious act of a biography—my aim was to gather a comprehensive picture of India over those eighty years when George was born and brought up, became a trade unionist, got affiliated with an ideology, developed a political ambition and then proceeded to attempt to fulfil it. The book is interwoven with the sad history of the Socialist Party of India, in its myriad of forms, from a hesitant yet promising start to the continuous hiccups of splits and mergers. Socialism today seems a dated ideology, but there was an epoch when it was a driving force. Socialists played a significant role in India retaining an ideological affinity with the mores generated during the freedom struggle. A critical appraisal of the socialist contribution to India's polity, though, remains to be written.

Unlike Jawaharlal Nehru, whose silver-spoon upbringing smoothed his path into the leadership of India's freedom struggle and its political life as an independent nation, George had a comparatively modest upbringing, and his life was one of hardship and toil. In this case, the father had no dreams about the son's career and future—the father's aim was simply working hard to make ends meet—but the son wanted to break free from the constraining aspiration of financial security and dreamt of a life driven by a purpose larger than survival.

George Mathew Isadore Fernandes, as his parents named him, was never a congressman in a country whose destiny had largely been shaped by the Indian National Congress. He neither had political pedigree, nor did he belong to India's dominant Hindu community. Originally coming from Mangalore, a coastal city in present-day state Karnataka in southern India, his region was of less political significance than many others at that time. His mother tongue Konkani is a language of a strip of land along the western coast. He still somehow rose to political eminence, it was largely because of his personal wit and grit. His political career is also a tribute to India's nation builders who generated the values and ethos that made his arrival and acceptance possible.

Chronicling George's political career is significant for other reasons as well. First, look at the major spatial choices that marked his rapid growth from regional to national leadership. Second, his political choices reflect the compulsions and compromises inherent in a democracy. It is surprising how little we know about the counter-resistance to the National Emergency of the mid-1970s—the state and its institutions attempted to erase the Opposition's actions in those nineteen months from social memory.

Writing this biography of a politician who led a fairly long and active political life was not smooth sailing. With the two most important protagonists of this biography, the central characters indeed—George and Leila Fernandes—missing from my oral-interview schedule, this book draws principally from the documentary sources, both personal and governmental, that George himself collected over the years. Though I recorded interviews with more than 200 people spread over the length and breadth of this country, including George's political and trade union colleagues and family members, the archival sources, newspapers, party documents, autobiographies and biographies, collected works, and repositories of private papers provide the book's basic ingredients.

George was an active politician till much recently, and contemporary political personalities generate contradictory emotions amongst their followers and colleagues. His erstwhile colleagues nurtured strong emotions; when they were friends, they were loyal, but once estrangement set in, they distanced themselves and warmth wore thin. The causes of estrangement were not solely ideological; they were also personal—many thought George in power did not return the favours they had bestowed upon him when he was in the Opposition. This book includes snippets from oral interviews that I had with people who had known and worked with George. How much of these oral testimonies could be taken at face value remained a dilemma. Memories are not just recollected but also reimagined, coloured as they are by later-day happenings and shifting human interpersonal equations. Memories also get shaped by the readings of similar situations at another location and another time. Oral testimonies become hard to completely rely on as historical evidence. They however made the narration colourful, and if they did correspond with other more verifiable evidence, they acquired the weight of being a historical fact.

A biography being largely a history recounts not just a life lived but also the atmospherics that nurtured, gave voice to, and brought the subject into multifaceted engagements. While history is mostly about events, biographies are studies of individuals, their struggles, inner turmoils, compromises and choices. The context is recreated as painstakingly as the life itself. The biography combines an exploration into both the human heart and the motivation. The importance of the author's intimate acquaintance with the subject over a long period in order to chronicle the life cannot be overemphasized. Often, journalists are well-suited to do a political biography. They adopt a style of reportage and bring anecdotal narration to make the personality comprehensible to the reader. The day-to-day familiarity does bring some kind of an understanding that quickens the writing process. While biographies written by journalists bring out contemporary facts and events, they seldom do justice to the subject. A life must be contextualized and seen through the currents of historical and contemporary events. Such contextualizing requires deep research and an understanding of the socio-economic environment in which politics is played out. Some journalistic outpourings are brilliant. Vast amounts of literature are consumed before the characters begin to take shape and start speaking. But the requirements of research are endless. A feeling of inadequacy constantly assails you. Have all dimensions been taken care of? Have the characters been fleshed out or do they remain disjointed, perilous skeletons?

There have been earlier attempts at chronicling George's life; there is a biography of his in Konkani written in Kannada script. There are also anthologies of his speeches and writings. When George was mentally agile and physically fit, he shrugged off suggestions that he write his memoirs. He had no time to reflect, so engaging was his life. Later, his mind caved in under the duress of age, and he was no longer capable of putting down his thoughts on paper. This is the first study that goes into the microscopic details of George Fernandes's complex life and times. It focuses on his ideological formation, political predilections, his professional coalitions and compromises, his personal relationships and romantic involvements, his family, party, and legacy.

In deciding the title of my biography of George Fernandes, I was for long in a quandary and requested suggestions from friends. Some thought as he was a socialist—and among the last of them—my book title must have the word in it, something like 'George Fernandes and the History of the Socialist Movement'. Some others, considering his trade unionism and actions during the Emergency, thought of George as a 'rebel' and desired that word to be in the title. A third category of people were intrigued by his move to the NDA and thought the title should capture his transformation from a socialist to a Hindutva camp fellow traveller. There were others as well who thought as his life was coterminous with post-Independence developments in India, his biography must be pitched as India's twentieth-century history. And because he was a politician who had straddled regions, religions and languages during his long political career, he must be seen as an embodiment of a model Indian; his Indianness underlined by a title such as 'India's George Fernandes'. But there were also those who, given the surcharged political atmosphere in which his biography is being published, thought he must be presented as a representative of minority aspirations. It is another matter that throughout his political career, even though the Christian section of the Indian population thought of him as their man to be approached at crucial moments in the community's relationship with the state, he never really presented himself so.

These proposals though well-meaning only caused confusion and despair. Finally, I decided, with the help of my publisher Meru Gokhale, on a straightforward title: *The Life and Times of George Fernandes*. This was, as Meru said, 'simple, confident and powerful'. Later, I saw additional merit in so naming the book: to choose any one word as descriptive of George would have limited his personality to just one peak. He was a patriot without doubt, a rebel who was also a trade union leader, an advocate of civil liberties, a socialist who ceaselessly opposed the Congress. From the time he left his coastal town of Mangalore and came to Bombay (now Mumbai), George's was a life lived with passion and, more importantly, a struggle against all odds. This book is a celebration of that struggle and his country's pangs in seeking to evolve as a humane, democratic and inclusive habitat.

1

All's Well That Ends Well

One Sunday afternoon in October 2009, I went to meet George Fernandes. Most of the time since the unexpected defeat of the Atal Bihari Vajpayee government in the general elections held in 2004, in which he was the minister of defence, he had remained cloistered in his ministerial bungalow in Delhi. He was no longer in the government, but because of his position as a senior member of Parliament (MP), he continued to retain the bungalow. It had been his home for over two decades, having been allotted first in 1989 when he was the minister of railways in the short-lived government of Vishwanath Pratap Singh (1931–2008). The bungalow was on Krishna Menon Marg in Delhi's power district. The tree-lined avenue was named after a man who, as the defence minister, was forced to resign in disgrace for India's military debacle in 1962. Incidentally, Krishna Menon (1896–1974) had given a helping hand to George's political rise.

It was a large house with colossal columns, high ceilings and long verandas. The colonial bungalow, located a mere 200 metres away from India's imposing Parliament House, was surrounded by acres of landscaped abundance of lush green lawns. Its architectural design conveyed the power and grandeur of the British rule. Although republican India had continued to retain the symbolism intact, the need of a democratic facade every now and then had sullied its form. It is said that the bungalow's gates during the times George lived there always remained flung open as a mark of socialist disdain for governmental trappings. It was a bungalow worth over Rs 100 crore then; yet his quintessential image of a man of the streets, fighting and thriving in adversity and living frugally, had perplexedly persisted.

My meeting with George was facilitated by his 'close personal friend and confidante', Jaya Jaitly (b. 1942). Back in the late 1970s, her husband, Ashok Jaitly (1942–2015), an officer in the elite Indian Administrative Service (IAS), had worked with George during his stint as the minister of industry in the Janata Party government. During this time, driven by many things, including her devotion to handicrafts and artisan communities, she became close to George. Over time, she would get estranged, separated and then divorced from her husband, and work with 'unshakeable faith' by George's side.[1] June Chettur, which was her maiden name, was just fourteen when her diplomat father, K.K. Chettur, suddenly died while on ambassadorial duty in Brussels, throwing her world into a spin. Leaving behind large diplomats' houses across world capitals, she returned with her widowed mother to Delhi to spend her teenage years in a one-room tenement and share mess food at Kotah House. She grew up with a sense that she had been on the receiving end of misfortune through no fault of her own. Her memoir, *Life among the Scorpions*, published at the age of seventy-five, reflects a personality that feels unfairly dealt with. Combative to the core, when Jaya Jaitly speaks, her speech has a way of flowing into you, sharp and pungent. Bitterness and anguish come together in equal measure, but seldom give way to self-pity. A tall and sharp-featured woman with an impressive gait, she retains an agility that belies her age. She was the moving force behind the founding of Dilli Haat, a carnival bazaar for craftsmen in the heart of Delhi.[2] She also founded Dastkari Haat, a cooperative of sorts for craft and artisanal workers. She delved into politics as well.

'George Saab!' Jaya Jaitly called as I went along with her through a long passageway into a claustrophobic study, our entry announced by the wreath of hanging brass bells on the doorway that jingled every time the door opened or closed. It was a small room, with closely arranged ordinary-looking furniture and a bookshelf. In the middle of the room was a set of sofas. Opposite the doorway, aligned with the wall, was a table with two plain chairs. One of those days, I would see George taking his supper there. The bungalow had a dining hall, but perhaps he liked taking his meal in the solitude of this inner sanctum. On the left was one more door that opened into his bedroom. I was never to enter it, but images carried by occasional media publications conveyed its modest size. The study's decor, now as I think of it, carried a lingering sense of having outlived its age; if it was still there, it was simply because its replacement was not possible, or even desired since it would have been an unnecessary diversion from the more important scheme of things. Draped over the room was a still air that had lost its whir many years before—as if an indubitable climax had arrived, and, for all those who were linked to it, by fate or passion, salvation lay in its natural decay and dissolution.

As I stepped inside, I saw George sitting upright in a sofa-chair encased in an unpretentious grey khadi upholstery. He wore the khadi kurta–pyjama that for a long time had been his everyday dress. 'Will you please talk to him? Tell him all you want to say,' Jaya Jaitly said to him with comforting authority, evidence of long, affable familiarity. In her voice was the sweetness often heard when one wants to make a child do one's bidding. George nodded, looking straight at me as I took a seat before him. His presence filled the room. A low table lay between us. As I collected myself, I saw Jaya Jaitly leaving, closing the door behind us, saying, 'I will let you both be alone.'

We both sat looking into each other's eyes for what then appeared to be a long time. It seemed as if he wanted to speak, but his words would not reach me. *How was he?* 'Fighting fit,' he replied crisply, his eyes still measuring me. Those were the only two words he ever spoke to me. His lips quivered, but said nothing audible. Seeing him making an effort, I was transported to the summer of the mid-1990s, when I had heard him speak at an informal post-dinner gathering at the Jawaharlal Nehru University (JNU) campus in Delhi. The venue was a small dining hall in a students' hostel. The air outside was thick with allusions to his swing into the saffron camp; his Samata Party had joined the BJP-led NDA as one of its thirteen constituents. Inside, a jam-packed audience listened to him with rapt attention. In that hall crammed with hundreds of fellow students, I listened to him while he moved from one corner to another, gesturing, gesticulating and growling. He was sweat-drenched, his khadi kurta-pyjama looked ordinary, but his firm face glistened and his eyes sparkled—he was a compelling vision. At the age of sixty-five, here he was, roaring at his highest pitch, reeling out facts, quoting reports, spilling beans—and, not a single scar of his tumultuous life visible on his taut face. He left a lasting impression.

That image of George—with a defiant fist of a shackled hand raised above the proud bespectacled face, jaw clenched, beads of perspiration trickling down his forehead, veins standing out on his throat—in that iconic black-and-white photograph reprinted years later in *India Today* magazine's 'The Decisive Decade' issue of 1985 (I was in school when I chanced upon it) had remained etched in my mind.[3] It was an Emergency-era photograph encrypting India's coming-of-age historical moment. A photo that was comparable if at all with one from another age—of a young sardar, pensive and determined, on death row yet full of life: of Bhagat Singh (1907–31) sitting on a cot in jail.

It was this photo of a chained George that triggered my desire to write a book on him.

It was, therefore, a terrifying sight to see him now fumbling for words. A fluent speaker of half a dozen languages, George, presently unable to speak, lowered his head, hid his eyes, mumbled some unmusical note and disappeared into a safe confine known to him alone. I noticed his eyes moistening. It made me uncomfortable. Just then, much to my relief, Jaya Jaitly breezed in and ordered tea for all of us. I saw biscuit crumbs falling off his lips, the tumbler of tea he held shaking in his hand. Not much was known of the affliction he suffered from; there was an obvious attempt to hide his illness from the public. When I met him, I recalled eerily, he was already in dire straits, taken over by Alzheimer's disease, rapidly losing his sense of self, his cognitive ability, his speech. George's mind was withering away, his memory was failing him, his mumbled words were unrecognizable and would not reciprocate to his thoughts.

Two months after that appointed meeting, on the first day of the New Year 2010, not only did his withered mind get cloistered for ever, but also ended a decades-old custom at George's Krishna Menon Marg bungalow. In the vein of a Biblical saying, the gates of the bungalow were closed forever at the end of the day because there was to be no day again. With the void in his mind becoming obvious, the unhinged body was an invitation to contrary claims. Those long lost returned to lay claim over him, and those who had been with him all through his ministerial days either disappeared of their own volition or melted away, fearing the new claimants. On 1 January 2010, Leila Kabir Fernandes, George's long-separated wife, and their only offspring, Sushanto (b. 1974), now with a new name 'Sean', appeared to make a familial claim over his ailing self. Sushanto had found affectionate mention in his father's circulars issued during those dark, depressing, underground days of the National Emergency (1975–77), but thereafter had remained invisible to the Indian public throughout his father's political career.

'In a clandestine and surreptitious manner akin to a medieval palace coup'—these are the words of George's brothers—Leila Fernandes packed George off to her house in Delhi's upscale Panchsheel Park.[4] The motives behind this swift, surgical takeover were hazy, though. Just days before, Sean Fernandes, who in 1993 had left India for the US, had countered an appeal from his uncle Paul Fernandes, George's Canada-based brother saying 'Are you also thinking about the other side of the coin—that my dad didn't even make it to my college graduation, that he visited you in Canada a few times over the years but never came to visit me in New York?'[5] The son was hurt and torn by filial expectations and a sense of betrayal. Two years before, in 2007, Paul Fernandes, in an attempt to heal the wounds, had implored New York resident Sean to visit his father who was in Toronto for a medical check-up. The son came, stayed for a night and left even before his father could be medically examined. But before he left, he let it be known that he held Jaya Jaitly responsible for their estrangement. 'Jaya,' Sean Fernandes complained innocently, if bitterly, to his uncle, 'stole my family.'[6]

As these events began to unfurl, Sean Fernandes, in public at least, appeared to have the right motive. He said that upon becoming a father himself (in April 2009, his Japanese wife, Chikako Egashira, had given birth to their son, Ken), he was filled with a rediscovered love for his father. But he carried a misplaced fear too: soon after taking George away, he revoked the power of attorney vested in Jaya Jaitly by George Fernandes—some say by forcibly getting him to thumb-impress blank sheets, barred her access to George or his official residence, and asked for police protection for him. 'I am apprehending,' he wrote to the police, his complaint finding wide media coverage, 'foul play/physical harm from some people who I believe have been looting whatever has been left of my father's assets and taking advantage of his poor health.'[7] He didn't specifically name Jaya Jaitly, but the implication for her was clear. She had become persona non grata. Leila Fernandes too, as if to reinforce her newly discovered conjugal duty, underlined how 'vested interests had been taking advantage of his poor health and their proximity to him to pursue their agenda'. But what made her return? George's brothers claimed it was greed. Jaya Jaitly thought it was revenge. Leila Fernandes herself said it was concern. 'Let me now take care of this man in his last days,' she said, unsentimentally, 'and let him die a dignified death.'[8]

Leila Fernandes' mutinous return stirred a storm in George's domestic establishment. In a false start or by some tacit design, Jaya Jaitly refused to come out in the open on the nature of the relationship she shared with George. Her diffidence made the takeover by Leila Fernandes a smooth if somewhat sensational event. Privately, Jaya Jaitly felt lonely, deserted and outsmarted. 'Maligning someone to get back personal or family revenge on loyal political colleagues is quite despicable,' she said with reason.[9] She was angry, frustration welling up in her, when one day she said of Leila Fernandes, 'Short of strangulating her, I don't think I can do anything'.[10] At the same time, she felt unburdened—'Now I am a free bird, though my mind is in torment'—and somewhat scared too that 'the wretched ones are probably sharpening their knives for the next onslaught.'[11] She feared that the 'thumb in their possession' might be used to make her out to be a cheat and more. 'If there is silence,' she warned close friends, 'my ultimate slaughter by these people will be through George's blank mind.'[12] She recalled, 'No one came to sit by his bedside in the past five years, let alone the past twenty-five years.' She spoke of many spurned invitations to Leila Fernandes, and how she acted 'as if she [Leila Fernandes] did not exist and did not care'.

'From 1985,' Jaya Jaitly said of her role in George's life, 'when his wife and son moved away from his home for reasons with which I was not involved, apart from being a political colleague, I looked after all matters concerning his establishment and continued to do so for twenty-four years till 2nd January 2010.'[13] That's the nearest she came to conceding some kind of commitment to their relationship, even if it was pretty poorly defined. What was she committed to— his household or his official positions? Worried about social tags that had come to be attached to her, she put it as if it were Leila's disappearance that had put the onus of managing his household on her. Jaya Jaitly was acting her political self, giving an inch and claiming a furlong.

Much before Leila Fernandes' return to George's household, Jaya Jaitly had become distanced from it. Mumbai-based Fredrick D'Sa said, in his post-ministerial years, 'Jaya would come in the morning, leave her dogs and go, come back in the evening, take her dogs and go.'[14] The sprawling residence provided her pets with a playground. 'A rhythmic and stabilizing factor in George's life,' repeated George's brothers, 'has been Jaya Jaitly's visits to him every morning and evening.'[15] They explained: 'From the onset of his illness, unless an emergent situation developed, Ms Jayalakshmi Jaitly would visit Mr George Fernandes at 9.00 a.m. and stay with him till 11.00 a.m. During the day she would be in regular touch with the staff to enquire about his lunch, rest and general level of comfort, and then return later in the evening at 7.00 p.m. to supervise his medical treatment, provide company and conversation and other special needs including dietary needs, after which Ms Jayalakshmi Jaitly would normally leave at about 10.00 p.m.'[16] It was an unabashed expression of a routine, concept and obligation. Filed in March 2010 in the High Court of Delhi, praying access to the ailing George, the language of this twenty-nine-page plaint with eighty pages of annexes was less theirs and more of Jaya Jaitly's lawyers, but it gave away more than it hid.

George's affliction with Alzheimer's had drastically altered his overall health—his deteriorating memory was diagnostically confirmed sometime in 2006. Nitin Kumar, a Central government employee who was reliable enough to figure as a witness to the general power of attorney (GPA) that George thumb-impressed in March 2009 in favour of Jaya Jaitly, recalled the day doctors had announced the diagnosis.[17] 'It was sometime in the afternoon. They had just returned from the hospital. George was standing in the middle of the room, limply, in his long kurta, forlorn, his body shrunk, his aura condensed. Jaya was sitting, slouched in a sofa, crestfallen.'[18] Nitin Kumar felt the tension in the air. After a fallout with Jaya Jaitly in May 2009, Nitin Kumar was one of those insiders who would help bring Leila Fernandes in and be present in December when George was made to thumb-impress the revocation of the power of attorney.[19] Jaya Jaitly called him 'the worst *saanp* [serpent] on earth . . . In front of Saheb, he tells I tried to sabotage his election. I told him, "You know what? You are talking about me to a man with whom I have shared thirty-five years of relationship." And Saheb was standing shocked, not knowing what to say. I said, "After you say such a thing, either you should be here or I."'[20] He left after George nodded when asked by Nitin Kumar whether he should leave. He hopped straight into Leila Fernandes' camp.

Looked after by untrained help in the absence of commanding authority, George's household came to wear a shabby appearance, with stinking toilets and leaking taps, and dogs' food crumbs and hair—grey, white and red-brown—strewn all over. By early 2009, his worsening situation had turned into a full-blown crisis of care. He would become aggressive and refuse to be calmed down. 'There were days when he would defecate in his pyjamas. Boys would ring me up and tell me, "*Saheb nahin sun rahe aaj.* Violent *ho gaye*. What to do? He is lying in filth,"' Fredrick D'Sa recalled.[21] 'It was an animal life.' Jaya Jaitly was the only one whom George listened to. But 'Mama-Sen', as he endearingly called her, was no longer at hand. 'In the last six months of 2009,' Fredrick D'Sa further recounted, 'she was very harsh with him. She hadn't expected that his health would take that kind of deteriorating turn. I used to ask her to help, and she would say, "I am not his nurse; I am only his political companion. I have other things in life to do. I can't be running to change his underwear. Let his family members take care of him. I am not his family.'"[22] His observations are corroborated by what Jaya Jaitly herself wrote to George's brothers in November 2009, 'I urge you to come urgently and handle all matters concerning his daily existence, healthcare and future.'[23] She was worried about George's longevity, that if he lived longer his caregiving might fall on her. His parents had lived long lives. Moreover, Alzheimer's disease is about senile decay—the body might remain robust for long. But her frosting had more to do with the growing interventions of George's brothers in decisions with regard to him.

In light of George's declining health, his brothers began to visit him more frequently. Michael Fernandes says he visited George in Delhi 'during the past five years (2005–09) a little over fifty times'.[24] During these visits, he stayed with George. He 'found George in complete thrall of Jaya Jaitly'.[25] In 2007, Paul Fernandes arranged a medical check-up for George in Toronto, but no sooner had he gone than there were pressures for him to return. There were plans to relaunch the defunct Samata Party. Jaya Jaitly was the moving force behind it. 'I insisted,' Paul recalled, 'that the medical check-up was more important. There was no point in making a tamasha of him.'[26] Paul Fernandes was keen that George bow out of politics, resign from Parliament. Being not in favour of such things, Jaya would not even put him in the hospital. 'Without her consent', said Fredrick D'Sa, who now carried a visceral dislike for Jaya Jaitly, which hadn't been visible when they were colleagues, 'I couldn't take him to the hospital. She wouldn't as she had no time. It was an unwritten understanding to allow him to rot, and he would die. But he was refusing to die.'[27]

Indian election laws now required candidates fighting elections to file a disclosure statement about their assets. At the time of the 2004 general elections, George's declared assets were about Rs 11 lakh in cash, bank deposits and bonds, and 22 acres of agricultural land at Nelamangala on the outskirts of Bengaluru.[28] The land had been bought by George in his mother's name sometime in the late 1980s.[29] In the early 1990s, he was keen to live his retirement years there. 'I have taken a vow that X'mas '92 will be in our house in Nelamangala,' he had written excitedly in December 1991 to his Calcutta-based Air-India stewardess friend, Sampa Das.[30] 'This does not mean one waits an entire year. Work on the house will begin in a few weeks,' he wrote. He never retired, nor was the house ever built. In 2006, the land's sale proceedings began, fetching a handsome amount to his account, which was disclosed at the time of the 2009 general elections. This disclosure left a murky trail.[31]

His brothers had remained largely obscured in his life. Jaya Jaitly wrote of his brothers, to a friend: 'They are what my father used to call mugwumps!'[32] A mugwump is a fence-sitting lackey, unable to take a firm decision. She was not agreeable to their plan for a trust in George's name with the money in his bank. Peeved, she let it be known that George's care was his 'family's responsibility'.[33] As if to spite her, and to liberate him from her control as well, his brothers decided that the onus of care be put on his immediate family, howsoever estranged they might be. 'Paul had gone to Leila,' Fredrick D'Sa revealed, 'and told her, "Jaya has destroyed him morally, destroyed him financially; please come and take charge of him."'[34] Paul also encouraged Sean Fernandes to sit up, take courage and get 'that woman'—meaning Jaya Jaitly—banished from the household. He demanded Sean's 'intervention' to 'end the callous neglect George was being subjected to'.[35] Sean later wrote to Michael Fernandes reminding him of his urgings and feeling apologetic about his own then reticence: 'You [Uncle Michael] kept telling me that I was the one person who could do something to help Dad in his current situation. As I now remember with some dismay, I was somewhat reluctant to get involved at the time . . .'[36] While all this was happening, with new alliances replacing the existing ones, every one of George's household staff, who had been ridden roughshod by Jaya Jaitly, now got back at her. Even Fredrick D'Sa broke ranks with her and, in December 2008, on Christmas Eve, went to meet Leila Fernandes.

All this yielded mixed results. Leila Fernandes gatecrashed into the Krishna Menon Marg bungalow, occupied it and banished Jaya Jaitly from its proximity. She said, 'I was least interested in the whole thing.

But his brothers came and implored me to take charge.' The ferocity of her return made his brothers feel like they were losing out. Shocked and dismayed, they reconfigured their loyalty to Jaya Jaitly. They accused Leila Fernandes of being an absentee estranged wife. She, in turn, accused them of being ignorant 'about the connection that George and I have shared over the years'.[37] They accused Sean Fernandes of greed. 'What he stands for is another extreme of what his father stood for,' Paul declared, forgetting that it was he who had first invited Sean to take charge.[38] 'What finally motivated them? When did that happen?' Paul Fernandes wondered. 'It happened when the assets were declared in April 2009.' Accusations of greed were mutually hurled. Leila Fernandes charged the brothers with being 'more concerned with his assets than with his health'. She said, '. . . whatever funds George has should be used exclusively, entirely, and absolutely to ensure that George who is helpless today is cared for optimally, holistically, with affection, with doors open to all those who wish to visit him but are debarred . . .'[39] But in spite of the professions, she debarred others from entering.

The contention among George's closest relations now opened up into a new realm. A war of positions was unleashed. There was a scramble among the contending caregivers to take possession of his ailing body. The prelude to becoming a bona fide inheritor was to become a bona fide caregiver. Each claimant not only questioned the other's right and rectitude, but also attempted to establish their credentials as a more qualified, sensitive and morally equipped caregiver. This was, to say the least, theatrical, and being enacted in full media glare. Here, Jaya, with her ambivalence, had only a back-door chance; Leila Fernandes, legally wedded wife with a son to boot, had her rights clearly established. The brothers claimed 'being related to George by blood and having been a continuous part of his life (without interruption) since our birth'. Their claims of an existing 'biological' bond were countered by the continued 'legal' status of Leila Fernandes: 'I am his wife.'[40] She was effusive in her newly discovered conjugal rights that had been lost on her a quarter century before. 'All the wishes of a person do not come true,' she said when asked to explain her long absence.[41] Not to be left behind, Jaya Jaitly pitched in with her 'moral' claim of having been with him for the past twenty-five years. Unable to assertively chip in, she quoted medical experts who advised keeping the patient in a 'familiar environment', which only she could provide. Of Leila Fernandes, she said, privately, 'She hates herself so much that she has to turn it into hate for everyone else. It is the only way she can rise in her eyes.'[42] Jaya Jaitly chose a proxy war, instigating his brothers to file a writ petition demanding access to George, which the court granted and Leila Fernandes conceded.[43] There was no clarity about what the brothers wanted. One afternoon in June 2010, six months after George was taken away, they were with Jaya Jaitly staging a televised protest before the closed gate of the bungalow on Krishna Menon Marg;[44] not long ago, they had been claiming she had destroyed George.

It was indeed cruel to remove George from his familiar environment. At first, in the new house, George showed signs of rebelling, looked 'distraught and behaved like an emotional wreck', his visiting brothers recounted, particularly Michael, who visited him quite frequently in those days.[45] He wanted to be taken out and he told them so. They would talk to him in Konkani and Tulu, his first languages, to rekindle his memories. He would be stirred, but not for very long. Jaya Jaitly kept up with her regular visits to George even when he was no longer in a position to recognize her. She attended to her craftwork in between, dealing with labyrinthine court cases following the *Tehelka* sting that eventually got her a legal conviction.[46] His brothers gradually lost interest and returned to their own lives, occasionally visiting him when they came to Delhi. And the care of a shrivelling George fell on the aged Leila Fernandes. Confined, he lay in bed, intravenously fed, turned every hour by hired medical assistants to avoid bedsores, and with Leila Fernandes watching from her upstairs room through a CCTV camera.[47]

George lay in a decade-long preparation for the inevitable merging with the elements. On 29 January 2019, when the news finally arrived, he was already largely forgotten by the world; even the claimants who had once contended fiercely over him had settled down in their respective routines. The news of his death brought him alive on TV channels and the front pages of newspapers more out of politeness than any realization of the irreparability of the loss. His former colleagues wrote clumsy, factually incorrect op-ed pieces extolling his role in Indian politics and in their own lives.[48] These were perfunctory tributes to his life and work.

If the communists remained muted and aloof, the BJP took command of his funeral that was spartan, silent and sparsely attended. At the home of Leila Fernandes, his portraits were dusted off and displayed in the sitting room which had been emptied of all furniture. His body lay in a freezer casket, placed in the middle of the room, his shrunken, final, terror-stricken face visible through its glass cover, as social and political dignitaries filed past, laying their condolence wreaths all around. Leila Fernandes, believing George was a born-again Christian, made arrangements for Christian funeral rituals. Jaya Jaitly (who had once said, 'If she phones me and says, "Jaya come and help me," I will leave everything and go because beyond a point nothing but humanity matters.') was the first to be told of his death by Leila Fernandes.[49] True to her word, she was the first one to arrive as well and inform all others. She said George's last wish was to be cremated, and Leila Fernandes agreed.

The body lay in state for three days. On the third day, after the arrival of Sean Fernandes, the embalmed body was taken to Delhi's Lodhi Road Electric Crematorium in a green army truck. As the vast oval furnace consumed his body, a sprinkling of political and trade union colleagues mourned his passing. On the final day of the funeral affair, an oversized and wasteful casket nailed with an urn of his ash was lowered into a trench with cemented floor and brick-laid walls. A little later, Leila Fernandes thanking Jaya Jaitly for the 'marvellous help' wrote, 'George has left us and found his peace and brought us all together.' And Jaya Jaitly reciprocated: 'It helped wash off the hurt and pain of these intervening years.' The Bihar government headed by Nitish Kumar (b. 1951) declared a two-day state mourning. The chief minister himself was present all through the funeral affair. Jaya Jaitly, angered by a legion of turncoats attending the funeral, wrote to Sean Fernandes: 'Some hypocrisy is indeed the only homage vice can pay to virtue.'[50]

* * *

Beur Jail in Patna's dusty outskirts is a gargantuan high-walled enclosure. Bihar's *bahubali* politicians, when caught at all, and further charged or convicted, which happens still less often, are incarcerated here. Despite its high walls, the jail is notoriously porous. With no fear of punitive action, imprisoned bahubalis hold regular durbars there, issue diktats and decide state elections. Its premises are frequently raided by the police. One such search in December 2004, not omitting its official part, yielded an alarming cache of contraband goods.[51] The cell phone records of an inmate, Pappu Yadav (b. 1967), a MP from Madhepura, revealed that he had been in touch with the state ministers.[52] In the run-up to the general elections of 2004, Pappu Yadav was escorted by jail personnel to Madhepura, ostensibly for a medical check-up (as if this backward Koshi bowl boasted of a super-speciality hospital not to be found in the state capital), but was caught campaigning.[53]

In early October 2007, a week before he left for Canada for a medical check-up, George visited Beur Jail to meet a bahubali politician inmate.

Anand Mohan Singh (b. 1960), Pappu Yadav's bête noire and a Koshi basin compatriot, was convicted for killing an IAS officer in December 1994. He was in jail serving a life term. Justice had taken thirteen long years to traverse its tortuous course. The murder of G. Krishnaiah, the IAS officer, was part of an intense social churning thrown up in the wake of the implementation of the Mandal Commission recommendations for the socially and educationally backward classes. Hailing from a landless Dalit family of Andhra Pradesh, Krishnaiah was an inspiration for India's 'untouchables'. He happened to be just passing by when a mob carrying the body of a slain upper-caste mafia don attacked him. He was stoned and shot dead. Anand Mohan Singh had led that bloodthirsty mob.

George's ten-minute visit to Beur Jail at the head of an upper-caste delegation exposed him to the charge of being insensitive to India's iniquitous hierarchy-ordained caste system.[54] The charge was ironical as all along his long political career, he had always stood for the cause of social justice. Years before, in 1978, on a visit to his constituency of Muzaffarpur, a furious mob had surrounded him, heckling him for supporting the reservation policy announced by Karpoori Thakur (1924–88) in Bihar. He was spat upon so much so that its wetness had weighed his khadi kurta down. But he had held his ground firmly and remained a steadfast supporter of the reservation policy for the other backward classes (OBCs). Anand Mohan Singh's rise in Bihar politics— or for that matter, that of his opposite number, Pappu Yadav's, from the other side of the barrier—was linked directly to the implementation of the Mandal recommendations. In 1990, he was elected to the Bihar assembly on a V.P. Singh-led Janata Dal nomination. Soon, however, the Janata Dal disintegrated into many regional formations. Anand Mohan too broke ranks and founded a 'forward' bastion: the Bihar People's Party. The murdered Krishnaiah's humble background and his own advocacy of the Mandal Commission should have made George shrink from venturing out to Beur Jail. Yet, a politically adrift George, already diagnosed with Alzheimer's disease, was paraded by interests inimical to his politics. It was widely believed that Jaya Jaitly organized his visit to spite Nitish Kumar, the Bihar chief minister.

In the aftermath of the 2004 general elections, a shell-shocked BJP found it hard to come to terms with its stunning defeat, but not George. He was confrontational as the new ruling alliance led by the Congress revived the controversies surrounding the Kargil war (1999), waged under him as defence minister, six years after its conclusion.[55] Wartime defence purchases were opened up to CBI scrutiny and judicial inquiries.[56] Controversies knocked at his door from the unlikeliest of quarters. He was ridiculed for opening an ordnance factory in Nalanda, an ancient centre of Buddhist learning. A book by an American diplomat revealed that he had been strip-searched twice on official visits at American airports.[57] George's problem, though momentarily unsettling, was not this attack of the successor government on his integrity and legacy; he called it a 'witch hunt in which witches are doing the hunting'.[58] The real problem for him had arisen from within: it was in his own Janata Dal (U) where disquiet was brewing against him.

On the eve of the 2004 general elections, Nitish Kumar forced George to shift his electoral constituency from Nalanda, where he had had three successive wins, back to Muzaffarpur.[59] Nitish Kumar desired to stand from Nalanda where his Kurmi caste mates dominated the constituency. In a television interview, some months after the elections, George vented, albeit haltingly: 'Nitish told me that he didn't want to fight the election . . . which made me believe he was worried about his situation in the election.'[60] Nitish Kumar had in reality been cruder, conveying the message by supporting the candidature of a jailed forgery kingpin, also his caste man, from Nalanda.[61] That was surreptitious; in public, displaying modesty, he said, 'I am a small leader in front of George Saheb.'[62] The shift crudely exposed George's political vulnerabilities and brought 'tears in his eyes', as vouched by Laloo Yadav.[63] George gave in to Nitish Kumar too easily and all the time, Jaya Jaitly would tell me. 'He would give in, because he felt Nitish is the only leader acceptable in Bihar.'[64] There was no doubting though who drove the politics of JD(U) in its core constituency of Bihar. It was Nitish Kumar.

After the defeat of the NDA government at the Centre, where he was a railway minister (1998–2004), Nitish Kumar was stirred by the goal of ridding Bihar of the Laloo–Rabri rule. He now wanted to 'take another road'![65] There was the Muslim vote still up for grabs; it needed to be assuaged though with an explanation why the JD(U) had trucked with the 'communal' BJP.[66] George's scapegoating could remove the blemish.[67] Flaunting his 'secular' credentials, Nitish Kumar said George had 'almost begun to accept Hindutva agenda'.[68] He desired a clean break from the BJP, and 'even better, dump George' to prove his secular salt.[69] George was 'kept out of the JD(U) campaign in Bihar'.[70] In November 2005, Nitish Kumar realized his ambition of becoming the chief minister. However, he formed a coalition government alongside the BJP! George felt 'betrayed' at his purging: 'I spent three years of my life in Bihar, to see that Bihar comes out of the situation in which it was, and when it came out I had to go out,' he said in that televised interview of 2007.[71] His slide into oblivion had begun. But before that would be sealed, his irrelevance was doubly underlined by the treatment Nitish Kumar gave to Jaya Jaitly's aspiration.

She was keen to be rewarded with a Rajya Sabha nomination. Earlier as well, it had been promised to her by the Vajpayee government but her name was removed from the list at the last minute. Once bitten, twice shy, Jaya although nervous kept her suitcase packed and documents ready, flight tickets safe in her handbag, waiting all that evening and the next morning for a call from Patna. Jaya Jaitly recalled: 'It was the last day of the five days nomination window.'[72] She was with George, sitting despondently, the time for nomination past, when the phone finally buzzed. It was Nitish Kumar. He told George that Jaya Jaitly couldn't be accommodated. He had instead nominated a certain King Mahendra.

A Bhumihar pharma-baron, Mahendra Prasad's wealth was close to Rs 700 crore, giving him the tag of the richest parliamentarian and the nickname King Mahendra. His parliamentary presence was evidence of all that ails the Indian representative system, particularly the House of Elders, the Rajya Sabha. King Mahendra had been in the Rajya Sabha once on Congress support, twice on Laloo Yadav's nomination, and now he was suddenly cosy enough with Nitish Kumar to get Nitish to back him up. George felt cheated, 'kicked in the teeth', as a journalist paraphrased his state. In that 2007 television interview, George, speaking slowly and with a lot of effort, said: 'I think it was something which I could not accept.'[73] The interview was a case in self-inflicted humiliation; a more disparaging public display of a political leader of George's stature was never seen on Indian television. George was not just humiliated, which was the object though, but ironically, he was pathetically complicit in his humiliation. By recalling instances when Nitish Kumar subjected him to curt treatment, George was not only underlining his pitiable position, he was asking for sympathy; his anguish was not a counter-attack but a plea for compassion. It was so uncharacteristically George.

George was ill, unable to speak, and yet his symbolic identity was enough for the purposes of warring groups. Upper-caste dons, under pressure from an image-conscious Nitish Kumar espousing 'speedy trials', disgruntled political rebels showing blatant ambitions of replacing Nitish Kumar as the CM—all began to project George as their leader, even while Nitish Kumar mouthed George being *sabka neta*' (everyone's leader).[74] But in truth, George was left with no one to call his own. Then, his long-time associates in trade unions began to desert him. The Hind Mazdoor Kisan Panchayat (HMKP) was broken into two, and he was shown the door by its dominant section. The Municipal Mazdoor Union (MMU) founded by him in 1954 moved under the control of his protégé turned bête noire. George felt extremely lonely and low. Sampa Das, his air hostess friend from Kolkata, met him in those days. 'Everybody has left me,' he said to her melancholically.[75] He was amazed by betrayals, astounded at the world around him falling apart. Weighed down by the spectre of facing life all alone, after long years of weary struggles, George became doubly dependent on Jaya Jaitly who, however, was more focused on using him to target Nitish Kumar.

Elections for a new party president of the JD(U) were held at Patna in April 2006. The tide was in favour of Sharad Yadav (b. 1947) who was backed by Nitish Kumar.[76] Yadav scored a convincing victory over George who polled only twenty-five votes against the 413 secured by the victor. Surrounded by minions, a colossus was dwarfed, and, sadly, he was taking part in his own dwarfing. The defeat diminished George beyond repair. On the rebound, George went for solace to his old socialist friend, Mulayam Singh Yadav (b. 1939). But despite some ripples in the media, the George–Mulayam friendship did not cross the threshold of platitudes, and even these shrivelled when Mulayam Singh Yadav's party demanded that George cut his ties with the NDA, resign his Lok Sabha seat and win a fresh mandate before they could open their party gates to him. Then, there was talk of reviving the Samata Party despite George earlier claiming it 'had ceased to exist'. Jaya Jaitly acted as the patron of the Samata Party revival operation, but the venture remained stillborn.

In 2009, when the general elections arrived, George's health was poor. The party president, Sharad Yadav, denied him a renomination from Muzaffarpur. George accused Nitish Kumar of 'belittling' him and declared his independent candidature. His defiance was seen as having been instigated by the 'vested interests'. The blame was put on Jaya Jaitly.[77] She was accused of holding him to ransom—a weapon to hit back at Nitish Kumar. Michael Fernandes told her making him fight the election was a 'blunder much bigger than all the earlier ones put together'. He worked on Jaya Jaitly to stop the charade, but to no avail. Holding her responsible for this 'terribly wrong decision', he urged Jaya Jaitly to not commit 'your biggest sin ever' and make George withdraw gracefully.[78] It is possible that even with tentacles of an Alzheimer's disease closing upon his mind, it was George who had put everything (including, in the words of Michael Fernandes, the 'persona he [had] become through honest and hard work and struggles all his life') at stake in the Muzaffarpur election when the party he had founded humiliated him by denying him a nomination. Startled, the only way open to him was to cling harder to his position. In the election, he polled so low he lost his security deposit. It was a humiliating blow in his twilight years.

Nitish Kumar, however, kept the promise of giving him a Rajya Sabha nomination. Jaya Jaitly was against George accepting it.[79] A socialist never goes to the Upper House, she argued. Hadn't Nitish Kumar humiliated him enough? Why take what he was offering now? But George flew down to Patna and, flanked by Nitish Kumar and a slogan-shouting mob, filed his nomination papers before the returning officer. The stress took a toll on him.

That night, he stayed at a suite in Patna's five-star Maurya Hotel. Fredrick D'Sa and his long-time help, Durga, were with him. Once in the room, he began to pace about agitatedly. He was in a terrible mood—angry, aggressive and audacious. He became uncontrollable. He tore his clothes away. He defecated in his pyjamas and sat in it, unwilling to budge. Strongly built, he stomped across the room, naked and filthy. He didn't sleep, nor did his companions, but he later relented, and helpers cleaned him up. The scrubbing went on till early morning.[80]

George's oath-taking ceremony in the Rajya Sabha in July 2009 brought to the fore two unpleasant details: first, that his health was undeniably bad—he was unable to read his oath; second, Leila

Fernandes' appearance next to him on the portals of the Parliament pointed to the simmering discontent within the household.[81] She posed happily with him and spoke of how close they were. After this, Leila Fernandes' visits to his residence gained in frequency while those of Jaya Jaitly declined drastically.

* * *

Not only did George's ministerial legacy come under merciless attack, but to bludgeon his politics also became a cause célèbre. In the *Asian Age*, M.J. Akbar reminded his readers how George had defended the Gujarat riots and absolved the Bajrang Dal of any role in the brutal burning alive of Graham Staines and his minor sons. M.J. Akbar, who in a few years would be a member of Narendra Modi's cabinet, attacked George trenchantly: he derided his politics, he derided his ideology and his humanity. Once upon a time, he had been a close confidante. Does it say something about the coarse nature of human frailty or the unreasonableness of human ambition?

'None of them,' George said of his colleagues, 'has any use of me, and I don't think they will miss me.' George's tragedy was that much before age sheared his vitality, his politics had lost its shine, his legacy its lustre. Much before age and disease crippled him and turned him into a relic, George already stood diminished, his ideas sullied, his image blurred. When was the peak conquered and when was the plot lost, when did the descent begin and what did the descent mean? These questions form the crux of his story. Herein is unravelled the life of a man, who not just rose from the streets of Bombay to straddle the power corridors of Delhi, but, as a sometime cabinet colleague Arif Mohammad Khan (b. 1951) said, he was so full of commitment and proved himself to be an indefatigable fighter. In the middle of 1984, in the face of acute personal and political desolation, he had written to Jaya Jaitly, in one of those notes they exchanged between them: 'There is a commitment to a cause that is much bigger than ourselves, howsoever hopeless that cause may look, and howsoever inadequate we may appear to be in fighting that cause—the cause of remaking our country.'[82] In it, there was no hint of personal gratification or desire for a legacy. From somewhere in the underground during Indira Gandhi's Emergency days, he had reminded the world of the prophetic words of Hermann Hesse:[83]

> Time and the world, money and power
> Belong to the small people and shallow people
> To the rest, to the real men belongs nothing.
> Nothing but death.

2

A Christian Beginning

On the now largely levelled hill at Bijey (or Bejai), in the city of Mangalore on the west coast of India, stands the grey building of a church dedicated to St Francis Xavier. Among the local notables who, following contemporary convention, had petitioned Rome for a parish church at Bijey was Jacob Fernandes, George's paternal grandfather.[1] Skirted by a high enclosure wall, much of the church edifice, first built in its concrete form in 1928, even today largely remains the same. A welcoming arch at the foot of the hill opens on to a busy thoroughfare. Inside, on the left, up the paved slope is the tile-roofed structure where George did a year of primary schooling. Opposite the school, on the right, is a cemetery with rows of palm-shaded grave markers stretching in all directions. In one of these lost graves are interred the remains of Jacob Fernandes. In India, like elsewhere in the world, a church within its sacred precinct invariably includes a school for the young and a resting place for the departed.

The people from Mangalore have been a peripatetic lot, moving in search of more promising destinations. After their feverish wanderings, they seldom return to the place where their dead are buried. At the beginning of the 1950s, George's parents moved home to Bangalore, never to return, nor did any of their six sons come back. As the urban Catholic dwellers in Mangalore leave for pastures abroad, the city space is refilled by Christian migrants from once salubrious rural stretches whose coconut and areca trees are fast disappearing as well. Their traces though are retained in parish chapels. No other religious administration in India keeps as detailed a record of the faithful as Catholic churches do. They throw illuminating light on the birth, life events, vocation and death of each Christian individual who has belonged to a parish from the earliest times. An enterprising chronicler in Mangalore has compiled encyclopaedic tomes on the genealogies of community members from records kept in church archives and from tombstones.[2]

A page in the register of birth kept at Bijey's St Francis Xavier Church gives 3 June 1930 as the date of birth of George Mathew Isadore Fernandes, son of John Joseph Fernandes and Alice Martha nee Pinto. Traditionally, birth alone has not entitled one to a religion; each faith has a set of rituals to initiate its followers. Without experiencing the rites of passage which are unique to every faith, no one bears a religion. Like Judaism and Islam initiating its followers by male circumcision, and Brahmanism by giving the sacred thread, baptism—meaning

Pages from the birth record book of the St Francis Xavier Church, Bijey, Mangalore.

Courtesy: Author

simply to wash ritually—is the way into the Christian fold. Two days after his birth, amidst much fanfare, a priest named and initiated the infant George into Christianity by a ritual dip in a tub of consecrated water. This ceremony was to wash away his original sin, make him a twice-born and foreclose any religious deviation.[3] Close to George's ancestors' place at Bajpe in Mangalore, at the spot where Pope John Paul II, visiting India in February 1986, addressed a pious multitude, stands a shrine commemorating that visit. One afternoon, many years later, the shrine's cassock-donning priest quoted the Bible: 'He that believeth and is baptized shall be saved.' He explained, 'Once baptized, your name is written in heaven. It never ceases.'[4] Through his holy dip, the infant George was made a follower of Christ for this life and after, of course with the possibility of being excommunicated if he went too far astray.

Christianity came to India in two events separated by several centuries, both times first on the west coast. Having been commanded by Jesus Christ to 'go and teach all nations', His apostles spread themselves. The Syriac-speaking Thomas is assumed to have come within the first century of the violent crucifixion of Jesus of Nazareth. The first of his converts were the Nambudiri Brahmins of Malabar, the erstwhile followers of the ancient Hindu sage Parashurama who is said to have scooped up Mangalore by throwing his axe into the Arabian Sea. Those first converts are still called Syrian or Thomas Christians. They remained secluded in Malabar, practising the faith in a form that retained the vestiges of Brahmanic rituals and caste norms.[5]

At the end of the fifteenth century erupted the second momentous event, when the Portuguese arrived, following a bloodbath that had reddened their peninsula, bringing along their version of Christianity. What had happened was that in distant Arabia a prophet founded a typhoon of religion called Islam, meaning simply complete surrender. In CE 632, the Prophet Muhammad (PBUH) died. Carried now by caliphs—simply, the Prophet's successors—Islam spread like wildfire, galloping across Asia, bringing divine illumination on those lost in ignorance and idolatry. Its knock at the frontiers of Europe made the custodians of Christianity cringe. Driven by a visceral hatred, they launched the Crusades, religious wars against the powers of Islam. Many of those royals from the twin Iberian kingdoms of Portugal and Spain who fought the Christian war were named 'Ferdinand'. Impelled by the religious conflagration and lured by a profitable trade, the Portuguese began to explore ways to reach a wider possible world by skirting regions of Islam. By the time Vasco da Gama anchored at Calicut in 1498, the Crusades were over and the royal 'Ferdinands' were much feted.[6] The Portuguese came expecting Christian allies and a share in the riches of India; instead, they found most of the coast already under Muslim rule and the spice trade under the control of Muslim traders. It unleashed a battle for supremacy in the Indian Ocean. Europe's protracted religious wars between the two sisterly faiths found a new theatre. With their huge ships, laden with guns and cannons and fortified by religious animosity, the Portuguese waged battles, drowned rival ships of Arab merchants, massacred coastal populations and married Muslim widows. In 1510, the Portuguese captured Goa from its Muslim overlord.

It is from the 'Ferdinands' that the name 'Fernandes' is said to be derived. Today, 'Fernandes', spelt differently in different cultural contexts, is a common enough surname in the lands from Brazil to Sri Lanka, once under imperial Portugal. Randomly chosen by the baptizing priests, the names built a pan-global identity of the converts, completely unconnected to each other and yet linked to one Portuguese culture and history. Even in India, 'Fernandes' denoted no particular family, caste or class identity; it was simply a surname given to converts without any linkage to ancestry. The new names were to erase the converts' original past and replace them with an entirely new set of cultural values. They carried an ideological veneer: caste names divided people, whereas the adoption of Christianity rendered everyone equal before God.[7] The Fernandes surname was a reminder as well of the historical role its royal bearers had played in upholding Christianity against Islam. It implicitly nudged the lay bearers of their existential competition with the followers of Islam.

In the 100 years after it was taken, Goa rose rapidly to prominence and then fell back into being ordinary. Goa's undoing was the religious zealotry of its Portuguese rulers.[8] They functioned under the belief that the Hindu faith was based on superstition, its customs immoral and idolatry its basest bane. As a result, temples were demolished, idols desecrated, people forced to convert to Christianity.[9] As more and more people came into the ambit of Christianity—pushed mainly by fear, force and favour, and seldom by theological fervour—the new converts in the privacy of their homes observed practices that were contrary to what the priests prescribed. The Portuguese responded to such sacrilege by taking a leaf out of their recent homeland practice against Muslims and Jews, and established 'inquisitions' against those lapsed converts in Goa. Across the sixteenth and seventeenth centuries, until its formal suspension in the middle of the eighteenth, the state-sponsored 'inquisition' played a disturbingly cleansing role in Goa.[10] As a result, the region's religious demography was transformed. Its landscape became dotted with tall white cathedrals. The lifestyle, names, attire and eating habits of the people changed. Festivals and carnivals, rites and rituals, and art and architecture changed.[11]

From Bombay down to the northern tip of Kerala, the strip of land between the resplendent Western Ghats and the frothy Arabian Sea is called the Konkan, literally, a sandy corner. Goa is its heart. As the heat of the inquisition mounted, a successive wave of Christians—mostly, but not exclusively, Gaud Saraswat Brahmin converts—slithered down the Konkan strip. They settled in Canara region, which houses Mangalore. Here, they carved out fields and became landlords, pushing the Tulu-speaking indigenous Billavas (toddy tappers) and Koragas (basket-makers and labourers) farther into the forest. In the middle of the seventeenth century, it was found, these new settlers were living a life of scandal 'without priests, without sacraments, without instructions'.[12] Still two centuries later, travelling German protestant missionaries were 'astonished at the ignorance of some Roman Catholics, for they knew not only nothing of the Saviour who had died for our sins on the cross and risen again, but could not even tell who the blessed Virgin was'.[13] The question arises: Why did these lapsed Christians not revert to their past religion? Contrary to what an authorized history of the Church in India vouches, first caste and then colonial power saved Christianity in Canara. Having lost caste because of their conversion denied them the opportunity to revert, and the colonial power finding in them a loyal group because of the common faith gave them the required protection. The converts began to nurture their new religion while continuing with elements of their cultural past. For long, beef was ritually shunned in Catholic-Christian homes in deference to their Brahmanical past. And sometime later, Brahmanical surnames were revived; for instance, a Prabhu after becoming a Machado reverted to the surname Prabhu and took pride in it. If caste let Christianity survive, it also ironically stifled its growth; most proselytizing missionaries found in caste their greatest and wiliest of enemies.

George is one of those whose ancestors had adopted Christianity either because of the Portuguese coercion in Goa or under their ecclesiastical influence at Mangalore. Whatever be the truth concerning his family's conversion—as facts are hazy and opinions varied—it could be surmised that his ancestors were of Brahmin or upper-caste origin. The socialist leader Rabi Ray (1926–2017), who served as presiding officer of the Lok Sabha from 1989 to 1991, tells an interesting tale. One afternoon in the early 1970s, Rabi Ray, Ladli Mohan Nigam and George lunched at Rajya Sabha member Balkrishna Gupta's house in Delhi. After the meal, George facetiously asked Balkrishna Gupta, who was a Marwari businessman, to give them the *dakshina* or gift that they as Brahmins were entitled to.[14] More than a decade later, in the late 1980s, when boasting of his Brahmanical past was no longer politically fetching, the matter of his caste would be raised. No amount of advocacy of the Mandal Commission Report would endear him to the OBC leaders of his party. On the eve of the elections in 1989, which would be followed by a social churning around Mandal, he was asked point-blank, by Haryana satrap Devi Lal, 'What caste are you?' George was so rattled that he would make long-distance phone calls to Richard Fernandes, his youngest brother, and vent, 'Look, they are asking my caste!'[15]

* * *

Squeezed between the rivers of Netravati and Gurpur, Mangalore from a hoary past was a principal seaport on the west coast. On the bank of the Gurpur river at Boloor, just before it disgorges itself into the Arabian Sea, a massive watchtower stands guard to the inland entry of ships into the river. Called Sultan *Bateri* (Battery), it is a miniature fortress with many mounting places for cannons all around. This was constructed during the reign of Tipu Sultan, the successor of the warlord Haidar Ali who had emerged as ruler at Mysore in the 1750s.[16] For sixteen years, Tipu Sultan ruled a continuously shrinking principality, yet, he was a threat so strong that a range of armies, both Indian and European, wanted to douse his ambition and scrap his kingdom. Sultan Bateri reminds us of his fierce determination to preserve himself. In one skirmish over Mangalore with the English, it is said, he was betrayed by his Christian subjects, who 'supplied men and material' to the enemy.[17] As was the practice, an angry Tipu Sultan ordered their eviction from Mangalore and transported them to Seringapatam, his capital, where they were kept captive, circumcised and converted to Islam. Estimates of the number of captives range from a high 60,000 to a credible 10,000. Only in 1799, following Tipu Sultan's defeat and death, were they released and given safe passage to Mangalore, where under protection from the victorious English, they began to flourish again.[18]

Even 200 years after his death, and in republican India, Tipu Sultan remains a deeply controversial figure and stirs extreme emotions, often leading to vandalism and violence.[19] He is much reviled among the Catholics of Mangalore, as the social memory of the forced march and the Great Captivity has been zealously kept alive, and is retold with 'awe and dread' and circulated through grandmotherly tales.[20] Churches display images related to the event on wall hangings. It has spawned a tradition of fertile historical imagination, intense equally among the lay and the learned. Books in varied genres—history, drama, fiction, poetry—reconstruct horror stories. The first doctoral work on the subject was done in 1931.[21] Much of these writings draw from English sources, notably the memoirs of the English prisoners of war at Seringapatam who escaped. They paint Tipu Sultan as a bigoted and cruel ruler.[22] On the other hand, at the grand mausoleum at Seringapatam where the remains of both the father and son are buried, travellers and tourists, devotees and seekers all congregate on the festival of Urs to maintain a night-long vigil in honour of the departed heroes. Viewed by some as one who challenged the British supremacy and by others as an oppressor, the state government of Karnataka since 2015 has been observing Tipu Sultan's birth anniversary to make him into a contemporary icon, and each year a bunch of people from Mangalore have risen in protest.[23]

In 1948, a monthly magazine *Mangalore* published a series of articles on Christians who were left behind when captives were taken to Seringapatam. Founded in 1928 and published by the Catholic Association of South Canara (CASC), *Mangalore*, since then, published something or the other on this sad historical event in every issue and kept the discussion on the wound fresh and close. In 1969, two years after George's victory in the Lok Sabha election from the Bombay (South) constituency, Praxy Fernandes, a Mangalorean career bureaucrat, wrote *Storm over Seringapatam,* which was published by George's friend Dinkar Sakrikar.[24] In explaining what motivated him to write a book on Tipu Sultan, the author alluded to the Great Captivity. It was an event, he wrote, 'which has left a deep scar in our racial memories . . . To us in Mangalore, the name of Tippu [sic] evoked dread and nameless fear.'

Born four years before George, Praxy Fernandes joined the IAS in 1948, and during his long career was also Mysore's municipal commissioner. He would become the finance secretary in the Janata Party government in 1977, in which George was the industry minister. Working from a personal background in which the social memory of a tyrannical Tipu Sultan was rivetingly alive, Praxy Fernandes, as the municipal commissioner of Mysore, began to discover a new Tipu. This Tipu Sultan had assisted Hinduism's holy Sringeri Math when marauding Marathas had looted and desecrated it. He was also found to have sustained by his munificence the Sri Ranganatha Temple that majestically stood in dark, rocky splendour not far from his palace in the Fort of Seringapatam. The temple could have been razed and a mosque built in its place, but not only did it remain intact, it also flourished, and many gifts are recorded as having been bestowed on the temple. This new Tipu was even seen in historical correspondence requesting the Portuguese of Goa to send Christian priests to his domain. Praxy Fernandes' book was his way to exorcize the ghosts of a prejudiced judgement of this ruler, even while the book was dedicated to the memories of captive survivors. Some years later, Praxy Fernandes' daughter Louise would marry the Congress politician Salman Khurshid.

In 1784, when Tipu Sultan had taken Mangalore's Christians captive, he had also simultaneously ordered churches to be demolished.[25] As the legend goes, Milagres Church (Our Lady of Miracles), one of the earliest churches in Mangalore, was demolished by him and Christians ordered to ferry stones of their demolished shrine to construct what is now an Islamic prayer house. This idgah, its roof presently of tin sheets, occupies a rectangular space just in front of the St Aloysius College campus. Every Friday, as prayers are held, the busy thoroughfare skirting the prayer house gets completely blocked, with rows of the faithful bending over in prayer, while the rest of the space is chock-a-block with their vehicles. It makes many resident Catholics silently fume. Michael Fernandes, George's younger brother, recalled the existence of marked segregation between Christians and Muslims in their childhood. Christian neighbours were never invited to Muslim *munji* (circumcision) rituals nor would Christians be keen to be invited. The interaction was limited to commerce and services that were the preserve of Muslims alone, such as tinning or *kalai* work on brass cooking ware, in which Malayali Khaskas excelled.

In 2015, Alan Machado Prabhu published *Slaves of Sultan*, which, despite its provocative title, absolved Tipu Sultan from the charge of bigotry. The author, while ambiguously hinting at the widely held account of the demolition of Milagres Church, argues that as stones were costly, many churches in those days were built of bamboo or mud, and would not have survived long in the torrential rains.[26] Milagres Church was rebuilt many times on the same site. It was rebuilt in 1811 when the captives returned. But reason has no place in matters of faith.

Religious competition and conflict have been part of the social fabric of Mangalore. Some 200 kilometres away, in its neighbouring district of Hassan, a massive rock statue of the Jain icon Bahubali Gomateshwara protrudes benignly from a hill at Shravanabelagola. Jainism came to the region in the third century BCE when a procession of monks from eastern India came to settle here. Similar monolith statues of Jain Tirthankaras dot the region's landscape. Their reaching out to the sky is not just evidence of the religion's magnificence or its pious call to the faithful, but also defiance against Brahmanism's subsuming revival under Adi Shankara. Some local traditions hold that the indigenous Tulu-speaking, Bhuta-worshipping Bunts faced similar attacks by a resurgent Brahmanism. Today, whereas Jainism is mostly confined to the annual televised consecration of the naked Bahubali statue by pouring tonnes of milk over it, the region remains a centre of Hinduism. Mangalore today is less known as a creation of Parashuram's prowess than indeed by the antics of Sri Ram Sene, a group of fanatics claiming for themselves a Hindu creed. Mangalore's Catholic population is just 15 per cent. Among them are men who publish a provocatively titled journal, *Persecution*, that chronicles India's vandalism against Christians.

For us, the relevant question is, did the memory of a grievance that his community suffered at the hands of Tipu Sultan, rankle in George? Did its existence prod him to become the first credible leader from a non-RSS background to join the NDA bandwagon? Towards the end of his political career but at the height of his executive power, just a month short of his 73rd birthday, George would stand on the floor of Parliament to make a speech that would expose him to attack in posterity.[27] It was a debate on the Gujarat violence. He would take up the gauntlet of defending Narendra Modi at his most vulnerable moment in 2002. 'These stories of atrocities on women, of the rape of women,' George would say to the gathering of lawmakers, rage welling up in him at the sight of Sonia Gandhi (b. 1946) chewing gum opposite him, 'they are nothing new. Slashing a pregnant woman's stomach to tear out the foetus . . . for the last fifty-five years, we have been hearing these tales . . . So why make such a fuss about it now? . . . People being hacked into pieces, being burnt and roasted alive, are also not new. So why make so much noise about them now?' He was stressing that the mayhem of communal violence was a commonplace affair in this country's history. It was more power politics than aggrieved conscience that was stirring the debate on the Gujarat riots. His speech provoked unceasing objections and was largely seen as lacking in taste, coming from a senior member. When in jail during the Emergency, as letters from the family would be withheld from him, he would send a petition to the court in which it was stated that 'he was born to Christian parents, that his wife is the daughter of a Muslim father and a Hindu mother, and while in his entire public life extending over twenty-seven years, he has a record of fighting against communalism in all its manifestations, even his personal and family background would preclude his thinking on communal matters'.[28] Why was a man who all his life fought against the virus of communal hatred saying that such violence was part and parcel of this nation and so might be taken as normal, momentary eruptions?

His speech, made while riots were still breaking out in Gujarat, would be considered by many as emanating from his anti-Congress stance, as he said: 'During the last forty-six years when the Congress Party was ruling the country, at that time what happened in the entire country, the same thing is happening in Gujarat today—nothing new is happening there.' Here, he was not absolving the Narendra Modi-led Gujarat government but was hitting at the Congress Party for doing what it had been doing during its long rule. A Congress that had imprisoned him, tortured him, vilified him and called him 'kafan chor' (coffin thief). A Congress that was dynastic, status-quoist, and responsible for India's all-round stagnancy. But by attacking the Congress, by exposing the faults in its decades of rule, he neither absolved Narendra Modi, nor did the victims of the Gujarat violence receive any solace, succour or support from him. So why did he do it? Was it sheer opportunism and conceit of power? Was he a turncoat working to endear himself to the Hindutva brigade? According to Govindacharya, the ideologue of the BJP in those days, George's political foray in Bihar made him realize the importance of the BJP: 'I had offered them a DMK-like formula in which they would play a dominant role in the state assembly while supporting and giving a lion's share in central Parliament.'[29] So was George's proximity to the BJP/RSS solely dictated by his need to be in power? If so, was he like any politician intent on exploiting opportunities as stepping stones? But a politician who doesn't isn't. Power for a politician is the deepest desire, and opportunism a stepping stone.

Towards the end of his political career, on the eve of the 2004 general elections, George claimed that his ancestors were Hindu, his son's name was of Sanskrit derivation.[30] 'We all had Hindu ancestors. So, my Christian name doesn't make a difference. My son's name is Sushanto. He has a father who was born to Christian parents. His mother was born to a Muslim father and a Hindu mother. So, I always tell him you are the real Indian, free from caste, creed and religion.' Being a real Indian was a kind of motif in his conversation in those days. In 1998, in a post-Pokhran interview, he claimed that there were no real Indians left any more.[31] Was his claim to be a 'Hindu Christian' a result of his growing proximity to the RSS—a fact brought uncomfortably into the open by his party colleague Nitish Kumar—or was it to underline the fact that India, in the course of history, despite having become a multifaith abode, had remained largely Hindu in its core ethos? She retained her cultural core even while a change of gods was not just permitted but also encouraged. Belonging to the same ethnic and cultural stock, the religious minorities in this country did not change by adopting a different religion. The proselytizers, faced with the prospect of inalienable bonding of religion and culture that restricted their influence, at first attacked the culture, then gave their religion and thereafter transformed the converts' culture to underline their separateness. Culture became a marker for segregation and then separation, but underneath nothing changed.

This ancient memory didn't create a communal-minded, Muslim-hating man who, to show his revulsion, sided with the RSS/BJP-led political front. Even in that late-evening speech in Parliament, in which he said 'what is happening in Gujarat is nothing new', he pointed out that many Muslims had remained in India after Partition as they didn't look at the country through the lens of religion. 'Therefore, we can never forget anyone who has been born in this country, is loyal to it.' In late 1975, on the run from Indira Gandhi's police, he would accuse her of being 'the most communal-minded person' and repeated a charge that she, as the home minister during the Bangladesh war, had ordered divesting of Muslims from key installations and vital positions. Accordingly, Muslims employed in the BEST Undertaking in Bombay, at drinking water installations, in the Bhabha Atomic [Research] Centre, were terminated from service with one month's pay in their hands. (One wonders if Mrs Gandhi was affected by this accusation. In 1984, she refused to change her Sikh guards despite being advised of the risk. But this is in the realm of conjecture.) He wrote in that pamphlet, written from the underground: 'I also repeat my charge that Muslims in India are denied equality and opportunity and in the matter of jobs in army, police and other public services, they are discriminated against.'[32] The same questioning of Congress's professed secularism was repeated in the 2002 speech in Parliament. 'I have been saying this right from the day of the war for Bangladesh— how the home ministry had written letters to PSUs and the private sector asking them not to employ Muslims.'

* * *

Many years later, when his slide into Alzheimer's disease was already noticeable and medically confirmed, George in a conversation would reminisce about his early childhood in Mangalore's Bijey.[33] He was born a year after his parents' marriage in 1929. His mother, Alice Martha Pinto, was just seventeen years old when she married John Joseph Fernandes, who was twenty-nine. Alice Martha had been born on 1 December 1912, a year after George V, the English emperor of India, landed at the Gateway of India in Bombay, built especially to commemorate his arrival. She was so enchanted by the proximity of her birth to the royal visit that when she became a mother, she chose George as the name for her firstborn. As was generally the norm, most Catholic children were named after Christianity's revered apostles, saints and martyrs. St George, for instance, had died pleading to the

Roman authority to nail him to the cross upside down, as to die in the manner of Jesus would be a deep sacrilege, a profanity he would not bear even in death. Thus, a twenty-two-year-old soldier was transformed into a martyr and a saint and inspired many namesakes. But when Alice Martha chose George as the name for her firstborn, it was inspired not by the faith of the martyred saint but rather by the pomp and show of that royal visit a year before her birth.

On 3 June 1930, when George was born, times were not such as to inspire devotion to the colonial ruler. In March, Gandhi had launched a month-long march to the sea at Dandi to publicly make salt. By doing so, he breached a law that gave the government a monopoly over salt manufacture. The government in reprisal let loose a reign of terror. Thousands were put behind bars, many were injured or killed. The whole country was in ferment, rising in rebellion against British rule, and here was a woman naming her son after an English royal! If it was a case of a young girl's fascination, it was also either a courageous act of conviction or more likely a family's acute political naivety, in keeping with the ethos of conversion to a new religion and culture. Having their origins in Portuguese influence and nurtured by the English, the Mangalorean Catholics had emerged as a Westernized community. Their cultural leanings were pronounced in the choice of their spoken language, which for most of them was English. For them, everything superior was 'yeropi' and inferior things 'gaunti'.[34] The community's feelings about the national liberation struggle were decidedly muted. When in February 1936 King George V passed away in distant England, at Mangalore, 'bells were tolled in all the churches and memorial services were held', and an assembly at St Aloysius College expressed 'poignant sorrow of the Catholics of Mangalore at the death of the king'.[35]

George would remember differences between his parents that marred happy memories of his childhood. In a chilling statement, eighty-year-old George recalled a scene he witnessed as an eight-year-old boy. 'Often my aunt would complain about my mother to my father. My aunt would start crying. Father would become angry. Taking his sister's side, he would beat up my mother. I had no clue. Being young

I did not understand why was that happening. I could see my mother crying. And I would see my father holding her against the wall.'[36]

John Joseph Fernandes' father, Jacob Fernandes, was primarily an agriculturist from Karambar village of Bajpe (literally, mother of vegetables) taluk. Jacob, after his marriage to Emiliana D'Sa, had settled at Bijey, on the outskirts of Mangalore town. By the time John Joseph was born, the family occupation had moved from farming to petty trading. He was the youngest of five siblings, the only boy. When still in his childhood, their mother passed away, leaving him in the care of the youngest of the sisters, Mary, seven years his senior. As Mary replaced his mother, he was dependent on her kindness in boyhood and remained obliged to her as an adult. Unmarried and insecure about her future, Mary felt a need to control her brother, the need accentuating after the arrival of Alice Martha as his wife. When she stepped into the household, the young bride found herself in a household run by her husband's elder sister. The house and the land on which it stood by way of inheritance had come to belong to Mary; John Joseph Fernandes was given the family's agricultural land at Karambar as his patrilineal share. The complicated situation added to Alice Martha's suffocation; her relationship with her husband became one of controlled truce. It was not a particularly peaceful abode; hostilities were mutual and intense. George attributed the discord at home to the presence of his father's spinster sister. 'My aunt and my mother did not get along.'

'My father's family was more sober and socially engaged. They donated liberally to the Church,' one of the sons would remember decades later.[37] Alice Martha came from a locally dominant landed family: 'They were more power-oriented.' She seems to have inherited some family traits. 'My mother was extrovert, domineering, and liked to be at the wheel. She would not brook any interference,' Richard Fernandes, her youngest son, recollected. And the father? 'My father played a role that the environment demanded from him: to be a strong man of the house and throw his weight around.' A family photograph of the 1960s shows Alice Martha as a contented-looking, slightly plump woman, while John Joseph has the posture of an imposing patriarch. And yet, decades later, when George was in jail, accused of

In this 1933 photograph (sitting ladies), first from the left is Alice Fernandes, the mother with infant Lawrence in lap; (children sitting on the ground) first from the left is three-year-old George.

conspiring against the state, it was Alice Martha, well into her sixties, who would pick up the fight against Indira Gandhi's government, writing letters, meeting authorities, pestering the mighty to reveal her son's whereabouts. It was Alice Martha again, who would campaign for the imprisoned George's election from a constituency that did not understand her language, which was interpreted by an intrepid Sushma Swaraj (1952–2019).

After George's birth, Alice Martha bore four more sons: Lawrence Vincent Cajatan Hasanth (1932–2005), Michael Benedict (b. 1934), Paul Boniface (b. 1936) and Aloysius Gregory who is known as Louie (b. 1939). In the later part of 1938, when Alice was pregnant with Aloysius, one Sunday after the mass at church, her brother came to take her to her natal home for her confinement. This was a ruse, as her family had come to know of her marital troubles. She would stay in her maternal home, which was just over a kilometre away, for the next eight years, leaving her four tender-aged sons in the care of her husband. George was eight; Paul was just two.[38] Nothing in Alice Martha suggested she didn't want to be a full-time mother or had any me-first tendencies. Domesticity was her world. Although the first institution of higher education for women in Mangalore, the St Agnes College, had had a

Family Portrait, 1967: (standing, L - R) Michael, Aloysius, Lawrence and Richard; (sitting) George flanked by parents.

fledgeling start in 1924, she had studied only up to primary school. It was noteworthy when she left her marital home, she didn't take her children with her. Her motive seemed to be more to spite her unfeeling husband rather than to risk her matrimony. By leaving the children, she was keen to give back to her husband in the same coin. The event throws some light on the personality of John Joseph Fernandes as well, who preferred eight years of lonely domestic drudgery, besides social condemnation for having a wife living separately, to reconciliation.

Years later, in the early 1980s, as a beaten but thoroughly busy politician working to re-establish himself in the aftermath of the Janata Party collapse, George would go through a similar experience. His chagrined wife Leila Fernandes would leave their ten-year-old son in his care and go abroad. George would complain to Jaya Jaitly about Leila playing truant, but would refuse to throw in the towel. 'What is she trying to prove? Does she really believe that I'll put up with all this because I have a public life to live? How mistaken she is!' he wrote to Jaya Jaitly in one of the notes they exchanged in those days, expressing as well how humiliated he felt at the ostracization he faced at his home.[39] George would read bedtime stories to his son, prepare him and drop him to school, asking Jaya Jaitly for help, whenever she could. And when Leila Fernandes returned and took possession of the child, setting conditions on George meeting his son, he would write, 'Does she not realize the damage she is causing to Sonny Boy? What kind of a mother's love is this that teaches a child to hate his father?'[40] But through all this turmoil, George would come to understand his father better. Not only did his father create no ill will against their absent mother, but his nurturing was also such as to draw George one day to ask his father to bring his mother home. In his own case though, by the time his son Sean Fernandes finally returned to fetch George, it was amidst a thickening cloud of bitterness rather than honest filial intent.

The physical distance between the four Fernandes boys and their maternal home was not much—barely a ten-minute walk, through uneven terrain and paddy fields and thickets and rain; but when love recedes, the distance gets bigger; hearts might long sometimes, but minds are stubborn. George grew from eight to sixteen and his mother was yet to return. The children would walk down to their maternal home occasionally. 'When she was away at her parents' place', Michael Fernandes recalled, 'we were still going there.' Michael had recurring health problems and needed a mother's care. Once, when he had eczema all over his body, he went and stayed at his mother's place. 'Our relationships were not sour in any manner.' George visited his mother as well, usually on the way to or from school. 'I would go straight to the place my mother was, and my father would get to know about my visit. He would say, "Why did you go? For what purpose?" And I would say whatever I had to say [by way of explanation]!'[41] In 1947, a determined George, all of seventeen, extracted a commitment from his father to bring their mother home, which he did, thereby bringing about a reconciliation. Richard Fernandes, the youngest child, was born thereafter in 1952. With no further marital problems, they lived together happily till 1983, when John Joseph Fernandes died on 1 June. Alice Martha would outlive her husband by a decade.

* * *

In those eight years of separation, John Joseph Fernandes proved to be a doting, if strict disciplinarian, father. Although his sister Mary helped him in carrying out domestic chores, he was kept busy cooking and cleaning, ferrying water pitchers and running errands, mending the children's clothes, etc. Besides, he did many things to earn a living. He needed the children as helping hands and kept strict control over their everyday routine. The father's strenuous schedule influenced them all. The four sons in a motherless home learnt not to shy away from manual work, to be independent in their needs, and to be publicly engaged. Nor did they learn any vices from him. John Joseph Fernandes was a teetotaller and non-smoker. He dressed simply; most often he wore a *mundu*, and never donned trousers or shorts. George too would neither drink nor smoke. Throughout his life, he washed his clothes himself and lived frugally, and as he grew older, he became still less concerned about what he wore or ate.

The family home at Bijey was built on a high earthen plinth. The earthen floors of the courtyard and rooms were regularly smeared with cow-dung paste. The walls were of brick. The roof was of baked mud tiles, held on beams of rosewood, widely found in the Western Ghats. Bijey was famous for its flower gardens and jasmine cultivation. A flourishing trade in flowers prevailed in the area. The flowers were used in the conduct of Hindu worship, and also to decorate wedding venues and to embellish women's long hair. Flowers figured a great deal in the Fernandes family's life as well; in fact, they were known as *phulavikteli* (Konkani for flower sellers). On the family's patch of land grew rows of jasmine and varieties of fruit trees. The proceeds from the jasmine sale were the mainstay of the family's income. Sellers would come home to snap up fresh jasmine, and the rest would be taken by a member of the family to sell in the market. Flower selling was usually a woman's job, but in some instances, men too would do this job, and Michael Fernandes recalled selling flowers in the marketplace. After the National Emergency was imposed in 1975, when George was underground, and the family home in Bangalore was pelted with stones and assailed by a barrage of accusations, Michael Fernandes, calling the attack 'opportunistic and utterly in bad taste', would remind his trade union colleagues in an open letter: 'Years ago, as a young boy, I used to pick cowdung [sic] for manure, draw well water for the flower and vegetable gardens, and (even as a college boy) sell flowers and vegetables in the market—all honest and hard work to help in making both ends meet!'[42]

Additionally, the Fernandes family cultivated fruits and vegetables in their garden. The home was ensconced amidst lush green and tall canopy trees: coconut and areca nut, mango and cashew, and a huge tamarind tree. There was also a pineapple and banana plantation—'we had many different kinds of bananas'. Fruits from these trees were sold in the market, while vegetables were grown for consumption. 'Throughout the year, we didn't have to buy vegetables.' Most garden work was done by the children. One had to climb the coconut trees and gather the fruit, clean up the debris of dead leaves and water the plants. Water was fetched from the in-house well. George being the eldest would organize fetching the water and climbing the trees. 'The time when we had to water those plants, especially the jasmine, and during the summer months, George used to organize us into some kind of assembly line carriage system. Someone filled the water into a brass vase, then George carried it till a certain point from where one of us took over and so on,' Paul Fernandes recalled.[43] The rows of jasmine plants were also sprinkled with human urine, the children's own or collected from the neighbours. 'It was the best nourishment,' as the plants flourished after they were given urine treatment.

The father made sure that they were brought up in a religious environment. John Joseph Fernandes went regularly to Sunday mass and took the children along. He was popular among the priests, a legacy of his father Jacob Fernandes, who had helped in setting up the parish church at Bijey. The priests were also partners in his business ventures. At first George, then his other brothers as well, helped the priests conduct the Sunday mass in which prayers from the Holy Bible were sung. They took turns to become altar boys at the church, and actively participated in the conduct of the Holy Communion. They were also active in the Sodality, a kind of gathering of Christian adolescents who offered themselves for religious and social service. Impressed by the church pomp, George regarded himself a 'church boy'.

The father was also concerned about his children's education. In 1939, close to the time when his mother left them, George was put into a church-administered, Kannada-medium primary school attached to St Francis Xavier Church. A year later, in June 1940, he was admitted into St Aloysius High School on the hillock, also run by the church. It was, and still is, a leading school in Mangalore. At St Aloysius nothing much has changed; the red building still stands at the same place. 'Near the school, on the other side of the road, there was a restaurant.' Father would drop him at school, pay for his lunch at that restaurant, and then head for his work.

'My father looked after me very well,' George averred. 'He gave me full freedom as long as I did well in my studies.' The father, however, regarded sports or other extracurricular activities a waste of time. No sports were allowed, not just at home but even in school. 'We all brothers were exempted from game classes which were held after the school hours as father had arranged for a doctor's certificate showing us weak and ill—incapable of undertaking strenuous physical work.' They had strict instructions to be back immediately after classes ended. They were not allowed to bring home storybooks from the school library either. At home, in the father's absence, children would organize sports at their own risk. They would collect neighbouring children and play cricket. 'We improvised the stiff rib of a coconut frond into a bat, and the ball was made out of solid, round stuff, wrapped around by a piece of cloth.' Even this was frowned upon by their father. 'We took the precaution and would cover up the telltale signs of our sport by spreading pebbles or grasses over the makeshift pitch. If he found us out playing, he would shout at us. Playing cards was absolutely no-no.' It was an old school of thought that believed children playing was a waste of time. There was no sparing the rod either. 'Father would use the stick to beat us.' Parents were encouraged by religious and other authorities to be strict in the matters of what children ate and wore, and the company they kept. Editorials in *Mangalore*, for instance, extol strict parenting, exhorting those perceived to be lax in their duties to nip in the bud the new-fangled habit of frequenting 'roadside coffee hotels'.[44]

In the absence of the mother, the father had his hands full. Each of his four sons was a target of his discipline, his anger, his reproach, and they all nurtured the resentment until late in their lives. His lonely ploughing of domesticity made him abrasive, and sometimes spurts of rage engulfed him with no one around to assuage his temper. The father's strict ways seemed frighteningly impersonal, but the boys devised their ways of coping. Sickly Michael was sent to calm their father down as he would rarely get thrashed because of his weak constitution. 'He would be less exacting with me,' Michael Fernandes recalled.[45]

* * *

In 1942, Mahatma Gandhi gave his 'Quit India' call. It was the year of 'Do or Die', of the 'August Kranti'. As a twelve-year-old, George participated in stone-throwing with other students from the top of the hill where the St Aloysius School's red building was located. Years later, while jailed at Hissar in a cage-like enclosure, he recalled what had happened on that particular August day in 1942.

> I was just twelve years old. Our school was at the foot of the hill on top of which was the St Aloysius College and High School. When I reached my school that morning, the boys from the college came down and told us to fold our books and walk out of the classes. I was one of those who ran up the long flight of steps to the college campus and with a few stones in my pocket quietly climbed atop the red building. The students had assembled in the rectangle below; the police were there in strength, with arms; the rector and other Jesuit priests were engaged in excited arguments with the student leaders. Slogans rent the air from all sides. I was then not aware of history, but I was a part of the excitement. There were three slogans that we kept reciting: 'Mahatma Gandhi ki Jai', 'Jawaharlal Nehru ki Jai' and 'Bharat Mata ki Jai'. Suddenly, a student produced a Gandhi cap and put it on the head of the rector. That was the signal for the police to act. They resorted to one of the bloodiest lathi charges and later opened fire. When we had emptied our pockets of the stones, some of us took shelter in the classrooms of the red building. Fortunately, for us, the police did not enter the room in which a few of us had hidden. After what seemed like ages, when the dust had settled down, we ventured out.[46]

The demonstration raised in him the first streak of differences with his father. He decided to learn Hindi. 'One day, after I returned from school, I went to my aunt and asked her to give me 2 annas (12.50 naye paise) to buy a Hindi book.' There was a small rivulet that divided his home from the rest. On the other side of this rivulet lived a Pandit who gave Hindi lessons at his home. George went to him and asked him to teach him as well. 'Somehow, I don't know how my father came to know about my visits to the Pandit. He took the Hindi text and tore it to pieces.' He let the Pandit know too that his son should not be allowed in his home. That brought an end to his Hindi classes. 'Then I began to learn swimming. My father put a stop to that too.' There was a wrestling arena on the other side of the house, and George decided he should learn wrestling. But by the time he had picked up one or two tricks of wrestling, his father appeared. Standing in the middle of the road, he growled at the wrestling guru to refrain from associating with his son: 'If I see him here I shall break your head.' 'I was made to give up wrestling too.'[47] But the wrestling lessons had a lifelong beneficial impact, giving him his famed endurance. The father's strict rule meant no deviation from their universe of house–school–church routine. However, if the father was strict and restricted their simple joys, he could also make exceptions. George was allowed to join the scouts, and his father bought shoes for him. 'He was the only one amongst us who wore shoes,' Michael Fernandes recalled. The family's tight-fisted economics didn't allow the luxury of shoes for all four children.

In 1946, when George finished his matriculation, the question arose about his future. Given the family's dire economic conditions, he desired to go to Bombay straight away in search of work, as most Mangalorean boys did. In that desire, there was also a wish to escape from the exacting discipline of the father. But his father was adamant—he wanted George to study further and go to college. A tense period at home ensued, and a compromise of sorts was worked out by the son himself. He proposed to go to a seminary to study for the priesthood. The father agreed. There was a seminary in Mangalore, but the sixteen-year-old George wanted to go to Bangalore. The father agreed and preparations began at once. In June 1946, when he left for Bangalore's St Mary Minor Seminary, his mother was still at her maternal home.

The church seminary was a residential theological school. The training was divided into two unequal parts, carried out by a minor and a major seminary. The training period could extend up to eight and a half years, two and a half of which were to be spent in the minor seminary and the remaining six at the major seminary before one qualified to be a priest. The Church language was Latin, which was primarily taught at the minor seminary, along with a course in philosophy. The seminary conducted examinations like any other educational institution to test a pupil's proficiency at various levels. A part of the budget to run seminaries came from the general public who donated at churches on Sundays. The other part came from Rome. Parents of the pupils enrolled in a seminary did not have to spend any money on their wards' upkeep; the institution offered free tuition and free boarding and lodging. This was a powerful incentive; however, it was religious fervour that led many families to dedicate their firstborns to Christ. At St Mary, when George joined, there were twenty-seven pupils in his batch. A photograph of the batch has survived with Lawrence Noronha, who was his batchmate.

The priesthood was not a profession but a vocation, a special calling to serve God and His people. A priest's duties were to teach, to sanctify and administer sacraments. He gave sermons about God, about the Son of God, Jesus, his life and his teachings to the laypeople entrusted to him. He was required to engage in deep and rigorous study and lead a life of privation. To bring God to others and be the instrument of

Courtesy: Lawrence Noronha

Group photograph at St Mary Seminary, Bangalore, George in blazer standing in the middle of the third row, 5th from the left. Among those squatting on the ground, 2nd from the left is Lawrence Noronha, from whose archive this photo is gift.

making others holy, he was to first sanctify himself, dedicate himself to God, be close to Him, have God in himself. A priest was a model for others to follow. To guide fellow human beings in their relationships and their everyday worldly affairs, a certain amount of interpersonal skills were required as well. Honesty, transparency, commitment and personal integrity were the needed qualities. It was, however, not necessary that to serve God, one had to become a priest. One could still serve God by developing integrity and love in whatever one did.

While still at minor seminary in Bangalore, George fell ill. Doctors at the seminary thought he had contracted tuberculosis and ordered him home. Once there, he recovered, but when the time came for him to leave, he asked his father to bring his mother home. His mother's condition at her maternal home had deteriorated and it was said she suffered from 'hysteria'. In the 1930s, 'hysteria' among women was the 'plague of our times'.[48] Hysteria was a routine diagnosis for women who deviated from the norm, many of them without opportunities, forced to spend their lives tending to domestic chores, and with selfish, prudish husbands who were unwilling or unable to make love to them. Isolated from her children and uncared for by her husband, Alice's behaviour had turned 'hysterical', requiring water treatment to cool her head, as was the general practice then. 'She would be brought to the brim of the well, and cold water drawn from the well would be poured on her head.'[49]

George's chosen vocation added to his decision to try and reconcile his parents. He was going to become a priest, and one of the priest's duties was to help build families. How could he from a broken home mend the pain of others? Such a contradictory situation played on his mind. George admitted that parental differences had made his childhood difficult: 'It was because of this situation that my childhood was a little hard.'[50] A now chastened and older John Fernandes conceded to his adolescent son's righteous imploring and brought his wife back.

George learnt Latin in the seminary. 'I did not just memorize words but managed to understand quite a lot of Latin phrases and words.' At the minor seminary, along with others, George produced an in-house journal. Contrary to the staid and serious nature of the seminary, it published jokes and humorous asides on priestly conduct. The establishment received it good-humouredly. After completing a year at the minor seminary, George pleaded with the Father–Rector to be promoted to the major seminary. Though he had completed less than half of the two and a half years required at the minor seminary, he felt confident enough to approach the authorities for promotion. 'I know everything; please allow me to appear in the examination,' George implored. When the Father–Rector declined, George insisted, 'Father, if I pass, you let me go up the ladder. If I fail, I shall be where I am. Nothing to lose!' He was allowed and he passed. He was to graduate to the major seminary when senior pupils who were studying there began to caution him against the move. 'I was told the rector of the major seminary, a French man, a veteran of World War II, was a tough, demanding man.'

George refused to be intimidated by the projected image of the rector. The first thing taught at the major seminary was not the theological nuances of Christianity but an introduction to comparative religions and how Christianity was distinct from the rest. After it, the student was instructed in Christian theology with all its accompanying ritual paraphernalia. George held some ideas on the way theological Christianity ought to be taught. He went to meet the Frenchman, the rector. He carried his work along and presented a chart of possible reforms to him. He explained. He illustrated. 'I was satisfied I had pleased him.' But the Frenchman was unhappy. He took it as an infraction of seminary rules. Some sixty years later, George recalled and explained his failure to convince the Frenchman of his ability. 'I had jumped. I might have sounded cocky. I had crossed the disciplinary line of the seminary because one is not supposed to override what already exists.' George's confidence was a breach of Church protocol. 'And from then onward, my plight was miserable.'

The seminary required reading from the Holy Bible before every meal, thanking God for each morsel of food received. The rector, to teach the cocksure young man a lesson, put the entire responsibility of recital from the Bible before meals on George. He understood it as a punishment for having crossed the boundary and would remember it even in his old age. The daily routine at the seminary comprised morning classes followed by indoor games after lunch, while in the evenings they played outdoors. Sunset was an invitation to prayers followed by the evening meal. By 9 p.m., pupils were expected to be in bed. George would take a book and read it under the bedclothes by the light of a candle. The warders did not find out, but obviously, the other students in the hall were aware of it. The books were borrowed from the seminary library, which had works on a wide variety of subjects besides religion. The only books forbidden were those with anti-Church content. He would use his stipend money to buy books for himself. In the cantonment area, where St Mary was located, books were always available from homeward-bound British soldiers who would sell them cheap, or sometimes even give them away if one cultivated their friendship. George cultivated a few such friendships and received many books as gifts, which enriched his stock. He later recounted, 'I had a very good library with about 300 books.' When he moved to St Peter's Major Seminary (named after the apostle who was given the key of the church by Christ himself, and who is considered the first pope), George took his books along. Even ordained priests would come to borrow books from him.

In the seminary, all activities were conducted in groups. Pupils would always hang out together. But George retained his individuality. Having learnt at home to do his own work, when night fell, while everyone slept, George washed his clothes. He was made one of the student-procurators, with the responsibility of procuring everyday provisions for the seminary. Along with other boys, he cycled to the market to buy the provisions. On such trips, George and his friends would sometimes visit theatres to watch films. In this way he watched some European and American movies which had content that bore the approval of the Roman Catholic church.

At the seminary, English was the medium of instruction; Kannada was seldom used; in fact, it was discouraged. George was disturbed by the closed-door, isolationist policy of the Church. He was further disturbed by practices within the seminary where there were corruptions of all kinds. Money that parents sent for their wards was kept with the rector or deposited in a private bank under the rector's control rather than in the seminary's bank account. Sometimes, the private bank would go bust and money would be lost. There was discrimination too: the food served to the seminarians was of inferior quality, whereas priests enjoyed sumptuous food at the high table. Priests were seen as representing Jesus Christ, yet here they were leading a hypocritical life. They had their place to meet; they would smoke and drink. They had a lifestyle that tended to be more 'exhibitionist than substantive'. George's true cognizance of discrimination, although the seeds had been sown at home, began at the seminary in Bangalore. 'I couldn't reconcile all these.' He decided to 'jump the wall'.[51] 'I do not like to sermonize', he would state many years later in a speech as a first-time minister in the Central government, 'I tried to be a priest once and gave it up.'[52]

3

The Revolutionary Road

From the earliest times, the papal church at Rome sent missions abroad for making religious conversions. One of the oldest such missions was the Society of Jesus—in short, the Jesuits. As the Catholic population in Canara increased, they invited Rome to send the Jesuits to their region. The Jesuits arrived in the middle of the 1880s and opened institutions for healthcare and education that are even today much admired. Soon, with every village having a church and a school attached to it, Mangalore became an educational hub, and the educated began to move out in search of opportunity and prosperity. Bombay was their most favoured destination. The Jesuits, however, were not the only missionaries to arrive in Mangalore. Much before them had come the Protestant Basel Mission, named so as they hailed from the German-speaking Swiss town of Basel. They found that the Brahmin population of South Canara did not favour their religion; their preaching to gatherings in a village square or a bazaar were much reviled and sometimes forcefully disrupted. As if in defeat, the Basel Mission turned their activities' focus on the Billavas, a numerically dominant Sudra caste.[1] After much negotiation and failure, across many tough years, the Billavas became the largest group of converts made by the Basel Mission. It is ironical that the Basel Mission, who, discovering caste to be the staunchest impediment to their work, had vowed to never compromise with it, found their religion, much to their chagrin, identified solely with this particular caste. But whatever their evangelical achievements, which many see as modest, the Basel Mission gave Mangalore several firsts. They founded many modern industries, the primary ones being tile manufacturing and the printing press. To overcome the caste-based occupational hierarchy, they worked to change the livelihood patterns of the Billavas, who traditionally were toddy tappers and mercenary soldiers. In due course, the Basel Mission became a single-caste theological branch on India's west coast so significant that Protestant Christianity was headquartered at Mangalore. The Jesuits had more success with the upper castes who, in order to identify with their origin, began tracing their ancestry to a village in Goa, a rediscovered family deity (*kuldeva*) or a pre-conversion family name like Prabhu, Kamath, etc.[2] It is not that the Jesuits did not work among the poorest and the lowest, some 'untouchable' castes were indeed converted by the Italian priests. But these remained unintegrated in the Catholic world, called (as they still are) the new converts or RC, a pejorative contraction for Rice Christians.[3]

Many sacrifices went into the making of Christianity in India. From early on, as missionaries who came from Europe's cooler climates suffered and even perished as brittle fries in the hot pan of Mangalore, hopes of expanding their religion went through cycles of optimism and dejection. As the Gandhi-led national movement began to take shape, the Mahatma criticized the missions' quest for religious converts. At a Catholic Congress, held at Nagpur, the session's president, one George Joseph, disagreed with Gandhi's 'view that Christian Missions while providing educational and medical relief should abstain from proselytization.'[4] Taking strong exception, he said, those works were 'not an end but only a means to the conversion of the human beings to the Catholic faith'. The Catholic Congress resolved that more 'systematic and organized efforts be made for the evangelization of "untouchables"'. At the same time, they asked from the British rulers constitutional safeguards to protect their 'special interests'. Requesting separate boarding facilities for Catholic girls in schools and colleges in order not to 'wound . . . our tenderest susceptibilities', an office-bearer of the Catholic Association of South Canara wrote, 'We have our own social rules and customs which manifest themselves in the food we eat and in other habits of life and in this we differ not only from our Hindu and Mohammedan brethren but also from the Protestant Christians who racially belong to a different stock from ourselves. Hence, living together with any of these is objectionable to us not only on religious but also on social and caste grounds.'[5] They were also against Christian participation in the freedom movement.

Many years later, while imprisoned in a cage-like enclosure guarded by an armed squad, George would recall the day of 15 August 1947 when he was training for the priesthood at St Mary's Minor Seminary. 'One of the regrets of my life is missing the thrill and excitement of 15 August 1947,' he wrote in the isolated confines of the jail.[6] 'The greatest day in contemporary Indian history passed by without as much as even causing a minor disturbance in the daily routine of our seminary life.' The 'distinctive culture' Catholics claimed was merely one, two or at most 400 years old in India, had supplanted one that had existed for millennia before. If they had desired, they could have reverted to their ancestral faith, but it was not to be. It was not just that the colonial power had nurtured a kindred religion and socially divisive ideology, narrow community interests had developed as well. A perusal of a list of 400 members of the Catholic Association reveals that they were landlords, tile manufacturers, government servants and other privileged groups who had a vested interest in the continuance of a system that outwardly at least was under threat from the socialist-minded Congress. They called themselves 'Catholics first and Indians afterwards'.[7] Doing well, in British rule's preservation, they saw their welfare and happiness. They were social conservatives as well. A Catholic women's conference held in December 1935 at St Agnes College, a premier woman's college in Mangalore, resolved 'to put up a determined fight' against the birth control movement. They described it as 'the most sinister, deadly and anti-Christian among the enemies of the home'.[8]

Even after 1886, when Mangalore became an independent diocese, the European priests continued to administer its major parishes. Around the time George was born, a great ferment arose when bishops of Indian descent began to be appointed. It was a matter of much rejoicing and pride for the community.[9] Soon, Mangalore became a breeding ground of Indian-origin priests. Learned priests from here were sent across the country to administer churches. It was said, 'There was no family but gave at least two of its members, and generally the best, to religion.'[10] Entirely a male bastion, the vocation carried both religious stature and high social prestige. A priest was a gossamer thread interwoven with others to hold together the world of the Church, from the tiniest of chapels in a village to the highest at the Vatican. He was part of the Church bureaucracy, and his position in the hierarchy conferred power and privileges on him. There was a social mobility attached to serving the Church, which was unavailable in other fields in the 1940s. A priest could aspire to not just the highest position as represented by the Pope, he could even one day be declared a saint if his piety was adequately documented and represented (and this applied to a nun as well).[11] This led to a tradition among Catholic families that one child would become a priest or a nun. In some cases, children themselves made the choice, much to the delight of adults: young boys would pray to be taken to a seminary or girls to a convent. It was a divine calling as you didn't choose to become a priest or nun; it was the Lord who selected you to be in His service. In turn, your choice won you the people's deference. At every location inhabited by Christians, priests and nuns had exclusive residential complexes in gated compounds where their needs were taken care of. At the same time, they abided by the discipline of the Church and acted according to the rules set out by the Vatican. Some such rules were harsh but were required to induce religious asceticism and piety. They were to be lifelong celibates and required to abjure family life. Any deviation was heresy, for which their voices could be muzzled and careers and creativity repressed. The Church, like any powerful institution, excommunicated people who did not align with it.[12]

In order to prepare himself for the priestly vocation, George attended (St Mary's Minor and St Peter's Major) seminary in Bangalore from June 1946 onwards, until December 1948 when he dropped out of St Peter's and returned to Mangalore. Dropouts were common, and could occur at any level for various reasons. A pupil could drop out due to parental illness, family duties or waning interest. Those who simultaneously pursued a secular education while also enrolled at a seminary for religious training sometimes dropped out when they found a job or saw better prospects in some other field. Ugly spats or sexual harassment made pupils drop out as well.[13] Although no longer a compulsory subject, learning Latin then was a deterrent that expedited dropouts.[14] A large batch by the end of the training could be reduced to just a trickle.[15] Yet, in the estimation of Catholic families, leaving the seminary midway was to invite fire-breathing hell.[16] Upon his return, George found his father sullen and bad-tempered. George had gone against his father's closely held religious principles. Many members of his extended family were in a religious vocation, and a priest in the family, he held, was God's visit to the home. Therefore, the abrupt return of George meant divine rejection, that he had failed the test of God. It was a lifelong stigma. Moreover, the seminary provided free education and boarding. For a family of humble origins, the economic burden of having a seminary-returned son was a worrisome prospect. Its repercussions went deep and wide. The father was well regarded in the church fraternity. The association fetched clients in his insurance work, and this could be affected by his son's defection. He felt let down by his eldest son, more so because it was George who in the first place had insisted on going to the seminary.

George lived in his father's home, but to avoid unpleasantness he spent time in his maternal home. He would also bicycle up to Bajpe to be with the people working on the family's fields. 'Some 24 kilometres away from our home, we had our ancestral land,' an eighty-year-old George gave words to his childhood angst against his father. 'Sometimes, disputes would arise about the quantity of produce or its share to us. Father would get extremely angry. He would call a thug and have these people thrashed. That in turn made me angry with my father. I used to think they were such good people, their children were so much attached to me, their parents had so much of love [sic] for me, why then should my father have them beaten up and thrown out.'[17]

George began to rehearse in a choir for a Christmas mass. The pomp of the Church still held an irresistible fascination for the young man. But something finally broke when the head priest decided that his nephew and not George would lead the mass. Humiliated, a day or two before Christmas in December 1948, he stomped out of the church. Sometime in the early 1960s, annoyed with the local Catholic community in Bombay, an irreverent George would casually speak of his intention to organize a bandh in the city on the day of the Pope's arrival. When concerned Catholics approached him, he told them that the thought did cross his mind but he had dismissed it.[18] Years later, he would write a polemic 'Why am I a Christian?'[19] A Christianity divided by caste, creed and wealth was not his, he wrote. He had become inwardly critical and was not moved blindly by the passions of dogma. The seminary experience had made him question social and religious priorities. There was growing in him—he would write of someone else, but the words befitted him equally well—'a tendency to dislike the excessive religious ceremony and orthodoxy'.[20] Once, in jest, it was insinuated in the church circle that if he had continued with the Church, he might have gone up the ladder but would have ended up breaking it. But that could be wisdom in hindsight, in the light of his later-day political activities.

Soon came the dilemma of what to do. He could just not while away his time. There were pressures from the family, and he was restless. At first, he followed in the footsteps of his father, taking up the work of an insurance agent, but as a separate entity, independent of John Jos Fernandes & Sons. Then, he dabbled in a few wholesale businesses; in one endeavour, Michael Fernandes remembered, young George, emulating their father's ventures, bought a carton of shaving blades of a non-branded make for retail sale. But because they were of poorly made, they remained unsold and became rusted and unusable. Finally, he heard of a monthly magazine attached to a weekly journal of the newly formed Socialist Party. Inspired, he launched *Konkani Yuvak*, a four-page magazine in Kannada script.[21] On advice from friends, he undertook a journey to Bombay and received a welcoming response from the Mangalorean community settled there. After a short stay, he returned with money to further his publication work. It was during this time that he began occasionally to contribute to Bombay's *Blitz*, which paid him as well for the pieces published.[22] After an issue or two of *Konkani Yuvak*, he front-paged a provocative article titled '*Dev Na?*' ('Does God Exist?'). The irreverent tone attracted attention, and during Sunday mass, in church after church, presiding priests asked the faithful to shun the magazine. 'If you have it in your house, throw it away. Keep it, and you will go to hell!' That's how George recollected the priestly negation of his publication venture. The rupture with his father having further deepened and widened, he spent minimal time at home. On 13 July 1949, while leading a vagabond life in Mangalore, he joined a fledgling Socialist Party, but not before putting some conditions on his membership.

* * *

Some 2000 kilometres north-east of Mangalore on the borders of present-day Bihar with Uttar Pradesh—in a plague-ridden, flood-prone region that changed its geography as the river flowing through changed its course—Jayaprakash Narayan was born. The village was Sitab-Diyara in Bihar's Sahabaad district, and the year 1902. He would become the star campaigner of socialism in India. In 1920, a young Jayaprakash dropped out of his Patna College in response to Gandhi's call for boycotting British-run educational institutions. Soon after this, he left for America to pursue self-financed higher studies. Once there, he worked at various odd jobs to earn enough to support himself. As his biographer tells us, Jayaprakash washed dishes and served food in restaurants, polished floors and worked in boiler rooms, coaling booths, barber shops, etc. He cleaned toilets and worked as a shoeshine boy, hawked creams and lotions on streets. But the hardships did not turn him into a tough or thick-skinned man. He retained his vulnerabilities, his mystique and, worse, his wooliness. In 1929, after a seven-year hiatus, he returned to India a confirmed Marxist, to find his wife Prabhavati Devi living in Gandhi's ashram at Wardha, having taken a vow of celibacy. This gave rise to a dichotomous situation that would weigh on him throughout his political career and cause him to flounder repeatedly at the altar of ideology. When he went to meet his wife at Wardha, he found himself gravitating towards Jawaharlal Nehru, who happened to be there. He later wrote to the Mahatma that his ideas were 'to a great extent similar to' Nehru's, and asked if he could work with the latter.[23] Gandhi consented, and Nehru sent an invitation. Jayaprakash (or JP as he popularly came to be known) was offered a position in the Labour Department of the All India Congress Committee (AICC) at Allahabad. There wasn't much he could achieve there though, as it was a short-lived tenure, cut short by the death of his mother when he resigned his position.[24]

But even in that short period, Jawaharlal Nehru showed remarkable hospitality towards the recruit. JP had taken his wife along and rented a bungalow to house them. It became expensive for him, living as he was on a salary paid from Congress funds.[25] A concerned Jawaharlal invited JP and his wife to stay at the Nehru ancestral home, Anand Bhavan. His acceptance within the Nehru household showed the confidence, mutual admiration and friendship that had developed between the two of them. Throughout their political interaction, even when disputes arose, their friendship endured; in his letters and conversations, JP always addressed Jawaharlal Nehru as 'Bhai' and was among the very few who could do so. There was a third axis of Ram Manohar Lohia (1910–67) who was also a Jawaharlal protégé, joining the Congress Foreign Department and working with him for twelve long years before parting ways on the eve of Independence. All his life, after his return from Humboldt University in Germany, Lohia would be called 'Doctor Saheb' by his followers and colleagues; yet, truth be told, he never submitted a printed copy of his thesis to the university and therefore was never awarded a degree.[26] It is in the context of Nehru's relationship with Jayaprakash and Lohia that some suggest, not unfairly, that the Congress Socialist Party (CSP) which came into being in 1934 was incubated not in Patna or Bombay, not even in Nasik Jail, as history books faithfully report, but at Allahabad, in Nehru's Anand Bhavan home.[27] Throughout the freedom struggle, and even after, most of the veteran socialist leaders remained deeply intertwined with Jawaharlal's politics. They received their politics as well as an ideology from him, and in their conception, socialism was something that Jawaharlal must put into practice when he came to rule India.[28]

Socialism is a beautiful word, so said Gandhi. The beauty of it had attracted India's young, educated and dynamic individuals as its ardent admirers in the days of the struggle for national freedom. When the idea of a socialist party within the Indian National Congress was mooted, however, a spate of critical voices was heard. When Acharya Narendra Dev, the venerable teacher of Kashi Vidyapith and erudite Marxist scholar, whose face always wore a famished look, sent a manifesto on behalf of the motley group of little-known young intellectuals who called themselves members of the Congress Socialist Party to Gandhi for his comments, the latter was bemused.[29] Finding the ideas in the manifesto trite and unconvincing, the Mahatma called it 'intoxicating', adding he feared all 'intoxicants'. Socialism then was a competing idea to divide the national wealth to achieve the equitable distribution goal.[30] The idea as such was not a novel one. But how it was to be done was. The socialist way was to let the wealth produced in society be owned by the state. Many in the Congress Party did not like this hankering after socialism, as they thought it was not an indigenous idea. Sardar Patel saw an espousal of socialism as a precursor to a split in the Congress itself. He said, 'Socialism could not be brought about by reading Lenin,' and asked the socialists to acquaint themselves with the reality of India by 'going to the peasant'. Then, the all-powerful Congress Working Committee (CWC) warned the socialists against 'loose talks'. S.K. Patil, by electorally defeating whom George would don the mantle of 'giant-killer', putting an end to the Congress veteran's political career, said, rather mockingly, 'A socialist party within the Congress is a meaningless thing.'[31] According to him, the Congress was already socialist, and Gandhi and Nehru its most ardent exponents.

In response, an indignant Jayaprakash, calling the Congress leadership 'reactionary', asked his comrades to redouble efforts to 'overthrow the leadership'.[32] But despite the bluster, JP recognized the threat to their nebulous organization, that the Congress might just 'drive us out'.[33] He was quick to defend the socialists against the insinuation of being 'disruptionists'. He lowered the pitch by declaring that their position was not that the Congress either accept their creed or they leave. In a conciliatory note, he said, 'We merely place our views before the Congress and the country and, through the most proper and legitimate methods, expect to bring the Congress to our point of view.' Jayaprakash claimed that although they remained within the Congress today, theirs was a venture for the future. 'We shall go to the peasants,' Jayaprakash responded to Patel with characteristic conviction, derived less from intemperate youthfulness than from the belief in one's ideological and moral superiority, a self-image that remained with him till his last, 'but we shall go to them not with a spinning wheel but with the militant force of economic programme'.[34] Claiming they were there to infuse 'content' into India's urge for freedom, Jayaprakash contended that the Congress had failed to adequately link the freedom movement with the everyday economic struggles of the mass of Indians.[35] Indicting the party, he said it had failed the workers and peasantry. Gandhi's khadi was 'totally inadequate and incomplete'[36] and its workers were completely unaware of 'what an economic approach to the peasant is'.[37] Jayaprakash in the 1930s was too much of a Marxist to toe the line of Gandhi. He was critical of Gandhi's views on several matters. Without himself being adequately informed of the Indian reality and being ideologically firm on Marxism, JP's criticism derived not just its content but also its language from Jawaharlal.

As Jawaharlal was the first among Gandhi's close colleagues to raise disturbing questions on his politics, he became a draw for young India.[38] A new politics was waiting to be invented, to interrogate internal socio-economic issues. This new politics had Jawaharlal at its fore. While Jawaharlal maintained a public silence, the opposition to Gandhi orchestrated by the socialists in 1934 mounted to an extent that the latter was forced to resign from the Congress. Gandhi, in the view of Nehru and others of his ilk, was not 'socialist' enough.[39] If socialism was to take roots, according to its advocates, not just Gandhi had to be reshaped—it was not a good idea, after all, to jettison him completely, given his mass appeal—but the organization, the Indian

National Congress, of which he was the leader, had to be captured as well. This was the first left-wing challenge from within the Congress to his leadership; in their conception, Gandhi was past his political expiry date. Hitherto, and later as well, the right wing was unrelenting in its opposition to him. While Gandhi resigned his primary membership of the Congress, Jawaharlal became the president for two consecutive terms, leading the Congress to victory in elections held under the newly enacted Government of India Act, 1935. Jawaharlal, therefore, was in the ascendant. Gandhi, in contrast, was in the deep morass, searching for ideological as well as spiritual solace in the wilderness of Wardha where, at a village Segaon, he established his new, fledgling idea for reinvigorating rural India in a hamlet he called Sevagram, the village of service.

The CSP was Nehru's firing line in his ideological tussle with Gandhi. In 1963, while outlining the history of the socialist movement in India, Lohia admitted that having regarded Gandhi conservative and Nehru radical, the socialists had sided with the latter.[40] Without engendering many recriminations, one may safely assert that the options before Gandhi were scarce. There were three categories of people to choose from: first, his close followers like Vinoba Bhave; second, his political colleagues including J.B. Kripalani and Rajendra Prasad; and third, those personally close to him but ideologically distanced, which included JP. But Gandhi's close followers were intellectually defunct. The 1948 post-Gandhi meeting of Gandhians at Sevagram, the chronicle of which until recently was in the custody of the Sarva Seva Sangh, an organization whose establishment was the outcome of that meeting, amply proved the intellectual bankruptcy of the Gandhians.[41] No one came anywhere close to Nehru, who remained independent while accepting Gandhi's leadership at his convenience. The socialists' relationship with both these top leaders of India's national liberation movement underwent perceptible change in later years. Although Gandhi would be respectfully critical and differ with their viewpoint, Nehru would not hesitate either to mobilize them under him or to castigate them for being reckless critics.

The socialists had to tackle the two most important political relationships that underpinned and determined not just their genesis but also their survival. To the Congress, they were organizationally bound, conceived and nurtured within the parent organization, and to the Communist Party of India (CPI) they owed an ideological kinship, both being Marxism-inspired. Seeing itself as a Marxist party, the CSP competed with the communists for the ideological niche, and bound as it was to the Congress, pitted itself against the parent for organizational space. The socialist quest for power was so self-righteously founded that they stumbled on both these two relationships that proved at first disorienting and eventually fatal. The serious flaw in their relation with the Congress was misjudging the significance of their foster mother. They forgot what an advantage it was to have the Congress's tacit tolerance and broad platform to their socialist credo. And with the communists, who sometimes were their fellow travellers on the road to revolution and at others the repulsive agents provocateurs of an international conspiracy, they proved as much opportunists as they accused the latter of being. The communists, with the Communist International and Soviets at Moscow on their side, proved more resourceful than them, causing much heartburn. JP wrote to Subhas Bose in 1940, proposing a new left party as 'Congress no longer remains an instrument for revolutionary action'. He asserted that the new party would not be anti-Communist International as it 'should indeed have contacts with Moscow and seek the aid of the Soviet in our revolution'. He further said the CSP was to be kept going merely as a cover to deflect Congress malevolence.[42] The socialists' overtures to the communists, either for power-sharing or just electorally, remained ambiguous, driven as they were from their frustration at having lost to the CPI in their bid to forge a relationship with Moscow. Their antipathy turned vituperative after the Quit India Movement, which, if for the socialists proved their nationalist credentials, established the communists as betrayers of the nationalist cause.

The year 1948 began on a bad note for the socialists. Gandhi, who had ironically been emerging in his last years as a bridge between them and the Congress, was murdered. Marginalized during his lifetime, reduced to a larger-than-life Congress emblem, he died a perfect death. Gandhi's mortal disappearance changed the fortunes of the socialists. In 1946, after JP was released from prison, Gandhi had proposed him for the Congress presidency, an idea vetoed, ironically, by Jawaharlal Nehru who harped on divisions among the socialists.[43] Their revolutionary role in the Quit India Movement had won them public acclaim. But despite this and Gandhi's advocacy, socialists—'Augusters' they were then called—were denied positions in the Congress hierarchy. Long accustomed to seeing Congress as a conservative bastion, they refused to mellow down, and persisted with their characterization of it being run by 'ancient people' with 'narrow, sectarian, static' views.[44] JP pitched for the organic assimilation of socialists in the body-polity of the Congress to infuse a new life in 'a machine that had stopped running'. But in the scramble for power, an ageing leadership, as Ram Manohar Lohia would opine years later, spurned their overtures.[45] Ceasing to be a movement, the Congress had crystallized into a parliamentary party.[46] Amending its constitution, debarring the dual membership, it first forced the socialists to drop 'Congress' from their name, and then, soon after Gandhi's death, ordered them to voluntarily dissolve or leave.[47]

So, in March 1948, a month after Gandhi's murder, the Congress Socialists gathered at Nasik to take a call on their ever quibbling, querulous relationship with the Congress.[48] Fifteen years before, in Nasik Jail, the blueprint for a socialist party within the Congress had been drafted. Now was the time to sever that connection. There were apprehensions among the socialists about life post-divorce. 'Who will listen to us? Will we not get isolated and crushed?' JP wondered.[49] Nehru, at whose behest—and, as some old-timers have claimed, at whose home, once again—the Congress Socialists announced their separation from the Congress due to 'ideological incompatibility', kept his silence at the development. If there would be anyone who drew political mileage from the severance, it was Nehru. He gained in the breakaway socialists a bulwark against his cabinet colleague and home minister, Sardar Vallabhbhai Patel, who had been at the receiving end of the socialists' political rhetoric since the beginning of their journey.[50]

Their first salvo after having largely decided on separation from the Congress was against Sardar Patel, accusing him of being lax about the Mahatma's safety and lenient towards the RSS. The new party called itself the Socialist Party and now aspired to replace the Congress as the party of government. Else, they would constitute 'a democratic, free, fearless, and healthy Opposition to the party in power'.

Many years later, this decision to separate from the Congress would still be subjected to scrutiny for its effect on the socialist movement in India; they argued over its necessity and fretted about its correctness. This decision breathed life in and gave a flying start to the new party, but simultaneously it sapped it, raised doubts on its motivations, generated mutual distrust among its adherents and gradually weakened it over the years, so much so that when it met its end, it was a relief to everyone around, to its flag carriers as well as to its pall-bearers. It was truly a momentous decision; it would inspire and caution, in equal measure, a series of political moves that would eventually end in the party's rolling over into the history books. Now, it can be said, safely perhaps and with impeccable historical hindsight, that the fate of the political organization, founded in 1934 and annihilated in 1977, was doomed at its very genesis. The ideological choices that it made, the political trajectory it took, the power games that it so ambitiously unfolded, had just one end and that was its end. Of course, between what was founded in 1934 and what went bust in 1977, two years before the death of its veteran leader JP (in that sense, it was with JP that the party was born and died), there were a series of tragic mishaps that define socialism in India.

* * *

It was this Socialist Party born in 1934 that a nineteen-year-old George joined on 13 July 1949 in Mangalore. His amateurish publishing venture had come to an unceremonious closure with the controversy it had raised on the existence of God. But it left a trail that opened newer opportunities. A printing press owned by a Socialist Party sympathizer that printed *Konkani Yuvak* also printed a magazine *Raithawani* (farmers' voice). It was here that George met Ammembal Balappa (1922–2014), who then was the secretary of the local Socialist Party. Impressed by the editorial content of *Raithawani*, and at Balappa's urging, George joined the Socialist Party. Initially, as he recalled much later, he was not particularly enthusiastic about it. 'I rejected it as much as I could and I made some jokes also what Samajwad means—if you have two *beedi*s, give me one.' In keeping with the initial socialist approach, George was an ardent and self-proclaimed Nehru supporter. One of the three conditions he put before his comrades for joining the Socialist Party was that Jawaharlal Nehru would be retained as the prime minister in case they defeated the Congress Party at the polls.[51]

> The first task allotted to me by the district party was to help in organizing a district-level conference of the agricultural workers and small farmers of the district. Ammembal Balappa who had been imprisoned in the 1942 movement and was one of the leading lights of the party in the district was my mentor in those early days. Balappa and I set out, visiting centres of party activities among the farmers and agricultural workers, from Mangalore to Coondapur in the northern tip of the district. It was a tour undertaken by bus and in some areas on foot and lasted about eight or ten days. This was within weeks of joining the party. I was a cub who had yet to learn a lot on what socialism was all about and, more so, on the organization.[52]

As they walked from one area to another, the landowning farmers on one occasion were waiting for them. Having heard of their intentions to organize the farm workers and small farmers, the landowners ordered their lathi-wielding guards to attack them. The police sided with the landlords, making the situation difficult for the socialists.

Then, George was also given the responsibility of a beedi-makers' union and unions of workers at two small eateries. His increasing involvement made his father angry as he thought, 'The devil has got into his head.' Trade union work across the world was a communist activity, which was anti-religion and therefore anathema to a Catholic family like his. And from that point on, the disagreements became unbearable and led eventually to George's ouster from home. If the father was intolerant, George did not help the matter either and became averse to going home. His mother was there, but fearing greater agitation if she intervened, kept quiet. Many years later, when he was more settled, he would speak of the chill he felt when he was 'thrown out of my house by my father. . . . I had only a short pant and a shirt on me.'[53]

When George left the house, not knowing where to go, he first went to the big maidan in the centre of the city where on one corner a radio station was located. He thought he would sleep in the maidan itself. But that was not to be. 'A little later, two-three policemen came and asked who I was. Why was I sleeping here?' He told them he couldn't go home and so was sleeping out. Unsatisfied, they told him to get up and move. He wandered away to Hampankatta, a busy marketplace, a little distance from the maidan. 'And I went climbing up a building which at that time housed a central post office.' He stretched out on the floor. 'Someone came and asked who I was.' George blurted out about needing a place to sleep that night. 'The wretched place was haunted,' he recalled an experience that had left him spooked. Next morning, he went to the party office in a back lane of the Felix Pais Bazaar. The party colleagues offered him a place to stay in the office itself. In the neighbourhood was a restaurant named Light of Persia, run by a Parsi gentleman, who called him and said, 'Have a bath in our bathroom. And you shall have your breakfast here.' Word about his predicament spread. A friend of his father's, Dr Naggappa Alva, later to become a minister in the Karnataka government, sent for him. 'You need not worry about your food,' Dr Alva told him.

After George took over editorial work at *Raithawani*, its so-far-small circulation began to increase. One day the printing press owner, a man of considerable means, came to the party office. When leaving, he left his coat behind. Next day he returned, said his coat had a Rs 100 note which he now discovered was not there and accused George of the theft. Balappa and others stood there silently while the man was accusing him. Hurt by the malicious allegation, an infuriated George stormed out of the office, swearing against the socialism of lies and promising to have nothing more to do with the Socialist Party.

Balappa came running after him. A teary-eyed George upbraided him for keeping quiet when he was being accused of stealing. Balappa tried to console George. He explained that after he had raised the circulation of *Raithawani* the man wanted it back. He was looking for an excuse. 'This man is wanting to get you out of the party and the paper. You have to fight back.' Balappa's words 'electrified' George. It was about midnight. Both friends retired to Balappa's house. 'I came to the conclusion that night that unless I fight, I cannot survive in public life. One cannot be sentimental about it.' From now on he would not take any personal slight, insult or humiliation as serious enough to merit attention in public life. The important thing was not the humiliation or insult thrown at you, but one's unwavering and continuous commitment to the cause.

Soon after, while he was working with the Socialist Party, George met Placid D'Mello (1919–58), who had come to Mangalore after being externed from Bombay because of his work among the dock workers in the city. A resident of Belmond near Chikmagalur, D'Mello after his matriculation had moved to Bombay in 1936, to look for gainful work.[54] A series of fortuitous encounters brought him to the Bombay docks and he took the job of a casual tally clerk in a stevedore company. Those days, most tally clerks were Konkani-speaking, English-knowing Catholic migrants from South Canara.[55] His job was to make an inventory of things loaded into the ship or unloaded on the dock. The plight of the *godi* (dock and port) workers impelled D'Mello to engage with the workers' issues. Soon, he was in the thick of trade union activities among them. He also became politically engaged, joining first a group led by ex-revolutionary Manabendra Nath Roy (1887–1954) and later, when it was disbanded, the Congress Party. In March 1948, when the Socialist Party established its independent existence, D'Mello became a socialist. While a Royist, he met many other trade union activists and budding politicians, important among them Yashwantrao Balwantrao Chavan (1913–84), the Maratha politician who in a decade would be the chief minister of Bombay. As a leader of the dock workers, D'Mello demanded a war bonus owing to greater profits and an end to the casual employment that entailed much exploitation. He did not just make demands but set deadlines for the authorities to act. A degree of violence was implicit in D'Mello's unionism. To take on a combination of dock officials and labour contractors (the *muqaddams* and *toliwallah*s), a mafia approach was adopted. In November 1947, matters came to a boil when the disaffected dock workers struck work. Keen to carve out space for themselves, the socialists became aggressive on the labour front. In the context of a newly independent country in the throes of political turmoil due to Partition and the migration of millions, the labour strikes became an irritant that the government was in no mood to tolerate. The socialists were clubbed together by Nehru under what he called 'disruptive forces' who were 'urging workers to go on strike causing suspension of work and production'.[56] Nehru called their industrial strikes in Bombay, despite a commitment to maintaining truce, 'very irresponsible'.[57]

D'Mello was jailed twice, and the third time, when the government wanted him out of its way, it decided to extern him from Bombay. Looking for total dominance, the Congress in 1948 carved out its trade union federation, Indian National Trade Union Congress (INTUC), from the existing All India Trade Union Congress (AITUC), which had come to be dominated by the communists. For his trade union belligerency at the Bombay port, D'Mello and some of his colleagues were arrested under the Bombay Public Security Act. Some were jailed at Nasik, and D'Mello, being from outside Bombay, was externed. In April 1949, he arrived in Mangalore, which then was part of Madras. In a eulogy written some years later, George wrote, 'A revolutionary is a revolutionary whether he be in Bombay, in Madras or for that matter in any part of the globe.'[58]

When D'Mello arrived in Mangalore, so small was the Socialist Party's spread that it took him a month to locate its office at Felix Pais Bazaar in a double-storey building. Describing the drama of his first meeting with D'Mello, George said he came to the party office and stood in the doorway with his imposing six-foot personality. He sat at one end of the hall, surrounded by Balappa and others. An irreverent but reticent George sat a little distance removed from the group. He had his pride, having fought his father on the matter of his political conviction and launched his journal. In his way, he was already a leader of sorts, having formed a trade union of workers at two hotels. He had also tried, unsuccessfully though, to organize the peasantry along with Balappa. Midway through their conversation, George cracked his joke about what socialism meant: 'If you have two beedis, you give me one.' D'Mello was taken aback by the insolence of the upstart. He shouted at him to remind him that this was the Socialist Party office and he would not tolerate any idiocy. Temperamentally the two men were quite similar; hot-headed and passionate with a strong sense of their destiny, although the senior D'Mello was graver and George a young adventurer. Their first meeting ended abruptly. D'Mello, who had momentarily lost his composure, was not one to hold a grudge, and Balappa had briefed him about the potential of the recruit. So, moments later, D'Mello followed him to the door of the printing press. George was hurt. He had left the seminary. He had left the Bijey Church. He had left home. But he had clung to a self-belief. D'Mello clambered up the steps and said, 'You are very angry, are you?' 'Yes, I am,' came the cocky reply. 'Come, let's go,' D'Mello commanded. George was reticent. 'I have work to do,' he said stiffly. But D'Mello would not let him off easily. They both went to Light of Persia. It was to lay the foundation of a relationship that would leave on George the greatest impression.[59]

On the eve of 'Independence Day', 26 January 1950, George gave his first public speech at Gandhi (Central) Maidan. It was organized by the party, and George spoke in Kannada. The country had been independent for over two years now. Elections were the talk of the town. George, who had all along been pro-Nehru, within a few months, in keeping with the Socialist Party's turnaround, got into Nehru-bashing. George said what the Socialist Party after its break from the Congress was drumming all over the country. Congress had done so little in so many months after Independence, he said. A man in rags stood nearby, smoking his beedi, listening to what George was saying, how very little had happened. And the man took his beedi out of his mouth and spewed, 'What would have happened?' Nonplussed, George left his speech midway.

D'Mello rented a house in Mangalore, and George took up abode with him. They were both so similar and yet their habits were poles apart. D'Mello, the chain-smoker (he used to smoke Cavender cigarettes), advised George against his habit of consuming coffee. George, the non-smoker, while still staying with D'Mello, regularly went out of the house late in the night. One day, a perplexed D'Mello asked George, 'What is this every night you go out for?' 'To have a cup of coffee to keep me awake for the nights of reading and writing,' George replied. 'Oh!' D'Mello said, and after a thoughtful pause, added, 'If you drink a glass of water, you will still be able to do your work.'

Of the three people for whom George ever used the word 'mentor', D'Mello was one; Balappa and Lohia were the other two. 'D'Mello took things very seriously—everything,' George recounted later. 'He was a well-read person. And, he had a special knack for organizing people. He could influence workers because of his speech.' The protégé was observing the mentor closely and making mental notes for his

The only photograph of Placid D'Mello that is in circulation.

Courtesy: Transport and DockWorkers' Union, Mumbai

own use. Describing D'Mello's negotiating tactics, George wrote, 'He gave another chance to the government to settle the dispute. But the "chance" carried a threat too. "If the government does not agree to the demand in a given time, the workers will be compelled to think in terms of direct action, though most reluctantly," he declared.'[60] In every one of the strikes George would conduct, he would never shirk from negotiating with the authorities, but at the same time, he would keep the workers united and fighting fit. He would set a time frame within which he demanded resolution of the issue at hand. His language would betray no weakness and contain always a 'threat of direct action'. The authorities would be left exasperated and confounded by this unrelenting aggression, which made them think he was not sincere about arriving at a settlement. They would suspect negotiations were a ruse to lull them into inaction, whereas he always prepared for a showdown.

D'Mello began testing the waters in South Canara's labour pool. In the towns were transport companies employing drivers and conductors to ply passenger vehicles. Canara Public Conveyance Company Ltd, a Kudva private concern, had the monopoly of road transport in the district. When D'Mello came to Mangalore, he was approached by aggrieved motormen. At D'Mello's prodding, George, Balappa and others went to organize the drivers, cleaners and conductors into a union and prepare them for action.

A motorman strike was fixed for 22 February 1950. According to George's brief written account of it, the strike was short and unsuccessful. It lasted for seven days, but its power had fizzled out on the second day itself. Some sabotage by filling fuel tanks with water was resorted to. But on the night the strike began, D'Mello was arrested under the Preventive Detention Act and sent to jail in distant Vellore. Still, the strike happened, the district transportation was paralysed, and for some time the buses remained idle. In his desperation, at Hampankatta, George recollected, he lay before a bus to stop its movement. But beaten by excessive use of force, the workers returned to work. The Kudvas, owners of a monopoly transport company, ruthless in suppressing the strike, would not allow any negotiation as the strike stood broken.

Another failure followed with the hotel workers. George organized a strike for better conditions at work, but the hotel owners simply dismissed the staff and closed down the hotels. Two disasters in quick succession! Although in a much worse situation with the closure of hotels, the workers who were thrown out of their employment got together to acknowledge George's work, telling him: 'It is better that you go to Bombay, get some qualification, maybe become a lawyer, and then come back and fight.' He went to Madras, where the Socialist Party held its annual conference in the middle of July 1950. It was chaired by Asoka Mehta, a Bombay-based socialist, upon whose insistence they had severed their relations with the Congress Party to establish an independent existence. In the conference, Jayaprakash Narayan presented his general secretary's report, and Madhu Limaye's organizational report was read in absentia. It was George's first exposure to national leaders, meeting and listening to the gingerly group. His own fellow Mangalorean, Kamaladevi Chattopadhyay (1903–88) was the chairperson of the conference reception committee as well. She was a rebellious and outspoken woman who had broken conventions, married a man out of her community, and become a favourite with the Mahatma. It was a momentous occasion. About 50,000 spectators, 380 delegates and 772 member-visitors attended it. Socialist parties from across the world sent their fraternal greetings. There was much hope in the air.

4

Bombay Days

One rain-drenched day in August 1950, a twenty-year-old George arrived in Bombay. He had left Mangalore just when it had appeared he was beginning to discover his moorings there. But he broke away from them abruptly and completely, carrying the essence of inheritance alone as his baggage to the new city. Mangalore's hotel workers provided for his journey. As a formal send-off, 'the hotel workers organized a meeting in Maidan and gave me Rs 20 and a bus ticket to Kadoor, from where one took a train to Bombay'.[1] They advised him to study further, become a lawyer and return to serve them. But he didn't become a lawyer, nor did he ever return. 'I let them down,' he would tell *Himmat* one day, 'not because I wanted to, but because Bombay was very cruel to me in the beginning.'[2] As initiations are seldom not brutal, he explained, 'I had no money. I wanted a job, any job, very badly. Without the job, I could neither live nor study.' These everyday torments of a recent migrant were recalled many years later when he was girding his loins ahead of his first Lok Sabha election campaign in 1967. As it was an experience in a conquered past, it is doubtful if he was not venting to make an effect; after all, Bombay was a city of migrants and he, one of their own, was now challenging S.K. Patil, a seemingly unshakeable fixture in its politics. That urge in him, however, could not obscure the spirited courage with which he had moved out of Mangalore. That venture conveyed a determination far more

73

powerful than the desperation of a migrant escaping poverty. Beneath the temerity of his scheme lay hidden the implacable resoluteness of his will and a raw ardour. Far from being a hungry migrant fleeing the hinterland, he was a lad pushed out by the exuberance of a life already lived among the toiling people. A couple of months before his departure, he had been in the thick of the transport strike organized in February under the leadership of D'Mello. In July, he was at Madras, along with Ammembal Balappa, as delegates representing their district, soaking in the proceedings of the eighth National Conference of the Socialist Party. And, then 'a few weeks later, I left for Bombay'.[3]

As a matter of fact, it was quite a bland statement, not revealing what made him suddenly decide on Bombay. A clue, however, seems to lie in his meeting C. Gopala Krishnamoorthy Reddy (1921–94) at Madras where they both had been to attend the national conference of the Socialist Party.[4] Ten years senior to him and about the same age as D'Mello, CGK had started his career in Bombay and had been distantly associated with the socialist trade union movement active there before he moved to Bangalore to work as the manager of a newspaper enterprise. He was involved in the Mysore unit of the Socialist Party and gingerly took part in party deliberations at the national level. They found much in common, as would still be clear some twenty-five years later when CGK sought him out in hiding and they worked together in the underground resistance to the National Emergency.[5] Spurred by the experience of the transport workers' strike, it is entirely possible they exchanged notes, and George asked for his advice about his future course.[6] CGK might have suggested or, more plausibly, steeled George's nebulous idea of going to Bombay to work in the organization of labour there. Bombay then was not just India's leading industrial site and a commercial and financial hub, but it had also become a 'most dramatic centre of working-class political action'.[7] Nothing that was done in its factories remained within them—its message invariably went deep and wide beyond and acquired national prominence. Further, chairing the Madras conference was Asoka Mehta (1911–84), famous for his work among the labouring class, and who soon after would spearhead a textile millworkers' strike in

Bombay. And, adding to the excitement, George knew that D'Mello would return to Bombay once released from jail.

Although he has said, 'I didn't have anyone,' when he arrived in Bombay, in S.R. Kulkarni (1927–2016) he had at least one acquaintance he preferred not to go to. Twenty-three-year-old Srikrishna Ramachandra Kulkarni of the Bombay Dock Workers' Union had been in Mangalore following D'Mello's arrival and had played a role in the transport strike in February.[8] During a lifetime of activism among the dock workers, he would never cross boundaries to step into the political arena.[9] Although George would later claim 'a bond of friendship', it would not be preposterous to assume an early rivalry between the two protégés of D'Mello. But rivalry alone didn't stop him from approaching Kulkarni. There was pride as well. Having rather dismissed S.R. Kulkarni, George veered towards the Socialist Party. In Mangalore, after he was expelled from home, he had found respite at the party office there. He assumed a similar reception here as well. Madhu Dandavate (1924–2005), whom he met, was then the secretary of the Bombay unit. 'I identified myself and said, "I have just come from Mangalore. I am also in the party there. Can I get someplace here?"' Instead of a welcoming hug, Madhu Dandavate 'just threw me out'.[10] Madhu Dandavate would later be his party and ministerial colleague, his younger brother Bal Dandavate (1929–81), a loyal trade union comrade. Yet, throughout their intertwined political careers, Madhu would continuously snipe at George, deride him for his political choices and compete for credits. Temperamentally, they were poles apart. In 1993, after he had retired from active politics, a mellowed Madhu Dandavate presented 'with revolutionary greetings to "the Extreme Leader" George' a signed copy of his book, *As the Mind Unfolds*.[11] The appellation was an instinctive endorsement of the way he saw George: an impulsive leader who crossed the reasonable limits all the time.

But the socialist rejection wouldn't collapse George's dream or falter his belief in Bombay's absorbing benevolence. Thrown out of the Socialist Party office, George went to the 'footpath opposite the Central Library' and took to living there. Bombay was the favourite hunting ground for the people from his region in search of a livelihood. The Bunts had a flourishing share in the city's eateries, running the ubiquitous Udupi hotels. Living in the vicinity of his pavement dwelling was a family of Mangalorean descent, running a corner shop selling some eatable items and cigarettes. The lady owner lent him a rug to stretch out on. She occasionally provided him with food too. 'She looked after me,' he would remember in gratitude sixty years later.[12] 'The nights of these terrible months I spent sleeping on the various footpaths,' he told *Himmat*. In the mornings, he roamed around the business district 'aimlessly, subsisting merely on *chana* (peanuts) and municipal water'. There were quite a few cinema halls in the area. On the advice of kindred people, he approached them for work. He also approached restaurants and hotels. 'I started going from hotel to hotel. I had been told how to ask for a job: *"Seth, nowkri hai kiya?"* Everywhere it was the same refrain: "Chalo" (get lost).' He wanted 'a job, any job', but it was proving painfully elusive. 'All his knockings at doors were in vain,' he would write a year later, recounting D'Mello's experience in 1935 when he had first come to the city looking for work. 'His fate also was that of thousands of others, a lot of them more learned than himself.'[13] The words he wrote for D'Mello befitted his travails too. Then someone, again a Mangalorean, suggested he approach the *Times of India*. He did, and got the job of a proofreader, helped by his felicity in the English language. He had no money to buy a dictionary or thesaurus, but discovered an ingenious way to overcome the limitation. There were bookshops lining the road in the vicinity of Victoria Terminus. When in doubt about a particular word or a phrase, he would rush out of his office and head for one of those, refer to a dictionary and run back to his working desk. In a slow, incremental way, life began to roll on, even if it was seldom without pain.

* * *

George's arrival in Bombay coincided with the tumult among the city's textile millworkers. As had been announced, led by Asoka Mehta, under the banner of the socialist Mill Mazdoor Union, they were on an indefinite strike from 15 August.[14] The Mill Mazdoor Union was formed recently, as a result of the socialist parting of ways from the Congress-controlled INTUC, which itself was carved out from the communist-controlled AITUC. A 2-lakh-strong workforce had downed tools and emptied factory floors, promising not to return until they were given a bonus. If the leaders campaigned chawl to chawl to steel the workers' resolve, Morarji Desai (1896–1985), the home minister of Bombay, threatened summary dismissals if they didn't return to work. Neither was necessary. The workers' lives in their urban hovels were so appallingly poor, their real wages so ravenously low, that their loyalty to the mill work had always been shaky. As a consequence, they kept alive their ties to their villages to which they intermittently returned to recuperate from the hard life in the city. They were habituated to it by the very adverse nature of their factory-floor conditions. Fifteen days after the strike commenced, workers across industries and sectors went on a general strike to show solidarity with the millworkers. The government was hoping that the strike would fizzle out, sapped by the futility of its heightened expectations. 'Let it continue for six months or even for six years. But workers will not get a farthing if they remain absent from duty,' Morarji Desai declared. He predicted gravely the strike would end 'only at the cost of the workers'. And he warned, 'The stage will be reached when the mills will be run with alternate labour.' To starve the strikers, he ordered shutting the ration shops in the workers' localities. 'If you are patient,' he advised the groping mill owners, some of whom seemed perturbed enough to desire a settlement, 'and do not submit to the strike, I am quite sure that labour will return to work soon.' For he viewed it to be a political strike, 'instigated' by the socialists. Taking advantage of their proximity to Jawaharlal Nehru, Asoka Mehta complained to him about Morarji Desai's intransigent attitude and demanded his intervention, but in 1950, even if he was willing, Nehru alone was not the Congress. When he asked Morarji Desai to settle as the strikers were in a majority, the latter countered, 'Would you like the law to be made by a strike or by the legislature?'[15] A quietened Nehru wrote to JP, who had proposed a meeting with the strikers, that it was 'completely out of the question'.[16] More than

Nehru's helplessness, it was JP's audacity of asking the prime minister to meet the strikers, ignoring the state government, that was significant. After sixty-two days of tense impasse, the strike was suddenly called off on 17 October. It ended disastrously for the workers, who had been tossed around among competing political camps since the beginning of their making.

Many years later, when a more rabidly militant labour leader Datta Samant (1932–97) would ring the death knell of the city's textile workers, Asoka Mehta lamented the absence of an exit route in his 1950 strike strategy. 'One should not launch a strike unless one knows how to get out of it,' he said, but displaying convenient amnesia, he blamed the workers, saying they had 'insisted on a strike'.[17] 'The Congress was not willing to strengthen our hands, so the strike didn't succeed,' he said candidly. He would also say, eager for a scapegoat, 'My failure was in not having sufficient workers trained enough to know how to launch a strike, run it and call it off.' A prefabricated exit route, authority's willing acquiescence and a trained cadre were three vital elements of a successful strike, he seemed to say, and which he lacked.

George timed his arrival purposefully to witness the strike first-hand, or even with an adolescent hope of playing a role in its making. In a few swift years, he would find himself in a political camp opposite Asoka Mehta. Though he would adopt every single strategy from Asoka Mehta's book when he led labour strikes in Bombay, he would also learn from Mehta's failures, not conceiving a strike without an exit route in place. Asoka Mehta, who had started with great promise, would die a bitter man in the mid-1980s in the seclusion of a Delhi farmhouse. In the late 1970s, George would inherit his electoral constituency of Muzaffarpur. But he maintained discreet rancour against Asoka Mehta, who was largely held responsible for the exhaustion of the Socialist Party because of his Congress-ward tilt. And George would hold an additional grudge against him for cutting D'Mello's politics short. But that alone, though significant, was not his biggest mistake; his sin was his arrogance, his pretence of being an intellectual politician and his dry deportment. A Shroff couple was doing for Asoka Mehta what a Kaul couple would do for Atal Bihari Vajpayee (1924–2018).

However, one day, suddenly, he abandoned them to consort with the widowed Maharani of Patiala.

On 6 October 1950, as the mill strike raged, D'Mello, having been acquitted and released from the Vellore Jail, returned to Bombay to a rousing reception. The acquittal stirred the government of Jawaharlal Nehru to bring about the first amendment to the newly enacted Constitution of India, which let it frame the Preventive Detention Act. 'Five thousand dockers crowded at the Victoria Terminus to accord a great welcome to their beloved leader,' George would record the scene for posterity.[18] Soon after, George left the *Times of India* to join a music shop, Furtados, where his job was to sort and arrange LPs, long-playing discs, into categories, indexing them in proper order to make retrieval not a matter of chance but method. At the shop counter worked two girls who were paid low wages. Instinctively, George voiced the injustice of it on their behalf to the proprietor, but its implication was harsh: he was ordered out. In quick succession, he took and left other jobs. At the same time, D'Mello was 'insist(ing) that I join the Bombay Dock Workers' Union'. In early 1951, he finally did so, and 'in D'Mello's small office I started my work'.[19] In the nights, the office doubled as his living quarters. It was a bare hall, with desks and chairs strewn in some careless pattern according to the convenience of the users. Amidst piles of brochures and leaflets and name registers, surrounded by gloomy, ageing walls with painted slogans, pasted posters and a suspended noticeboard with typed sheets pinned on it, he slept his nights on a long wooden table. His initial responsibility was primarily secretarial: typing D'Mello's correspondence and managing official documents of the union. He worked as well to revive the publication of a newsletter, *The Dockman.*[20] As someone would vouch, basing herself on hearsay, George 'did not have the desk inclination', unlike those in the Dock Workers' Union who were sophisticatedly attired and carried an air of self-importance.[21] S.R. Kulkarni and others wore their safari suits seriously. George was eager to get engaged with the dock workers, and opportunity for the same would arrive soon.

About 10,000 sturdy men, more than half of them from far-off Uttar Pradesh and all of them employed casually by private companies and through middlemen, worked on the docks as stevedores—simply, those handling cargo aboard ships—and as shore workers.[22] Marathi-speaking workers making up less than 10 per cent, the dock workers presented wide diversity in faith and tongue. Their wages were so low and work so erratic that sometimes they pledged even the clothes they wore to a Pathan to borrow money for food. Mostly without families and with no social security, they lived in a neighbourhood that was filthy, risky and hungry. These street-inhabiting footloose workers had regular run-ins with the police who picked them up on charges of loitering which was a criminal offence. In the last week of May 1951, a few of them got involved 'in heated arguments' when the police came or were called by the aggrieved party.[23] In the ensuing melee, the officer pulled out a whip from a stationary hack Victoria and whipped one of the men 'till the whip broke into pieces'. When the workers at the docks heard of the fracas, they stopped their work in protest. 'I took a horde of them to the Yellow Gate Police Station,' George would recall.[24] A meeting was held there, and a demand for the 'immediate suspension' of the offending officer was voiced. This happened just weeks after he had joined the union.

At the docks, food-laden ships were waiting to empty their hulls. The situation was of urgency as riots around the country were breaking out over scarcity of food. The work stoppage on the docks couldn't be allowed to fester. After the police assured them that the complaint against the officer would be investigated, the Dock Workers' Union called for the resumption of work. But something not so unforeseen was to happen just three months later. On 31 August, D'Mello, along with other top-ranking leadership, S.R. Kulkarni among them, was arrested again.[25] It fell partly upon George to see that the union performed its chores in the absence of the leaders. This was about the time when the first-ever general elections based on unprecedented adult franchise were held. D'Mello was put up by the Socialist Party as a candidate in absentia for the Bombay Assembly. He was defeated despite giving a close fight. Not only was he locked up and unable to campaign, the constituency he was nominated from by Asoka Mehta, the Bombay Socialist Party chief, was also not entirely to his liking. It was George's first experience of elections.

He wrote a memorable paean to celebrate the work of D'Mello, whom he called *Sher-e-Docks*.[26] A year after the arrest, when the detention of D'Mello persisted, a procession of 200 dock workers, led by George, walked a distance of around 240 kilometres by road for four days from Bombay to reach Poona, the monsoon headquarters of the government, only to be turned away empty-handed by Morarji Desai, the chief minister.[27] The pilgrims in protest wore no footwear, slept on the road and ate what they got on the way. George walked the full distance; by the end, his clothes were tattered and his feet swollen with painful blisters oozing blood. After the ordeal, he spent a few days in a hospital to recover.[28] Weeks later, he would take a group of womenfolk from the docks to occupy Morarji Desai's chamber in Mantralaya and burn a straw effigy of him. D'Mello was released in March 1953, after eighteen months of imprisonment. Sour ever since 1949 when D'Mello was first externed, by a fiat of Bombay government's home department headed by Morarji Desai, George's feelings against him further hardened. He harboured a perpetual resentment against the man he would work with in his first government days in the late 1970s.

* * *

At home in Mangalore, troubled by conjugal discord, distracted by the immediate needs of sustaining a large family and driven by a quest for proving his self-worth, George's father's pursuit of material success never really came through. He lacked the equanimity to build an enterprise. He ventured into many, but would not win the steady income required to run a household.[29] But the failures would not harden him, and, untouched by bitterness, he would still be kind and compassionate towards all his children. Impressed by Michael passing his matriculation examination successfully, John Fernandes gifted him a wristwatch. It was a conspicuous accessory when Michael went about in a pair of worn-out and patched-up shorts and with feet bare of sandals or shoes. Hence, it was never worn. One evening, a group of agitated men barged into the house demanding to see John Fernandes. Intimidated by the commotion, Michael could gather just

enough courage to tell them his father was not home. They told him his
father had bought a wristwatch that still wasn't paid for. Embarrassed,
Michael went in and brought out the wristwatch to hand over to
them. It was not an isolated instance of money falling short to buy
a small happiness, but such worries scarcely dampened John's forays
into risky ventures. A new financial enterprise, a chit-fund company
from Kerala, was making the rounds of Mangalore. Seeing it offered
attractive returns, many invested their hard-earned money in it. Always
on the lookout for opportunities, John took a cue from it and with a
group of friends started his own chit-fund enterprise that promised
even more attractive terms. It did not work. The family's land at Bajpe
was mortgaged.[30] Michael dropped out of the college and even carried
a written note around to raise money for his education. In May 1952,
while in the middle of his two-year graduation course, he went to
Bombay to look for work. On the pretext that he was underage, he was
refused. He, however, found a benefactor who sponsored his education
for a year. Meanwhile, abashed by a legion of business failures and
harassed by creditors who seemed to have even approached the police
to get their money returned, the ever-enterprising John Fernandes
made an ignominious exit from the city of his birth and decamped for
Bangalore, where he took work as an accountant in a firm and settled
down. Later, he would get some success when he became an agent for
Peerless Insurance.

The family faced hard times. Sometime before George left for
Bombay, Lawrence had dropped out of school and gone to work with a
Catholic institution in Kerala. There he trained in mechanical welding.
But within a year or so, George called him to Bombay. In 1953, a
seventeen-year-old Paul came as well. In May that year, after finishing
his college, Michael arrived for the second time. He first worked at
the Bombay Port Trust as a clerk, but soon got an appointment at
the auditor general's office. Michael lived with George, sharing a
tiny terrace room they took on rent on the fourth floor of Engineer's
House, a building in the Fort area. It was an irregular quadrilateral
of a building with each of its four sides of different lengths and a
narrow staircase. It had slabs for its roof, and its low height wouldn't

allow George to straighten up. As for furniture, they had a double cot and a small corner-piece to keep things on. There was no space to move around. They shared the expenses. 'George was paying the rent and I was looking after the breakfast,' Michael Fernandes recalled.[31] Spreading the Polson-brand butter over the raw sliced bread, sprinkling it over with sugar crystals to make it palatable, and drinking cold Aarey packet milk while munching the unmelted granules of Bournvita they had put in, they would have their only meal together in a day. They had moved into Engineer's House in November. Michael recalled an event that occurred soon after on Christmas Day 1953, the intensity of which so many years later still moistened his eyes. Having bought a Christmas cake, he sliced it into pieces and waited for friends to arrive. 'But before that could happen, the man responsible for cleaning the building turned up.' As a gesture, Michael offered the tray for him to take a piece of cake, but instead he took all of it, emptying the slices into his dirty shawl before he left. For a nonplussed Michael, it was a sad hit in already hard times of scarcity. In March 1955, he received an offer of technical apprenticeship at the Indian Telephone Industry's (ITI) founding unit at Bangalore. He accepted it and left Bombay. He was just twenty. In Bangalore, he moved in with their father. Their mother, along with their two youngest sons, Aloysius and Richard, arrived as well. In June the same year, a sixteen-year-old Aloysius (Louie) left for Bombay, accompanied by Paul, who had come to fetch him. Richard would grow up in Bangalore.

In 1952, Frank Buchman (1876–1961), an American evangelist with a penchant for delving into international diplomacy and an ambition to change the world, visited India. He was the founder of the Moral Re-Armament (MRA) ideology, that preached reconciliation and the primacy of 'guidance, not gun' in class relations.[32] He spoke of a world in which people lived led by conscience, not ambition.[33] The MRA was seen as an American-sponsored body with pro-capitalist ethics, as many of the world's wealthiest supported his endeavour. Although *Blitz* would name J.R.D. Tata and other industrialists among those who brought the MRA into India, many of Jawaharlal Nehru's cabinet colleagues and Congress trade union leaders were at the forefront in according Frank Buchman a warm welcome.[34] He stayed in India for about eight months during which he was much feted. With a 200-strong theatrical troupe, he travelled the subcontinental length and breadth, performing to packed audiences. Bombay was his first stopover. The only group that aggressively attacked him were the Marxists. For them, he was part of the American soft-power propaganda against communism. Just as Frank Buchman left Indian shores, Aneurin Bevan, the left-wing leader of the British Labour Party, came visiting. The only public meeting addressed by him was organized by the Bombay Dock Workers' Union on 23 February 1953.[35] The militant oratory of Aneurin Bevan and the conciliatory ideology of Frank Buchman both left a lasting impact on George albeit with some confusion of thoughts. A decade after Bevan's visit, George, now in jail allegedly for violating the Defence of India Act, would still be interested enough to ask for his biography by Michael Foot.[36] But it was the MRA that would give him lasting moorings. Moral Re-Armament was headquartered at Caux, where Frank Buchman conducted conferences for world personalities and activists. In mid-1954, George was invited to attend one such conference. His brother Michael went to see him off at the airport. It was his first foray into internationalism and competing post-war ideologies. He travelled through European capitals. At London, the city's prosperity brought tears to his eyes. Years later, while being taken in a police van to a Delhi court for resisting against the government's Emergency declaration, he would think of that visit prompted by the sight of New Delhi's palatial grandeur. 'I had wept while walking on the streets thinking of the blood and sweat of my countrymen that has contributed to the affluence of London. On every wall, every brick I saw, the blood squeezed out of the Indian people by the colonial rulers,' he would write that evening in his prison journal.[37] At Caux, Frank Buchman was sufficiently impressed by the young, confident trade unionist to invite him to the US. George wrote a piece which was published in German in a journal called *Caux Information*. Its confessionary nature makes an interesting revelation about his ideological struggle.[38]

Here in Caux, I have decided to put my will—the strong will to do bad things—in the service of the higher will. I took this decision after much deliberation and argumentation. And I won't regret it.

Since then I have seen some of Europe and my conclusion, to live according to the four absolute standards, has deepened, as I have seen the Moral Re-Armament there at work. I saw how the practical application of Moral Re-Armament, be it in private, in industry or politics can solve problems. I believe, if it can solve problems for individuals, it must be able to do so with problems of peoples and the world as well.

When I decided for absolute standards, I had to make all kinds of amends towards quite some people.

I always saw myself as a good unionist and socialist. But only when I saw my life in the light of absolute moral standards, I realized that I have not much to show in both fields.

That was a hard nut, it was not what I had wanted—but I had decided for myself to follow a higher will. I allowed this Will to work against my own, and I decided to openly state to my general secretary, at a reception in Dr Buchman's house, that I regret my behaviour.

I don't know what consequences this will have on my trade-union or political future. But I am clear in one thing: That I am happy to have opened up my thinking and heart towards this man.

In our previous-year national union congress, I had brought resolutions against Moral Re-Armament. Today I know, that during the next meeting of our socialist union, I'll support Moral Re-Armament.

It is a great task, but anyway I have taken my decision. It demands sacrifices, quite some: my aspirations, my secret wishes, and my ambition. But my decision stands firm and after the journey through the European continent, I am more than ever determined, to fight for this ideology.

He wanted to support the ideology of Moral Re-Armament during the next annual gathering of the Socialist Union (Hind Mazdoor Sabha), an ideology he had opposed the year before. But soon, George would be sufficiently cautious to cordially part ways with the MRA. In August 1958, Lohia's iconoclast *Jan* announced to the world that Mahatma Gandhi's grandson Rajmohan had become the MRA's Southeast Asia representative, deriving a handsome monthly pay and perks of unlimited expenses.[39] *Jan* called the MRA a CIA-funded organization, an insinuation that, many years later, when pointed out, would be shrugged off by Rajmohan Gandhi in a light-hearted way.[40] George remained formally associated with the MRA only for a short time, but it would leave a lasting influence over him, and his friendship with Rajmohan Gandhi too would remain unaltered.

* * *

In the general elections held in 1951–52, with a harvest of a mere ten seats in the 497-strong Parliament, the socialist dream of replacing the Congress came crashing down.[41] But the defeat was not electoral alone. With a powerful will, and after a healing gap of time, it could have been reversed. However, not just the will went amiss, the desperation made them hard-hearted and impatient. They found it easy to turn against each other. And they found it even easier to propose a return to the parent body, the Congress.[42] One man who violently opposed the thought of returning was Ram Manohar Lohia. He rebuked the party for the absence of a socialist doctrine that was independent of communism and capitalism.[43] In order to build a distinct identity for the party, he spoke of launching a perpetual struggle against injustice, whenever, wherever. His vigour made colleagues look intellectually inept and politically naive. JP, the party's long-serving general secretary, who, since its foundation, had raised finances, established provincial branches and chosen people, felt the barb when Lohia said organizations aren't raised but they evolve in the crucible of action.[44] In response, he began to recoil from a party he had spent a lifetime building, ostensibly to engage with the new-age Sarvodaya movement, but actually to bide his time to revengefully inflict wounds on it. He ultimately got his wish when some twenty-five years later, he forced the socialists to merge into the Janata hotchpotch. It was a pedicide that went largely unnoticed in the exigent times of its accomplishment.

In desperate confusion, when their bête noire, the CPI, despite plenty of vilification, had won more seats, even while fighting on a far lesser number, the socialists went for a quick-fix solution. Immediately after elections, in 1952 they merged their party with another Congress breakaway, the J.B. Kripalani (1888–1982)-led Kisan Mazdoor Praja Party, to have a consolidated strength of nineteen MPs and a new name, the Praja Socialist Party (PSP). Soon after, driven by something as basic as the congenital birthmark, they got into a sort of dangerous involvement that eroded the new party's viability and sounded, as it seems in hindsight, the beginning of its end. It all began in February 1953, when at the top of the heap Jawaharlal Nehru invited JP for a 'cooperation at all levels' dialogue. It was simply unbelievable why an all-conquering prime minister would seek cooperation from a defeated outfit. A section of the socialists was enthused at the invitation, whereas another section was equally dismayed. Led by Asoka Mehta, the enthused section felt futility in continuing independently when Nehru at the helm was doing all they intended to. Led by Lohia, the dismayed section was aghast at those pining to return home. Dissipated by indefiniteness, egotistic men turned quarrelsome and a loosened djinn left them in convulsions while Nehru relished their flapping death wish.

This was vintage Nehruvian politics to which JP had willingly played. The bluntness with which he had retorted to Sardar Patel about going to the peasant 'not with a spinning wheel, but with a radical economic programme of transformation', the impetuosity with which he had told the Mahatma of his 'inadequacy', with the same reckless abandon JP now wrote Nehru to accept a fourteen-point socialist programme if he desired their cooperation.[45] As a result, Nehru publicly rescinded the talk, and for the socialists the damage was done. The loosened djinn whirred more rapidly. Twenty years after he had found Gandhi uninspiring, doing the same odd job, speaking the same language, JP admitted how false his discovery was. Twenty-five years after this failed talk with Nehru, maybe to join his cabinet, JP would admit again how misplaced his charter of prerequisites was: to implement them, one would have needed a dictatorship, not democracy. Although no tears were shed on the futility of the Nehru–JP talk, it left a lingering shadow on the intentions of interlocutors. Motivated by the chagrined egos of two men, Nehru and JP, their talk was meant primarily to slight Lohia, who was actively stirring people's struggles, wherever, whenever, that embarrassed Nehru and annoyed colleagues. If the invitation to JP, leaving Lohia out, was Nehru's way of insulting Lohia, JP's acceptance of it was to cut Lohia down to size. He found Lohia insufferable because of his 'extraordinary vanity'.[46] About the rumoured levels of intimacy of the three socialist leaders (JP, Lohia and Asoka Mehta) to Nehru, it was said: Asoka's was limited to Nehru's study, JP's to his dining hall, but the deepest access of them all had been availed of by Lohia whose reach went up to Nehru's bedroom.[47] Nehru and Lohia knew each other intimately and the level of intimacy bred matching contempt. Lohia knew his colleagues as well. As early as July 1950, he had written to JP, 'The way you have begun to talk to different people about me is good for nobody, neither for you nor for me. If you dislike me so much, keep your dislike to yourself. We are not children anymore, and we have, after all, to stay together.'[48]

The socialists were now in a fratricidal war. In June that year, Asoka Mehta gave a theoretical cover to the deep-seated urge to rejoin the Congress, calling it a 'political compulsion in a backward economy'.[49] It was a plain argument under which what had earlier been said to sever from the Congress was now turned upside down and presented as the new reason for rejoining it. The Congress that had earlier repulsed them enough to break away from it was now to be changed by re-uniting with it. 'Reform of other political parties should never become an aim of one's political action,' a livid Lohia said at the specially called party conclave. Exactly a decade later, these very words would be thrown at him, but here, when spoken, they sounded convincing and made him heroic and dauntless. But his words cast a dim shadow on JP's integrity, and the cause was lost. Asoka Mehta faced so much opposition from the rank and file for his pro-Congress thesis that it took him almost a decade to muster the courage to finally cross over to the Congress.[50] In July 1960, still waiting in the wings, he would spearhead a Central government employees' nationwide general strike. Prime minister Nehru would look straight into his eyes across the aisle in Parliament and speak, deriding those 'trying to ride a tiger when they cannot ride a donkey'.[51] But the indictment wouldn't stop him from worming his way into Nehru's power circle. He became the deputy chairman of the Planning Commission and joined the Congress. Years later, turned out of Indira Gandhi's kitchen cabinet, he found himself in a camp he had always derided. It was an ironical twist to his political career, which would end in bitter solitude.

Nehru was still not satiated. In January 1955, at the Congress Party's sixtieth annual conference, held at Avadi, he announced his aim of building a 'socialistic pattern of society'.[52] He had been the prime minister for more than eight years now; still, the declaration made headlines. It was a consolation in rhetoric, but the anxious socialists took it as an actual concession. There was a renewed clamour to join the Congress. From then on, it was an inexorable march to a point where the party's moral right to exist would no longer remain. The coalitionist termite would relentlessly nibble at its inner core, making it lose its soul and paralysing its body. While the rest of the party got deceivingly embroiled in a false debate about who between the Congress and the communists was the greater enemy, a dauntless Lohia would liken the communists to the maggots that bred on the dung heap of the Congress. 'To want to destroy that maggot without wanting to demolish the dung heap is absurd' was his way of underlining his primary target of removing the Congress from power.[53] He wanted the socialist focus unflinchingly set on wiping the Congress off the face of Indian politics. Soon, the socialist fraternal tension reached boiling point. A series of conflicting views culminated in a cusp where its unity could no longer be held. JP in a final salvo suspended Lohia from the party.[54] And, in Lohia's evolving conception, the only redemption was in the party's further diminution. He chipped away to establish a new Socialist Party at Hyderabad in December 1955, and began a painful, slow ascent to a vague and vagarious electoral success.

* * *

Madhu Limaye (1922–95) of Bombay was one man who sided with Lohia.[55] At the tender age of seventeen, he had become a full-time socialist activist. He turned out to be a prodigy and was taken by the party bigwigs under their wings, which won him loads of encomiums and opportunities. In the early 1940s, while conducting an anti-war campaign, he was arrested, but the sentencing magistrate gave him a 'light' punishment of a two-year jail term because of his youth. Years later, when he was impetuous enough to charge the party chairman with having a convenient memory, the latter would curtly retort, 'You are protected by your age.'[56] When still young, he was JP's blue-eyed boy, and he admitted years later, when his relationship with Lohia hit a rough patch, that by joining Lohia he had 'parted company with other big leaders with whom I was no less close'.[57] He knew that going out with Lohia would mean a life of privation and isolation. But he still did it because he believed in Lohia's policies. So much so that the belief became a garb. Attacked by Lohia's consort Rama Mitra in a letter to George, the 'hysterical outburst' of which left him amazed, Madhu Limaye wrote a reply simply because 'supporters of seven revolutions must take women seriously'. In 1950, at Madras, George had heard Madhu Limaye's bleak organizational report, read in absentia. When he came to Bombay, a friendship blossomed, and that only grew more intimate in due course.

Limaye hailed from Chitpavan Brahmin stock and would suffer from a sense of caste superiority that others felt but he would not admit to. Sometime after Independence, he met Champa Gupte, whom he married in 1952. They had a son whom they called Poppat (b. 1954). One day in July 1955, money-strapped Madhu Limaye, deeply anguished by the developing fracas in the party, would pack his satyagraha bag and, leaving his wife and one-year-old son behind, cross the border of Bombay at the head of seventy-nine others and enter Goa to liberate it from the Portuguese. He was captured, tortured and given a punishment of twelve years' rigorous imprisonment.[58] In Bombay, protesting against the repression, George led a procession to the Portuguese Consulate: 'I climbed the wrought iron gates of the consulate compound, jumped across to the terrace of the consulate building and pulled down the Portuguese flag. When I climbed down, the police stopped us from proceeding further and when verbal persuasion and a lathi charge failed to dissuade us from marching towards the secretariat, a police officer took out his pistol from the holster and jabbed it against my chest.'[59] Such shared acts of daring made George and Madhu fast friends. Advocacy would win Madhu Limaye clemency. During his time in Goa Jail, George would visit his home and play with the toddler, perhaps the first child he ever held. By the time Madhu Limaye came out of jail twenty months later, Bombay had become a piping hot bone of contention.

Originally inhabited by Kolis—a Dravidian race and the aborigines of western India, whose principal occupation was fishing—Bombay's fortune had begun to change a hundred or so years after its transfer to the English.[60] It had emerged as a mercantile centre, leaving its fishing past burrowed deep in a few clusters of beachside frond-roofed hovels. The city was built by the sweat and passion of migrants who came from across the Indian subcontinent. If the money to unleash this transformation came from Gujarati banias, Bohras or Parsis, the labouring classes came from its continuously expanding hinterland. Bombay was cosmopolitan while it retained a Maharashtrian cultural core, and that fact made its belonging a complicated puzzle. After the revered activist Sri Ramalu starved himself to death demanding a Telugu-speaking Andhra, Nehru instituted a State Reorganization Commission to look into the linguistic basis for redrawing India's political map. Acting under intense pressure from various groups, the Nehru government was in quandary about the position of Bombay City. To overcome its indecision, it forged a bilingual state of Bombay, incorporating both the Marathi- and Gujarati-speaking contiguous regions. The proposal left the people discontented. A movement to demand a unilingual Maharashtra with Bombay as its capital began. Two Maharashtrian men, Shripad Amrit Dange (1899–1991) and Shreedhar Mahadev Joshi (1904–89), both long-standing trade union leaders, were at the forefront of the Samyukta Maharashtra Samiti-led agitation. When it was still going on, one day, George, who had been convalescing from a feverish affliction in the house of his friend William Pinto, near the iconic Churchgate station, would rise from his bed to join a passing procession shouting slogans and demanding Maharashtra. He was arrested.[61] But it was not his first arrest. He had been arrested before for leading a satyagraha against rising prices under the auspices of the new Socialist Party, and imprisoned for fifteen days. 'I repeatedly courted arrest in that satyagraha. The subsequent arrests generally ended with imprisonment from one day to three days,' he wrote while remembering his friend Dinkar Sakrikar.

At the height of the Goa satyagraha in August 1955, coinciding with Madhu Limaye's departure, the Transport and Dock Workers' Union, which George had established under the tutelage of D'Mello in January 1954, forced an embargo on ships carrying cargos to and from Goa.[62] Coinciding with these activities, substantially proving his organizational mettle, the dock truckers led by him went on a strike to demand better wages, amenities and paid leave.[63] Around 4000 employees worked in various capacities on about 1500 trucks owned by transportation companies, both big and small. The week-long strike/agitation brought cargo movement in the docks to a standstill. The stretched dock officials resorted to bullock carts to ferry cargos. Eventually, some truck operators signed agreements, conceding the demands. Whether the gains were substantive or not is clouded; in any case, only the large fleet-owners could be pressurized, but there were also trucks run by owner-drivers who were outside the ambit of the strike. The strike foregrounded George, which made D'Mello's other colleagues envious, seeing in him a rival best nipped in the bud. But there was another unexpected outcome. The news of him organizing footloose and privately employed truckers spread fast. Many more employees from different sectors came asking him to lead them, among them a group of drivers of refuse trucks of the Bombay Municipal Corporation.[64] The fact that workers of an institution in no way associated with him asked for his leadership of their organization clearly indicated his emergence as a militant union leader.[65]

It was Noor Mohammed Karim Mohammed who came to me with money which he had collected to give to the ongoing union. I was reluctant to start a union just for municipal transport workers. But these municipal workers insisted. I then told him, 'If you want to have a union you will have to start another one. You can't be represented by the Transport and Dock Workers' Union. But having a small union serves no real purpose.' They agreed. Soon, we started a process to register an independent union of municipal workers.

A Municipal Mazdoor Union (MMU) was established in December 1955. Meanwhile, George felt suffocated within the dock fraternity. Despite D'Mello, S.R. Kulkarni et al. had made his life difficult and constrained his growth. He was keen to have an independent existence where he would wield influence, design action and be a leader. The municipal workers gave him deep and wide access across the metropolis. D'Mello, who was requested to be the president of the MMU, at first was reluctant. The Oxford-returned Maniben Kara (1905–79) complained to him about the turf war unleashed by George's entry into the arena of municipal workers.[66] In 1930, she had established a Municipal Workers' Union, and two years later in 1932 had been elected a councillor to the Bombay Municipal Corporation. D'Mello, a fellow Royist, was scarcely in the mood to displease her. But George was determined, and D'Mello, seeing it, agreed to head the nebulous organization.

Maniben Kara's Municipal Workers' Union wasn't the only trade union of municipal workers. There were ten others, feted and patronized by the authorities. One of the first municipal workers' strikes in post-Independence Bombay was led by the Municipal Kamgar Sangh, an organization founded and formerly headed by B.R. Ambedkar (1891–1956). They went on strike indefinitely on 13 May 1949.[67] The Sangh claimed to have a large following; 12,000 of 18,000 municipal workers were on its rolls. But in the end, they failed to get any of their demands satisfied, and after a futile 154 days' show of belligerency, the strike was called off. Moving strategically, and working in tandem, the provincial and municipal authorities adopted a multipronged approach to create panic, break morale and confound issues. If Ambedkar's status as the law minister in Nehru's interim cabinet was one supporting factor, the nature of their work, whose non-performance could jeopardize the public health of a burgeoning city, was their strength. Yet, the municipal administration refused to give in. In the end, leaving everything aside, the workers were reduced to pleading for the reinstatement of their dismissed colleagues, which was a crowning victory for the authorities. At first, the government had found the strike simply 'irksome', then it thought it would fizzle out as it lacked 'public sympathy', but when it still persisted, they declared it 'illegal'.[68] Ambedkar was under much pressure to intervene, but he refused. Arrests and dismissals followed.[69] The families living in the municipal quarters were ordered to be evicted. A posse of journalists was taken to report on the city's hotspots. 'The only place,' they reported, 'which was filthy was the municipal chawls where a section of the sweepers stay.'[70] But the fact that the living quarters of the sweepers had always been so—filthy, stinking and a hazard to public health—was ignored.[71] The tone of the report said it all: it was a war, striking sanitation workers were the enemies of the state and their living quarters not just a part of the city. To further pressurize the striking workers, the corporation began recruiting substitutes from Ahmedabad.[72] It boasted of a phalanx of 'loyal workers' whose ranks were steadily swelling.[73] Unveiling a mechanization plan, giant exhaust pumps were purchased.[74] Cornered, the workers resorted to pinpricking. They sabotaged the drainage system at a few joints by dumping obstacles. But the hard-line approach, in the absence of alternative employment or accumulated income, yielded results for the beleaguered authorities. A full five months after it had begun, the strike was withdrawn. The failure, however, would not be forgotten.

George was making a bid to organize the municipal workers six years after this tragic fiasco. Of course, the 1950s was not the most propitious decade for work among a class of workers long regarded as untouchables. In the riveting 1930s, the issue had acquired centrality in both creative and activist fields, and a social revolution was unleashed. In 1932, Gandhi founded the Harijan Sevak Sangh to spearhead a nationwide attack on the pernicious social practice of untouchability. There were people's struggles around the issues of temple entry and access to waterbodies, one of which was famously led by Ambedkar. Films like *Achhut Kanya* (1936) and novels like *Untouchable* (1935) were outcomes of that intense churning.[75] In contrast, the 1950s was a muted one, and at best legally spasmodic, with Article 17 (1949), the Untouchability Offence Act (1955), the Barve Committee Report (1958) producing such sarcasm that a MP counselled the 'Harijan Sahebs' to behave.[76] It was thought that legal empowerment and political entitlement could herald social justice. But what it yielded was a reservation policy that was never, or at best grudgingly, implemented in slow and small doses, a pathetic schooling system that was exceedingly difficult to access, and the politicization of occupations that only strengthened the stigma without providing commensurate relief. Independence had brought more isolationist, rigid social behaviour.

In the months leading to Independence and in the immediate aftermath, when the British were departing, when Hindus and Muslims were killing each other, many Christians, perturbed by the orgy of violence and prodded by the teachings of Christ, were simultaneously questioning the 'colour of God'.[77] As Joseph D'Costa, the fictional rebel of *Midnight's Children*, would say, 'Leave white gods for white men. Just now our people are dying. We got to fight back; show the people who to fight instead of each other, you see?' George was not the only yield of such a revolutionary quest. His leadership of the municipal workers was inspired as much by Christian theology as by socialist ideology. Just two words defined socialism for Lohia: prosperity and equality. There was this socialist school shaping George's thinking and the more ancient teaching of Christ influencing his deeds. In taking up work among the municipal workers, those 'outcastes' performing the menial services of the urban metropolis, he was largely prodded by his inward journey. He was a casteless Christian, which reassured the municipal workers who were pejoratively called '*bhangis*' to accept him. The divide between them and others among the untouchable classes was so deep and fractious that even Ambedkar was dubbed a Mahar. But soon, despite at first calling it a thousand-year curse, George would see the untouchable occupation as a more modern phenomenon, a growth so recent in origin that it obscured very many things. Shorn of caste, the municipal sanitation workers were an urban occupational class, to be redeemed by a proper wage structure and improved working conditions. The government too saw them not as a caste category but simply an occupational group of recent origin, gaining in number as urban dwellings augmented economic power and population density.[78] George knew society's prejudices were such that he would get no sympathy from the middle classes in his fight for the rights of municipal workers. Many years later, in a lecture he delivered abroad as a minister, George would recount, 'When I first organized the municipal workers of Bombay, the municipal commissioner of the corporation, a very senior civil servant belonging to the Indian Civil Service, refused to allow me and the union's managing committee who went to talk to him to sit down in front of him.'[79] But as he organized them, forcefully articulating their demands for work–life dignity and making their wages and working conditions central to their struggle, his militant ways brought a modern city face to face with its ugly reality.

His expeditious emergence was facilitated by an altered social and political environment in Bombay. The delegitimization of untouchability and the making of its practice a penal crime, and Ambedkar's recent conversion to Buddhism and his much-mourned death, all produced a new sanitized social space. It prodded the authorities into giving a more calibrated rather than a prejudiced response to the demands of the municipal workers. The existing regimes in Bombay as well, at both the corporation and the state levels, carried by the discontent brewing over the Marathi and Maharashtra issue, gave way to the friendlier ones. The newer ones revealed their soft spots, even while remaining ranged against George. At the corporation, in May 1957, the Congress yielded to the Samyukta Maharashtra Samiti, a political conglomeration that included the dominant PSP and CPI along with many smaller parties. Because of its leadership's trade union background, the new regime provided a breach that George would not fail to avail of. And, at the state level, the change happened within the Congress; Yashwantrao B. Chavan became the chief minister of a still bilingual state, replacing Morarji Desai. He had been a fellow traveller of Royism with D'Mello. On account of that, George shared an affable relationship with Chavan; some have even vouched that it was of the 'uncle–nephew' kind. Also because Chavan had a keen desire to rein in the communists who were dominant then in the labour arena, it was largely perceived that his interventions helped George. The ambiguous political environment, with the Lohia socialists working to carve out an independent path, would further George's enterprise as well. The PSP people were former colleagues who could still be, as unity talks were on. With Madhu Limaye in jail, and with D'Mello as city chairman of the Lohia-led Socialist Party, it was George who had begun to call the shots. But all these were only favourable factors that he used in his own way to make himself. 'George made himself entirely from A to Z on his own,' a colleague would recount years later. 'Don't be under the impression that D'Mello made him or Chavan facilitated his growth. He became what he did entirely on his own.'[80] Aggression, commitment and dedication would be staples on which he would build one success after another. His passionate commitment, his sharp oratory, his diligence, unmindful of personal comfort, all drew municipal workers in a body, undivided by primordial loyalties or professional categories.[81] Within a very short time, with an iron-hot determination, by overcoming their constricting categories, he succeeded in welding a disparate municipal workforce into one dedicated organization. Nothing could stop him any more, not even the challenging condition of massive unemployment.

But his first challenge was to win official recognition for the MMU, which would enable them to negotiate and be called for negotiation on the demands of workers. When they presented a charter of demands comprising fifty long-pending items in 1957, eighteen months after their establishment, with 16,000 workers on their rolls, official recognition was still denied to them.[82] They were ignored, their complaints given scanty attention and their letters failed to elicit replies. 'To the municipality, we didn't exist,' he wrote midway through the intense face-off.[83] 'Recognition', the municipal commissioner said, was a courtesy not deserved by the MMU. George lacked 'decorum and due restraint'.[84] It was a charge that would be thrown at him repeatedly in these years. In return, he gave a strike notice. It caught the authorities on the wrong foot. The union had the strength behind its slogan. It could flex its muscles. The authorities veered swiftly to make an oral promise on the union's principal demands and assured grant of recognition within the next six weeks. The swift coming around of the authorities was also possible because of the change of regime, which was now run by the Samyukta Maharashtra Samiti. The MMU had resubmitted a demand list reduced now to five points including recognition of their representative status. The oral understanding was a last-minute outcome of a war of attrition whose actual manifestation was averted but not without much drama. As the municipality had no power over the police, they depended upon the fire brigade personnel to back their orders. One evening, while inside the corporation building negotiations were taking place, outside gathered the slogan-shouting workers. The fire brigade was summoned, and its boot-stomping steel-helmeted personnel in their blue jersey uniforms, entered the corporation building. After six hours of back and forth negotiation, the corporation relented, but only stingily. It made oral promises only under duress and dilly-dallied. It took a lightning strike from the municipal workers on 13 July, therefore, for the mayor to solemnly pledge the validity of the oral agreement reached on 24 June. Although all of George's politics in the years to come would be centred on the needs of the small man, its beginning truly had the small man at its centre. In the first week of August, when the six weeks' deadline expired without bringing the much-touted recognition to the MMU, Marco Aranha, a cook in a municipal hospital, was suspended from service on the charge of collecting fees for the MMU, a still unrecognized union. George tried to reason but in vain. It was then that the menial staff of the municipal hospital where Marco Aranha worked went on strike. Two days later, workers in all other municipal hospitals went on a solidarity strike. But it was only when the city civic workers threatened to withdraw from work that the authorities were brought to their knees. The recognition to the MMU finally came at a culmination of a protracted slugfest.[85] Represented by weak organizations and divided within, the municipal workers had found in George a militant leader who had made a 'splendid organization' (S.A. Dange's words) out of them. Their earlier subdued self was not solely because of their beaten state but because of the absence of a leadership that was unafraid and unfazed. George's militant language was to indict not just employers but also the competing unions who had a penchant for 'giving slogans without backing them with action'.[86]

In 1958, the municipal issue opened up again in a pattern that would become a usual course in the years to come, and every time during the onset of monsoon. This time the issue was the dearness allowance. An agreement on it had been arrived at in June 1957 itself. However, the corporation, instead of coming true on its promise, decided to refer the agreement to an industrial tribunal for correct interpretation. George feared it would not favour them. On 14 June 1958, the MMU went on strike. It was really the first major strike spearheaded by George. Some would even call it 'the first serious and successful strike of post-Freedom India'.[87] Earlier, whenever S.A. Dange or S.M. Joshi had led a strike, they were incriminated, arrested and made to spend time in jail; their action was called illegal, calculated to instigate 'gullible' workers and spread disaffection. Now, they were employers by virtue of being the heads of the ruling party in the corporation. Would they behave in exactly the same manner they had deplored all along? Would they victimize workers for their insistent demands? Even though their lesser colleagues at the corporation still called the workers' leaders names, branded them saboteurs and threatened to teach them lessons, there was this speck of ambiguity about these two top leaders' attitude that provided a hopeful opening. In private, their lesser colleagues said they knew how to break a strike, but in public, even they took a position of injured innocence. Mercifully, they would not ask for the arrests of workers' leaders or declare a strike illegal or hire blacklegs as substitutes. It was a major difference in approach that contrasted well with that of the Congress regime. Sticking largely to the trade union ethos, S.A. Dange, for instance, was against letting the strike fizzle out through a long-drawn engagement without arriving at a settlement. They did stipulate the withdrawal of strike as a condition for negotiation. Hoping to get public sympathy, they resorted as well to the ultimate blandishment about letting the people judge the genuineness of workers' demands. There was, however, a begrudging acceptance of George's organizational prowess: no one denied his uncompromising commitment to the cause of municipal workers and his total identification with their demands. His strategic moves were his strong points; setbacks and insults failed to dent his straight-face confidence. And it was his staying power that won the day. The Samiti leadership procrastinated, declared their financial insolvency, offered concessions with a view to spilt the workers' unity. When they asked for police protection for new recruits and encouraged volunteers to protect themselves, which was obviously a call for street fights, it was left to Y.B. Chavan to draw a line. His government declined protection for substitutes and assured it only to regular employees desirous of resuming work. After Chavan's intervention, the settlement came about speedily.

That Chavan played an important role, inadvertently or otherwise, in the rise of George became clearer when in the latter half of 1959, now leading the workers of the Bombay Electric Supply and Transport (BEST) Undertaking, George conducted a strike.[88] Here too, the municipality was the employer, Dange and Joshi the final appellate authority. In October, when the demands were raised, the Samiti leadership made some concessions, with a 'take it or leave it' offer.[89] The workers rejected it. Noting that personal animosity was hindering a settlement, George resigned from the union's office and took over as the convenor of a struggle committee that held within it not just representatives of all factions but also those from other city trade unions. It was an innovation to weld the faction-ridden union together and balance out contending forces. The tactic would be harnessed by him again and again. He also let the pressure mount when he said the MMU too would join the strike action in solidarity with the BEST workers. On 26 December 1959, he said he didn't want a strike but the adamant authorities were pushing towards it. Two days later, the strike was on. And four days later, a midnight negotiation brought about its end on 2 January 1960. Chief minister Chavan once again played a significant role. He hasn't left any record, but George has.[90] It is said that Prime minister Jawaharlal Nehru was visiting the city, which was under siege because of the strike, and Chavan was keen that the red city buses run by the BEST begin to ply to signal normality. 'Mr Chavan summoned the officials of the BEST to his residence on 1 January and told them to get the buses and trams on the road by the following morning,' George wrote in a report on the face-off. By the wee hours of 2 January, a settlement was hammered out. The Samiti leaders, knowing that the game was up, signed on the dotted line. At 3.50 a.m., the first 'workman special' bus rolled out of a BEST depot, bringing to an end a four-day strike. 'When Chavan gave settlement to us it was a nail in Samiti's politics in Bombay city,' observed a colleague of George years later.[91] But in this face-off, Madhu Limaye was with George, in place of D'Mello.

A year before, on 20 March 1958, D'Mello at thirty-nine had been found dead on a street in Calcutta.[92] He died young and a bachelor. D'Mello had played both the roles of a frontal leader and back room strategist in George's struggle against the municipal authorities. He had used his friendly contacts with the Samiti leaders to bring them to the table when George's aggression derailed the talks. In Bombay, where D'Mello was buried at Sewri cemetery, the news of his death was received with profound shock and sorrow. *Blitz* carried a photo with the caption: 'Mass demonstration of grief such as the labour world of India has never witnessed before was seen at the funeral of the Dock Workers' beloved chief P. D'Mello in Bombay. Workers—Christians, Hindus, Muslims, Sikhs—broke down and wept at the funeral.'[93] Trade union flags were flown at half mast at the union offices, and workers stayed away from work.[94] His mentor's sudden death left George shattered and distraught. In close to nine years of their deep and intimate relationship, D'Mello influenced all his political style and aggression and negotiating skills. His apprenticeship under D'Mello had begun in 1949 at Mangalore. A day after the mortal remains of D'Mello were laid to rest, Madhu Limaye, who considered him to be 'the greatest working-class leader of India', visited George, but 'it was difficult to say anything and we remained speechless', and, consequently, left a note for him:

Comrade D'Mello's death has been a grievous blow. I know he meant everything to you, as his sudden death has a poignancy which cannot be described but only felt by sensitive minds.

His loss is irreplaceable but you can have this satisfaction that while he made you what you are today, you also partially repaid the debt, if such debt can ever be repaid, by pushing him to the fore, and practically forcing him to function not only as of the leader of dockworkers but on the wider stage as a great working-class and party leader.

However deep the sorrow, and time alone can mitigate it, in this hour of gloom and despair, we must collect ourselves and act like men. A great responsibility especially devolves on you, and the fighter that he was he would not have liked us to let our sorrow to deflect us from the path of duty. So, George, hold yourself together and try to regain your equipoise as quickly as possible.

I have told you not to keep away from Bombay for a long time. Try to get back, if possible on 27th March but definitely before the end of this month.[95]

Madhu Limaye, with support from a faction of workers of the BEST, of those originating from northern Indian states, led by one Sobhna Singh (also Parasnath Pandey), engineered George's control over the BEST Workers' Union. On 27 March, in place of D'Mello, George was elected president of the BEST Workers' Union. 'One can say that those Uttar Bhartiya bhaiyas who already controlled the representative union of BEST workers gave him a big union on a platter after the death of D'Mello,' recalled a colleague many years later.[96] At the age of twenty-eight, George had Madhu Limaye, a seasoned face of Maharashtra, fresh from his Goa imprisonment, not just consoling him but also acknowledging his role in building D'Mello. When the PSP split, George's role in persuading D'Mello to take up the leadership mantle of the Lohia-led Socialist Party in the city was visible. Most others among the dock workers' leaders retained their affiliation with the PSP. To overcome the political opposition George faced from a splintered socialist movement, he resolved to continuously expand his area of influence. In contrast to Madhu Limaye, who primarily rose in party hierarchy because of his grasp of world politics and his proximity with party seniors, George emerged in his own right by virtue of hard work, commitment and passionate advocacy of the workers' cause. Their friendship was mutually beneficial and was based on faith, trust and conviction.

In less than a decade after he had arrived in the city, George had become one of its most known labour leaders. In 1958, as he was preparing for a showdown with the Bombay Municipal Corporation on the issue of workers' dearness allowance on a par with Central government employees, and after having been made the president of the BEST Workers' Union, he began to intervene in the city's other labour hotspots. In July that year, he would force the city unions to bring about a 'Bombay Bandh' in solidarity with the striking workers of Padmini Automobiles. For about three months, workers at Padmini Automobiles had been on strike. The management had adopted every trick in the book to break the strike; they had hired new workers, used repression, given extra protection to the loyal workers. George gave a call for a one-day Bombay Bandh. At first, the communist- and PSP-sponsored unions were reluctant partners, but after he gave a rousing speech at a gathering of the city unions he won approval for the first-ever shutdown of the city on 25 July.[97] This raised his profile and gave him political clout. Thereafter, one after another, in quick succession, remarkable for its vitality and purpose, George organized workers belonging to many manufacturing and services sectors such as those from engineering, tailoring and hotel work. His work in organizing the hotel workers was his biggest achievement. He would pay back the sponsors of his journey to Bombay by building a powerful Hotel and Canteen Workers' Union in the city. In the middle of the night, when restaurants and canteens would shut down their services, he went around the city's eateries to speak to their employees. It was so effective with constant *morcha*s and sit-ins that the government would be forced to take cognizance of their unfair conditions.[98] All these efforts to organize the unorganized made him found the Bombay Labour Union (BLU) by merging four separate unions, prominent among them that of the hotel workers.

Most of his organizational cadres came from a stock of young men who had migrated to the city in search of work. Poverty was a recurring theme cutting across all protagonists—poverty that was less a product of injustice than a compelling factor that pushed people to explore a wider world that was uncertain, but with an abundance of opportunities. As more migrants came in, Bombay became more inviting: it expanded and became livelier. It never actually became a waiting-to-explode urban squalor; it always was soothing, providing the means to those who had the guts to dig in for small personal glories. If Calcutta was a city of joy, Bombay always was a city of gold. Over the years, George grew into a living legend. 'People came to believe that he could do and undo things,' is how a contemporary summed it up.[99] Literary novels and theatrical plays were written to extol his virtues. He would be in the MMU office at Charni Road every morning by 8 a.m. Seeing him so early in his office, his other comrades too began to come in.[100] Soon, when the new Socialist Party read its report, it was George's work among the working class that found pride of place. He became more politically active as well. In April 1959, he led a demonstration at the Chinese Consular General's office against the repression in Tibet, and released two pigeons to mock Nehru's Panchsheel. Cyclostyled copies of a memorandum addressed to Chairman Mao were thrown into the premises. Thereafter, a picture of Chairman Mao was pelted with ripe tomatoes and rotten eggs.[101] The news of it went directly to Prime minister Nehru as the Chinese took umbrage at the insult, and it found a mention in the white paper the government laid in Parliament on India-China border clashes. Thus, 1959 was a busy year even from the standard of the yields it gave for George's career.

The elections for the Bombay Municipal Corporation were held on 26 March 1961. George fought and was elected a ward member from Umerkhadi. The hub of the city government was located in an iconic colonial building just opposite the Victoria Terminus, now called Chhatrapati Shivaji Maharaj Terminus. Here was convened the first meeting of the newly constituted House on 10 April 1961. At the very outset, even before the chairman of the House could be elected, George raised the issue of the language of the House. He requested that the proceedings be conducted in Marathi or any language other than English. He broke convention by speaking in Marathi when corporations' deliberations were held in English. He was told that under the existing rules, the House proceedings could only be conducted in English. In 1957, even when the Samyukta Maharashtra Samiti was pushing its demand for a Marathi-speaking state and its exponents dominated the corporation, the proceedings of the House were still not conducted in Marathi. George was asked to resume his seat. When, disobeying the Chair, he continued to speak on why the proceedings ought to be conducted in Marathi, he was asked to withdraw from the day's meeting. Pandemonium broke out. The more he spoke, deriding the colonial and elitist mindset, the more chaos churned the House. Unable to control him, the mayor ordered marshals to take him out of the House. When George still didn't budge from the meeting, and as 'great disorder prevailed making it impossible to conduct the business before the House, the chairman suspended the meeting'. Taking a cue from George, the rest of the socialist members also raised the question of the language of the proceedings. Soon, other non-socialist members too voiced their Marathi preference. But when it came to electing the city mayor for which George was one of the three candidates, he received zero votes.[102] Still he ploughed on. On 10 October 1961, he raised the issue of how 'flies managed to get into two vials of antibiotics supplied in the city hospitals';[103] in December, he staged a walkout when prevented from speaking on the demolition of hutments in different parts of the city, which had rendered families homeless.[104]

* * *

Courtesy: Fredrick D'Sa, Bombay Taximen's Union

Young and dashing George, on the eve of founding of the Municipal Mazdoor Union in 1955. He was fond of cars and movies, and even in those conservative times, had love interests.

He was fond of cars and aspired to emulate Henry Ford. 'My childhood asthma is partly attributed to a late-night drive through Mumbai with George to see the Republic Day lighting in his very dilapidated kind of jalopy,' Madhu Limaye's son Poppat recollected.[105] This car of George's was an old convertible; it would start and stop, in fits. He was also fond of movies. In 1953, George watched the movie *Niagara Falls* in which Marilyn Monroe's character throws tantrums but ultimately falls in love with the man. He saw it with a girl in Bombay whose name we don't have. At Caux, the enchanting beauty of its undulated, snow-covered hilly terrain would, however, not suppress his fond memories of her, the tremulous nostalgia making him write to her, reminding her of *Niagara Falls* that they had watched together, one afternoon, a year ago in a sweaty theatre, and lamenting that he was now alone in the chilly Alps. This was a fact revealed many years later in a letter to his wife he wrote from jail.[106] The memory of that old love interest still stirred his dreary life in jail. But a verse he had then written had left her unimpressed.

In July 1962, George visited Delhi for the first time. He found the city 'hot, very hot'. 'I was sweating when the train steamed into Delhi at 8.30 p.m.'[107] For the night, he put up at a hotel called Regal just opposite the station. In the morning, he ate his breakfast at the railway restaurant and found it 'excellent' enough to recommend it in his letter to Madhu Limaye. They had been communicating on an everyday basis, writing about everything they did and everybody they met. Having become a city councillor, George was keen to visit Delhi's municipal corporation. He found the Delhi municipal office located, just as in Bombay, opposite the railway station. He went in to see if the mayor was in, but 'the chap was out'. He also went for a look into the Corporation Hall, 'a cosy little place' that was 'better than our own'. But he was disappointed that most of the officers, including the chairman of the Standing Committee, were not in their seats even by noon when he was there. He shuffled through the telephone directory and found 'there are so many Chuddhries—and they spell their names in at least a dozen different ways'. But then there was a similarity in experience in the two cities. He hired an autorickshaw. 'The first scooter driver I met in the morning after hearing that I wanted to go to Karol Bagh turned his face away. The second one took me to the place, found the house for me, waited for fifteen minutes, brought me back to the station, and when I paid him Rs 4, returned me Rs 2 with thanks. They are the same wherever you go, isn't it?'[108]

* * *

In the early years of Independence, Bombay witnessed many strikes, sometimes spontaneously declared, long-drawn and often total. The motives driving labour strikes were many, and not exclusively related to workers' rights. The world wasn't, isn't and will never be divided into a binary of oppressed and the oppressor; such an understanding was part of the Industrial Revolution social science that simplified the world in comprehensible categories. If the industrial force joined the strikes, it wasn't solely because they felt oppressed; many extraneous reasons dictated their choice. The strikes were also occasions to settle inter-trade union and political rivalries, suffused as the arena was with labour organizations sharply divided on ideological and political lines. Some strikes were solely to establish one's hegemony. Violence, leading to murders and mayhem, and the destruction of state property, normally accompanied them. Some strikes did yield considerable gains for the striking workers too.

A successful strike—in terms of its continuation as well as demands—proved the influence of a trade union. In Bombay, accumulating tonnage on the dock, putrefying filth on streets or the silent chimneys of textile mills were signs of a successful strike. A conspicuous sign of a strike was the sight of traffic-empty streets where either children played cricket or cows squatted in the middle of the road. Rhetoric was generally used as a measure of a strike's power; the more belligerent the speaker, the greater was the visible power. The longer the strikers held their ground, the greater was the trade union's rising stature. But one lost if the force of the strike petered out and workers resumed work.

A trade union calling a strike attempted to prove how 'complete and peaceful' was their action. The opposing unions, on the other hand, battling for the same slice of workers' patronage and employers' attention, worked to deflate their claims by attempting to break workers' solidarity and get at least some 'loyal' workers on the factory floor as show boys of a functioning system. Such workers were derisively called 'blacklegs'. State agencies actively collaborated in mobilizing 'blacklegs' for the embattled workspaces. Other methods such as employing substitutes were resorted to as well. The idea was to browbeat workers into submission, irrespective of the justice of their demands. Questioning the strike's legality was another ploy to control the militancy, and arrests of leaders were common. The striking workers did not withdraw into their ramshackle cocoons after announcing a strike. Picketing to restrain 'blacklegs' from entering the workplace was a common sight. In such cases, police bandobast and private militia offered protection to those who were cajoled to join work. The state often sided with the employers. Bombay being a crucible, its workforce came from varied backgrounds even while they worked under the same roof. The authorities played on these divides to keep the workers on a leash. The effect was the diminution of their strength and continuance of their misery.

A strike did not become successful on the strength of the workers alone. Workers' strength, despite the rhetoric, never really won rights or dues for them. The union had to cultivate relations with state authorities for its strike to succeed. It was imperative to have a siding state all along to win the battle of nerves. In the event of the state's unwillingness, reprisals were swift, brutal and destructive. Counterclaims were commonly heard and made. The media was handmaiden to the contending parties, propagating partisan concerns. It was a matter of tilting 'public sympathy' one way or another. Various insinuations were deployed to discredit the other. With the government commanding the information system and coercive apparatus, it was suitably placed to discredit its enraged opponents who sometimes took the law into their own hands or destroyed public properties. The power vested in it to recognize a trade union's right to represent workers' demands on workers' behalf was a tool of unfair and divisive advantage to it. The management obviously preferred a pliant trade union to a militant one.

'We had tremendous success,' reminisced Dada Naik, a contemporary of George. Not only were they able to get a fair wage, but on the question of work–life dignity too they were fairly successful. Socialists were the first to demand a timeline for the complete eradication of the practice of carrying night soil as head load. However, George's redemptive role in the lives of the city's municipal workers remains largely unacknowledged. His rise was phenomenal and quick. By the time he was in his late twenties, he was among the foremost trade union leaders in Bombay. His call for a strike often had elements of coercion in varying degrees, but he knew exactly when and how to withdraw a strike action. He could mobilize workers out and out for their demands without overtly reaching out to a political purpose. It is another matter that each of those strikes ended with expanding his own area of influence. He was also determined to ensure protection of workers mobilized for a strike against attacks by the state or by opposing parties. The strike as a weapon of political battle could not be harnessed if workers were threatened with violence. In time, he became a sharp negotiator and always kept his politics in mind. He made it clear from the very beginning that he would not be contained by mere labour issues, rather he would use labour issues to explore wider fields. It created an equally determined opposition who were keen to preserve their dominance and influence.[109] The face-off happened sooner than expected.

5

A Man More Dangerous than the Communists

A little after midnight on 4–5 April 1963, George was arrested in Bombay. That night, coming straight from a taximen's rally to his home at Pan Galli near Kemp's Corner, he noticed a large number of police vehicles patrolling the area.[1] Although he later said he hadn't expected the police to have come for him, there had been enough signs in the days before that they would. That morning, in the legislative assembly of Maharashtra, his name had cropped up in a heated discussion, and a few lawmakers had called for his arrest. Under pressure to show who wields the stick, the government acted in the manner as is usually anticipated. George had written, ten years before, recollecting an event that had happened five years further removed (in 1948), 'the men in power took note of the man who dared to defy their unlimited authority and strength'.[2] Those words, written then as a tribute to his mentor Placid D'Mello who had been arrested and ordered to be removed from Bombay, now described his predicament. After his arrest, and until he was released on 13 December, while he remained in jail for eight months and eight days, at first feeling abject misery and angry with 'the fools, goondas, eunuchs who run the state government', and later claiming he was 'happy and ready to spend another twelve months here', during those tense months the city of Bombay would feel as if it was a tinderbox.[3]

* * *

It was his leadership of the Bombay Taximen's Union (BTU) that led to his arrest. On Bombay roads, taxis were a relatively recent apparition, introduced in 1949. The cabbies were thought to be prosperous, as they drove motor cars, which until then were the exclusive preserve of the rich. For a society that ran on a bare minimum means of conveyance, the emergence of taxi drivers was confounding. Curious voyeurism prevailed about the taxi among the people, most of whom could afford neither the driver's nor a passenger's seat. The Bombay film industry, to satisfy such voyeuristic interests, made several movies with a taxi driver as the protagonist, which turned out to be blockbusters.[4] In the suave *Taxi Driver*, a vagabond girl, on seeing a mansion before which the taxi ferrying her halts, asks the taxi driver who rescued and sheltered her, 'Is this your home?' Nonchalantly, he replies no, his is a small rented room in the building. She is intrigued, as she had thought he was rich, with a bungalow, servants, etc. What made her think so? he asks. 'Motor-owning people are rich, aren't they?' 'But it is a taxi.' 'Taxi is also a motor!' she chuckles. He gets serious and explains, 'A motor for a rich man is a plaything. But for a poor man, it is his livelihood.'[5] For a footloose migrant, who might have already spent time in jail for a crime of hunger and poverty, a taxi was a socially respectable acquisition. Here, one worked according to one's whim, away from the grime of a factory floor or a queue of head-loaders waiting for work. Cinematic renditions of a taxi man's life by swashbuckling actors, with rings of smoke billowing from a cigarette held in the curl of their lips, haughtily refusing a patron, thrashing a villain or saving a damsel in distress, made the taxi trade a tempting livelihood option. As a consequence, George wrote, 'A large number of men working as drivers in reputable firms or the BEST Undertaking quit the security of their jobs and all the benefits which they enjoyed to opt for the "prosperity" of taximen.'[6]

But the everyday reality was a life of colourless struggle in urban squalour.[7] Taxis were not easy to come by. They had a hefty price tag, investments for which came from private financiers who exacted a high rate of interest. No public-sector bank, already scarce, would lend in the absence of collateral. Some people mortgaged their wives' jewellery or sold the little patch of land they owned back home to secure the necessary capital. Even then, earnings from the taxi trade were not commensurate with the time they worked behind the wheel.[8] Regulated by the city government, taxi fares kept a laggardly pace with the rising cost of living, and response from the authorities to their periodic demand for a fare revision was always tardy. They lacked even the sympathy of commuters for all the troubles they endured. Not many members of the public agreed when George said it was a loss-making trade. If people still came into the taxi trade, he said, it was largely because of unemployment or because 'taximen have never cared to understand its economics'. They were not a strong political community either. In a city of 5 million, taxi drivers were a minuscule 15,000. Although they played an important role in moving the city, they were a marginal group of the newly arrived, lacking regional and linguistic cohesion or spatial stability. But George took up their cause with a gusto that had come to be associated with him. It explains why, years later, he would say, 'My political life was based on the deep convictions that I held and the hard work I did.'[9] The BTU was established in January 1960. Since then, he had set about resolving the anomalies in the taxi trade. He was negotiating a deal on revised taxi fares with chief minister Yashwantrao Chavan when, in late October 1962, China attacked India's northern border. India lost badly and agreed meekly to the unilateral ceasefire announced by the invading army. As a consequence, a weakened Jawaharlal Nehru unwillingly sacrificed a discredited Krishna Menon, who was replaced by Yashwantrao Chavan as the defence minister. In Bombay, one M.S. Kannamwar took over as the chief minister, who was not enthusiastic at all about the negotiations that George was brokering.

Although a warlike tension had existed for a long time, the actual international clash was a short affair. In its wake, the Central government imposed a National Emergency, increased taxes to mop up more resources and introduced a compulsory deposit scheme (CDS). These controversial measures were not eased even after the threat at the borders subsided. Together, they stirred a rise in prices, and that in turn aroused general discontent. The Defence of India Act and the Rules under it, widely known by its acronym DIR, a set of Emergency laws for preventive detention, when enacted for the first time in the post-war India of 1918, was called the Rowlatt Act. During the China conflict, it was re-enacted with wide powers given to the state. Whether it was scared or not because of the conflict over the border, Nehru's state was in a perpetual state of fearmongering and did become severe in dealing with its people. The law came in handy to serve the partisan ends of the ruling Congress Party and to wreak vengeance against its critics.[10] In Parliament as well as in the streets, as much among politicians as among the lay citizens, misuse of the DIR became a cause of concern.[11] Some five months after the conclusion of the border clash, on 18 March 1963, George led a demonstration to Bombay's governor demanding a rollback of harsh measures. 'You have no right to tax the poor,' he said in a memorandum to Governor Vijayalakshmi Pandit, Jawaharlal Nehru's sister, 'if you don't stop pilferage, luxury, tax swindling.' It was a two-page petition, drafted in Hindi by Madhu Limaye and signed by George on behalf of the Socialist Party. Demanding repeal of the CDS, the memorandum said, 'The people are greatly perturbed over the mounting cost of living,' and asked '. . . when there is no actual fighting with the Chinese, why is this Emergency continuing?'[12]

The BTU had temporarily shelved its demand for taxi fare revision because of the war. In January 1963, it took up its case again. On 31 March 1963, at a rally of taximen, George reiterated their demand for a public inquiry into the existing fare structure.[13] The government remained unmoved: it neither instituted an inquiry nor drew up a new taxi fare structure as demanded. Tired of waiting, George gave the government a fourteen-day ultimatum to act, failing which, he said, they would unilaterally declare a revised taxi fare structure. It was an impulsive challenge the government was least inclined to brook. Thereafter, events gained momentum. On 4 April, there was a shouting match in the Maharashtra Assembly over George's challenge. Eager to corner the government, the legislators asked if it was aware of his open threat. It was, said the state's deputy home minister, and added they knew how to deal with such disagreeable matters suitably. 'The deputy home minister,' as Raj Narain, the Socialist Party chairman, wrote to Lal Bahadur Shastri, the central home minister, 'in his eagerness to

Courtesy: Fredrick D'Sa, Bombay Taximen's Union

At the beginning of 1963, George was campaigning for supporting the war effort by requesting the city's working class to make liberal contributions to the war fund. Here, George is seen addressing the BEST workers. On his left is the BEST Workers' Union's Sobhna Singh.

prove himself, lost intellectual and constitutional balance and planned to arrest George under the DIR on the night of 4 April.'[14] The arrest was made that very night; with him were also arrested Sardar Parsbag Singh and Janardhan Upadhyay, the two other office-bearers of the BTU.[15]

* * *

'Fernandes Is Arrested: Anti-National Work' was the headline of a small news item published in the City page of Bombay's *Times of India*.[16] As the police apprehended trouble from his supporters, they ordered arrests of what they called 'anti-national elements', prohibited 'rallies, marches and protests across the city' and banned 'carrying lethal weapons, stones, explosives, swords and corrosive substances from now for four days'. Immediately, the taxis went off the roads in protest on 6 April for a full day. In the evening, workers affiliated to the George-headed Hind Mazdoor Panchayat (HMP) collected at Kamgar Maidan at Parel in the labour district, but their protest march was cordoned off by heavy police presence.[17] The arrest, the state home minister explained on 7 April, had become a necessity; his public outbursts were seditious; he had unilaterally proposed a 'schedule of taxi fares in utter disregard of the public interest and the law'.[18] Claiming that to reveal any more was not in the national interest, the minister refrained from giving more details of his inclement activities. When in the Bombay Municipal Corporation (BMC) the socialist members raised the matter, they were denied a response.[19] At the same time, in a confused gesture, the government announced a new fare structure for the city taxis.[20] If the announcement was conciliatory, the continued detention of George made the BTU offer explanations on his behalf. The Union said 'it had no plans of taking the law into its own hands or in any way disturb the public peace'.[21] It was ready to negotiate. It asked for his release, as the new fare structure showed they were right on their demands.

His arrest was not an unusual affair. He had been arrested several times before. So regular had his jail visits become that they no longer worried the family back in Bangalore. 'There was a time in Bombay,' Michael Fernandes recalled jocularly, 'when policemen would serve an arrest warrant on him at his office and, after finishing his work, he would walk into the police station and get himself arrested.' But there were also serious prison terms he had endured. On 5 May 1961, he was sentenced to two months' rigorous imprisonment for leading a protest at Dadar railway station on 13 July 1960. He was held at Bombay's Arthur Road prison for nearly a week before being shifted to Visapur Jail. When he came out, he wrote to Yashwantrao Chavan describing how 'conditions in the Indian jails of today are as bad as they were during the British days'. He was humiliated by the jail officials, there was corruption among jail staff, and ordinary amenities such as newspapers were denied to political prisoners who were treated on par with criminals.[22]

Courtesy: Fredrick D'Sa, Bombay Taximen's Union

E. Bandookwala, the Mayor of Bombay (1963–64) had this photo taken with George on 1 April 1963, just three days before his arrest under the charge of anti-national activities. The Mayor would write to him, inquiring of his health and wishing his speedy release, while George remained in jail and wrote requesting his corporator's salary to be sent to his jail address.

This April, George's whereabouts in the days immediately after his arrest were kept a secret. Only about a week later, it became known that he was at Nasik Central Jail.[23] On 5 April, soon after he was brought to jail, George wrote to H. Shiva Rao, his trade union colleague, requesting a list of things he needed and inquiring about Leela Bai, his landlady. Two days later, Shiva Rao sent a consignment through a courier to Poona 'under the presumption that you were at Yerawada Prison', as he wrote on 22 April by way of explanation. The consignment was returned and Shiva Rao resent it, this time to Nasik Jail. The items were: (1) bedding; (2) one pair bedding covers; (3) two *lungies*; (4) two bath towels; (5) one thermos flask; (6) two bush shirts; (7) one pillow with two covers; (8) three bottles of pickles; (9) mirror and shaving things; (10) one tin of biscuits. 'Leelabai,' Shiva Rao wrote, after listing the things in the dispatched consignment, 'has been somewhat upset about your arrest.'[24] He had taken her to a doctor, and wrote later, 'She is alright now.'[25]

Leela Bai, however, was not 'all right'. She felt 'upset' and scared too. Her tenant's reputation was being embellished every day as the government justified the arrest and newspapers faithfully reported what it said. It came to be said that he was a threat to 'national security'. Any other number of epithets that scared her were used to characterize him; he was 'more dangerous than the communists' and he was an 'American-style gangster'. The landlady wished that he vacate her flat but feared telling him herself. She solicited the help of one B.V.K. Alva. The messenger in turn took a winding route to convey the message. Writing with some hesitancy, he hoped that George with his 'tremendous power of appreciating the other man's point of view' would understand the motive and purpose of this letter'. A few days before, he had gone to Leela Bai and found her 'extremely confused and sad'. 'Since her depression was rather pronounced', he had persuaded her to confide in him, 'hoping to be of some assistance to the good lady'.[26] The letter's roundabout tenor and apologetic tone conveyed an impression that it was written to someone feared. The message was clear even if it took a long winding path to be conveyed to the recipient: Leela Bai wanted the man imprisoned under the DIR to vacate her house. B.V.K. Alva, who had given the first court surety for George but now regretted it, was stoking her fears rather than dousing her anxiety. The house, however, was not vacated, and, as is evident from letters he wrote, George remained solicitous of Leela Bai all through his months of imprisonment. He made sure the rent and other dues were paid to her on time.[27]

At Nasik Jail where he was kept in an isolated ward, the food was of low quality. He was not allowed any visitors. Nor was he allowed to spend his own money. As a consequence, he fell ill. He wrote to his trusted doctor Ravi H. Dastur that he was suffering from piles. The doctor wrote back, complimenting him for his 'unlimited capacity to endure' and prescribed: 'Take Isebgul 2 tablespoon full twice a day, and apply Boot's H.P. ointment for piles.'[28] Ravi Dastur's was among the first letters that came directly to Nasik prison. His envelope bore a stamp 'Censored' emblazoned in blue, countersigned by a jail official. All letters that George wrote or received had to go through the scrutiny of

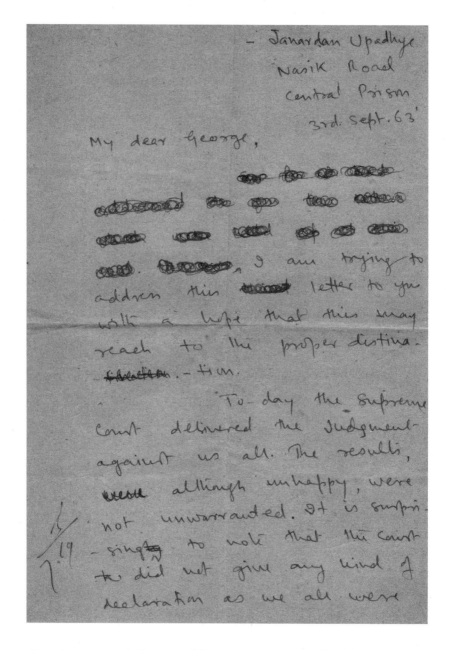

the jail censor, and objectionable content was made illegible by repeated overwriting with a blue ink-pen. He wrote to the government seeking permission to be medically examined by Ravi Dastur, his physician

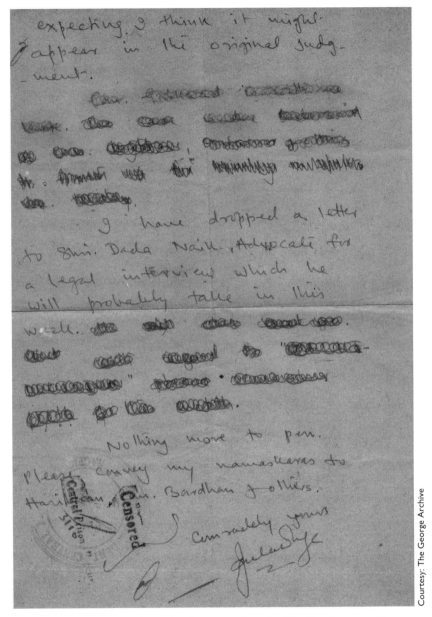

Censorship in Nehru's India, 1963: Co-prisoner Janardan Upadhyay's censored letter dated 3 September 1963 to George. The words have been made illegible by repeated scribbling over.

who had been treating him 'for over twelve years now and is conversant with my conditions'. He listed ailments he suffered from. 'For some time before my arrest,' he wrote, 'I was undergoing treatment for some severe pain in the right knee joint as also in both wrist joints. I have a longstanding complaint of migraine headaches which recur now and then. I also have occasional shooting pain in the chest in the region of the heart for the past several years.'[29] All these complaints had been troubling him again. He was prepared to meet the expenses that would be incurred in his medical check-up.

For some, he was 'the first public man to raise his voice against this frivolous piece of legislation called the Emergency'.[30] But there were also those whose understanding remained 'clouded' and thought his action on taxi fares was ill-advised. Prabhakar Kunte (1924–2007), a colleague from the PSP, thought the taximen's reduced income wasn't such a 'basic' issue as to force an ultimatum. 'The taxi is public convenience, and hence the risk to the passenger must be the minimum . . .'[31] A taxi driver, in his opinion, could not be given the right to refuse his service, whatever his grievances. Agreeing that George had simply asked for an inquiry committee to look into the fare question, Kunte was unhappy with the way it was asked. His actions under constant scrutiny, such aspersions on George's judgement were commonplace. To his detractors, whether he broke the law in self-interest or on principle was of no consequence. But Kunte's letter was a spiteful one, as evident from its biting sarcasm in reminding George of his Visapur experience and asking if 'the jails have improved after fifteen years of freedom'.

Citing his arrest as a result of inter-trade-union rivalry, George filed a 'habeas corpus' petition on 22 April at the Bombay High Court. The government favoured the Congress-controlled INTUC, which was envious of his rising stock among the city's labouring class. In his criticism of the Nehru regime, George had stressed that the government had not done enough to fight the Chinese, and this was hardly an act prejudicial to the defence of India, public safety and maintenance of public order, for which he had been allegedly detained. On 2 May, his case came up for hearing but was deferred to 17 June. The experience of attending the adjourned court session was physically exhausting. He fell sick. On 7 May, he wrote to Yashwantrao Chavan detailing his travails and venting his frustration.[32] His earlier letter hadn't elicited a reply, yet he wrote again but with 'an assurance that during this term of incarceration I shall not bother you another time'. It was the kind of letter you would write to your parents, with a mix of disappointment, anger and lurking hope. He intended to make sure Yashwantrao Chavan knew who the real culprit behind all his trouble was: 'I only hope that the report of this breakdown in health will have been conveyed to the deputy home minister [of Maharashtra] and the police officers, for theirs is the pleasure of my suffering.' More than the physical trauma, what he had endured was emotional turmoil because of a horrid picture the police had painted of him in their reply to his 'habeas corpus' petition. 'The substance of commissioner's rejoinder is,' George wrote, 'I am an anti-national person whose freedom spells national disaster.' But he was not a 'traitor', George wrote. 'I am [in jail] to enable a small frog of the deputy home minister of Maharashtra to bloat himself into a big "strong man".' He said he was in a 'position to tear to shreds all the so-called evidence' against him. But at the moment, he knew, his was a cry in the wilderness. 'No one but the old cat that prowls around here in my barrack will listen to me in my present condition.' George reproached Yashwantrao Chavan for sitting 'so very nonchalantly and watch[ing] this tragic comedy as a disinterested spectator'. As perhaps expected, Chavan did not reply, nor did George ever write again during 'this term of incarceration', keeping his promise. At about the same time, George wrote to S.M. Joshi, who in June would be anointed chairman of the PSP, expressing hurt at being called 'anti-national'. The sacrilegious charge hurt him to the bone. He pleaded for some action to get him released or he would begin to act on his own. S.M. Joshi, who at the time was working towards socialist unity by getting the splinter groups to merge, replied, 'Let me try my hand and, in my way, if we fail, you will be justified in taking any course to vindicate your honour.' He advised patience: 'Do not allow yourself to be excited and provoked in the face of gravest provocation', signing off affectionately as 'Anna' (elder brother).[33]

S.M. Joshi (third from the left) was a senior socialist and played an important role as the co-convenor of the Samyukta Maharashtra Samiti.

Courtesy: Fredrick D'Sa, Bombay Taximen's Union

* * *

High courts across the country believed that to a prisoner under the DIR, 'no right is conferred, because the remedy is barred'. This was the position of the Supreme Court as well. The government was still more clear: it simply argued that 'detention cannot be questioned' in a court of law.[34] This was insufferable as Emergency laws were meant to preserve people's freedom and expand it, not restrict or abolish it. As was expected, George was not given any relief on the grounds that he was not entitled to any relief as his fundamental rights in an Emergency remained suspended.[35] Now, approaching the Supreme Court was the only legal option left to him. Not one to give up, he tried that, but returned empty-handed. Outside, sporadic demonstrations were equally sterile. When no remedy was in sight, the street, of which he was a master, had to be conjured up as the theatre of justice. His last hope of being released from the claustrophobic confines of jail now hinged on a total shutdown of Bombay. From early July, a new plan was afoot to bring the roaring city to a grinding halt.

The simmering plan was led by Madhu Limaye who was on the warpath and defended George as no one ever did. In quick succession, he wrote an angry missive to M.S. Kannamwar and a conciliatory one to Yashwantrao Chavan apprising him of the 'harmful consequences' of George's arrest.[36] To the chief minister, it was long and aggressively worded.[37] It was a misnomer to say George had played a 'disruptive role'. Not just had he asked the unions under his command to contribute a monthly sum to the defence fund 'till it hurts', it was the same government who had made him a member of the Citizen's Defence Committee (CDC) and ministers had taken him around addressing the people. The socialists were at the forefront to arouse mass sentiment against the Chinese aggression. As far as the taximen's agitation was concerned, Madhu Limaye vouched, 'George was prepared to discuss it.' He advised the government to call a meeting of the CDC and invite George from jail to participate. In keeping with his aggressive posture, he warned, if not done by 18 April, they would withdraw their support to the war effort: 'It is the end of a united effort of the past few months.'[38] When the government remained unmoved, Madhu Limaye and George tendered their resignation from the CDC.[39] And various trade unions affiliated to the HMP, prodded by Madhu Limaye, began announcing the stoppage of their voluntary contributions to the defence fund. On 11 April, the MMU declared so;[40] on the 13th came the announcement from the Bombay Labour Union;[41] on the 14th from the workers of the BEST Undertaking; on the 17th, from the BTU came an appeal to not make the arrest a 'prestige' issue and release George.

In a cascading stream, events began to follow one after another, taking a rehearsed path. Prices of commodities had certainly risen and people were feeling the pinch. 'Bombay's rice eater,' the *Times of India* reported in mid-July in a front-page news item, 'is today paying 20 per cent more for the main item in his daily menu than before the Emergency.'[42] It was decided George's continued imprisonment would be hinged to the discontent produced by the price rise. Naturally, the municipal workers would be the fulcrum of the movement against the soaring prices.[43] On 4 June, they held a meeting to pass a three-point resolution. They asked for, first, a raise in dearness allowance (DA) by linking it to the Cost of Living Index; second, as they believed the computing method to be obsolete, a change in the method; and third, pending settlement on both these counts, an immediate 25 per cent increase in their DA.[44] The municipal authorities were angry at the demands.[45] To the deputy municipal commissioner's comment about increasing production in the times of National Emergency, his colleague Bal Dandavate wrote, 'I do not think municipal work has any bearing on the defence effort.' Claiming demands were out of their purview, the authorities accused the municipal workers of making an 'annual threat of a strike to hold the city to ransom'.[46] An angry M.S. Kannamwar expressed a desire to take up 'broomstick' (*jhadu*) to crush the strike, which gave rise to a mocking slogan: 'Kannamwar Jhadumar'. Focus on the obsolete method of computing the Cost of Living Index and demand for its change brought about a wholesale transformation in the character of the protest. It no longer was a shrill cry to get an imprisoned George out of jail. Enlarging the ambit of discontent, the demand went beyond the realm of the individual to acquire a political purpose of a systemic change. There were some industries in which DA paid was already linked to the Index, and the accusation that the Index was wilfully manipulated served to bring in workers belonging to those industries. The protest demanded and, as would be clear in days to come, it received, the loyalty of a cross section of workers beyond organizations, beyond sectors and the colours of collars. As positions began to stiffen, Madhu Limaye laid the responsibility of simmering discontent squarely on the government: 'Government is sitting on the top of a live volcano and if it did not act quickly there might be an eruption soon.'[47]

Finally, it was all in the open. Madhu Limaye adopted the same fierce attitude towards fellow trade unions that he had adopted against the government. At the national level, the PSP and the SP were again in talks for a possible merger. Taking advantage of the leadership change in the PSP and the unity efforts, he forced the PSP and its trade union wing, the Hind Mazdoor Sangh (HMS), to rally behind his plan. The Bhartiya Mazdoor Sangh (BMS), the Jan Sangh labour wing, with a nominal presence among the city's workforce, was easily persuaded. The biggest labour federation, however, was the Congress-run INTUC that, in keeping with the ruling party ethos, was against agitation in the time of National Emergency. At the second rung came the communist AITUC that had a strong following among the city's textile workers. With HMS and BMS behind him, and with no hope of INTUC ever joining them, Madhu Limaye's attention veered to the AITUC. In the later part of July, he wrote to Shripad Amrit Dange, who was the AITUC and CPI boss, inviting his support. Dange would 'not let little children like Madhu Limaye dictate the form and date of mass action!'[48] But whatever were his public utterances, the real war was about the turf as the socialists were the enemy in the trade union and political fields. He wanted the municipal and BEST workers which were under the socialists to fight alone and get smashed in the process. As if to frighten him into lending support, Madhu Limaye wrote, somewhat menacingly—threats would become a hallmark with the arrival of the ubiquitous Shiv Sainiks—'It is never pleasant to appeal to the ranks above the heads of their leaders, but it is not as if you are exactly unfamiliar with the technique . . .'[49] To force him, he announced a Textile Struggle Committee; this was a breach into the communist fortress, textile mills being their stronghold. Dange, although furious at Limaye's audacity, was mature enough to assure support to working-class unity.[50] Not convinced, Madhu Limaye expressed the confidence that the 2-lakh-strong textile workers would join the movement irrespective of Dange's approach; 'the rising tempo of the movement will either force him to join it or isolate him.'[51]

A Bambai Mazdoor Sangharsha Samiti (BMSS) was established.[52] Madhu Limaye kept the steering wheel in his hands. A six-point charter of demands—withdrawal of CDS, payment of 25 per cent DA to municipal workers and the release of George among them—was put before the government to respond.[53] The BMSS worked on a twin programme of action: to hold a 'big *morcha*' on 9 August—an auspicious day for the socialists, given its link with their glorious role during the Quit India Movement in 1942—and a 'token general strike' on 20 August. Madhu Limaye warned the government and rival unions against sabotage. 'Strike-breaking tends to lead to breaking of heads,' he said. Still, M.S. Kannamwar prodded the Congress-led INTUC to debunk the strike plan, which they dutifully did by saying there was an 'ulterior motive' behind it. Unconcerned about the machinations, Madhu Limaye wrote to Rama Mitra on 5 August: 'Slowly, the tempo is rising.' When fair-price grain stores were opened in workers' localities, he dismissed it as 'patchwork solutions'.[54]

As anticipated, the 9 August mammoth morcha of workers was a grand success. It was 'one of the largest and most disciplined witnessed in the city since Independence', observed the *Times of India.*[55] An enthused Madhu Limaye declared that the 20 August 'Bombay Bandh' too would be a success. The phrase was long in the running but acquired real gravitas now: 'Bombay Bandh' became an iconic action-packed phrase, a weapon to announce the people's power. Despite his initial reticence, seeing the success of the morcha, S.A. Dange came around. He announced the support of textile workers to the 20 August Bombay Bandh. It was a turning point. On 11 August, the 30,000-strong municipal workers went on an indefinite strike. With the municipal workers off work, as the strike progressed, stink rose from rotting garbage, clogged drains and unclean streets. The humid weather and unceasing monsoon rain added to the woes. Pestilent air began blowing over the city, only relieved, ironically, by torrents of rain.[56] Hospitals were shut down. Police took to manning the water installations. Myopically declaring the strike illegal, the government brought the DIR into force. Hundreds of workers' leaders were arrested, scores under the DIR. The chief minister demanded the strike be called off if negotiations were to begin. While the city reeked, a confident Madhu Limaye asserted that the strike was 'total and will continue to be total as long as a settlement is not reached'. On 16 August, five days into the strike, he was finally arrested.

In Delhi, on the same day, Ram Manohar Lohia took the oath as a first-time member of the Lok Sabha. He wanted to raise the issue of the Bombay strike even before his oath-taking, but was restrained. The Lok Sabha had been dodging demands for a debate on the strike as the matter pertained to a state. This was a thin-edged plea when the 'matter happens to be of such importance as the paralysis of the normal life in the industrial capital of India', a member argued. Lohia with others moved the first-ever No Confidence motion against the Nehru government. In Bombay, the BEST buses went off the roads, bringing the city to a complete halt. If the municipal workers held the key to civic life, the BEST transport system was the lifeline of the city.[57] Its coming to a stop paralysed a pulsating metropolis, just as municipal workers had put the city's sanitation in jeopardy. The field was now wide open for the national leadership of the Socialist Party to wedge in. On the night of 17 August, Raj Narain flew in from Delhi to negotiate with the state government. From the Arthur Road Jail, Madhu Limaye was steering the strike, and Raj Narain would not make a move without consulting him. Madhu Limaye, who smuggled out handwritten directives, wrote in one such:[58]

Maratha should repeat in every issue, morning and afternoon, the six-point [demand]

Vinayak Purohit and others should meet the Governor Mrs Pandit and request her to interfere

Piloo Mody should speak to Rajaji on trunk telephone requesting him to approach the PM

S.M. Joshi be requested to break the ban on a procession at Shivaji Park on 18th

S.R. Kulkarni should persuade his colleagues to start the waterfront strike from Monday, the 19th. This strike should be for 2nd day [sic] up to Wednesday morning (21)

Taxis, hotels should be called out from the midnight of 18th, i.e., for two days, 19 & 20

Bombay branch of Republican Party should be asked to support the municipal strike openly

Meet Dange immediately and persuade him to give a call to textile workers to come out on 19th

Our trade union workers should not court arrest, political workers may continue defiance everywhere

> Advocates committee be formed to give relief to arrested employees
> If a general strike of docks, textiles, hotels begins from 19th, I will
> wire Chavan offering to cooperate in reaching a general settlement,
> without this broad-based action, I will not move.

Madhu Limaye's handwritten note showed lurking players behind the scenes. On 19 August, the *Times of India* screamed a scary headline: 'Taxis Off Road: Protest Strike by Dock Men Today: Hotel Staff to Follow'. With the dock workers on strike, it now attained a critical mass and pulled in the Central government as the Bombay Docks were its concern. Ram Manohar Lohia, during a raging debate on the no-confidence motion, spoke for the House when he said, 'An explosive situation has materialized in Bombay. It is going to burst at its seams.' More than a lakh of workers had gone on strike, he said, ruefully adding, 'The tone with which the striking workers are being dealt should have been the language against the Chinese aggressors.'[59] The members demanded Yashwantrao Chavan's intervention. He was eager but remained uninvited. His message to Madhu Limaye, in which, according to the plan, he had asked for withdrawal of the strike and had owned moral responsibility towards the workers' demands, was not allowed to be delivered in prison. Such was the fickleness of power that the state government under Kannamwar would not let Chavan intervene. Soon, Yashwantrao Chavan would strike back, but in circumstances dictated by providence.

If pressure was mounting on the government, the trade unions also felt a meltdown. They abhorred a situation of no return. On the eighth day of the municipal strike, Madhu Limaye wrote to Vijayalakshmi Pandit: 'I write this to you not as one prisoner to Head of Maharashtra State but as one freedom fighter to another.' It was the right way to begin, tugging the heart strings rather than building a rational case of injustice. The strike could still be called off, he said, even the 'Bombay Bandh' be averted, if she intervened. He wanted to meet her. 'But I am a prisoner and I don't know how to obtain an interview with you.'[60] But the olive branch was too late in coming. Other leaders, worried about the absence of a road map, resorted to issuing bellicose statements. 20 August was the day of conclusion. It must all end, anyhow, on this day. The socialists were now prepared to 'withdraw strikes only on the condition [the government] releases all those arrested'. They had climbed down. It was obvious. But the Kannamwar government would have none of it. It was keen to force the strike through its course. It wanted to wear the trade unions thin, show them their place and dent Yashwantrao Chavan irreparably.

And then, on 20 August, a roaring Bombay fell silent. It wore a deserted look. The 'Bombay Bandh' was not a reverberating call any more, it was a resounding reality. It was a front-page lead story in all major dailies in the country. The *Tribune* of Chandigarh reported: 'Life in the city, rocked by waves of strikes in the last eight days, was completely paralysed today.'[61] From all accounts, the strike was the most massive demonstration to date against the rise in prices. But at the same time, a cartoon by R.K. Laxman showed the Maharashtra government, the BMC and the MMU fighting while the issue of price rise went for a toss. George was at the centre of it all: his imprisonment the key to contention, his release the main demand. But it all came to nought. The government refused to bite the bait, slash its wrist or bend its back. At midnight of 20 August, on the ninth day of the municipal strike, Madhu Limaye from jail announced the withdrawal of strike and asked workers to resume work from the morning: 'There is no point in continuing,' was his message.[62] But to keep up workers' morale he also said, 'There is no cause to be disheartened and no reason to be desperate.' That Madhu Limaye wrote this statement in prison for others to sign on only showed how tightly leashed the movement was to him.

On 21 August, while a gloating M.S. Kannamwar declared the end of strike 'in a fiasco early this morning', Madhu Limaye (at 9.40 a.m.) wrote to the state home minister requesting the government to not oppose his bail application at the high court later that morning. 'It would be helpful for all concerned.' On the same day, Ram Manohar Lohia took to the floor in Parliament: 'George Fernandes is in jail for the last four months. Who is this George Fernandes? A man of such exemplary nationalist credentials that on his question, the prime minister himself had offered apologies to the Chinese prime minister. What is his crime? He is leading the municipal workers of Bombay to

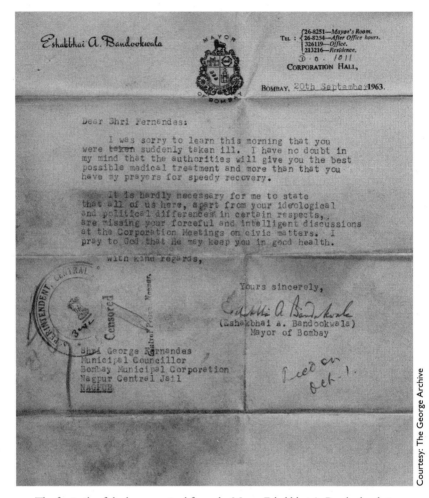

Eshakbhai A. Bandookwala

TEL : 26-8251—Mayor's Room.
26-8254—After Office hours.
326119—Office.
213216—Residence.
D.O. /011
CORPORATION HALL,

BOMBAY, 20th September 1963.

Dear Shri Fernandes:

I was sorry to learn this morning that you were taken suddenly taken ill. I have no doubt in my mind that the authorities will give you the best possible medical treatment and more than that you have my prayers for speedy recovery.

It is hardly necessary for me to state that all of us here, apart from your ideological and political differences in certain respects, are missing your forceful and intelligent discussions at the Corporation Meetings on civic matters. I pray to God that He may keep you in good health.

With kind regards,

Yours sincerely,

(Eshakbhai A. Bandookwala)
Mayor of Bombay

Shri George Fernandes
Municipal Councillor
Bombay Municipal Corporation
Nagpur Central Jail
NAGPUR

Courtesy: The George Archive

The facsimile of the letter received from the Mayor Eshakbhai A. Bandookwala is noticeable for at least two things: one for its stamp of 'Censored' and another for its content, which coming from the Bombay City Mayor, shows how authorities were divided over George's arrest.

demand a better deal. The same sweepers of Bombay who were getting Rs 90 in July 1962 began receiving Rs 85 a month after September 1962. Could anybody say that the cost of living in Bombay was reduced proportionately?'[63]

George continued to languish in Nagpur Central Jail, where he had been shifted by June end. On 3 September, in another setback, a Supreme Court bench, while ruling on George's plea, reiterated that a person detained under the DIR had no right to challenge the validity of detention.[64] On the same day, George began a letter to Ram Manohar Lohia which was written in bits and pieces and sent after many drafts. An earlier letter to Lohia was not delivered. 'I asked for reasons. They had none.' In June, George had expressed resentment at Lohia's 'unprincipled' alliance-making, and both he and Madhu Limaye had contemplated resignation from the National Committee of the Socialist Party to inject 'shock treatment' to the party and to bring the 'doctor in line'.[65] 'My Dear Doctor Saheb,' George wrote now, effusive about Lohia's determination 'to make the Lok Sabha the mirror of the suffering and aspirations of our people'. He approvingly cited a report of Vidharba's Marathi daily, *Tarun Bharat*, which said, 'All Opposition leaders in the Lok Sabha are now trailing behind Dr Ram Manohar Lohia, who is also the most sought-after MP, even by the ministers.' But the letter was understandably about himself. He wanted the Maharashtra government to prosecute him on the charges made or else he would go on a fast-unto-death.[66] His frustration was mounting and crossing the threshold of tolerance. On the promptings of A.B. Bardhan (a fact mentioned in the first draft of the letter, but deleted subsequently), who was with him in prison, George requested Ram Manohar Lohia to highlight the state of lawlessness in Maharashtra. 'Putting the Maharashtra government in the dock will earn you the gratitude of many people in this state.' He was enticing his leader by underlining the political dividend he might get by taking up the issue of detainees.[67] George was never prosecuted. Outside, though, rumours of his imminent release circulated freely. Shiva Rao was so confident of his release in November that he did not even renew the subscription for newspapers George received in jail.[68] But George was not so optimistic, as is evident from a list of things he asked for: (1) CREST aftershave lotion: 1 bottle, (2) CINTHOL soap: 6 cakes, (3) PALMOLIVE brushless shaving cream: 2 tubes, (4) Colgate toothbrush—medium: 2, (5) NIVEA cold cream: 1.

Accidents constitute history. Mundane matters prod historical movements. On 24 November, two days after an assassin snuffed out John Kennedy's life in Dallas, in Bombay, M.S. Kannamwar, the belligerent chief minister of Maharashtra, died of cerebral thrombosis at the city's St George Hospital. His disappearance from the scene brought Yashwantrao Chavan back into the reckoning. His nominee V.P. Naik took the oath of office on 7 December. In the evening of 13 December, George received his release order. He was reluctant to leave A.B. Bardhan and asked the jail superintendent if he could stay the night. When told there was no such possibility, George hugged A.B. Bardhan and left the prison, exactly eight months and eight days after his arrest. The prison authorities gave him a railway warrant to travel from Nagpur to Bombay by a mail train. At Bombay's Victoria Terminus when he disembarked, surrounded by admirers and followers, he quipped, *'Jalaanewale jal gaye'* ('The fire-bearers got burnt'), an oblique reference to his tormentor M.S. Kannamwar's death.[69]

Throughout George's imprisonment, Madhu Limaye remained in Bombay, not even going to Farrukhabad to campaign for Ram Manohar Lohia's election, and led an insistent campaign against his arrest. It was he who made strategies, forged alliances and spearheaded the workers' movement. Although underlying it all was the riveting issue of George's release, Limaye never let this demand come to fore for strategic reasons. He was adept in using Machiavellian strategies to line up allies and force them to accept his lead. His strategy was so persuasive, his rhetoric so transparent, his aggression so pronounced and his motive so subtle that he ultimately took the upper hand. But it didn't lead the socialists anywhere, nor did it give their trade unions any firmer footing. Slowly, louder demagogues came to the fore, and the Shiv Sena's parochial approach to the working class pushed the socialists into oblivion. In 1963, however, it was the socialists and the communists who set the workers' agenda in the city of Bombay.

The friendship between George and Madhu Limaye was already a decade old and would endure for two more, during which they would act in complete tandem. In contemporary politics, a friendship of this kind has seldom been witnessed. Madhu Limaye was a decade older than George and, after the death of Placid D'Mello, took him under his wing. He had found George disconsolate on the death of D'Mello and wrote movingly, 'His loss is irreplaceable,' but also asked him to brace himself for the battles ahead.[70] Madhu Limaye would send him books from outside for his reading in jail. While maintaining his functional autonomy, George along with Limaye even took on Ram Manohar Lohia. They both kept each other informed on political and trade union developments almost daily. In the days when the long-distance telephonic conversation was difficult and cumbersome, they wrote lengthy letters to each other, posted from wherever they were. They had a common vision to the extent that they both pursued power, but if for Madhu Limaye it was more an intellectual/ideological understanding of power, for George it was more emotional and instrumentalist. They complemented each other, forming a close partnership of punch and subtlety. It therefore would be a sad end when they parted ways in the mid-1980s. Madhu Limaye had by then retired from politics, having been defeated in the 1980 general elections, and would not fight any elections thereafter. In the 1980s, with their friendship still enduring but on its last legs, George would lead a public campaign to raise funds to send an ailing Madhu Limaye for a medical check-up to the United States. But their relationship would hit a block. The toddler who had clung to George's bosom and played many evenings with him would grow up to accuse him of insensitivity. 'One of the things that made me very sad, then angry, but not anymore,' Poppat would recall many years later, 'was when my mother was suffering from cancer and we were living at New Delhi residence, George never visited once, never called once, nor did he come for her funeral in November 2003.'[71]

Dissent within a democracy is always within the parameters defined by authority. This explains why a successor government to Yashwantrao Chavan would go against George. The speed with which George had risen in the 1950s was much attributed to the helping hand of Yashwantrao Chavan as the chief minister of (then) Bombay. Placid D'Mello was a fellow Royist with Chavan. After his untimely death, it was said, Yashwantrao Chavan took it upon himself to look after George's interests. Probably, he saw his political interests served in George's rise. An impression that gathered steam in Bombay was that Yashwantrao Chavan had feathered the socialist nest, by giving wings to George, to hatch his own eggs.[72] It was this impression that his successor M.S. Kannamwar was keen to demolish, besides his wish to curb the defence minister's influence in Bombay. Kannamwar, a Vidharba politician, would not brook the continued dominance of a Maratha in the affairs of the state. George paid the price for his perceived closeness to Chavan. By jailing George, the new CM was signalling Yashwantrao Chavan that times change!

* * *

We have A.B. Bardhan's testimony of life in prison.[73] Later to become general secretary of the CPI, Bardhan was a prisoner for some months together with George in the Nagpur Central Jail. They were lodged in a big yard. 'In the beginning,' he said, 'there were three of us: me, George and one person of Jamaat-e-Islami.' They had a set routine. They spent time reading and in improvised sports. He had never played cards; George taught him to play rummy, and they kept accounts of their wins and defeats. At 7 p.m., after they were served dinner, it was time for lock-up.

In jail, George was mostly doing two things: writing letters and reading books that he procured from outside. He retained a handwritten copy of each letter he wrote to friends, colleagues and family members. The solitude in jail gave him ample opportunity to devour an enormous amount of reading material.[74] Noting that 'the time of my life is here to read and study', he kept a list of books that he read. Being a multilinguist and a voracious reader, his need for books knew no bounds. He wrote to Shiva Rao asking for books in various languages and even indicated where to source them all from. 'I had asked for some Kannada, Konkani & Urdu books. What happened to them?'[75] He read William Shirer's *The Rise and Fall of the Third Reich* 'twice over to find out how such a disciplined and intelligent people like the Germans could allow themselves to be swayed by a fascist maniac'.[76] He read on the British labour movement. He liked Michael Foot's *Aneurin Bevan*, and wrote to Madhu Limaye, 'Foot always gives his hero the benefit of the doubt and pours sarcasm, ridicule and contempt on the labour leaders he does not like—Attlee, Morrison. Will you please send *In Place of Fear* over? After the biography, the autobiography will be good reading.'[77] Many books on the communist movement were withheld from him on the grounds of their 'suitability'.[78] In protest, he wrote to Jawaharlal Nehru and copied his letter to Maharashtra's home minister.[79] Seeing his interest, editors sent him books for review and asked for contributions for their journals. He reviewed *The Theory of Wages* by Hicks.[80] In October, 'the monthly symposium' journal *Seminar* invited him to contribute 'a most incisive and thought-provoking piece' on the 'poser' *The Workers' Share* in their upcoming issue.[81] George wrote a piece titled 'Increasing Poverty'. With an uncommon determination for which he was already known, he began to learn Urdu script, first by using Munshi Premchand's *Karbala*. His enclosed residence didn't give him claustrophobia. On the contrary, he utilized the opportunity well in intellectual pursuits. A friend though wrote, 'It has, in that sense, been a good thing. But there is also something like "too much of a good thing" which can engender surfeit.'[82]

While in jail he received newspapers sent by colleagues although initially there were considerable hiccups.[83] The cost of the newspapers was added to his account, which left no reserve for him to make any other purchases.[84] After he returned from the futile trip to Delhi to attend the Supreme Court hearing, George asked Shiva Rao to send him Bombay newspapers of August.[85] He asked for almost all the English, Marathi and Hindi newspapers published in Bombay. He wanted Shiva Rao to send him 'in one bundle . . . all Bombay papers from 1 August till the date you receive this letter, and also arrange to have the subscription copies for future.'[86]

One day, sick of a jail superintendent's regular rounds, George and Bardhan planned some mischief. At the appointed time, when he was to visit the yard, they decided to strut around in their underwear in the barracks. 'When he saw us in our semi-nude state, he hurried back never to come on his visits again,' recalled Bardhan. But the jailer was furious at their disrespectful behaviour. He ordered a restriction on the number of books they could keep in their cell even if sourced by themselves. His limit was twelve, when George had close to sixty books in his stack. The superintendent also imposed a ban for a fortnight on their interviews and correspondence. They petitioned against both orders in the Nagpur High Court.[87] Arguing his case himself, George said books received from private sources could only be restricted on the grounds of 'unsuitability'. As they were needed for study, it was difficult to know how many books were needed at a time. Further, a similar restriction was not imposed any time in jails they had been formerly detained (Arthur Road, Nasik and Delhi). The opposing counsel argued that 'the detenus had no legal right to books except the books from the jail library'. The restriction on the number of books was imposed as somewhere a line had to be drawn and also due to security aspects. The court held that both orders of the jail authorities were unwarranted and the rights were restored.

Aloysius Fernandes (Louie), his brother, wrote regularly to 'Jerrybab' (George), keeping him informed with small but spicy family tales. Sometimes, Louie typed letters to avoid delay due to censors; typed letters made the job of deciphering easier and therefore reached George faster. 'My Dear Jerrybab,' Louie wrote on 12 June, 'Gopal informed me over the phone . . . that there was a general improvement in your physique . . .' George's tendency to gain weight was a joke among family members. On 25 September, cousin Cliffy Saldana wrote to George, 'It was nice to hear that you are quite hale and cheerful, but I do hope you don't go and put on weight—too much of it, as Placid D'Mello did while in detention.' They were aware of the sacrifices he was making for the cause of human dignity. Louie wrote, 'I sincerely hope your period of (ar)rest does not go beyond October or November.'[88] The health of their parents was a constant cause of worry for the brothers situated at various locations in the country.[89]

Being in prison for so long was difficult, particularly for him who had been so active and alive outside. Allowed as he was one fortnightly visit from family and friends, George made sure that he met everyone and no one was inconvenienced. His handmade calendar kept track of visits. By November, he was settled enough at the Nagpur Jail to tell the Home Department to leave him alone when they planned to transfer him to Yeravada. He longed for the outside world but at the same time was in a state of mind that made him 'ready to spend another twelve months here'.[90]

On 3 September, George wrote a pensive but poignant letter to one Bina, perhaps a love interest. He signed off by writing the enigmatic 'May I tell you something?', an unsaid something that lovers generally coo to each other. She was the one whose health George was worried about—he wrote to Dastur to take care of her. She had a son, Pappu, for whom George expressed parental concern, inquiring about his studies and sports: 'Your mother desires that you come first, but I shall be happy if you are there among first ten. Study a little late in the night, get up early in the morning.' George invited them both to visit him in jail during vacation. The content of the letter is a poignant reflection of his state of mind in jail. 'Outside, I made news, but inside I have to hear news from you all,' he wrote to Bina. And then added, 'It is not good to write that I am fine in jail, nor is it proper to say that I have difficulties here. Once you are inside the walls of the prison, your world changes a little, the strength of mind and body is sapped as if it has been drained off outside the walls. I can only say this much that even these days shall pass.'[91] Bina in all probability was the wife of a journalist.[92] In those days, given the circumstances under which dedicated public figures worked, such multilayered relationships were more accepted. It gave the political figure a family with no strings attached. It has not been possible to ascertain from scant available sources the nature of relationship George shared with the family, but he certainly shared a warm relationship with them. This journalist, who wrote aggressively against the smugglers in Bombay, was murdered in the late 1960s, the time when George won his first parliamentary election. George took up the anti-smuggling drive in Parliament and wrote many letters to prime minister Indira Gandhi demanding action.

How helpless is a person before the might of the state! No quarters help him. Did this experience contribute to George becoming such an indefatigable fighter for civil liberty and against wrongs done by the state? The insinuation of being anti-national, and the pain it caused him, surely made him an uncompromising soldier of non-Congressism. He was jailed at a time when the state, due to the scare at the borders, had become severe on its citizens. He would, however, not let the experience crush his faith or shatter his exuberant belief in the individual's capacity to effect change. The experience would strengthen him emotionally and morally. It would bring him maturity, and his urge to take sides against injustice would remain ever raw. When as the defence minister of India he would learn of Iftikhar Gilani, jailed for allegedly violating the Official Secrets Act, George was to remember his distant midnight arrest. Iftikhar Gilani, journalist and son-in-law of Kashmiri separatist leader Syed Ali Shah Geelani, was tortured and wrongfully detained for seven long months in Delhi's Tihar Jail. Upon Iftikhar Gilani's release, not least due to George's intervention, George would spend hours with him, even cancelling his attendance at the President's reception on Republic Day. Gilani recalls George telling him 'to put the pain and the anguish I had suffered behind me and look forward to a bright future'.[93] George understood the helplessness and isolation of a man accused of an act he had never committed, incarcerated solely because some bungling mandarins in the government wished so. He had learnt the hard way to forgive, even while not forgetting the experience at all.

* * *

Nothing explains George's arrest. While he was detained allegedly for threatening the administration, Shripad Amrit Dange, who had advised the workers not to work free an extra day in aid of the national defence fund, got off scot-free.[94] In contrast, George had urged members of his trade unions to contribute 'till it hurt'. In fact, after the Chinese attack, he had temporarily suspended all agitations. As Raj Narain wrote to Lal Bahadur Shastri, pointing out the injustice of it all, 'between 22 October 1962 and January 1963 the ministers used to tag George along in all their government meetings'. It was ironic that after his arrest the same ministers had the gumption to call George anti-national. Moreover, three days after his arrest, the government revised the taxi fare structure, meeting the demand raised by him. And, also, a month after the Bombay Bandh of 20 August, the CDS was eventually withdrawn. The government also instituted the Lakdawala

Committee, named after the economist who headed it, to look into the issue of Cost of Living Index and its computing method.

Was George's arrest a result of inter-union rivalries? Or was it a result of political rivalry between one who had recently shifted to the Centre and the one who remained in the province, at first as an obedient follower and then as a rebel eager to carve his own space, an eerily repetitive story in Indian politics? Not that the Government of India was at all serious about enforcing Emergency conditions. These were Nehru's last days, rattled by the swift defeat that the Chinese had inflicted. Jawaharlal Nehru was more worried about making a success of his succession plan. As George's acquaintance wrote, 'It is amazing how stupid the government can be. The entire defence effort and zeal of a year ago have fizzled out beyond recall, and not a bloody minister thought about sweets and sweaters for jawans this Diwali. The bloody fools are deeply involved in their squabbles.'

There was a moral courage in George that gave him the strength to take on the mightiest in the land. In the first week of December, while still in jail, he was elected president of the Maharashtra branch of the Socialist Party. By the end of the month, he would be in Calcutta, taking on Ram Manohar Lohia himself on the issue of political alliance. Some years ahead, he would take on the mightiest of all, S.K. Patil, on his own turf.

6

Stepping Up

A decade after George's release from jail, someone not particularly known for friendliness would still be obliged to call George the 'most dynamic trade union leader of the country'.[1] These words would be spoken on the floor of Parliament, when he was in jail again for having caused a strike on railways. Over the years of the decade, he would lead many a strike of Bombay's working underclass to bring the city to a repeated stop. And, built on his profile as militant labour leader, he would craft his stupendous first-ever victory in the parliamentary election, and also lose it four years later in the next. If his friendship with Madhu Limaye got further enmeshed, they lost their indomitable leader Ram Manohar Lohia to an unforeseen death and an intrepid colleague Raj Narain to political rivalry. Eventually, George would head a united Socialist Party without the affix of united but, by then, it was too late to resuscitate the party long set on an inexorable slide into oblivion. Twice he was bludgeoned to near death, but each time he not just survived to tell his tale, he also augmented his steadily growing political weight. And after a series of 'involvements', he finally got married to Leila Kabir, but as he would say later, the day he got married was the last day he ever smiled.[2]

* * *

On 13 December 1963, when George stepped out of the jail, a riotous welcome awaited him in Bombay. Thereafter, he went to Calcutta to attend the Socialist Party's convention where he rose to speak in a conscious challenge to his leader Ram Manohar Lohia. It had so happened that when he was in jail a few by-elections to the Lok Sabha had been held in May. One of those constituencies was Farrukhabad, for which the party proposed Ram Manohar Lohia as candidate. In March, when Madhu Limaye visited Farrukhabad, spending a fortnight gauging perception, he found the constituency bereft of any party organization, but, he wrote to George, 'the people here say that the general climate is favourable to Doctor'.[3] Even while the party drummed up support for him, Ram Manohar Lohia until April remained unsure. Keeping true to the rules he had himself framed, Lohia insisted on having a people's committee in every village before he agreed to contest. Ultimately, he gave his consent, and that made a chagrined Madhu Limaye lament, 'Why did Doctor insist on conditions when he knew that their fulfilment could only be a fraud?'[4] It was not an isolated case of his 'silly conviction' about which they were much agitated. Soon after he filed his nomination, Lohia spoke of how the by-elections had acquired high stakes. 'I know that nothing short of a people's soul is at stake.'[5] Ever critical of the Nehru government, he was more so since the border clashes with China. After the war had concluded in a swift and severe humiliation of India, remembrance of which is unpleasant, while Asoka Mehta found one more pretext to push the PSP socialists into the Congress, Lohia took an aggressive and contrary posture, arguing for an electoral alliance of Opposition parties to defeat the Congress whose rule he called a national shame. To inaugurate such a design, he resolved to campaign for Jan Sangh president Deen Dayal Upadhyay (1916–68) who was a candidate in the by-election from Jaunpur.

Lohia knew there were 'walls of misunderstanding and suspicion' between the Jan Sangh and the Muslims. He blamed Nehru and the Congress for the same. In January 1948, Jawaharlal Nehru had reasoned with a civil bureaucrat who asked his advice on dealing with the remnants of the Muslim League that it was 'bound to disappear' sooner than expected and therefore might safely be left alone.[6] It was dying by itself—why kick it now to give it martyrdom? The prime minister didn't favour the Muslim League's disbanding. 'Muslims', Jawaharlal Nehru wrote to this Madras deputy commissioner, exactly four and a half months after Partition, are a 'beaten community'. His worry was 'chiefly the RSS', Nehru wrote to the Bombay chief minister, B.G. Kher (1888–1957).[7] He accused the RSS of fanning the communal clashes, of being the agent provocateur. In the wake of Gandhi's murder, however, the RSS was banned, its leaders jailed, and despite lofty outbursts of the murderer, a pall of gloom hung over the nation. Suddenly, after these two vile acts of India's Partition and the Mahatma's murder, the communal tension in the country had considerably weakened. Electorally too, if there was any meaning in the first general elections, it was in the total decimation of the communal parties.[8] Yet, Jawaharlal Nehru continued to harp on about communalism, more so on its Hindu variety. The more he attacked it, the more he evoked a spectre of its monstrous rise, not only making the Muslims distrust Hindus but also herding them favourably into the Congress fold. If the Congress survived by fanning mutual distrust, by raising the bogey of the Ugly Hindu, reasoned Lohia, its defeat required correcting that mischief, and it would eventually happen if he succeeded in bringing 'Jan Sangh and Muslim minds towards each other'. Hence, his resolve to campaign for the Jan Sangh president Deen Dayal Upadhyay in the Jaunpur by-election. This was a brand new Lohia.[9]

In his older form, he had advocated going alone in order not to contaminate the radical purity of his outfit. In 1955, at the time of the Socialist Party's foundation, Lohia had laid an ambitious road map to political power within seven swift years. Calling it the only genuinely radical party, Lohia refused to have any truck with other existing parties and denounced political alliances as crutches. However, the political power he was seeking failed to materialize. His rigid, puritan politics only reaped defeats. His theory of equidistance—to keep equally aloof from both the Congress and the communists—not only made him chip away from the Congressward-tilting PSP, and form an independent Socialist Party, but also forced him to scuttle repeated subsequent attempts at socialist unity.[10] 'Had we been a little flexible in 1957,' Madhu Limaye wrote to Rama Mitra, Lohia's partner, 'I cannot say of others, but I could certainly have won a Parliament seat for myself.'[11] The defeat was more galling as he had returned a hero from Goa after a jail term. Madhu Limaye, despite toeing the Lohia line, would not forgive him for the slight he had felt at his odious defeat. Even in 1962, in the third general elections, Lohia had forced a no-alliance policy. His shift, therefore, from a rigid 'going alone' to his now ardent advocacy of 'all-in' alliance surprised and angered his colleagues.

Lohia won the by-election at Farrukhabad, despite being maligned by the Congress as both anti-Brahmin and anti-Muslim.[12] At the age of fifty-four, he fought his way into the Lok Sabha.[13] Madhu Limaye thought Lohia's Jaunpur campaign for the Jan Sangh president made his victory a 'tainted thing'. He wrote to Rama Mitra: 'Do we have any fixed principles or is it all a matter of expediency?'[14] On 18 June, from inside his prison cell in Nagpur Central Jail, George wrote to Madhu Limaye, 'Doctor has shocked me, as he has shocked so many others.'[15] It was a long letter describing in detail his disenchantment with 'Doctor'. The cause of his resentment was Lohia's flinging 'to the winds principles for which we have sacrificed so much'. He suggested resignation from the national committee to administer 'shock treatment' to bring the party in line, or as he wrote, to actually bring the 'Doctor' in line. 'I believe it's time the Socialist Party got wedded with an ideology which is more than just what Doctor says.' But even while he wrote, 'I know the ideology is there,' he knew as well that 'minus Doctor', there was no party! Aware of the party's dependence on him, Lohia showed no compunction in unilaterally dictating its choices. As the two friends were unhappy with Lohia, they both resigned, George sending his resignation from jail.

In 1963, Lohia was at the peak of his political career, having finally arrived after many years of desperate wandering. The by-election victory put him in a happy and marauding mood. He was a firm believer in the dictum 'Out of chaos, only good can emerge'. He earnestly set upon churning chaos. On the very day of taking oath of membership in Parliament, Lohia in association with others moved the first-ever no-confidence motion against the Nehru cabinet alleging all-round failure.[16] It was moved by J.B. Kripalani, the prime minister's old colleague. But its main ammunition was provided by Lohia, whose speech on the motion was original, incisive and laid bare the innards of the Nehru government. His was a harsh assessment: 'The winds that have blown over the country for the past eighteen years have been ill, very ill.' Those years coincided with the period of Nehru's regime. Lohia spoke on a devastatingly sarcastic note, ripping the Nehruvian myth of development to shreds when he said his was a government of, by and for just 50 lakh people in a country of 34 crore. As he spoke, if the House was spellbound, the press gallery was at the edge of its seat in excitement.[17] It was a scene-changer. The next day, for the first time in his career perhaps, he was on the front page of most newspapers. With Lohia coming in, Parliament became a livelier arena of action; the Opposition was more legitimate and audible. Many of Lohia's ideas were erroneous at their foundational core, yet the sheer force of the eloquence, courage and conviction with which he aired them, and the irreverent manner and the apt timing of their airing, all provided a great ballast to his words. Nehru, in turn, poked fun, even insults, at his audacity, and cautioned the new member to observe parliamentary decorum.

The Socialist Party met at Calcutta in the last week of December for its national convention. Fresh from an eight-month-long jail term, George hogged the limelight. He was in such an unbeatable mood that he spoke against the political resolution moved by Raj Narain, the party chairman.[18] The resolution was a verbatim reproduction of Lohia's inaugural speech, making it in effect Lohia-sponsored. It envisaged a coalition of political forces against the Congress. George attacked it for espousing the idea of 'all-in' political alliance. Some ten years before, when the controversy of coalitionist politics was raging, when it was said the acceptance of JP's fourteen points would give the Congress its much-needed vitality, and therefore the socialists would do well in joining it, Lohia had said, 'Reform of other political parties should never become an aim of one's political action.'[19] He was now proposing to do exactly what he had derided all along, George said. It was not their task to remove the barriers between the Muslims and the Jan Sangh. Though the resolution was endorsed and carried through, George's opposition created intense ill feeling. Days later, he went to Delhi, to Lohia's home for lunch, where Rama Mitra and Raj Narain joined him. 'The atmosphere is, to say the least, suffocating,' he wrote to Madhu Limaye. 'Even if you sneeze, people read meanings and purpose in it. It's hell.'[20]

Lohia went on with relentlessly pursuing his idea, which came to be called non-Congressism. In order to build a stronger socialist force, he proposed, against his well-known position, an 'unconditional' merger of the Socialist Party (SP) with the PSP, the two warring splinters of socialism.[21] In June 1964, both groups, after almost a decade of separate and mutually wrangling existence, merged to form the Samyukta Socialist Party (SSP). The democratic compulsion weighing upon them brought them together, but it was an uneasy alliance of leaders who until recently had been famously berating each other. In the letters exchanged between them even on the eve of the merger, and in the months leading to it, there was a marked proclivity to score points, to snipe at each other, in a soft, unhurried way, while at the same time making a show of urgency.[22] Each tried to show how the other was more confused about the issues involved. They conveyed a meaningless rancour, duelled over vapour-nothings and argued endlessly about what came first, hen or egg. While conveying anxiety about socialist unity, they were unyielding and took pleasure at each other's discomfiture. The SP and PSP were a wrangling couple pushed into a compromising position by circumstances; given a chance, they would have preferred to remain longingly apart, even if coming close enlivened them. It was an awkward way to break the ice after a long, frosty relationship. The marked immaturity in their exchange was one more reason why a party of socialism did not survive in India. The frontline leaders were cavalier about the task at hand, that is, of the merger in the face of depleting strength. There was much reminding of the past, and, instead of planning a future together, there was gingerly digging up of the deeds of the other. Ultimately, they were proving that their differences were nothing but their inability to get rid of the 'petty small-town politicking' they had grown accustomed to.[23] Such things happen when the larger aim eludes you and you have no notion of an unfolding future because of the pettifogging in the present. Not surprisingly, when the unified party met for its first national conference at Varanasi in January 1965, it ended up coming unhinged at the very spot into its pre-unified formations. While the PSP returned to its old form, although a little shrunken, the experience of merger augmented the SP which became the SSP, the Samyukta Socialist Party.

* * *

In the fourth general elections held in February 1967, Lohia's non-Congressism yielded handsome results, but not so much for the SSP; it was the RSS-hoisted Jan Sangh that benefited the most. George fought his first parliamentary election ever and was rewarded for his exceptional courage by a remarkable victory against incumbent S.K. Patil. Known as an uncrowned king of Bombay, Patil was Bombay City mayor for three consecutive terms when George had just arrived, and in 1956, when he had begun his Municipal Mazdoor Union, Patil's life-size portrait was unveiled in the Corporation Hall.[24] A member of the Congress syndicate, S.K. Patil was the railway minister in Indira Gandhi's cabinet when his dream of becoming India's home minister after the elections was shattered by his crushing defeat at the hands of George. In the run-up to the elections, when S.K. Patil reminded 'Dear Voters' that he had served the city for over thirty-two years, George quipped that given his prolonged service, he deserved a period of retirement.[25] Around this theme—that S.K. Patil needed a rest—George wove his electoral campaign. South Bombay, where the contest took place, was the smallest of Lok Sabha constituencies. He had been preparing for the combat for long. One day in 1962, after the third general elections, when George and a colleague were sitting on the tetrapods strewn along the seashore of Marine Drive from where they could see the celebratory mood in Patil's house, George conjured up a happy augury of defeating him in the next.[26] If he pursued his dream zealously, S.K. Patil too didn't leave a stone unturned to return victorious. In the times when the holy cow had gained political traction, he projected himself as 'a champion of the cow, a good Hindu and a staunch Maharashtrian' in contrast to George who was 'a Christian, a Mangalorean and a trade unionist'.[27] Promising a total ban on cow slaughter—'If I fail in that, I will quit public life'—Patil proposed a provident fund for aged cows. In Bombay, where providing for hungry and homeless, old and infirm humans was an immediate necessity, his attempt to communally divide the electorate didn't work.

George's electoral triumph came at the climax of a busy decade (1957–67) during which he had not only emerged as a trade union leader in his own right but also inched higher into the echelons of a fledgling Socialist Party. Still, it was hard to believe Patil could be

The *Free Press Journal* (Bombay) of 7 February 1967 that front-paged the above picture said in its caption: 'QUICK WORK—The poster at left came up all over South Bombay one fine morning. That night a lot of people must have been busy. For, the next morning, same poster had become as shown on right.'

defeated. A cartoon depicted him leaping from the top of the Bombay Municipal Corporation building to that of Parliament. S.K. Patil believed in his own invincibility. Defeating him was an impossible dream. In one presser, as the campaign began to heat up, Patil was asked, 'What do you think of this challenge from George? Can he defeat you?' Patil snapped back with the known arrogance, 'Even God cannot defeat me!' This boast was suicidal. The following day, it was headline-grabbing news: 'Even God Cannot Defeat Me, says S K Patil.' It became the battle cry of George's campaign. He unleashed a poster war.[28] A sympathetic South Bombay Citizen's Committee issued a poster bearing the inscription, 'Now, It's the People against S.K. Patil: George Fernandes for Parliament'. Overnight, a similar-looking poster appeared in the adjoining spaces that said, 'Now, It's the People who vote for S.K. Patil: George Fernandes for Parliament'.[29] It was obviously a Patil supporter's doing, but it generated some amusement for the electorate. George benefited as well from the internal Congress crisis in which a rookie Indira Gandhi was hoping for freedom from the syndicate bosses. All the anti-syndicate forces, including Indira Gandhi herself, it is said, ganged up against Patil. Everyone wanted Patil to be defeated.

A decade later, while he was jailed at Hissar, facing a charge of conspiring to overthrow a duly elected government, George recalled V.K. Krishna Menon's role in his election victory.[30] Denied a Congress nomination, Menon fought independently from North Bombay but was defeated, drowned by the vitriol of the Shiv Sena's parochialism that made the election campaign poisonous. But he helped George by sponsoring candidates against the Congress that diverted Patil's resources and distracted his attention from his own battleground. Menon was called an outsider. Speaking one day many years later, as a Central government minister, George remembered how he himself had 'often come up against the same problem'.[31] Without referring to S.K. Patil's 'outsider and Christian' jibe that had hurt him, George said, 'I have often heard that I am an outsider. Some say I am a Christian. Well, I did not have the choice to select my parents.' But it was openly insinuated then that, despite S.K. Patil's professed love for the cow, and despite the Jan Sangh having its candidate in the fray, the RSS had backed George in his fight against Patil.[32]

'It was a miracle. We had no money. We had no organization,' recalled a colleague of George's giant-killing election victory.[33] His determination had enthused people and support poured in.[34] Olga

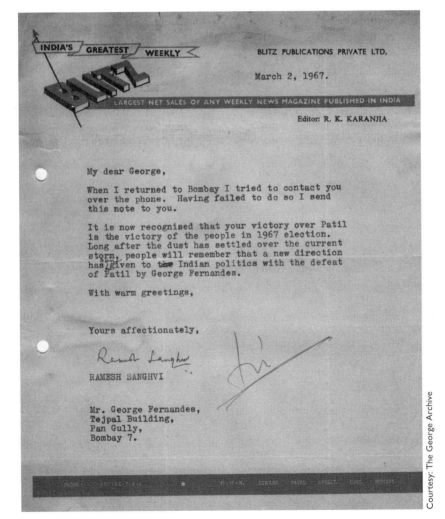

Facsimile of a letter among the hundreds of congratulatory messages received by George on his electoral victory over S.K. Patil. There was much hope in the air. Not only was he a voice of democracy, it was felt he would change the political destiny of India in the years to come.

Tellis, who worked in the *Statesman* but wrote a column in *Blitz* under a pseudonym, constituted a group called Youth for George Fernandes. She would become a lifelong friend who would remember how he was always without money in his wallet.[35] When his victory was announced, a cacophony of congratulatory messages arrived from across the country, from unknown people and family acquaintances, from trade unions and ex-politicians. There were prefabricated telegraphic messages and handwritten ones in Marathi, Hindi or English from unions of hotel and pharmaceutical workers, from bodies of railwaymen and insurance agents. In their enthusiasm, senders mixed up emotions and sent messages meant for occasions other than an election victory. The enthused party units offered their 'revolutionary salute'. They hoped his 'victory will advance working-class interest'. One called it a 'success of God over a fiend', while another congratulated him 'for overpowering Congress bull in country's china shop'. The president of the Karnataka Catholics' Association informed him, 'Kanara,

Courtesy: Fredrick D'Sa, Bombay Taximen's Union

In the aftermath of his election victory there was much feting and felicitation in Bombay. Here, George is speaking at a felicitation function held in his honour at Maratha Mandir. Also seen in the picture are his closest comrades: (to his right) Bal Dandavate and Dinkar Sakrikar.

Catholics, Bangalore rejoicing.' A professor from Kolhapur wrote, 'By defeating Patil you have not only saved democracy but taken it one step ahead.' A Goan ex-minister wrote, 'News greeted with crackers throughout Panaji.' From Calcutta came congratulations for 'routing minister of accidents'. Meghnad Bhatt of Bombay wrote: 'If I were a schoolboy I would write an essay on the happiest day of my life. We waved at you when you moved in the mammoth procession from our side! Durga says: "May the smile on your face ever be the index of the happiness of the generations to come."'[36] Someone from Delhi wrote, '*Dilli kabhi bhi door nahin thi.*' 'My Dear George,' wrote Madhu Dandavate, 'Parliament will provide a new forum to you to serve the cause of socialism.'[37]

The small margin (of 500 votes) of Lohia's re-election at Farrukhabad in the general elections was, however, of concern for the party. In March, Rama Mitra wrote, 'Doctor is physically and

Courtesy: Raghu Rai / (sourced from Richard Fernandes)

This expressive face of George at a victory
felicitation rally in March 1967 was captured by
India's ace photographer Raghu Rai.

mentally completely worn out. Suddenly he is looking so aged.'[38] She took him to Kanyakumari for some much-needed solitude to calm his ruffled nerves. In October, he died. When Lohia was on his deathbed, a botched-up operation draining the life out of him, many socialist-supported state governments were in the saddle and there was a scramble to fetch doctors to look into his ailment.[39] George brought one from Bombay to Delhi's Willingdon Hospital (renamed Dr Ram Manohar Lohia Hospital) where the leader lay motionless. But it was already too late. 'The doctor who had operated upon Lohia had caused so much damage that it would be a miracle if he is saved,' a still affected George would write from somewhere in the underground when an imprisoned Jayaprakash Narayan stared at a similar irreparable threat to his life. 'The doctor later even received an award from Indira Gandhi.'[40] A week after Lohia's death, George wrote to a colleague, 'When I met him in Delhi on 21 September, he wanted me to spend some time with him. I was so busy with the small problems that I could only ring up from the airport on my way to Bombay to say why I could not meet him. That's going to eat at my conscience for the rest of my life.'[41]

Throughout 1967, there were rarely any occasions when in Parliament George asked questions on his own. The street fighter was in a rarefied environment that boasted of set mannerisms, etiquettes, norms and rules. He looked at first ill at ease in this company. His combative instinct, his spontaneous repartee, his ready wit, his confidence, the elements in his nature that made him who he was, were rarely in evidence in this year. It would be some time before he discovered his moorings. He was cautious, circumspect and restrained in the presence of Lohia. He became more voluble after the leader's demise. All George's interventions, his budgetary speeches, his verbal salvos in his first term in the Lok Sabha were in Hindi, keeping with the Lohiaite tradition. His grip over the Urdu language that he had acquired during his long incarceration vested in him a rich vocabulary that he used in his speeches.[42] In due course, he would come to acquire a parliamentary persona that would be singularly his own, when he spoke, quoting data, citing anecdotes, in a modulated tone, bringing his command over multiple languages to the fore.

If anything, his parliamentary interventions—the din and dash, the scathing and surreal, the witty and wishful—bear an imprint of his earthy nature and a raw anger. Springing forth from his socialist convictions were subjects he passionately believed in. Corruption in the licence-permit-quota raj, violation of norms by large industrial houses, the nexus between politicians and smugglers, SC/ST vacancies in services, labour victimization and apathy to the plight of the common man were themes on which his parliamentary interventions revolved. The weight of deplorable conditions of railway porters or city scavengers were brought to bear on the parliamentary consciousness. His constant espousal of workers' rights, his sharp attack on ministerial or bureaucratic misdemeanours, his speeches during budget discussions— most often on the railways—brought a common-man perspective at the macro level. Anyone making anti-workers remarks, even if asking for efficiency and productivity, raised his hackles. 'What punishment,' he asked, 'does the government contemplate taking against the mill owners who plundered the mills and made it sick, the mills in which now the government is going to invest crores?'[43] The industrial sickness in his opinion arose owing to the incompetencies and corruption of owners rather than from strikes and agitations of workers. J. Mohamed Imam, a member from Chitradurga, sarcastically appreciated George's sensitivity towards workers' issues as only natural: 'I can understand his feeling towards the workers with whose help he has been elected to this House perhaps.'[44] His concerns were national, although he was partial to issues arising out of Bombay. He repeatedly raised the problems of commuting in Bombay's suburban trains. He skirted the issue of the Shiv Sena's communal actions, calling it a nationwide phenomenon, not limited to Bombay alone, where at first there was a clamour for public-sector units and then the demand would arise for restricting opportunities to the sons of the soil alone. Such parochial organizations were sprouting all over the country due to growing unemployment. His drumming up of support for the oppressed humanity in Tibet, Africa or elsewhere reflected a restless but sensitive mind.

George mastered the art of citing the government's own sources in his speeches to expose it. It became a pattern: first trash the statistics and then thrash the government for the claims that didn't match the ground reality. The treasury benches squirmed under his onslaught. Creating a frustrating commotion, they would ask, 'Where did you get all these data from?' That was the moment he would be waiting for, as he would reply, undeterred, 'From your yearbook.' When ministers replied in monosyllables to parliamentary queries, it made him angry. On 15 May 1969, he asked 'whether the Planning Commission have prepared any data of the total number of persons who will be rendered unemployed during the next five years'. Bhagwat Jha Azad, the minister of state in the Ministry of Labour, Employment and Rehabilitation, answered simply with a 'No.' An indignant George addressing the Speaker said, 'The minister should feel some shame in answering in such a manner.' Azad did not take kindly to this, and rising to his feet said, 'He should learn some decorum while speaking.' But George shrugged him off haughtily, and echoing Lohia, said, 'Please do not teach how we should speak here; do so outside.' The socialist dominance over the parliamentary proceedings was so complete that a member vented his exasperation when he noted, 'Sir, for the last ten years this is how it is going on: Hem Barua on Nagaland, George Fernandes on Bombay and Madhu Limaye on Jayanti Shipping Company have been asking questions related to these and have been wasting public money. Why don't you for once and all finish their queries?'[45] None of the named members had a decade-old parliamentary presence, yet, their presence seemed so overwhelming, dominance so substantial, command so proficient and interventions so learned that the socialists created an illusion of permanence. On 24 April 1968, even the Speaker said to George, 'I wonder how old parliamentarians like yourself can get up at any time and move motions like that,' forgetting he was just a year old in Parliament.

George was an angry young parliamentarian. When two UP ministers in Delhi, where they had come to protest, were thrashed and arrested, their demonstration dispersed and harassed, George observed, 'If such barbarity can be exhibited against two ministers whose arrest is newsworthy, then it is beyond imagination what is happening with the common people in courts, by the police. I am more concerned about this.'[46] For him, the security paraphernalia around ministers was revolting; being stopped to let the prime-ministerial cavalcade pass first was a violation of democracy. 'Go to Sweden, Belgium or Norway, countries whose incomes are much higher than India—you would see their prime ministers standing in queue for the bus to go home after work. But here, traffic is brought to a halt so that the prime ministerial cavalcade can pass.' And when two fellow MPs were censured for walking out during the President's address, George was reminded of a rickshaw wallah who was hauled up and imprisoned for getting too close to visiting prime minister Nehru in Nagpur. 'In place of Babu rickshaw-wallah, today is Hiren Mukerjee and Ishaq Shambhali, and in place of the prime minister is the president of the republic. What dignity remains in the president of the republic if members of Parliament cannot even bring to his notice the discontent prevalent in the country?'[47] He was concerned about the police firings to quell people's protests, but it was also not surprising if he asked about the number of schools run by the government or missionaries in the NEFA (North East Frontier Area, now Arunachal Pradesh). When a jhuggi in Delhi was allegedly burnt by the police who went to apprehend the man dwelling in it 'as a result of which his wife got serious burn injuries, gave birth to a dead child in a hospital and ultimately succumbed to the injuries', he raised the issue in Parliament. He asked for support to artists fallen on bad times. One Jitendra Burman, 'a famous musician, a big artist of Delhi Akashvani', died a destitute, so much so that his still working colleagues made contributions to carry out his last rites. Another, 'a famous clarinet artist' removed from Madras Air due to old age, died in a pitiable condition. In his last days, he was reduced to playing his clarinet at funerals to earn his living. A third was Istiyak Ahmad, a sarod player who had earlier represented India abroad, whose family lived miserably in a corner of Old Delhi after his death. Such instances of concern were not few, but parliamentary etiquette didn't permit sustained argumentation.[48] Ministers answered only to the extent they were prepared by notes provided by bureaucrats. He was so disillusioned and frustrated with the dilatory, sterile and wasteful procedures that, a year after coming to Parliament, he contemplated

Courtesy: Fredrick D'Sa, Bombay Taximen's Union, Mumbai

Four years after that stupendous victory at the South Bombay
constituency, George stood defeated, losing even his deposit,
so humiliating was the defeat. It was said he had supported the
Indo-Israel friendship, and therefore Muslims who had supported
him overwhelmingly in 1967 deserted him in 1971.

resigning his membership.[49] He stressed it was no substitute for mass
work but only a platform for airing public grievances, frustrations and
hopes. In the absence of vigilant public pressure, remedial measures
were scarcely available. Moreover, elections were expensive, nor did
victory mean any respite. S.K. Patil after his defeat went to court
against him, and the defence required money and time that could well
be used in more productive ways. 'How can any ordinary person put
up with this harassment?' George asked, in his statement denying that
he was resigning.[50]

Four years after his 'giant-killing' Lok Sabha debut, George
stood abjectly defeated in the same constituency of South Bombay.
The year 1967 had seen his peak in Bombay after which, according
to his trade union colleagues, the pace slackened. Earlier, he used to

work eighteen hours a day. That thrill went missing once he became a parliamentarian. In 1971, the fervour was lacking. His union colleagues saw him transformed into a self-occupied politician. In the fifth general elections held midterm in March 1971, Indira Gandhi gathered a brute majority. The SSP and all other Opposition parties were defeated by her rise. His defeat was attributed to his neglect of the constituency. He had promised much, like the municipal councillor he was when he had stood up in the fray, but as an MP he seldom had an opportunity to fulfil his word. He fumbled in his electoral strategy as well. His making pro-Israel remarks, when his constituency had a significant Muslim population, went against conventional politics and was a strategic failure, contributing to his defeat.[51] Critical of Sheikh Abdullah's continued arrest for fourteen long years on unexplained charges, George had asked for his release. 'You arrest him, then leave him, then again arrest him. There is no justification in spending so much money on a person who indulges in anti-national activities. There have been several people under detention, Balraj Madhok was under detention, I was under detention for long, big leaders of all political parties have been under detention sometime or the other, everybody has tested its [the government's] hospitality, but is there any other person in the country on whose detention so much money was spent?'[52] His pro-Sheikh speech in Parliament was not taken kindly to by the Congress. 'In the 1971 election campaign, the Congian Muslims subjected me to vicious and poisonous abuse for speaking up for Sheikh Abdullah,' he would note in his prison journal during Indira Gandhi's Emergency.[53] He was still obsessed with S.K. Patil whom he accused of hobnobbing with smugglers. Patil did not take the insinuation lying down. Congress was now divided, and Patil's Congress (O) took up the battle in Parliament. In a personal letter to the Speaker read out on the floor of Parliament, S.K. Patil said, 'Even Mr Fernandes can be in a photograph with me and that does not prove that he is connected with me except in the sense that he wants to abuse me.' But in his eagerness to nail S.K. Patil, George only strengthened Indira Gandhi in her factional feud with erstwhile Congress colleagues. His anti-smuggling drive in Parliament and outside failed to yield any results. In his many letters to her, he accused Indira Gandhi of sheltering smugglers. His defeat was also attributed to his drive against smugglers such as Haji Mastan and Yousuf Patel. When attacked by Opposition trade union leaders in October 1975, Michael Fernandes underlined this as the main cause of George's defeat in 1971. George's drive against smugglers and his fruitless appeal to Indira Gandhi for action made him believe that the Congressmen were hand-in-glove with the smugglers.[54] Actually, the moneybags in Bombay no longer thought highly of S.K. Patil, as a new claimant to their patronage had sounded the bugle in the form of the Shiv Sena who would fight the socialists to wrest their hold over the city's labouring class.[55] Defeat would make George return to Bombay's trade unionism, but it would not be long-lasting. From being a local leader and Bombay-based trade unionist, he was now a national leader. Since he was acquiring a national image, he began to organize trade unions on a national scale; his national labour front Hind Mazdoor Panchayat (HMP) absorbed his attention along with the All India Railwaymen's Federation (AIRF), of which he was elected president in October 1973.

When George came into Parliament in 1967, although not a novice in legislative work, elected as he was before to the Bombay Municipal Corporation, the Lok Sabha was an arena loaded with stalwart speakers, with accomplished reporters in the press gallery noted for their incisive and eagle-eyed observations. Lohia was brilliant in playing to the gallery, his rejoinders were bold, fresh and provocative; he could stir Parliament by his quick repartees or lighten its tension with wordplay. Madhu Limaye's responses demanded attention due to being grounded in the Book of Rules and in his reading of constitutional history; his range of sources as well was remarkably large. In front of Madhu Limaye's constitutional command and Ram Manohar Lohia's theatrics, George's responses seemed to lack vigour if not punch. It was largely perceived he was doing what Madhu Limaye bid him to; 'tell your *chela*' or 'make him understand' were some phrases thrown at Madhu Limaye to rein in George. Not formally educated in political philosophy or legislative history, his parliamentary anger spewed out from his trade union work and his personal history. His interventions, therefore, went largely unnoticed, so much so that he would exasperatedly declaim, 'I studied the budget presentation for 150 hours, spoke for two hours in Parliament and then the *Times of India* reported, George Fernandes also spoke.'[56]

* * *

His political emergence coincided with the consolidation of power by Indira Gandhi. Not that they were competing against each other, but her politics was so motivated by her own survival needs that the force of it impacted everybody else, creating confusion and newer unexpected constellations. Since 1966, when she became the prime minister, she had faced restrictive impositions from the party seniors, called the syndicate, while on the outside she faced ridicule and much mocking from the Opposition who took her to be a rookie. Indira Gandhi wrote to George, even when she had nearly established herself, 'Many members of your party have indulged in a sustained campaign of personal vilification in Parliament and outside. In Kanpur, I was told that you made such a speech.'[57] Running a minority government, she deftly manoeuvred the outside political space to cut short the opponents within. Another strategy was to present herself as a more radically pro-people prime minister than any of the contenders inside her party would ever have been. Her efforts to establish total control over her party created ripples across the political spectrum. If it broke her party vertically into two, every other party irrespective of their ideological make-up was similarly affected, creating disarray and irrelevance in the ranks and files. Indian politics was caught in the quagmire of the Congress split into the Ruling and Organization factions. After leading a precarious coalition for two terms (1966–67, 1967–70), Mrs Gandhi ultimately gained political eminence by registering an awe-inspiring parliamentary presence through the March 1971 general elections. The Opposition stood decimated.

Soon after the death of its founder-ideologue Ram Manohar Lohia, the SSP began its rapid slide into oblivion. A last-ditch attempt to infuse vibrancy was made at its Jabalpur convention when George, the rising star, was made its general secretary and Karpoori Thakur, the backward castes leader from Bihar, the chairman.[58] The party had played its most shrewd as well as suave move. But when George got down to work, although he tried putting some method into the madness of the party organization, the results were meagre.[59] Creating a database of the dwindling party membership or raising finances to pay rent or clerical staff salaries was one thing, to gain supreme allegiance across regions and affiliations quite another. It was then he realized how difficult it must have been for Lohia to build a party from scratch. He might have realized as well what degree of endurance it took for JP to raise the party from its foundations to its formidable presence twenty years later in 1950.

Apart from his unflinching passion, powerful oratory and a determined will, with no linguistic or regional base, no caste solidarity and even less the primordial connect of religion, George's basic vision was chiselled in the urban metropolis, around the issue of industrial workers' rights of wages and working conditions. The vast country was waiting to hear and feel a vision that affected them more directly. By 1968, he began to be seen as one who took up cases of injustice, whenever, wherever. He was on the mailing list of civil rights activists.[60] People wrote imploring him to take up their case in Parliament or invited him to address them. His focus now was not limited to Bombay or Maharashtra alone; he had countrywide appeal. 'We were completely mesmerized by his constant talk of India and change theme,' remembered a woman journalist who had been part of a group in 1968 who were taken for a round trip of Bombay in his 'big, black car' that he himself drove. 'We heard that he would sleep on bare benches and lived frugally. We were much impressed. We were electrified in his presence.'[61] George scribbled every day twenty to thirty letters to comrades and correspondents located across the country. He undertook many travels, addressed many meetings, never denied any invitations, and indulged in theatrics as well. Around May that year, a Kutch movement erupted against the award of certain portions of land to Pakistan after the 1965 war. He devoted a large chunk of his time there, spending two months in prison, hoping for some nationalistic aura to stick on to him. 'There is no success in trying to put life in a corpse,' an exasperated colleague expecting much from him as Patil-vanquisher wrote to him. On 6 April 1970, while leading a demonstration of Adivasis in Delhi, the police beat George up so thoroughly that when, after a gap of twenty-one days, he came to Parliament, he was still bandaged and disoriented.[62] The traumatic head injuries that he received here would lead him to suffer years later from Alzheimer's disease, robbing him of his memories. In August, they launched a land-grab movement, whose epicentre was Bihar; some arrests happened, but the yields again were very low. At a public meeting in Bettiah, in Bihar's Champaran district where Gandhi in 1917 had launched his political career in India with satyagraha against the unjust land relationship forced on the peasantry by the white indigo planters, George said belligerently, 'The SSP would face all resistance from the vested interests and would see that the Harijans and other landless people get possession of land even by applying force, if necessary.' He told a largely attended public meeting (at Forbesganj, on 31 August) it was a movement to de-grab land grabbed by the landlords during the British Raj. 'We simply want that all unused, fallow and illegally grabbed land must be given to the landless for cultivation. It will never be possible to achieve it through acts of Parliament or of state legislatures.'[63] This was a position that was also militantly advocated by the Maoist rebels called Naxalites. He spoke of raising a 'land army' to organize the landless and small peasants. But soon the tempo was lost as the CPI too launched its land struggle, and they ended up accusing each other of taking up the struggle at the behest of Indira Gandhi.[64] It was not that the Hindi heartland, where the socialists had some electoral presence and to which he was slowly shifting his political base, was not accepting of him; he won some comrades, he campaigned in some constituencies and he became a troubleshooter in the factional disputes, but even the combination of these factors was way short of the potion that was needed to infuse the party with any vitality.

Frustration got him entangled into a debilitating trap of reining in a boisterous Raj Narain (1917–85). This was his first major mistake that would go against him, but its effect would be more visible on the health of the party. Raj Narain was equally self-made and a senior, and practised his politics from the depth of his guts. At the age of sixteen, during the Quit India Movement, Raj Narain, a student of the Banaras Hindu University, had disrupted a talk by Vice Chancellor Dr S. Radhakrishnan to ask students to join the movement. It was he who at the very first had launched a movement for dismantling the statues of colonial viceroys, an act that was picked up by George a little later when he led the dismantling of such statues in Bombay.[65] In 1965, despite Lohia's injunction against electorally defeated candidates nominating themselves to the Rajya Sabha, Raj Narain won a seat in the Upper House, leaving Lohia so livid that he didn't talk to Raj Narain for months. Raj Narain was a fearless man, who, when decided on something, would go for it lock, stock and barrel. He ruled the party in UP.[66] Why would George, who single-handedly and tactfully built his trade unions under the nose of adversarial politicians of the PSP, want to discipline Raj Narain or control his whimsical ways? It is quite possible that, threatened by the invasion of leaders from Maharashtra on his turf, Raj Narain might have spoken sarcastically or done something causing humiliation that would have rankled in George's heart. Raj Narain called George *padri* till his last; he was even more derisive about two other socialists: Surendra Mohan was 'a worthless man' and Prem Bhasin a *chaprasi*, a peon. A more plausible reason was their temperamental differences. Raj Narain was a rigid, inflexible man, whereas George with his long trade union experience was willing to see the compulsions of the other side to hammer out a compromise.[67] As early as February 1968, very soon after Lohia's death, 'the unseemly duel of words between Raj Narain and George' was becoming a source of consternation among colleagues.[68] By 1971, 'It was said openly that George Fernandes and his ilk cannot work with Raj Narain and his ilk.'[69]

Not just did George take on Raj Narain in amazing futility, castigating him for enrolling bogus party members and fomenting rebellion in UP against him, the party like a fistful of sand began to slip imperceptibly from his hold. Indiscipline began to define the party. Rampant infighting came into the open.[70] Conventions and rules were

Courtesy: Fredrick D'Sa, Bombay Taximen's Union

Despite his own defeat in the election, George here seen coming to felicitate his old
comrade Mrunal Gore, who had won her first electoral victory in 1961 along with
George to the Bombay Municipal Corporation. And, in 1972, she won her first legislative
seat in the Maharashtra Assembly.

openly flouted. The office-bearers resigned, protesting what they called
the 'dictatorial attitude' of the leaders.[71] 'We are becoming imprisoned
by uncertainty,' an old-timer said to another.[72] The inexhaustible
hostility the factional feuds engendered was to finally sap the party's
vitality, despite efforts one more time to bring about socialist unity.
The recurring theme of unity so exasperated the party that instead
of enticing the cadres it engendered cynicism and resignation. The
party treasurer, who was close to Rama Mitra (b. 1919), wrote to her,
'If as much energy that was put in unity effort was directed towards
the movement, something more worthwhile would have been the
outcome.'[73] Even the new Socialist Party, outcome of the latest bout of
unity, was faction-ridden, mutually acrimonious and with no hopes of
ever rising again. It was divided into at least three dominant factions:
the Raj Narain, the Madhu Limaye–George, and the Karpoori Thakur
factions. A wearied JP was to write lamenting, 'the kind and level of
party behaviour, disputes and quarrels'.[74] George shared the anguish

but didn't know the way out. 'I am completely at a loss to find a way out of this mess,' he wrote to JP.[75]

Many political changes ensued with the temporary weakening of the Congress in the initial years of Indira Gandhi. New forces with a little following gained ascendency at the cost of the Congress. Mutually bickering but hungry Opposition conglomerations took over the reins of power in many states. They were short-lived. Indira Gandhi soon wrested the initiative by nationalizing the banks and abolishing the privy purses, which created a socialist halo around her. The purging of those perceived to be conservative within the Old Congress helped her underline her distinctiveness. If the split in the Congress made all parties experience tectonic shifts in their allegiance to the ruling Congress Party and also within, it left the socialists confused and directionless. How do you respond to a regime that you always thought was a conservative, dynastic and slow-moving bureaucratic monolith but was now not only mouthing radical policies that you had a monopoly over but also insisting upon their implementation? This was a question that stared at the socialists. What Indira Gandhi was doing was to squeeze the Opposition space by not just adopting their radical slogans as her own but also taking measures to fulfil them. Caught in a bind, the Opposition felt compelled to side with her. For most of the time, since she began to purge the Congress of conservative elements that the socialists had mocked at, berated and targeted, the socialists found themselves in an unenviable position. If they opposed the measures, they would be seen untrue to their protestations, but if they went along they faced desertion and disintegration from within. There was another dilemma that stared at them. With Indira Gandhi forming an outfit owing allegiance to her alone, called then the Congress (R), those who were left came to be called Congress (O), who now occupied the Opposition space. The same people who the socialists had opposed hitherto now became the official Opposition for the first time since Independence. Some among the socialists believed in Indira Gandhi and advocated support to her, whereas some others retained their allergy to her, regarding the breakaway as the real Congress.[76]

Indira Gandhi had taken over the left mantle. As a result, the SSP was witnessing active depletion in its ranks in favour of an Indira Gandhi-led ruling Congress. In September 1970, faced with the prospect of the abolition of princes' privy purses, a move that was long demanded by the socialists, the SSP sided with Indira Gandhi in opposition to the conservative parent Congress. In May, George had put up a Constitutional Amendment Bill seeking abolition of privy purses and princes' privileges for consideration, but it was prevented from being taken up. Although the home minister would later call the measure 'a compulsion of history', the onus for scuttling his Bill, George said in a letter to the Speaker, lay on the 'unholy alliance between the Swatantra Party Maharajas and Mrs Indira Gandhi's Congressmen . . . and the presiding officer'.[77] When Indira Gandhi proposed legal abolition, the socialists were caught in a bind. Which way they leant was a moral dilemma of deep consequence for them. A coalition of forces whom they had called the rightists opposed the Bill. Morarji Desai, the breakaway Congress leader, opposed the Bill and called it 'deceptive and dishonourable'. He demanded compensation to princes whose privy purses were being withdrawn by the Bill. Socialists along with communists and ruling benches interrupted Desai's speech and made derisive comments, ridiculing Morarji Desai for being solicitous to the princes. They believed privy purses should be abolished without payment of any compensation. They went with the government and voted for it.[78] The party MPs were directed to vote for it since its defeat 'will be worse than its passage'.[79] It created an organizational hara-kiri.

At the end of 1970, Indira Gandhi played a fresh gambit. The Lok Sabha was dissolved in the last week of 1970 and elections were announced to be held in February 1971. Once again, the Opposition, having first divided itself under the banner of left and right, was forced to bind together, forgetting their name-calling, into a grand alliance. Despite doubts about the efficacy of non-Congressism, the SSP chose to go along with the conservative Congress rather than make common cause with the Indira Congress or forge a partnership with its own fissured half—the depleting but still surviving PSP who had sided with

Indira Gandhi. They were caught in a trap. They became part of the grand alliance with the Jan Sangh, the Congress (O) and the Swatantra Party. George was a vocal critic of this conservative combine. He did not favour an anti-Congress alliance that included the Jan Sangh. It was also the opinion of Madhu Limaye. A colleague wrote to George, 'In this caste-ridden society which is now free from any political monopoly, the Jan Sangh has become a potent danger. The idea of left unity is the only answer to this. Hope that you would go ahead with this idea.'[80] But the SSP didn't heed this. Nor was their siding with the old Congress to yield anything tangible to them. When the alliance had come about, a sceptic wrote to him, 'Do you suggest that Mr S.K. Patil and Mr Morarji Desai would ever agree to have a common programme with you? I can very well understand if you abstain from supporting Indira. But to support syndicate?!'[81] It was cataclysmic. The SSP and the PSP both lost ignominiously, the SSP reduced to just three wins and George bit the dust at his South Bombay constituency.

'It is no longer a secret that our party is facing a severe crisis,' George the general secretary wrote to Karpoori Thakur the chairman in June 1971.[82] The party was yet to recover from the despairing

Courtesy: Fredrick D'Sa, Bombay Taximen's Union

George's friendship with Madhu Limaye grew in strength. In April 1973, he campaigned wholeheartedly for Madhu's Banka election.

shock of election defeat. Disappointed at the failure of the party, George began to focus on his trade union work. The electoral defeat further accentuated his need to reach out to his trade unions, neglected because of his parliamentary preoccupations. Established now as a strongly mandated ruler, Indira Gandhi also gained a further halo of a nationalist by undertaking a war to carve out a new country of Bangladesh. This melted into submission the whole of the Opposition. George issued statements of support to a free Bangladesh and identified with the government's defence efforts. Even at the trade union level, he did not take a position contrary to the government line. A meeting of the trade unions and employer organizations held in Delhi, in which he participated, 'pledged unconditional and wholehearted support to the national effort in protecting our frontiers and making this subcontinent safe for democracy'.[83] The idea was to lessen industrial strife during National Emergency and increase production in factories across the country.[84] The war undertaken in December 1971 cemented her power by giving sweeping victories in the assembly elections held in states.

In the year 1973, devastating electoral defeats compelled the already depleted forces of the SSP and the PSP to forge a new Socialist Party at Bulandshahr with George as the chairman. They had come together, but integration was forced and out of compulsion to survive. But George taking over the chairmanship of the beleaguered party also fired imagination of some people. Hans Janitschek of Socialist International was delighted with George becoming the chairman of the united party. 'Your choice signals the beginning of a new chapter in the history of the Indian Socialist Party, if I may say so. There is a dynamic leader, a man with charisma and international reputation. A man who has the confidence of the trade union movement and a man who is young enough to have time to turn the Indian Socialist Party into the dynamic and powerful element which will make it a decisive factor in Indian politics. . . . I hope that your election will also lead to a reassessment of relations between the Indian Socialist Party and the Socialist International and eventual membership of your party in our movement.'[85] It was, however, a tough job, George knew, 'with the size of my country and the problem of communication and what have you, it is indeed heartbreaking if not back-breaking . . .'[86]

Madhu Limaye fought and won a by-election in Banka in April 1973. Raj Narain, who had been suspended from the party for indiscipline a year earlier, fought against Limaye, but despite support from Karpoori Thakur, was not just defeated but stood fourth in the league.[87] When differences between Raj Narain and Madhu Limaye came into the open, culminating devastatingly in a straight electoral battle between them at Banka, George was with Madhu Limaye. Local party workers felt elated at the coming of George to campaign. Lauding his 'magnetic speeches', one of them wrote, appreciating his contribution, 'The credit of this resounding victory goes to you. Despite your leg trouble, you toured the constituency extensively. You were the source of our inspiration during electioneering.'[88] Banka lacked any party organization. But the victory provided a hope to party workers all over the country that the socialist movement could be revived.[89] Once again, the Socialist Party seemed on the ascendant, but the hope proved deceptive.

The party had been continuously breaking, with splinters joining others, more mainstream, deserting the party's ideology and promise. Its affairs continued to engage him even five years later when there was already the talk of a new federal party by subsuming individual party identities. 'Five years ago today,' he would write in his prison journal on 9 August 1976, 'the reunited Socialist Party was born . . . It's foolish to speculate on the "ifs" of history. Yet I cannot help thinking about the lost opportunities, the petty quarrels, the heart-corroding jealousies that have brought the socialists to such a sorry pass. Will we ever learn our lessons? Or will we go the same way as we have gone during the last thirty years? I wish I had an answer.'[90] They could never build an enduring ideological infrastructure or even a robust organization. 'Believers in self-centric politics have destroyed the entire Socialist Movement,' rued a party worker angrily.[91] They were political leaders with strong individualistic traits but their charisma was constrained by their inability to build a cadre or work together in an organization. Their lack of understanding of power and its constituent elements was so conspicuous that it hurt their existence. They failed to learn even from their trenchant enemy, the Communist Party, which had party offices scattered across their strongholds that were attended to by the committed workers. With each successive general election, as prospects of them ever coming to power receded, socialist leaders scrambled to bargain with the powers that were.

Years later Laxmi Narayan Yadav (b. 1944), a BJP MP from Sagar, Madhya Pradesh and a former socialist, would speak about what made him join the BJP. He reeled off tales of frustration and penury while he toiled his life away for the Socialist Party and its various formations. 'The path was extremely difficult. How long one could keep furrowing a lonely battle? There is a limit. You see your family always hard-pressed against needs. There comes a point when your family begins to see you adversely and that is the breaking point, beyond which one can go no more.'[92] The socialists were for too long in the Opposition, and desired some positions of power and leverage. Those who received them left others an indignant lot, and such acceptance of official patronage became the bone of contention and also cause of cleavage in the party. They adopted vain methods and forked tongues, and resorted to mutual distrust and bickering and name-calling to sully each other, some to ingratiate themselves with the powers that were, others to distance themselves from it. Still others, dispirited with party politics, positioned themselves independently to bring themselves to the fore in a post-Nehruvian scenario. In the aftermath of his retirement from politics, when dispirited socialist colleagues visited him for advice, Madhu Limaye told them to join whichever party was dominant in their state. Finally, Madhu Limaye was proposing something that Asoka Mehta had already proposed under the high-sounding theoretical exposition of 'political compulsion of a backward economy'. What Asoka Mehta had anticipated about the party's longevity in 1954 when he pined to rejoin the Congress, Madhu Limaye, the rebel of the time, would veer around to after his retirement from politics.

* * *

Margaret (Margo) Skinner, a journalist from California, who had a recurring problem with the Government of India in receiving her entry visa, was an editorial member of the Ram Manohar Lohia-edited Socialist Party journal, *Mankind*. *Mankind* described her as a 'socialist of over twenty years standing, beginning with her membership of the Young People's Socialist League of America'.[93] A lady friend of Margo Skinner lauded her 'completely honest attitude to all things, and your total lack of malice, jealousy, all those hurtful and stupid traits'.[94] She had an enduring romantic interest in Lohia whom she called 'my boy'.[95] She is found to have repeatedly expressed, in phrases differently formed, her amorous desire for 'my boy, who, it seems to me increasingly, is the only man I ever knew with both a soul and a body'. In September 1961, she was deported from India, the Nehru government sending her a curt note that she 'shall depart from India forthwith for New York by air from the port of Bombay; she shall not thereafter re-enter India'. In the interim, she was warned not to associate with any political party. Her association with Lohia's ongoing satyagraha movement was the cause of her expulsion. In desperation, she even scouted for a teaching assignment in Burma for 'Burma is fairly near India'. A year before, in June 1960 in London, she met Rama Mitra, a history professor at Delhi's Miranda House College. She was also on the editorial team of *Mankind* and, Margo wrote to her friend, she was in Europe to do a 'PhD, just like my boy; from Germany too, just like him'. *Mankind* in its 'Communication' section published extracts from Rama and Margo's letters to Lohia with the heading 'Two Editors in England'.[96] But what the journal didn't publish was what the women thought of each other. These are contained in Margo Skinner's letters to her London-based friend. Rama Mitra had been virtually living-in with Lohia in Delhi. She had been taking care of him and he would die almost in her keep while at the hospital. Margo Skinner had mulled marrying him but was told 'marrying a Westerner . . . would ruin him in public life as far as ever getting elected to anything'. Thereafter she had kept the idea to herself. But when she met 'that Indian girl' Rama Mitra, who fancied being an exclusive Lohia consort, Margo Skinner, belittled by her own 'only an MA' tag, found her a 'nondescript sort of person' but wondered

if a PhD had made her more desirable. They talked of what else but
Doctor, and Margo Skinner felt a pang of pain when she was told that
Lohia was suffering from angina, and piercing anger when she heard
of a stone from an anti-Hindi demonstrator in Tamil Nadu hitting
him on his face. 'I wish I had been there and it had been me instead,'
she wrote to her friend. They both wanted to own him. A month after
they met, Margaret Skinner wrote to the same friend, describing Rama
Mitra, cheer swelling in her chest, 'She is a little thing, about four-foot-
something. Not pretty. Lovely eyes, but thirtyish, and lots of Indian
women don't age well.' Not content with this unappetizing portrayal
of Rama's attributes, she went on, 'Ugly, straightline mouth and bad
teeth, which, had she been in the West, would have been straightened.
Very plain hairdo, not too nice.' Not just her physical features were
unremarkable, her psychological make-up was of low esteem. Rama
Mitra had no confidence in herself as a woman, lacking in 'grace and
secret'. She spoke disparagingly about herself.[97] Although not 'a pretty
woman'—no, that was not the reason why Lohia had asked her to do
a PhD from a foreign university, a ruse to get her off his back—and
despite the sisterhood Margo felt in their common love for Lohia,
Rama Mitra's total lack of 'bloom and warmth' made her squirm. She
cringed at the implication when she wrote there was 'a certain dearth of
womanhood' in Rama Mitra, and yet she was so sure of her devastating
portrayal, she soon unfettered herself to elaborate it further: 'She is not a
girl who would ever know how to flirt, either consciously or, what is far
better, instinctively as one does with men one likes.'

Jayati Leila Kabir hated herself, and she fell in love with George.
The strange thing about love is that you know nothing of it until you
have possessed the object of affection. Leila had been taught by Rama
Mitra while she was at Delhi University, and they had become friends.
Self-hate which is said to be a mental disease is most often rooted in
deep psychic dislocations that make one feel acutely inadequate. Born
in an elite family and educated abroad, for Leila Kabir to show traits
of self-hate is difficult to believe. But there it was. A decade after her
wedding, her marriage flailing, when she contemplated living 'anything
between two to three years' all alone in the US, where her brother

was, Leila Fernandes slid into a remorseful, reproachful yet spirited self-analysis, writing to her brother how they both had the 'same basic stress–anxiety–tension-ridden' childhood when 'I was never ok—dark, stupid, petite, fool, ugly etc., plus a female'.[98] This exhausting letter of hers, twenty pages written on both sides of the paper, in her relatively small handwriting, would be used by George's brothers years later as evidence of her 'bipolar personality' to throw doubts on her ability to care for George's decrepit, Alzheimer's disease-stricken body.

Leila was the only daughter of Humayun Kabir (1906–69), an Oxford alumnus, who was a minister in both Nehru's and Lal Bahadur Shastri's cabinets. 'A distinguished writer, administrator and politician, Kabir was closely connected with education and cultural matters,' an obituary said of him when he died in 1969.[99] He broke away from Indira Gandhi to first associate with the Bangla Congress, and then to form his independent Lok Dal. In 1969, as an MP, he introduced a private member's bill asking for demonetization of certain high-denomination currency notes.[100] His proposals were not taken seriously, even by Opposition members, including George, who too was in Parliament. It was the last hurrah of a scion of the East Bengal zamindari system, who

George and Leila Kabir in their silk fineries on the day of their wedding.

Courtesy: Fredrick D'Sa, Bombay Taximen's Union

had revelled in his Oxford days, and whose marriage to Shanti Dasgupta (b. 1904) in 1930 had caused much social consternation, requiring the Mahatma's intervention. As was the case in those days, this put the final stamp of approval on such unions. About Leila Kabir's mother it was said, with an elitist pride again, when she studied at Santiniketan she gently awoke Gurudev Tagore every morning by her sonorous singing and veena recital.[101] A Brahmo, she would not change her religion after marriage, providing a religiously syncretic atmosphere to their two offspring, Prabhahan (1933–2004) and Leila (b. 1937).[102] But their expectations of their children were high indeed.[103] It was a frightful load the Kabir children were made to carry, and both of them floundered at the constant critical parental evaluation and disapproval. Burdened by the parental expectations, unable to deliver on them, and diminished in her own eyes, Leila Kabir felt 'it was a disaster to be born' and contemplated suicide. While her brother eventually killed himself one day by drowning in a shallow sea on the east coast of India, she suffered from depression all her life, surviving on pills, and with wildly extreme mood swings. She was never happy in her marriage, always angry, always complaining. She was unhappy with George going underground during the Emergency, seemingly unconcerned about her and their toddler. After he became a minister in the Central government, Leila Fernandes' most frequent complaint was that 'rustic people from Bihar and UP come up to our bedroom'.[104] She was not happy playing wife; as she wrote in that letter to her brother, she needed a 'wife' for herself. Five years after his wedding, when he was arrested and kept in a cage-like enclosure, open to the elements and guarded at all hours, George would ask the visiting Shanti Das Kabir to bring all the books written by and on Humayun Kabir, for he desired to write a biography of his father-in-law. In one unaware moment, he even wondered why Humayun Kabir and Lohia didn't work together. But that was a weak moment in his reasoning. Kabir was an elitist politician who believed in the enrichment the English language had brought to India, whereas Lohia, just to take this point alone, was not just fighting for the entitlement of the excluded but also the removal of English.

Leila Kabir studied nursing at Oxford and taught it at the College of Nursing, Delhi University. It was during these years she became friends with Rama Mitra, who was living with Lohia. It was at Lohia's home, often in the company of Lohia himself, that George and she met. She would later join the Red Cross and would get involved with the refugees pouring out of East Pakistan. According to her, 'Our fate was sealed on a flight from Calcutta to Delhi in April 1971 while returning from our separate missions to East Pakistan.' In three months they were married. There wasn't much time between his announcement at home and the date of the actual wedding. The news of the marriage was widely reported in newspapers. Yusuf Beg wrote from Varanasi: 'Last time when you had come to Banaras and had indulged in a spirited shopping for Banarsi saris, the mystery of that shopping expedition opened before us today when we read in newspapers about your impending marriage with Ms Leila Kabeer.'[105] A.B. Shah from Poona: 'I think this is one of the wisest decisions you have taken in your life.'[106] Among the plethora of other messages, one came from Bombay, which is significant only because what happened was the opposite of the expectation expressed: 'Behind every great man, they say, is a little woman . . . I am glad to know that you will soon have the gentle, guiding hand of a little woman which will, I am sure, take you on to greater achievements in your chosen field.'[107] His brother Richard Fernandes, who arrived in Delhi a week before the wedding, which took place on 22 July 1971, and was the only other male, besides George, to be invited to Leila Kabir's bridal shower, said, many years later when much rancour had crept into their relationship, 'George was unconcerned about the wedding.'[108] The wedding preparations frustrated him, frantic hullabaloo exhausted him, so much so that Leila Kabir wrote on 'Wednesday, 7 July 1971 at 6.15 p.m.' assuaging him, 'What is sacred and intimate between us no one has touched, people only want to share with us our happiness, and if there is all this excitement, it is a measure of the love, affection and regard that people have for you . . . so you shouldn't grudge it nor fume . . .'[109] She was excited, rather nervous, over preparations. She fussed over the seating of guests, as chairs were stiff and formal and could accommodate only a few of a guest list that was daily expanding. She finally decided to make sitting arrangements on the floor covered with a white chaddar.

The day of the wedding began with George and Leila visiting her father's resting place at the Jamia Milia Islamia cemetery to pray. They had worn the fineries in which they were to get married, but a sudden downpour left them drenched. They got into simple daily clothes: he in his old trousers and bush shirt and she in her old used sari, for their registered wedding. Later, a ceremony was held at Delhi's India International Centre where a Quaker couple pronounced them husband and wife in Hindi. It was the misery of Bangladesh that had brought them together, and therefore Bangladesh was very much present at the ceremony, with the yet-to-be-born nation's anthem *'Amar Sonar Bangla . . .'* sung on the occasion.[110] George had his forehead pasted with a shining, whitish substance. There was a huge card wherein the guests were all requested to sign their names. Most guests were from the bride's side.

A few years later, on their fifth marriage anniversary, when he was incarcerated in isolation at Hissar Jail, George recalled his wedding day to fill his solitude: 'The dictator who was then PM was there. Spent a long time with the guests and, from what everyone told me later, enjoyed herself. Most of the cabinet was there. But it was Sheikh Abdullah's presence that had delighted me the most! I will never forget his mischievous smile and still more mischievous comment when he put a simple garland of sweet-smelling jasmine round my neck at the reception: *Mujhe laga thha daal main kuch kala hai jab inko le aaye thhey uss din khaane par.* I had a meal with him about six weeks before our wedding and Leila had accompanied me.'[111] George's father didn't come. He was not very happy with the non-Christian marriage and asked what this India International Centre was and if there was a church there. His mother came with mixed emotions, being in tears during the whole ceremony, and the brothers who were there as well were all on the sidelines, 'feeling a little out of place'.[112] Unfortunately, tears were the only outcome of this alliance as far as George's mother Alice Fernandes was concerned. A few months later when Leila Fernandes delivered a baby boy, George called his mother to tend the baby, but she would return sad, with tears and tales of mistreatment at the hands of the abrasive and abusive daughter-in-law. 'Treating her like a servant almost, being the boss, do-this do-that kind of ordering around,' her sons recalled years later.[113] In the mid-1980s, now a lonely and depressed widow, Alice Fernandes would distribute her gold jewellery among her daughters-in-law, Leila Fernandes' share being a set of five bangles which Alice would give George to pass on to her. Unfortunately, this would be exactly the time when Leila Fernandes sent divorce papers for him to put his signature of mutual consent on the parting of ways. He not only returned the papers without signature, but also sent his mother's gold bangles along. Many years later, this would be claimed by Leila Fernandes as evidence of his enduring love for her, in a riposte to those questioning her reclaimed status of a wife twenty-five years after she had deserted him. 'You see,' she said, 'when I sent him a divorce paper, he sent it back along with gold bangles.'[114]

They went for a honeymoon to Europe immediately after the wedding. They met Edgar Snow (1905–72) in Geneva in the first week of August and heard him talk about the India–China relationship. Upon their return, Leila Fernandes was keen to give up her Red Cross job. George was keen as well to keep her engaged, and she was brought in as the publisher of *Pratipaksh*, a journal he had recently founded.[115] But she soon began to feel lonely as he moved from one place to another at a frantic pace, and George began to drift, unable to find 'purpose' in the woman he had married. Friends who met her in the aftermath of their wedding found her always angry, sulking and complaining.[116] His busy schedule left her to fend for herself, although it wouldn't be entirely correct to say that he was obdurately aloof. Marriage, however, made no difference to his schedule and failed to domesticate him.

Leila was singularly incapable of playing what she understood as the gendered role of a 'wife', as seen from her letter to her brother, explaining to herself perhaps the cause of their spousal estrangement. And, George too, many times, as he wrote obituaries of departed colleagues and leaders, eulogized the wives of those men, a kind of wife he perhaps desired and missed. Incarcerated in the maximum-security Hissar District Jail during the Emergency, he would hear about the death of Usha Tai, wife of the venerable S.A. Dange, and write in his diary about a letter he had just written to the communist comrade, not sure it would reach him, as 'after all he is one of the crutches on which dictator walks'. He wrote, 'There was something very youthful about Usha Tai, like Dange. I never really got to know her well; she seldom sat down whenever I was with Dange at their residence whether in Bombay or Delhi, but she always used to be around, bright and cheerful carrying her rather enormous frame lightly. I always felt that her frequent appearances in the room where we talked were meant to keep an eye on her husband. There was something of the mother-hen about her. Usha Tai is a part of the communist movement in India, and she played her part well, though her greatest role was in looking after the man who played perhaps the most key role in the communist movement in our country.'[117] A few years later still, George now in the political wilderness and struggling to re-establish himself, with Leila Fernandes having deserted him, wrote of S.M. Joshi's departed wife, 'Tarabai may not have been the purpose of his life, but she was a part of his life as none else could have been, and a friend, philosopher and guide.'[118] Leila Fernandes with her acute need for a 'wife' for herself would never become 'friend, philosopher and guide' to George. What he was seeking in her was 'a goddess, seeing all, forgiving everything and being calm throughout', something Ram Manohar Lohia had asked his consort Rama Mitra to be.[119] But Leila Fernandes carried an irredeemable rancour against George, resenting his busy political life and her own struggle with solitude that she spoke about freely. She came to be in a debilitating spousal competition with him. In his own search for an emotional anchor, although not as acute as Leila Fernandes' need for the same, George would continue to look for woman of substance radiating emotional warmth. This need would only grow with his growing distance from Leila Fernandes.

7

The Strike Man

'Never in the history of civilization,' said a letter to the Editor in June 1974, 'have any people paid so heavy a price for a mere quarrel between a man—George Fernandes and a woman—whose name I cannot disclose because of the DIR.'[1] In the just gone by May, the so-called 'quarrel' had fetched a nationwide strike on the railways. A year later, when the woman—Indira Gandhi—suspended democracy and enforced her authoritarian regime, she claimed the railway workers whose action had made the nation pay 'so heavy a price' were actually paid to go on strike. In fact, she didn't stop there, but added, as 'our trade unions are not rich', the money for the purpose came from abroad.[2] But, in those twenty-odd days in May when the strike was on, it was not the nerve-racking immobility but the sheer audacity of it all that captured the imagination of a nation at war against its government. Yet, the May Strike was not a sudden outburst of workers' militancy. Nor had its cause sprung forth urgently in October 1973 when George was elected to spearhead the All India Railwaymen's Federation (AIRF). But if ever an affliction at the inception of a thing could bring the whole edifice crashing down with an opportune gust of wind, the May Strike was it, the seeds of which lay in that distant train journey of a mere 30 kilometres from Bombay to Thane in 1853. The railways were made by a mass of workers employed under a wage structure that was biased against them.[3] It affected them when their work extended for indefinite hours or they were denied a bonus or their career lacked growth. It affected them when the minimum wages they received were not need-based and less than those in the new-fangled public-sector industries. But their voice that was the AIRF had fallen in estimation. A George was needed to rekindle hopes in its ability to fight for the workers' cause. A year after the May Strike, when he was underground to resist the National Emergency, the now-estranged AIRF would still admit he was that gust of wind which had blown at the opportune time.

* * *

George's relationship with the railwayman had started only in 1960. In July that year, the railway workers, along with other Central government employees, went on a nationwide indefinite strike against falling wages and soaring prices.[4] It was the Nehru regime's twilight years. The strike started on 12 July, but five days later, on 17 July, it was called off unconditionally.[5] Although an advocate of industrial democracy, Nehru had refused to meet the workers' representatives, calling the strike a 'civil rebellion'. His administration unleashed unprecedented fury; thousands were arrested, dismissed and suspended. On 13 July, at Dadar in Bombay, while leading a demonstration, George lay on the tracks to block the movement of trains and was arrested. Aroused by his surreptitious arrival, the police pounced upon him and beat him up thoroughly. They bodily lifted him from the tracks. He was seen bleeding and reports said his hand was fractured. A picture of a subdued George in soiled vest and torn trousers lying flat on his back on the platform was published in the *Times of India*. It showed him surrounded by a horde of police constables.[6] Police denied he was beaten.[7] But at the same time they admitted, 'In order to clear the track a cane charge had to be made. In the melee, Mr Fernandes also received some blows.'[8] Going ahead, the police charged him for obstructing trains and, after a year of trial, he was convicted with two months of rigorous imprisonment.[9] Most of those days he spent in a lonely cell at Maharashtra's Visapur Jail. Before being taken there, they handcuffed him. 'I resisted,' he would recount many years later when he was retired from active politics; though his memory was largely eroded, he retained a remarkable lucidity that showed the hurt he had repressed all those past years.[10] 'Still, they handcuffed me and took me in a van alone to Visapur Jail. When I was brought up there, I was beaten up by convicts and undertrial prisoners. I was made to stand near a tree and asked to hang on to that tree and I had to do as I was ordered. Then I was asked to remove all my clothes. A set of jail clothes were given to wear there itself. It stank.' During his rigorous imprisonment he was made to dig up soil with whatever tools he was given. Two months later, after he had served his sentence and was released, he wrote a letter to chief minister Y.B. Chavan, and copied it to the President and prime minister, complaining of the awful conditions in jail that so many years after Independence still prevailed.[11] Steeled by his experience, his tryst with the railwayman had begun.

Soon after the Lok Sabha election in which he defeated the incumbent railway minister S.K. Patil, he was nurtured by his party to be its spokesman on the railways. He spoke on the four successive railway budgets, until December 1970, when Parliament was prematurely

Courtesy: Fredrick D'Sa, Bombay Taximen's Union

After the audacious leap and police beating, George being taken away from the Dadar railway station platform on 13 July 1960 by the police.

dissolved. In those speeches, he cited reports and figures to make his critique scathing. The railroad accidents that occurred with an eerie regularity, killing and maiming scores, caught his attention. On 2 April 1968, he declared he was not in Parliament to speak in a condolence meeting but to point out failures of the system, mistakes of individuals, and demand accountability. Quoting extensively from government reports, he said if only recommendations had been implemented, there would not have been any accidents at all. The commercial losses of the Indian Railways were mounting, but it chugged along, claiming it served a social purpose. But even among the Class IV employees, the presence of scheduled caste and scheduled tribe persons in the railways was below the sanctioned level. Besides, they were scarcely present in Class I and II categories, and only sparsely in Class III. The Indian Railways was indifferent to its workers dying of tuberculosis.[12] On 19 September 1968, the railway workers went again on a one-day token strike. As a result, some 1,600 employees were dismissed on disciplinary grounds. The official recognition to the AIRF was withdrawn. A year later, Parliament debated the fate of those dismissed workers, and while most speakers asked for mercy and lenient treatment, George's reply was definitive. He called for reinstatement of them all. 'Whatever strength we might have at our disposal,' he spoke stirringly, 'and I admit, today, we don't have much, but whatever strength there is, let me warn you, we can still use that outside this House to get their reinstatement.'[13] The labour movement was past the stage of supplication, he said. The government suffered from a class bias in dealing with labour strife: when medics went on strike, emptied OPDs, left patients unattended, the government mollycoddled them, gave them concessions, but with striking railwaymen, it resorted to violence, intimidation and mass dismissals without compunction. 'Rekindle hopes in his life,' George said when they debated the low efficiency of the railwayman.[14] 'Today, there is not a section of employees that is not angry and frustrated.'

Throughout the 1960s, the trade union fame of George continued to echo. Whether he was keen or not, and why he wouldn't be is questionable, the railways attracted him like iron filings to a magnet. He had for long been inching inexorably towards leading the railwaymen. His defeat in the March 1971 election failed to dent his morale. Instead, he readied himself, concentrated indefatigably on the target. The railway workers' trade union, the AIRF, was there, raving and ranting, sometimes threatening, sometimes threatened, but always there. Of late though, it had stiffened into a self-serving bureaucracy and was ignored by the authorities. It preferred cultivating official patronage to remain afloat. Founded in 1924, it was for long the only one putting forth the railway workers' demands. Gradually, the socialists had come to dominate it.[15] But soon after freedom, the ruling Congress desiring one of its own, created the National Federation of Indian Railwaymen (NFIR).[16] Both unions were recognized by the railway authority—vested in a 'big octopus' called the Railway Board—to negotiate on the workers' behalf, but whereas the AIRF wielded the weight of the workers' aspirations, the Congress-sponsored NFIR had the backing of the railway officials.[17] Every time the AIRF rose to take up workers' demands, the NFIR would rise from its officious slumber to pooh-pooh it. The NFIR was universally called a federation of the strike-breakers, the scabs, a derisive stigma thrown at it but actually relished by it as a badge of honour in the service of nation.[18] But the AIRF obviously had developed its own weaknesses. Not only had it turned against its own militant worker-leaders, the workers had begun to desert it to build their own tiny, more vulnerable category unions. On the railways now were many outfits espousing demands of category workers. Their emergence had blunted the AIRF's edge. In June 1972, George wrote to Peter Alvares (1908–75), the AIRF president, a letter that revealed the malaise as well as his intention:

> Frankly, I do not know whether you have been applying your mind seriously to the various problems that the AIRF is now facing. I believe that we still have some very fine cadres on the railways, though their number must be dwindling just as it is happening at the party level. However, it is easier to create trade union cadres and then give them political orientation than to create party cadres. I, therefore, believe that with some central planning and coordination, the AIRF could still be built into a powerful organization.[19]

'It is no bed of roses,' Maniben Kara (1905–79) cautioned George on his election as president of the AIRF.[20] When in the 1950s he began his trade union work in Bombay, she was already an established labour leader. Later, she was president of the AIRF from 1963 to 1968. In her letter to George, she hoped he would succeed in rebuilding 'this organization step by step and lay a sound foundation for one of the oldest, largest and vital organizations in public sector'. Almost as if she was warning of the dark portents ahead, she admitted, 'I tried and I failed.' But what of her commitment? On 19 September 1968, railway workers went on a one-day strike. Maniben Kara, the AIRF president, not only sulked and withdrew herself, but also held back her Western Railway Employees Union (WREU) from participating in the strike. 'I'm not one to abuse Indira for everything,' she'd say.[21] In return, the government rewarded her with an honorific of Padma Shri. It was left to S.A. Dange—the Bombay-based communist patriarch, who when accused by the AIRF of sponsoring rival unions parallel to it—to rub salt on its wound by reminding it of the betrayal of Maniben Kara.[22] 'You,' Dange wrote to George, weeks before the May Strike, 'yourself know that the AIRF has been nothing but the handmaid of the Railway Board so far.'[23] S.A. Dange was unsure if George's election would help the AIRF acquire 'a new look', because 'the president, that is, you alone do not make the whole AIRF'. He wrote ominously, 'even if you try to do it, there will be many hurdles.'

It was not that the AIRF had turned itself over to officials. Actually, it adopted aggressive resolutions, and took them up with the Railway Board in a fashion and under a machinery founded after long struggles. But the reality was that the negotiations had become a 'mockery'.[24] Engrossed in its rarefied splendour, the Railway Board even failed to acknowledge letters from the AIRF office-bearers. Pushed by the restive members, the AIRF in December 1972 organized a demonstration before Parliament to demand early submission of the Third Pay Commission Report. In January 1973, going a step further, it conducted a strike ballot to gain workers' endorsement of the intended strike action. The agitated workers favoured a strike.[25] The battle lines were drawn, just the trumpet was to be blown, when hopes came crashing down and it proved a damp squib.[26] The call was withdrawn when the government gave some vague assurances.[27] Not just did it expose the AIRF's propensity to be browbeaten, it also proved to be the last straw on the back of the railwayman's proverbial camel.[28]

While the AIRF remained groping in the dark, the year 1973 was a 'tough year' for the government. It was the Strike Year of post-Independence India. A cursory glance at the year's *Times of India* reveals a bleak scenario with strikes being reported on its first page almost on an everyday basis. Similarly, a perusal of the Lok Sabha debates reveals at least one case of labour agitation raging at one or the other corner of the country being discussed every day in its august chamber. Hospitals and factories, airports and railway stations—they were all getting emptied of people working therein. Politics was in tumult as well; students in Gujarat and Bihar had risen in rebellion against their state governments. In February 1974, the President's opening address to Parliament raised a tense spectre: 'You reassemble at a time of difficulty and trial,' he said.[29] On the railways, for long, the locomotive running staff—of engine drivers, firemen, shunters, those who kept the engines of trains alive and running—had been asking for reduction in their working hours and recognition of their All India Loco-Running Staff Association (AILRSA), among other demands.[30] In 1973, even when strikes were banned, the illegality of it failed to constrain them.[31] They repeatedly went on strike in May, August and then again in December. Although their fiery determination didn't win them a concession on their main demand of an eight-hour work schedule, some concessions were made. They felt the AIRF was hand in glove with the Railway Board to debunk their demands. The AIRF, contrary to that perception, felt the locomotive staff's agitation was sectional, subversive and done at the behest of officials. But the truth was, caught in a cleft, the AIRF was irrelevant to the rising crest of workers' militancy. Not just the loco men but also the other categories of railwaymen began to put their demands and go on strike independently of the AIRF. The category unions' emergence acquired an uncontrollable swell. No longer could the deluge be dodged. The AIRF urgently needed to stymie its own withering. It needed someone who could give the workers' demands a decisive edge. Known by the strikes he conducted, the militancy he exuded, the workers' strength with him he exhibited—united and powerful that yielded results as well, the zonal leadership of the AIRF saw in George a panacea for the ills that afflicted their organization. The AIRF needed him in order to survive with dignity, lost because of its subservience to the Railway Board and stiffening in its bureaucracy. Its needs were dire. If they would get in him a right prescription to pull them out of the morass they had fallen into, his needs were equally urgent. Contrary to what he would say some months later, the strike was not a fait accompli given to him along with the presidentship of the AIRF. In reality, he was elected to bring about a strike that the incumbent leadership had failed to make. The strike was a call, an inevitable culmination of a logic that infused life in both the AIRF and George's own career, a little disarrayed by his election defeat in 1971. A combination of factors made the railway workers vote an entrenched leadership out and bring George in, with a simultaneous endorsement of a strike. He was the much sought-after Strike Man they were awaiting to revive their plummeting spirits.

* * *

At Secunderabad, from 15 to 18 October 1973, the AIRF held its annual convention to elect a new set of office-bearers. Although his victory was by a thin margin (277 to 210 votes), George won the leadership contest by defeating Peter Alvares in a straight fight. His opponent was a soft-spoken Goan freedom fighter, a party colleague and a JP follower. A long-serving railways leader, Peter Alvares was elected to the Lok Sabha from Goa in the first election held after its liberation from the Portuguese. Being long with the AIRF had made him privy to the problems within, but he was ineffectual in arresting the slide. He would rant and rave, write many letters to Indira Gandhi and to V.V. Giri (1894–1980), the only labour leader ever to become the President of India. But the flurry of letter writing didn't win any concession for the railway workers. He had also antagonized some of the zonal leaders. V.R. Malgi, the general secretary of a Central Railway union, National Rail Mazdoor Union (NRMU—CR), for instance, was one of those. He had been belittled by Peter and denied a position he desired. As a consequence, Malgi replaced Peter Alvares with George as president of the union he controlled and backed him for the AIRF presidentship as well. He was George's most influential and ardent supporter. V.R. Malgi's salvos proved that history is moved by feelings, more so by personal slights.

Once he was elected president of Malgi's railways union, everyone expected George to stake claim to the leadership of the AIRF as a logical next step.[32] Days before the actual outbreak of the May Strike, Malgi would be arrested and die of a heart attack. In his letter to Malgi's son from jail, George acknowledged how V.R. Malgi 'more than any other single individual is responsible for giving me this opportunity to have the privilege of leading the railwaymen.'[33] But most others as well were keen to rejuvenate the AIRF by bringing George in. It was a foregone result, his election, even before a vote was cast, as not only was he a candidate in the fray, he had been invited as well to inaugurate the AIRF convention at Secunderabad.[34] A.V.K. Chaitanya of the South Central Railway Union that hosted the convention was a protégé of Peter Alvares. It was therefore disheartening to see him shout slogans against, and before, Alvares, who was keen to continue for one more term into 1975, the golden jubilee year of the AIRF. But the zonal leadership was unwilling. Alvares would be feted by George's opponents in Parliament during the May Strike. The railway minister Lalit Narayan Mishra (1923–75) himself would set the tone of accusation by sympathizing with 'the way Mr Peter Alvares was thrown out . . .'[35] His party colleague Yashpal Kapur, Indira Gandhi's shady aide-turned-troubleshooter, called George 'a naughty and indisciplined [sic] person, I should say, who fought elections against his own leader . . .'[36] Actually, George had a morally anguished fight against a respected party colleague. The contest was not taken kindly to by the party; those loyal to their JP salt contemplated action against him, but somehow the hurricane that had begun to blow over the Indira Gandhi regime swept that threat away. George by then had ingratiated himself to the JP camp, becoming its prominent supporter, so much so that he advocated disbanding the Socialist Party in order to establish a federal party that JP was working on. So shocked would Peter Alvares be by his defeat, he died an untimely death a year after, where else but in a railway bogey.[37]

At Secunderabad, while George was elected president, the AIRF resolved to indefinitely go on strike from 27 February 1974, if their demands were not settled by then. Speaking to the congregation, he mapped the hidden strength of the railwaymen. 'Seven days' strike of the Indian Railways will cause every thermal station in the country to close down. A ten days' strike of the Indian Railways—every steel mill in India would close down and the industries in the country will come to a halt for the next twelve months. A fifteen-day strike in the Indian Railways—the country will starve.'[38] He spoke it as a caveat, but it was bandied as evidence of his subversive intentions and anarchic ethos. Shedding all ambiguity, and with the knowledge that a capacity, more than its exhibition, was enough to wring out a settlement, George began to work to build a united platform of railway workers. Enthused by his election, many railway unions invited him to visit them, in different states and districts, towns and cities, placing much hope in his leadership. He undertook what came to be called whirlwind journeys to every nook and corner of the railway system. He travelled incessantly, with an utter disregard for personal comfort, to those scattered locations, addressed meetings and exhorted railwaymen to shed reticence. He told them to acquire strength by forging solidarity across categories and overcoming divisions within. Two weeks after his election, on 8 November, George, as president of the AIRF, wrote a letter outlining workers' demands to the Railway Board. Most of it was about wages and allowances, and one specifically demanded wage parity with the public sector.

He said the railwaymen were for a 'negotiated settlement', and although he never retreated from this position, it is true, knowing government and its intrinsic nature, he never stopped preparing for a strike.[39] The authorities were told to open negotiations at the earliest.[40] Long accustomed to supplications from the unions, a language of

Facsimile of *Blitz* front page of 11 May 1974, which in its usual style makes a blaring announcement, telling the world the nature of the strike on the Indian Railways.

intransigence was jarring to the railway authority. His critics cited his verbal salvos to charge him with a political motivation. But unmindful of all the calumny, he was. On 26–27 December 1973, he called a meeting of the representatives of the AIRF affiliated unions. He followed it up with another meeting with a still larger invitation list on 24–25 January 1974. Impelled by the force of speed, even the NFIR said they too stood for bonus, they too were unsatisfied with the Pay Commission award, and they too were worried about the soaring prices. They offered to work in tandem on joint action, but to their misfortune, events had gone beyond their design and they were left holding a 'loyal workers' tag.[41] When the negotiations actually ensued, and finding George dominating the dialogue, the NFIR would spar with him and work to put him down.

The Secunderabad Convention had decided on a strike from 27 February 1974. But George, citing lack of preparation, wouldn't agree to it. When he said, 'It is not the date that is important', some AIRF comrades ridiculed him. But he gathered support from other quarters. In the first week of November, the Bhartiya Railway Mazdoor Sangh (BRMS), the Jan-Sangh backed labour federation, said a unilateral decision about the date of strike was 'unfortunate' if a united platform was desired.[42] They said so after a discussion with George. Similarly, Dange who was the AITUC chief also favoured a new date. In the beginning of February, in keeping with George's view, the AIRF ultimately fell in line.[43] A national convention was held on 27 February, where the decision to establish a National Coordination Committee for Railwaymen's Struggle (NCCRS) was taken by a gathering of 2000 delegates representing more than 100 unions on the railways. The NCCRS was a tactical master stroke, akin to George's earlier labour strikes when he worked to build a broad-based alliance. He invited all the central labour organizations, those having affiliations to political parties, to be represented on the NCCRS. He wouldn't even run down sectional or category unions on the railways. He invited them all. It ensured widest unity and lessened mutual hostility and criticism. It transformed the nature of the railwaymen's movement. It no longer was an AIRF phalanx, but of all railwaymen, above organizations, categories and ideologies. Unlike Peter Alvares who had attacked the locomotive running staff for their divisive, disruptive and sectional pursuit, George vouched he stood 'foursquare' behind them, and won their hearts.[44] It made JP, himself a former AIRF president, 'happy that after years of hibernation, the AIRF under its present dynamic and yet wise leader has regained some of its old strength and vigour'.[45] Years later, it was this NCCRS that was most fondly remembered as a grand coalition George conjured up with a wave of his wand. Such unity of the working class was seldom attained.

The railway authority was still not taking the threat of a nationwide strike seriously. In the first week of April, however, the labour minister, a Congressman who was an ex-communist, took note of the labour disquiet on the railways. It was a meaningless gesture as the labour minister had no mandate to negotiate. Two days later, demanding the railway minister's immediate intervention and expressing shock at his casual approach, an indignant George wrote to 'Dear Lalit': 'In my twenty-six years of trade union work, I have hardly come across an employer who displays such a contemptuous attitude towards the workers' organizations as the Railways are presently doing. And those who display a similar attitude are some village yokels who have struck it good in towns and though catapulted into the role of employers are so full of an inferiority complex that they must take their workmen and their organizations for granted to feed the ulcers of their ego.'[46] He would be closing in on the authorities from any number of quarters and through methods ranging from bare aggression to righteous indignation to relentless groundwork.

On 16 April, distressed by the laggardly pace of negotiations, the NCCRS decided it was time to announce the launch of its indefinite strike. The date was to be 8 May, when the railway workers were to down their tools and withdraw their labour at exactly 6 a.m.[47] No railwayman was exempted. In three weeks, they were going to launch 'biggest ever action'. George knew once the strike began, the government would not be in a hurry to negotiate at all, and issue false promises, small concessions and partial acceptance of demands, 'but these should be considered as measures to break the strike'.[48] 'I would appeal to you not to get involved in disputes,' George wrote in an open letter to the railwaymen. This hinted at many discordances within. Competing coordination committees had sprung up at many places, which were inevitable in a people's movement. Unmindful of it, he focused obdurately on the militancy alone.

Prefabricated forms were sent to employees' unions so when it came to the crunch, they should hold meetings, fill in names and send their letters of affirmation to strike to the authorities. As the tempo rose, if there were enough supportive letters, there were also angry ones. Letters from opponents were basically driven by a few general themes: one, the strike would greatly inconvenience travelling people, it was a callous disregard of millions of commuters and transporters; two, the strike was a misadventure that would fuel the price rise in a worsening economic situation; three, how fair was it to privilege railway workers, whose demand for more was an anti-national and unpatriotic act. Innumerable letter writers questioned the timing of the move, even made open threats. 'Interest of the country' involved calling off the strike. Such themes were publicized by the government through its communication channels and ministerial speeches. Many had imbibed the government's version. There were letters also from cranky, self-important individuals who offered themselves to mediate between the strikers and the ministers. Some even enclosed lengthy proposals, whereas a few others proposed to reveal them at the appropriate time when they were called in by the government. Fence-sitting, ambiguous people advised restraint, as if the government was a helpless victim of its workers' intransigence. 'I have been watching closely the protracted negotiations between you and the government authorities on the railway strike issue,' wrote the newly elected MP P.G. Mavalankar (1928–2002), whose only claim to fame was that he was the son of the first Lok Sabha speaker, Ganesh V. Mavalankar. 'Judging from the press reports it seems to me that the government is taking a rather stiff attitude, but I may point out that political parties and trade unions are also unfortunately using their weapons for their own party and political ends.'[49] Everyone had an opinion.

The government began to organize its reprisal machinery in earnest. It ordered punitive transfer, intimidating raids and preventive detentions.[50] The workers' leaders' properties were attached by the police. On 17 April, the authorities restrained officers from holding any negotiations or even meetings with staff representatives.[51] Any 'demonstration, agitation or behaviour of any sort that affects the working in any working area' was banned. Sanctioned leave was cancelled and orders were issued to grant no special casual leave to visit any offices. The intensity of the victimization became so harsh that the George-led Action Committee decided to take it up first on 15 April when they met for talks with the railway minister. On 21 April 1974, even when talks were being conducted, the NCCRS served a mandatory fourteen days' notice of their intention to bring the wheels of the Indian Railways to a complete halt by withdrawing their labour. This strike notice was served by each of the affiliated trade unions at five railway divisions, thirty-three subdivisions and 7000 stations on the Indian Railways. Still, the government behaved as if it didn't matter. Taking a plea that the deputy minister's father had expired, requiring Mohammad Shafi Qureshi's presence in his native village in Kashmir for the last rites, the negotiations were temporarily shelved. This was a tragic subterfuge. Not only because the minister's father had died, but more significantly, vital time was lost, as they waited for the minister's return rather than make an alternative arrangement to continue negotiations. The government woke up in fits and starts and went back to its lethargic sleep time and again. Whether this slothful behaviour, like the Indian Railways' slow-moving locomotives, was a natural outcome of its long-founded organizational inertia or had some political purpose we will have to leave it to the story's own intrinsic power to unravel. But one indication of its intention came when it began to cancel passenger trains, at the rate of hundreds a day, and store coal in its power plants.

Three tactical ways had come to be identified with George. First, he would not shirk from a 'negotiated settlement' or shut doors to negotiation, any time. Even when the demands were presented in aggressive language, their refrain was to reach a settlement. Second, he would not let the workers' solidarity be breached by rivalries among workers and their organizations or by divisive moves of authority. He was not leading the AIRF but a movement of the railway workers. He was continually broad-basing the movement. Each of the category unions were impatient about their own demands. The All India Train Examiners Association, Telegraph Staff, All India Guards Council and others rose to threaten sectional strikes. But instead of browbeating them into submission, he took up their cause, and wrote to the Railway Board putting the onus on it to address and settle the issues 'immediately and avert the otherwise inevitable crisis'.[52] Such an attitude bonded the railway workers in one unitary thread. 'I am gratified with the steps being taken by you for ensuring the involvement of the sister trade unions in the railways in the ensuing general strike,' a comrade wrote him.[53] Third, he would keep the reins of action strapped steadfastly in his own hands. He would not expend much energy on known detractors but occasionally got them sidelined and the message was conveyed forcefully. If his own general secretary, Priya Gupta (1921–79), was playing hard to comply, he had others take up cudgels

Courtesy: Fredrick D'Sa, Bombay Taximen's Union

George addressing a workers' meeting in Bombay, leading to the strike on railways.

on his behalf. M. Namasivayam of the Southern Railway wrote to Priya Gupta, when he was giving more weightage to participation in the Permanent Negotiating Machinery, 'In my humble opinion, the AIRF should not only be serious but also appear to be so in its effort to make the strike a success.'[54] The NFIR was first invited to participate, and when it showed disinclination, it was marked and shunned. But when negotiations began and the NFIR was invited too, George decided 'if the NFIR raises issues outside our charter of demands, they should go for separate negotiations'.

Someone not to take personal slurs seriously, he would not let a comment pass unaddressed if it reflected upon his relationship with workers. 'You,' he wrote to Mukul Banerjee, a Congress MP, 'told [a group of railwaymen who had come seeking support], among other things, that I am taking money from foreign countries and that I am enemy no. 1 of the country.' He asked Banerjee for proof to back this allegation.[55] Then, like a consummate trade union leader, he would not let personal difficulties come in the way of his commitment to workers. In January, when Leila Fernandes went into labour and had to undergo a Caesarean, he found the doctors and the nurses in Delhi's government hospitals were going on strike. 'This will mean tremendous agony and anxiety to me personally,' he said in a press note, poignantly detailing his family's travails, and himself in the midst of preparation for a strike on railways, 'but we shall undergo it all and support the causes of the doctors and nurses.'[56] And, as if he stood for workers worldwide, irrespective of their national affiliations, he wrote to the Japanese prime minister to address the problems of the railway workers in his country who too were going on strike.[57] Whatever be the cost, he was not ready to disown the workers, be they the medics in hospitals or workers in railways. If in leading them, his leadership claim climbed a notch up the ladder or attained a national recall value that his current political standing didn't command, it simply was incidental and served a dual purpose rather than being politically motivated.

* * *

Early in the morning of 2 May, George was woken up at Lucknow station's retiring room. He had slept after midnight, having come late in the evening from Delhi to address a May Day congregation of the railway workers. And now, a police team from Delhi knocked at his door, and asked him to get ready. He was brought down from his first-floor room to the station platform, which was emptied of people and filled with uniformed men. A government plane was at the airport tarmac to take him to Delhi. At about the same time, the driver of the railway minister knocked at Leila Fernandes' Delhi home. Annoyed, due to sleepless nights with her infant son, she opened the door and was given a letter from Lalit Narayan Mishra. In the letter, he blamed George for the failure of talks, which was the cause of his arrest; George would call it a 'treacherous act'.[58] The blame game had begun, but as would be evident soon, in Parliament and across the country, the railway ministry, rather than George, was seen as provocateur. That the arrest was a 'treacherous act' was an opinion held by most.

Hours later, as news of his arrest spread, spontaneous action broke out sporadically throughout the country; at places, the railway workers emptied their workstations and walked out in processions. The strike was breaking out much in advance of its due date of 8 May. In the Lok Sabha, agitated Opposition members, from the Jan Sangh's Atal Bihari Vajpayee to communist Indrajit Gupta (1919–2001), disrupted proceedings and demanded a discussion on the arrest. The same was the case in the Rajya Sabha. His arrest had cemented the Opposition into a momentary unity. Congressman C.M. Stephen (1918–84) recognized this. Himself a trade unionist, but believing that the strike was politically motivated and wrong, he mockingly vented, 'I am reminded of that anarchist-syndicalist who spoke in terms of a general strike for the purpose of bringing about revolution. It is this anarchist-syndicalism that I am finding in Mr George Fernandes and his gang of people. I must congratulate Mr George Fernandes because he has played his cards very well. A person who is nobody in this country has now got all this bunch of people in his hand and made them dance to his tune and put the workers to strike, not for the purpose of bonus, not for the purpose of parity, not for the purpose of a particular demand, but for the purpose of protesting against the arrest of this very great man of the twentieth century, no less than Mr George Fernandes of India. To protest against his arrest, these great parties, the Communist (Marxist), the Communist Party of India, the Jan Sangh, the Swatantra, the whole lot of them are ganging up. The strategy of this man deserves to be appreciated indeed!'[59] There was an obvious note of exasperation in his tone owing to the slipping of initiative from the hands of the government.

The arrests of their leaders evoked serious resentment among the workers. At places they went on immediate, sporadic strikes; employees' gatherings passed resolutions condemning arrests and endorsing workers' strike from 8 May. On 2 May, as Bombay City and its railway workers went on a spontaneous lowering of tools in protest against the arrest of George, V.R. Malgi, General Secretary, National (Central) Railway Mazdoor Union, died when in the morning he was taken into custody. He suffered a massive heart attack and didn't recover (he was a heart patient and had been operated upon twice before). Paying a tribute later in the day in Parliament, the railway minister, Lalit Narayan Mishra, said that everyone came with a fixed count of breath, and life and death was in the hands of God. The stock of Lalit Narayan Mishra was so low he had to repeatedly claim it was he who had ordered George's arrest. This was rather doubted by his fellow politicians who held the prime minister responsible for it. A few days before, the Railway Board had met the prime minister, without the consent of their minister, to apprise Indira Gandhi of the emerging strike situation in the railways. They were worried that their minister would give in to the demands; whereas they, the Railway Board, wanted the workers to be disciplined by letting the strike take place and then wreaking vengeance on them for doing so.[60]

The Opposition was angry with the railway minister and said so. It called him corrupt, fumbling and inept, and busy with Bihar affairs to smoothen his brother Jagannath Mishra's ascendance to its throne. Being the face of the government on railways, Lalit Mishra's action produced hostility that refused to subside even after the strike was called off. Seven months after the strike ended, with an embittered and sullen workforce, Lalit Narayan Mishra would meet an inexplicably gory end, detonated to death by a bomb thrown on the dais from which he was to address a public meeting at Samastipur, near Muzaffarpur in Bihar.[61] It was a sad death and largely went unmourned. Indira Gandhi, though, at the condolence meet startled everyone by claiming that if she was killed too, it would be said that she had organized her own killing. At another condolence meet held at Baroda House, the headquarters of the Northern Railways in Delhi, there was expression of 'jubilation and joy instead of horror'.[62] Mishra had become a hated figure, so much so that when Kamlapati Tripathi (1905–90), a supposed right-reactionary, succeeded him as the railway minister, George wrote congratulating him for his newest ministerial assignment and hoped he would prove friendlier than the 'progressive' Lalit Mishra ever was.

Zonal and branch office-bearers of the AIRF wrote of the arrests of colleagues or the repressive police action the administration had resorted to. 'On hearing news of your arrest, the railwaymen of the Eastern Railway burst with resentment, held demonstrations, processions as a mark of protest almost everywhere', a letter told George.[63] 'In our Integral Coach Factory, the General Strike is a total success. As soon as we received the message of the arrest we went on (from 3 May onwards) strike and continue till today.'[64] 'Strike has started in Gorakhpur Loco Shed in advance from 5 May and the strike in the shed is complete.'[65] The general secretary of the All India Guards Council directed all its members to 'unconditionally' take part in the ongoing strike. 'Attempts should be made to paralyse entire movements with active cooperation of the Loco Running Staff, even if they do not adhere to our proposal, no guard should work any train with any consequence whatsoever.'[66] At Mughalsarai railway station, Asia's biggest railway yard, 'strike was cent-per cent', departments shut, movements of trains stopped and employees gathered in procession in violation of prohibitory orders. But while the strike raged and trains came to a dead stop in their tracks and yards, hoisting the spectre of an industrial shutdown across the nation, the argument that it was a political strike resounded in the twin chambers of Parliament.[67] The Congress-led NFIR, dissociating itself from the strike, accused George of leading a political strike. The charge of political motive was not a nebulous innovation. Each time before when he had led trade union struggles for labour rights, for their sheer intransigence, fighting organization and unity of purpose, charges of such nature had always been hurled at him. But there was something sinister behind the focus in Parliament on his personality and his deeds. When he became the centre of parliamentary debates and adjournment motions and even one no-confidence motion against Indira Gandhi's government, when Opposition MPs were still debating when to take up the motion and Indira Gandhi stood up and said 'now', politicians across the benches and divides were sadly sidestepping the real issue of the railway workers' plight. Before his rising stature, the railways workers' demands and issues were dwarfed. Politicians vied in shielding him, in eulogizing him. N.G. Gore said he was the most dynamic trade union leader; George was the new Mahatma.[68] Instead of forcing the government to resume negotiations and arrive at a settlement, the Opposition geared itself to corner it on the arrests. If it provided an easy way out for the government and allowed the Opposition to show a momentary solidarity, it provided George and his supporters a centrality that they would not abjure but would also not relish either.

Taking advantage of his arrest, the CPI and others who were opposed to his rising stock among organized labour got busy to find a way out of the deadlock. From jail, George wrote repeatedly to Indira Gandhi and to Lalit Narayan Mishra to not consider the strike political but settle the economic demands of workers to avert the strike from 8 May. George wrote to the prime minister, whose progressivism he considered a sham, about her 'blissfully ignorant' railway minister. In the letter to her, two days before the formal launch of the strike, in which he requested her intervention, saying, 'You can still avert the catastrophe, if you wish,' he also said, 'but if the idea is to have a trial of strength, then, this time, I hope, the railwaymen will not be found wanting in proving their mettle.'[69] This was the language the government cited in support of its crackdown. But it had also been preparing for this eventuality much before the talks had started and continued with the preparation all through the talks as well. Charitably, one could say that it was unable to understand the language used by a trade unionist. Both parties at the negotiation table had been apprehensive about the other's intentions and doubted if talks would lead to an amicable resolution. They both, however, not just continued to talk but tried to position themselves as the victim of the talks' failure. And, yet, they both were preparing for the strike, the government by ordering the steel and power plants to hoard coal and the NCCRS by forging strike committees, by issuing guidelines and by advocating their cause both nationally and internationally. Both sides were talking about the paralysis of economy owing to the railway strike, but their invocation of the economy was for contrasting purposes. While the government side wanted the strikers to shun the strike in order to reactivate the economy in the times of oil crisis, rising prices and worldwide depression, the strike leaders wanted a 'negotiated settlement' as the strike would be 'catastrophic'.[70] Strangely, worsening impact on the economy was the concern of both, and still the strike was happening. Worried that his letters to the prime minister and to the railway minister were reaching the press even before they arrived at the addressees' desks, the government got an injunction from the court to not permit George, without its clearance, 'any interview or telephonic communication with any person or to send letters to any person'.[71] Madhu Limaye, who was working behind the scene, sought an appointment from the prime minister to know 'how far the PM was prepared to go', but was denied. His repeated efforts scuttled, he wrote to V.V. Giri about the unhelpful attitude of those in power.[72] But Indira Gandhi was more focused on the nuclear test blast at Pokhran which would happen soon in the middle of the strike.

The communists were caught in a bind, the CPI particularly. Having been solidly behind the prime minister, it suddenly lost all relevance and direction. The CPI had characterized the JP movement raging outside a fascist enterprise supported by the Jan Sangh, and now they had to stand with its supporters in Parliament in order to demonize the Congress government. They had been supporting Indira Gandhi, and now they had to move a no-confidence motion against her government on a working-class agenda, in the making of which they hadn't really played even a peripheral role. They had been made into a tail, whereas all along they had thought they were the bulldog of the workers' movement. Reduced to being the cheerleaders, they were actually uncomfortable all along. In March, S.A. Dange had blessed the formation of a competing federation of railway workers, the AITUC-controlled Indian Railway Workers' Federation. Dange, the AITUC chairman, was elected president of this new federation. It was not clear if he wanted to prop up AITUC or its newly created railway federation or was genuinely worried about the workers going home beaten. Dange spoke in the strike's initial days of the government's aim to divide workers' unity by making selective arrests and by leaving out the communists. In carrying out the 'selective arrests', the government desired to dent the trade union solidarity. But when Madhu Limaye pointed out the case of 'selective arrests', feeling insulted Dange wrote a stinging reply. Their exchange at the height of the strike was released to the press, and that made the waters murkier, making the category unions who had been supporting the strike feel embarrassed and used. It was not clear as well if Madhu Limaye was trying to protect George when he insisted upon negotiations being held with the 'entire Action Committee, including those members of the Committee who are in jail, and not with the truncated committee', or he was simply delaying any truce.[73] Dange had been calling for negotiations with those members of the Action Committee who were outside. George, however, while writing a tribute to Madhu Limaye many years later would recall his glorious supportive role during the railway strike.[74]

A three-point formula emerged: the simultaneous withdrawal of the strike, the release of railway leaders, and the resumption of negotiations. George sent a message from jail recommending the formula's acceptance, with the addition of a fourth issue of no victimization of workers.[75] But his message was withheld by his colleagues working to prolong the strike and shelve a settlement. His general secretary Priya Gupta was alleged to have done so. But was he alone? Or was Madhu Limaye behind it? The formula eventually got rejected by the thirteen-member Action Committee, of whom six were in jail, and after this the government's stand became more rigid. It ordered railway colonies to be evicted of their worker-residents. The Opposition demanded that those in jail be released first, so that they could consult those outside and take unanimous decisions. George asked for resumption of negotiations even if it meant jail was the place for talks. Lalit Mishra retorted, 'George Fernandes is not a Mahatma that the venue of negotiations should be where the Mahatma is.' Maniben Kara arrived in Delhi from Bombay, 'to find some solution to the deadlock created by the rigid attitude of the government'.[76] Instead of engaging with the government, she caused a flutter by insisting that the strike be immediately withdrawn as workers had already begun to rejoin work. On 17 May, in a letter to George, she informed him that the strike had 'started deteriorating all over the country, excepting Bombay and parts of southern railways. The workers had begun to drift back to their work.' She wanted the strike called off 'to save the organization and our cadre amongst the workers'. She wanted it withdrawn by that evening itself, whether there was a respectable way out or not. She further lamented that the railway workers had lost control over their fate. 'I was all along afraid that this will happen, and I regret that my fear has come true—I think most of those who are today deciding the fate of the railway workers have hardly any connection with the railway workers. This is most unfortunate.' It was a euphemism for incursion of politics into the workers' movement, but that was a partial and partisan view, as she was herself working towards withdrawing the strike without seeking consent from the workers. She was careful enough to write that she was there only at the invitation of Madhu Limaye. Lest she was misunderstood, she further mentioned that her own Western Railway Employees Union (WREU) was 'actively working for the success of the strike. We shall continue the same till you decide to withdraw the strike.' But she was, she said, 'not one to abuse Indira for everything'.

The government was not keen on any steps to resolve the crisis. Its strategy was to wear the strikers thin by breaking their morale and organized strength. In response, almost caught in a bind, the railway workers' leaders decided they had no choice but to 'carry on their valiant struggle'. The government was aware of deterioration in the strength of the strike. On the seventeenth day of the strike, the government remained adamant about its lack of capacity to pay what was being demanded by the railwaymen. But the employees of the

Indian Airlines were given a second interim increase to their wages, and when George got to know of it, he wrote Finance Minister Y.B. Chavan a stinging missive, asking him, 'have you lost all sense of justice and fairplay? Should railwaymen forever be treated as slaves?'[77] In order to keep the motivation high, he went on fasting in jail. He had created a situation in which everyone else was made to fall in with his design. Others, even those reluctant, were led by the nose to the suicidal pit to make them silently jump into it, according to the timing and direction decided by him. Dange had been dragged into it; the Jan Sangh had their own objectives but they too had been made to fall in line. The idea behind the nationwide strike was to inflict so much damage on the government by the total stoppage of transportation that it would be forced to negotiate with the workers and arrive at a settlement favourable to them. Most industrial strikes happened on that premise. But the government was refusing to give in. It was not worried about the consequences of the strike. Its capacity to bear the losses was immense, it seemed, certainly much more than the capacity of the railway workers to endure an indefinite strike. The government was not a municipality which was worried about the pestilent air generated by piling, rotting garbage on the roadside, at marketplaces and in slaughterhouses, spreading immediate hazards to public health. Here was an impervious elected government, with a seemingly deep pocket, supremely confident of its capacity to tide over a minor distraction. It remained unmoved. Not just did it refuse to negotiate, the Indira Gandhi government, unmindful of all the transportation stoppages, even went on to conduct an experimental nuclear explosion at Pokhran in the midst of the ongoing strike, as if everything was normal. Its gloating over the explosion hogged more limelight than the economic disorientation caused by the strike. The attitude of the government exposed the weakness in the workers' strategy. A government could not be made to give in merely because of mounting economic losses. To make it climb down, it had to be hit on its moral right to rule.

The strike, which the government continued to call 'illegal', was called off 'unconditionally' with immediate effect from 6 a.m. on 28 May. The AIRF general secretary Priya Gupta submitted a dissent note on the decision to withdraw the strike. He wanted it to be prolonged as he had felt the government was on the verge of tottering.[78] Taking a cue from Priya Gupta's dissent, workers at many places in the North-Frontier Railway continued to hold out for a few more days. The government took a hard-line approach. Following its 'no work, no pay' principle, it denied payment to employees for the strike period. Those who had taken part in the strike were made to suffer a break in service that deprived them of many benefits they were entitled to had their employment been continuous. 'The employees who indulged in acts of instigation, intimidation of other workers, caused obstruction to working and / or against whom there are any charge for acts of violence, sabotage or crushing damaging to railway property etc. should be dealt with firmly under the provisions of Law, including the Defence of India Rules,' a government order read.[79] Somehow the government had succeeded in spreading a countervailing message that the strike was an unreasonable tantrum from an already privileged class of workers who because of their organized strength were asking for more to the deprivation of all others. Although the people at large retained their bewildered neutrality, the perception that the strike was a selfish act on the part of the organized employees had taken root and did bother them to an extent. As the government regrouped, George, accepting the moral responsibility for all that had happened, needing 'neither scapegoats nor alibis', said:

> Those who are either lamenting or gloating (and, both species exist in abundance in our midst) over what they call the 'defeat of the workers' should know that the strike has been called off by the workers' leaders who were charged with its conduct. I do not subscribe to the political and trade union theory which believes that workers lose their struggles. In my opinion, workers never lose in any struggle as long they keep fighting to the best of their ability. Each struggle takes the working-class movement a few steps forward, even in a fascist and police state. The workers came out victorious. In Franco's Spain, in Pinochet's Chile and in Indira's India, the workers are fighting what to the traditionalists may appear to be losing battles,

but it is both lack of understanding and absence of vision that makes these men see defeats in workers' struggle.

After their heroic action, I would like to know who would dare again challenge the railwaymen for another strike. On our part, we shall do everything to restore normalcy in the running of the trains. But normalcy cannot be a one-way traffic. Much depends on what attitude the railway administration and the government take in the coming days.[80]

* * *

It was in nine straight months that the denouement of the biggest strike in Indian Railways was reached. It undid India's working-class movement for a long time to come. But when it was galloping to its finale, it was like nothing that the Indian working class had ever witnessed. In its scale and the inspiring bonding it forged, it was unprecedented. Its influence was widespread given that its mammoth base was scrambled through at a momentous pace. In October, when it had all begun, there had been wholesale apprehensions but also a sullen, silent hope of realizing workers' long-gestating demands. And, when it was really raging, despite allegations of opportunism, it was not a political struggle for power, but an economic battle of India's organized labour. And, the charge was that it was the Prime Minister Indira Gandhi, who had brought it about, not George, the man accused of doing so; the phrase 'this is a government strike' explained all the hidden hands behind it. Throughout the countdown, there was an uncanny sense as much among the movement's rank and file as among its leaders that the strike might not actually come through. Yet, it happened.

The state reprisal, its fury culminating in arrests, mass dismissals, punitive break-in-services, emptying of railway colonies, was not unprecedented in AIRF history, although George would later say it was a 'dress rehearsal' for something more sinister. These measures of repression were certainly not devised during the 1974 strike, a fact overlooked by him.[81] Those victimized for taking part in the 1960

Courtesy: *Himmat*, 1 June 1974

In its caption to the photograph, *Himmat* wrote, By George . . . George is
left holding the baby not the railwaymen's but his own, soon after his release,
last week at the Socialist Party office at Vithalbhai Patel House, New Delhi.
He was welcomed by his wife Leela [sic] and George II.

Central government employees' strike and in the one-day token strike
of September 1968 were still to be fully rehabilitated, and some were
reinstated after a long gap, with a break in service, throwing them
into financial and career losses. They had been penalized for 'active
instigation', a phrase under which came not the acts of sabotage and
violence, for which there were more stringent statutory provisions, but
such normal trade union activities as organizing a workers' meeting,
slogan-shouting, going in a procession, demonstrating or engaging in
any kind of picketing.

With characteristic optimism, George said that in spite of the
withdrawal of the strike, the railwaymen's movement had proved

itself and was 'poised at the threshold of achievements that may have no parallel'.[82] His repeated avowing that he didn't want a strike, but a negotiated settlement, was significant. A strike, as Lenin said, is a school of war, not a war by itself. In it and while being a participant, a worker learns what a state is. How enslaved and helpless he is. To lead a war to gain real liberation, a worker or a band of workers needs to take a leap beyond the conduct of a strike, to get involved with other aspects of society as well. Even while he was leading a countrywide strike by railway workers, George was simultaneously also thickly involved in the raging JP movement. For the political class, his simultaneous involvement with the railway workers and with the people's movement in Bihar and other places under the JP movement came in handy to brand his action political. He was never given due credit for envisaging a bigger scenario. Not by railway workers themselves, who having lost their jobs, having seen the barbarity with which the government had imposed its repressive machinery over them, accused him of leading them to nowhere or not fighting enough in the aftermath of the strike to get their jobs back. A week after the strike had been called off and workers were beginning to feel the pinch of their audacious leap, their wives had surrounded George and torn his clothes and demanded wages to keep them going.[83] Nor by the communists, who even after ingratiating themselves to the regime of Indira Gandhi still thought themselves true leaders of workers, and were therefore surprised at George doing what they couldn't. The communist support to the strike extended only till the strike ended, and even then, it was lukewarm at the central level and cold and disruptive at the provincial and cadre levels. S.A. Dange was even prone to think of displacing George from the leadership position, and argued with Madhu Limaye for opening up negotiations with the government even when a large part of the leadership was in jail. The communists, the CPI and the AITUC mainly, both headed by Dange, despite the involvement of some of its branches or individuals in the strike, remained waiting at the margins, as if on instruction. In fact, they were keen to sabotage the strike and rob initiative once the ground was ceded by George's arrest. Years later, writing his autobiography, Jyoti Basu said the strike should not have been withdrawn. It was a betrayal, the revered Marxist observed.[84] However, George knew his timing well. George's leading the Railway Strike as the president of the AIRF, his leading the Socialist Party as its chairman, his being an indefatigable warrior of the JP movement, all combined to build a tempo that went beyond the strike as a school of war, almost reaching out to the society. The communists, on the other hand, were already a compromised lot and had a coalition with the ruling Congress. When they, in support of their approach, pointed to the 'progressive elements' within the Congress, George asked, 'Who is the progressive and democratic in the Indira Congress Comrade Rajeswar Rao?' He continued,

> What an irony that when the progressive, left democrats led by the greatest progressive, left democrat of them all, Mrs. Indira Gandhi were a privy to the killing, raping and other brutalities against the railwaymen, it is the right reaction of your quixotic imagination, the Jan Sanghis, who were your allies in the NCCRS and in resisting this onslaught. It is the Congress (O), Swatantra, BKD, Jan Sangh, SP who formed a solid phalanx inside Parliament and outside and used what little moral authority and political leverage they had to stand by the beleaguered railwaymen![85]

A few months later, he would go underground to escape Indira Gandhi's dragnet. He would then discover the ephemeral nature of railwaymen's loyalty that during the May Strike was so overwhelmingly intense that even a dismal failure to achieve what they had aspired would scarcely douse its fiery blaze. In the underground, he would arrange clandestine meetings with zonal leaders of the AIRF to drum up support for his resistance against the Emergency but would soon be appalled by their cold shoulder. He would even get to know that the AIRF leadership, at the behest of the ruling Congress, was conspiring to overthrow him, their fugitive president, and invite a Congressman to head their organization.[86] In the end, it was Priya Gupta, the general secretary who had been envious of him, who had sulked all through while the strike preparation was being made and was conveniently allowed to stay free, only to emerge when the strike was called off to write a note of dissent on its withdrawal, who was chosen to replace him. George contemplated replacing Priya Gupta as the AIRF general secretary in 1975 but didn't succeed. The loyalists of Priya Gupta would strike back. Priya Gupta would become the first one to rise from the ranks of railway workers to head the AIRF. The AIRF rank and file would always perceive George as an outsider, whereas Priya Gupta was one of their own. However it has been said in Priya Gupta's favour that when Kamalapati Tripathi asked him to change the AIRF president, he turned around to ask the minister how would he feel if they asked him to change the prime minister.[87] It was the time of a National Emergency when words spoken were carefully weighed, and therefore his courage in speaking so directly is applauded by his fellow railway workers to this day.

George became anathema to the railway workers. When immediately after the strike, George would get busy with the JP movement, he issued a letter to the railwaymen asking them to give their might to it: 'Obviously, the government would expect the railwaymen to drive the trains over the dead bodies of the people. But I do not have to emphasize that the railwaymen must do nothing that will alienate the general masses of people from their own movement, or any way cause any physical harm to the people who are struggling against injustice in Bihar.'[88] The Railway Board saw his statement as an exhortation to the railway workers to identify with the political movement and threatened the AIRF with derecognition.[89] Ironically, his overlapping roles as the chairman of the Socialist Party and the president of the AIRF saved the day. But it created issues within the AIRF, and they began to object to the telephone bills that he was incurring due to his many involvements.[90] In his dogged years of the 1980s, when he was down and out, the AIRF would spurn his overtures to reclaim its leadership. They would shout slogans against him, throw rotten eggs at him, show him black flags and would not allow him to address them. '*Rail ka neta, rail-mazdoor, bahar-wale bahar jao*', he would hear in their war cries. He had become an outsider. Why would the railwaymen show such intense dislike to someone who just a few months before had moved them enough to abandon home and hearth, and risk their lives by declaring a war on the state and abstaining from their duty? Was it because the traditional leaders of the railwaymen who had brought the AIRF to a state of complete limbo, of idle existence, were so staggered by the intensity of his engagement, unity of purpose and dedication to the cause that they decided to put an embargo on him in order not to expose themselves? This was not the first time they had got into a spartan repartee, but he took advantage of the opportunity provided by his blockage to show how unjust, how ungracious they were, and got embroiled in a bitter, acrimonious wrangling that stirred up in both of them, the AIRF and him, the rancour that had lain dormant all through when he led the organization. They had invited him to lead the AIRF in order to infuse a dose of hope, activism and enthusiasm that had been stripped of them by a compromised existence of a lacklustre leadership. They accepted him for what he really was: a man passing through, but he, down in the dumps in the 1980s, wanted it to prop up his sagging political career as a return gift for his services to the railway workers. The spurning would long rankle him, it would continue to the time he became, ironically, the minister of railways in the short-lived government of Vishwanath Pratap Singh (1989–90). During this period, when in pursuit of a meaningless memory of that rancour, he tried to smother the AIRF into oblivion, by stripping it of its life force, the recognition of the Railway Board, his malevolence would be fought against gallantly by the AIRF to preserve itself.[91] It was only then that he would finally lay to rest his past as the AIRF leader.

A person who would win the hearts of railway workers was Madhu Dandavate, who just five days after the installation of the Janata government in 1977, when he presented the rail budget in Parliament, would announce the reinstatement of all workers dismissed or victimized during the 1974 strike. This would win him a permanent place of gratitude among the railway workers.[92] But against George they would continue to hold a grudge. In 1999, in somewhat muted preparations for the Silver Jubilee Year of the May Strike, there would not be a single reference to George in any of the AIRF publications and communications. In truth, as George was told in 1974, 'It is time you perceived that the trade union movement is no longer a revolutionary force. Its primary function today is to get better terms for workers. Changing governments or social systems is far from their dreams. They have been neatly fitted into the present order, not only here but in every industrialized country of the world.'[93] The working class was not interested in making a revolution to loose its chains, and was certainly not imbued with the passion to inherit power. 'They may support a revolutionary activity but cannot initiate it. You made a brave bid, but the course of events must have given you food for thought.' The workers were no longer the vanguard of revolution. Even the NCCRS that had brought workers' unity and was the reason for the successful beginning of the May 1974 strike was in shambles within a month after the strike.[94] The AITUC broke from it; the Hind Mazdoor Sabha (HMS) disowned it; George was left alone with it. It was a sad end to a dream, a lifetime saga of fighting for the rights of workers. In 1959, a year after D'Mello's death, George had written to Madhu Limaye,

Yesterday was D'Mello day! We had a meeting at Kesar Baug. Unfortunately, it was a poorly attended meeting. A few hundred workers were present. The dockers had a programme of procession from Carnac Bunder to Sewri cemetery. There were about 5,000 men in it even though there was a complete 'hartal' in the docks and there were about 15,000 men idle. I think all this goes to prove that the workers' memory is rather short lived.[95]

8

The Most Hunted Man

The hunt would last a full year. At the end of it, when the investigating sleuths pieced together bits of evidence, they discovered a trail that had its nebulous beginning in the sleepy hamlet of Gopalpur-on-sea in Orissa (now Odisha) where Leila Kabir Fernandes had prevailed upon George to spend some time with the family. Here, in June 1975 when it had all begun, she, along with their seventeen-month-old son Sushanto and her mother Shanti Das Kabir, had been awaiting George's arrival. And here, on 26 June, within hours of his arrival, George would resolve 'to spare nothing, nothing at all, my life included, to fight and overthrow this dictatorship'.[1]

* * *

Life had been frenetic since their wedding in July 1971. The swirling political and trade union campaigns kept him on the move, barely leaving them time together. A fortnight before their wedding, she had pleaded with him to settle the Bombay taximen's issue without a call to strike so that he could come on time. With a disconcerting innocence, she had then asked, 'Do you have some time to be with just yourself in the midst of all your hectic activities . . . just you and your thoughts?'[2] The nudge must have baffled him, he who revelled in action soaked in the sweat of the working people. But perhaps the soothing warmth of a newly fashioned love and promise of a wedded future together made him, and her as well, overlook the seedling of divergence between them. It didn't help, though, when the marriage failed to slow him down. She felt increasingly lonely as he most often was not there. 'I am thinking of you, . . . my beloved husband,' she wrote unhappily a year after their wedding, 'sitting on my bed . . . wondering where you are, what hectic programmes are being arranged.'[3] The letter is a litany of loneliness. She wrote of chirping sparrows that gave her company and of movies she saw to pass time, including a Czech film *A shop on the high street*. In order to get him interested, she provided a synopsis of the movie: it was about the 'poignancy of human dilemma when the individual gets trapped in the soulless machinery of state policy'. Was this a cue for her politician-husband, a hint that he should slow down and savour the moment? Or was it simply an indication of her own desperate life which she wished he would notice? One other movie she saw was the Japanese film made in 1967—*Portrait of Chieko*. This experience was a disaster. The movie, as she wrote to him, was a 'very romantic true story of a sculpture's love for a girl who lost her mind after failing to qualify for some art competition'. But halfway through the movie, the newly married Leila Fernandes felt sick and rushed out of the theatre. She managed somehow to reach home, where she had a severe bout of vomiting. It was a vital bodily sign calling attention to her complicated emotional state. But she shrugged the symptoms away as caused by a possible overdose of medication she was on against a bacterial infection. 'These modern drugs,' she wrote, as if to provide a persuasive cover to her explanation, 'are too toxic. In curing one condition they give five new diseases.' But that she was ridden with anxieties and laden with restlessness was an inadvertent revelation when she wrote with some dread, 'I have no business to be low but I am.' Her misery made her take notice of death occurring in the vicinity. A neighbour who had married late and had three young children died of a heart attack at a relatively young age of 52. Terribly shaken, she wrote, 'The widow is in a daze, weeping bitterly.' The neighbour's death made fears of mortality creep into her. They too had married late; George was 41 and she 34 when they were married.

'Darling, what is it all about?' she inquired, in confusion, and perhaps also seeking some consolation, '. . . True we make our own destiny, but it is in some kind of a framework not entirely in our control.' The starkness of truth saddened her more in his absence and, as time went by unceasingly, on his refusal to surrender to a conjugal fate: 'I missed you ever so much last night. I would have snuggled myself in your arms for comfort.' And yet, knowing him, she would not ask him to return from wherever he was. She only wrote: 'whatever I am doing I am always by your side, walking along with you, praying for success in all that you undertake to do.' She expressed undying love and a lifelong commitment to stand by him 'so that some of the dreams for this land and its people can be made into realities.'[4]

Soon, she was pregnant. In those months when she carried Sushanto in her womb, tough as they were, she had struggled consistently against her inner demons. She expected a 'lot of patience and optimism' from George but he was rarely there. In January 1974, Sushanto was born. In May, she carried little Sonny Boy in her arms to meet his father in jail. It was in the midst of the railway strike. Many years later, with their marriage floundering, but still refusing to blame him, she would think of those dreaded 'post-1971' days as mainly born of her own 'nameless doubts and anxieties', aggravated—and, this was as far as she would go in holding him responsible—by his 'total absence of time investment' in their marriage.[5] He too would realize this and be remorseful. 'The longest period' they had spent 'together uninterruptedly' in the five years that they were married—he would recall in July 1976, sitting in a cage-like solitary cell in Hissar Jail, exposed to the elements during the day and kept under a scorching searchlight at night—was the four months in 1972 when they had toured the United States and Canada meeting members of the extended family.[6] Jail is a strange place; it makes time weigh heavily on the conscience, so much so that the only relief one finds is in whipping up memories. Unsure how long his incarceration would last, he was apologetic: 'Even when Sonny Boy was born, I could hardly spend a week with her.' He would wonder if she had 'bargained' for all that when they had married: 'My life and my work are not fair to her and Sonny Boy but she has borne it all, though

I know at what cost.' What she could not succeed in making him do when they were together, the jail's solitude did. But it was a remorse that was late in coming and in prison where the seclusion made him think of what might have been rather than was.

It was therefore at Leila Fernandes' insistence that a sort of family union was planned in the blissful isolation of this little fishing village of Gopalpur-on-sea. Little did she know that the family vacation she had long been planning would come to an abrupt end and in such a manner that she would be forced to stay away from her husband for the next 22 months. During those months, he either was a runaway, or in jail; and she, thousands of miles away, at first seeking a breather in a foreign land, and then getting sucked into a worldwide campaign to save his life. Months later, after he had successfully escaped the dragnet, he would reminisce in a moment of solitude: 'That day, when I was getting ready to enter the underground, Sushanto was constantly calling out Daddy, as if he had sensed that it was a long, long war which we were getting involved in and it [would] be a long, long time before he would see and talk to his Daddy again.'[7] Thereafter, his life was dangerously hinged and precariously lived: evading authorities, writing resistance, inciting action against the 'dictatorship' of Indira Gandhi. Yet, as the hunt gathered heat and he thought fondly of his family far away, although he was advised to escape, to give up this lone battle and join them abroad, he was even more resolute to not do so because his 'work was in this country'.[8] Seven months in the underground, with a reward on his head and Leila Fernandes' passport impounded, he would write to a friend, 'In the event of my arrest, Leila is not to return—no matter what reports are put out.'[9] Someone sheltering him during those dangerous days recalled, 'He used to say that he did not care if he was killed or what happened to his wife and child, but he would see to it that Indira Gandhi was forced to step down from her office.'[10] And, in this, there was 'no retreat nor any room for any compromise'. He knew his mind well: 'It is either freedom or death.' He had made his choice long ago, 'long before Madam became dictator when her emissaries offered me all that I would care to have except the prime ministership. In fact, my choice was made when I joined the [Socialist] Party, now more than twenty-seven years ago.'[11]

* * *

Although she denied her disqualification from Parliament was the reason, it was clear Indira Gandhi declared the National Emergency to preserve herself. In December 1970, sensing her rising popularity, she dissolved the Lok Sabha a year ahead of schedule. In the general elections held in February 1971, the Congress Party with a pledge to eradicate poverty swept the polls, winning 352 of 518 parliamentary seats. The Opposition, with a Grand Alliance of four parties, one of them the Samyukta Socialist Party (SSP), was routed. The SSP registered a paltry three wins. George lost his deposit in a constituency that four years before had given him a memorable, first-ever parliamentary victory. Indira Gandhi fought for her election at Rae Bareli in Uttar Pradesh. Contesting against her was the indomitable Raj Narain, the SSP strongman. She beat him by a margin of more than one lakh votes. But refusing to give in, he petitioned the Allahabad High Court to get her victory annulled, alleging unfair practices in her win. Among a slew of charges, one in particular was about the use of special imported ink from Russia in the ballot papers. It was alleged that the ink magically changed every vote cast into a Congress vote. Everybody had laughed it off. But not Raj Narain![12] The legal battle went on famously for four long years. On 12 June 1975, Justice Jagmohan Sinha delivered his judgment holding Indira Gandhi guilty and disqualified her from Parliament.[13] She was given a twenty-day window for appeal, but within a mere fourteen days she made the acquiescing President declare 'a grave emergency exists whereby the security of India is threatened by internal disturbances'. When the Allahabad verdict was delivered, the Opposition asked for her resignation, but as George said a few weeks later, 'None of us even remotely implied that the Congress government at the Centre resign or be dismissed.'[14] A month later JP would write to her, 'You seem to act swiftly and dramatically only when your personal position is threatened.'[15]

At Gopalpur-on-sea, the Kabirs owned a seaside bungalow on a four-acre plot. It was a double-storeyed structure built of mortared stone and brick, standing majestically like a frontier fort on a sand dune at the foot of a tall lighthouse. From here one got an unhindered view of the sea and heard its irresistible roar round the clock. Many years later, when Leila Fernandes along with her now-adult son would be making claims over an ailing George in Delhi, she would receive a call one afternoon from Gopalpur-on-sea informing her of the discovery of her brother's lifeless body on the beach. The locals say Dadabhai, as he was fondly called, had returned from abroad solely to die here. How else could one explain an expert swimmer drowning in knee-deep water?[16] It was a sad insinuation. He was newly married, for the second time. His mortal remains were first buried within the bungalow's premises but later on, when locals objected, they were shifted to the nearby Muslim cemetery.

But in June 1975, the bungalow was protected from any such sad spectre of the future. Swathed in the sweltering pre-monsoon heat, it awaited George's arrival in anticipation of family fun and frolic. On 16 June, Leila Fernandes wrote to George, of how 'thick rain clouds loom threateningly and then blow over without any shower'.[17] The dry spell made drinking water scarce. Their well dried up, making them borrow water from anxious neighbours. Prickly heat led to rashes on Sonny Boy's body on which talcum powder had little effect. The toddler, she wrote, 'perspires dreadfully—like you'. He kept himself cool by playing on wet sand by the sea during the low tide. With feigned annoyance she wrote, 'he is best off in his birthday suit—I've hardly used those fancy clothes you got him.' This expectant letter, while describing the bleakness of the Orissa horizon, was political in nature. 'The twelfth of June,' she wrote with biting sarcasm, 'was indeed a memorable day.' She was naturally elated over the judicial indictment of Indira Gandhi and called the verdict 'a three-fold hit for that woman who has shown her true colours to the whole world—as an utterly shameless, brazen and power-crazy person who cares two hoots for the country's name or welfare'. She scarcely expected her to voluntarily melt away into oblivion after the verdict. She believed that Indira Gandhi, now with 'no legs to stand on', would be pushed 'into tearing up the constitution and clamping a dictatorship'. Her prognosis was eerily prescient. But eerier still was her evaluation of Indira Gandhi's personality. She expressed amazement at 'the total amorality of the person', adding, 'it isn't even immorality—for that implies a consciousness of doing wrong.' In her opinion, Indira Gandhi's brazenness was 'her primary source of strength, but will also ultimately result in total nemesis'.

Born in a political family, Leila Fernandes had her reasons to characterize Indira Gandhi as 'almost a psychotic person'.[18] Her father Humayun Kabir was foremost among those who had rebelled against Nehru's daughter and had established a political party in opposition. After her marriage to George, any warm-hearted feelings she may have had for Indira Gandhi went missing. George was opposed to her politically and 'to a considerable extent as a person'. The only time he exchanged smiles with her, he said, was on the occasion of his wedding. But to say that Leila Fernandes' animus towards Indira Gandhi or to her son, Sanjay—'a plain coward who rode on Mommy's back'—was coloured solely by the politics of her husband would be untrue.

She was preparing for his arrival in an intimate way, aware though unmindful of the evolving political scenario. She wrote again on 18 June, inquiring if he would have time to shop for groceries, either in Delhi or at Calcutta, and then on her own wrote a list of things to be bought: 'A few desirable items—peanut butter—1 bottle/tin, Marmalade, Amul Cheese—1 packet, from Calcutta's main market (or Vidya/Rajni will tell you where), a basket of fruit—long-lasting type—mosambi etc and a few vegetables—not more than ½ kg each—there is nothing here from which we can make a green salad—tomatoes, capsicum (simla mirch), cucumber, lemons, cabbage, carrot, beans—will do fine—but if all this is too much trouble, don't bother—we will manage with whatever this place has to offer.' In her typical way, even while expecting him to do a few errands, she was accommodating of him. Complaining that quality ghee was not available even at Berhampur, a commercial town close to Gopalpur-on-sea, she further requested, 'If that ghee-tin in our fridge is still unopened—and if you can manage, please bring it along. Also, 2 kg good quality basmati for yourself—[bring] a pair of swimming trunks for sea-bathing.' After this sizeable inventory, she wrote of the arrangement to pick him up from Berhampur railway station on his arrival: 'Anusheela Bhavani, a resident plies here her car as a taxi—and we usually use it. If it is working, we shall send it to the station—a small old blue coloured car with a baggage carrier over the roof. Otherwise— if you find no such car—take a cycle rickshaw to the main bus-stand— and you will find Berhampur taxi right there. Fare anything between Rs 20–25.' Evidently, she relished micro-managing his life. Did this trait of hers worry him? Ignoring his public persona, she assumed he would arrive by himself at Berhampur. She even planned a return journey on 27 June. Like a cautious housewife, counting her pennies, Leila Fernandes wrote, 'The train would save us some money since you and Sonny Boy wouldn't need tickets—and AC is very comfortable.' Since he became the AIRF president, he held a first-class pass on the railways. Moreover, the train provided a longer time together, a consideration no less significant for her. Her mother Shanti Kabir was to return, too, but she wanted to travel separately by chair car, not willing to intrude into her daughter's family. Leila Fernandes didn't like the suggestion though, wondering 'how can she be in chair car and we in the AC'.[19]

The day after the Allahabad verdict, George wrote to her of how unsure he now was about joining them. Things were not sanguine in the party. It was in deep crisis. Every cure they suggested helped only further disease it. The party considered piggybacking on the JP movement but feared losing its identity.[20] They were indecisive and that produced a contradictory and self-serving approach. George and Surendra Mohan (1926–2010), the two topmost office-bearers, weren't on the same page. A reconciliation was nudged, as had become a morbid pattern, by letting the issue remain unresolved. But now, politics was on the cusp of transformation. It acquired an urgency. A meeting of the four Opposition parties to discuss the formation of a new federal party was called in Delhi on 21 June. As the Socialist Party chairman, George was in the thick of negotiations. Could he take some days off? This was not the most opportune time for a family vacation. George's dithering message was received even before Leila Fernandes had dispatched her 18 June letter, and she would add a page and mail it. She wrote with an abiding faith and fortitude in that added page: 'I know what a pivotal and historic role you will be destined to play in the coming months and years. So, I suggest you should be right there where the compelling circumstances require your presence.' If there was a touch of irony, she hid it well, writing simply, 'we miss you'. The next day, she went to Berhampur and booked two train tickets for 29 June to Delhi.

* * *

In Delhi then, prevailed an uneasy calm. JP (Jayaprakash Narayan) was at its centre. The crisis enlivened him, catapulted him into a centrality he was missing for long. Way back in the 1930s, he had advocated capture of state power necessary to construct socialism.[21] But Gandhi's murder so overwhelmed him that from a 'bloody commie' he became an exponent of the Sarvodaya movement.[22] In the twenty years that followed, he was a non-party social worker, striving to make non-violence the basis of a new society. His regard for Jawaharlal Nehru, at first, would not let him stake claim to power; but by the descent of the post-Nehru era, his time had passed. Reduced to a caricature of his earlier self, his slide was underlined at the cremation of his wife in April 1973 when barely a hundred admirers attended it. Indira Gandhi's receding popularity, since her victory in 1971, gave way to restive streets. Signs of public disenchantment first found expression in Gujarat. The students led a mass agitation. At many places in the state, food riots broke out in January 1974. In March, as Gujarat students got a scent of victory, Bihari students reclaimed the streets. They pulled JP in, and the nation was 'afire'.[23] In November, while leading a gherao, JP was assaulted at Patna, which only inflamed the conflagration further.[24] Five months later, on 6 March, he led a people's march to Parliament House in Delhi.[25] The political atmosphere had stiffened so much as to make George write to an acquaintance, 'It is not possible for me to move into Bihar till 6 March, because either they will extern me or they will detain me.'[26] Over 70 years old and always an enigmatic personality, JP now acquired the halo of people's hero who aspired once more to capture the state. Coming a full ideological circle, he had the RSS cadres as his foot soldiers.[27] A man who had once denounced the 'RSS machine'—'It is a secret or semi-secret organization'—now found common cause with them: 'If you are a fascist, then, I too am a fascist,' he told them.[28] The bulk of the Opposition lost in 'small squabbles and foibles' found in JP a rallying point. Suddenly, as George observed, he became the Prophet who would lead his flock to the Promised Land. 'Everyone jumped on the caravan.' A determined Congress, on the other hand, rallied behind Indira Gandhi. Showing no leanings to resign, she asked the Supreme Court instead for an 'absolute and unconditional' stay on the Allahabad judgment.

On the evening of 22 June, George and Madhu Limaye drove to the Ramlila Ground in the heart of Delhi to address a political rally. In the car, they discussed their possible response 'if the lady should decide tonight to tear up the constitution, arrest all those who are opposed to her authoritarianism and proclaim herself a dictator'.[29] After the rally, they went to Madhu Limaye's place to have a frugal supper. Late in the night, when George reached home a source in the army informed him of major troop movements around the capital. He tried to telephone Madhu Limaye, but the line was out of use.

Not willing to disappoint Leila Fernandes, George had decided to go to Gopalpur-on-sea the following day, 'And precisely for that reason, while going home that night, I had borrowed Madhu's alarm clock as I had to catch an early morning flight to Calcutta.' Later in the day, Madhu Limaye would leave Delhi for a Chhattisgarh (then part of Madhya Pradesh) tour. JP was unhappy at their leaving Delhi at such a crucial time.[30] There was a plan to establish a Lok Sangarsh Samiti to mount a campaign for Indira Gandhi's resignation. Moreover, on the following day, 24 June, the Supreme Court was to rule on her appeal. A newspaper had called it the 'most-exciting legal battle since independence'.[31] On reaching Calcutta, George boarded another flight for Bhubaneswar. The same night he reached Gopalpur-on-sea.[32] Leila Fernandes' transport arrangement remained unused, carried as he was by his trade union comrades.

On 25 June, Delhi's air was 'tense right from the morning, portending something sinister'.[33] Indira Gandhi had got a conditional stay on the high court judgment. On the east coast, at Berhampur's centrally located Giri market, George addressed a public meeting at the Prakasham Hall.[34] Ramachandra Panda (b. 1949), a correspondent of the Odiya daily *Samaj*, vividly remembers George's speech.[35] He spoke of the military movements in Delhi. He asked for support to the JP movement. Critical of the prime minister's authoritarian ways, he called for her resignation. In Delhi, later in the evening, at a mammoth public meeting at the Ramlila Ground, JP exhorted 'the army, police and government employees not to obey any order they consider illegal'.[36] It was a cue for Indira Gandhi to act swiftly and surgically. That night, the prime minister made President Fakhruddin Ali Ahmed sign an ordinance that said 'a grave emergency exists whereby the security of India is threatened by internal disturbances'.[37] By the early hours of 26 June, it was all over. Even before her cabinet or the nation was told, the arrests were made, the voices muzzled, and the Emergency declared. It became so intense that a frail and diseased JP, now in solitary confinement, his kidneys failing, his morale low, his 'world in a shambles', and under sustained attack for unleashing chaos, would wish it had not happened.[38] 'You know I am an old man. My life's work is done . . . I have nothing and no one to live for,' he wrote in an appeal to prove his innocence.[39] More evidence of his state of mind was given by the one who visited him tied to a dialysis machine in a Bombay hospital: 'I started a movement but it has brought about fascism—I feel guilty for all those who are hunted for their lives and all those in jails,' JP said.[40]

'The President has proclaimed Emergency,' the prime minister told the country over the radio on the morning of 26 June.[41] An hour before she had called the cabinet to tell of it. 'There is nothing to panic about,' she told the nation now in her broadcast, blaming the parties in Opposition for hatching a 'widespread conspiracy' to destabilize the country. And then she said, 'This is not a personal matter,' as to pre-empt the charge that it was a step in self-preservation alone. At noon, a radio bulletin announced sharply, which amounted to:

A National Emergency has been declared. Some antisocial elements have been arrested and peace prevails everywhere in the country. It was surreally Nazi-esque, George would write later.

At Berhampur, the Telephone Exchange supervisor Y.L. Sitaramayya, a leader of the post and telegraph employees' union, was at Prakasham Hall, too, to hear George. Later that night, he eavesdropped on a message to the Berhampur District Magistrate. According to it, George was to be arrested after his rally of railwaymen in the evening. The next moment, a heavyweight Sitaramayya was on a bicycle, frantically peddling to reach Gopalpur-on-sea in order to alert George. At about the same time, Ramachandra Panda tuned in to the BBC on the radio and heard of arrests. Shocked to the bone, he immediately thought of George, as one leader after JP who was a case for an arrest. He too rode his motorcycle to Gopalpur-on-sea. The day had already broken, and the sun had risen on the eastern horizon. He found George on the first floor of the Kabir bungalow conversing with a few fishermen. No public transport plied between Berhampur and their beach town, they were ruing. Panda saw Leila Fernandes wringing out washed clothes while Sushanto crawled nearby. Taking George aside, he told him what he had heard over the radio. With the experience of an earlier Emergency still vivid, George at that very moment decided not to give in easily this time. Gopalpur-on-sea is a small village hemmed in by the sea, with just one road linking it to Berhampur. At one end of the sandy shore by the sea is a stream of a backwater, stretching more than a mile inland. At the other end stands the tall lighthouse. The escape was not easy. The same people who were vying to invite him to their homes now refused to lend him a vehicle.[42]

Turned into a trophy, he still would have to escape the police dragnet rather quickly. He recorded a speech for the evening's scheduled public rally and asked for the publicity to continue. Then, he wrote a defiant and trenchant statement, to be given out later by Leila Fernandes, condemning Indira Gandhi's 'final and mortal blow' to 'Indian democracy or whatever was left of it'.[43] In it, he appealed to 'the youth, the working people and the toiling masses everywhere [to] rise in peaceful revolt'. Finally, after bidding a sad and 'hasty' goodbye to Leila, George hugged his son and left in a taxi driven by Anwar, a Telugu-speaking resident of Visakhapatnam. A socialist colleague Tarini Patnaik sat beside him. They arrived at Bhubaneswar's quarters for legislators, where he found in Mira Das (b. 1941) the first of many female allies who would help him evade the police. The 34-year-old Mira Das was married at seventeen. Her husband worked in the Talchar unit of the Fertilizer Corporation of India (FCI). She had been at JP's Sukhodeora ashram to train in social action. She was cutting her teeth in politics as well. Although she had been the president of the Orissa unit of the SSP, her party had a small footprint in state politics. The residential colony of the legislators was swarming with police. In consultation with her, a plan of escape was hatched. George became the servant who carried her apparently ill daughter Pranati on his shoulder. They sat in a car that took them on-to the national highway to Calcutta. Some 50 kilometres from Bhubaneswar, at Badchana village near Chandikhol, they stopped. Here, in the wilderness, a few yards off the highway, they waited for a bus. When the bus came, a vacated seat was occupied by an unobtrusive George. He did not move even once from his seat for more than 560 kilometres of the journey. It was past midnight when the bus reached Calcutta.

Not fate but his desire to please his urging wife had brought an unwilling George to Gopalpur-on-sea and that saved him from arrest. Everyone who helped him escape was hauled up, tortured and harassed by the police. Within a week, Y.L. Sitaramayya, Tarini Patnaik and Santosh Mahapatro, organizers of his escape, were arrested under the Maintenance of Internal Security Act, 1971 (MISA). The driver too was put in jail.[44] When chief minister Nandini Satpathy (1931–2006) came to know of the role of Mira Das, she was harassed as well and her husband was transferred to faraway Ratlam. She would run from pillar to post to get the transfer order withdrawn, even meeting Sanjay Gandhi. Ironically, this meeting would be held against her to deny her a Janata Party nomination for the post-Emergency state election. She would then ingratiate herself into Biju Patnaik's charmed circle on the strength of their common caste.[45] Many months later, George would write a note in his prison journal, 'If there is one get-together that I would love to have, it is in Gopalpur-on-sea.' He desired to write the story of his escape and about those who helped, but it was never written.

On the morning of 27 June, George knocked at the door of the Alipore residence of Vidya Sagar Gupta (b. 1932), a Marwari businessman.[46] He was dressed in the costume of a fisherman—lungi and shirt, with a *gamcha* tied around his head, his face unshaven. The Gupta family had been politically active, and their Marble House in Joda Bagan was a socialist adda. Originally from Rajasthan, they had made their home at Forbesganj in Bihar, bordering Nepal. Here they owned rice mills and a sprawling *kothi*. Balkrishan Gupta (1910–72), the family's eldest scion, had studied with Ram Manohar Lohia in Calcutta. In the 1920s, they both went to Europe for higher studies: Ram Manohar Lohia to Germany's Humboldt University and Balkrishan Gupta to the London School of Economics. By the time Balkrishan returned in 1939, Ram Manohar Lohia was already a known face of the Congress Socialist Party (CSP). In the Quit India Movement, those socialists spearheading the underground resistance took shelter at the Forbesganj kothi as well as in the Marble House. Balkrishan Gupta was 'ferociously political,' and was often cited as the power behind Ram Manohar Lohia's sharp repartee.[47] Lohia's Hindi journal *Jan* was edited by him. Margo Skinner, the American admirer of Ram Manohar called Balkrishan Gupta 'a rich industrialist, and a friend and a caste-mate of my boy [Lohia]'.[48] In 1968, after Lohia's death, he wrenched a Rajya Sabha nomination from the crisis-ridden party, which went against a Lohia principle of not giving nomination to those defeated in an election. It was the cause of much consternation in the party. Vidya Sagar Gupta, the youngest of five brothers, after Balkrishan's death, would maintain the family tradition of political friendship, if not of engagement. When George appeared at his doorstep, a mortified Vidya Sagar moved George to a safe house and provided a car to take him up north.

Before he left Calcutta, George wrote a cryptic message of uncertainty for Leila Fernandes, 'I don't know, when, how and where this fight will end for me. Our son will give you company.'[49] Next, he arrived in Varanasi. He was housed at the Institute of Gandhian

Studies, founded by JP and located on the banks of the Ganga. His first circulated pamphlet of 1 July 1975, was written, typed and cyclostyled at Varanasi.[50] S.A. Haque, a stenotypist at Mughalsarai railway division, who had been dismissed from the service because of his involvement in the railway strike, helped him in making the pamphlet.[51] It was circulated widely, reproduced internationally, and translated and printed into many languages at home and abroad. Indians for Democracy at Michigan, USA printed this 'historical document' as the 'first underground paper from India'. It was put up as an exhibit before the US Congress committee hearing on human rights violation in India. What on 26 June had been 'something resembling martial law', in a week took on a definite nomenclature of 'fascist dictatorship'. It would be George's unflinching characterization of the Emergency. Briefly, his pamphlet said the coming of Emergency had 'benumbed the people, section by section, group by group'; 'there is no rule of law any more'; 'crass lies and tendentious propaganda . . . is broadcast a hundred times over in true Goebbelsian style'. It also noted the absence of resistance. Accepting it as a fait accompli, the people had suddenly become good, harmless, obedient citizens who abided by the law and seldom acted in haste. All the cacophony of upsurge was subdued, gone were the days of rallies, protests and processions. 'We are now living under cold, calculating and ruthless fascist dictatorship,' he wrote.

But all this was a prologue. The real message of the pamphlet was to 'defeat fascism and to restore democracy'. With incredible clarity, within days of the Emergency proclamation, it unveiled a plan of resistance, with elements drawn from India's freedom struggle. In August 1942, when all the nationalist leadership was arrested in one fell swoop, the socialists had sustained an underground resistance. The colonial state, according to them, survived through surveillance. Infiltrate the institutions carrying surveillance and subvert the infrastructure supporting it, and it will come tottering down. In pursuance of such an understanding, they tore up railway tracks, burnt down police stations, detonated bombs at post and telegraph offices and blew up bridges. They did not kill individuals—it was not even intended, 'non-injury and non-killing' was the motto.[52] But their actions sent tremors across the veins of an oppressed nation, inspiring valour. JP and his friends became cult heroes. George, citing them, called for the revival of 'spirit of 1942'. He too wanted to make India heard. If it had to be achieved by 'sabotage and blowing up bridges', so be it.[53] What other means were left for the people to express themselves? Some of those ingredients of his plan were as under:

> Production and distribution of underground literature
>
> Production and pasting of posters . . .
>
> Whispering Campaign . . . remember, 'three raised to the power of eighteen' . . .
>
> Organizing strikes, *hartals* and *bandhs* . . . will have now to become the order of the day . . .
>
> Paralyse the functioning of the government . . . Transport and communication must be choked. The functioning of the radio, post and telegraphs and railways must be made impossible.
>
> . . . (T)he armed forces must not allow themselves to be used to subvert the constitution, to destroy democracy, to impose a dictatorship.
>
> Set-up as many underground radio transmitter stations as possible . . .
>
> Make this fascist [Indira Gandhi] an outcast in the eyes of the civilized world . . .
>
> This is no time for ideological quibbling or personality clashes . . .
>
> Mahatma Gandhi will be the unseen leader of our movement. It will be Mrs Nehru Gandhi versus Mahatma Gandhi.

George arrived at Patna in the early hours of 5 July wishing to connect with Rewati Kant Sinha (1928–79). He was a party colleague, who was a leader of the government employees. In 1958, he was elected general secretary of the Bihar State Non-Gazetted Employees' Federation and later, in 1960, became its president. He welded together category unions of government employees into a formidable single union. In August 1965, during a Patna Bandh, the police fought pitched battles with the demonstrating public. and Rewati Kant Sinha came into the forefront.[54] Leading an agitation of over three lakh non-gazetted employees he caused the ouster of the chief minister K.B. Sahay. But this led to his termination from service and a term in prison. An ardent follower of Ram Manohar Lohia, this ordinary government clerk rose quickly to political prominence. He was elected to a short Rajya Sabha stint in 1967 when George was elected to the Lok Sabha from Bombay. In 1970, when he was elected to the Bihar Legislative Council, George would invariably stay at his R-block government house during his visits to Patna.

That morning at 5.30, George in a 'handloom *lungi*, collarless *kokati* [saffron] colour kurta and a *gamcha* hanging around his neck' knocked at Sinha's door.[55] A cloth bag hung over his shoulder contained cyclostyled copies of the 1 July pamphlet. 'George was in disguise, operating underground and evading arrest,' recalled Rewati Kant Sinha. Not just did he welcome and shelter him, Rewati Kant Sinha readily became an ally and accomplice. He would become deeply complicit in the underground operations and in distributing George's clandestine circulars. Yet, a few months later, he would betray him, provide the sleuths graphic details of his involvement and become an approver to nail him. The betrayal would not rest lightly on him, however. Weighed down by it, a humiliated, tortured and finally insane Rewati Kant Sinha in a couple of years would die a social pariah in penury. More than the physical torture he had endured, what made him sell out was his nine children, some of them minors, whose future he thought would be safe if he informed against his erstwhile colleagues. The Central Bureau of Investigation (CBI), the agency charged with the probe, warned him that he should either accept the pecuniary bribe they offered or 'all my family members including minor children would be put in jail'.[56] He caved in. George would send emissaries to him, assuring his family would be looked after, and pleading with him to retract his statement, but Rewati Kant Sinha would remain unconvinced. He was never bodily harmed by those he sold out, but an unkind fate and his guilty conscience would bring his agonizing end. No one would remember his children.

But that morning, he stood by George as a loyal ally. At his behest, the railway union leader Mahendra Narain Bajpai (b. 1941) came with a few others to meet George. As a parcel clerk at Patna Railway Junction, Mahendra Narain Bajpai was with the Eastern Railwayman's Union. During the railway strike, participation in it resulted in his dismissal from the service. He arranged George's onward journey. 'There used to be a coach going to Allahabad and there it was attached to the Bombay Mail. In that same coach, I arranged an upper berth for him.'[57] George was brought to the station through a relatively deserted side. He wore a reddish handloom woven kurta and lungi and had a red jute bag over his shoulder. He was unshaven, a ten-day-old beard covered his face. For doing what he did in the underground, a year later Mahendra Narain Bajpai would be caught and tortured. The police kept him 'standing for hours, and when my feet got swollen, they would tie my one hand to the ceiling and when that got swollen, too, they untied it to tie the other'. This went on for many days. He was told 'my sister and I would be stripped naked and kept in the same room'. He was given half an hour to decide if he would speak. A seemingly friendly sentry on duty outside his cell advised him: 'Become an approver now and then you are free to withdraw before the magistrate, or else they will finish you off.' Taking the counsel seriously, he gave in, thereby indicting himself and his comrades.

During his first month in the underground, George went from Orissa to Bengal, then to Bihar, Uttar Pradesh, Rajasthan and finally to Gujarat.[58] He had been there before, campaigning for the Janata Morcha, a four-party conglomeration of which his Socialist Party was one. A Janata Morcha government had taken the oath of office on 16 June, and the chief minister Babubhai Patel was lax about the Emergency restrictions. Somewhere between Patna and Ahmedabad, George made contact with Ladli Mohan Nigam, a party colleague from Madhya Pradesh, who gave him a non-political door of Dr Davendar Mahasukhram Surti (b. 1924) at Ahmedabad to knock at.[59] George didn't stay long in Ahmedabad, however. By the middle of July, he was at Baroda (now Vadodara), along with G.G. Parikh (b. 1923), the bearded socialist from Bombay. He met K. Vikram Rao (b. 1938) of the *Times of India*, who was with the Bombay edition before he was transferred to Baroda. He had worked for George's election campaign against S.K. Patil (1898–1981).[60] Since his arrival in Baroda, he was active in the city's union of journalists. In a signed statement, he demanded the Emergency's revocation and vowed not to shave his beard until press freedom was restored.[61] Born in Madras (now Chennai), he was educated in north India where, at Lucknow, his father Kotamaraju Rama Rao (1896–1961) was the editor of Jawaharlal Nehru's *National Herald*. Congress Party chronicler Dr B. Pattabhi Sitaramayya (1880–1959) was a relation of theirs. In 1942, the fearless K. Rama Rao was jailed by the British for writing an editorial supporting the cause of the nationalist prisoners at Lucknow Jail.[62] Later, in 1952, he was nominated to the first Rajya Sabha. Vikram Rao had inherited both journalism and politics as family legacies. He was in student politics, and in the 1950s had been president of the Lucknow University Students' Union. He was also an office-bearer of the Indian Federation of Working Journalists (IFWJ), whose constitution had been drafted by his father in 1952. In 1971, on his prodding, the IFWJ took a pledge to 'bear upon their professional duties a positive bias in favour of the weaker and underprivileged sections'.[63] Vikram Rao was tall and imposing, with a booming voice. He lived with his wife Sudha, a practising doctor with Indian Railways, and their two small children. For Vikram Rao, it was as if he had a premonition of George's coming. On 16 July, he took two journalist friends along to meet George: they were the 'wheatish complexioned, short-statured, and bald-headed' Kirit Bhatt (b. 1933), a correspondent with *Indian Express*, and Satish Jay Shanker Pathak (b. 1939), the Chief of Bureau of UNI that had then been renamed 'Samachar News Agency'. They belonged to the English press, and as journalists, had links in Baroda society. Their immediate task was to find a safe house for George. That evening, Kirit Bhatt called a local industrialist Bharat Chhotabhai Patel (b. 1936) to ask if he could house 'an important person'.

Bharat Patel was one of the many directors in the family-owned Sayaji Iron and Engineering Pvt. Ltd at Baroda, which manufactured construction equipment and owned stone quarries. He looked after the company's export division and was a frequent traveller to Dubai where the machines were assembled and sold. The student-led anti-corruption movement in Gujarat, was for him a moment of stirring. He worked for the Janata Morcha, and through Vikram Rao invited George to canvas for its candidate in Baroda, in May elections. When told of who the 'important person' was, Bharat Patel readily agreed to keep George in the air-conditioned guest suite attached to his house. Chaperoned by the three journalists, George came wearing saffron kurta and lungi, a saffron cloth tied around his head, and carrying a cloth bag in which were his meagre belongings—a few clothes and books. 'He had grown a beard and by his disguise, he looked like a *sadhu* and was being addressed as "baba" accordingly,' recalled Bharat Patel.[64]

That evening at his house while they discussed politics, Vikram Rao brought up Bharat Patel's entrepreneurial interest in stone quarries. 'I told them that we used gelatine for blasting the stones. Gelatine is also called dynamite.' Next day (17 July), his nephew Atul Patel arranged a 'blasting demonstration' for George in an abandoned quarry on the outskirts of Baroda. He brought dynamite sticks, fuse and wire for a live show. The three journalists went along to witness it. They saw 'how blasting operation is done, how holes are made in the quarry, how gelatine sticks were put in the hole and caps are arranged and the fuse is connected'.[65] The UNI journalist Satish Pathak recalled, 'I could notice that George was taking a keen interest in the whole process of blasting.' Asserting that 'he had certain other uses of gelatine in his mind', George spoke of dynamite as publicity material. 'By using this gelatine, we can blow up the rail and road bridges, then the public would come to know that the resistance movement has started,' Bharat Patel paraphrased George saying.[66] George would build a web of his trusted trade union activists in the railways and elsewhere to distribute the contraband. Bharat Patel's role was to provide the most basic ingredient—'I was to supply gelatine.' An elated George desired explosives to be removed immediately from Baroda to Ahmedabad for safe keeping.

It was at Bharat Patel's place that George wrote an open letter to MPs who on 21 July were gathering in Delhi to put their stamp of approval on the Emergency. Bharat Patel arranged for the paper, typewriter, correcting fluid, stencils, etc. He got a typist friend to type handwritten sheets and cut stencils for cyclostyling. In his letter to the members of Parliament, George urged them to not acquiesce in giving legitimacy to Indira Gandhi's dictatorship. Dictators were known to be ruthlessly paranoid. 'None who made the revolution in Russia lived to tell their story. Stalin saw to that. Hitler was even more ruthless.' Nor does proximity to the dictator ensure survival. Lalit Narayan Mishra was detonated to death. He thought he knew too much to be shunted out of the cabinet but he forgot 'dead men tell no tales'.[67] He urged the members of Parliament to not reduce themselves to being the show boys of Indira Gandhi's democratic facade.

In the evening of 19 July, George with the three journalists drove to Ahmedabad. They first went to the house of Purushottam Ganesh Mavalankar (1928–2002), who since 1972 was an independent member of the Lok Sabha from Ahmedabad. He was the son of Ganesh Vasudev Mavalankar (1888–1956), the first Lok Sabha Speaker. On 26 June, he had been in Bangalore to attend a meeting of the Parliamentary Consultative Committee. While the likes of L.K. Advani (b. 1927) and Madhu Dandavate were arrested, he was not. On 21 July, he was going to Delhi to attend the special Parliamentary session. George's arguments made no impression on him. He would later publish a book titled *No Sir*, containing his parliamentary speeches during the Emergency. The book is dedicated to 'freedom and democracy'.[68] A jailed Madhu Limaye would resign from parliament protesting the extension of its legal term, and so would a 28-year-old Sharad Yadav, whose emphatic win in the by-election at Jabalpur had enthused the Opposition. Purushottam Ganesh Mavalankar, 'the distinguished son of an illustrious father', his conscience untouched, would continue to hold on. George, who was looking for a safe house and had come expecting shelter, was refused.[69]

He found himself again at the house of Dr Davendar Mahasukhram Surti. That night, after they had settled George in, the three journalists went to meet Chimanbhai Patel (1929–94), the target of the anti-corruption movement and an Indira Gandhi discard. He was now the crutch on which the Janata Morcha government of Babubhai Patel survived. He had recently been to Varanasi. There, the hotel he was staying in was hosting a meeting of the local Rotary Club and he was requested to make a speech which he did. Just when he was about to fly out, he was arrested and sent to jail where he was lodged among criminals. Only when the Rotary Club president certified that he hadn't spoken about the Emergency at all, was he released.[70] Chimanbhai was an educational entrepreneur. He showed them a place, a students' hostel, Sardar Chhatralaya, to store explosives, Satish Pathak recalled.[71] George and Chimanbhai Patel were to have a meeting, too.[72] Many years later, in a Lok Sabha speech, George would give Chimanbhai Patel his due: 'When we were underground in Gujarat, he used to take us around in his car. A man of ordinary calibre would not have dared to do that under the Congress regime.'[73]

21 July was a rainy day in Baroda. Two cars—a white Fiat Safari and a yellow Ambassador—were driven to Bharat Patel's Timba Road guest house. There, each car's boot was loaded with ten gunny sacks. Preparations to collect and transport explosives and accessories to Ahmedabad had begun soon after George had left Baroda. The dynamite sticks, about the size of a palm in length, were generally licensed to be sold only to a registered user. The manufacturers were bound by law to keep a proper inventory of the same. But now, the original cases were broken open and the manufacturer's stickers removed. They were then packaged in a hundred shoeboxes, but as they proved unwieldy, gunny sacks were bought to hold them. These were loaded into cars that had the three journalists, besides the two drivers. At Ahmedabad, they arrived late in the night and stopped in front of a house with a garage. An old man Prabhudass Patwari (1909–85), a politician close to Morarji Desai, opened the gate and let the cars in. The UNI journalist Satish Pathak saw 'about ten gunny bags full of material' being unloaded from the two car boots. He noticed 'a sharp and pungent smell' and caught unawares, he asked Vikram Rao, 'What is there?' 'Dynamite,' he was told. After having stored the gunny sacks, they went to Dr Davendar Mahasukhram Surti's place where they found George, Ladli Mohan Nigam and others having supper. The operation's success was reported to them. On the urgings of Chimanbhai Patel, a part of the consignment was stored at his Sardar Chhatralaya. Everyone was an accomplice now; irrespective of who was more deeply involved than

others. The knowledge of contraband bound them in a secret pact, and the clandestine act made them brothers in arms.

In Delhi, the government laid a sixty-page white paper titled *Why Emergency?* before Parliament.[74] An underground pamphlet with the same title would be printed later in October. 'It is a tirade,' the anonymous authors of it said of the government version.[75] The target of the government's *Why Emergency?* was JP. One of its chapters though was on the railway strike, which it said, was 'a plan to disrupt economy'. It cited extensively from George's speeches to prove its contention. He had called the railwaymen a 'sleeping giant' and exhorted them to wake up to fight for their right: 'Seven days' strike of the Indian Railways— every thermal station in the country would close down. A ten days' strike of the Indian Railways—every steel mill in India would close down and the industries in the country will come to a halt for the next twelve months. A fifteen days' strike in the Indian Railway—the country will starve.'[76] The white paper said the strike was a political act to 'unseat the present Central Government'. But more devastating was its claim that 'substantial amounts of money were received in May– June 1974' from abroad through a foreign bank to carry out the strike. It was an attack on his integrity, also on his patriotism. George had written to China's Mao Zedong, the government's *Why Emergency?* said, complaining about the repression of the railway workers.

The government's version was given wide media coverage. The *Times of India* carried the news on its front page, 'money flowed from abroad during May–June 1974 railway strike, George wrote to Mao'.[77] All India Radio carried the news even more prominently.[78] *Blitz* made it into a screaming headline. He had been singled out. George responded with a stinging letter to 'Mrs. Indira Nehru Gandhi' telling her 'all dictators are congenital liars, but you, Madam, excel them all'.[79] The letter was cyclostyled, and a courier carried a bunch of copies to Bombay to post. It was printed at Baroda and translated into Marathi and Hindi. In the end, it had some ominous words: 'No dictator has died an honourable death—No man has ever mourned a Dictator's death.' A fortnight later, Sheikh Mujibur Rehman was assassinated at Dacca (Dhaka), his family wiped out with him. The Dacca massacre on 15 August left Indira Gandhi shaken. George challenged her to 'produce the evidence, put me on trial, and get me shot if what you say is true'. The AIRF which was also cast under a cloud, repudiated the allegations that it received money from any foreign sources.[80] Indira Gandhi had been speaking in many tongues. 'I don't think the railway strike itself had anything to do with the declaration of the Emergency,' she said to London's *Sunday Telegraph*, 'though it was clear that it was not just an ordinary strike for a better deal for the workers.'[81] This was some improvement, given *Why Emergency?* alleged it was 'essentially a part of the movement of national disruption' necessitating a clampdown. But, she repeated, 'Those who went on strike were being paid. Where did the money come from? Our trade unions are not rich.' With 80,000 of the workers dismissed during the strike, and thousands still out of employment, eighteen months after the strike was called off, the charge that they were paid for remaining out of work was cruel. George said it was 'naked lies'. 'Madam Dictator,' he wrote, 'you are ignorant of the conditions of our working people. They starved madam dictator, they starved to death.' It pained him that his letter to Chairman Mao, which was a protest letter against the Chinese repression of their railway workers, was given an unpatriotic spin. 'Someday, in the near future, when you and your dictatorship have been swept into the dustbin of history,' he wrote, 'I shall be able to vindicate myself. But what about you?'[82]

* * *

In the middle of July, Bombay-based Fredrick D'Sa (b.1948) found in his mailbox a cyclostyled circular 'from somewhere in the underground'. A week later, a young man came to the petrol pump managed by him to deliver a handwritten note from George that asked him to go to Ahmedabad. On the morning of 23 July, D'Sa was at Davendar Mahasukhram Surti's house. Hailing from a farmer's family in Udupi, D'Sa was the eldest of four brothers and four sisters. In 1966, after he finished school, he came to Bombay in search of work. He began as a helper in a private mechanic shop, then worked as a waiter in a restaurant, but soon joined an electronic firm. This frequent change of job continued for a while. Simultaneously, he enrolled in an evening college for graduate study. By then, he had become a member of the BLU. George hired him to head Taximen's Services Ltd. The company had a few petrol pumps and retailed motor parts for taxis. 'I felt obliged to George for having given me this job,' D'Sa would say.[83]

At Ahmedabad, Fredrick D'Sa was asked to go to Delhi to fetch Captain Rama Rao Prahlad Rao Huilgol (b. 1915). He was also to meet Leila Fernandes and pass on George's instructions to wrap up *Pratipaksh*, whose editor Giridhar Rathi was already arrested. Born in Karnataka's Bellary district to Brahmin parents, Rama Rao Huilgol was educated at Benaras, Bombay and Poona. His family had been 'staunch Congressites' but he was never 'a member of any political party'. Beginning his professional career with the Air Force, in 1969, he was working as Indian Airlines' planning manager when he was suspended following an allegation of bribery in the purchase of aircraft. He remained suspended for four years from 1969 to 1973 when he retired from service. During these testing times, he met many politicians to canvass support. Convinced of Huilgol's innocence, George raised his case in Parliament and followed it up with letters to the concerned ministries. To the minister of Civil Aviation, he asked 'how anyone can justify the kind of victimization to which Captain Huilgol is presently being subjected to'. George's fight on his behalf would endear him to the Captain. 'I felt much obliged to George Fernandes due to his efforts to get me a clean chit,' he admitted.[84] There developed an enduring friendship. After his electoral defeat in March 1971, he moved into Huilgol's house in Vasant Vihar. At Ahmedabad, he told Captain Huilgol to post a letter addressed to Hans Janitschek (1934–2008) of the Socialist International at Bombay Airport.[85] A baffled Captain could merely ask him why for so minor an errand he was called from so far.

About the same time, Ladli Mohan Nigam arrived at Patna to sound out Rewati Kant Sinha about the imminent arrival of 'literature', a code word for explosives, to be used to 'create a state of violence'.[86]

On 8 August, Jaswant Sinh Chauhan (b. 1945), 'of wheatish complexion, aged about 30/35, well-built and about 5'8" height', along with two party workers from Baroda, arrived at Rewati Kant Sinha's house. Mentored by local politician Sanat Mehta, Jaswant Sinh Chauhan, of Kshatriya caste, worked in trade unions in Baroda's many public-sector units. One day after the National Emergency had been declared, the pacifist Prabhudass Patwari would urge him to get a gun and shoot the prime minister.[87] Chauhan was hot-headed and a little conceited as well, having an inflated sense of self-importance. 'I first met George just before the Railway strike,' he would relate many years later. 'We were never friends but working comrades who had come together to fight the Emergency.' Before Chauhan left for Patna, he scoured the local market at Ahmedabad for second-hand suitcases. They carried 'literature' to Patna in 'one tin box, an attache case, a briefcase and one cloth bag'.[88] Chauhan explained the 'suitcases were full of explosive in the form of dynamite sticks and that the cloth bag contained detonators besides fuse wires'. Rewati Kant Sinha divided the consignment into two parts, kept one 'tied in one cloth bundle' in his house and the rest in suitcases at an acquaintance's place. Ten days later, Mahendra Narain Bajpayi came seeking 'literature'. Later (in September), the part kept at the acquaintance's house began to ooze a yellow substance. Wasted, this part was thrown into a roadside gutter.

Meanwhile, George prepared to leave Ahmedabad, and by 16 August, he was at Sharad Patel's house in Baroda. A friend of Bharat Patel, industrialist Sharad Patel was the owner of the Standard Radiators Company. On a visit to Bharat Patel's guest suite in July, he had recognized George. 'I had asked him "have you not gone underground?" He said that he was.'[89] When Bharat Patel left for Dubai, he extracted from Sharad Patel a promise to accommodate George whenever he visited Baroda. The former nonchalantly even shared the dynamite plans with him. Sharad Patel not only accommodated George but provided his chauffeur-driven Ambassador car to drive him to the outskirts of Surat, where Fredrick D'Sa and two others, one among them being George's cousin, Sofy, were waiting in a Fiat. 'Baba' was on his way to the south and they were to travel with him to deflect police suspicion. They reached Bangalore in the third week of August. The driver, an employee of the Bombay Labour Cooperative Bank (of which George was chairman), remained to ferry him around in the city, and noticed 'a beautiful lady, aged about 40' who was George's prime contact in Bangalore.

She was Snehalata Reddy (1932–77), whom Lohia had described as 'a statuesque beauty with accomplishments in the mobile arts of dance and drama'.[90] Of her film-maker husband, Pattabhi Rama Reddy (1919–2006), Lohia had said, he 'is a man utterly at peace with himself, and I have met no one more relaxed than him'. While she was a film actress and theatre personality, they both worked in the film industry. They were Lohia devotees, so much so that when their son was born they named him Konark Manohar. For the Socialist Party, Snehalata Reddy was more than a showgirl from the glamour world. When Ram Manohar Lohia had felt deserted by his closest colleagues, it was she who provided a soothing balm to the frayed tempers. 'Do go and meet Doctor,' Snehalata Reddy exhorted Madhu Limaye, counselling caution. 'It's essential you both understand each other—especially at this juncture.'[91] Even before this, during party squabbles, hers was a calm voice of reason. Founded on the rhetoric of inner-party democracy, the Socialist Party was soon mired in the disciplinary urge to suppress dissent, and this produced shock and dismay in the party. 'A group of people, who belonged to us yesterday can very well belong to us tomorrow—we have their fates in our own hands. Let us examine ourselves again before we dispense justice,' Snehalata Reddy had written to Madhu Limaye, who was the party chairman in 1959.[92] Ten years later, when a young U.R. Ananthamurthy (1932–2014) wrote a short novel *Samskara*, situated in a Brahmin *agrahara* somewhere very close to George's Mangalore, the Reddy couple took it upon themselves to produce its cinematic rendition. In the novella, there were two principal protagonists: a learned Brahmin priest Praneshacharya and a low-caste woman, Chanderi, played by Snehalata Reddy, who had been living with a tradition-bashing fallen Brahmin Narayanappa from the same agrahara. Narayanappa's death and the issues thrown up by it bared the soul of a corrupted tradition and a decaying vocational identity. In keeping with Lohia's anti-caste rhetoric, it was thus a novel that appealed to the sensibilities of the Reddys. The film won critical acclaim and was awarded the President's Gold Medal for the best film in 1971. George inherited the Reddys' devotion to Lohia, and nurtured his friendship with them further. In 1967, after his maiden parliamentary victory, the Reddy family visited him in Bombay and he took them sightseeing in his ramshackle car, of which their daughter Nandana Reddy, then just eleven years old, carried fond memories. 'George asked us to stay at his Kemps Corner flat. It was for the first time I witnessed a public meeting of his. I was completely floored. I had decided, at that moment, that I am going to be trade-unionist.' So on a day in the third week of August, when 'George came with this call for the underground resistance movement, we—my mother, my father, we all—agreed to it'.[93] They would all pay for their fateful decision.[94]

C. Gopal Krishna Reddy or CGK was another of those Lohia devotees. He too had named his two sons after the leader: the first was Manohar Reddy (b. 1948) and the younger one Ram Manohar Reddy. CGK was an 'irreverent, extrovert and somewhat flamboyant character,' Manohar Reddy would recall of his father.[95] In 1952, CGK was nominated to the Rajya Sabha by the Socialist Party. He thereafter dropped out of politics and rejoined the newspaper industry. By the end of June 1975, that George had evaded arrest and was underground was generally known. CGK rose out of his comfortable middle-class slumber to search him out. He contacted Snehalata Reddy. On 22 August, CGK was asked 'to attend the wedding which had been fixed at short notice'. It was a coded message. CGK immediately left for Madras where a rendezvous with George was fixed. 'From then on till my arrest on 28 March 1976, George and I were in continuous and close touch,' CGK wrote in a book on his underground days.[96] George remained in south India for almost two months, travelling to various locations, but making Bangalore his headquarters.[97]

George's sojourn in the South was as secret as was possible. His disguise was sufficiently foolproof, however. Twenty-four-year-old Richard Fernandes was then in the third year of his PhD in theoretical physics at Bangalore's Raman Research Institute. He was the last of the

Fernandes sons, born in 1951, which made George twenty years senior to him. On his occasional visits home, George had taught his little brother to use nail clippers and also the paper-punching instrument. On being told of his presence in Bangalore by Michael Fernandes, Richard at once went to the West End hotel, where George was holed up. There was some fear of being followed; however, when he knocked at the door, he failed to recognize George. 'He was a perfect Sardar.'[98] George gave Richard his passport for safekeeping, and a stack of letters to post. Although he was in touch with Lawrence and Michael Fernandes, the latter bringing home-made food for him, the Reddy family remained his main contact. For some time he stayed at Nandana Reddy's one-room rented accommodation. It was here that he wrote one of the most pensive underground pamphlets penned by him. It contained emotional references to Herman Hesse's poems and love and longing for his toddler son.[99]

Girija Huilgol, the young daughter of Captain Rama Rao Huilgol recalled, on the night of 28 October, 'George appeared at our house along with Mama [C.G.K. Reddy]:' George had come from the South. It was a biggish house with a courtyard in the centre with rooms around. Born at Secunderabad in 1951 and educated at Gwalior's Scindia Kanya Vidyalaya, Girija Huilgol in 1975 was on the threshold of graduating in medicine from Delhi's Maulana Azad Medical College. Her sense of history sprang from Lapierre and Collins' recently published *Freedom at Midnight*. Interested mainly in 'music and dramatics' while growing up, she would be drawn into the resistance struggle due to her family's association with George. She had seen George fight for her father's innocence when he was accused of bribery in the aircraft deal. She found him a bold and outspoken leader. If she admired George, he as well gave her an identity by calling her 'Doc' even before she was one. George's circulars would reach the family also, and she read them.[100] During his stay at the Huilgol house, in its back room, George mostly kept himself busy with reading and writing.

Soon after, CGK left for a trip abroad. But before he went, he introduced George to R. Chandrachudan (1915–2009). Sometime in the first half of November, CGK 'after dark came to my flat and there was a bearded gentleman with him', R. Chandrachudan remembered.[101] A former Congressman from Tanjore, R. Chandrachudan, like CGK, worked for *The Hindu*. He had had a varied experience that took him from Madras and Bangalore to Simla, and finally to Delhi. He had been brought into *The Hindu* fold by CGK and lived in accommodation provided by his employers. 'I am a believer in Gandhism and non-violence. I have stayed with Gandhiji in 1937 and I have been closely connected with Gandhi's sons and their families. Because of this association my belief in nonviolence and orderly Government remained strengthened,' R. Chandrachudan would vouch. At the age of 60, at the urging of CGK, a khadi-wearing, Gandhi-loving Chandrachudan was tempted to hide a fugitive George at his home while CGK went abroad to canvass support for the resistance movement.

In Europe, CGK met Hans Janitschek who, as he wrote in his hand-written diary, was 'extremely helpful—in fact, but for his wholehearted support, what has been achieved in Europe would not have been possible'.[102] Janitschek wrote to the member parties of Socialist International informing each of them of CGK's (he went by Krishna Rao) visit and appealing for assistance. CGK remained abroad for a month. He started by attending a meeting of the Bureau of the Socialist International that was held in the last week of November at the Belgian capital of Brussels. Here, he presented a 22-page booklet *Indira's India: Anatomy of a Dictatorship*. This had been written by George, smuggled out by CGK and swiftly printed in London by Hans Janitschek.[103] It gave details of events preceding the Emergency, provided an analysis of Indira Gandhi's political gamble and predicted why she would never give up the power she had appropriated. CGK appealed to the socialist bureau members for 'publicity, solidarity and monetary assistance'. Another person whose help was vital but whose mention was glossed over by CGK was that of Mohammad S. Hoda, a Bihari settled in London, who was secretary of the International Transport Workers Federation (ITWF). CGK and M.S. Hoda together worked to get a resolution on the Indian Emergency moved at the meeting of the bureau. CGK received some monetary support, mainly from Dutch and Belgian socialist parties that enabled him to buy tickets to travel around

Europe. Monetary support also came from socialist parties in European capitals he visited. He also met several newspapermen. But CGK did wonder during his whirlwind tour 'whether it was worthwhile for me to have come this far at such expense'. Everywhere he went, according to the report he hand wrote to George, he asked for monetary support that largely went towards his travel. 'The support for my travel has been rather skimpy so far and phones, taxis and sometimes a hotel have all been very expensive,' he wrote, explaining his drawing money for his expenses from the funds collected for the cause. He also went across the Atlantic and met Leila Fernandes at Charlottesville.

George spent parts of December at R. Chandrachudan's place. On 17 December, with Girija Huilgol and her father, he took an evening flight to Bombay. They went straight to the house of Chander Kumar who was Huilgol's son. Fredrick D'Sa arranged a car for George to go around the city, and he met Viren Shah (1926–2013), who was the chairman of Mukund Iron & Steel Co. Ltd and a member of the Rajya Sabha from Gujarat. Viren Shah's secretary recalled a man 'with a beard and long hair, wearing spectacles of golden frame, and wearing kurta and lungi' being ushered in to meet Shah. Later, on 20 December, George shifted to a Christian Orphanage at Babasaheb Ambedkar Road. When Mrunal Gore (1928–2012) was arrested soon after, the news disturbed him so much that he decided to leave Bombay at once. Early morning on 24 December, an Ambassador car from the BTU left Bombay, driven by 'Sikh' George, with Chandra Kumar and Fredrick D'Sa accompanying him. When they reached Vikram Rao's residence in Baroda, the house was locked. They decided to watch Hema Malini starrer *Jheel Ke Us Paar*. Midway, George got restless and decided to leave. Vikram Rao this time was home, and Kirit Bhatt and Satish Pathak were called. Satish Pathak saw 'one tall Sardarji in a red turban' who called out to him, 'Hello, Pathak, Sat Sri Akal.' Pathak noted George's 'appearance was completely changed' and yet his voice and eyes were a giveaway. At Baroda, Sharad Patel again sheltered George in an under-construction house of his. He brought a mattress and other things to make his stay comfortable. It was the night of 25 December, and they all left after wishing George a happy Christmas.[104]

Next day, Sharad Patel went early in the morning to meet George. The door of the room was left ajar, and there were a few people in an animated discussion. He overheard the conversation about 'explosions to blow up important bridges and about chemicals like Ammonia Nitrate etc.'. The planned transfer of explosives to different parts of the country was long delayed, despite a few acts of daredevilry. Satyadev Tripathi was a student leader in UP and an activist of the Samajwadi Yuvjan Sabha, associated with Raj Narain. He was flown to Ahmedabad from Delhi, his ticket paid for by CGK, and driven to the airport by Girija Huilgol in her car. At Ahmedabad, Vikram Rao gave him a bag containing a consignment of dynamite sticks and accessories. He returned by air to Delhi with the consignment and kept it with Kamlesh Shukla, a party colleague.[105] In October, Satish Pathak had accompanied Vikram Rao and Kirit Bhatt to Ahmedabad in a car. The driver noted that when he reported at Vikram's house, two suitcases were brought out and put into the boot of the car. On the way, two more persons were picked up from the Baroda bus stand. They were from the BLU. The car raced to Ahmedabad. The two later riders were dropped at the railway station and asked to wait there. The three journalists then went to Prabhudass Patwari's garage, where two sacks of dynamite sticks were packed into the suitcases and loaded back in the car. They also picked up detonators from Dr Surti's house. 'The policy was,' Satish Pathak recalled being told by Vikram Rao, 'not to show to anyone the place of storage of the material.' At Ahmedabad Railway Station, those two waiting were picked up, and given a ride back to Baroda. At Baroda station, they got down, took the suitcases from the boot, and went to take a train to Bombay. So much for national security under a fascist police state! But George 'the most hunted man' was not satisfied with these efforts.[106] That morning on the eve of Christmas, when Sharad Patel had been eavesdropping on his conversation, he was lamenting to Vikram Rao: 'Work is not being carried out properly. The persons to whom money is paid do not show their face again. I am not doing anything for my interest. If this continues like this I will have to give up. I am now running short of money also.'[107] It was at this moment of low feelings that Sharad Patel offered to work for

George and give him a place from where he could operate freely. He took him to his farmhouse Sayed-Vasna on the outskirts of Baroda. On the way, George asked him if he could arrange for the transport of the explosives from Baroda to different destinations across the country. 'I said that it would be easy to do if properly packed and documented and should he so desire I would gladly undertake the job.' George liked Sayed-Vasna and expressed his desire to stay there whenever he came next. That evening he left for Ahmedabad in Sharad Patel's car driven by Atul Patel, nephew of Bharatt Patel and accompanied by Kirit Bhat and Vikram Rao.

9

Where Is the Underground?

When she was told how George was not safe even in the Janata Morcha-ruled Gujarat, an intuitive Girija Huilgol would rush out to fetch him to a rather safer Delhi. This happened at the beginning of the new year. When weeks later she would be hauled up in 'never-ending interrogations' to explain why she did what she did, she would say it was because she admired the man and his commitment 'to restore democracy to our country'.[1] With circumstances as they were, her words still incriminated him, but it was not long before she stood up to say her declaration was forced.[2] But by then, the trust between them had broken down. Weighed down by abject guilt she would implore him, now behind bars, to let her 'atone for my mistake'. Indeed, she promised 'to try to be the kind of person you want me to be, with no secrets from you, and to lay down my life rather than betray you'.[3] She thought her lapse was ephemeral. But in the underground, once you are in, you are eased only by your blood. Shared criminality is its throbbing life and forbidden boundary. Just the way coming in binds you into indissoluble compact, going out irredeemably defiles you. The only way to survive the underground is to stake everything on it. If you are halfway into it, you end up nowhere.

* * *

Since that evening in late October 1975 when George had knocked at her door, if he was in Delhi, he either stayed at her place or at R. Chandrachudan's, where Girija Huilgol would visit him every morning on her way to medical college. Lying in his electrically heated bed, waiting for the sun to climb, an arthritic R. Chandrachudan recognized her voice in the adjoining room.[4] All the while, she was a courier and conduit to pass on messages. Caution prevented George from posting his letters from the place where he was staying. They were dispatched from a place distinctly removed. At times, they ran into a thousand and more cyclostyled copies. In Delhi, it was Girija Huilgol who wrote addresses on their envelopes before they were dispatched. She also travelled with him, as his practice was to talk as little as possible on journeys because he risked being identified by his voice. On journeys, he always wore the attire of a Sikh, with a turban, safari suit, chappals and all. And changed into the garb of a 'baba' once he arrived at the destination. She became deft in handling his disguises. In the middle of November, she was with him at Ahmedabad to attend a Janata Morcha public rally. He was keen to be there, even when he wasn't a scheduled speaker. At Cama Hotel, where they stayed for a while, she signed bills 'for the supply of two chicken sandwiches, two mutton cutlets and two teas'. At Prabhudass Patwari's house, where George arranged to meet others, she came into contact with those who came to meet him— Baroda journalists, Mrunal Gore et al. She hid her identity and told them she was a student of English literature. A month later, she went with him to Bombay where they stayed at her brother's place. There, she met Fredrick D'Sa, who arranged a car for him to go around the city. At places, she noticed, he revelled in doing the obvious and often got out of the car to take a stroll, unmindful of risks in this city that knew him well. In Delhi, she drove him to his clandestine meetings that took place on the sprawling IIT campus or, occasionally, in the seclusion of the ruins of medieval monuments. Her car's old engine tired easily; it required switching off at regular intervals. During such waits, he would amble about near the car and continue his conversation with companions. To those she fetched to meet him at her home, she was introduced by the fictitious name of Gita. In mid-December, she brought Vijay Narain (b. 1941), who had contacted her at the hospital where she worked. She gathered 'Vijay Narain was close to George'. She heard him brief George on their activities in Varanasi and ask for more funds, which were promised. On one occasion, when she heard the word 'dynamite' and was curious, they explained how it worked. She heard them discuss doing 'something spectacular in Delhi itself'. They fussed over the targets, whether to detonate electricity junctions or telephone boxes, as the former required complicated technical expertise. 'It is true,' Girija Huilgol admitted, 'by this time, George had begun to show trust in me.'[5] Many confidential conversations happened in her presence. In many clandestine rendezvous she accompanied him.

He trained her well and trusted her completely. He regarded her as his most 'trained and experienced' young colleague.[6] Although a student of medicine, she was generally acquainted with the politics of the day. At Maulana Azad Medical College, where she earned her degree, she had participated in students' strikes. She was 'a little outraged' by the declaration of Emergency as to her there hardly were any reasonable grounds for it. She felt too 'a sort of restraint' on free expression. From the day George had spoken for her father in Parliament, she had held him to be an 'honest and upright leader'. So, one day in November, when he casually asked her if she would do him a favour, despite some reluctance she readily agreed and became a willing accomplice. To prepare her, he prescribed a list of literature for her to read.[7] These were mainly accounts situated in a downtrodden Europe—stories of resistance in Paris, in Warsaw, in Norway during the World War and Nazi occupation.[8] They drew from true events, like *MILA 18* by Leon Uris, a story of the uprising in a Warsaw ghetto in which a ramshackle army of emaciated Jews collect arms, make bombs and dig in bunkers to wage a violent guerrilla war against the Nazis. In it is laid bare the underground resistance in its varied forms. He found *Is Paris Burning* by Lapierre and Collins, the authors of *Freedom at Midnight*, 'more gripping though, perhaps, not as inspiring'. It is a story of Paris in the face of competing forces trying to take her over from the evacuating Nazis who are hell-bent upon destroying her before they retreat. On the other hand, John Steinbeck's *The Moon Is Down*, another he recommended, envisaged aerial dropping of dynamite sticks in an occupied area to help the resistance forces. Here, murder and mayhem are mutually resorted to by both the invaders and the occupied alike. Finally, help comes from the sky. One fine morning, people find in fields and forests, on rooftops and in the streets, tiny little objects standing upright like seeds in the snow. They are 'the ten-inch packages of dynamite' brought floating down by their tiny parachutes. He listed these books as recommended reading in one of his circulars as well. Once he did so, he wrote to her, copies of *The Moon Is Down* were seized from book stalls by the police. After her reading, she was to pass on books to those in the underground or to potential recruits. He asked her to read in such a way as to 'enter those characters which fit you or appeal to you'. She was to read relevant parts 'again and again till you emotionally identify yourself with some of the characters'. In *MILA 18*, there is Gabriela Rak, a Catholic girl in love with a Jewish man, standing unshakeably with him in the underground rebellion. Did George wish Girija Huilgol to model herself on Gabriela Rak?

Further, he put together a manual of startling instructional clarity on the rules of the underground for the others to follow. Among the rules, the first was, inquire not; another, never use the telephone. Mails were not to be received directly either, always through an intermediary: 'It is best to have some reliable and trustworthy friend's address as cover.' And, the decoy must be protected from exposure. 'Whatever tidbits of information come your way from any part of India,' he instructed her, 'jot them down for me.' She was his 'hearing aid'. He mentioned, perhaps not entirely in jest, 'working underground didn't mean growing beards'. He urged her to shun ego, but the most important lesson was to not be credulous. Cautioning her about CGK, he warned her, 'Just now, he is the greatest threat to your security with so many people having come to your house through him.' He proffered advice on her health as well. She complained of body aches and mood swings. To mitigate them, he prescribed a regimen of simple exercises to do every morning. As for diet, he asked her to scrupulously avoid 'curds and anything prepared with curds and stop eating bananas'. Conscious of how silly he sounded advising a doctor, he wrote, sharing his experience: 'In the mornings after you are up, never take liquids—tea, coffee, milk, water—on an empty stomach.'[9]

Girija Huilgol was a professional from the social upper crust, members of which seldom took to the torturous underground and were generally above police suspicion. It explained his investment in her. In her involvement with his activities, something seems to have developed between them, and this worried her family. When her brother found out, he told their father about her having 'too much interest in George and his activities' and, also said, 'I did not like it'.[10] In the first week of December, the father came down from Bombay to confront his daughter. 'With a view to assess her involvement I had a talk with her about her interest in George,' the father told the sleuths later, accusing her.[11] If he was angry, he kept it to himself. He had married twice and had two families. Girija Huilgol and her ailing mother lived in Delhi, occasionally visited by him. His second family was in Bombay. With reduced moral authority, the father faced the facts: his daughter looked after George when he stayed at their home in Delhi; she visited Ahmedabad along with him; she was visiting Bombay with him and staying at her brother's flat. 'She told me she was accompanying him, as George did not want to travel alone.' Free of parental counsel, Girija Huilgol was acting on her own. Huilgol realized how his whole family had been pulled by George into his covert affairs. Knowing this, he fell in line. If Rama Rao Huilgol nervously acquiesced, it was partly because of the prospects that association with George yielded. But that lay in a distant future. At present, George was a fugitive, fated to implicate everyone touching him, intentionally or inadvertently, and apportion to each a culpability equivalent to his own. A few months later, when a desperate Rama Rao Huilgol discovered all of his family seized by sleuths, with a cowardly violence welling up in him he laid all the blame on his daughter, thinking it would protect him and his son from any dire repercussions. But Girija Huilgol, true to her calling, didn't wince or retract from anything she did.

* * *

In early January 1976, when Girija Huilgol was told that George was not safe even in Gujarat, the messenger assumed she would take immediate measures to save the situation. Indeed, she rushed out to find him at Sharad Patel's under-construction house in Baroda. There was, however, no escaping the bad news. On the eve of Christmas, he had scrambled out of Bombay when Mrunal Gore was arrested from her hideout.[12] Now, he was told, she was kept imprisoned in a dark, ill-ventilated and windowless solitary cell, sharing the yard with two other woman inmates, one of whom was insane and the other suffered from acute leprosy. They shared the same toilet facility.[13] An underground leaflet stated, 'The lunatic wore no clothes and kept shrieking in shrill voice day and night.'[14] Disturbed, George wrote to Amnesty International to adopt Mrunal Gore as a prisoner of conscience.[15] At about the same time, his younger brother Michael Fernandes too was arrested in Bangalore. On the night of 23 December, called by the police, Michael went to meet the Deputy Commissioner but was detained. 'There is a witch hunt against my family,' George wrote to Mohammad Surur Hoda. 'My Delhi house is under police watch. My parents' residence in Bangalore is under police watch. Michael has been detained. My other brothers in Bangalore have to report to the police if they have to leave the city, and are trailed most of the time.'[16] And, a few days later Snehalata Reddy informed him that his home in Bangalore had been pelted with stones by unidentified urchins. But his most corroding worry was about the safety of his wife and child. In Delhi, R. Chandrachudan recalled, 'He used to say that if he was caught she [Mrs Gandhi] would destroy him and cause even his wife and child to suffer.' On 5 January, on the grounds that she threatened 'national security', the government withdrew Leila Fernandes' passport.[17]

After she had returned from Gopalpur-on-sea, Leila Fernandes faced a bleak world in Delhi all by herself. Their home was raided and *Pratipaksh* was wound up after its editor was arrested. To draw some solace, she occasionally visited Huilgol's place. Then, in the first week of October, she left for her brother's place at Charlottesville in the United States. Before she flew out, she visited Bangalore, and although Lawrence Fernandes was keeping an eye on her, she felt her in-laws were not welcoming.[18] At Charlottesville with a supportive brother, she finally felt settled.[19] Their son in his short life had seen more new places and met more new faces than was good for him. It worried her that he always clung to her. 'I know that my brother's presence will, in the absence of his father be positively beneficial,' she wrote to Surur Hoda, who was in regular touch with her.[20] Although George kept himself informed, his letters were what she craved most. His not writing was because of his extreme caution.[21] Even in normal times, a small percentage of all foreign mail was subject to scrutiny. Now, some said, it was more than half. Leila Fernandes was keen on a work permit to keep herself busy and be financially independent. In his report back home, CGK conveyed, 'I was in a position to tell her that she doesn't have to work for the money and that she may rest confident that she will not be a burden to her [brother] or to your brother.'[22] Yet she wanted to work. When he got to know about the withdrawal of her passport, George was disturbed, convinced that the government wanted to make him surface. Although a junior minister patronizingly said, 'I am giving him a long leash,' it was intriguing why Leila Fernandes had been allowed to leave the country in the first place. Once abroad, she had kept a low profile so as not to draw attention to herself. George did not want them to return even 'in the event of my arrest (which is most unlikely)—no matter what reports are put out'.[23] But, as he reconciled himself to the fact that there was no turning back from the path he had chosen, he told his wife, 'the time has come for you to speak'. 'You and Sonny Boy could symbolize the millions of Indians whose voice has been muffled.'[24]

Bharat Patel after his meeting with George in the middle of July 1975 had left for Dubai. Although he was to make return journeys many times, he avoided George despite many messages. George had given him a bunch of letters to be delivered to world personalities and international organizations.[25] One of those was to Hans Janitschek who was told the courier was a special emissary and could be trusted: 'He carries a statement which I hope you will be able to use all over the world, through press and radio.' Bharat Patel, however, developed cold feet. His involvement was against his commercial ethos, and the regret kept growing in him. In January, when he was once again back from Dubai, the fellow businessman Viren Shah persuaded him to meet George. On 30 January, he was received by CGK at Delhi airport. They were meeting for the first time, and he was chaperoned to a meeting with George at Girija Huilgol's place. They were received by her, 'a young lady wearing salwar, kamij'. George had a completely changed look from when he had seen him last. He had grown long hair and big beard which was separated at the middle of the chin from the two sides of the face in Rajput fashion. George briefed him, repeating what Viren Shah and Vikram Rao had already told him, about explosions taking place in Bihar, Karnataka, Bombay and Delhi. They faced no shortage of explosives as they had discovered new sources. A Japanese trade union had promised radio transmitters free of cost. But the issue was to get them smuggled in. George desired Bharat Patel to the provide legal cover of his company to bring them in. On 2 February, Bharat Patel flew back to Dubai. Once there, he cabled his inability to do the job.

Meanwhile, in Baroda, Sharad Patel replaced a now reticent Bharat Patel in their scheme of things. When George was there in December, he had been taken to Sharad's farmhouse at Sayed-Vasna, in the outskirts of town. It was a place, he was told, from where he could do whatever he liked. Sharad offered as well to arrange transport of explosives to destinations across the country. That offer cemented George's faith in him. Soon, explosives from Ahmedabad were brought back to Baroda, kept in the custody of Sharad Patel at his farmhouse. But apprehensive of the intentions of the Gujarat government, George contemplated shifting the explosives to Varanasi, where Vijay Narain promised a safe place.

* * *

The beginning of the new year came laden with challenges and trials. Indira Gandhi was at the peak of her power.[26] She had completed a decade in power, her admirers called it a 'decisive decade'. The Opposition wanted to engage her in a dialogue to ease the stiffened situation. A competition of sorts ensued among them to approach her with an olive branch. Contemptuous, she was not ready to relent, imperiously saying that the climate for dialogue was still absent. Putting the onus for normality on the parties in Opposition, blaming their 'path of obstruction and violence' for what followed, she dismissed them saying 'because a few people have been detained, they think freedom is in peril'.[27] George, however, was against brokering any deal with her. He said the only way to open negotiations was when pre-Emergency conditions were restored. Until then, he wrote to JP, 'we should stop all talk of talks with Mrs Gandhi' and 'dig in for a long fight'.[28] JP was in agreement with him. But he faced opposition from other fellow politicians in the Opposition. There were differences over methods of resistance. One was satyagraha—'simple civil disobedience'—that required dissenters to crowd prisons. It might have yielded results if it received wide publicity, which was hard to come by due to censorship. The other method of 'underground resistance' believed in subversion and sabotage of the government machinery. Its existence, even symbolically, was its real heroic achievement. It fed on rumours, the mythical imaginary and occasional daring. But diehard politicians were against it. The motley group of individuals George had collected, although committed, were on the margins of the political canvas. But despite criticisms, he stood firm. 'I believe that from the early hours of 26 June 1975, all obligations of a "purely peaceful" movement ceased to exist. Therefore, we should not condemn even those who may take to the road of Bhagat Singh and Chandrasekhar Azad or Netaji Subhash Chandra Bose,' George wrote in a widely circulated note.[29] He thus unrepentantly positioned himself in the revolutionary tradition of the freedom struggle. When he said he was for the 'non-killing, non-injuring' methods of 1942, there remained a lot of ambiguity about his ideological position.[30] At the house of Girija Huilgol, in an interview, he said he believed in 'selective sabotage and selective violence' to achieve his end of dislodging the prime minister. 'There are those who say "OK, as long as it doesn't hurt people or take human life". I'm against that,' he told the interviewer.[31] This meant he was *for* violence, not only against goods and property but even human life, when necessary.

It made JP angry. Ironically, in 1942, it was JP who had been accused of leading a violent movement and Gandhi had to protect him. In an oblique riposte to JP, George simply wrote, 'A veteran of 1942, now with stiffened bones and loosened muscles, would not go for subversive ways. But let no one advise a young man either that fires do not brew over the cold water of Ganges or Kaveri.'[32]

The first target of the resistance was to remove Indira Gandhi. How it was to be done might be left to individual discretion.[33] It was a waste, he believed, to quibble over the ideology of resistance. He reiterated its irrelevance when it came to resisting the Emergency as everyone irrespective of ideologies came under its juggernaut.[34] 'A dictatorship does not recognize the ideologies of its opponents.'[35] The government declared him 'India's most wanted man'. It was rumoured that a 'shoot-to-kill' order was given against him.[36] Some feared he was already dead. With a long beard and the garb of a mendicant, he resembled one of those outlawed Anand Margis, the prime suspects in the murder of Lalit Narain Mishra. It was as dangerous to be mistaken for one of them as it was if he was recognized. Snehalata Reddy was genuinely concerned, 'Please be careful, very careful. I'm scared for you. Please don't trust anyone except the very close ones—keep away from everyone for a while.'[37] She informed him cinema halls were playing 'a terrible newsreel with you during the railways strike threatening to starve the people'. Indira Gandhi's government was his enemy, but even among his friends there was a 'vicious campaign' against him. 'Just now, all of Karpoori's men are engaged in a similar task in Bihar and elsewhere,' a contact informed him.[38] Karpoori Thakur, in an underground meeting in Calcutta, had attacked him, and others attending it had returned to whisper against him.[39] The RSS mouthpiece *Panchjanya* denounced him as a crazy singleton and reported the Opposition stalwarts were ready to disown him.[40] He knew as well that all that bravado was leading to his isolation. The chorus of criticism, he wrote to a party colleague, was designed 'to isolate me for a start and then perhaps to get rid of me'. But 'for a man like me there is no room for compromise with the dictatorship of Mrs Gandhi or for that matter of any other person'.[41] He pleaded for defence, 'Of all those who are engaged in the struggle, even if you do not agree with the words and deeds of some of them.' He added they were still 'more patriotic and less harmful than the best of the dictator's myrmidons'.[42]

Facing isolation, he became mocking, provocative and biting in sarcasm towards those who had taken to silence for survival. He wrote to friends and foes alike, scathing, urgent letters, castigating them for not doing enough, or exhorting them to do more. He asked of old men like Gulzarilal Nanda, twice caretaker prime minister and minister of many things, from home to labour, what use it was being 'terribly concerned' if he didn't act. 'The worst that can happen is that he will be jailed. That will be a glorious finale to his life,' George wrote.[43] Niren De argued before the Supreme Court, in a habeas corpus case that despite his being temperamentally against a law that impaired liberty, as a lawyer he had to defend it as he found no other way. 'The way is,' George wrote to him, 'do what your conscience tells you is right. Have you heard of a man called Rabindranath Tagore? You know what he said about walking alone?'[44] On 18 February, he wrote to an ex-Central minister, 'How is it that otherwise sensible men like you have become so spineless as to accept not only the dictator but also the son of the dictator? Shame on you!' To his old friend, Rajmohan Gandhi, baiting him to hold a dharna outside the captive Parliament, 'stand out and not just stand up', he wrote, 'I do not know what Rajaji would have told you, but I have no doubt whatsoever that Gandhiji would have asked you to go out and fight.'[45] He was politically isolated, but his woes were not limited to that alone. He heard the socialists were breaking down. Snehalata Reddy, who called him 'Professor' to camouflage his identity, informed him, 'Everyone in jail thought it's all worthless. Everybody outside felt the socialists have no resources—moral or otherwise—to fight the dictatorship.'[46] He too felt he was nearing the end of his run. The crackdown seemed imminent, what with the exit of the DMK government in Tamil Nadu on 1 February. He assumed the Janata Morcha government in Gujarat would be the next on the chopping block.

A conjunction of several factors enabled him to send a recorded message to a convention of Indians for Democracy in New York. 'I am speaking to you on behalf of the underground from somewhere in India.'[47] It was stirring just to hear him. 'Across the country, hundreds of us are hunted and hounded . . .' He spoke of political prisoners being subjected to torture. He didn't want trains to run on time if the cost was so high as to barter freedom. 'During British days . . .' was harped on. He evoked memories of the revolutionaries abroad of those days. 'Another generation of Indians fought British Imperialism to wrest the country's freedom . . . It is now given to our generation to pay the price.' The activities of Indians for Democracy on foreign soil, their publications, the debates, the sit-ins, the demonstrations, the long marches, brought cheer to fugitives. He asked them to meet often, keep informed, launch campaigns, produce literature, undertake advocacy and raise funds. 'The wealthy who have money to spare [are] on the side of Mrs Gandhi.' He asked for sanctions against India, as harsh as those imposed against the apartheid practising South Africa.[48] To American businessmen, who came to attend a meeting of the India–US Business Council, he appealed to shun India. 'No considerations of business and monetary gains should, therefore, make you oblivious to the happenings in India.'[49]

* * *

Towards the end of February, he called a meeting of his comrades to reassess the underground. Held at the home of Kamlesh Shukla (1937–2015), a Socialist Party joint secretary and the founder editor of George's *Pratipaksh*, it was attended by select individuals to whom he had sent letters inviting them. Girija Huilgol fetched people from pre-fixed places and arranged for lunch. At this meeting, while bemoaning a sluggish North, George spoke of a better, sturdier network in the South. But his assessment was more to infuse enthusiasm in his comrades than a statement of fact as the reality in the South was not rosy either. Snehalata Reddy was its linchpin.[50] She wanted to court arrest as, she said, 'Our people here were doing nothing so I felt I should do something.' They held a meeting and, as she wrote, 'what a sorry sight we were—so few of us'. George advised her against courting arrest. 'You should not offer satyagraha under any circumstances', he told her. Prison was for those who believed they couldn't work outside. Further, to get arrested while distributing contraband literature or scribbling profane slogans or delivering protest speeches in a crowded bazaar served some purpose. Bare arrests none. 'Even if you should not be able to do anything big and spectacular,' he told her, 'what you are doing now is enough to justify your involvement.'[51] She fed him whispered tidbits. She collected handbills for him to see. She was also distributing cyclostyled clandestine bulletins, which would be known as Emergency literature. News items that found no place in newspapers, and his insistent circulars inciting rebellion were put together in crisp, single-leaf releases in ways not apprehensible by the authorities. When the Tamil Nadu government was dismissed, a shaken Snehalata Reddy wrote, 'Why don't they do something drastic when MAD [Madame Dictator] visits there soon.'[52] It was a state of desperation in the cesspool of stagnancy. She sincerely felt the lie of living as if everything was normal was oppressive. But she would overcome such sentiments when told her arrest could jeopardize the chances of her son Konark Manohar ever getting into Canada to train in music.

Ten days after the meeting at Kamlesh Shukla's home in Delhi, the underground went bust.

It was the night of 8 March. At Baroda, a police party seized seven wooden crates from the godown of a transport company. The crates contained a cache of 900 dynamite sticks along with detonating accessories. They were roadbound to Varanasi, but the departure was delayed due to the confusion over required papers. The investigation and arrests began the same night. First to be arrested were Jaswant Sinh Chauhan and Kirit Bhatt, who were arranging for the dispatch. The news of seizure and arrests was not reported the next day. On 10 March, Manubhai Shah (1915–2000) raised the issue in the Rajya Sabha. Viren Shah who was present in the august chamber slipped out of it to inform Girija Huilgol. She moved with great haste to R. Chandrachudan's place where George was. On hearing of the exposé, George took out a plain paper to jot down names, inquiring, 'Now, Doc, let us see who all will be affected by this.'[53] Then turning to her, he asked, 'How long you would be able to stand the interrogation?' How would she know? CGK who had just arrived witnessed a solemn pledge of secrecy between them. With words given and oath sworn, he drove George to the airport for a flight to Calcutta. Just before he boarded, George posted a telegram to Asha Singh, wife of Vijay Narain, at Varanasi. It was a cryptic, coded message that said, 'Be careful about your health, Baba.'[54]

Vijay Narain at Varanasi had a decoy to receive the consignment from Baroda. This was at a medicine shop, owned by one Radhey Shyam. To gain currency, Vijay Narain boasted of his familiarity with George. 'He also used to collect money in the name of George Fernandes.'[55] When the news about the Baroda seizure broke, a shaken Radhey Shyam went in search of his friend. Vijay Narain was holed up in a hostel room at the Benaras Hindu University. It is a plant, he told Radhey Shyam, and as a proof of all being well showed him George's telegram! On 18 March, a police party from Baroda arrived at Radhey Shyam's house, but because he had escaped, they took his mother and wife to the police station. Next day, pressure mounting, he surrendered and was brought to Baroda, where on 23 March he recorded his first confession, blowing Vijay Narain's cover.

In the beginning of March, Vikram Rao was transferred to the Nagpur edition of the *Times of India*. He was on his way to Nagpur to take up his new position when he got to know of the bust while at a stopover at Delhi. On 17 March, he called Girija Huilgol and spoke of his plan to surrender. His journalist friends were already in police custody and they had spilled the beans. His house in Baroda was searched in the presence of his wife, and incriminating documents such as phone diary and travel tickets were seized. The police were after him now. Girija Huilgol protested at his plan; wouldn't it put her at risk, she argued, but he was unrelenting and said, 'he was a family man,' although he also said he would cut Delhi out from his statement. He returned and surrendered before the Ahmedabad police on the 19th. His doctor wife who worked with the Indian Railways would be transferred to a punishment posting at a godforsaken place Kamli Ghat in Rajasthan, and then, when she lodged a protest, to Gandhidham in

Kutch.[56] Satish Pathak already had a premonition, 'something bad is going to happen'.[57] So sour had he become, he even refused to attend Vikram Rao's send-off party. Friendship had waned under the stress of clandestine activities. He was arrested on 11 March, and in the next three days unravelled the whole saga before the Baroda police. The police made him stand in a line-up to be identified by plumbers, blasters, clerks and accountants, all those who had a role either in the storage or carriage of the explosives. His confession provided the basis to apprehend and interrogate many others. The information he reeled out, complete with names, disguises and action plan, showed he was a careful observer and possessed a graphic memory. A weak link and easy prey, he identified the handwriting of George from letters he had received. A careerist, with no ideological roots, he was happy he had moved up from being a private tutor to a news stringer to a full-time journalist. Vikram Rao and Kirit Bhatt were carried away by their momentous cause, its illicit and clandestine nature, and its anti-state posturing. Their adrenaline rush possibly led them to be recklessly boastful. Satish Pathak had been for the most part a passive escort. Eager to save himself, he gave away the most. They paid the price for confiding in him, trusting a non-participant and keeping the company of a flab like him.

Bharat Patel returned from Dubai on 10 March. His first intuitive act that very day was to destroy the drilling and blasting record books at Timba Road Quarry. Next day, the police arrived and he was taken into custody. His first statement was recorded on 12 March, wherein he tried to wash his hands of it all. He spoke evasively hoping the investigation would not be able to reveal the full picture. He feigned ignorance of many things that he would later confess. He admitted to having sheltered George, but the rest he rebutted. He denied he arranged a stenotypist for George's convenience or made a recording of his speech. He was ignorant of the trip to his quarry by George in a car driven by his nephew Atul Patel. After this initial attempt to obfuscate the investigation, Bharat Patel gave up, and his damaging full confession was recorded on 3 and 4 April. But before his statement was recorded, his testimonies were used to snare others. He gave up easily.

Beginning first with small doses of revelations he opened a horrendous, incriminating flow. He spilled every bean, produced every shred of documents, and named everyone. Overwhelmed, he opened up 'in the larger interest of the country and truth, irrespective of the consequences I may have to face'. He was promised a legal laxity if he turned himself into a state approver, to which he readily agreed. He gave a blow-by-blow account of what had transpired when George stayed at his place in the middle of July. He surrendered the material evidence such as the Olivetti typewriter, trunk-call bills, mileage register of his car, letters and notes written by George, etc. In his confession to the police, Bharat Patel said, he realized the help he rendered to George 'to carry out sabotage with a view to threaten and overthrow the government was against the national interest and I now earnestly repent . . .'[58] The police recorded his confession but left him at large.

After George left for Calcutta, Delhi for some time fell quiet. On 25 March, CGK was contacted by Bharat Patel. They met at a five-star hotel in Delhi. Patel had already squealed, but he hid that fact from CGK. Instead, he asked CGK for George's help to get his nephew Atul Patel political asylum abroad. It was a ploy designed by the police. Bharat Patel was laying a trap for George to fall in. CGK dodged his request to meet George, claiming his whereabouts were secret, but still conveyed the message to George. On 28 March, when CGK went again to meet Bharat Patel, the sleuths were waiting. He was arrested. Bharat Patel had been so trustworthy George would not yet believe he had betrayed them. On 31 March, he wrote separately to Hans Janitschek, M.S. Hoda and the British Foreign Affairs minister seeking political asylum for Atul Patel who was somewhere in Europe then. He even wrote to Bharat Patel informing and enclosing a copy of each of those letters.[59] The letter signed by 'Videshia' arrived at Bharat Patel's house while his interrogation by the local police was on. He promptly handed the letter over to the sleuths. Bharat Patel would be given a pardon and made a state approver against George and his underground activities.

On the day of CGK's arrest, 28 March 1976, Rama Rao Huilgol was taken into custody as well. He underwent custodial interrogation, but his statement was recorded only on 31 May. Clearly, police

interrogation preceded the judicial recording of confessions. His son
Chandra Kumar was also arrested, and his statement too was recorded
much later on 21 May. They both underwent torture, intimidation and
illegal confinement. The nightmare of Girija Huilgol had begun. She
was taken into police custody on 30 March, but it was informally done,
not shown on record, and she was not produced before a magistrate.[60]
If she was not arrested, it was in the hope that she would lead them
to George.

Inevitably, the bust couldn't but have been an insider's job. When
Sharad Patel overheard the conversation in his under-construction
apartment at Baroda that Christmas Eve, it made him offer his farmhouse to facilitate the work. 'Do what you wish to do from here', he said
warmly to George. But simultaneously, it had set him thinking: 'I am a
builder by nature and I could not withstand the idea of destruction.'[61]
A more compulsive factor for his turnaround was a CBI case against
him: he was under investigation for forging permits for iron and steel.
The matter was reported in newspapers. Seeing it as an opportunity
to clear this stain, he decided to delve deeper into what he had heard.
In the middle of January, exigencies acting upon them, Vikram Rao
and Kirit Bhatt under orders from George went to Ahmedabad in a
car driven by Sharad Patel and brought the explosives back to Baroda.
With the explosives in his possession, Sharad Patel sat over the heap,
storing them in a dark, locked room at his farmhouse. Eager to disclose
his secret to the right person in Delhi, he even thought of confiding
in the prime minister but the improbability of such a scheme working
out made him abandon it. From then on, he was in touch with a Rajya
Sabha member from Gujarat, who directed him to sleuths at the central
agency, CBI. He tempted them with the offer to net their prize catch,
George Fernandes. They asked him to 'hold [the explosives] as long
as possible as a bait'. He, therefore, delayed their dispatch to Varanasi
despite many desperate reminders, but George would still not come
to Baroda. Vikram Rao had advised him to keep off Gujarat. 'The
mercury is shooting up in this island,' he had sent a coded message.[62] In
January, when George had left along with Girija Huilgol, he had felt the
changing mood of the Gujarat government. The state was a bastion for

Opposition politicians, and Indira Gandhi had known of it. Initially, she made a virtue out of it, telling the world how the non-Congress government in Gujarat was eloquent evidence of India's functioning democracy. But at the same time, she was looking to clip its wings and bring its flight crashing down. The Babubhai Patel government to buy peace perhaps decided to sell out George, who got a whiff of the design and kept away from the state. However, a rogue businessman facing heat for his foul deals brought a house assiduously built crashing down. On 12 March, a cocksure Sharad Patel was arrested. He held an opinion that nothing would happen to him. His statement was recorded on that very day.

On 23 March, a fortnight after the seizure of explosives, the CBI took over the investigation. It dug up trunk-call details from telephone exchanges, train reservation charts from railways, air travel details from Indian Airlines, leave records of private organizations, etc. More arrests took place in Gujarat, Bombay and Bihar. On 14 April, Prabhudass Patwari's house at Ahmedabad, in whose garage the explosives had initially been kept, was raided. On 16 May, Rewati Kant Sinha, in police custody, squealed on Jaswant Sinh Chauhan who had brought explosives to Patna. These were seized by the CBI. They even scoured the gutter to retrieve what explosives had been thrown into it. The sleuths made witnesses record a statement to the effect that the 'plan was to create chaos and panic in the country to over-awe the central government and put an end to the dictatorial rule of Indira Gandhi'.[63] Another common refrain in all confessional statements was their absolute abhorrence of violence. If the first statement was to show the political purpose of their act, the second was to absolve themselves of its doing. It was as if they were all gullible people brought into the vortex of the underground only by a violent-minded George!

Secrecy and faith are two important ingredients of the underground, but by their nature, they are in conflict with each other. They rarely coexist. While to run an underground utmost secrecy was needed, to win the confidence of comrades adequate doses of information had necessarily to be passed on. Fear was only a partial glue to keep the wavering bound in a secret pact; it could not bind them perpetually.

As Satish Pathak said, 'I thought it prudent to keep quiet having taken some part in these matters.' But secrecy alone was not enough; people must as well have faith in what they were doing. So, a degree of a bluff, a dose of whispering, a whiff of the high and mighty, boastful stories and bloated tales were the ingredients that built camaraderie in the underground. It also sowed the seeds of its eventual collapse.

The underground functioned under the premise of indicting all who were drawn into it, as the more implicated the people, the safer the leadership. The trick was to let everyone know a little but not more. As the web of little-knowing people enlarged, the greater was the time required to bust the underground. Many were brought in but with no stake in it. They would be briefed about him, his close associates and their activities, but it made no material difference to the underground; it only led to dangerous leakage. George relied too much on a very few. His team was of ordinary people, from the railways and municipal union, from journalism, and a very few from politics. It lacked a robust character. This was not because of 'any lack of training or experience', but because of obvious secrecy involved in recruiting cadres. Believing the struggle to be a 'fairly long-drawn one', it could only be carried out by constant replenishments in cadre strength. Without expanding the popular base of the resistance, success would be short-lived. The criticism about his path attenuated his options. Inviting a young daughter of a political colleague, whose parents were both already in jail, to join him in the underground, he wrote, 'Of course, if you feel that the kind of activities I am engaged in are not to your liking, then there will be no purpose in meeting.'[64] Moreover, those who were still at large lay in their cocoon, not wishing to be reminded of their roles.[65] Further, he found a people habituated to democratic freedom less attuned to the rigours of the underground. 'They could never keep a secret. If I went to a particular place and stayed with a certain person, it was only a matter of time before everyone everywhere got to know about it.' Deception was the pivot on which the underground moved. Secrecy, its lifeblood, made the underground endure. Identities of the people involved must always remain in the closet. In this case, however, deception was a sham, secrecy at best casual. Every one of them knew

चुनाव चिन्ह

चुनाव चिन्ह

जार्ज फरनांडिस

एवं सभी राजनैतिक बंदियों को रिहा करो

जनता पार्टी की ओर से

८ मार्च शुक्रवार रात्रि ७ बजे, चौक हौज़ काज़ी पर

—विशाल सभा—

वक्ताः श्री कैदार नाथ साहनी   श्री विजय कुमार मलहोत्रा
     " सिकन्दर बख्त   " सांवल दास गुप्ता
     " राजकुमार जैन   " पी.के. चान्दला
     " प्रेम दास शंकर   " सुदर्शन राही
     " श्याम गम्भीर   " रविन्द्र मनचन्दा

निवेदक:-   संयोजक सभाः-
रघुवीर सक्सैना   वहीद उद्दीन

जनता पार्टी जिला चान्दनी चौक, दिल्ली

प्रकाशक:- सांवल दास गुप्ता

Poster by the newly formed Janata Party demanding release of George and other political prisoners under the Emergency rule, March 1977.

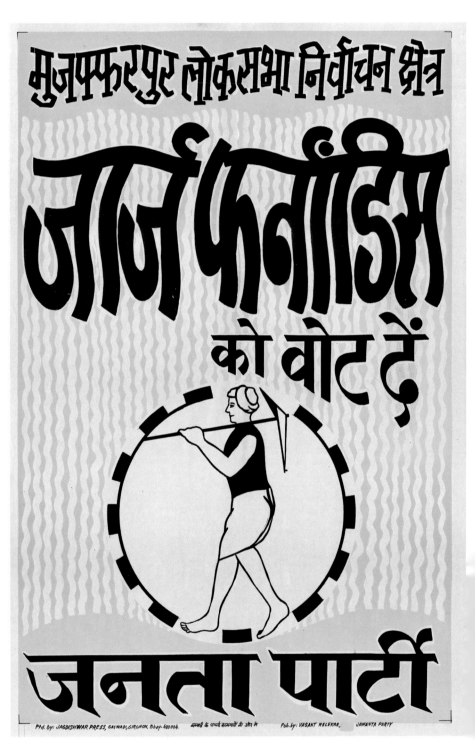

Poster for 1977 election campaign: Note the sponsors. Similar posters with different sponsors were printed and sent from Bombay to Muzaffarpur.

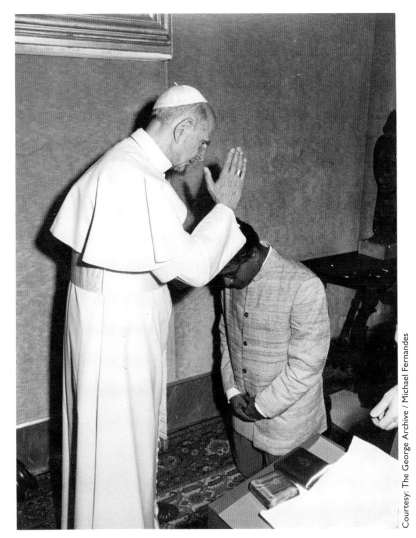

George as a minister in the Janata Party government visited Rome in early 1978 and met Pope Paul VI (1963–78). Contrary to what the photograph conveys, George despite being approached by Christian correspondents from across the country, never let himself be known as a denominational leader.

एक और दरबारी या
एक हक्कलाखी

जार्ज फर्नांडीज

सही समय पर सही फैसला कीजिए
जनता पार्टी को वोट दीजिए

PUBLISHED BY RAMCHANDRA BHARJ, GENERAL SECRETARY, JANATA PARTY, BIHAR
PRINTED AT BHARAT PRINTS, ROYAL INDUSTRIAL ESTATE, BOMBAY 400031

A defence minister of Jawans.

With Vishnu Bhagwat, the Chief of the Naval Staff of India, who was later (in 1998) dismissed by George under a controversial glare.

With Jaya Jaitly at home, 3 Krishna Menon Marg, New Delhi, during his days as the defence minister.

With Bihar chief minister Nitish Kumar at Patna, 2009. George was there to file his Rajya Sabha nomination.

every one of those involved, including their name, profession, origin and closeness with George. Only seldom were they introduced by some assumed name; and in subsequent meetings, even that minimal caution was thrown away. Once the heat was on, those vital links turned brittle.

Few could survive the sustained interrogations. Satish Pathak spilled even the most inconsequential of details. Men like Vikram Rao, who had shown some ideological mettle, caved in the moment arrests began.[66] The people already in the CBI net uncovered every person they had met and every act they had played a role in. By opening up they implicated themselves as well as their colleagues. They thought revealing statements would win them mercy, an honest confession a fresh lease of life; but the more truthful they were, the more they implicated themselves. If Snehalata Reddy wanted to protect her family from any harm, Girija Huilgol had the same concern. Their confessions were meant to get a pardon for their families.

But a confession wins you no reprieve, you still have no escape, as your honesty begins by deceiving others who once were your comrades in arms. If deception in the underground held you to your comrades in an absolute bond, once you are enticed by sleuths to truthfully render your deeds, you deceive your comrades and betray your cause. The deception you practise in the underground, being for a bigger good, energizes you and gives you the resilience to endure it. But once, upon interrogation, you deceive your comrades by giving identities to dots, by helping the police to connect the dots, you have diminished yourself. While the underground works to erase all traces of its existence by mastering deception, the police are always on the trail, just sniffing distance away. One straw, one clue, one link left carelessly can do you in. The exigencies of the underground led them to throw caution to the wind, engaging men of weaker resolve, wobbling beliefs, and of doubtful tenacity in the wake of custodial interrogation.[67] This made everyone vulnerable and the network prone to bust.

The underground movement reveals George's personality. He was scarcely the ruthless type. His letter to Bharat Patel about his nephew's political asylum, his allowing Vikram Rao to carry along flab like Satish Pathak, his putting a lot of eggs in Bharat Patel's basket, all undid him.

It was not that he was credulous, but the fact is that those closest to George brought the pack of cards crashing down. Barely a few days in custody, and they were singing to the CBI sleuths.

His was a political movement with militarist methods, not a militarist movement with political intent. It was not a hardcore underground that foisted militarist strategies to gain political ends. It was a movement to bring about a political change through militarist adventurism. It ran underground but its basic character was political, dialogic and dissipative, not destructive and decimating. It was a disruptive effort to awaken the slumbering masses. In the absence of a people's involvement at the popular level, it came to depend on a select few—journalists, businessmen, politicians, trade union activists, and some idealistic young men and women. Those who sheltered or supported him were partially in awe of his political aura and basked in its reflected glory. They were mostly non-political, a set of amateurish individuals, with no idea of the underground—its rules, its demands, its ruthless scrutiny.

George primarily depended on his trade union colleagues to build his network. It was they who had carried the contraband and distributed it at various places. It was largely presumed that workers, more so railway workers, played a major part in his underground activities, given that he was the AIRF president and his escapes were facilitated by his contacts among railwaymen. As a journalist remarked, 'He is known as the underground underground. But still above the ground are thousands of railway guards under his command in his other capacity as railway union boss; these are the couriers for the 72 underground newspapers which carry the anti-government word beyond the censor's reach.'[68]

However, George's repeated overtures to the railway workers did not stir the 'sleeping giant', tranquilized by the dose of 'order' that Indira Gandhi had administered. The organization of the AIRF had come to a complete standstill. Fearing retribution, some branch offices had even downed shutters. The workers were behaving like 'frightened chickens'.[69] At Rewati Kant Sinha's house in Patna, George could elicit only a lukewarm response from the railway leaders. In July, at Baroda, his secret meeting with the leaders of the Western Railway Employees' Union didn't go as expected. Just a year before, he had led the railwaymen's unions to a glorious shutdown. But the repression and retrenchment in the aftermath of the strike were massive and unexpectedly harsh, and this had a lasting effect on the workers' morale. They had been beaten black and blue by the state and thousands were still out of jobs.

George wrote letters to workers, exhorting them to participate wholeheartedly in the unfolding battle, 'pack the jails till the jail walls break at their seams'.[70] He reminded the AIRF of its historic role and also the embarrassing allegation made by Indira Gandhi. He wrote of JP who in May 1975 had inaugurated their fiftieth annual conference at Jodhpur but now was languishing in jail. He asked them to not be 'meek spectators' to loss of democracy and through 'mass action and underground activities serve notice on the fascists'.[71] He rued the capitulation of trade unions before the 'fascist Indira Congress' as a 'measure of the weakness of our movement'.[72] The CPI-run AITUC was moving closer to the Congress INTUC, just as the CPI and the Congress were gloating over 'emerging cooperation' between them. S.A. Dange, the CPI chairman and also the AITUC boss, was looking for opportunities to expand their activities under the protective shadow of Indira Gandhi's Emergency.[73] Dange called the Emergency a link in the unfolding chain of 'democratic revolution'. Responding to a bonus law amendment that adversely affected the workers, he said cynically, 'bonus is important but Emergency is more important.' Dange once had said that workers' unity in India would come about 'when India went through a period of dictatorship when all trade union leaders belonging to various ideological hues found themselves in prison and decided to so organize the workers in future that they could act as the strongest bastion against future dictatorships'. Unfortunately, when the dictatorship finally arrived, Dange ended up being the one defending it.[74] In Bombay, George's former colleagues at the Port and Dock Workers' Union championed the renaming of the Alexandra Docks as Indira Docks. And Manohar Kotwal, his old envious adversary, paraded a statue of Indira Gandhi on the streets.[75]

The indifference of the working class to building resistance against the Emergency was a painful revelation. Marx's statement that workers have nothing but labour to sell fomented proletarian revolutions across the world. But now workers were prepared to sell their labour to anyone who could pay a suitable price. Their vision didn't extend beyond their own needs. The 'sleeping giant' when stirred from its slumber by organized prodding was simply concerned with its feed: raise my wage, allowance, bonus and gratuity, give me more holidays, give my children jobs after me. It seldom thought beyond its close-knit group of kith and kin. It was single-mindedly focused on joining the middle class rather than being a revolutionary force to emancipate humanity from its cycle of inequality and servitude.

* * *

Giving us a peep into his state of mind during the first year of the Emergency, George said he was not feeling gloomy or desolate, but 'never was loneliness so cruel and oppressive, though strangely enough, the few real moments of joy have been when I have withdrawn deep within myself. With cheer in my heart, I had looked forward to the coming of spring and even "conspired" to have a brief "holiday", but it is already summer, and except for the chirping of another generation of little sparrows which I enjoy, there was not even the whiff of spring for me. But I suppose that is the way the wheel of life keeps turning, grinding slowly, pitilessly, exposing the fragility of most people and relationships, calling someone's victory as another person's defeat, converting one man's pleasure into another man's pain, some one's happiness into another one's sorrow, when it has come to a full turn, levelling everyone into the uniformity of nothingness—the nothingness of death.'[76]

In eleven months in the underground, and more urgently after it was busted, with scores arrested and himself forced into claustrophobic hiding, he acutely felt the 'protecting hand of God' guiding what he was doing.[77] To 'say everything and for all times' to his long-away wife and child, he penned a touching verse—only the third he ever wrote. It was titled, 'A Home in My Heart', and it went . . .

> Someone said,
> His wife and son are ten thousand miles away.
> He doesn't know,
> Or does he,
> of a place called the
> Human heart,
> Which is bound neither by space nor by times,
> Not as long as it ticks.
> That's where they are,
> In my heart,
> Even while they are ten thousand miles away.
> I talk to them every day and hear them talk,
> We even play our little games
> When we are alone, just the three of us,
> And laugh,
> Every night I lay my Sonny Boy on my breast
> And sing
> And tell him stories!
> See his dazzling smile,
> Hear his joyous laughter,
> As Peshi girl looks on
> With eyes that are overflowing with
> Tears of love.
> Who said they are ten thousand miles away?
> They are here,
> Right in my heart!

Six weeks after the first exposé and arrests, when the dust temporarily seemed to have settled down, George wrote a melancholy if defiant letter that exhorted that the 'struggle must go on with unabated vigour and with a conviction that we shall triumph'.[78] He wrote how arrests had crippled his network. Although Indira Gandhi claimed she was unafraid of anything, George believed, 'no one in our country today [was] more frightened than the dictator'. He said fear and freedom do not go together, but the exposé and arrests had lent him new experience. If the courage and endurance of many had gladdened his heart, he at the same time felt saddened and pained by the treachery and betrayal of those 'who claimed to be my friends'. 'There are still a few who, by their conduct, constantly keep reminding me of what Dr Lohia had written about those brave socialists and communists of Europe who scurried around like rats for shelter when Hitler came to power in Germany.' That brought him to pay the finest tribute to Ram Manohar Lohia—'A great son of India, a man who will be honoured by history when the present-day ruling cliques of this country will be spat upon, a man who loved India as few are even capable of loving her'—the architect of a vision for the country George claimed he shared. 'It is a vision of an egalitarian India, a democratic and socialist India in which exploitation and repression will be bad dreams of the dark days of the rule of the Nehru Dynasty.'

On 12 October 1975, when asked if there was any kind of organized underground movement, Indira Gandhi said there was 'no regular underground movement. They do produce some literature but not on a large scale and is diminishing.'[79] Then, a piece titled 'Yes, there is an underground' was published.[80] Still, Russi Karanjia provocatively asked her how when the national scene was quiet, the international bodies were making a scene. Referring to the Socialist International, she asked: 'Who are their backers? I want to know where they are getting their money from?' Just when Indira Gandhi was confidently asserting that the common people were 'liking' the effect that Emergency brought, the Baroda Dynamite case made an appearance on the front pages of newspapers. The Babubhai government was reduced to a minority by the desertion of his party MLAs to the Congress Party. Tensions prevailed in the Gujarat House during the debate on the Opposition-sponsored motion condemning the discovery of explosives at Baroda. The Janata Front ministry was accused of total failure in curbing the violent forces within the state. Some MLAs alleged that the discovery of explosives indicated that the Front government was out to wage a war with the Centre. The nine-month-old Babubhai Gujarat ministry was dismissed and central rule imposed. Whereas parliamentary proceedings were selectively allowed to be published by the censors, the Congress attack on the Janata Front government for its alleged coalition with the Dynamite conspirators began to get first-page appearance in the national dailies. Fettered as it was by censorship, the press did not have much space; it only acted where it was allowed to. The exposé was a validation of the government's claim that the Emergency was to preserve democracy from political irresponsibility and indiscipline of the Opposition rather than extinguish it as alleged by the Opposition. It provided an opportunity to further build up the propaganda that the Opposition was 'obstructionist and violent'. After completely denying the existence of the underground for many months, finally, the tone of the government changed. It now claimed that its existence showed how violent the Opposition was.

His family under threat, the explosives he had collected seized, his most trusted colleagues trailed, arrested and interrogated, he himself betrayed, yet he refused to give in.

10

Chained and Fettered

In the afternoon of 10 June 1976, finally, without much ado or gore, it all came to an end. George was arrested from St Paul's Cathedral on Chowringhee Road in Calcutta. A posse of CBI men barged in and found three men sitting in a back room of the church auditorium.[1] The church ran a social organization called The Samaritans. Vijayan Pawamuni was its operational incharge. He was one of the three men. The second was Vijay Narain from Varanasi, who had just arrived from Delhi. While coming in, he had noticed 'many strange-looking people around the church'. There were men positioned even on the roofs of adjoining buildings. He asked the third man to leave immediately. But as this man dithered, the raiding team broke in. Amidst a swirl of commotion and plenty of shouting, they asked each of them to give their identities. Vijayan Pawamuni responded, and said the two others were his guests. Did he have a guest register? There indeed was one in which the third man had signed as Professor Raj Sekhar from Allahabad on a research assignment. They asked for his luggage. He had kept a suitcase with Vijayan Pawamuni, who, thinking it safe, gave that over to them. Rummaging through it they found a photo identity card of George Fernandes, president of the AIRF. George though was not one to give up easily. With a deadpan face, he disclaimed he was whom they in their spurt of euphoria had assumed him to be. But having got their prey, they would not let it slip away so easily. It had been an unprecedented manhunt, that intensified greatly after the Baroda group was busted.

Many years later, when asked why a man in his circumstances would carry anything that gave away his identity, he explained, 'If the police were to gun me down, someone should know who the person was.'[2] Some years before, D'Mello had been found dead and unclaimed on a pavement in Calcutta, and it helped identify his body when a badge of the Port and Dock Workers' Union was found on his person. This had so affected George that the memory of it had made him carry his identity even in times when it was least expected. 'These eleven months of underground life,' he wrote to his wife days before his arrest, meditating over life and death, 'have given me further evidence of the working of God's hand in most of what I am doing. But for His protecting hand, I should not have been around.'[3] Death had followed him all these months, yet something saved him from the clutches of its claws. He had ignored advice nudging him to leave the country. In response, he would say, 'This is my country. I shall work here, live here and die here. If it is given to me to die in the struggle, I shall welcome death.'[4] When urged to save himself to be able to fight another day, he would say unequivocally, 'Well, if it comes to that, let me leave it to others to fight another day. For me, the struggle is here and it is today.'[5] Years before, he had been at Kohima's War Cemetery and had seen a rock memorial on which was engraved:

When you go back home
Tell them about us, and say
For their tomorrow
We gave our today

The words had brought tears to his eyes.[6] But in this struggle, the certainty with which he had carried on gave him a mysterious immunity and made him invulnerable to the risks.

The arrest, contrary to what was long prophesied, didn't end in an instant slaughter. He was taken to the police office at Alipore, where till the morning of the following day, he was made to sit on a 'hard wooden chair' and not allowed to sleep. A flurry of intelligence men took turns interrogating him. They needed him to confess. He said nothing. 'In the hours immediately after my arrest,' he recollected a month later, 'I told the police that I would make no statement whatsoever concerning my activities and movements for the period from 26 June 1975 to 10 June 1976.'[7] He was served with an arrest order under the Maintenance of Internal Security Act (MISA). A special Air Force plane from Delhi brought the order, pending execution since July 1975. Repeatedly, the Delhi Police had sent confidential circulars to the police across the states for his arrest. An August '75 order had even enclosed a photograph of him for ready reference and identification. Later, they declared a reward for his capture, dead or alive. After the Baroda hideout was busted, the Intelligence Bureau (IB) renewed the 'secret/immediate' order on 18 March 1976, for 'a vigorous drive launched with a view to securing his apprehension'.[8] Presently, he was flown to Delhi by the same Air Force transporter that had brought the arrest warrant. The authorities were seemingly undecided about where to keep him in the capital. They drove him first to the iconic seventeenth-century Mughal Red Fort, with secret chambers to interrogate those charged with sedition. Then, he was taken to the Tihar Central Jail. A little before dusk, after a metropolitan magistrate had committed him to police custody, he was brought back to the Red Fort.

It was the sultry month of June. The air was humid and heavy. When the door was slammed shut behind him, he found himself in a 'dark, ill-ventilated dungeon'. It smelled bad. It hadn't been cleaned for years. He was not allowed 'even my handkerchief with which to wipe the sweat in this hot oven of a lock-up nor an old newspaper with which to fan myself'. He was given two coarse blankets to sleep on. As he made a 'dirty, rough blanket spread on the cement floor' his bed, he readied himself for anything. In one corner of the cell was a clogged hole in the name of a toilet that bred stink and a swarm of mosquitoes. The overpowering stench and incessant whirring of insects would not let him rest. To protect himself, he would use the other filthy blanket as a cover. However, seconds later suffocation would make him throw it off. But the heat, stink and insects were not all that gave him sleepless nights; the interrogation sessions added to them.

The interrogation room, in contrast to his cell, was presentable, the walls wore fresh paint and the chairs were inviting. Sleep-deprived, at regular intervals he was brought in, questioned and returned to his dungeon. He was kept here for three days and three nights before being moved again. Though brief, the stay would haunt him; two months later when on the occasion of the 28th Independence Day Indira Gandhi stood on the ramparts of the Red Fort to hoist the flag, he noted in his prison journal, 'just a few feet away [from her] is the dingy, stinking black-hole' where he had been lodged 'without bath and without civility'.[9] More than this, he didn't leave any record of what happened in those three days and three nights. Was it too humiliating for him to say it all? Or would talking of it be an indulgence in self-pity? At the CBI office where he was kept for a week soon after, he found himself in a large hall with armed guards inside and outside. The sentries were fiercely wordless, showing no emotions. He was not allowed a bath, although never was the request denied. Stale and insipid food from some small roadside vendor was served to him. These were ruses to tire him out. His refusal to engage provoked volleys of obscene and vulgar language from the sleuths. The veiled menace of violence was always there, but some even threatened him with assault then and there. A heavy chain and handcuffs were always kept in the car when they transported him from one place to the other.

On the evening of 23 June, he was driven to Tihar Jail and kept in an isolated cell. Two days later, he was brought to the District Jail at Hissar in Haryana, some 180 kilometres north-west of Delhi. There, before being admitted, he was strip-searched, 'with the jail staff trying to find out if I was carrying anything clandestine or incriminating hidden in the private parts of my body'. Feeling humiliated, he wrote to the Union home minister describing the ordeal he had been through.[10] The letter to 'Dear Mr Reddy' was returned as its tone made it an unofficial communiqué, and he was advised to rewrite it on an official letter form which had sixteen ruled lines. He did so, beginning with a formal 'Dear Sir'. The books and medicine bottles he had brought along were confiscated. The medicine bottles were returned the same night. The books—a set of six by Alexander Solzhenitsyn, one each by Fredrick Forsyth and Norman Mailer, a copy of *The Bermuda Triangle* and the latest *Reader's Digest*—were not. They were sent to the censor for permission. He was kept in a cage-like enclosure, made of iron bars and pipes, in a courtyard ringed by a high wall and guarded day and night by men in the watchtower. When it grew dark, powerful electric bulbs floodlit the entire yard to give it a look of a night sports ground. One day, a barrack guard told him that the gun of the man on the watchtower was empty of its firepower. He understood the trap in the message: 'Should I try to escape, I would be shot.'[11] The enclosure did not protect him from the elements. 'Hot summer winds capable of melting the grey matter in one's head blow through these barred doors which, after repeated requests, have now been covered with old blankets', he wrote to 'Dear Sir', the Union home minister Brahmananda Reddy (1909–94). The blanket, while acting as a windbreaker, in turn, flared the heat of the cell greatly. His cot was chained to an iron bar of the cell. In consequence of his letter, the angry authorities removed the blankets. He was told to sit under the neem tree in the yard if the heat in the cell became unbearable. Then came the rains and flooded his cell.

A week after his arrest, when Leila Fernandes sent frantic telegrams to know of his whereabouts, she received a cryptic reply from India's Home Ministry. 'How can you not be aware of the activities of your husband,' the brusque message read, 'who has for the past several months been moving about instigating people to commit acts of violence, subversion, sabotage and other serious crimes prejudicial to public order and security of the country.'[12] When she asked the Indian ambassador in New York where her husband was, he shot back, 'In India.' His arrest made worldwide news.[13] With Hans Janitschek and Mohammad Surur Hoda working behind the scenes, the Socialist International issued a statement signed by German Willy Brandt, Swedish Olof Palme and Austrian Bruno Kreisky appealing to Indira Gandhi to be fair 'in the interest of India's reputation in the democratic world'.[14] They were apprehensive he would be tortured, even beaten to death. Immediately after his arrest,

Michael B. Fernandes.
MISA Detenu No 168.

Central Prison, Belgaum.
February 8, 1977.

To: George Fernandes,
Tihar Jail, Delhi.

By Regd Post / Ack. Due.

My dear Jaykal,

I've not had yet a single line from you in response to my telegram of last June 18 (sent to Alipore prison, presuming you might have been taken there), letter of July 30, and a registered letter (ack. due) of Sept. 21 (also enclosing a copy of an earlier letter), both to Hissar, and New Year greetings sent to Tihar on Dec 29. I had also sent a telegram to the Union Home Minister asking for your whereabouts which too has remained unanswered. I shouldn't have known the fate of any of these, but for Ricky informing me some time ago that you had received my telegram and also written to me. But all that I have seen so far is three or four of your letters to Kitte and to Levi. I hope that atleast this letter will reach you and fetch me a reply (which actually comes to my hand). If it doesn't, I think I shall give up attempting any more to correspond with you in prison, ...

I was overwhelmed by grief and shock on seeing in the Deccan Herald of Jan 21 that Sneha was no more; and I couldn't help thinking of how the news would shake you down. But what could we do from prison except sharing in silence in the sorrow and gloom her family and friends had been drowned in? I wrote to Ricky my thoughts and a message of condolence to be passed on to Potteli. She died indeed a martyr in the struggle for human dignity and freedom of conscience. Cruel death has cheated her, and all of us, by not letting her be a witness to and participate in the developments that have taken place since her untimely death. Somehow I just can't get myself to believe even now that she is dead. Truly, Sneha is only gone, but her spirit lives on!

While the gloom cast by Sneha's death still persists, the recent developments have greatly lightened our slow dragging days in prison. Last week Monday (Jan 31), I completed one year and one month and one week and one day in prison, ...

when he let it be known 'I would not say a word, even if I were to die' the police treatment became rough. But then an incredible thing happened. The commanding officer called him to ask if he had any complaints to make about his treatment. 'I was surprised, and said, "well, I was not

Censorship during Indira Gandhi's India, 1977: Michael Fernandes' letter, written from Central Prison, Belgaum, to George, who was in Central Jail, Tihar, is made illegible in its major portions by the government censor.

treated very politely—as a matter of fact, I was threatened with torture."
" The officer asked if he would like to register a formal complaint. 'Rather
bewildered, I replied, "Not at this moment.""[15] Word of his arrest was
already out, and there were pressures to be fair with him. Besides, he
wasn't of any use dead, but alive he was a potent demonstration. Indira
Gandhi had been calling the Opposition leaders violent disrupters and
destroyers of democracy, with a penchant for solving political problems
in the streets. His arrest gave her a further handle on these leaders, most
of whom were already in jails. While Amnesty International refused
to adopt him as a prisoner of conscience for his was a criminal case,
the House of Representatives of the US Congress began its hearings on
'human rights violations in India'. One of the witnesses to appear before
it was Leila Fernandes, presenting with a heavy heart 'my husband's
case which is intertwined with the destiny of India'.[16] She launched
herself actively into mobilizing public opinion in the USA, and travelled
to Europe in October to meet and speak to the socialist leaders of the
continent. She sounded resolute and unruffled. 'I'd like to tell him I am
with him, every inch, every moment', she said.[17]

* * *

Most men sold themselves for petty gains and small favours. But what
about George? In the underground, he put everything, his family and
his life included, at stake: 'I was willing to die.' He travelled incessantly
and often incognito, 'from the big cities to the very small hamlets';
while travelling, he kept mostly to himself, and seldom spoke or
indulged in pleasantries. At places where he lodged, he confined himself
to reading and writing. Even that was not easy, as he wrote, because he
was 'on [the] move from one part of the country to another'.[18] Still, he
thrived on work, churning out challenging pamphlets and cyclostyled
one-page leaflets with crisp news items that no newspaper published.
Avoiding conversation, as a rule, he found enduring companionship
among books. He read works of literature to draw solace but he also
read chronicles of other people's experiences in fighting dictatorship
or alien occupation. Turmoil and defeats never sagged his spirit,

dampened his smile or dented his confidence. Fear stalked the world outside, but he remained unruffled. No inner conflicts, the bane of lesser men, ever tore him into indecision. At places, his words bore 'deep frustration and sadness at the poverty of commitment' but he carried on without malice.[19]

Once in a while, he seemed to need the warmth of a soothing voice. While hiding at St Paul's Cathedral, he was visited by one Kanen from New York, who returned carrying sacks full of letters for his correspondents abroad. They had been romantically linked earlier. In April 1971, she had written in a tone of informal familiarity, not knowing perhaps of his impending marriage with Leila Kabir, to complain of him being 'a bad correspondence' [sic]: 'I think it's because you fool yourself into thinking that you don't have time to sit down and write to a non-politically involved WOMAN about non-political matters. But you do . . . Please write, lazy-busy one,' she had written.[20] Now, he employed her as his trusted messenger to the world outside. But he had been visited by others as well, Girija Huilgol included. Was this urge for human warmth, even while dwelling in the solitude of the underground, his undoing? Some would think so.

Vijay Narain, always disrespectful towards women—in the 1990s, he would paint Jaya Jaitly disreputably, telling the world that she and her daughter were pimping themselves to politicians—would repeatedly state that this weakness of George was his undoing.[21] When he had gone to visit George at Girija Huilgol's house in Delhi he had noticed the closeness between them. He blamed her for George's arrest. It was she, he said, who led the sleuths to his hiding place in Calcutta. Girija Huilgol's convoluted letter to George in January 1977 would give traction to Vijay Narain's pointed fingers and simultaneously indict her. 'George,' she wrote in that long letter, the purpose of which was to seek redemption, 'don't you see, it is bad enough betraying one's comrade, but it becomes unforgivable when the comrade in question happens to be you and is betrayed by his closest and most trusted associate.'[22] She said her act had got him arrested but the manner of it is not told. A little more light is thrown in subsequent lines: 'When I asked you in my last letter to help me find the reason for my taking

Ashok Patel to Calcutta with me, it wasn't so much the reason for taking him to Calcutta, as the reason for not giving you his true identity. I wish I had had the courage to do so at that time.' Ashok Patel was the police officer who had interrogated and later befriended her. She had taken him to meet George at his Calcutta hideout. She was repentant now and, knowing his trust had worn thin, wanted to win him back. 'Believe me, George,' she wrote agonizingly, 'I would have picked up the thread of our movement after your arrest, had it not been for how you were arrested.' And then comes a revealing line that to a large extent should have settled the matter, 'After realizing how I had been used in your arrest, how could I carry on?' But it didn't.

George was not expected to make the error of inviting Girija Huilgol to his hideout when he was aware of the tortuous terrain of the underground and its rules well. A girl in her mid-twenties, studying to be a doctor, Girija Huilgol was roped in as a travelling companion and conduit to ferry information and fix meetings. During their time together, they had developed feelings for each other. Vijay Narain had noticed it. Her parents' anxiety at her closeness with George was also known. Slowly, her whole family was sucked into the vortex of the underground as silent, if not active, accomplices. In March, when the underground came unstuck, her father and brother were arrested, and she was under pressure to become informer if she wanted them alive. George knew she was in the police net, her father was, her brother was he knew it all. How was it possible that she, made vulnerable by arrests of her close relations, would not have caved in and spilled all that she knew, and she did know a lot! Was he, therefore, being plain credulous or was his faith in Girija Huilgol so complete he would not imagine the danger inherent in inviting her to Calcutta? Among the axioms on which the underground worked was one about not trusting any man or woman. The man who formulated the manual was scarcely expected to be negligent of its rules. In it lies the explanation for Vijay Narain's damaging insinuation.

A decade later, in 1985, George would relate how he was 'discussing strategies with one of his underground contacts who had just arrived from Delhi when the police pounced on him'.[23] They had followed the contact all the way, knowing he would lead them to him. He doesn't give us a name but it was Vijay Narain who had just arrived when the police barged in. He was a trusted colleague, as Girija Huilgol well knew. On 10 March 1976, after being dropped at Delhi airport, before boarding the Air India flight to Calcutta, George had telegrammed Asha Singh, wife of Vijay Narain, at Varanasi.[24] His friend at whose address the dynamite consignment was to be delivered was caught and interrogated. He exposed Vijay Narain to the police pursuit. It was a practice with the police to let the suspect loose after interrogation to make him/her contact other fugitives and snare them. Was he that loose cannon fired by the police to apprehend George? Years later when I was piecing evidence together, though Vijay Narain's resistance was diminishing with age, his response to my persistent questioning was decidedly irascible. His narrative was a mix of self-projection, of how it was he who had found a safe hideout in Calcutta for George, and self-righteousness, insisting it was George's weakness that led to his arrest. He spoke in fits and bouts, and hinted how he was first sent to Delhi but was constrained to back off without meeting Girija Huilgol when he saw her under police surveillance. He cautioned George on his return. But George, instead of heeding the advice, sent Vijayan Pawamuni to Delhi with a note for her. Vijayan met her at the hospital where she worked. And the note having fallen into police hands, they followed Vijayan when he returned to the Calcutta hideout. We could settle for this version provided by Vijay Narain, as he is the only one in a position to remember a bit of it. But there was inconsistency in his account, as we know that on the day of arrest, according to Vijay Narain himself, it was he who had just arrived when the police came in. Was he shifting the blame on to Girija Huilgol to absolve himself of complicity in George's arrest?

Then again, many years later, when I asked Jaya Jaitly if she knew Girija Huilgol or if George ever talked of her, she said, feelingly, that Girija was the one person who was 'completely erased from his conversation'.[25] Months after his arrest, when with the restoration of democracy he became a minister in the Morarji Desai-led government at the Centre, Girija Huilgol was unable to get hold of him. A sister of hers, 'Veena Tiwari nee Huilgol', would write to him for an intervention to stop the vindictive transfer of her uncle-in-law—'virtually my father-in-law, since he brought up and educated my husband', but it cannot be ascertained if the request was addressed at all as her letter is marked simply 'File M(I) (personal)' by his redoubtable secretary and is found in his archive, without any accompanying document.[26] At least one knowledgeable source spoke about Girija Huilgol approaching Surendra Mohan to complain that George, having promised her marriage, was now proving elusive; Mohan told her to forget about it and go home.[27] But Surendra Mohan was never friendly towards George, being jealous and bitter about his popularity and political success, even when they were in the same party and together occupied positions of responsibility in the party structure. When I contacted her during the course of my research, Girija Huilgol told me on the phone, 'I am suffering from a memory loss.'[28] She had been a significant factor in the resistance movement. And more than 35 years later, she claimed memory loss and said that she was on medication. It was a ruse, obviously; she didn't want to share her past.

One underground pamphlet circulated two days after his arrest claimed George had prior intimation of his arrest.[29] His whole underground network, so assiduously built in all those months, was completely shattered. The nodes in police custody had ratted out all that they knew. In the letters Kanen carried to friends across Europe and North America he admitted how the police action had depleted his network. Despite a boastful 'At the time of my arrest, we had more than 2000 people—mostly new and young cadres—recruited from all over the country', in the aftermath of the busting at Baroda, the attrition of the underground was a hard reality.[30]

Not only had the police arrested all his accomplices, but they had also begun to close in on the sacred realm of his family. On 1 May, his brother Lawrence Fernandes was arrested in Bangalore. He was not concerned with politics at all; as Leila Fernandes said before the representatives of US Congress, he was 'a small businessman, a bachelor looking after his aged parents and got caught in the torture chains, only because he was George Fernandes' brother'. Having failed to track down George, the police made his brother pay. On that evening, a police team came to their house and asked Lawrence Fernandes to accompany them. He was required to answer some queries related to Michael Fernandes, who had been in detention since December 1975. The police jeep drove Lawrence straight to Carlton House, the office of Corps of Detectives (COD) of the Karnataka government. The officers first asked him about family affairs, their sources and amount of earnings. 'After about half-an-hour they left, leaving me alone in the closed room.' Then, he was taken to an adjacent room fitted with flashlights, recording mikes, etc. A force of eight to ten policemen surrounded him. They asked him about George. He denied any knowledge of him. He was ordered to be stripped. They tied his hands and legs and stretched him out flat on the ground. Two constables stood on his body. They used whatever was handy to thrash him, resorting lastly to a Banyan root. Next day his worried old parents approached everyone in the police and civil bureaucracy to know where he was. Frantically, they telegrammed anyone who held a power string. Lawrence Fernandes was held in illegal custody till 20 May, when his arrest was recorded, and he was brought to Bangalore's Central Prison with his bones fractured, a tooth broken.[31] His case became a telling example of the Emergency's excesses. 'I suffered mental and physical damage on account of my treatment in police custody and jail', Lawrence Fernandes wrote to the Shah Commission on 3 August 1977, requesting an inquiry into his case in the interest of justice.[32] On 1 May, the day he was taken in, Snehalata Reddy's family was also interrogated. Brimming with anxiety, she agreed to tell 'everything I know' on the condition that her family would be sent home. She was taken into custody. She remained in jail, confined in a solitary cell in the Bangalore prison, to be released on parole in January 1977 when her health deteriorated, only to die a week later. George had got to know of their arrests in May itself.

So, did he use a vulnerable woman and a compromised man to facilitate his arrest? Although there is little evidence of a prior understanding with the police, he had indeed run out of options. Running on loyalty, binding and unflagging, rather less to the cause than to the ring-leader, those arrested and in police custody were all his chosen people, hand-picked from trade unions he had founded. They were people not very resourceful or capable on their own, and dependent on him for their livelihood and work. They, however, were no trained guerrilla warriors. Their endurance had limits. Money was in short supply, too. Vijay Narain would not wait but pester R. Chandrachudan for 'lack of money is hampering our work', he said. 'Sudama', the man whose real name was Surendra Kishore and who was a Patna-based correspondent of George's *Pratipaksh*, repeatedly went to Kanpur to draw money from a contact there (possibly, Veena Tiwari nee Huilgol).[33] Vikram Rao had Baroda industrialists who fed him money, but an irritated George would one day reprimand him that this couldn't go on indefinitely. The tightening condition, here only surmised and not substantiated, might have induced George to think politically and to use a legal trial to vent his politics.

* * *

George at Hissar District Jail for some time battled to receive the minimum courtesy within the rules of imprisonment. The first few weeks were exhausted in writing letters of complaint to the authorities, who perhaps never read them, or to members of his family, who never received them. In the middle of August, he petitioned the High Court of Delhi, seeking direction to prison authorities to return letters withheld from him. But before he did so, he sent a chiding missive to the jail superintendent that he didn't 'grudge the dictator and her myrmidons all the sadist pleasures they may desire from blocking my family members from hearing from me'.[34] To the High Court, he said not letting him have letters was a 'part of the systematic and brutal torture' he had been subjected to since his arrest.[35] It was not the intemperate content because of which his communications were withheld. There were indeed lawful restrictions on a prisoner's correspondence if they referred to political or communal matters. To prove his were clean from prejudicial taint, he wrote of his family's religious composition, 'The petitioner submits that he was born to Christian parents, that his wife is the daughter of a Muslim father and a Hindu mother, and while in his entire public life extending over twenty-seven years, he has a record of fighting against communalism in all its manifestations, even his personal and family background would preclude his thinking on communal matters.' He was worried about his seventy-six-year-old father, a heart patient, and a despairing mother, whose three sons were in prison. To his mother, he wrote he was not receiving her letters because of 'boys whose mother must never have written to them'. Towards the end of August, however, things turned a little better as his mother Alice Fernandes and mother-in-law Shanti Kabir both visited him separately after making long and eventful journeys.

Dauntless, unencumbered by any guilt, ideological or real, he largely remained healthy. When Shanti Kabir met him, she noted, despite some loss of weight, he was cool and calm.[36] He had acclimatized well to jail life. After he had complained repeatedly and been ignored equally repeatedly, he left things as they were. 'It's fine,' he would say whenever anyone enquired. If that attitude gave him peace, it made the officials jittery. One afternoon, when it rained all through and his cell was wet with pools of water on the floor, he decided it was not a significant enough matter for protest. With long-winding hours weighing heavily upon his fettered self, he discovered howsoever he befriended a hurrying squirrel or made acquaintance with a nesting bird there was no stilling of his thoughts. When he was visited by someone and was returned to his cell after the meeting, he dwelt on every word spoken, every gesture made, every pain expressed, to pass his time. His thoughts swung from occasionally upbeat to downright dumps. Not that he always mulled over the lows, but those highs he thought of were often sullied by a remorseful emotion as if even in those moments his vivid memory brought up something reproachful to make him feel guilty or wasted.

As a consolation to his solitude, he began to write a journal. In it, he meditated on jail life, humiliation and turmoil within. He deliberated over the evolving politics of which he was either told by visiting friends or read about in newspapers. Although personal matters do appear, politics constituted in essence the content of his life, and therefore references to it fill the pages. He was allowed loose sheets of plain paper, each leaf stamped and signed by the jail superintendent. He could also buy exercise books. When writing paper ran short or was denied, he used the reverse of advertising brochures that newspapers brought along to write on. A sheaf of these handwritten sheets has survived in his archive. Although in 1984, while reviewing Vijaya Lakshmi Pandit's *Prison Days*, he referred to his journal, it would never be in the public domain.[37] Written between 21 July and 20 September 1976, when he was at Hissar Jail, the authorities were reluctant to let him carry the pages along on his transfer to Tihar Jail. They agreed only when he refused to budge without them. Once at Tihar, he was much preoccupied with daily court appearances and also as he felt whatever he wrote might be used against him and his colleagues in the trial, he put the journal on hold. But finding himself at the bottom of an emotional pit when a copy of the charge sheet, with witness statements and all, was given in November, he began writing once again the last pages of the journal.

Letters, visits, anniversaries are some of the core themes covered in it. His feelings are largely repressed though some words are giveaways of his implosions. On 22 July, their fifth marriage anniversary, he wrote with longing, 'Ten thousand miles away, Leila too will be thinking, and scattered all over the world, many others who care for us and love us and think about us.' Generous to a fault, he held himself alone responsible for the things that had inadvertently gone wrong in their marriage and hurt that had been imperceptibly caused. Feeling guilty, he wondered 'if Leila bargained for all that I am'.[38] Then again when he read his mother's letter to the President of India, on Lawrence Fernandes' illegal custody and torture, disturbed and indignant as he was, he was also anguished that his brother had risked his life to save the underground resistance.[39] He handwrote copies of all his letters in exercise books. He read the Bhagavad Gita 'at least one hour every day in the morning' and learnt Sanskrit grammar to read it expertly. He worked on speed-reading and English language vocabulary. When Shanti Kabir came visiting, bringing things he needed, he wrote, 'like hawks, the jailor looks at everything'. Richard Fernandes, his youngest brother in Bangalore, sent Irving Wallace's *The R Document*, and after reading it he thought it was written with the Indian Emergency in mind.[40] 'Must write to Leila asking her to meet Irving and to thank him for this book.' He was amused when his brother Aloysius informed him of Eva Vaz ('who has some relation to my father'), a Congress minister in the Karnataka government, stating that George had disgraced the Christian community by his underground resistance to the Emergency. 'Poor girl,' he wrote, 'doesn't seem to be literate enough to understand the meaning of her statement. Get into your knickers and frock back to your Sunday school and study your bible, Eva.' He narrated how adulatory police officers and decrepit politicians were sent to him to make him talk but he was conscious enough to avoid the trap. When his 'naturally anxious and worried and reduced to half her size' mother visited him on the last day of August, he told her to 'feel proud that she has the unique distinction of having her three sons in prisons'.[41] His father sent a bottle of Chyawanprash with an admixture of gold and calcium, a jar of ginger pickle and advice. 'Pray and work hard and you will win the battle.'[42]

Shanti Kabir brought a letter from Leila Fernandes and three paintings by Sonny Boy. In her letter, Leila had enclosed a 'portrait of our son, whose childhood is rolling along without the presence of his father'.[43] On seeing the paintings, he enthused, 'They are simply beautiful. I couldn't do them no, not even at 46.' An excerpt from his journal, written on 16 September, reads thus:

Since yesterday morning I have the presentiment that there was either a letter or visitor round the corner. This morning, this feeling becomes very intense. Letters are a rarity, and there was no intimation of any visit. But there he was, the lambardar with a note at the strike of twelve. There was a visitor. It was the mother[-in-law]. She had driven by car to Hissar, gone straight to the District Magistrate's office and sought and secured permission to interview me. Like Santa Claus, she unpacked the gift packets the first thing she came in. What a lovely picture of Sonny Boy smiling away, what a happy face. Then were unpacked Sonny Boy's artefacts: these paintings and two fish cut out of white paper with multi-colour paper designs. The 'lion with the tail' is a (pardon the father's pride) collector's item. What a range of colours, what masterful use of the brush. An unnamed item shows a maturity that can only be called 'fantastic'. I hope Peshi [Leila] is keeping all the pictures. Someday, we could have an exhibition of child art. The Gillette tech metic razor sent by Leila has been detained by the jail authorities. No reasons were given. I know one: cussedness. The one hour with mother passed off in exactly 59 minutes and 60 seconds. Not a minute more, not even a second more than one hour. Mother said that today they made her wait outside for over an hour and that despite her telephone call informing the Superintendent that she was coming in fifteen minutes. The fellow came during the interview, looked at the tech metic razor and said to no one particular: 'I hope it is not dynamite'. That must be his sense of morbid humour. He had his underlings rummage into the knick-knacks that mother had brought for me. Three cakes of CINTHOL soap were stripped of their wrappers and allowed to stay naked. Even a 50 gm glass pack of Nescafe had its foil seal torn off. The paper bags were emptied of contents their dry fruits and then filled again. I suppose this performance make the Jailor realize their importance.

If Leila Fernandes sent paintbrush drawings and indecipherable scribbles of their toddler son, he, in turn, wrote short stories of longing for them. A story he wrote for his son was rendered sensitively. It was short story of longing and heartache:

A little boy lived in a little town in a far-off land. His mummy was with him. She did everything to make the little boy happy. And the little boy was happy. But he was also sad. Because his daddy was not near him. His mummy told him that his daddy was in another far-off land. The little boy and his mummy knew that Daddy loved them and thought of them all the time. One day, it was Christmas time. The little boy made a beautiful star with shiny sparkles on it. He made a hole in it to hang it up. Then he hung the star and went to sleep. When the little boy was fast asleep, the star climbed up in the sky. Up and up it went and like all the stars in the skies, it began to go round and round. And, from behind the bars of his 'house', the little boy's daddy saw that star. And he was happy. Now every night when the little boy goes to sleep, the star he made goes up in the sky where it shines bright so that the little boy's daddy can see it.

On 20 September, he was driven to Tihar Jail in Delhi. Just before he was to leave Hissar, the jail superintendent, asked his 'opinion about his prison'. Like all prisons it was cold, and having spent time in ten prisons in four states, he could say this jail came 'at the bottom but one'. He found 'a singular lack of warmth in Hissar Jail, and a deliberate attempt to subject me to harassment and torture'.

* * *

On 24 September 1976, the CBI filed a charge sheet in a Delhi magistrate's court accusing George and twenty-four others under various provisions of the Indian Penal Code 1860, the Explosive Substance Act 1908 and the Indian Explosive Act 1884.[44] The charge sheet was given worldwide publicity by the government.[45] It accused him of wilfully sabotaging the economy through 'violent, agitational and subversive' trade unionism and conspiring to 'overawe' an elected government.[46] A version of it was published by *Blitz* a month before its judicial appearance; they called it a media trial and made the tabloid liable for contempt of court for selective leaks, but even the court wasn't interested in it.[47]

The CBI made two exhaustive lists; the first composed of twenty-five accused of hatching a conspiracy, and the second was of 526 witnesses who were to support their conspiracy theory. Of the first, all but two, who were absconding, were arrested from different locations in the country and put together at Tihar Jail's Ward No. 17. Ahmedabad-based Congressman Prabhudass Patwari (1909–85) was the oldest of them all; Tulu-speaking Kannadiga Padmanav Shetty (b. 1954) the youngest. A twelve-year-old Padmanav had fled his village to 1960's Bombay, where he found a bearer's work in a hotel. During the day, he worked taking orders, serving food and cleaning tables. In the evening, he attended a night school. In February 1974, he was recruited by the Bombay Labour Union as a full-time organizer.[48] Curiously, Girija Huilgol didn't make to the list of accused, nor did her brother or father. Contrary to the assumption that the railway workers were the force behind George, only two of the accused belonged to the railways. Most came from his trade unions. Gujarat's share in the list of accused was seven, whereas Maharashtra with eleven had a majority presence.

In the second list were witnesses, including the star approvers, the turncoats Bharat Patel and Rewati Kant Sinha, who both were given amnesty. A large number of witnesses came from Gujarat, mainly Baroda, and understandably so, as the explosives were procured and distributed from here. They were employees of the quarry, helpers, wiremen, blasters, drillers, carpenters, record keepers, storekeepers, clerks, drivers and others. Some five hundred and more pieces of documentary evidence were collected. Among them were copies of bill books, invoices, fragments of letters and notes, train and air tickets, diaries, pamphlets, newspaper clippings and magazine stories, telephone records, car-mileage book, guest registers of hotels, the daily collection of cinema halls, etc. Petrol pump books, explosive registers, typewriters were seized as other material evidence. The Gujarati statements of witnesses were rendered expeditiously into English. The alacrity was exceptional; it suggested political motives.

Although the CBI worked hard to unravel the plot, the evidence was mostly circumstantial and drew from statements of accomplices who proved brittle under custodial coercion. The sleuths admitted absence of direct evidence but also their inability to establish the existence of conspiracy without the statements of witnesses.[49] George had adopted fictitious names and disguises and hadn't left any proof of those. Those who met him in hiding were forbidden from taking his picture. The charge sheet simply portrayed several people donning disguises and running around with assumed names and carrying explosives but failed to throw illumination on acts of sabotage that killed or maimed people or destroyed properties.[50] If nothing was executed, what was the conspiracy for?

* * *

The trial began from 4 October 1976, on which date he made his first appearance in public since going underground. They were all produced handcuffed and fettered for a criminal case called the *State of India versus George Fernandes and others.*[51] Reports of their handcuffed appearance

This iconic photograph of George in chains, encrypting India's coming-of-age historical moment, triggered my imagination to do a book on him. For many others, it represents not just what the National Emergency meant but, more significantly, the defiance Indians put against its imposition.

made a worldwide splash but were cursorily mentioned in the Indian media due to censorship. The sight of them handcuffed and tied by a rope to the belt of accompanying policemen became an iconic frozen moment of post-Independence Indian history. The world saw a scintillating George, seizing the moment and making it his most effective vehicle of propaganda. He was transformed into a charismatic individual who had overcome constricting categorical boundaries to go national.

'We, and the chains we bear before you today,' George stirringly read from a prepared statement before Mohammad Shamim, the Chief Metropolitan Magistrate of Delhi, 'are symbols of the entire nation which has been chained and fettered by a dictatorship which has established itself in our country.'[52] If the government had thought handcuffs would make them criminals in the public eye, the strategy backfired. George's fettered raised fist became the most telling image of resistance to the Emergency and its most enduring memory.[53] The humiliation of being chained like a common criminal apart, their rights as prisoners, food in the court, legal interviews with their lawyers were all denied to them. In Malwa's Narsingarh sub-Jail, when he came to know of all these facts, Madhu Limaye lamented, 'Whatever be the reality, but whatever is happening is damaging and dangerous.'[54] At the same time, an elated Richard Fernandes wrote, 'the case was covered by VOA and BBC yesterday very extensively—including your statement to the reporters at the Court.'[55] Internationalizing their predicament was a way to counteract what was happening to them locally. Peter Rindl, an Austrian Communist Party member and trade union activist, visited George at Tees Hazari Court. 'In the bulge of his pocket he carried a small tape recorder, and every time he managed to stand or sit beside me, he would switch it on and signal me to whisper into it all that I had to convey to the world outside.'[56]

Every morning, they were driven in enclosed trucks, escorted by armed guards, to attend court, and returned in the evening to Tihar Jail. While driving through the environs of New Delhi in a police truck, George relived nostalgic memories associated with each of the places rushing past. When he passed the YWCA Hostel on Ashok Road, he wrote in his prison journal, in the last of its pages, 'I first went there twelve years ago, in 1964, with Gloria. Then in 1971 with

Leila.'[57] He was thinking of Gloria Arora, with whom he had lived at his North Avenue house after he became a member of Parliament. Of mixed descent, Gloria Arora, separated from her husband, was a journalist with *Blitz* when they had begun their 'involvement'. She had a minor foot deformity and was hospitalized in Delhi in the late 1960s; Vijay Narain remembered visiting her in the hospital. When George decided to marry Leila Kabir, he had merely dropped a postcard to Gloria informing her of his impending marriage.[58] It had left her bitterly distraught.

A young Swaraj Kaushal (b. 1952) with his newly married firebrand wife Sushma (1952–2020) had arrived in Delhi from Chandigarh to begin their legal practice in the capital's courts. However, the ambitious couple were more inclined towards politics than professional success in the legal arena. Struggling to establish himself in the new city, simultaneously also working to provide legal and other assistance to George in jail, Swaraj Kaushal wrote to him: 'You can take me as the last man with you.'[59] He provided a reasoned rejoinder on handcuffing a prisoner for him to 'cut, mould, or fold the arguments to your choice' in order to present it before the trial court.[60] Years later his visits to jail would still be a fresh memory, when Swaraj Kaushal said, 'I never saw George having even a streak of fear in him. He didn't regret anything. He was ever cheerful and always confident'.[61] But the prison hardships did exist. When asked by a foreign correspondent, 'How are things in jail, Mr Fernandes?' George with a pondering look replied, 'Well, there is not much to bring home, except that the only tap installed in the ward has no water'.[62] But everyone was not equally accommodating and spirited. When Vikram Rao was terminated from service by the *Times of India*, he replied cravenly that he had expected his employers to show 'consideration to my present situation that has come about due to no fault of mine'.[63] Viren Shah contemplated turning an approver to get a reprieve. Arguing separately, Viren Shah said he was a heart patient, a sitting member of Parliament, an executive member of the FICCI, and 'a peaceful and respectable citizen', and hence handcuffing was 'undue humiliation' to him. Such individualistic proclivities apart, kept in two large barracks in a gated yard with a small garden, they remained jovial, played games, read Bhagavad Gita and other sacred books and cooked together in a makeshift kitchen.

They formed a community and shared each other's pains and pleasures. On 29 November, which happened to be the fifth marriage anniversary of Vikram Rao and Sudha, they made a greeting card signed by all twenty-one of them for the couple and their two children. CGK cooked a sweet delicacy Mesur pak to celebrate the occasion.

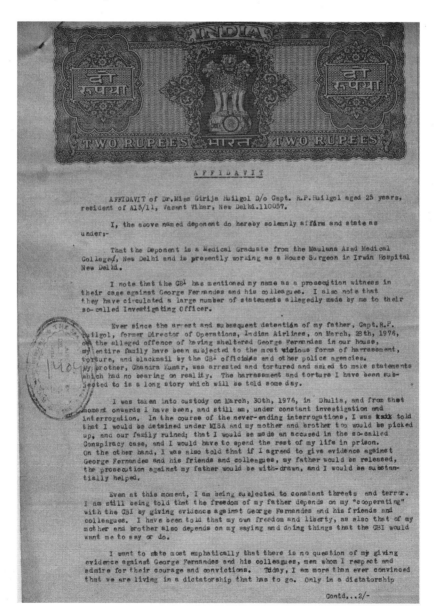

AFFIDAVIT

AFFIDAVIT of Dr.Miss Girija Huilgol D/o Capt. R.P.Huilgol aged 25 years, resident of A15/11, Vasant Vihar, New Delhi.110057.

I, the above named deponent do hereby solemnly affirm and state as under:-

That the Deponent is a Medical Graduate from the Maulana Azad Medical Colleges, New Delhi and is presently working as a House Surgeon in Irwin Hospital New Delhi.

I note that the CBI has mentioned my name as a prosecution witness in their case against George Fernandes and his colleagues. I also note that they have circulated a large number of statements allegedly made by me to their so-called Investigating Officer.

Ever since the arrest and subsequent detention of my father, Capt.R.P. Huilgol, former Director of Operations, Indian Airlines, on March, 28th, 1976, on the alleged offence of having sheltered George Fernandes in our house, my entire family have been subjected to the most vicious forms of harrassment, torture, and blackmail by the CBI officials and other police agencies. My brother, Chandra Kumar, was arrested and tortured and asked to make statements which had no bearing on reality. The harrassment and torture I have been subjected to is a long story which will be told some day.

I was taken into custody on March, 30th, 1976, in Dhulia, and from that moment onwards I have been, and still am, under constant investigation and interrogation. In the course of the never-ending interrogations, I was told that I would be detained under MISA and my mother and brother too would be picked up, and our family ruined; that I would be made an accused in the so-called Conspiracy case, and I would have to spend the rest of my life in prison. On the other hand, I was also told that if I agreed to give evidence against George Fernandes and his friends and colleagues, my father would be released, the prosecution against my father would be with-drawn, and I would be substantially helped.

Even at this moment, I am being subjected to constant threats and terror. I am still being told that the freedom of my father depends on my "cooperating" with the CBI by giving evidence against George Fernandes and his friends and colleagues. I have been told that my own freedom and liberty, as also that of my mother and brother also depends on my saying and doing things that the CBI would want me to say or do.

I want to state most emphatically that there is no question of my giving evidence against George Fernandes and his colleagues, men whom I respect and admire for their courage and convictions. Today, I am more than ever convinced that we are living in a dictatorship that has to go. Only in a dictatorship

Contd...2/-

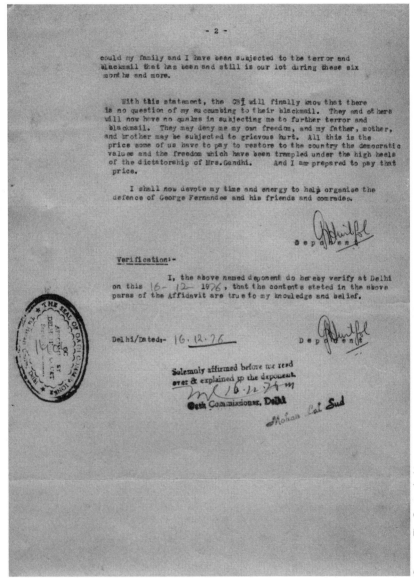

- 2 -

could my family and I have been subjected to the terror and
blackmail that has been and still is our lot during these six
months and more.

With this statement, the CBI will finally know that there
is no question of my succumbing to their blackmail. They and others
will now have no qualms in subjecting me to further terror and
blackmail. They may deny me my own freedom, and my father, mother,
and brother may be subjected to grievous hurt. All this is the
price some of us have to pay to restore to the country the democratic
values and the freedom which have been trampled under the high heels
of the dictatorship of Mrs.Gandhi.   And I am prepared to pay that
price.

I shall now devote my time and energy to help organise the
defence of George Fernandes and his friends and comrades.

                                                    Deponent

Verification:-

          I, the above named deponent do hereby verify at Delhi
on this 16-12-1976, that the contents stated in the above
paras of the Affidavit are true to my knowledge and belief.

Delhi/Dated:- 16.12.76   Deponent

          Solemnly affirmed before me read
          over & explained to the deponent.
                    16.12.76
          Oath Commissioner, Delhi

                                        Mohan Lal Sud

Girija Huilgol's hush-hush affidavit of 16 December 1976 before the trial court accusing
the CBI of torture and harassment to extract information on George went a long way in
disowning the culpability as well as absolving herself from the damaging statements she
had earlier given to the sleuths.

Courtesy: The George Archive

Someone lent George a copy of Eva Forest's *From a Spanish Jail*. A mother of three children, she was a victim of Franco's police for holding a viewpoint contrary to the dictator's regime. While in prison and undergoing interrogation, she started writing a journal to fill her time in a cell that was so restricted as to not allow her to stretch her legs when lying down. Writing therefore was cathartic, easing her repressed emotions on to paper, but necessarily within a boundary set by the censors.[64] While reading her book, George underlined a sentence that read, *I am really very optimistic,* a sentiment that he could truly say for himself as well and identify with. It was while he was still reading her book that he was served with the charge sheet, containing confessions of former friends and strangers. He read them all—'The approvers' statements, the liars' declarations, the renegades' testaments'. But when he read 'two sentences in two statements by two members of one family' it hurt him terribly. Not only her father and brother but Girija Huilgol too, under fear or duress, had given damaging confessions. He least expected this return gift for standing by her father in his difficult days. The element of physicality which existed between them had brought him her loyalty and devotion. Their betrayal brought forth a surge of words and he began to write his emotion-ridden journal, suspended since his transfer from Hissar Jail.

The betrayal weighed upon Girija Huilgol as well. George's legal team was making attempts to win over crucial witnesses, make them retract their testimonies. Rewati Kant Sinha was told that his needs would be taken care of if only he pulled away. But he remained uncertain about the promise. Worried about Fredrick D'Sa, George asked his brother Louie Fernandes to find out what he was up to as 'he is a key witness'. But their greatest success was in winning back Girija Huilgol. In the middle of December, just when the trial was to begin, she turned hostile. She submitted an affidavit, accusing the CBI of coercion, torture and threats.[65] 'In the course of never-ending interrogations,' Girija Huilgol said in a statement secretly drafted and surreptitiously presented in the court, 'I was told that I would be detained under MISA and my mother and brother would be picked up, and our family ruined; that I would be made an accused in the so-called Conspiracy case, and I would have to spend the rest of my life in prison.'

She was told her well-being depended on her 'cooperating'. Having shed the fear of the CBI, she said in a stirring sentence, she would now stand by George, whatever be the consequences. Her statement left the CBI befuddled. The government banned it from publication.[66] The deed done, she won praise from George but it didn't endear her to his comrades, who persisted in blaming her for his arrest. She continued to visit him in jail or court, and provide for his needs. In one of her letters, she wrote, 'Give the trousers and the chappals (if not of the right size) to Ravi so that I can exchange them. I've got the stuff ready—only to be dispatched. The delay was thanks to people you thought would help.'[67] But whatever she did, she would never regain the trust he once reposed in her.

In the underground once you are in, you are tainted. The taint keeps you glued as long as it is humanly possible. Rewati Kant Sinha thought he could sell out his comrades and save his children's future. Bharat Patel thought his blow-by-blow account would give him respite. They all paid in their way. Rewati Kant Sinha died a destitute in 1979, reduced to beggary towards the end of his life. Girija Huilgol slipped into anonymous existence.[68]

The Socialist Party held a special national convention at Bombay in November 1976 to deliberate over the formation of 'a single party out of various democratic parties and groups'.[69] George from inside Tihar Jail expressed his disapproval of the design and urged them to 'continue the struggle against the dictatorship'.[70] In his and Madhu Limaye's absence, the leadership of the party had fallen in the hands of N.G. (Nanasaheb) Goray and Surendra Mohan. Goray was never arrested, while Surendra Mohan was arrested and then released. Neither of them had a charismatic personality or popular base; both thoroughly abhorred Lohia's activistic politics and possessed a marked dislike for the people's struggle. George's rejection of the one-party idea made them silently fume and see in him an obstacle. They also feared that the rising inferno of his trial would consign them to oblivion. Consequently, there was a move to dislodge him from the leadership, a move that was finally scuttled after 'intense lobbying and fierce speeches, threats and ultimatums'. When he was asked to lend his weight to the fund-raising drive for George's defence, an emotionally challenged N.G. Goray muttered insolently, 'Did he ask us, before he started all this?'[71] N.G. Goray's 'hostility' was well known, but the whole of the 'Poona Brahmin' gang was playing a 'deep game' against George.[72] Besides, Surendra Mohan declared that as the general secretary he was the last word on the party policy. Madhu Limaye, however, remained true to his support for 'political prisoners, no matter what their ideological hue or methodology'. 'The new party,' Madhu Limaye anticipated well in advance, 'may not agree with the views of George Fernandes and other co-accused. But they are our comrades. It would be disgraceful to disown them. I certainly own them, and applaud their courage.'[73]

A Baroda Dynamite Case Defence Committee was constituted on 23 December 1976, under the aegis of the venerable J.B. Kripalani.[74] JP appealed for contributions to the defence fund.[75] Finances were needed to pay legal fees. Ram Jethmalani who had located abroad fearing arrest 'advised the appointment of his daughter' for legal services.[76] His daughter Rani was based in Bombay and the trial was taking place at Delhi, so he demanded money for her expenses. 'He told us that his daughter had to resign her job as a lecturer to take up this case,' Surur Hoda wrote to George from London where negotiations with Ram were taking place. Jethmalani's demand became so persistent that George eased him out. As for other things, the AIRF removed him from presidentship but more worrying were the actions of trade union organizations founded by him in Bombay.[77] 'Let me put it very frankly to you', a source informed him, 'you have very few friends left in Bombay.' The Bombay Taximen's Association captured by a group inimical to his interest expelled him from its body.[78] The Municipal Mazdoor Union though continued to express loyalty. 'Wherever you are, the municipal workers are always remembering you. You are in their hearts and will be their guiding star forever', they wrote to him.[79]

If he felt betrayed by his closest comrades in the underground, fearing a 'sell-out', George roped in JP, who agreed with him on continuing the struggle against the Emergency.[80] Indira Gandhi desired the Opposition to admit that 'what they did in the past was wrong', but also accept that 'everything she has done since 26 June

1975, is all in the best interests of the country'. But the democratic Opposition parties were in an unseemly hurry to merge into a single entity and to establish a dialogue with the government. George was 'against the merger and dialogue' obsession until the pre-Emergency conditions were restored.[81] His party's general secretary, Surendra Mohan responded that the four parties were equal participants in the struggle against the Emergency and made ample sacrifices equally, and therefore to doubt their credentials would be unjustified.[82] He gave a clean chit to the RSS: 'There have been aberrations in the behaviour of RSS leadership though the younger elements have stuck to their guns.' He even held a wishful vision when he warned that leadership of the unified party would be taken over by the militant socialists if it wavered in their opposition to the Emergency. He dangled a carrot before George, saying these parties were associated with his Defence Committee. Even as Surendra Mohan wrote this, the leaders of the Socialist Party itself, leave alone of the other three Opposition parties, were even more keen to isolate George. 'Despite the opportunities that were available,' he wrote to Surendra Mohan, 'you have not briefed me, let alone consult me.'

Just when he was writing this to Surendra Mohan, Indira Gandhi announced the general elections. Muffled for nineteen months, the Opposition was unfavourably placed in the electoral fight, he felt. 'Evidently, she believes that whenever she calls the tune and whatever the tune she calls, the Opposition will dance to it.'[83] He called for boycott of elections, but his letter was not placed before the Socialist Party's National Committee. Making a 'humble and personal' request, Surendra Mohan wrote to him, 'At this juncture, we might have to go unitedly.'[84] Before the Emergency, Surendra Mohan had opposed the merger plan but was now all for it. It seemed ironical if not lamentable. Going a step ahead, Surendra Mohan entreated George to offer himself as a candidate for the new Janata Party (that by that time had magically come into being) from 'Bombay or anywhere else'. George was unwilling to give in, even refusing to be assuaged by a scribbled note from JP, which said, 'The country, particularly the youth are with you.'[85]

One of the youth, Girija Huilgol, established Youth for George Fernandes and Others to campaign for his release. She wondered, 'how the Socialists can talk of elections when their own party chairman is still being held a prisoner under a case to overthrow the government!'[86] She announced her resolve to sit in a fast unto death in front of the house of Morarji Desai (who had been released from prison on 18 January 1977). The party's desire to have George fight the election from jail was not liked by her, making her wonder, sardonically, 'The man because of whom they are getting this chance should be inside, while all the other nincompoops should be outside?' She vented a generally perceived sentiment when she said, 'they are trying to isolate you.' Many thought being bogged down by the daily court proceedings of the Conspiracy Case would prove his 'political end', but, as Swaraj Kaushal wrote, 'the lifelong dedication of a man cannot be made futile so easily'.[87] His close comrades began to pester him to 'contest to win', but there were many others who advised him against taking the plunge. 'Lok Sabha would not add any substantive feathers to your present stature. In fact, boycotting the elections would.'[88] A 'deeply depressed' George, still keen on the Socialist Party's independent existence, resigned from chairmanship of the party that was soon going to disappear because of the march of events.[89] He declined to contest, stating that the 'question does not arise'. The news of his resignation, however, enthused party cadres as he was not alone in holding a view that it was going to be a fraudulent election.[90] Lacking in organization, the election could only be won by the Janata Party by building on the passion unleashed by its announcement.

But after Jagjivan Ram and others announced their upsetting severance from the Congress at the beginning of February, an enthused George congratulated each of them for the courage shown. He had been critical of the Communist Party's role during the Emergency but now asked for its rehabilitation in the Opposition camp, perhaps due to his desire to counterbalance the RSS-backed element in the newly formed Janata Party. It had widely been perceived that except for the RSS-backed Jan Sangh, the rest of the political parties had turned non-entities. Snehalata Reddy had written to him: 'It should not be forgotten that outside the RSS cadre there is not much material in terms of dedicated youth which can be brought forward to national politics.'[91] Many people had their reservations about the Jan Sangh. Leila Fernandes for one was unhappy about it and said so.[92] Finally, it was Madhu Limaye who convinced George to fight from Muzaffarpur, a constituency that was a socialist stronghold nurtured by JP, and from where Asoka Mehta and J.B. Kripalani had been formerly elected.

With the fierce temerity with which he had been through several other occasions in the past, with the blind passion with which he had gone into the underground, with the same burning intensity now he pitched into elections. Even while the star approvers deposed before the court and George attended the trial unfailingly, listening, taking notes, crafting legal strategies, from inside the prison cell, he also ceaselessly directed his campaign in Muzaffarpur. 'I have to fight the election from prison. I need your help' was a common refrain of the numerous letters he wrote to friends and colleagues outside. He wrote pamphlets and designed posters, sent messages for funds and directed colleagues to go and camp at Muzaffarpur. A pamphlet in Hindi with a biographical sketch of his journey from Mangalore to Bombay, of his early struggles and emergence as a trade union leader, his inter faith marriage, his underground resistance to the National Emergency and continued incarceration, his felicity with many languages, and his love and reverence for the Gita as much as for the Bible, was printed. The emphasis was on his self, not on any party. Except for P. D'Mello and Ram Manohar Lohia, no other leaders were named. He was so intensely concentrated on campaign work that even his wife wondered at his earlier fierce rejectionist posture. She thought his agreeing to fight had something to do with Jagjivan Ram coming out of the Congress. The socialists had held Ram in high esteem. When Kamalapati Tripathi said Jagjivan Ram's departure from the Congress was the bursting of an abscess, George from the Tihar Jail sent a rebuttal to 'Panditji' in stinging terms: 'When did Babuji grow into an abscess? Is the fact that because Babuji belongs to a socially downtrodden caste made you call him an abscess?' He reminded Tripathi, who had been waiting in the wings hoping for the political demise of Mrs Gandhi, of the upper-caste arrogance of Lalit Narain Mishra who had referred to Ram as a 'Kala Bhoot'.[93]

On 26 February 1977, he wrote to the Shahi Imam of Delhi's Jama Masjid, who replied the next day.[94] Each complimented the other for his patriotism and obedience to the call of conscience to electorally defeat Indira Gandhi. The correspondence was translated into Urdu, printed and distributed widely among the constituents, when it was found it was effective with Muslim voters who viewed the merged party askance.[95] Sushma Swaraj went with George's mother Alice Fernandes to Muzaffarpur and translated her speeches at public meetings. With three of her six sons in prison, she was a mother on the prowl. Her 'A Mother's Appeal' was printed and released. After detailing all that the family had already gone through, she asked the voters of Muzaffarpur to vote out the Congress Party. In its publicity, that party claimed, 'You vote for yourself when you vote for Congress.' For Alice Fernandes, however, it was an invitation to barbarism. 'She has done it to us. She will do it to you if you give her another chance,' she told people in her speeches.[96] The trade unions founded by him in Bombay sent printed posters, including one of George in chains and behind bars, which was used popularly. Labour leaders and political activists from across the country came to Muzaffarpur to lend a hand in the campaign. The local lawyer Sharda Mal played host to visiting people. Usha Mehta raised funds through her contacts among the industrialists. 'Finally,' she wrote to him, after giving details of collections made and through whom, 'children have allowed me to proceed to Muzaffarpur—their condition is theirs will be the first house you will be visiting in Bombay', leaving unsaid the obvious: after he had won and was released from jail.[97] The young socialist Mohan Singh (1945–2013) after his release from jail went straight to Muzaffarpur. He found the euphoria infectious and concluded, 'victory is certain'. Amazed, he wrote to George, 'I don't know what has happened. Don't ask about the trend. Had you been out and here, you would have been astonished.' When Indira Gandhi was visiting

Muzaffarpur, George wrote to her asking to be taken along, as her government was not heeding his plea for parole.[98] That he was not released to campaign went to the heart of the electorate and tilted the balance in his favour.[99] The election campaign donned a decidedly moral overtone, and the battle was seen as a war between forces of good and evil, in which good would undoubtedly emerge victoriously and evil would be exorcized. He was seen as a virtuous man who would bring about a fundamental change in this flood-prone constituency. 'Our George is certainly in jail, but every child, youth or old here will play the role of George. They will snatch you out of jail by giving you a momentous victory', wrote a young boy. Many people signed printed pledges and offered their services. The young collected funds by selling tea and polishing shoes. The letters he received were full of eulogizing salutations. He had become a 'symbol of revolution' and Muzaffarpur the 'seat of revolt'. When denied even a request for transfer to a jail in Muzaffarpur, he decided to go on hunger strike, stirring JP to write, 'not to risk his life'.[100] George, however, decided to go through the ordeal. 'It is the only way I can express my solidarity with all those who are fighting against such heavy odds', he replied to the revered leader.[101] The fast began on 11 March, and he remained without food for five days. He lost weight and when he suffered from dehydration and nausea, he was taken to hospital.[102] Telegrams poured in from his constituents, assuring him he would not just win but win with a record margin. In the evening of 16 March, the election day in Muzaffarpur, he accepted a glass of orange juice from his mother, who had just returned from week-long campaigning. A telegram from Leila Fernandes that read, *Terribly concerned. Please do not endanger your life. Love,* was delivered to him at Tihar Jail, two days after he ended his fast.[103]

After many false hopes, Lawrence Fernandes was finally released from Bangalore prison on 8 March. He carried signs of torture on his body and walked with a limp. On the same day, Michael Fernandes was also released from Belgaum Jail. Their release received wide publicity. Aloysius (Louie) Fernandes felt a little left out, writing to an acquaintance, 'The whole family has been busy hitting headline

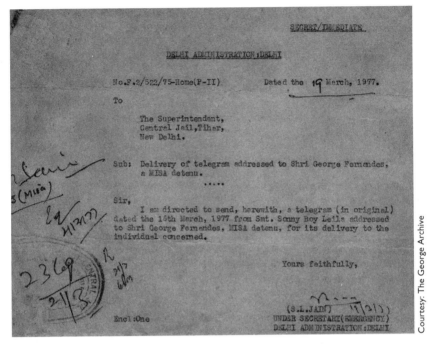

The covering letter to Leila Fernandes' accompanying telegram of 16 March 1977 that expressed concern over her husband's fast in jail took five days to reach her husband.

after headline.'[104] He was the one running errands from one jail to another or taking Mother to meet them. Both Fernandes brothers were taken straight to Mangalore to join the election campaign of the Janata Party. They were given a hero's welcome, taken in procession around the city and exhibited as live examples of Emergency excesses. Soon, Lawrence Fernandes, with a stick in his hand, took a flight to Patna en route to Muzaffarpur, where he reached on 16 March, the election day.

Two months before this, Snehalata Reddy was dead on 20 January. In prison since 1 May 1976, she was released on parole when her asthma grew acute.[105] George's reaction to her death is not recorded, although after he became a minister in the Janata Party government, on his first visit to Bangalore, he would go directly from the airport to the Reddy home to offer his condolences. They might have been romantically involved. Her relationship with her husband had been a rocky one, tending to improve in her last months. Snehalata Reddy had kept George informed not just about Karnataka politics but also sought his counsel on her family affairs, while he was underground. Soon after Leila Fernandes' passport was impounded in January 1976, an envious Snehalata Reddy had written, 'poor, Leila, where would she get asylum', somewhat mocking, somewhat pleased. 'In 2006, when my father died,' Nandana Reddy, the daughter, summed up, 'George did not come.' 'I think,' she said with empathy, 'he felt guilty in getting my family involved. He held himself responsible for my mother's death.'[106]

* * *

Why did the Emergency's authoritarianism fail? Why would Indira Gandhi order elections? It failed, George said, because it lacked an enduring infrastructure to sustain itself. In India, responsibility for maintaining an authoritarian regime fell on the 'storm-troopers' of the Youth Congress, which was not the same as the discipline of rule by armed forces.[107]

George's underground resistance—its rhetoric and objective, means and method, aims and objectives—were inspired by Europe's experience in resisting the Nazi occupation. Therefore, his steadfast identification of Indira Gandhi as an Indian version of Hitlerian dictatorship was a situational necessity. In his view, the Emergency was a unique experience, not comparable even to colonial British rule as the latter were not 'fascist dictators'. Further, the British had 'a conscience, a thing that Mrs Nehru Gandhi either was not born with or learnt to live without a long time ago'. Third, the British colonial rulers were answerable to their own people back home, but Indira Gandhi was to none. How fair was his comparative assessment is debatable, but his spontaneous resort to the underground resistance is indicative of the 'cold, calculating and ruthless' power she had come to acquire. The Emergency was not a democratic aberration, as many would make it out to be, but according to him it was a dictatorship. Like the Europeans who thought the Nazis would have an empire extensive and long-lasting as those of Rome, Babylon or the Ottomans, in a similar vein George thought Indira Gandhi was here for perpetuity. Once he had drawn the contours of that dictatorship in his mind, he was pretty sure the ideology of resistance was secondary to resistance itself. He would not waste time on the violence vs non-violence debate and was a trifle impatient with those who raised it.

His characterization of Indira Gandhi's regime, although evocative, was not appreciated, both in domestic politics and international diplomacy. At the Socialist International, some member states asked to be dissociated from a report made by George and sent through CGK that likened Indira Gandhi to Hitler.[108] Internationally, she was still admired. The Emergency's excesses failed to dent her popularity. Mario Soares, the socialist prime minister of Portugal even invited Indira Gandhi to visit Lisbon. British Labour Party leader Michael Foot and Jennie Lee, the widow of labour leader Aneurin Bevan, visited India and sang paeans to her. Amnesty International which had adopted several prisoners to work for their release and advocate their unjust incarceration, was not keen to adopt George and those under the shadow of the Baroda Conspiracy case as they were charged criminally. It was therefore important for domestic dissenters to discredit her in the eyes of her admirers. In December 1976, George wrote to Mario Soares dissuading him from inviting her and telling him how she had adversely affected the Indian socialists. He was sour at their overlooking the excesses.[109] Indira Gandhi had successfully painted the Opposition stalwarts to be the anarchists. When told repeatedly by the Opposition members that her government was fascist, Mrs Gandhi took to defining the term on the floor of Parliament. 'It means a situation where a small group of people want to enforce their views, their desires on the larger group through force, through intimidation, through coercion.'[110] Clearly, having won majorities in elections, she considered the Opposition to be that small, unrepresentative group who were making an illicit scramble for power. It was JP who was fascist, she said, as his movement was asking for the dissolution of elected state assemblies!

The 1970s saw an enduring dream rudely broken. India's Gandhian innocence was finally stripped from her body politic. No longer was man unblemished, a mute victim of a satanic system, as Gandhi had said. If that man was not with the ruling regime, if he didn't side with it, wasn't committed enough to it, he was satanic, was the new ruling dictum. It was a decade in which India's moral claims generated during a long-drawn freedom struggle were finally shed. Parties in contention took to legal technicalities to beat each other. The Opposition claim of electoral malpractices hid the stark reality that neither had Indira Gandhi received the state government's support in the constituency she fought against Raj Narain in 1971, nor was her victory by a slender margin.[111] On the other hand, Indira Gandhi's claim that the Emergency had nothing to do with the Allahabad judgment did not sound convincing either.

It was a decade when to dream was treason. JP was accused of sedition when he asserted the people's right to recall their elected representatives. Sanjay Gandhi ridiculed the communist reds, saying, 'If you take all the people in the Communist Party, the bigwigs—even the not-so-bigwigs—I don't think you'd find a richer or more corrupt people anywhere.' He slammed the public sector for its inefficiency, corruption and mounting losses, and extolled the enterprising private sector.[112] Indira Gandhi on one occasion said her father was a saint in politics whereas she was a real-time politician, and therefore knew how to be Machiavellian. The vices that Nehru described as grievous became to Indira Gandhi virtues of 'pure politics' practised with all the required elan. The Emergency, Vinoba Bhave innocently said, was a celebration in discipline. But he ignored how it infantilized Indians into delinquents meriting no right to free expression.

While the Opposition cited Indira Gandhi's authoritarian and corrupt rule as the reason for their agitation, she sought to put the spotlight on 'the circumstances which created chaotic conditions in the nation before the Emergency'. In her detailed reply to the Shah Commission, instituted by the Janata government to inquire into excesses committed during the Emergency, she said, 'For two years preceding the Emergency the country was in the grip of grave crisis.'[113] One of the dominant features of her eighteen-year-long rule, interrupted only nominally by the Janata Party's two-year reign, was her tendency to blame others for the ills that afflicted the nation. She always had a foreign hand to crib about. Blame displacement is a symptom often found in deeply frustrated personalities. They lack the faculty to own responsibility for events occurring under their domain. Why Indira Gandhi would fall victim to such a deep psychological malady is difficult to understand. After all, she was the only prime minister ever to be hailed as 'Durga', and 'the only *man* in her cabinet'. Her biographer Katherine Frank points to her deep sense of inadequacy that often made her stubborn, insensitive and harsh, while at the same time brought out her motherly instincts for mute victims.[114] Indira Gandhi's exemplary policy on wildlife that gave India her Project Tiger and national parks was an example of her sensitivity.[115] In his analysis of Indira Gandhi, Ashish Nandy also makes a similar point.[116] She openly admitted her compatriot politicians' lack of faith in her. She generated fear as long as she seemed all-conquering, but that fear degenerated into vitriolic confrontation once her power seemed to slacken. Each of them who once crawled before her and sang paeans in her praise, turned into abusive adversaries as her popularity seemed to wane. Not just D.K. Barooah, who coined the phrase 'Indira is India, India is Indira', a slogan that always reminded George of her Hitlerian trait, but other former stalwarts of her regime as well were the first to jump out. Jagjivan Ram—powerful, rich, resourceful—whom Indira Gandhi always had in her cabinet (though she never trusted him), was one who not just piloted the Emergency through the Lok Sabha and poured out eloquence in its favour but also remained throughout the Emergency glued to her cabinet and meekly swallowed humiliation. The same man, when he sensed the direction of the wind, jumped the line, crossed the fence and formed what ironically came to be named 'Congress for Democracy'.[117] Or Y.B. Chavan, the man perpetually in doubt about when to show his real face, kept dangling between being a supporter in public and a challenger in private. In that duality he lived and died, as he unfurled the banner of revolt soon after her defeat in 1977, only to make a homecoming with the return of Indira Gandhi after the Janata debacle.

The Emergency was an inauguration of a new India, an India that had finally overcome its reticence generated in the crucible of the freedom struggle. Indira Gandhi's state was not just committed to removing constraints on consumption but it also made an audacious leap to control people's libidos. Its penetration was so deep and wide that if it raised expectations, it also scared people. It sought to see people merely as producing machines: raise production on factory floors and in fields, but limit your reproduction, was its most defining claim to national efficiency. India would never be the same again. She would be Indira Gandhi-like: Machiavellian, scheming, ruthless or, as George said, a 'congenital liar'; after all, as the Congress slogan put it: India was Indira, Indira was India. Emergency was a coming-of-age event for India, after Indians, having been treated for so long by her feudal kings and colonial masters as juveniles, needed regulation.

It was Indira Gandhi's fear-inducing power, her perpetual, pathological tendency to displace blame on to her opponents, that frustrated her political colleagues and made them swear against her as much as fear her retribution. It was in this context that George's letters to her from the underground, marked for their vitriolic tone, for their direct attack on her moral standards, were to be gauged. 'What is one to do with a congenital liar like you?' was George's opening salvo in a letter written to 'Mrs Indira Nehru Gandhi' on 14 October 1975. The letter to 'Madame Dictator', if of any historical worth, is evidence of the man's political frustration at a prime minister whose ways were not always morally explicable and who led a 'campaign of lies' against her fellow politicians. It was this frustration against a quicksilvery, slippery prime minister that made him resort to the underground to register his protest at her 'fascist dictatorship'. If his inspiration came from the underground led by JP, Lohia and others during the 'Quit India' movement of 1942, it got strengthened by his reading of the history of the American trade union movement. *Dynamite: The Story of Class Violence in America* by Louis Adamic was first published in 1934.[118] As its title reveals, the book deals with violence as a means used by the underdog. During his first ministerial tenure in 1977–79,

George received two copies of the book, first in 1977 and another in September 1979, sent by the same person. It is not certain whether he read the book or was informed about its content. But knowing George, and given his involvement with militant trade union activities, it would not be mere speculation to state that he was aware of the phenomenon of violence in the labour movement in America and took inspiration from it.

11

Janata Days

In the fifth general elections held in March 1977, George registered an impressive victory. It was when the Emergency was still in force and he in jail; it was an election he had at first refused to participate in and called for his party to boycott as well. While he was exercised over it, it was Madhu Limaye who presented him with a fait accompli. In a five-short-sentence letter, endorsed as well by JP, Madhu Limaye urged him to contest from Muzaffarpur 'in the interest of party unity and for political considerations'.[1] Seconding his proposal were the two others who though they could have been candidates themselves wouldn't fight because they wanted him to win. The Bihar strongman Karpoori Thakur, too, endearingly scribbled, 'If you don't [fight] there will not be any relationship left between us.' Armed with such goodwill, urging him to take the plunge, Madhu Limaye predicted, 'You will win with a thumping majority'. Leila Fernandes, who was unsure if he should contest at all, was unhappy at the turn of events. 'I read your long statement urging a boycott of elections', she wrote from Charlottesville, 'and learnt later that you are contesting.'[2] More than surprise, her words were dipped in sarcasm that he chose to ignore. She was uncertain about the outcome as well. 'Well, I certainly shall be keeping my fingers crossed that your friends' campaign on your behalf will get you elected.'

He was elected, his nearest Congress rival trounced by a margin of more than three lakh votes. Although the newly formed Janata

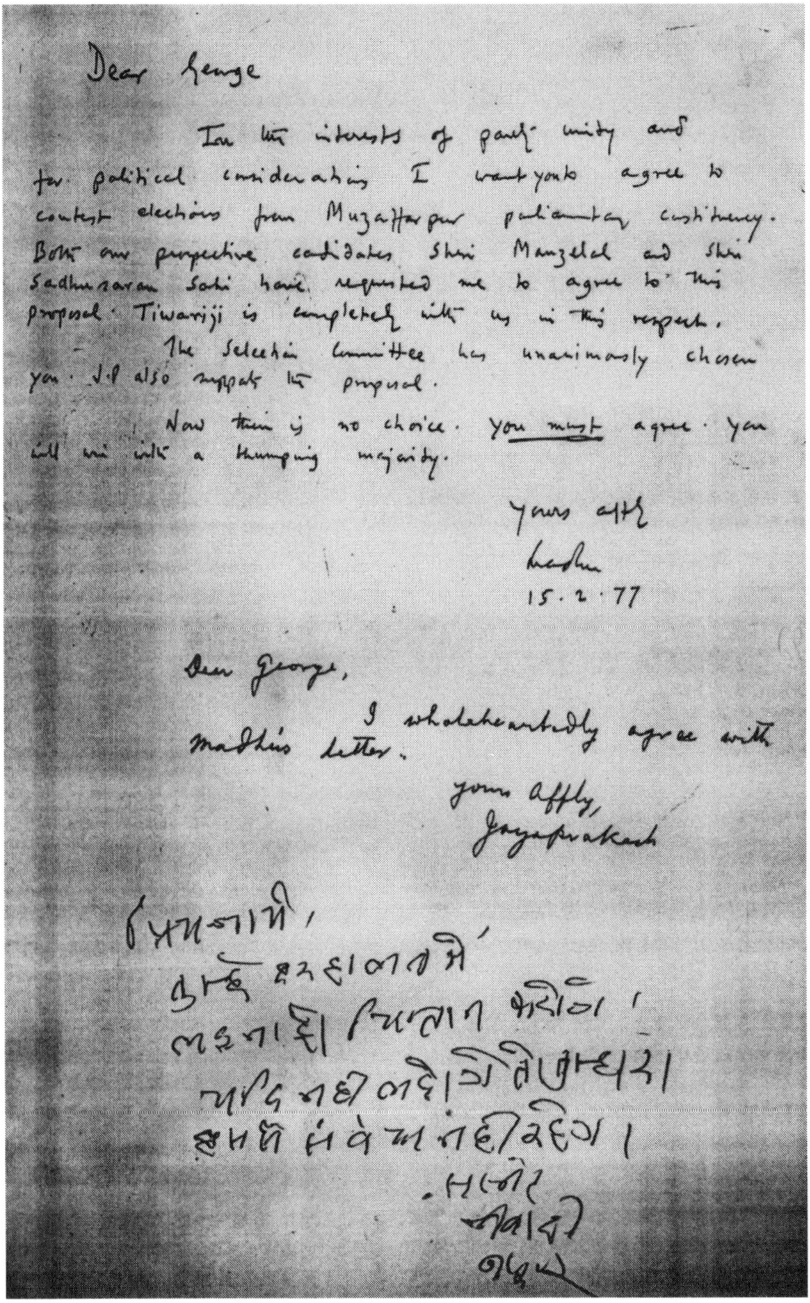

Dear George

In the interests of party unity and for political consideration I want you to agree to contest elections from Muzaffarpur parliamentary constituency. Both our perspective candidates Shri Manjelal and Shri Sadhusaran Sahi have requested me to agree to this proposal. Tiwariji is completely with us in this respect.

The Selection committee has unanimously chosen you. JP also supports this proposal.

Now there is no choice. You must agree. You will win with a thumping majority.

yours affly
Madhu
15.2.77

Dear George,
I wholeheartedly agree with Madhu's letter.

yours affly,
Jayaprakash

(भूमिहारी,
हरे हरदीवानमें
लड़गादी बिहान करेंगे।
गाँव नहीं बड़ेंगे तो पाएँगे।
हमें मने मन नहीं रहेगा।
.मेरे
ग्वावे)
ल(ब्द)

Madhu Limaye's proposal of George's candidature from Muzaffarpur in the 1977 general election was endorsed by Jayaprakash Narayan and seconded by Karpoori Thakur and Ramanand Tiwari from Bihar.

Party swept the north Indian scene, the manner of his victory in a constituency he had never been to, voted by a people who had never heard him speak, established his invulnerable charisma. He was a hero, an anti-authoritarian fighter who had put at stake his everything in the fight to restore democracy. Contesting from inside jail, refused parole, even his request for transfer to a jail in the constituency denied, it was indeed a victory sweeter and more emphatic than his first-ever win in 1967. But from inside the prison, it had seemed the odds were stacked against him. However courageous his mien, he feared as well. In an imploring letter to a socialist comrade in Bihar, he wrote of his wife and toddler son who were in exile and declared: 'For me, this election is the only way to save myself from a hangman's noose.'[3] His was truly a people's campaign, run on an inexhaustible enthusiasm and

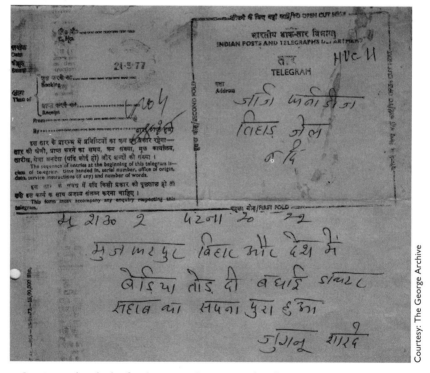

Courtesy: The George Archive

One among hundreds of enthusiastic telegrams sent by admirers and sympathizers on George's victory at Muzaffarpur in the 1977 election, expressing happiness at the the crumbling of the chain before the mass upsurge of voters in his favour.

transparent sincerity. Later, he would acknowledge it as a 'peaceful and democratic revolution' brought about by the common man.[4] Even though young men sat at the town square with shoeshine boxes and makeshift tea stalls, funds were not much required. His constituents were 'overwhelmingly proud for having a leader of your stature to guide us'.[5] Many worked voluntarily for his election campaign. To prove that they had a role in his victory by working as agents of his, they sent him agent passes issued by the presiding officers at polling booths.

* * *

From early on it was clear that the Janata Party would never become a cohesive unit. Although its coming into being had set forth great enthusiasm and generated terrific hope, its formation was essentially a reaction to the Emergency. Having come together under exigent circumstances, it was at best a simmering cauldron, of all but one steel-clad Congress breakaways, distinguished not by what had brought about their respective splits but by the timing of it. They were united in their common antipathy to Indira Gandhi's rising power. The socialists, who once had visions of being an alternative, now after long years of daunting existence were depleted, facing ideological, organizational and electoral meltdown. They were a much-shrunken lot. The expansive one, the Jan Sangh, without the Congress roots and with the backing of Rashtriya Swayamsevak Sangh (RSS), itself a fifty-year-old organization providing a trained, purposeful cadre to build upon, was in the ascendant. It was confident of its organizational prowess and ideological conviction, and although prone to flex its muscles, was willing to bide its time. There were others, caste- and personality based ambitious formations. They, working most often at cross purposes, made the Janata Party a motley group. In March 1977, when Morarji Desai (1896–1995) became India's fourth prime minister, he was at eighty-one an old man, hardened by the rigours of lifelong self-discipline.[6] If any one group had contributed to the making of his image as a politician on the right, it was the socialists.[7] Chandrasekhar (1927–2007), a socialist Congressman who had been instrumental in casting shadows on Morarji Desai's integrity, was now president of a party that had Desai as prime minister.

Still another, Madhu Limaye who was now Janata Party general secretary, had been a determined bête noire of Desai's. Chandrasekhar and Limaye had consistently raised the issue of his son's controversial business links in Parliament and outside. Several people who at various times had hurled mutually disparaging accusations, called names and demanded inquiries against each other were to work together in a new government. Their present was heavily laden with an acrimonious past, rankling memories and grievous grudges. Of course, Morarji Desai was the first of the 'Big Three' in the Janata Party. But other two of the triumvirate, Charan Singh (1902–87) and Jagjivan Ram (1908–86), would not think any less of themselves. Like Morarji Desai, they were also lifelong Congressmen, having chipped off in Indira Gandhi's time: Charan Singh in 1967, while Jagjivan Ram was a minister in her cabinet almost until the Emergency ended.[8]

Faced with such a constellation of friends, it was no wonder George got into the charmed circle of Morarji Desai even while it was Madhu Limaye who pushed him into the cabinet. He had seen the old man staking his life to get Indira Gandhi to dissolve the discredited Gujarat assembly. Impressed by his iron will and resolute character, George would also pick up Morarji's practice of urine therapy. One of the first acts of the new government was to drop all charges against George, including that of hatching a 'deep-rooted criminal conspiracy to overawe the central government'. It was a controversial measure, spinning forth a frothy censure.[9] However, Rajmohan Gandhi who edited *Himmat* extolled, 'The man who was painted as a conspirator has become a national hero.'[10] On 28 March, he was made the minister for Post and Telegraph (P&T), but the portfolio was not to his liking. He saw his responsibility not commensurate with his halo. It was such a put-down that he wept. 'At Surendra Nagar P&T guest house where he was staying, I went to see him at breakfast,' recalled a long-time colleague.[11] 'What does Morarji think?', a fuming and slighted George asked Arun Kumar Panibaba (1941–2016). 'What insult you can inflict on George who had come after so much struggle, and after so many beatings to the national platform. From that benchmark he climbed into Morarji Desai's trusted group.'

Two different men were now to work together. A correspondent noted the anomaly, 'I think of your background with the prime minister and how fate has brought you together. You may have a very great role, being a true friend to him and thereby helping him to fulfil his destiny and India's.'[12] As a minister, he began to work at a 'killing pace', but was advised to, 'with your characteristic militancy, claim and fight for a daily spell of solitude'.[13] It was to no avail. On 31 March, he outlined in Parliament, 'certain broad policy changes which I am contemplating'.[14] The emphasis was on providing postal services in the rural areas: 'hilly, tribal and backward areas will receive special priority'. A fortnight later he was at Amsterdam to attend a meeting of the Bureau of Socialist International. Before leaving, he wrote to Morarji Desai, 'For any messages you want me to carry and for any assignments you wish me to undertake, I am at your disposal.'[15] The next day, he wrote again, 'My Ministry is presently concerned with examining the question of selecting the telephone exchange switching system for manufacture in the country. Messrs Phillipe in Holland is one of the important manufacturers of the electronic switching system in the world. I propose at Amsterdam visiting their factories.'[16] His practice of keeping the prime minister in the loop brought them close. Soon, he would claim to have with Morarji Desai 'a tremendous rapport, a rapport I have with few others'.[17]

Leila Fernandes returned two months after the elections, and when at first little Sonny Boy shrank away from the arms of his father before nestling into them with the gusto of a toddler, she noticed her husband was a strangely changed man. It was a wife's gaze of suspicion. However, a friendly reporter from the outside feelingly wrote, 'After all the sufferings you and your family have been through I hope you and they will be fully restored. "I make all things new" Jesus promised.'[18] The suffering and its befitting vindication by a massive electoral victory was a constant motif in the correspondence he received in those days.[19] There were those shunted or superseded by the previous regime who wrote exposing the skulduggery of those still occupying official positions despite the change of regime. 'MISA detenue during Emergency' was a qualification to claim patronage.[20] Anonymous

Courtesy: Fredrick D'Sa, Bombay Taximen's Union

Leila Fernandes return to India after the Emergency: Leila with their son Sushanto being
received by George upon their return from the United States.

letters tagged with photos of 'Prince' [Sanjay Gandhi] with persons
complained against were signed simply as 'one who suffered during
the DARK DAYS'. Demanding reparation, they wrote, 'God has saved
you to do justice'.[21] George, too, kept their past behaviour in mind
while responding to them. To one V.L. Shanbhag, who sent a long list
of policy priorities for the Janata government, he asked, 'Were you so
scared during the emergency that you refused to take a picture of mine
to Bombay for an election poster? I am surprised.'[22] Invited to speak
at a commemoration ceremony to release a postal stamp, he called
industrialists 'rats' for 'kowtowing to those in authority' during the
Emergency. Malice would be the dominating theme in the functioning
of the Janata Party government.

    Suddenly, on 7 July, he was given the charge of Industry, replacing
the incumbent, a Jan Sangh nominee with a controversial tenure. The
move to a high-profile ministry was not a simple tale of talent-hunting
or compulsions of a coalition. Morarji Desai's choice of George to lead
the Industry Ministry underlined a deep level of confidence the prime
minister came to possess in him. But the appointment sent 'shudders

down the spine of India's industrial establishment'. The chips in the stock exchange dived. The very next day, he made a 'few introductory observations' in Parliament about the industrial policy while moving a Demand of Grant resolution.[23] In outlining the thrust areas in an economy, as he said, 'devastated during the last 30 years', he sounded so convincing, his policy pronouncement so befitting the Janata manifesto, that amazed members exclaimed 'but you have only just taken over' to which he retorted, 'no, you forget, we took over some three months earlier'. It was a commanding performance. He spoke for twenty minutes. He laid down the salient features of a new industrial policy. He was for an emphasis on tiny and cottage industries to generate employment. He favoured expansion of the public sector and a more limited role for the private sector because 'resources of the big houses come from public financial institutions'. Moreover, the large houses seldom expended their resources on research and development. But even here there was no dearth of malice. Citing Sanjay Gandhi who had said, 'let the public sector die a natural death', George said, 'the people who held this view themselves died a natural death in so far as the public life of this country is concerned'. His party would develop the public sector, make it more efficient, and divorce from it the bureaucratic hangover. Wondering why industries were not commissioned in the backward, rural areas, he thought it was perhaps because of the 'active nightlife in the big cities'. He desired taking industries to 'those areas which have been treated as some kind of internal colonies by the previous government'. In his speech there was no shrinking from expressing rancour against the predecessor government when he told of regions where mail was still delivered by runners. 'Thousand years ago there were mail runners and now even after 30 years of freedom, we still have mail runners.' He was all for foreign collaboration, but he would not encourage it 'for brassieres and biscuits'. He proposed a workers' sector in addition to the private and public ones, and asked the trade unions to present plans for management of 'sick' companies. Howsoever powerfully he indicted the previous regime, his was, a Congressman said, a cry of a 'widowed Gandhian', a phrase that was identified with the Lohia socialists. Congress refuted that the agriculture sector or the public sector had ever been neglected. But his dynamism was contagious and in response to his speech enthusiastic members took to the floor with 'constructive suggestions'.

The debate in the Lok Sabha went on for three days. One discussion was about the Coca-Cola Company. At the beginning of the 1970s, Coca-Cola had become an issue of animated discussion in Parliament, with questions on its operation repeatedly raised by left-leaning members, who argued that it was 'a prosperous company selling positively harmful drink . . . robbing poor India'.[24] Starting in 1958, the company had grown in India from a one to a twenty-two bottler concern. The attack on it was in keeping with a worldwide trend that considered the beverage a symbol of Americanism and anti-communism.[25] But the rancour against it was also because in the political corridors it ran a powerful lobby, giving parties and gifts to influential people. Its bottlers came from elite families: President V.V. Giri's son-in-law was one, running a plant at Madurai. Some members did not like the taste of it, no, not of the beverage, but this repeated broaching of its name in the august chambers of Indian democracy. It gave the company a publicity that could well have been avoided. Was it a ploy, they wondered? Who is interested in Coca-Cola, they asked? It was after all a very small fraction of the national economy.

In one such discussion in March 1974, apprehensions as well as adulation poured in. A few members were at a loss to understand 'what is fundamentally wrong with this sort of consumer commodity'. But many others said India was not yet ready for such frivolous consumerism when other priority sectors were crying for attention. It was harmful to children, caused tooth decay and hypertension. But this litany of woes and hoarse disapproval was suddenly calmed when Atal Bihari Vajpayee stated that nothing harmful had happened to him, none of his bones had weakened, even when he had preferred the drink and had been consuming it for over two decades.[26] H.M. Patel had been another of its supporters. With both of them now his cabinet colleagues, George lamented that whereas Coca-Cola could be found everywhere, there were two and a half lakh villages that didn't have drinking water. Coca-Cola was a 'much wider problem of priorities and planning, of the concepts of progress and the standards of progress'. He opined that the company brought no know-how, only a marketing blitzkrieg to earn profits.

The next day, even as the Lok Sabha debated the ministry's priorities, a secret document was submitted to George by his mandarins. It contained confidential information on the Coca-Cola Company's operations in India. They knew if Coca-Cola was asked to divulge the formula of its concentrate, it would prefer to fold (rather than reveal it), forcing bottlers to shut down and retrench workers. On 8 August 1977, George declared that Coca-Cola was a 'multi-national corporation operating in a low-priority, high-profit area in a developing country that attained runaway growth in the absence of alertness on the part of the government concerned'.[27] He demanded indigenization of the company. As anticipated, the inevitable happened. The company decided to wind up its operations and leave. The banishment of the company in the hope that it would spur indigenous soft drinks firms to build their products and brands was soon belied. The government came out with its own drink that initially gained some popularity. Its Double Seven, named so to commemorate the Janata Party electoral success in that year, although launched with much euphoria, did not live up to expectations. Many years later, though, entrepreneur Azim Premji would admit that George's giving marching orders to IBM, another of those multinationals to pull out of Indian shores, created the necessary environment for the indigenization of the computer industry.[28] Still, the Coca-Cola Company's departure was viewed as evidence of accumulated malice. Throwing Coca-Cola out was bad publicity. It made the Janata government suspect in the eyes of the international business community. Soon, George would be going around the world capitals inviting investments and, at a meeting of trade unions in Europe, he requested them to adopt villages in India to provide drinking water to the inhabitants. In September, industrialist Viren Shah wrote to George, 'As you are keen to invite foreign capital to India it may be desirable to brief our missions, particularly in USA and Canada about the facts and policy on Coca Cola. I understand there are two ex-Coca Cola persons in the Centre's cabinet.'[29]

On 23 December 1977, drawing from the election manifesto of the Janata Party, George presented a Statement on the Industrial Policy to Parliament. It was the last day of the session, and therefore no discussion could take place.[30] The statement's importance lay not in its content, for many such statements had been made before and all of them, including George's, were based on Nehru's Industrial Policy Resolution passed by Parliament in 1956. It was, therefore, not the content that demanded applause but the dynamism with which it was presented. After he had read from a written statement, an uninterrupted rendering in pin-drop silence, members mobbed him with hope and adoration. The policy paid special attention to the small-scale sector. It decried the concentration of wealth in a few industrial houses and favoured rural-ward tilt of the economic policy. The iconic sentence was: 'Whatever can be produced by small and cottage industries must only be so produced.' In it was inherent many thoughts, besides of course the idea of giving a fillip to 'cottage and small industries widely dispersed in rural areas and small towns'. To ensure that whatever could be produced by small and cottage industries 'must only be so produced', the policy announced a big increase in the number of items reserved for production by the small sector.[31]

The central concern of George's industrial statement was to create more jobs by spurring industrialization in the rural areas. It gave an independent place to rural industries. He asked big industrial houses to withdraw from producing commodities of mass consumption to benefit cottage industries and the small-scale sector. It was decided no more industrial licences would be issued in and around metropolitan areas. The handicrafts sector received much-desired attention. A dedicated cadre was to be built to cater solely to the development of handicrafts.

To give teeth to the policy, he envisaged what came to be called the District Industrial Centre (DIC). The ambitious DIC programme was launched on 1 May 1978. He determinedly went about achieving the presence of DICs in all districts as quickly as possible. By the end of January 1979, 246 DICs were approved as against the targeted 180 for the year 1978–79. Characteristically, he focused on making a robust, efficient and networked organization, from central to district level. But despite all the flurry of activity, the DIC programme failed to achieve its goals. Some months later, when he was no longer in the government, George wrote an assessment of it. Despite having a promising start, the programme didn't take off. He laid the blame for its tardy performance on bureaucratic lethargy and the scramble for positions: the bureaucracy failed in taking bold, quick decisions, while 'we are in hurry'. But there were more intricate issues that led to its tepid performance.

Either because of his socialist ideology or the Janata Party's manifesto which spoke of Gandhian heritage, or a combination of both, George's term turned out to be controversial and generated much sound and fury. Very few people held a neutral notion about him. Consequently, every policy measure he spoke about proved greatly disconcerting to the placid waters of the industrial sector. He was applauded for his boldness and freshness but, at the same time, he produced discomfiture among the industrialists. No industry minister was ever talked about so much or stirred so many policy debates as he did during his two-year tenure. No other economic ministries during his time garnered so much front-page news. He plunged head-on, without fear or favour, generating controversies. Even before he took over, he had raised the issue of industrial magnates' proclivity of 'kowtowing to those in authority' and called them 'rats' scurrying to oblige an undemocratic regime. And, then, he attacked large family-owned industrial houses. George proposed that the large houses be broken down, and private enterprises of steel, aluminium and automobiles nationalized. He went hammer and tongs to demolish the mystique associated with large houses. He said, if the bulk of their assets were financed by borrowings from public institutions, what was the rationale behind leaving their control in the hands of a family? This unleashed a wave of protest, and he vented, 'hell was let loose on me by the big business houses and their hired mafia in the political world of our country'. Adverse stories were floated in newspapers. 'Hardly a day goes by when the chief of some organization and some distinguished columnist do not warn the people about the calamity that would befall this country if the action were taken to reduce the power of a few families.' V. Balasubramanian, a columnist writing in the Birla-controlled *Hindustan Times* was continuously writing harshly headed critiques. For him, George was either a 'fanatic or charlatan', who had unexpectedly found himself in a position of authority. His motives were questioned. The public sector's record was assailed, its efficiency questioned, its losses mocked at. 'That was Big Business at work, out to malign a man they could not buy and for that very reason they feared.' He was perceived to be largely against the Birlas, whose patriarch G.D. Birla (1894–1983), a man who had financed Gandhi and given scholarships to many socialists, including JP and Ram Manohar Lohia at the behest of Gandhi, was harnessed to speak up against the 'deteriorating industrial environment in the country'.[32]

The large business houses had supported the Emergency. Concurring with Indira Gandhi's slogan of 'discipline makes a nation great', they had retrenched workers, announced lockouts and denied bonus. J.R.D. Tata in January 1977, just before the elections were announced, had spoken extolling the Emergency for having speeded up economic progress and social justice. When, partly out of malice and partly for a righteous cause, George took up the gauntlet against the large houses, the attack on him was sharp and swift. He was called a demagogue, someone who was a rabble-rouser and an irresponsible trade union leader. His proposal opened him up to accusations of discriminating against Tata and Birla concerns. George's words, said newspaper edits, smacked of his trade union background rather than providing evidence of the 'serious intent of country's industry minister'. They accused the government of speaking through many mouths. If George was threatening to split up the large houses, the law minister denied any such intention.[33] He was accused of going beyond the party mandate. A Laxman cartoon in the *Times of India* showed him in medieval fighting gear drawing a tiny sword—denoting Janata policy—from a disproportionately large sheath—denoting George's policy.[34] All these generated a huge debate and much calumny but yielded little. His proposals had sound reasoning. The private sector did not invest in the development of technology. 'Look at this Hindustan Ambassador,' he wrote, 'after 30 years of producing cars, we are not in

Courtesy: Fredrick D'Sa, Bombay Taximen's Union

The Minister George

a position to prepare a die for the shell, forget the engine. This is true of most Indian businessmen.'[35] He was sour that when Indira Gandhi had nationalized banks it was seen as heralding socialism, but when he tried to introduce similar policies he was badgered for encouraging public-sector inefficiency and taking a 'populist posture'. Morarji Desai himself was against 'nationalization for the sake of nationalization only'. Under pressure, though, from George and a few others, the Janata Party constituted a committee to examine aspects related to the large houses. Constituted at the end of January 1979, the nine-member committee that included George was to submit its report within a month. But it was still holding its inconclusive meetings when six months later in July the government, reduced to a minority, fell apart. The committee had, however, drawn attention from industrial magnates, who wrote espousing principles of mixed economy wherein 'all sectors were to emerge and expand together'.[36]

Throughout these months, George projected 'an image of business-like minister' and avoided political controversies.[37] He issued sage-like statements about not frittering away the opportunity, about not betraying the people's mandate.[38] In all the pettifoggery that was going on in the Janata Party, rife with prime-ministerial ambitions pitting one against the other and toppling games played by factions in states and at the Centre, George kept himself above all these and focused steadfastly on making constructive policies. If he generated discomfiture among the industrial houses, it scuttled his chances of ever getting their backing for a larger leap into power politics. For his political funding, he largely drew from his trade unions in Bombay. If this gave him a degree of independence, freeing him from quid pro quo deals with the industrial giants, it also constricted his political expanse. His independence proved his Achilles heel.

* * *

George's victory heightened the expectations in Muzaffarpur. The hopes in him emanated from a depressing reality of the constituency, located in a rural, flood-prone and industrially backward region of north Bihar. The vital infrastructure needed for a region to become industrially developed was absent. Less than one-third of its villages were electrified. Only 18 per cent of its people were literate.[39] Civic amenities were scarce. Underground water, pulled out with the help of eight borewells, was stored in low-lying overhead tanks. This untreated water reached homes through pipes laid along open drains. Sometimes those pipes cracked and drinking water and sewage got mixed, spreading diseases that were (and still are) endemic in the region. Some distance removed from Muzaffarpur existed Barauni, north Bihar's sole industrial zone with an oil refinery and a fertilizer factory. But their giant presence didn't give a fillip to a much-desired industrial surge. The ancillary units they had spawned were lying sick. The only power plant at Barauni was inadequate to feed the needs of the whole of north Bihar. The region had a concentration of handloom weavers. Although some of these weavers were organized under cooperatives, these were mostly defunct and weavers were left to fend for themselves. Cotton came from outside, its supply inadequate, dilatory and costly. The handlooms needed technological upgradation but bureaucratic apathy and financial scarcity would not permit it.

George tried to leverage his position to initiate developmental activities in Muzaffarpur. He sent many committees comprising both social activists and bureaucrats to study its needs. They went around, met the local mandarins and submitted similar-sounding reports, each chronicling the existing ills in more nauseating detail. They exasperated him. But whatever the worth of those reports, reading them perhaps strengthened his resolve to have centres, one in each district across the country, to encourage industrial development in backward regions. The idea of the DIC was thus born. His team identified some growth centres, mainly populated by traditional artisanal classes, for targeted development. Power was the most important requirement. He initiated a thermal power station at Kanthi near Muzaffarpur with serious intent. When land acquisition got delayed, he implored Bihar chief minister Karpoori Thakur to intervene.[40] The power plant eventually came up at Kanthi and was to generate electricity by the mid-1980s.

As agricultural development was to precede industrial growth, the focus was on developing tube-well irrigation. Energy-intensive, in the absence of electricity they were run on diesel. While at Delhi the work was smoothened by Ashok Jaitly (1944–2015), his secretary, at Muzaffarpur the activities were supervised by Vinod Kumar Singh (d. 2017), the local MLA.[41] Many skill development and training programmes were initiated. The Khadi and Village Industries Commission (KVIC) was roped in to encourage low-technology enterprises in matches, soap and handmade paper.[42] The artisans were given credit facilities, raw materials and tools and implements. Many non-government organizations (NGOs) pitched in with specific expertise. The Social Work & Research Centre at Tilonia offered technical help. The Rashtra Seva Dal conducted training camps on leadership for local youths.[43] George wrote to Suresh Kalmadi (b. 1944) of Giants International at Poona who had shown interest in undertaking some work, 'We need roads, bridges over rivulets and rivers, schools, dispensaries and a host of other things. We also need a small scale, rural and cottage industry. Will it be possible for you to depute one or two of your leaders to go over to Muzaffarpur with me and identify specific areas of activity?'[44] His early forays in Muzaffarpur made him realize that artisans as a class could be developed into a target political group, beyond caste and community affiliations. He would carry the idea further in the following decade.

George received numerous representations from his constituents drawing attention to their respective needs. He was an eager respondent to every bit of every letter received from any quarter on any subject. Each response from him was dictated, read and edited before it was finally signed and sealed for dispatch. His archive is stuffed with letters people wrote and copies of letters he wrote on their behalf to concerned authorities. The piles of correspondence exchanged in the period 1977–80 reveal the quality of political relationship he shared with his constituents.

Most representations were about private grievances or individual aspirations. There were jobseekers, loan seekers, or complainants of official mistreatment. Almost every letter hinted at corruption in the bureaucracy and roadblocks they put up due to people's inability or unwillingness to meet their underhand demands. One letter writer, for instance, talked about a bank loan that was officially sanctioned under a scheme but never released to the potential beneficiary, and yet officials were now knocking at his door for the recovery of the said loan.[45] It was ignored that the complaint had its origins in a time when George was not the representative of the area. If the MP believed the bank was culpable, as such instances of embezzlement and manipulation were commonplace, he either took to a protest against the bank or asked the very same people to investigate whose guilty dealings were the cause of complaint. But it could also be that the complainant was colluding with the bank officials to loot public money through a scheme that was not adequately fortified against such embezzlement. In such situations, an MP had to do a tightrope walk. Some correspondents pointed to the nexus between politicians and vested interests who dislodged rightful owners from their private lands and homes.[46] Often they demanded shifting the head of an institution/department. Writers of long letters expected him to sift through the maze of allegations and side with them extralegally. Interested parties worked to politicize issues to persuade him to advance their control over an institution.[47] Some demanded his intercession to speed up investigation into the death of kin, in which they suspected foul play. Others asked for his help to recover stolen goods. Those on the receiving end of routine violence recounted atrocities by various perpetrators, expecting him to bring justice. Requests for a loan to build a house or seed money for an enterprise, which were the abundant part of correspondence, were routinely forwarded to the District Magistrate. They were replied to, stating lack of any such fund at the minister's disposal. However, they were still forwarded to the relevant ministries such as health, education or small-scale industries, depending on the purpose for which assistance was sought. To many who were seeking financial support for medical care, he wrote back regretting his inability. To one he wrote, 'If you desire state to support you medically, please write an application. I shall try my level best to arrange state support for your medical care.'[48] The nature of demands made on him may be gauged from the content of a letter George wrote in reply to one: 'I agree with your proposition that the medical needs of the people in public life must be served with the help of people itself. It applies equally in the case of your colleague. In his case I was ready and still am to donate my body organ. But if you expect that I cover the total expenditure for his heart surgery then it is beyond my means.'[49]

Loan seekers for small enterprises were invariably directed to the Laghu Udyog Sewa Sansthan (an organization providing loans to small industries). One Panchuram Barwa, a 'Harijan', requested a loan to open a shop for shoes and sandals, and George forwarded his first request of 30 August 1978, for necessary action to the Laghu Udyog Sewa Sansthan. No action was taken. In response to Barwa's second letter, George simply wrote, 'Please contact the concerned authority. They would offer you complete help.'[50] Individuals in the category called 'educated unemployed' also wrote requesting financial assistance to launch some enterprise. Some complained that even after the sanctioning of their project and grant of loan by the Sansthan, funds were not released. Several jobseekers claimed their current destitution was due to their having taken part in the JP agitations or because of the Emergency. Even while there were constraints concerning the Kanthi Thermal Power Project, hundreds of letters were received from aspirants seeking employment there. When one Ajay Kumar Gupta complained about 'outsiders' getting jobs, George asked him to write with documentary evidence.[51] He wrote, 'My effort is to provide youths in Muzaffarpur maximum possibilities for gainful employment. I have made an arrangement by which those who have been displaced from their land would get the first opportunity. The rest of the local applicants would be given employment based on their merit.'[52] Many demands pertained to subjects on the state list and, accordingly, they were directed to the state authorities. One significant set of letter writers were the party MLAs who requested the provision for temporary residence at Delhi for visiting people from the constituency.[53]

George made it a policy to write recommendatory letters only to government authorities: 'Please do not ask me to write letters to private-sector factory owners.'[54] It was not that writers were only asking; they were also advising, proposing and taking initiatives. Many wrote simply hoping to come closer to him. Others entreated him to visit their areas. Most letters placed demands on him for things that seemed trivial but, for the constituents, were of vital importance to life or livelihood.

There were grievances also of public nature. Being a rural hinterland, where accountability was scarce, irregularities in infrastructure projects were often brought to his notice by representations signed by many.[55] Endorsed by over a hundred signatories from a Dalit village, a correspondent wrote of a conspiracy to deprive them of a sanctioned irrigation project. They even threatened to launch a peaceful struggle against 'your government' if the alleged shifting of the borewell was not stopped.[56] Others signed letters demanding regular supply of electricity to their village, still others for repairing the dilapidated roads. Some on their own constituted inspection committees and desired his attention to any information they sent. Public causes centred on demands for metalled road, hospital, post office, Kendriya Vidyalaya or drinking water to a 'Harijan' hamlet. Such representations carried signatures of many of the village. He forwarded them to the concerned Bihar ministries for necessary action, but they did not always draw the desired results. The secretary of Muzaffarpur Eye Hospital wrote a poignant letter: 'On 2 February 1978, Bihar's Governor visited us and after inspection agreed to become its chief patron. In March, British High Commissioner too visited our Hospital and put emphasis on introducing mobile clinics for eye care in the rural areas. On our approaching you, you were kind enough to write to Raj Narain, the Union health minister, putting across our request for mobile eye clinic. But unfortunately, nothing substantive has been achieved in this regard to this date. May we request you again to write to Bihar health minister to allot us two equipped ambulances to carry out eye-care in rural areas.'[57] Sometimes, however, the concerned ministry wrote back informing him of initiation of action. The minister of communication informed him of departmental action on opening a post office at the village Madho Patti. The minister also arranged a job of postman on compensatory basis for a candidate who had requested a relaxation of rules regarding age.[58]

The correspondence gives us an idea about the kind of work undertaken in the constituency. George got clothes distributed to people affected by the floods. He launched a scheme to instal hand-pumps in Dalit hamlets.[59] He wrote to the Bihar government requesting allotment of funds to instal a chlorinator in every handpump to make the water potable.[60] The correspondence also provides a measure in the extent of bureaucratic apathy and failure of routine governance.

The work of an MP is to represent issues of public importance and formulate legislative responses. Although administrative sanction for individual initiative from MPs is restricted, most get burdened by the aspirations of their constituents, and failure in reaching out to such aspirations constitutes the failure of the MP. Perception of his performance is largely based on his ability to address individual demands. A parliamentary constituency comprises some fifteen lakh voters; in a situation of scarcity, vying even for the tiniest of privileges is a perpetual pastime. An MP can be asked to recommend a ward's admission into a school or a hospital or to facilitate a gas cylinder or rail reservation, all requests that George received. Stalled freedom fighter's pension or passport or facilitation for departure to the Middle East: each of these needed his intervention. To address and satisfy the personal needs of such a large multitude is not possible without addressing policy and administrative issues. Why a person from an obscure Muzaffarpur hamlet, locally maybe significant but nationally a speck, would approach a minister in Delhi for college admission or for a health check-up at the capital's hospital must have worried the establishment, yet the acute need for medical or educational infrastructure at the district level was not addressed. The mismatch between the aspirations of constituents and the capacity of the elected representative to meet such aspirations, both private and public in nature, have grave consequences for all those involved and for the democratic system. But politicians, despite being aware of the problem, were not inclined to find a solution. Such clamouring for their attention served them well. Until the 1960s when elections to Parliament and state assemblies were held simultaneously, people generally thought of the MP as one with a distinct set of jobs, whereas the MLA was approached for personal favours. In the 1970s, when elections began to be separately held, the nature of representation grew murky. With political parties intensely divided, state and Central governments ruled by separate political formations, often bitterly opposed, and the performance of MLAs or the state government could no longer decide the electoral fate of an MP. The MP began to be evaluated independently, and electoral strategies were designed accordingly. The MP found it easier to selectively satisfy a few resourceful individuals in return for electoral loyalties. Non-satisfaction sometimes led to massive defeats culminating in humiliating losses of deposit. George experienced such a defeat in 1971, just four years after the same South Bombay constituency had given him an overwhelming mandate. Some politicians found ingenious solutions to their predicament by choosing different constituencies each time they contested an election.[61]

Disillusionment with George began to set in early on, within a year of election. People began to express their disappointment and threatened this could be their last letter. Most writers only desired that he visit their area and be accessible; they were unhappy at not being given an audience. 'People of the village Mirapur, particularly the elders, desire your presence. During the fateful Emergency period, the people of my village hinged their hopes on you and sang paeans in your praise. They have great expectations from you.'[62] The correspondence proved his image of availability among the people. The affectionate and definitive words used showed the esteem and familiarity in which people held him as an MP. Still, complaints of letters gone unanswered or vain attempts to have an audience also abounded. With dripping sarcasm, they wrote bitterly of his unapproachability and reminded him he was first their representative and then anything else. 'I am at wit's end to fathom whom should we approach,' wrote one from Pusa, adding, 'even George who calls himself a labour-leader and is representative of the constituency has failed to visit the area even once.'[63] Another wrote that he still carried a 'weakness' for George's 'Emergency Image' asking how could a man quoting Herman Hesse's poems turn 'callous'.[64] 'For reasons quite inexplicable, you have to bear it in mind that no single leader has aroused so many expectations as you have done in the people. The stage has come when we ask you Sir Fernandes, "who gave their yesterday and for whose tomorrow"?' The sense of ownership that the people felt over him was unprecedented and hence their bitter disappointment and exasperation at being excluded from his proximity. Most blamed the breed of rudderless sycophants who according to them now encircled him and kept him distanced from his real supporters, the common people without influence. Many of those who had earlier hero-worshipped him, now, distanced by official protocol or by a mob of the more resourceful, felt sidelined and vented their anger in letters. Frustration mounted and they began to see a changed George. To one such complainant, he wrote, as if in apologia, 'We have lived a life of struggle. The present situation has not brought any change to that reality.'[65] But such entreaties went unheeded. One Ali Mubarak Asmani wrote an angry letter, in Urdu script—which George was careful enough to get translated into English, 'You call Morarji a hypocrite, but when I look into the mirror of hypocrisy, I see your face.'[66]

In March 1978, an awkward incident occurred at Muzaffarpur. Chief minister Karpoori Thakur had announced a reservation policy for the backward classes. Students, both supporters and opponents of the said reservation policy, took to street fighting that turned casteist, as the criterion defining backwardness was caste alone. George thought that it was a case of 'a right decision taken at the wrong time and in the wrong way'.[67] His upper-caste constituents were unimpressed. At a function he was attending in the constituency, the protesting students gathered around him and blocked his car. It turned ugly when in order to show revulsion they began spitting on him, demanding he rescind from supporting the reservation policy. But he remained unmoved. A local teacher feeling guilty later wrote: 'I appreciate your firmness in the face of the crowd of hostile upper-caste students.'[68] George did not take umbrage at the humiliating incident. Instead, he replied, 'The shameful behaviour of a handful of people either provoked by a momentary eruption of emotions or by others should not unduly upset us. Such things happen in a family. These people are ours and we are theirs.'[69] His loyalists however continued to hinge hopes on him. They wrote feelingly. 'Your commendable activities have raised the hackles of the non-socialist elements. They are feeling threatened. In the history of the constituency, no representative before you had either devoted any thought or possessed the capacity to undertake any worthwhile work. In these circumstances, we express our gratitude to you for having undertaken a range of developmental activities in the constituency.'[70]

George's past had established a kind of connection with a people who had never seen or heard him. They wrote pleading, advising, commanding, congratulatory or condemnatory messages. Common people wrote letters on bits of paper in unconstructed sentences and posted these envelope-less to just 'Udyog Mantri, Nayi Dilli'. One letter was addressed to 'Udyog Pita' (here the reversal in the people's consciousness had already occurred: one who was in battle with 'Udyog Pati', large industrialists, throughout his career was now the 'Udyog Pita', the protector of industries).[71] He had a kinetic personality in which many had reposed their faith. He was above appeals to region, religion or race. He was casteless. This made him acceptable in

Muzaffarpur. But, as someone wrote to him in February 1979, some six months before the fall of the Janata government, disillusionment had set in. 'The feeling about you has not undergone any substantial change from what was prevalent in July 1978. Only they don't feel so keenly about it any more. The disgust and disappointment with the party and government as a whole are so much greater today, with an undercurrent of resignation and hopelessness, that the "failure" of one MP—their own—fits into the general picture. Some people are making a shrewd guess that you have no intention of facing Muzaffarpur electorate again.'[72] It was a people who, in another time and locale, had convinced him of pervasive injustice and given strength to his adolescent self in raising his voice against it; it was the same people in a new setting now convinced of his perfidy who would force him to contemplate shifting his constituency.

* * *

Disillusionment with the Janata Party government was turning out to be a countrywide symptom. As the Janata Party's internal crisis ripened, George's response was to blame the prime minister. In November 1978, he offered his resignation from the cabinet but not before he had told Morarji Desai that he was not playing his role. He wanted to free himself from the responsibility of government and devote himself to party-building to 'at least postpone, if not avert, the disaster that I see ahead'.[73] He wrote his decision was self-taken because there was an impression that he did things under the influence of Madhu Limaye.

Although his resignation was rejected, George soon found himself at the centre of a controversy when he asked for a 'powerful people's movement' to make the government deliver. Even when there were people who felt elated at his statement, the prime minister was said to have stated that those who wanted to go could leave the government.[74] On the premise that they had come together and desired staying together, the prime minister said, but 'how can one get over the old habits'. But Morarji Desai's management of the factional contradictions in the party was not above board. To control one group or the other, he or someone close to him was leaking confidential information to the press to embarrass ministerial and party colleagues. Citing a news item in the *Tribune*, Biju Patnaik, the minister of Steel, wrote a sad letter that revealed the level of distrust that had crept in among the colleagues. 'It is surprising,' Patnaik wrote to the prime minister, 'that the account as given in this report could have been virtually picked up from a tape-recording of discussions that you have had with me.'[75] George himself was disturbed by many 'inspired reports' in the media for which he sought an explanation from Morarji Desai. Having come to such a sorry pass, weighed down by its web of intrigues, the government's collapse was just a matter of time.

The Janata Party remained at best a coalition of erstwhile parties in which the Jan Sangh element was gradually gaining strength and organizational control, spreading discontent among others. It was said that wherever they were in command of the organization, the Jan Sangh element conducted 'its affairs in [such] a manner that no other should and could feel involved'.[76] The fear of being overwhelmed by the Jan Sangh had compelled the party mandarins to delay organizational elections. The Janata Party had many power centres, some active and some biding time to bare their fangs. Even someone like JP, though the inspiration and instrument behind its formation, couldn't hide his aspiration to be the adviser, leading the disgruntled to approach him. Writing to Morarji Desai when the chips of his government were down because of its internal squabbles and resignation dramas enacted by its important ministers—in which even George was involved—JP reminded the prime minister of continued instances of pervasive corruption. Sadly, he wrote this letter when he was lying gravely ill at Bombay's Jaslok Hospital. In those days it was rumoured that JP put his signature on any document that was brought before him by any interested party. It was also the time when media outlets such as *Blitz* were running obituary-sounding pieces recounting JP's legacy. Ignored by the Janata government for the last two years, impaired by the slowly swallowing disease that made him bedridden and tied to a dialysis machine, when ministers showered platitudes without intention or substance, JP was much hurt. But although he said he was writing as a friend, he had much anger, and in his anger he lost the sense of his shifting ground. Now on his deathbed, he said the RSS was dominating and was fomenting communal troubles and Morarji Desai had failed in containing its perfidy.[77] It was not the first time JP had lost his sense of self, but now he had been exposed, and except for the reverence reserved for a decrepit, old relation with the expectation that he would soon depart this world, nothing remained either in or for him.

In the death wish that had come to grip the Janata Party, the factions were holding their respective conventions. Each of those streams secretly nurtured a wish to use the governmental sojourn to fatten itself independently of the united party. It was an infantile wish and lacked political maturity. They wanted the prime minister to remain weak, all in the name of consensus. Even George organized a meeting of socialists on 7–8 July 1979 in Delhi to take stock of the unfolding political polarization.[78] The decision that they arrived at after two days of deliberations was to remain in the Janata Party. But in a week's time that solemn pledge would be reduced to wishful thinking.

Twenty-seven months after the formation of the Janata government, a no-confidence motion, moved half-heartedly and perfunctorily, brought its premature collapse. For all these months, its saga of a divided self, mutual bickering and power struggle had gone on unabated. On 11 July 1979, its moment of truth arrived. The no-confidence motion moved by the Congress breakaway Opposition leader Y.B. Chavan had a lacklustre beginning, whereas a more serious affair was nibbling at its strength from the inside.[79] As the motion began to be deliberated in Parliament, the Janata members began to desert the official block to sit with Raj Narain, the lone ranger who had revolted. In a resolute display of his intentions, Raj Narain rechristened the parent body Janata Party (Communal), while he led a flock that called itself Janata Party (Secular). It was true that intercommunity relationships in the country had deteriorated in this period of Janata rule. Not only were RSS followers accused of indulging in anti-Muslim riots at Jamshedpur and Aligarh, but their ministerial nominees in the Bihar cabinet were thought to be erasing all signs of their participation in those riots. The Freedom of Religion Bill, moved by O.P. Tyagi, a Jan Sangh member, had come as a 'rude shock' to the Christian community as its object, contrary to its name, was to prohibit religious choice and conversion.[80] Diocese after diocese of the Christian church sent representation deploring the bill and questioning its motives.

On 12 July, it was George's turn to speak on behalf of the government. It was the second day of the no-confidence debate. Desertion from the party had already gained momentum. A packed Lok Sabha heard an hour-long hard-hitting speech by him. It was not his first foray in defending the government. In April 1978, he had lauded the government's performance: 'By all accounts, we are running a good government,' he had said then.[81] In May the same year, he campaigned tirelessly, providing life and vigour to the electoral campaign at Chikmagalur against Indira Gandhi who was looking to re-enter Parliament after the ignominy of March 1977. In the midterm by-elections held in December, he campaigned vigorously, asserting: 'The battle has just begun.'[82] Now he was again defending the government and its performance. Rebutting the Opposition charges, George wondered by what standard they wanted to judge the achievements of the last two years. 'What's the benchmark?' he repeatedly asked, raising the hackles of Congressmen. Quoting statistics from official publications brought out by the former government, he asserted that the results under Janata rule were far superior to those during the so-called dynamic decade of Indira Gandhi. The Janata government in a short period, by increasing investment in the rural sector in a big way, had reduced poverty, he said to the thumping of desks from the treasury benches.

George's defence of the Janata regime was much appreciated across the country. But soon a speech that had ignited hope in the survival of the government ended up bringing him much disrepute. On 15 July, a host of ministers, George included, tendered their resignations from the government. Seeing the tide turning against him, Morarji Desai tendered the resignation of his government without going through a vote of confidence in Parliament. The crisis that besieged the Morarji government was generated wilfully, but neither was the country prepared for it, nor were the circumstances such as to permit its eruption. It was sudden, shocking and dishevelling. The President for an alternative arrangement toyed with many ideas, including the one of a national government headed by Sheikh Abdullah. Although George's resignation letter to Morarji Desai didn't talk of the communal threat posed by the Jan Sangh element, the RSS and its ideology were at the centre of the great divide, even if just for politics' sake.[83]

By the last week of July, a new government headed by Charan Singh took the oath of office. The truncated socialists led by George supported it from the outside but he decided against joining it. The socialist support to the Charan Singh government despite his seeking Indira Gandhi's backing baffled many. They felt it was 'dangerous and ridiculous'. Even George was agitated at the prospect but his feelings were eventually assuaged by Madhu Limaye.[84]

Numerous letter writers saw in George's resignation from the government led by Morarji Desai a betrayal of mandate. The intensity of revulsion felt at large was simply boundless. Having supported the government so eloquently, his resignation was a shock for most people who still held him in high regard. G.G. Parikh, his jail mate, was dismayed, and thought he was innocent of Madhu Limaye's machinations. His daughter Sonal, who had also gone to jail during the Emergency, sent a message, decrying the fall of the 'one time hero of Indian democracy'.[85] Industrialist Viren Shah's son sent another scathing message, 'You seem to have thrown all principles to the winds. Still cannot understand how a man like you supposedly strong could behave in such a despicable manner.'[86] 'In the present political scenario, no one more than you has become a subject of ridicule,' he was told by a Barmer-based correspondent.[87] He was perceived to be 'a man who has makings of a Statesman, and enough character to be our prime minister. You had a singleness of purpose, loyalty to principles and a tremendous capacity for leadership.'[88] But by his 'startling actions . . . you destroyed yourself. And destroyed the faith in you of many people like me. How could George Fernandes join this band of politicians who have no principles, no morality and no loyalty, and who shamelessly believe that the people who elect them are too dull to notice their vulgar actions.' The angry letter writers reminded him of his image during the Emergency resistance: 'People by their votes had severed your chains, broke the jail that had imprisoned you, but what did you do? What they'd think of you and what did you turn into? The same people who had broken your chains will now blacken your face.'[89] The letter demanded to know how their representative could shift allegiance without consulting his electors. Posted within the agonizing week after the fall of the Janata government, it was a long energetic letter, full of angry, abusive words.[90] George's reply to the correspondent was short and circumventing, asking him not to get swayed by the moment.[91] But such entreaties were in vain. Many expressed their belief that what he and his family had suffered under the Emergency was a preordained punishment for the sin of betrayal he was to commit in future. Jayant R. Shah from Vadodra made criticism personal when he expressed his anguish mixed with irony: 'I got hold of the final report of Shah Commission only yesterday. As you know the first chapter deals with your brother Lawrence Fernandes. It brought back the gruesome memories of the said episode reported earlier. It gave me and like-minded friends of mine a great pleasure to read and hear that you were joining Charan Singh who is forming a government with the help of Indira Gandhi. How do your mother and tortured brother feel? They might be very happy of course.'[92] He was urged to commit suicide as he had murdered democracy.

People were angry and wrote expressing their feelings. Most writers lamented the lack of character in the political leaders, and considered the Jan Sangh element as more responsible and disciplined. They laid the blame squarely on 'professional party breakers like Madhu Limaye and Raj Narain' but were aghast at the cynicism displayed by George. 'Now, the public wrath is against you. You may please resign from parliament and contest again from your present constituency. I am sure you will lose your deposit as it had happened in Bombay.'[93] The secularism argument came unstuck. They did not buy the bogey of communalism as represented by the undigested element of the Jan Sangh. 'You know who had worked tirelessly during the Emergency? The Jan Sangh. They worked ceaselessly during the elections of 1977. Due to the foolish act of our leaders, the Jana Sangh would grow more in strength in the years to come.' Even his core admirers thought he was party to bringing back the 'Emergency scoundrels'. His friend P. Lankesh from Bangalore wrote, 'I just don't know how you countenance this unless you are keen on your moral and political suicide. Please come out of this dirty, vicious circle—kindly don't worry even if we are to start our socialistic or a broadly radical group all over again.'[94] Such advice came thick and fast. He was under ferocious attack, and so starved was he for support from any quarter that when Bhai Bhosale wrote appreciating his ministerial tenure as beneficial to the working class, he wrote back profusely thanking him for the 'sentiments expressed'.[95] According to many, he had fallen prey to the voracity of regional politicians, an allusion to Charan Singh's ambitions. A letter from an underground comrade is so apposite in the circumstances that an excerpt needs reproduction.

Dear George . . . Restlessness and embarrassment created by the people's anger, frustration and sense of contempt over your stand taken as 'overnight somersault, opportunist to the core, ever-shifting and shameful in the eyes of those' for whom you were the only hope, inspiration and leading light in today's vulgar exhibition of naked power-game, has compelled me to write this though it is both unpleasant and difficult.

Some close friends very deeply feel you have betrayed history and the revolution you led against the dictator has become irrelevant and meaningless resulting in a big zero. Had you just kept away from the dirty show by resigning the Lok Sabha seat you could have symbolized the massive discontent and wrath of the people over the vulgar selfish drama. But your clubbing with Choudhry has only led to the rise in regard for Mr Morarji Desai and also Jan Sangh-RSS.

Some people went to Bhagat Singh statue yesterday and pasted rubbish on your name on the plate, put old cycle tyre round the neck of the statue. I was telephoned by someone to find out how I feel about it.

People are not so much sorry for Morarji's departure as they are against Charan's take-over. A friend's remarks: Sharad Patel did

'gaddari' for gaining CBI case withdrawal, what is your stake? I am
afraid it is as if we have lost all image and credibility . . . This is how
it is here today . . . Kirit Bhatt[96]

Most held Madhu Limaye responsible for what had happened and
advised George to free himself from this malevolent influence. In
the first half of 1978, as Charan Singh had mounted pressure on
the prime minister demanding an inquiry into his son's affairs,
Morarji Desai sought his resignation from the government. In the last
week of June, along with him, a few others were dropped from the
ministry. Raj Narain was one of them. Charan Singh's rehabilitation
was campaigned for by many others in the party who were afraid
of the increasing powers of Morarji Desai, although this aspect was
disguised under the desire for party unity. Everyone in the Janata
Party was keen that the prime minister remain weak. It was during
these manoeuvres, when Morarji Desai thought he was in control,
that he made a disparaging remark about Madhu Limaye, who was at
the forefront of those working to clip the prime minister's powers by
forcing a truce with Charan Singh. A harassed Morarji Desai, lonely
at the top, accused of sheltering a wrongdoing son, told an interviewer
in one of those weak moments when men show their unvarnished
colour that Madhu Limaye was the 'dhobi' of the Ramayana who had
questioned Sita's chastity.[97] Limaye was 'the main trouble maker'.
The interviewer was George, and he seems to have relayed the affront
to Madhu Limaye. Understandably, the comment went straight into
the inferno of Limaye's Brahmanical ego. Incensed by the disparaging
remark, he wrote to Morarji Desai, demanding an explanation.[98] 'Am
I the dhobi of Ramayan? Is Kanti [Desai] a Sita?' And, four days later,
a still burning Madhu Limaye directed his fire at George, pestering
him to resign from the government.[99] On 16 August, he made his
final appeal. 'If you do not heed it, I shall have nothing further to
say to you,' he wrote expressing his ownership over him, reminding
him that it was he who had pushed an unwilling George to join the
government. He now needed proof of loyalty, and resignation would
be this proof.

Like George's constituents, distanced from him and accusing him of having changed, Madhu Limaye in a similar vein berated him for not being 'the same person that I knew and loved'. George was not just undecided but went on to defend Morarji Desai on the issue of his son, an act that further infuriated Madhu Limaye. He castigated him for defending the 'father and son', and further asked, 'Where is your old spirit? Willy Brandt, Kriesky and Palme did not risk the displeasure of the then powerful Mrs. Gandhi to back a mere supporter of the prime minister. They spoke out for a fearless fighter for democratic freedoms.' After this emotional appeal, Limaye made sure to recount the capitalist bent of Morarji Desai as well. 'What is his attitude to your proposals to bring automobile, aluminium and steel industries under public sector? He is for the status quo or worse.' In that letter of 16 August to George, a full year before the Janata government eventually collapsed, Madhu Limaye also predicted the imminent fall of the government. 'The process of erosion is gathering momentum,' he said. 'The government can drag on for weeks, may be, for months. But the outcome is not in doubt. Then why hang on, I ask.' And before he fired his salvo—'if you do not get out—what issues you should highlight I leave it to you—your position will be compromised'—Madhu Limaye harnessed the weight of JP to buttress his appeal: 'I warn you that JP also will not keep quiet any longer.' At the same time, Limaye was working to drive a wedge in the rapport between Morarji Desai and George, who then were close. On 29 August, he wrote to George again, giving him no quarter and taunting him mercilessly, 'have you decided not to assert on any issue?' When George squirmed and spoke of a compact with his cabinet colleagues, Madhu Limaye questioned his sense of loyalty, bluntly saying he had lost 'all self-respect and sense of honour'. Feeling betrayed and let down, Limaye threw a volley of accusing questions at George. His final one was about the compact they had shared: 'What about your 30-year old compact with your closest colleagues?' So driven was he by his aggrieved self and his sense of ownership over George, he believed George couldn't be allowed to exercise independent discretion in his choice of alignment. Limaye felt if George was with the prime minister, it was because of some frame-up. He asked naggingly, 'What has made you attach yourself to this autocrat? What is the source of your weakness?'[100]

A still undecided George, incessantly pestered by Madhu Limaye, in November 1978 offered to resign from the cabinet, but this was rejected by the prime minister. George then attacked the performance of the government and the leadership of Morarji Desai but was silenced when the prime minister harnessed Subramaniam Swamy and others to attack his ministry's poor performance, on declining industrial growth and labour troubles. Madhu Limaye continued to be critical of Morarji Desai, writing to him that he disliked being 'bullied'. His target remained focused on Kanti Desai. In January 1979, Morarji Desai brought back Charan Singh as his finance minister but refused to take in Raj Narain. The destructive forces ganged up together. Madhu Limaye changed tack and wrote a long letter to the prime minister accusing him of not doing enough for the Muslims. As if the destiny of Indian Muslims was inextricably linked with the state of Urdu language, the Aligarh Muslim University and a National Commission for Minorities, he outlined the government's failure in meeting the Muslim aspirations.[101] But by then Morarji Desai had accrued strength. Charan Singh had sheepishly accepted whatever he was offered. Refraining from disturbing the apple cart, he was keen to settle down to enjoy the return to power. There were, however, indignant others on the prowl.

Madhu Limaye was restless. There was no well-thought-out plan of action; he seemed motivated simply by his rage against Morarji Desai. In the last week of April 1979, he again wrote to George, this time bringing to fore the question of 'political line'.[102] He was working to persuade George to ditch the prime minister under whose dispensation, he said, the Jan Sangh element was gaining ascendance. 'The RSS group,' he wrote, laying out a design that would burst through in the next two months, unleashing total hara-kiri, 'has taken an anti-national position on all issues affecting the integrity and unity of the country.' He wrote of O.P. Tyagi's 'anti-conversion bill', which according to George was a private member's bill with which the government had nothing to do, but for Madhu Limaye it was a 'pre-planned RSS manoeuvre'. Thereafter, things moved swiftly and factional competition came to rest on the issue of dual membership in the Janata Party. It concerned those who held political membership in the Janata Party even while expressing allegiance to the RSS. To lull Madhu Limaye's relentless urgings, George called a socialist convention that decided against leaving the Janata Party (on 8 July), and accordingly, he then supported the government in a fiery display of loyalty (on 12 July). But on 15 July, he inexplicably submitted his resignation from the Morarji Desai cabinet and broke away from the Janata Party to join Raj Narain's Janata Party (Secular).

It was rumoured, G.G. Parikh would tell George a little later, that Madhu Limaye had 'threatened you and got you to fall in line'. Not just that, Limaye in fact 'had "triumphantly" announced this to one of his friends on phone'.[103] On 25 July, on behalf of his socialist comrades, George wrote to Charan Singh to inform him that they had already intimated the President of their support to him. He, however, made it clear that 'our group is extending its support to you on the clear understanding that this fight against authoritarianism referred to in your statement includes expeditious pursuit of the various cases against Indira Gandhi and her associates'.[104] But, as G.G. Parikh said, 'It was either wishful thinking on your part or height of immaturity to think that you can get Charan Singh to commit himself to the things you desire'. Charan Singh asking for Indira Gandhi's support to survive the confidence vote in Parliament made a lot of people 'sad, helpless and worried'. They advised George to withdraw his support. But things had moved too far ahead. As Parikh wrote: 'Your toying with the idea of getting Charan Singh to be prime minister was so immoral that now what you do is just political rehabilitation. At present secularism is not "the issue" of Indian politics. You had said so.'[105]

Throughout its career, a theory of non-Congressism had been at the centre of the Socialist Party's political existence, but in the end it saved the Congress by breaking the Janata Party. It paved the path for Indira Gandhi's triumphant return to power and its own fall into oblivion. The Socialist Party's was the ultimate sacrifice; by merging its identity, by coalescing its ideology, by sublimating its repugnance, it had hoped to emerge stronger, purified by the ordeal, strong enough to claim the Janata Party to itself, and when it was outflanked and outmanoeuvred, it had to hit back in frustration and blind fury. But when you are furious, you don't think beyond the present second; you live in the moment and die in it as well. Madhu Limaye and Raj Narain came to symbolize 'professional party breakers, who cared for their self-centred politics and selfish motives'. The Jan Sangh somehow escaped reprobation. Its stigmatization as a communal group was seen as Congress handiwork, as it was the Jan Sangh that was slowly emerging to challenge the Congress. Madhu Limaye played along with the Congress by mud-slinging against the Jan Sangh group. He 'burnt the house fearing the rats'. George was advised to 'not get clouded by the eclipse of Madhu Limaye'.

Being an intellectual, memories had a stranglehold over Madhu Limaye. They produced a great anger in him. He had never forgotten the slight when Morarji Desai as chief minister of Bombay declined to provide state security to him and others crossing the border into Goa for satyagraha in 1956, just the way he never forgave Lohia for a political line that shunned electoral alliances, leading to Limaye's rout in the election upon his return from the Goa Jail. And now he would never forget George's veering towards Morarji Desai, leaving him to 'wolfs'. He never thereafter spared an opportunity to ridicule him. If Limaye defended Charan Singh, it was ideological politics but if George defended Morarji Desai it was because he had been flattered by him or the prime minister held something incriminating against him. Two years later, Madhu Limaye would finally sever ties with Charan Singh, calling him an autocrat and retiring from politics altogether. George too would drop out of the Charan Singh-headed Lok Dal to begin an arduous backward journey to rehabilitate himself into the rump Janata Party headed by Chandrasekhar. He would remain a loyal friend to Madhu Limaye, sending him to the United States for a medical check-up by raising a public fund, in which the largest contribution came from his Bombay-based trade unions. Madhu Limaye returned from America to live a dozen or so more years; during the time he wrote a dozen books dealing mostly with Indian politics, socialism and Gandhi-Nehru relationships. Among these was a two-volume insider's account of the Janata Party experiment, wherein, rancour overcoming him, he repeatedly reduced George to the margins of the narration, and at the times when he did bring him to fore it was to disparage him, demean and sully his record, mocking him for his ambition to be the first Roman Catholic prime minister of India. In his final analysis, George's weakness was allowing himself 'to be dominated by stronger personalities momentarily at the head of the government or the party'.[106] So, in Madhu Limaye's dissection, George's loyalty to him was a case of his innate good sense, but his loyalty to others was a result of his weakness for domineering personalities!

Charan Singh was an exponent of rural-oriented economic policy. In January 1979, he was reinstated in Morarji Desai's cabinet as finance minister, whereupon he published a treatise called *India's Economic Policy: A Gandhian Blueprint.*[107] Six months later, Charan Singh would realize his ambition of becoming the prime minister with the help of Indira Gandhi. Congressmen who were accused of supporting the Emergency or acquiescing in it without a whimper were now made ministers in his cabinet, who would upturn all the features of George's industrial policy announced in December 1977. A disturbed George, who supported the Charan Singh government from outside, wrote an imploring letter reminding the prime minister of his contribution in the making of that industrial policy. He complained that members of his cabinet like Petroleum Minister T.A. Pai and Industry Minister Brahmananda Reddy were openly repudiating features of his erstwhile industrial policy and asserting there were to be no restrictions on the growth of large business houses. There is no evidence of Charan Singh's reply; in any case, his government became a caretaking one as it failed to face Parliament and prove its majority after Indira Gandhi withdrew her support. Political compulsion, opportunism and ambition are ingredients that go into seeking power. Yet, power is not constituted of those. Great executors of power are those who have an ideology, a purpose larger than vainglory. Charan Singh in the ultimate analysis proved himself to be a petty, regional-level politician. 'What surprises, shocks and makes one's blood boil,' wrote a correspondent, 'is that he has no principles in life.'[108] But George was left with a limited, lamentable choice. For him now there was no other alternative to the socialists than to join the camp of Charan Singh.[109]

On 12 August 1979, George was in Bombay, speaking to a jam-packed audience of trade union workers. He came dressed in a mundu and accompanied by Leila Fernandes. He unleashed a series of volleys at the RSS. 'You run the organization the way you like but keep away from us,' he told the RSS. Indignation was writ large on his face, as he spoke about the 'continuous attempts made by the RSS to malign him and tarnish his image'. He spoke of how Nanaji Deshmukh invited and feted him and his family, while his Sangh associates ran a smear campaign against him. Outlandish insinuations were brandished about him in the motivated media: it was said, he held a green card, his home had been raided, he had been bought over by the multinationals. 'They called me corrupt. And when this systematic undercutting was going on to finish me, Nanaji Deshmukh confided in me that the three old men [meaning Morarji Desai, Jagjivan Ram and Charan Singh] were no good. His all hopes were focussed on A.B. Vajpayee, Chandrasekhar and me. And since Vajpayee was not keeping good health and Chandrasekhar was uncouth, so only me! Well, I was not a fool to be taken in by his words.'[110] There was a character assassination campaign against him at the people's level while at another they tried to flatter him as possible prime minister.[111] In the pecking order created by journalists for those in the race, he did find his name mentioned.[112] It was asserted he was at his political peak and he had taken a suicidal step by jumping off the Morarji Desai cabinet; many said, if he had just stayed on with Morarji Desai after that glorious defence of his government in Parliament, nobody could have stopped him from succeeding Desai. Morarji Desai had almost made up his mind of nominating George as his successor. Although Madhu Limaye said the breaking of the Janata Party government was a 'historical necessity', he had been driven simply by an act of revenge, and his actions consumed even George in the inferno. A great lover of music, Madhu Limaye was told by his prison authorities during the Emergency that he would not be allowed to keep his radio-player with him. Hurt and humiliated, Madhu Limaye preferred to destroy the appliance rather than surrender it to the authorities.

When one remembers George's famous fight against S.K. Patil and then four years later his rubbing shoulders with Patil's party under the banner of the Grand Alliance, one is tempted to conclude that he had 'a tendency of undoing the good work and land yourself in fresh crisis'. This time, after returning a hero from prison to occupy a key ministerial position in the Central cabinet and doing a substantially good job in that position, his abrupt resignation from the government was again a case of 'undoing the good work'. He allowed himself to be emotionally blackmailed into resigning from the Morarji government and lost his pre-eminent position in Indian politics. His last-minute somersault at the behest of Madhu Limaye closed all his chances of getting the top job forever. In some sense, George's bowing to his friend's wishes would show him to be loyal and mindful of human relationships. But at the same time, some would see him as being innocent of power politics.[113] A few years later he would say, 'The events of mid-July 1979 had a dynamism of their own, and all of us were sucked into the vortex, not having the requisite forces at our command to chart out a different course, we could not play any decisive role.'[114]

The Charan Singh-led Janata Party (Secular) turned itself into the Lok Dal. Most socialists, including George and Madhu Limaye, joined the Lok Dal, and their presence provided a national presence to Charan Singh's UP-centric politics and outlook and the party. They on their own established state branches of the Lok Dal. The whole of 1979, governments everywhere, at the Centre and in the states, were on tenterhooks. At first, the political instability of the Morarji regime sapped its delivery capacity, and then the Charan Singh government scarcely had any potency in it. With the disintegration of the Janata Party, the dejected forces ranged against Indira Gandhi lay in shambles. The betrayal of the mandate brought about their ignominious exit in the elections that followed. The Janata Party lost deposits in 114 constituencies out of the 431 it contested, the breakaway Lok Dal in 151 of 291 (more than half), while the victorious Indira Congress was routed in just 8 of 480 seats. In 1977, despite the Janata Party riding a wave, Congress had lost deposits in only twenty-one seats.[115] The defeat meted out to the Janata Party and its breakaway Lok Dal was greatly more devastating in 1980 than the drubbing Congress had received in 1977. This was evidence of the intense feeling of betrayal among the electorate which was obviously of a greater force than the anger felt against the Emergency. The public apathy and revulsion were so pronounced that Raj Narain, the most talked-about figure of the passing decade, took to wearing a crash helmet at his election meetings. George visited Muzaffarpur. He received a welcome, was requested to contest again, but there were also instances of brickbats thrown at him, stone pelting at his meetings and hoisting of black flags against his volte-face. As the Lok Dal gave tickets to many socialists, George was approached to raise funds for their campaigns. After the elections, many defeated candidates wrote or personally visited him with the plea for further contribution to clear off debts incurred during the election.[116]

It is often said George was more a doer and less an ideologue; ideology was not his forte. He was not Raj Narain, the demagogue, nor was he Limaye, the schemer; Lohia he never was, although he did try to mould himself in his form, at least.[117] Courage alone does not ensure one's political effectiveness or even longevity. George had latent anger against poverty, exploitation and exclusion, borne out of his own tortured past, of the long incarceration and police brutality that he had experienced, and hence he needed the power to redress such repugnant forms of human relations. Seeking power could become an end in itself, however lofty the purpose it might have been mobilized for. Power needs an ideology otherwise it can turn either way, good, bad or a sullied grey. Dismantling the Morarji government, on any pretext, when the purpose for which the mandate had been given was still far from being achieved, would have been viewed by George as unfair, unethical, un-christian. He could not run away from responsibility. Hence, the conclusion is that, left to himself, he would not have rocked the Janata boat but would have paddled along as part of his Christian duty. It is a conclusion that does injustice to George.

After the Janata government fell to pieces, he stopped wearing trousers and took to kurta-pyjama. He even tried to adopt a dhoti but could not sustain it. He unfailingly responded to issues concerning Christians or even those specifically concerning the Catholic Church.

The prime minister trusted him to look into the affairs of the minority community; representations from the community were invariably directed to him. One such instance was when Fr Rosario Stroscio, 'an asset to the Catholic Church and our country in our effort to serve the poor and the downtrodden irrespective of caste, creed and colour', was asked to leave the country as his residency was to expire. An appeal to the prime minister to allow him to continue to stay in India was signed by the president and general secretary of the Catholic Bishops Conference of India. A copy of the appeal was sent to George, too.[118] The case was settled, and George wrote to Fr Jose Maliekal, 'He will continue to stay in India, the country he loves as his motherland.'[119] George's involvement with issues concerning the church revealed not his religious side, as is most often assumed even by his closest confidants; he didn't see the use of his ministerial power to bring some kind of material support to the church as part of his religious duty. He helped many churches in north India procure some sacks of cement that they had requested from the government, cement then being a commodity under government control.[120] He also wrote to the concerned authorities to expedite clearances or grant-in-aid payable to churches for their 'laudable service to the people'. Banarsi Das, the chief minister of Uttar Pradesh was asked to look into the 'problem of grant-in-aid to the Diocese of Varanasi Education Society for the four junior High Schools they are running at Azamgarh, Ghazipur and Ballia'.[121] Patrick D'Souza of the Diocese of Varanasi while asking for help in expediting the grant had written, 'Knowing as you do, how the State government functions, it will not be enough to tell Chief Minister but to ask him to let you know when the grant is sanctioned.'[122] To Paul J. Mannemplavan of Jyotiniketan Ashram at Bareilly, George wrote, 'I would like to meet you at some convenient time to discuss the role of the Church in the development of man.'[123] There were attempts to pull George into fraternal disputes between the Orthodox Churches. One such instance was when the dispute between the two orthodox factions in Kerala, the Orthodox Syrian Church and the Jacobite Syrian Church, had turned violent and George was requested by the latter's secretary to mediate.[124]

Even when George as a minister in the Central government acted on the issues of religious agenda, he did so as a national leader without worrying about the denominational divides. Emphatically asserting that 'my party and government will do nothing that in any way hurts the religious and other rights of the people, including this of the minority', he sought to downplay the significance of the Freedom of Religion Bill, a private member, bill introduced in Parliament, that had generated much controversy even before it had been brought before the august House for debate.[125] He repeated umpteen times to the Christian delegations that visited him to implore dropping of the Freedom of Religion Bill that the 'Janata government will not do anything that will affect the rights of the minorities or in any way infringe upon the secular character of the constitution'. This restraint was a responsible way of dealing with a socially sensitive issue in a divided polity. When the Arunachal Pradesh government passed legislation regarding religious conversion, George simply said that the President's assent was required for a Bill to become an Act and he hoped that the President would consider the opinions of citizens before giving his authority to the Bill. In passing, he also mentioned that as industry minister he had nothing to do with the Bill as it pertained to the home minister's domain.[126]

12

The Dogged Years

The end of the nineteen-eighties saw the second non-Congress government at the Centre. It was short-lived like the one before, and headed by Vishwanath Pratap Singh, again an ex-Congressman. In the months leading up to the new government, George was seen playing with Singh's dogs on the lawn of his house while waiting to be called in.[1] Although his love for pets was widely known, this act would be seen as his way to ingratiate himself with the rising leader. True, he was fighting a dogged battle to rehabilitate himself after the fall of the Janata Party government and his tangled role in it. But in a situation of splintered Opposition he had long concluded that ending the Congress dominance would necessarily have to be an insider's job. In the entity of Vishwanath Pratap Singh the insider who had revolted his faith was complete; he believed that if Singh had not been there, the dispirited Opposition would have had to conjure up someone like him to enliven itself.

* * *

The decisive return of Indira Gandhi in the seventh general elections held in January 1980 surprised none. It was the natural outcome of disgust voters had felt at the self-annihilation by the Janata government.[2] Consequently, in the elections, the Janata Party was ravaged, its tally stood at a lowly thirty-one, of which more than a half were those with Jan Sangh affiliation. The Lok Dal with forty-one MPs emerged as the second-largest party, reaping its largest bounty of thirty seats in Uttar Pradesh. Fighting on a Lok Dal ticket at Muzaffarpur, George scraped through to win a second successive victory. His opponent was Digvijay Narain Singh (1924–91), a grandson of legendary Langat Singh, who enjoyed iconic status among Muzaffarpur's dominant Bhumihar caste. Digvijay Narain Singh who had represented Muzaffarpur twice before, once in 1962 and then again in 1967, was a formidable foe. To counter him, George mobilized resources, caste groups and manpower, a euphemism for those who were up for hire. He played the caste card as well, successfully mobilizing the 'backward' as well as the breakaway 'forward' who resented Bhumihar dominance. A local, who was closely following his journey, made a telling observation when he remarked, 'George in 1980 singlehandedly raised the cost of an election in Muzaffarpur by infusion of resources'.[3] Still, he could only win by a slender margin of 20,000 votes. Soon after, a group of lawyers accusing him of corrupt practices filed a writ demanding his election be declared void. In an affidavit, complete with names of recipients, they accused him of distributing thousands of *ganji* (vests) to induce voters and having spent money beyond the permissible limit. But things such as these failed to rile him. In the very fortnight of his chancy victory, he began espousing Opposition unity to take on the 'common enemy,' the Congress. If Indira Gandhi could be forgiven for her Emergency excesses, he reasoned optimistically, their bungling of the mandate would be forgiven as well.[4]

His guileless sincerity encouraged a Bihar MLA to invite him to test launch his cobbling formula for Opposition unity from his state. 'Most MLAs from Janata Party believe that both parties must join hands', the Lok Dal MLA wrote to him.[5] But George realized how difficult the task was and said there wasn't any chance of unity as long as the RSS element remained in the Janata Party. In March, Jagjivan Ram, who was the Janata's prime-ministerial candidate, made the presence of RSS members a reason for his splintering away.[6] A month later, the RSS/Jan Sangh members left the Janata Party to form their own

Bharatiya Janata Party (BJP). Following this development, a political worker advised George to 'join the Janata again', but, as he said, the existence of 'reticence and misgivings on both sides' would not let it happen. He said only a fiery ordeal of joint struggles would bring about political unification.[7] It was the language of his mentor Ram Manohar Lohia. His approach too was that of a Lohiaite. His failure to evolve an enduring structure for the Socialist Party rankled in him. True, however exigent the circumstances and however reluctantly, he as the chairman of the party had let the Socialist Party merge its identity into the Janata Party. 'Parties are only instruments,' he had averred in those euphoric days, as if to disguise his failure and also to underline its temporariness. As a man of ideas and ideals, he believed it was possible to build 'a much wider platform of political thought and action in the country' without a party structure.[8] It was not to be. The socialists lost both the party and the government; and, it didn't add anything tangible to their embattled ideology. Scornful letters poured in accusing him of being callous and rash. One such angry missive came from an old colleague who wrote soon after the general elections. It was biting and bitter. 'I hope the new year will be less disastrous for you,' it said. 'You will be perhaps a little untrue to your claim about breaking more parties. You said you needed a party to "scratch your balls". But see how great this nation is? Have you heard the echo . . . B..A..L..L..S?'[9] In a short span of three years since arriving triumphantly from Tihar Jail, George found himself dented, deserted and diminished. His long days in the wilderness, which would stretch to become years, had begun.

The RSS mouthpiece *Panchjanya* called him a revolutionary who changed his colour like a chameleon. Writing a decade later, even Madhu Limaye made a mockery of his beliefs. Alluding to his July speech on the no-confidence motion against the Morarji Desai government and the quick somersault thereafter, Madhu Limaye wrote, 'The great speech did not even influence George's own decision.'[10] Coming from Limaye, who had a compelling role in the enactment of that theatre of the absurd, it only showed how far his stock had dipped. George became a nowhere journeyman. But scarcely someone to whine in a ditch, he readied himself for an uphill climb. 'Darkness of the night only indicates the unfolding day and its light,' George wrote to a distraught correspondent. But in reality, he was a dockless free-floater. Continuing with his trenchant non-Congressism, he urged the socialists out there to join the Lok Dal and make it their own.[11] By 1980, in whatever form they existed, the socialists were reduced to a marginal influence among just two socially demarcated groups of the middle castes and the industrial working class. Caste identities were in the ascendance, but determinedly standing beside those native claimants to partake in its leftovers made the socialists seem like interlopers. With the working class at its gasping end, there was urgent need to engineer a new constituency. One idea was to target rural artisans and craftspeople. They were a definite interest group, politically fetching and a breeding ground for party cadres as well. But the idea was short in the application; craftworkers, driven by their immediate livelihood needs, proved unreceptive. Another option was to align with the still surviving constituency of farmers. 'The urban situation has several angles. It will take us a long time to take the urban masses with us', he wrote to a colleague outlining why they should all join the Lok Dal. But farmers as a political constituency were on their last legs as well, dying less due to political neglect than from the afflictions wrought by the economic crisis. Villagers were abandoning villages. Farmer leaders were old, and no one as powerful and indigenous had emerged to replace this withering lot. Charan Singh was the only leader who spoke of a rural ideology; he was not identified with caste alone but with issues of rural India and wedged himself in the ideological tussle between rural and urban India. The socialists aimed to inherit Charan Singh's mantle of rural leadership in the politically sensitive heartland by aligning with him. A large group of provincial socialists did join Charan Singh's Lok Dal but they were sceptical of its utility. 'What do you expect from Charan Singh?' a colleague asked George.[12] By July, the gloves were off as Charan Singh got Raj Narain, who called himself Singh's 'Hanuman', expelled from the Lok Dal.[13] Every one of the socialists, including George, was complicit in his expulsion.[14] In 1987, Raj Narain would die of old age and George, despite urgent entreaties from colleagues, would fail to attend his cremation. A year before, in a by-election at Banka, where George was a candidate against a resurgent Congress, Raj Narain, calling him *padri*, had gone campaigning against him.[15]

On 31 December 1980, Bindeshwari Prasad Mandal (1919–82) as chairman of the Backward Classes Commission, appointed by the Janata Party government in 1979, submitted his report to the government. Indira Gandhi shelved it without much ado. But Lok Dal politics began to veer around it. In many states, particularly in Bihar, demonstrations to demand its implementation were organized. The ground beneath Indian politics was shifting, and George shifted in alignment with it. He called for a massive agitation to get the Mandal Commission recommendations implemented. On-street and in Parliament he was strident in his demand. But that constituency was not his, nor was its slogan his. He was in the Hindi heartland, with indigenous leaders addressing constituencies drawn from caste loyalties. The call to the class collective, a valid front in Bombay, had no takers in the largely rural heartland. Even if he survived here, he felt electorally imperilled, politically confused and personally questioned.

Insecure about age catching up with him, keen that his political legacy should pass on to his progeny, and prodded by the greed of his family, an eighty-year-old Charan Singh would not tolerate an alternative leadership in the Lok Dal.[16] He would not let his 'fanciful ambitions' wane or gracefully retire. His insistence on holding on to the leadership hampered the progress of merger talks to form a larger party.[17] But that alone was not the issue. As George confided to a socialist colleague, 'The real problem is the absence of ideological clarity and ideological politics. I do not know if we can restore ideology to our political life in the short run.'[18] The very same people who had broken away from the Janata Party and stood by Charan Singh, now began breaking away from him. Accusing him of being authoritarian, surrounded by a self-seeking family, they left him to embrace a new farmers' leader, Devi Lal of Haryana. In July 1982, Charan Singh after months of stonewalling the unity agenda, despite claiming he was all for it, expelled Devi Lal from the Lok Dal. Taken aback by this unilateral, 'incorrect, unnecessary, unjust and against the Party' action, George, along with others, called for a party conclave and declared Karpoori Thakur as their president, thereby irrevocably forcing a split in the Lok Dal. George became the general secretary of the breakaway group. Holding Charan Singh responsible for the split, he asked him to retire from active politics in order to save himself from further humiliation. There was an element of personal bitterness in George's attitude, as the old man had treated him shabbily and berated him for having an affair with his secretary's wife.[19] Getting rid of Charan Singh, however, didn't create the necessary conditions for unification. Chandrasekhar's desire to remain at the helm generated much mirth and hampered the effort. The antics of the Opposition politicians, a letter writer from Kerala vented, were more distressing than the authoritarian traits of Indira Gandhi's rule. The fission in the Lok Dal was a sad event. Perhaps, Charan Singh's authoritarian ways, his being captive to his family's interests, his clinging on to leadership, could be blamed for it. Perhaps George and others, who were the moving force, with age catching up with them as well, were an impatient lot. Whatever the cause, the split was a climactic tragedy. More than personal prejudices, at its root was the contrary pull of social constituencies. George was a votary of the class path to greater democratization; despite growing up with Lohia's Sudra revolution, he now stood perplexed by the adoption of the caste path to the same goal.

George realized that the Opposition parties were 'wasting a lot of our precious time and energy in an exercise of political self-abuse which is naturally both unedifying and unsatisfying', and yet he was at the centre of all peregrinations. His strong feelings against the Nehru–Gandhi dynasty unabated, he was drafting proposals, agreements and press releases, coaxing talks, pandering egos and organizing meetings. But the march of history had sidelined him, reduced him to a minor player. 'Your efforts at consolidation of the Opposition would, in my view, be meaningful if your own identity is well established—not merely as an individual but as a distinct ideological group,' he was told.[20] Couldn't there be a socialist consolidation? In January 1983, amidst more confusion, he moved out of Karpoori Thakur's Lok Dal and rejoined the Janata Party. Although anticipated, his move surprised

people. He had been talking of reviving the Socialist Party but instead
returned home to the Janata. His supporters were rattled. 'We think
this is the third major mistake we have committed as socialists in the
last five years,' a socialist comrade wrote, listing the three mistakes.
'First, the dissolution of the Socialist Party in 1977 to merge with the
Janata Party; second, parting of ways with the Janata Party in 1979 and
joining the Lok Dal; and, now this is the third.'[21] George responded by
saying he agreed that the 1977 decision was wrong. 'I also agree with
you that the 1979 break was wrong. However, our re-uniting with the
Janata Party is only correcting the wrong that was committed in 1979. I
believe we have to start where we left.'[22] This provided no solace. A step
taken in confusion, driven by the exigency of survival provided no clear

Courtesy: Sridhara Tumari, Bangalore

George had started to think of shifting his political base to Karnataka after his narrow
victory in the fiercely contested 1980 election at Muzaffarpur. Here, flanked, on his
right, by J.H. Patel (1930–2000), who would go on to become Karnataka's chief minister
(1996–99), and, on his left, by S. Venkatram (1924–81), joint secretary, trade unionist,
socialist ideologue, and the short lived HMS President (in 1981), George is addressing a
state-level convention of peasant and farmers' leaders at Karnataka's Nargund (District:
Gadag) in September 1980. However, his shift to Karnataka would be disastrous, defeated
in his very first electoral foray in 1984 by Congressman C.K. Jaffer Sharief (1933–2018).

road map for the future. A distraught supporter vented his feelings: 'A 35 years of hope for the socialists have vanished. Even communists who ally with identical parties for the sake of elections never wiped off their parties. Without the cadre's consent, you people are habituated of joining various parties, breaking away, then joining with some other party only to break away again.'[23] George tried to explain, saying now at least socialists were together in one outfit and how non-Congressism remained a driving political ideology. 'For socialists, the removal of the Congress (I) is a must if any ideological oriented politics in India is to take shape.'[24]

When George rejoined the Janata Party, the party president Chandrasekhar was on a nationwide padayatra, which he had launched at Kanyakumari to conclude at Delhi in June 1983. Since the time Chandrasekhar had taken the helm, the party had moved nowhere. George was not enthused by the 'educative' intent of his padayatra.[25]

Courtesy: Sudhendra Bhadoria

With Chandrasekhar; their relationship was typical of those between peers, marked by mutual competition as well as warmth. Sudhendra Bhadoria who gifted this photo was present when Chandrasekhar said, *George, Kaash main bhi tumahre tarah bol sakta!* (George, only if I could be orator like you!) Sudhendra who is the son of socialist leader Arjun Singh Bhadoria (1910-2004) was a child when in 1967 George won the parliamentary election and was frequent visitor to his father's North Avenue residence in New Delhi.

'I have very strong reservations on Chandrasekhar's Bharat Yatra,' a sceptical George wrote when he was invited to participate in it. 'This is not to say that the exercise per se is bad. My concern is that instead of discussing solutions to the problems and taking them to the people, senior political workers should now want to go to the people and find out what the problems are. I have spent my whole life among the have-nots of this country and struggled against the worst odds to set right what is wrong. If I and many others have failed so far it is not because the solutions were wrong but essentially because there are always forces that try to divert attention from the real solutions.'[26] After the loftiness of political ideals in the 1970s, the causes espoused by politicians in the 1980s seemed designed only to keep themselves afloat. In 1983, however, good news began to pour in for Opposition parties as Indira Gandhi began to lose state elections. But in October 1984, Indira Gandhi's assassination by her Sikh guards, in retribution for her ordering army action in the Golden Temple at Amritsar to cleanse it of the extremists hiding there, altered the political scene drastically. The elections held in December 1984 saw the expected massive sympathy wave swaying voters in favour of the Congress now led by Indira's son, Rajiv Gandhi, who had come into politics after the demise of his younger brother in a plane crash.

Every one of the Opposition stalwarts bit the dust. George shifted his constituency from Muzaffarpur to Karnataka's Bangalore. It was a last-minute change, though perhaps he had started to think of shifting his political base to Karnataka after his narrow victory in the fiercely contested 1980 election at Muzaffarpur. Karpoori Thakur who was electorally influential among the backward castes was now in a separate camp. He did not want George any more to stand from a Bihar constituency. The relationship between them had never been smooth.[27] In the immediate aftermath of the Janata government collapse, they became more estranged. Karpoori Thakur had never aspired for national leadership; his heart and soul was in Bihar politics.[28] Despite his avowed approval of OBC reservation politics, George concluded that Bihar would not stand by him in the long run. He also anticipated a strong sympathy wave for the Congress following Indira Gandhi's assassination. Many north Indian towns, including some in Bihar, had witnessed anti-Sikh riots, in those dark days and darkest nights in the first week of November 1984. An election held in that surcharged political atmosphere contained limited possibilities for him. But motivations for a change of constituency primarily came from his differences with Karpoori Thakur. In April itself, prompted by the discovery of an old election poster from the 1980 election in her cupboard, Jaya Jaitly had written him to visit Muzaffarpur: 'You should make a trip before you decide on Bangalore.'[29] He had begun to prepare for a shift but he kept the decision to himself. In a list released in the last week of November, he was named Janata Party's nominee from Muzaffarpur. But at the last minute, he switched and filed his nomination from Bangalore (North). His choice was ill-fated, though. He faced Jaffar Sharif, the Congress candidate, and despite giving a spirited fight, was defeated. Jaffar Sharif (1933–2018) had earlier defeated his brothers also in different elections held in the city when they contested against him.[30]

While most Opposition members remained dispirited after the resounding defeat of 1984, George carried on his fight against the Congress, unmindful of the potent mix of catastrophe and charisma that had propelled the party to an unprecedented electoral success. Refusing to be enfeebled by the setback, believing in the cyclical turning of fortunes not as a matter of fate but result of one's perseverance, he attempted twice in quick succession to win a parliamentary seat. Both attempts were made at Bihar's Banka. The first was in a by-election against the Congress candidate Chandrasekhar Singh who had been the chief minister and was being touted now as a minister in waiting at the Centre. Banka was an old socialist fortress, a constituency known to him since 1973 when he had campaigned for Madhu Limaye in a by-election held here. The young George had then attracted the attention of the region's youth with his powerful oratory and charismatic appeal. Young boys and men had taken to writing to him and inviting him to address their gatherings in Banka. But when he fought his election, he lost. The victorious Chandrasekhar Singh (1927–86) died within a year of his election. His widow Manorama Singh was given the Congress nomination for the by-election held soon after. George decided to field himself for the seat once again. He filed his nomination from inside Bhagalpur Jail, evoking the nostalgia of 1977 when in similar circumstances he had filed his nomination from Tihar Jail.[31] This time, George gathered Opposition parties to support his candidature. His unflinching ardour won him accolades and support, though also some heartburn and back-stabbing. Even Morarji Desai, who hadn't met him since their split in 1979, and who was so bitter at George's somersaults that he had thrown a spanner in the works every time the Janata Party discussed merger with the Lok Dal, wanted him to win. The widespread expectation was about George's win. It was said, 'he can make a corpse rise with his speeches', but the talent proved ineffectual against the state's combined might that was bent upon retaining the seat for the Congress.[32] He was a target of much vilification; he was called an outsider, his support for Indira Gandhi's alleged assassins and campaign against their capital punishment made the Congress accuse him of being with the separatists. He lost this time as well. He laid the blame for his loss on the electoral rigging done at the behest of the ruling party. However righteously aggrieved he might have felt at the loot of democracy at Banka, he was not without blemish either. Taking the Dalit widows of the Arwal massacre along to his public meetings he worked to convey the heinous nature of crimes under the Congress regime.[33] He got dummy independents to contest to help him overcome limitations imposed by the Election Commission and use their resources for his campaign. His trusted lieutenants were election agents to these independents. So hurt was he at the two successive defeats at Banka that when in December 1988 Rajiv Gandhi talked of a new electoral reform bill on the anvil, George sent a copy of his 'compilation of what the press reported on the rigging and booth capturing by the Congress (I) in the by-election in November 1986' for his perusal.[34]

Many thought George made these repeated election forays because he was desperate to enter Parliament. Rajiv Gandhi's popularity was still not sullied; he had not become 'as unpopular as we think he had', G.G. Parikh wrote to George, purportedly to provide consolation. He continued, 'in this country, people do not like those who wish to snatch power from the rulers. They instinctively are with the ruler.'[35]

In short, according to Parikh, George was being a usurper. To a man who had just suffered the second consecutive defeat, G.G. Parikh offered little consolation. Bitter at his irrelevance, although nurturing an inflated sense of being a socialist ideologue and a recurring grudge against George with whom he had been co-conspirator in the Baroda Conspiracy case, Parikh said, 'only when an exceptionally moral person challenges the ruler, the people respond'. He crudely implied that George was not that 'moral person'. Parikh wrote, 'I suppose someone among our leaders will have to achieve that stature, and I should add as a rider, he should also learn to work with others.' It was a crooked way of admonishing him and undermining his morale, when after the defeat, in a public pamphlet, a strident George wrote, 'Politics to me is not a profession. I have nothing to get from it. It is a mission. The cause is the country and its millions. As those involved in the struggle, we have no time to mourn.'[36]

Rajiv Gandhi began to bungle badly and propaganda against him began to stick. In July 1987, military contingents were flown into Sri Lanka to disarm the LTTE (Liberation Tigers of Tamil Eelam) cadres.[37] In October, Jaffna, capital of the Tamil-dominated North Province, was bombed by the paradoxically named Indian Peace Keeping Force (IPKF). It resulted in unprecedented mayhem even in this war-torn region. Rajiv Gandhi was hoping to lift his sagging domestic popularity by this action and make his geopolitical presence felt. But military intervention turned into a mire from which he couldn't extricate himself. LTTE leader Prabhakaran wrote heart-rending letters to Rajiv Gandhi who ordered that the LTTE leader be brought to him; to be precise, that Prabhakaran's severed head be laid at his feet.[38] The arrogance and inexperience of Rajiv Gandhi (1944–91) not just challenged a determinedly built resistance movement for dignity and freedom, but would lead to his own horrific death at the hands of a suicide squad in May 1991, detonating him so badly that remains of his head was sewn just to retain its fragments. A shrill cry to recall the forces began to be heard in Indian politics. Although the BJP and the communists supported the military action, George called it a foolhardy misadventure and demanded the withdrawal of forces.

'The time to get our men back from Sri Lanka is now,' he wrote and spoke ceaselessly.[39]

Earlier that same year, under a darkening cloud of corruption charges, Rajiv Gandhi had expelled Vishwanath Pratap Singh and a few others from Congress. VP, as he would be known, launched a series of nationwide tours giving strident speeches to rouse the people against his former boss. He became a rallying point for dissidents and opposition to Rajiv Gandhi. As his acceptance grew in the Hindi heartland, he began to be projected as the contender for the top job. George not only came to position himself as his close confidant, he went abroad to undertake investigations into many scandals that gripped the Rajiv Gandhi regime, at the centre of which were the alleged kickbacks in a defence deal with Bofors, the Swedish arms manufacturer.[40] George was the only politician who, much like the journalists breaking stories in *The Hindu, Indian Express* or *The Statesman,* undertook international trips to collect evidence against the Rajiv Gandhi government. He wrote pieces that were published in the *Illustrated Weekly of India* and other periodicals.[41] On his tours abroad, he held meetings with international players, investigating sleuths, parliamentarians and journalists. After a forty-day 'investigating' tour of Europe and America, he returned home in the middle of June 1987 to claim he had proofs of kickbacks that the Gandhis received from Bofors and other deals. Based on information collected, he gave damning interviews to the Indian press.[42] In one such interview, he talked of the inbuilt nature of kickbacks. In every defence deal, he said, the defence minister received a percentage of the total transaction; it was on them to reduce or increase the percentage.[43] George also began prodding the President, the soon to retire Giani Zail Singh, who was also miffed with Rajiv Gandhi, to order the latter's dismissal for his 'involvement in arms deals'.[44] He was brave enough to name the London-based, Indian-origin businessmen brothers, the Hindujas, as having played a go-between role in 'the greatest ever scandal in free India's history'.[45] In George's scathing language, Rajiv Gandhi had graduated from being 'a surviving son' to 'an illiterate' to 'a liar'. He was always for him simply, 'R. Gandhi'. His attack on the prime minister was direct, sharp and merciless. But his investigative forays also revealed to him the frailties of human nature. Olof Palme, the late Swedish prime minister who had intervened to save George's life after he was nabbed at the church in Calcutta on that fateful June day of 1976 at the height of the National Emergency, had also been the man who in contravention of all Swedish laws had acted as 'Sweden's biggest arms pedlar'.[46]

The encircling net around Rajiv Gandhi and the emergence of Vishwanath Pratap Singh generated rambling hopes in the leaders of Opposition parties ranged against the Congress. The death of Charan Singh in May 1987, if it cleared some hurdles, also gave rise to new ones. George broke tangentially away from the Janata Party line, in which Chandrasekhar had allied with the Lok Dal, now headed by Ajit Singh, Charan Singh's America-returned son, to fight the breakaway Lok Dal group headed by Devi Lal. George campaigned for Devi Lal in the Haryana state election. Favouring a larger coming together of the Opposition parties that included Devi Lal, George asked, even while he was in the Janata Party, for the withdrawal of the Janata Party from the fray in favour of Devi Lal's Lok Dal to defeat the Congress. For his pro-Devi Lal advocacy, he was again seen as someone not bound by party discipline and a wrecker of parties. Chandrasekhar's limpet-like hold on the Janata Party without an electoral base of his own annoyed George who forgot that he himself lacked such a base. In 1987, he was with Chandrasekhar at Ranchi, together addressing a public meeting. George, in the course of his full-throated speech, gesticulated at Chandrasekhar, declaring that if he had the power he would make even Chandrasekhar the prime minister. This was menacingly demeaning to Chandrasekhar, showed him as someone yearning for prime ministership at any cost. George derided him for the political choices he was making because of his insecurities and ineptness, limiting the party's expansion. Seeing Chandrasekhar's allergy to VP, George was prepared to move forward to unification even if it meant splitting the erstwhile Janata Party.

Not just did he give a call to support Devi Lal but openly sided with him, saying only he could bring justice to Haryana. In a long letter that he wrote to Chandrasekhar from Kolhapur, where a Marathi–Kannada border divide was being assiduously fanned, George advised his party president to take politics 'with greater seriousness than you have done in the recent past'.[47] He urged Chandrasekhar to 'not tolerate deadwood, and do not let hangers-on try to jump on the bandwagon'. They had an uneasy relationship. Both lacked a stable political base and were simply biding their time for some wave to pick them up. George often prodded Chandrasekhar to do more activist politics. Worried that the party was shrinking in its social base in the important Hindi heartland, George desired focus on farmers and working-class issues. He proposed the Janata Party's merger with the larger section of Lok Dal led by Devi Lal. Chandrasekhar instead brought Maneka Gandhi's Rashtriya Sanjay Vichar Manch into the Janata Party. After Sanjay Gandhi's sudden demise that left his mother distraught, a situation had risen where his widow Maneka Gandhi (b. 1956) left the prime minister's home. She had founded the Sanjay Vichar Manch, and just when successive electoral setbacks were making her a stale leftover, Chandrasekhar offered her a lifesaver. Opposing this fiercely, George said there was nothing in common between Maneka Gandhi and the Janata Party which was born out of the resistance to Sanjay Gandhi's Emergency.[48] Maneka Gandhi felt George's opposition to her entry into the Janata Party was mainly due to his ongoing hostility towards Chandrasekhar. 'I think Fernandes finds he gets a lot of press coverage when he talks about me, which he doesn't when he talks about economic issues,' she said.[49] She had been equally hard hit by the Congress arrogance. In the 1984 general elections, Maneka Gandhi faced Rajiv Gandhi at Amethi and was shouted down by the foot soldiers of Congress. *Beti Hai Sardar Ki, Desh Ki Gaddar Ki* (Daughter of a Sikh, traitor to the nation), she was told. If George had been a victim of the Nehru–Gandhi dynastic rule, she too projected herself as having suffered at its hands. If Maneka Gandhi, the dynasty's estranged daughter-in-law, could be reduced to belonging to a seditious community, there was nothing to stop them from calling George an outsider or an anti-national for showing sympathy to the assassins of Indira Gandhi. But George's indignation at the merger of Maneka's outfit into the Janata Party was caused also by personal pique. Maneka Gandhi had alleged in a piece published in her journal *Surya* that Leila Fernandes had played a role in the decline of the Red Cross in India.

At the beginning of 1988, the cause of Opposition unity was adopted by the newly installed chief minister of Haryana, Devi Lal (1914–2001). Chandrasekhar meanwhile brought Ajit Singh, who was electorally compromised since taking over his father's mantle, into the Janata Party and offered him its presidentship. This move was seen as calculated to scuttle a larger consolidation of Opposition parties. When George reacted unfavourably to Chandrasekhar's gambit, the greenhorn Ajit Singh (1939–2021), whose only claim to fame was being Charan Singh's son, crudely expressed his displeasure, saying, 'George is a kind of a gadfly.'[50] Devi Lal would send invitations written in English for conclaves of Opposition leaders. He spoke of the 'Devi Lal-V.P. Singh phenomenon' and was hoping that VP would be beholden to him. In July, at Allahabad, George spent many days addressing meetings in support of V.P. Singh's candidature in the by-election. V.P. Singh won here, and his victory provided a momentum to the cause of Opposition unity.

George's proximity to VP angered Devi Lal and those close to him such as Sharad Yadav (b. 1947), a one-time George protégé but now firmly in Devi Lal's camp. During the tedium of unity talks, George was sometimes invited and other times ignored. Ajit Singh's presence in the Janata Party contributed to George's temporary eclipse. At the end of September 1988, prominent Janata Party members met in Bangalore to take stock of the unity efforts. In the same month, the National Front held its inaugural rally at Marina Beach, Madras. George was among the special guests invited but he declined to participate. In these times, although playing an important role, he was mentioned only in passing, even when people like Ajit Singh, Maneka Gandhi and Chandrasekhar were hogging the limelight either for their obstructive ways or untrammelled ambitions. In the newly formed Janata Dal, George was one of the four general secretaries under the secretary-general Ajit Singh, who had still less claim over his father's legacy than Rajiv Gandhi over his mother's. But George didn't take it amiss. His consuming passion about defeating the Congress, bordering

Election poster at the time of the 1991 general elections.

on hysterical obsession, entailed negligence of all other issues, even if he was edged out to the sidelines. His outlook drew from Lohiaite non-Congressism but had been hardened as well by his brushes with the Congress governments, even if he admitted that all governments, irrespective of the regime, were bad per se. His attitude was something like, 'let the country face chaos but defeat the Congress'.

But by the beginning of 1989, he had regained some respectability, when he was made the chairman of the National Campaign Committee of the Janata Dal. George emerged as V.P. Singh's main troubleshooter.[51] He had believed that V.P. Singh was 'the alternative'. 'If there was no V.P. Singh we have to invent one.'[52] In the elections held in November, the Congress lost in northern India, whereas in the South it registered sweeping victories, dislodging even N.T. Rama Rao (1923–96) and Ramakrishna Hegde (1926–2004) from power in their respective states. George returned to Muzaffarpur and was elected. For a week, the country saw scenes of political manipulation at its worst, and ultimately V.P. Singh was unanimously chosen as prime minister by a sleight of hand. George for the second time became a minister in the Central cabinet. After having initially been considered for Home, V.P. Singh gave him Railways, when it was said he desired Industry. On the first day, he went to Delhi's Rail Bhavan in typically dramatic style, driving up in his old Fiat and asking the security man where the minister's office was before identifying himself.[53] Although his determined pushing through of the Konkan Railway project was celebrated in the region, some were opposed to it and in later days they would adopt every trick in their book to derail it. VP made him also a minister of Kashmir Affairs, some say at the suggestion of Rajiv Gandhi, but ditched him just when it seemed he was getting a grip of it. About his foray into Kashmir, his secretary Ashok Subramaniam recounted, 'V.P. Singh sent an all-party delegation. Two planeloads of people, numbering about forty, were put in a hotel called Sher-e-Kashmir International in Srinagar. The team arrived in the morning and left by the evening. Complete curfew prevailed in the city. George desired knowing the ground realities by interacting with militant groups. There were people from Intelligence Bureau and police and journalists but we slipped away from the hotel and interacted with a cross-section of people.'[54]

* * *

Soon after the Janata government collapse in 1979, a politically isolated George had desired returning to full-fledged trade union activism. Shanti Kabir his mother-in-law cautioned him against it.[55] 'You have an established reputation as a Trade unionist,' she told him, propping up his ego but actually with the tendentious purpose of dissuading him from going back to the streets. She wanted him instead to aspire for political positions. His resignation from government was the outcome of exigent political circumstances, she consoled him. 'Does that mean you must get back in haste to your old trade union activity,' she wrote, explaining, 'Trade unionism in organized sector is well established

where there are long-serving hard boiled men with vested interests.'
He was much needed among the 'exploited, downtrodden and starving
villagers', and should not get 'locked up again in trade unionism'. It
was a homily delivered more from her elitist desire to see her son-in-
law placed in more respectable government positions with trappings of
power. She was self-conscious of his striving, sweating days in the street
among the municipal, hotel, taxi, railway workers. Actually, going back
was not really an option, or the path leading to it any easier, but ignoring
Shanti Kabir's advice he repeatedly reached out to times gone by that
he had long outgrown. The trade unions were no longer in awe of him.
The break-up of the Janata Party had cast ominous shadows over the
trade union field as well. The always simmering fraternal rivalries had
surfaced in the Hind Mazdoor Sabha (HMS), with which in 1979 he
had merged his own Hind Mazdoor Panchayat (HMP). The HMS
now was a quagmire that rivalled the confusion in the Lok Dal. He
desired taking over its leadership, but the socialist labour front was
against it, repeatedly rejecting his overtures, even while it allowed his
nominees to become its presidents. Here as well he was unfortunate as
both his nominees, S. Venkatram (1924–81) and Balasaheb Dandavate
(1929–81), died in quick succession while in office. When the pressures
on it mounted to take him in, the HMS split itself in order to reject
him. His response to the continued boycott of him by the HMS was
typically socialist: he now designed a new labour federation called the
Hind Mazdoor Kisan Panchayat (HMKP) by splitting from the HMS.
The idea of a split didn't go down well with the trade union fraternity.
'You are perhaps aware that Lok Dal leaders particularly the socialist
group are being blamed throughout the country for splitting the Janata
Party, and if HMS is split, the entire blame would be attributed to you
and the socialist group by the general public,' a colleague wrote.[56] His
ground for splitting the HMS was not the ideological differences but
the inaction of the incumbent leadership. He was advised to capture its
leadership in the next election rather than split it. Expressing the futility
of uniting the fragments of the HMS, he said unpleasant feelings were
mutual. 'In any case, the HMS people have no use for me and treat
me as an untouchable, though they would like to have my unions,' he

responded. In the middle of 1982, those with him in the HMS met at Ahmedabad and decided to form the HMKP.

Whatever was George's initial motivation in splitting the HMS, it was not entirely primordial. He was convinced that the trade unionism had drifted away from the pioneering adventurism of yesteryears. The unions had become service agencies and organized labour self-centric. Those who were to have been the vanguard of a proletarian revolution had moved far away from the predicament of the unorganized workers.[57] The trade unions demanded uniforms made of fashionable terry cloth, without thinking about its impact on the handloom sector, which provided livelihood to millions in the unorganized sector. Their leaders were simply pleaders in local courts, who because of their knowledge of labour laws had taken on the mantle of labour as well. They now hired knifers and petty lawyers, pushing the leaders to the margins. George

Courtesy: Fredrick D'Sa, Bombay Taximen's Union

George with Datta Samant, Trade Union leader of Bombay.

had been fired upon quite a few times during his work to organize labour. One such incident happened at Modinagar, near Meerut, where he had gone to address a congregation of striking workers. The situation was already tense after the murder of a trade union leader and he wedged himself into it to show solidarity. After years in the workers' movement, George now lamented the laxity, the careerist attitude and corruption in the trade unions. Yet, refusing to give in, he felt he must take initiatives. 'The national trade union scene has the smell of the graveyard,' he wrote to Bal Dandavate.[58] 'The initiative has to come from Bombay and again, as usual, we have to provide it.' The new HMKP was to restore meaningful trade unionism. It was intended to organize 'agricultural labour, small farmers, artisans, craftsmen and other sections of the working people who are untouched by the urban-based trade union leadership'.[59]

Around that time, George was also aiming to regain the leadership of the All India Railwaymen's Federation (AIRF). But his attempts here as well were stonewalled by its traditional leadership. In August 1980, the AIRF organized a railway workers' convention at Bikaner. Although uninvited, he landed up in the city. When he arrived at the venue of the convention, he was booed down and had to make an unceremonious exit when he was shown black flags and 'go back' banners. G.G. Parikh wrote to him that the ignominy he suffered at Bikaner was because people hadn't forgotten July 1979 when the Janata government fell and his role in its fall. George retorted it was not July 1979 but October 1974, when he was elected the AIRF president against the wishes of socialist leadership, that the people hadn't forgotten. Stubbornly his supporters went ahead with their plan to instal him in the leadership of the AIRF. In September, as part of the plan, he was made president of the South Railway Mazdoor Union (SRMU) in the southern railway; and the South Central union (SCRMU) also nominated him their president. Reassembling its forces, the AIRF leadership struck back, engineering splits and dissensions in these railway unions. 'I notice that the AIRF leadership is working overtime to attack the two southern unions and all my friends on railways,' he wrote ruefully.[60] A few weeks after his election as SRMU president, a man emerged from retirement claiming he was the elected president and that George had been duped to occupy a position that was not vacant. The AIRF supported the resurrected president of the SRMU. The result was a split between factions, but eventually, the issue ended in a truce at the cost of George, who resigned quickly, matching the alacrity with which he was made the president. The Congress hatchet man Yashpal Kapoor and the Railway Minister Jaffer Sharief actively nipped his bid at leadership in the bud. In a candid letter to a comrade, George explained: 'The AIRF is bluffing the workers, though I am sure a large number of them are seeing through the game played by this colourless leadership. I do not believe the AIRF leadership will lead any struggle. But they have the immense capacity in collusion with Mrs. Gandhi to destroy the militant sections with the sole purpose of ingratiating themselves. I need to speak about such leadership.'[61]

The AIRF's bid to keep George out of the railways continued. 'All this means that we have to do much more work at the grassroots. I am doing whatever I can,' George wrote to a workers' leader.[62] In September 1981, the AIRF held its national convention at Mathura. This time a chagrined George avoided it, but egged on by his supporters, soon after the convention, he wrote a general letter to the railway unions, drawing their attention to the fact that 'the AIRF by itself cannot lead any struggle of the railway workers'. The government was tightening the noose around the neck of railway workers by enacting laws such as the Essential Services Maintenance Act, but the AIRF was still wobbling, he said. 'Let me state that the government will do everything it can to keep the railwaymen divided and there will be enough people in the movement who will be willing to play the role of stooges of the government in such an effort.' He called for a revival of the NCCRS, that magic potion that had galvanized the 1974 movement. He attacked the established leadership of the railway workers with much vehemence. Their lethargy, co-opted position, scrambling for small gains came under repeated attack from him, but this did not lead them to reform or see the reason behind his criticism; instead, they came together to stonewall him with a greater resolve. Although he said there was no room for the 'chicken-hearted', it was they who controlled the AIRF and they were determined to not let him in again.

In November, he gave a call for an alternative convention of railway workers. Someone responded acerbically, accusing him, 'a shrivelled politician', of being wrecker of workers' unity, a self-serving careerist who cared not a hoot when workers were dismissed after the 1974 strike. He was 'terribly disappointed' by the accusations but refused to be drawn into the slinging match. The AIRF leaders who were invited to his convention did not even acknowledge his missive, and the unions associated with communists, Janata Party and the BJP also refused to participate. The only response, he said tongue in cheek, came from the sleuths of the Intelligence Bureau. The disappointing show left him with no option but to chart out an independent path by forming a Rail Mazdoor Union (RMU), which was founded in Bombay in January 1983 as an alternative to the AIRF.[63] This step, instead of consolidating the railway workers, ended up further splintering them.

* * *

During the 1980s, George was everywhere, constantly on the move, taking part in political agitations, showing up in solidarity, unforgiving of sloth, resentful of the duplicity of governments. On 8 October 1984, Viren Shah, the Bombay industrialist and part-time politician, a co-accused in the Baroda Conspiracy case, wrote, amazed at his busy schedule: 'You continue to move like a whirlwind, making it difficult for ordinary mortals like me to see you.'[64] Someone who was young at the time but a keen observer said, 'he could carry three plane tickets in his pocket, so well endowed he was. He never had a dearth of money, but he had very different use of money, it was always for a purpose, mostly political, but never for personal aggrandisement. Some people have a knack for being resourceful, George was one such person.'[65] Sometimes pre-decided programmes were cancelled at the last minute, causing much indignation. Mama Baleswar Dayal (1905–98), working among adivasis of central India, wrote crisply: 'Look, leader . . . whenever I search for you I am told you are in Bombay. How long that can continue? How do you expect people like us to keep pursuing people from Bombay.'[66] He was expected to address a rally at Sagar on 3 April 1980, but he skipped it without letting the organizers know why he couldn't be there. An angry letter arrived from the chairman, District Yuva Janata, Sagar (considering he was in the Lok Dal, it is interesting he was being invited by the Janata). It said: 'The party workers despite being hamstrung with bare minimal resources were working day and night to make your programme a success. Your time is so precious that you can betray thousands of people who await your arrival and it costs you nothing. Socialism will arrive in this country even without you. And if the opportunity arrives we shall be eager to welcome you next time with black flags.'[67] Similarly, when George failed to turn up at a party workers' camp in Bihar organized by Kapildev Singh, the latter sent a biting reproof: 'Instead of devoting full time in Lok Sabha please spend some time regularly in building organization.'[68] Socialist Raghu Thakur from Madhya Pradesh was equally furious at his inability to keep to scheduled engagements and accused him of being a serial offender when it came to first committing to a programme and then abandoning it. After narrating a series of such mishaps, Raghu Thakur wrote, 'I have concluded that our unconditional love and selfless work for you have no value in your eyes.'[69] In 1981, a public meeting was organized at Bhubaneswar, which he and Biju Patnaik were to address.[70] He consented to be there, but when the final invitation came, he was already committed to be at a meeting of the Socialist International in Paris. 'This is an important meeting,' he wrote to the organizers of the Bhubaneswar meeting, 'hence I am proceeding to Paris.'[71]

Lonely but undaunted, he was never shy of taking up battles. On 4 July 1980, Parliament discussed the enactment of the Essential Services Maintenance (Assam) Bill. George called it a 'lawless law', which made the Congress members tauntingly demand that the provisions of the Act must certainly be used against people like him. His sympathy for the Assam student agitation was held responsible for fomenting trouble there. He himself left no opportunity to go Congress-bashing. He reminded the Congressmen that he had always been at the receiving end 'of all your laws'. 'For thirty-one

years I have overcome them and I shall overcome them for the rest of
my life also. Do not threaten me with your laws. I have experienced
your laws in the darkest days. I have had handcuffs on me; I have
had chains on me. I have experienced your laws in the darkest of days
and I am still alive. So, don't threaten me.'[72] Even his Indianness
was questioned. When he was speaking on the violence against SC/
ST in Gujarat, ruing the fact that so many years after Independence,
violence against a weaker section hadn't abated, and bringing to the
fore the fact that the violence was not limited to Gujarat alone but
was endemic throughout the country, underlining the brutality of
the establishment, he was told to go abroad if he was so unhappy
being in the country. The odious suggestion made him roar at the
offending Congressman, that such a power as to throw him out of
India hadn't yet been born. 'India is my country. No one can ask
me to go out of it.'[73] Whether questioning his Indianness was a
game in provocation or a serious innuendo was difficult to fathom.
However, the grimness of George's response made the presiding
officer intervene with a platitude of 'India belongs to everyone' and
then to admonish him condescendingly, 'Mr. Fernandes, why don't
you speak with a smile.'

George reached out to victims of injustice, travelled to the
scenes of injustice, and seldom shirked from speaking and writing to
authorities and forging campaigns to redeem the injustice. If there
were people who wrote to George desiring his channel to raise issues
of their interest in Parliament, he wrote to people as well seeking
reports, documentations and information to help him raise issues of
injustice.[74] People from across the country felt affinity and believed
he would take up their issues personally and work to provide them
justice.[75] A village sarpanch from Bihar's Saharsa district wrote a long
letter detailing how trusting labourers from his area were taken to
Gujarat and tortured to work as bonded labourers. George sent that
letter to both the chief ministers of Gujarat and Bihar, chiding them
for the prevalence of this practice. 'To any civilized government, it is
a stigma.'[76] In July 1981, a thousand lives in Bangalore were lost by
the consumption of illicit liquor. 'All those who died were workers,

Harijans and other indigent sections of society,' George said in a pamphlet, and organized a conference of working people with the 'primary purpose of dissuading workers from consuming alcohol'. He wrote an appeal to Gandhian institutions inviting participation in his activities, and picketed liquor shops.[77]

He stood for everything that opposed Indira Gandhi; whether he stood with a Farooq Abdullah dislodged by her or against the military action at the Golden Temple, he was hopping from one trouble spot to another. His relationship with Kashmir was not limited to the Abdullah family alone, with whom of course it was thick. Socialists in the state regarded him well. Elections to the J&K assembly were held in June 1983. In October 1983, Farooq Abdullah organized a convention of Opposition parties at Srinagar. Indira Gandhi didn't take kindly to it. In July 1984, she dismissed him and installed an alternative government of defectors. George was at the forefront of those who protested, attending meetings organized in Srinagar and taking Farooq Abdullah along for the nationwide public protests. 'Farooq is under attack essentially because he refused to compromise with the Congress (I),' was his refrain. When N.T. Rama Rao, the matinee idol who had become chief minister of Andhra and was pursuing Opposition unity, was dismissed by Indira Gandhi, George was there. When Assam exploded, he was there. When Punjab burnt, he was there. Believing passionately in the dictum that battles were never lost till death, never faltering from his path, even when frayed and fatigued fellow travellers decamped, he was everywhere, standing with victims and against injustice.

From the time trouble broke out in Punjab, he was involved in providing a healing touch. In February 1985, he took a team of Opposition politicians to Panipat in Haryana to hear horrid tales of atrocities against the Sikhs and record acts of arson. After the visit, in a letter to Giani Zail Singh, the President, he wrote, 'It is my considered opinion that there is no Hindu Sikh confrontation in Haryana. The entire anti-Sikh operation has been engineered by the Congress (I), and the State machinery, up to the District level has been used to carry out the nefarious designs of the ruling party.

Chief minister Bhajan Lal has orally said to several people the Sikhs need to be taught a lesson.'[78] By his acts of solidarity, he was brought close to Punjab leaders. Prakash Singh Badal (b. 1927) who was in Tihar Jail in March 1984 wrote a poignant letter informing him of the marriage of his only daughter. 'I wanted to celebrate the auspicious ceremony with great joy in the company of friends like you. But for me, party work is always on priority. As I am in Tihar Jail, I will not be able to attend the ceremony. My absence can be covered only if friends like you grace the occasion to bless your daughter.'[79] George attended the marriage and a profusely happy Badal wrote thanking him 'for the trouble you took to attend the marriage. We are proud of you.' He also worked to get Badal's New Delhi flat vacated by a Bombay firm to whom it was rented out. A week after the Golden Temple army action called Operation Blue Star, George wrote to the home minister seeking facilities to meet the jailed Akali leaders. 'The purpose of the meetings is to discuss with them ideas about the restoration of normalcy in Punjab and finding solutions to the many vexing problems confronting the state.'[80] He was denied permission to visit them in jail. In October 1988, he arranged a visit of Sukhbir Badal and his mother to Prakash Singh Badal's place of incarceration at Coimbatore. He himself had gone to meet him there in July with the permission of the state government. He campaigned, though to no avail, for the commutation of the death penalty awarded to Satwant Singh and Kehar Singh, convicted in Indira Gandhi's assassination.

With no hope of returning to government, he revived *Pratipaksh*. Though ignored by mainstream media, following the precedent set by Lohia himself, George in 1982 launched an English monthly magazine *the Other Side*. Its main advertising support came from his unions in Bombay. He solicited articles from writers and advertisements and subscriptions from all. When he asked industrialist Rahul Bajaj (1938–2022) to place advertisements in the journal by way of support, the latter wrote back expressing his inability. 'Advertising in any such magazines, especially one which is or may be deemed to be political in nature, is difficult for a company,' Bajaj wrote.[81] The argument failed to appeal to George. He replied exasperatedly, 'How are political journals to survive if companies do not advertise in them? And for that matter, which journals are not political? *the Other Side* is a journal of thought and action and is not at all concerned with what goes as politics in India.'[82] He told Mulk Raj Anand that he regarded *the Other Side* as a 'continuation of the work done by *Mankind,* edited by Dr Ram Manohar Lohia'.[83] (Mulk Raj Anand had been on the editorial board of *Mankind.*) If he was seeking approval for his venture, he was also showing concern for others. He encouragingly wrote to veteran Congressman S. Nijalingappa on his forthcoming autobiography, telling the 'angry old man' that he had great expectations from his book.[84] Marxist S.G. Sardesai who wrote a book *Progress and Conservatism in Ancient India* in which he attacked 'mysticism, obscurantism and Hindu Chauvinism' wanted George to request Atal Bihari Vajpayee and L.K. Advani to read his book. George not only reviewed the book in *the Other Side*, but he also assured Sardesai that 'both Atal and Advani [would] get the book so that there could be a debate on the issues raised by you'.[85]

George became sensitive to deaths around him and unfailingly sent condolences to the bereaved and wrote obituaries. He wrote to R.K. Karanjia on the death of his wife, Aileen, joining him 'in sharing your grief' and urging him 'Do look after yourself'.[86] His own father died in 1983. Though a natural death, it left in him a void and the feeling that now it was his turn to go. He began to meditate on the legacy he would leave behind when the great reaper arrived. This feeling of mortality became more overpowering when he returned from the cremation of Karpoori Thakur in April 1988. It was strange—he was just fifty-seven—to have such thoughts but then, Lohia, his mentor, had passed away at the same age in 1967. He wrote a touching obituary for Karpoori Thakur and published it in *the Other Side*.[87] It was a long monologue, portraying a troubled relationship, marked by both rancour and mutual warmth. Karpoori Thakur had visited his home at Bangalore and met his mother, and eaten supper with the family. They had been competing politicians, although it was felt, and Karpoori Thakur perhaps willingly fanned such an impression, that George had survived on Karpoori Thakur's largesse and magnanimity. But he refuted it, quoting facts and citing anecdotes. He wrote he hadn't achieved much, with a feeling of having reached the peak perhaps, with no turning the clock back. The spectre of retirement began to raise its head. He began to plan a life in retirement, desiring to build a home on the land he owned on the outskirts of Bangalore. Hans Janitschek of the Socialist International desired to write a book on his life. But this didn't mean he was wrapping up his activities. He desperately wanted to make history happen once more, to re-enact the role which had made him a national name. He even spoke of the possibility of going underground again in the eventuality of another Emergency being clamped, and at a convention to protest the enactment of the 59th Amendment to the Constitution that under the state of Emergency in Punjab gave absolute rights to the state to imprison without prosecution, he spoke of his readiness to use dynamite again as a people's material of protest.[88]

* * *

If people were aggrieved about his inexplicable disappearances and unexpected changes in formerly fixed engagements or public rallies, organized with great effort and expenditure and accompanying publicity, he took flak from them without ill-will. He had his reasons but was seldom in a position to air them: while his political career was in ideological disarray, his personal life was no less adversely hit. Leila Fernandes had gradually grown estranged from her husband. After George became a minister in the Janata government, her most frequent complaint was that she had 'to witness people from Bihar and UP come up to our bedroom'.[89] But the rift had begun even before, when he was underground and she in exile. She had met Subramaniam Swamy in the USA, and he had told her of George's infidelity.[90] By the early 1980s their marriage suffered a serious rupture. In sudden spurts of emotion, Leila Fernandes would take off for a visit abroad, leaving him to take care of a young son.[91] It was at first her way of taking revenge on him. His mother had done the same, leaving her four boys of various ages in the custody of their father and going to her mother's home. She had stayed there for ten long years, during which time the children grew up with their father. George's own experience with Leila Fernandes' wilful absences may have helped him understand his father better. He was scarcely capable of taking care of a growing child all by himself given his political engagements. He harnessed Jaya Jaitly's help. Leila Fernandes was a gutsy and volatile woman, careless of social etiquette and prone to emotion-filled implosions.[92] Contemporaries have recalled her in unsavoury anecdotes. Calling her 'ill-tempered', Swaraj Kaushal said, 'I was not exposed to foreign university system then. Leila had come to my house and we were having dinner. There was some talk related to London universities. She snapped at me for not knowing that Trinity was not part of Cambridge but of Oxford. She said, "Fool, Trinity is not in Cambridge."'[93] In fact, both Oxford and Cambridge

In October 1982, his man-Friday Fredrick D'Sa married Emilda at Udipi. George whose marriage with Leila was already on the rocks and one who was not known for attending marriage ceremonies, made an exception of it and attended it along with Leila and Sushanto. With anger and distrust having already replaced love, the photo is ample evidence of the distance growing between them.

have colleges named Trinity! Swaraj would only feel redeemed when many years later he sent his daughter to study at Oxford's Trinity.

By the mid-1980s, however, George's conjugal relationship collapsed completely; it so deteriorated that one day Leila Fernandes left his government bungalow and moved into her own home, leaving him in the lurch. The government house they were living in had long since ceased to be a home. She left, upbraiding him for cavorting in 'the company of other people's wives'. Madhu Limaye who had come to meet George happened to witness the incivility of Leila Fernandes' angry exit. He repeatedly questioned a shell-shocked and visibly mortified George on the matter, further embarrassing him so much that George would write that evening in a note to Jaya Jaitly (whom perhaps Leila had in mind when she made that insinuation), 'M. Limaye had come and he repeatedly kept asking me if Leila had "shifted".'[94] It was sad that the soured friendship between them had reduced the name to a crude initial. The events of immediate past years had cast a dark and ominous shadow on their mutual regard. When Madhu Limaye developed a heart ailment, which needed corrective surgery in the USA, George circulated a letter among friends and in social circles to raise money for his travel and surgery. The surgery never happened, as doctors declined to operate owing to the adverse condition of sharply fluctuating blood pressure, but the waning of warmth between them was visible. Madhu Limaye had extracted his price for nurturing George, and damaged their friendship and the complementary role they had played together in Indian politics by forcing him to resign from the Morarji Desai government. Having paid his price, George broke away from him and they had gone their separate ways by the time Leila Fernandes made her uncivil exit.

As after his defeat in the 1984 election he had to vacate the government bungalow, he moved into a small flat in South Delhi that doubled as his political and editorial office. The relationship with Leila Fernandes worsened as they lived separately. She would even send him a signed divorce writ, but he returned it without signing it, along with four gold bangles that his widowed mother had wanted him to pass on to Leila. With him being busy as usual, his promises often failed to materialize and that stiffened their estrangement. Soon after his Banka debacle in November 1985, when he promised to drop his son to his school, the child was excited but his mother was disapproving.[95] She wrote to him a chiding note. 'Quite frankly, the idea is somewhat impractical,' she wrote, 'since he has set routine every morning—catching his bus, and being responsible about getting himself to school on time.' His schedule, on the other hand, she complained, was erratic and subject to last-minute alterations. She was against him instilling such irregularity into their son's 'steady, daily routine'. She remonstrated, 'You can always drive him around for your mutual pleasure and go places and do things, hopefully more frequently than once in two or two-and-a-half months.' Leila Fernandes wanted a price to let him love his son, she wanted his domestication, she wanted to curb his free spirit for which she hated him, but he refused to give in.

Frustrated at not being allowed to freely visit their son, he would write to Jaya Jaitly, she unhinged from her IAS husband, liberated from the bounds of marriage and willing to lend him an ear. He would tell her Leila was teaching their son to hate his father. 'What kind of a mother's love is this that teaches a child to hate his father?' he asked her, not knowing what to do now.[96] It would be agonizing for him to realize the hostility in Leila, but still with his individuality intact, with that streak of ardour that made him reach out to streets as if he had been in eternal preparation for it, unafraid of losing any more, he wrote to Jaya Jaitly, 'Does she really believe that I'll put up with all this because I have a public life to live? How mistaken she is!'[97] Through the years of a life so piercingly concentrated on fulfilling a destiny that had been first conceived when he had asked his aunt to lend him four annas so that he could buy a Hindi text to learn the language, reaffirmed when he had hidden himself on the roof of the red building of the St Aloysius college and shouted 'Mahatma Gandhi ki Jai' and 'Jawaharlal Nehru ki Jai', then fortified still more by that audacious leap into the unsettled world of Bombay to witness a strike of millhands and remaining there to conduct many more, his relationships with women, including his own wife, had been a fleeting acknowledgement of his amorous needs, that is if he only had time to acknowledge them. Now, in his fifties, he had found Jaya Jaitly, younger than him by a decade, ready to explore a world beyond the boundaries of regulations and discipline, beyond the prestige of positions. They would find love, a realization that was as primordial as the urges of their bodies. She wrote that she realized the meaning of true love, 'just as one feels for one's children', with him alone, and he reciprocated with an equal intensity, by writing back, 'If sacrifice of my life means saving yours, my life is available as it is available for my son.'⁹⁸ He called her his 'life partner', felt 'a sense of fulfilment in your company whether you are present or not', and gave her free run of his home and total access to his pocket and whatever was his, without seeking apologies or thanks. 'You don't do such things on what is yours.'⁹⁹

June Jayalakshmi Chettur was born on 14 June 1942, to a diplomat Keralite father and a housewife mother. As a child she travelled to different countries, studied in schools abroad, before being jolted by the sudden death of her father when she was just fourteen. She with her mother returned to Delhi to live in a charity home run by the government and eat the mess food and attend Miranda House College, before getting an opportunity to study at Smith College in Massachusetts. While at Miranda she met Ashok Jaitly, whom she would marry soon after her return following graduation. She began to call herself Jaya Jaitly. It was her husband who introduced her to George. Ashok Jaitly became George's assistant secretary during his tenure as industry minister in the Janata government. After the collapse of the government, Ashok Jaitly was called back to Jammu and Kashmir, his IAS cadre. Jaya Jaitly remained in Delhi, campaigning for George at Muzaffarpur in 1980 and four years later at Bangalore. She travelled abroad with him, a practice that gave rise to heartburn and anger in Leila Fernandes and brought much discord in his household. She got into craft and artisanal work, and worked for some time with the Gujarat State Handicrafts Corporation. Although a righteous Charan Singh is said to have repeatedly disparaged George for having an affair with his secretary's wife, they—George and Jaya—saw themselves in the mould of Jean-Paul Sartre and Simone de Beauvoir, the French literary couple. 'See,' she wrote to George in July 1984, 'between you and me we do not need any kind of relationship superimposed on us by society.'[100] She said she felt liberated and demanded respect for her 'right to use my body and mind and thoughts'. Encouraged by George, she was talking with Leila on a regular basis to help with her widely swinging moods, and taking occasional care of their son. They were all in some way entangled with each other. Seeing it as an opportunity, she proposed a new arrangement for them all that had faint hope of accomplishment but at the moment seemed most natural for her to act upon. 'We are interdependent, obliged and grateful to each other. I think Ashok has reconciled to this new me who gives of her herself and her love to others, no matter what. I had mentioned that I had discussed with him my future in mainstream political work. He is in a very receptive frame of mind so why not all of us have a discussion together? It will enable us all to work more closely together without any discord.'[101] But it was a castle in the air that soon collapsed along with her misplaced hopes. There came about a permanent rupture in the lives involved; George and Leila Fernandes separated, and Jaya and Ashok Jaitly arrived at a mutually consensual legal divorce.[102]

Jaya Jaitly loved George and also determinedly pursued her own career ambition under his mentorship. She left behind everything and had too much at stake to simply love George for all that it meant and settle for a new domesticity. Moreover, the initial euphoria of love does subside slowly into a routine. She was genuinely looking for some form of self-realization, not in a spiritual but in the existential sense. As her husband would not lend her his personal car or let her use the official one, she travelled in Delhi by buses run by the DTC which was wildly whimsical in providing services to the waiting commuters. One day, while waiting for a bus that was playing truant, she mobilized other commuters to discipline the offending driver. It thrilled her so much that she compared her boredom as an IAS officer's wife with the exhilaration she felt even as a nebulous activist. 'I was more thrilled with my first brush with a successful agitation and people's power, than I was at being the wife of a supposedly important IAS officer', she recalled the emotions her activism had evoked even many years later.[103] The ambitious Jaya Jaitly stayed the longest with George, even longer than his legally wedded wife, and therefore proved she was not a quitter. She would not 'get fed up and run away' come what may. Although many a time she did express exasperation at uncouth politicos, she was always calmed down by a detached avowal from George who said there was no compulsion for her to stay put. She clung on, despite humiliation, political and personal, despite the presence of other women coming and going into George's life, despite always being under harsh scrutiny for being George's consort, the other woman. One day, the writer Khushwant Singh chaffed her, 'Jaya, he had been seeing other women even when you were with him.' The impetuous Sardar, sipping his drink, with his legs stretched on a *morha*, expected a wimpish reply but was left stunned by what she said, 'Yes, Khushwant, I know it. I fetched many of them.'[104]

In that sense, she was not the possessive, obsessive woman that Leila had been in her prime. In those days of 'pure love' she had written in one of those notes they exchanged between them how she would like to treat him: 'I do not want to grab, cling, monopolize, wrap around like a selfish octopus, chaining you to me in some ghastly vice! I want to care for, nourish, gladden, share, grow and add to your work and dreams for our country.'[105] She remembered George had told her once that he was never happy after his marriage, and, she said she wanted to make him happy. 'I have a letter in which George Saheb writes to me that in July 1971 he stopped smiling. He started laughing and relaxing when I was there,' she recalled. Soon, she would play a dual role, that of a colleague and a consort, taking care of him and managing his home and also being a political colleague.

Ambition has many facets and forms. While an ideologically imbued ambition makes you mobilize humiliation to your advantage—remember George's shackles and his statement linking his humiliation with that of a chained nation—naked ambition, shorn of a social purpose or just self-centred, on the other hand, makes you blind to many things as you pursue it. You don't struggle to restore your lost humanity but for the time being you swallow humiliation in order to survive and then nurture a permanent grudge, against the person, against the society, against the whole world. Slowly, in your perception, you become a person against whom everyone is ranged. Jaya Jaitly's trajectory transformed her into an angry and tormented woman, surviving among scorpions, who if they often stung her by baring their fangs were not spared by her either.

13

They Hate My Guts

No government's demise was ever more clearly foretold than the one headed by V.P. Singh. Supported from outside by the BJP on the one side and the left combine on the other, it fell because it assumed from the very beginning, even before its birth, that it could make its crutches convenient fall guys, in the contemporary parlance, political untouchables, and still expect to survive a full term.[1] Soon after its fall, after Chandrasekhar became prime minister, supported by Rajiv Gandhi's Congress, in a repeat of what his mother had done earlier to Charan Singh, Rajiv Gandhi pulled the rug from beneath Chandrasekhar's government of defectors, forcing an election that killed him. In this quicksilvery rush of events, topped by the coming of the minority Narasimha Rao government, George, unwilling to hang up his boots and walk into the sunset, was on fire, wrestling against his fate. In 1990 he turned sixty. Finding himself isolated by the politics of caste, George worked to organize his forces under the aegis of Hind Mazdoor Kisan Panchayat (HMKP). He launched a Samajwadi Abhiyan to struggle against the new economic policies of the Narasimha Rao government. Together, these forces waged a struggle against the Cargill multinational company in Kutch where many acres of land were allotted to this American company to produce salt. Calling the signing of the Dunkel Treaty a surrender to American interests, they surrounded Parliament on 30 March 1994, to restrain the government from going ahead with it. They shouted *Dunkel hame Manjoor na hoga—phir se desh gulam na hoga* (Dunkel is unacceptable—India will not be enslaved again), making clear their opposition to the multinationals. They put up banners urging boycott of foreign consumer goods. The prime example was George's stand against Pepsi-Coca-Cola. Although it was the government in which he was a minister that had sanctioned the entry of Pepsi into the Indian market, now his supporters threatened to physically stop the sale of foreign aerated soft drinks in India. *Cargill Company hari hai—Ab Coke-Pepsi ki bari hai* (Cargill has lost—now it's the turn of Coke-Pepsi), they asserted. From that day in 1991 when a new economic policy was unveiled by the government, a group of individuals would march down daily to the Parliament House from George's house on Krishna Menon Marg, some 2 kilometres away, to get arrested in protest. He launched his campaign on the *swadeshi-svavalamban-rozgar* (indigenous production, self-reliance, employment) plank as he believed the new economic policy threatened the country's economic security and would bring in its wake job losses. George roped in Gandhians and Naxalites, trade unionists and politicians, as allies in his protests. In May 1992, he invited Laloo Yadav (b. 1948) to inaugurate the HMKP's fourth national convention held at Bombay. Although the posters announced his presence, Laloo Yadav skipped the occasion. In the absence of wider political investment, the HMKP's backbone remained George's unions in Bombay, who provided men and material for its various campaigns. Although the *Azadi Bachao Andolan*, a non-government people's organization advocating Swadeshi, was an offshoot of a combined effort, the failure to forge a broad platform had grave consequences as it reduced all such protests to being of merely 'symbolic significance incapable of compelling the India government [sic] to change the suicidal course on which it has launched the country'.[2]

At a time when he was busy opposing the new economic policy, the Sangh Parivar led by the RSS was leading a campaign of cultural reparation by focusing on the Babri Masjid at Ayodhya. L.K. Advani's Rath Yatra from Somnath temple to Ayodhya, undertaken to spread the message of building a Ram temple there, was actually a desperate act for survival in order to counteract the fallouts from the implementation of the Mandal recommendations. Two years later, on 6 December 1992, the disputed Babri structure, to use Advani's words, 'finally suffered extinction as the outcome of mass frenzy' mobilized by the Sangh Parivar.[3] George called a meeting of the HMKP-affiliated trade unions at Bangalore. From its platform, he called the demolition 'one of those historical events which demonstrated the depths of human intolerance'.[4] Not just did he release a hard-hitting video statement titled *Yeh Desh Kiska?*, the HMKP issued a statement signed by him.[5]

Events preceding and following the demolition of the Babri Masjid in Ayodhya have caused us deep distress, as they would have to every patriotic Indian, no matter whether he professes any faith or not. The hurt caused to the sentiments of the Muslim apart, what causes us the greatest concern is the utter cynicism displayed by the Sangh Parivar. In one foul stroke, the Sangh Parivar has said it loud and clear that the constitution and the rule of law are matters of convenience and the law of jungle would be invoked whenever their political objectives may command it.

We believe that the Ayodhya issue is but one aspect of the fight of the Indian Establishment against the people of the country. The way it fought and continues to fight against the content of social justice is another. The economic exploitation of the people of India particularly of the workers, farmers, artisans and craftspersons is also a part of that. The so-called globalization of our economy and the invitation to multinationals to take over our economy is one more aspect.

That is why we assert that this fight has to be fought on an ideological plane. The divisive ideology of Hindutva as enunciated by the Sangh Parivar can be defeated only by an ideological confrontation and not through the banning of the RSS and its Parivar. We believe that the use of Art. 356 to dismiss the governments in Madhya Pradesh, Rajasthan and Himachal Pradesh were wholly uncalled for. The dismissal is not only against the spirit of the Constitution. It also implies that the bureaucratic machine of union and state governments is the final instrument to protect the secular character of our polity. We reject this idea as absurd and unacceptable. Moreover, we do not accept the secular credentials of the Congress, certainly not on Ayodhya.

We wish to make a special appeal to the working and toiling masses and particularly to the youth—employed or unemployed— not to be carried away by the spurious catchwords of the BJP. Ram, Roti and Insaf helped the BJP get the votes. But it has been a story of the betrayal of the election promises. We believe that the vested interests will use the Mandir-Masjid dispute to drive a wedge among the workers and create a lasting divide among them. But we are sure that the working people will give them a fitting reply.

The demolition of the Babri structure was such a huge defining moment that the whole of 1993 went into absorbing the shock waves that emanated from the act. Just 3 per cent of the population, comprising upper castes, monied classes and the western-oriented elite, the Indian establishment, and common both to the Congress and the BJP, George surmised, was powerful and ruthless. He reviled the Sangh Parivar for speaking in many voices: for supporting Narasimha Rao's new economic policy on the one hand and for taking over the mantle of the *Azadi Bachao Andolan* to advocate swadeshi on the other.

* * *

V.P. Singh's crusade against corruption and the Janata Dal's victory in many states of northern India drove the Congress to margins in the political scheme of these states. In Bihar, in the elections held in March 1990, Laloo Prasad Yadav came to replace the discredited Congress regime of ten years. He hadn't won on his own, but soon, as the chief minister, he acquired a persona independent of the Janata Dal. After initially supporting him, V.P. Singh was reluctant to prop him up into the chief ministerial chair. George was sent to Patna to push for Ram Sunder Das, a Dalit leader, in the leadership tussle. Laloo Prasad won and George's assigned role perhaps continued to rankle the new chief minister. Whereas at the Centre the Janata Dal government crumbled within a year, Laloo Yadav went on to become an enduring image of Bihar. His regime came to be identified during the very first term with a lax administration, common crimes such as kidnapping for ransom that became an industry in the state, and caste killings. His success lay in establishing a single-caste dominance in Bihar's polity that produced heartburn among the state's other backward castes. He was personally 'domineering' and his colleagues, not just ministerial ones in Bihar, but also seniors such as George, felt humiliated in his presence.[6] He would not ask visiting senior colleagues to take a seat before him, and kept his feet up on the table directed towards them. Even at public functions, while he sat in a high chair, the rest of his colleagues were made to squat on the rug laid below. 'He has no use for any decencies in public life and private relationship,' George wrote in one of his angry moments after fending off an attack on his life.

In May 1994, a year ahead of assembly elections in Bihar, fourteen Janata Dal MPs, left-leaning secular individuals under the leadership of George, broke away to lay the foundation of a new political outfit, the Samata Party. Although most of those fourteen MPs came from Bihar, there were also a few from other states, which provided the Samata Party a national outlook and George's leadership an instant recall value. Laloo Yadav took up the challenge with the kind of roughness his regime had come to be known for. He organized a murderous attack on George on 17 July 1994, at Fakuli, on the highway to Muzaffarpur, soon after the presiding officer of the Lok Sabha granted recognition to the breakaway block of MPs.[7] George said that two days before the attack, Laloo Yadav at Muzaffarpur had held a 'closed-door meeting with some of the criminals of the district, including those who are members of his party'. Describing the premeditated attack in graphic detail, George wrote, 'These goons carried with them iron rods, spears, lathis and a few countryside pistols. They smashed to bits the front windshield of the Ambassador car, jumped on the roof and bonnet of the car and made dents into it. Some of them tried to drag me out of the car, but the locked door and half raised window glass held them back. They punched me on the face and chest, pulled out my spectacles and crushed them, and kept abusing me in language that raped my mother (who is dead) and my sister (though I don't have one).' George was running sixty-five. The octogenarian former chief minister Abdul Ghafoor, one of those fourteen MPs, sat beside him in the car expecting his end. But both were saved when the rest of the cavalcade of cars carrying Nitish Kumar and others reached and 'staked their lives to save mine'. In a harsh indictment of Laloo Yadav, George concluded his report by observing that 'four years and six months after he was catapulted into the chief minister's chair in Bihar, he has not only achieved the dubious distinction as the most corrupt man to occupy that office, but he has succeeded in converting the state into one big hell for the law-abiding people, in the process making it a haven for anti-socials and criminals whose undisputed head he has now become'.

Laloo Yadav's replacement was electorally sought. The Samata Party, for all practical purposes a Bihar-based party, had a slow start, almost meeting its end even before it had shown signs of life. In March 1995, in the state elections Laloo Yadav registered a momentous victory, reducing the Samata Party challenge to a miserable six seats in an assembly of 324. He established his electoral supremacy, and in January 1996 he was even made president of the Janata Dal. The Samata Party began a rethink on its future. Nitish Kumar was keen that their nebulous party be wrapped up and they return to the Janata Dal. 'Nitish Kumar was crestfallen and demoralized,' Sambhu Shrivastava, a contemporary, held.[8] George disagreed. There was no going back to the Janata Dal under Laloo Yadav. This was typical George. His long-time political acquaintance Sharad Pawar would observe in the course of a speech in Parliament, portraying a character that drew its sustenance from struggles and fights: 'When he finally decides, it is his nature to fight till the end . . . If he decides to support somebody, he can support him very well but if he wants to demolish someone, whether there is some fact or not, whether there is some base or not, he can also demolish him aggressively.'[9] But more than the refusal of George, it was Laloo Yadav's resistance to their re-entry that sobered Nitish Kumar. George, on the other hand, went around the offices of left parties in a bid to make them allies against Laloo Yadav's Janata

Dal. But they all refused, on the pretext of an existing alliance with him. He even went to the Samajwadi Party of Mulayam Singh, which had broken away from the Janata Dal, but failed to convince him as well. The Samata Party called itself 'democratic, secular and socialist' but now began to contemplate allying with the BJP. In November 1995, while George lay hospitalized at Bombay, recuperating from brain surgery, the BJP who had gathered a lakh of its members from all over the country for its national convention invited the Samata Party leaders to attend it as special invitees. Nitish Kumar attended with the approval of George, who was the party president, but it was clear it was the former who had pushed for it.

Laloo Yadav succeeded in forging an unbeatable electoral coalition but he faced allegations of favouritism to his caste group. He brought the politics of Bihar to a stage where only those among the numerically strong backward castes could contend for power. Even Nitish Kumar who rose against him, alleging his dictatorial behaviour, chose to raise an array of forces drawing from caste affiliations. Domineering behaviour of a leader is often the cause of personal affront to many others, and allegations of dictatorship are almost always bandied about by disgruntled and ambitious elements to bring about a change in the leadership. Nitish Kumar succeeded in mobilizing a steadfast support of his Kurmi caste against Laloo's Yadavs. Although Laloo Yadav would later say his whole energy was directed in keeping the fires of social justice burning while at the same time also dousing the embers of communal fires, his rule came to be pejoratively referred to as Jungle Raj. Laloo Yadav was attacked morally for being corrupt, intellectually for being a buffoon, and electorally for being just a leader of Yadavs. It was a strategy that eventually worked. Instances of corruption in his administration began to tumble out of his closet. His very visible family and its extended branches began to show ugly sides by crass flaunting of acquisitiveness. Nitish Kumar positioned himself as an alternative to all that Laloo Yadav had come to be identified with. He played his politics deftly and proved himself a consummate schemer, who had already set his aim on the crown. A year after becoming the Janata Dal president, Laloo Yadav was forced to resign as chief minister after months of audacious refusal when the CBI filed a charge sheet against him in the fodder scam, alleging his kingpin role in it. The Inder Kumar Gujral government at the Centre was protecting him to save itself, dependent as it was on Laloo Yadav's support. By the end of July 1997, when Laloo Yadav was arrested by the CBI, he had successfully brought continuum to his regime by handing over the charge of the state to his wife, Rabri Devi. He broke away from the Janata Dal and formed his own outfit the Rashtriya Janata Dal. During these simmering times when Laloo Yadav was much assailed for sticking to power, George again asked the left parties to ally with his Samata Party to wage a nationwide struggle against the social sickness of corruption. But they refused, claiming George's association with the BJP had tainted him beyond redemption.

During Rabri Devi's rule, caste violence and crimes such as kidnapping and killings gained notoriety, giving credence to the charge that Bihar needed to be rid of Laloo–Rabri misrule. As attacks mounted, Nitish Kumar kept his focus on Bihar, and he worked to chip away Laloo Yadav's electoral support bit by bit. If George came in handy in that design, Nitish Kumar would use him; and when he became a liability he would dispose of him. In November, the Congress withdrew its support to the Gujral government, paving the way for fresh general elections in February 1998. The BJP–Samata Party combine won twenty-nine of fifty-four parliamentary seats in Bihar. However, the new government at the Centre headed by Atal Bihari Vajpayee ruled only until April 1999 when a supporting party—the Jayalalitha-headed AIADMK—withdrew its support. She had been demanding the dismissal of the DMK regime in Tamil Nadu as a price for her support. A similar demand had been made by the Samata Party for the dismissal of the Rabri ministry, to which the NDA regime had capitulated. George was the defence minister and the NDA convener and pulled his strings well. Under pressure from his Samata Party, he wilted to alter one of his long-held convictions and demanded the dismissal of the Rabri government under Article 356. Having reduced Bihar to a jungle raj, he said, Rabri Devi held no moral authority to remain in power; Bihar's deliverance lay in dismissing her. George, who had even opposed the dismissal of the BJP-run state governments in the wake of the demolition of the Babri structure, supported the demand this time on the plea of lawlessness. It was a wayward turn from his lifelong position. In the last week of February 1999, the Rabri government was dismissed and President's rule imposed. But the decision was abortive as the Congress defeated the move in the Rajya Sabha, and the Rabri government was reinstated.

George had fallen prisoner to Nitish Kumar's deft politics and electoral arithmetic.[10] A new crop of politicians had come to the fore, and his dependency on Bihar for his continued political relevance became acute. In the 1996 election, Nitish Kumar had made George shift his constituency from Muzaffarpur to Nalanda, a bastion of Kurmis and therefore more amenable to Nitish Kumar's appeal. It was far more difficult to nurture a secular constituency than to piggyback ride on an existing one, sanctified by primordial loyalties of caste and creed. With Madhu Limaye long gone from his side, and the new people, narrow and self-centred, surrounding him, they gaining from his stature and he advancing their cause in return for their support to his little needs, George was now, not so unwittingly though, ransom to others' ambitions. Nitish Kumar let the Anand Mohan couple merge their upper-caste outfit of the Bihar People's Party into the Samata Party to take advantage of its identity. In calculated fashion, he laboured to steal away one constituency after another that felt dissatisfied with or ignored by Laloo Yadav. Traditionally, the upper-caste bastion was the Congress dominated by Brahmins and Rajputs, but now with its decline setting in, the BJP, George's alliance partner, was staking claim over them and eventually succeeded in decimating and replacing the Congress for all time to come. In July 1999, George signed an agreement to unite the Samata Party with the Janata Dal, which was headed by Sharad Yadav. The newly merged outfit was called the Janata Dal (United) and George fought the state election under its symbol. In the Lok Sabha elections, fought under the aegis of the NDA, they registered an impressive victory, winning twenty-two parliamentary seats on their own and reducing Laloo Yadav's Rashtriya Janata Dal (RJD) to a mere seven. But six months later, without affecting the intended unity, twelve members of the JD(U) broke away to form a separate bloc in the Lok Sabha, claiming their unity move had come unstuck and they should be recognized as a separate group. It was a short-lived rebellion against Nitish Kumar. 'We are even allergic to see the face of Sharad Yadav,' dissidents said. The group called itself Janata Dal (Samata). In July 2002, they cemented the split and began calling themselves the reborn Samata Party, a move that was not liked by Nitish Kumar, who would soon strike back and make the Samata's merger into a smaller Janata Dal (U) a reality by his sheer dominance. Nitish Kumar wanted to keep the party confined to Bihar alone. It was clear George was completely beholden to Nitish Kumar.

* * *

Courtesy: Fredrick D'Sa, Bombay Taximen's Union

Facing revolt in his Municipal Mazdoor Union by the ambitious general secretary, George was called urgently from abroad to redress the situation. On 28 August 1995, he addressed a mammoth gathering of the municipal workers before the iconic headquarters of the Municipal Corporation in Mumbai. It began to rain but he kept on addressing the crowd. Drenched, he caught pneumonia. In Delhi, washing in his bathroom he fell and injured his head, leading to hospitalization. In November, he was admitted again to a hospital in Mumbai for a second brain surgery.

The 1990s brought George the realization of his declining health; he was now in his sixties, and whatever may have been said about a politician's agelessness, one day his weakened limb caved in and he had a fall in the bathroom, leading to the development of a clot in his brain requiring surgery. In the middle of November 1995, at the BJP's Maha Adhiveshan, held in Mumbai, where party president L.K. Advani emotionally declared '*Agli bar*, Atal Bihari', George, who was convalescing after brain surgery in a hospital nearby, sent Nitish Kumar and Jaya Jaitly to witness the rising crescendo of saffron aspiration.[11] They returned smitten, but the move created an unseemly situation in the party, leading opposing factions to expel each other. Eventually, a truncated Samata Party announced reaching an electoral understanding with the BJP. In the eleventh general elections held in May 1996, they fought as allies. If the BJP became the largest party nationally, winning 161 seats and throwing off the Congress for the first time from its pre-eminent position, in Bihar, the combine of BJP–Samata won a respectable victory. But it was a hung Parliament. On 15 May, Atal Bihari Vajpayee took the oath of office as prime minister but his government survived for just thirteen days and died without proving its parliamentary strength. The BJP proved politically untouchable, being perceived communal. In the confidence motion that was moved by Atal Bihari Vajpayee, George having reposed his faith in the Vajpayee government, spoke gallantly and provocatively, stirring uproarious scenes in the august House. He questioned the intentions of the parties that were ranged against the Vajpayee government. He read from their manifestos to cite their acute differences with each other and their vitriolic outpourings against one another. The United Front constituents, touted as the next government, had accused the Congress of peddling scandals and corrupt deals, and now they were to form a government with its backing. They had accused the Congress of having damaged secularism, and now they had all come together with its backing to save it! He indicted the Congress for being anti-Muslim since Independence. 'In Nalanda constituency that I represent,' he said, pointing to the presumptuousness of the secular parties, 'there is a town called Bihar Sharif. The Muslims who live there have around

50,000 votes. Half of them are weavers and Bidi workers but have been starving for the last 3 to 4 years. There is nobody to enquire about them. There is neither any arrangement of employment for them nor there is any arrangement for selling their produce. All those people have voted for me. They did not ask from me if I was secular. They raised the issue of livelihood. They asked me how we will be able to provide them employment. All of us and this House know in what conditions the Muslims of this country are living. Who is responsible for it? They were pushed towards handicrafts and on account of the new economic policy even the handicraft is being abolished. Then they give the slogan of secularism to win votes and run the policies of the country? I oppose it. I have been opposing it and will continue to do so.'[12]

Two years later, in February–March 1998, with Congress having played its naturally self-serving role, having brought down two successive governments led by the United Front, a general election to constitute the twelfth Lok Sabha was held. Atal Bihari Vajpayee again took the oath of office and George was made the defence minister in his cabinet. Speaking against the confidence motion moved by Atal Bihari Vajpayee, Mulayam Singh Yadav berated George for joining the communal forces. 'George Saheb you could have taken anything from Mulayam Singh but should not have preferred to sit with communal forces', he said patronizingly.[13] 'Whatever differences you have with Laloo Prasad, I was with you, you should have joined us. You would have been remembered for that. Whether you would have become a MP or defence minister or not, whether you wear Kurta Pyjama or not but you would have been welcomed with the slogans of "Zindabad" by lakhs of people. Forget about the Defence Ministry, it is not a very big achievement for you.' However, opportunism couldn't be an allegation against a politician; it's their life breath, it drives their pursuit to power. To hold George an opportunist was to deny him his growth, his quest and shifts, his maturing, and demand an irrational consistency. Mulayam Singh moreover was playing to the gallery; not just had he spurned George when he had approached him for support, but he would do so again. George responded by citing again the desperate name-calling that the United Front partners and the Congress had indulged in against each other.

In May 1998, the Vajpayee government tested a nuclear device at Pokhran. Twice on two days, 11 and 13 May, explosions took place at Pokhran. The last nuclear explosions had been conducted here in 1974 when George was leading a strike of railway workers, and it was largely thought that Indira Gandhi had ordered them to deflect the country's attention from the crippling effects of the strike. But this time, when Pokhran shook again, George was visible at the desert site with Vajpayee. If it invited retaliatory sanctions from countries that were already nuclear powers, within the country the government faced a barrage of questions on its motives. Within a fortnight after the India explosions, Pakistan exploded its own device, thereby diluting the impact and instilling a fear of competitive nuclearization. On 27 May, Atal Bihari Vajpayee gave his statement in Parliament on why his government had gone ahead with explosions. The Opposition took the stand that it was a futile waste of precious resources. Veteran parliamentarian Indrajit Gupta thundered, 'in the Capital City of Delhi, thousands and lakhs of people are going without power and water, and we are going to go in for producing nuclear power now and saying that this is a great achievement. There is nothing to get too euphoric about it.'[14]

It was not a progressive step, the Opposition said, as the conscience of the world had renounced nuclear weapons as weapons of mass destruction that could not serve any military purpose. The economic cost of producing nuclear weapons was enormous, what with the retributive sanctions and all. As defence minister, George needed to respond. He was accused of going back on his commitment to a non-nuclear world. He was accused of going back on his principles. He had been a lifelong opponent of nuclear bombs, and now, under his watch, India exploded them. He, therefore, was a turncoat who had unthinkingly gone along with the ultra-nationalist BJP for whom nuclear weaponry as a deterrent was a long-standing demand. In his response, George said he was opposed not just to nuclear weapons, but all weapons. When in 1974 the nuclear device was exploded for the first time in India, he reminded the august House, he was in jail as it was at the height of the railway strike he was leading. In response to the Pokhran explosion then, he had written an article titled 'India's Bomb and Indira's India'.[15] 'Since 1968, I had been against it, but in 1996 the matter regarding C.T.B.T. was discussed here. At that time I had stated that I was against it all my life, but now I have concluded that these five nuclear powers want to dominate the future and safety of our country.'[16] A few days before this parliamentary intervention, in an interview, when tauntingly asked if he was a former socialist, he had said, 'I am not a former socialist; I am a socialist. I am not a former pacifist; I am a pacifist. I am even today an anti-nuclear weapon man.'[17] When the interviewer persisted, he added, 'but as a defence minister of the country I will do whatever is best to protect its border, and if that means nuclear bomb, then why not?' But was it not at the cost of contradicting principles he had stood for all his life? Without batting an eyelid, George responded, 'yes, even at the cost of contradicting oneself, even at the cost of dying. If the security of the country requires me to die, I shall die. It's about being realistic. It's about being patriotic. It's about caring for the country.' In Parliament, he responded to Indrajit Gupta's rhetoric. 'Many problems like shortage of electricity and water etc in Delhi have been linked with it. I had been of this opinion. But when the question of national security is there, all other things become small. Therefore, it hurts me when such things are weighed in terms of money. Is it due to the nuclear explosion that people of the country are not getting electricity and water for the last 50 years?'[18] He spoke about China being India's 'potential threat number one'.[19] When someone said he had a personal agenda of China baiting, he said, 'My agenda is the agenda of our nation, our Government's agenda. I would like to state clearly that no personal agenda can be presented by a defence minister of a country.'

George, for whom the country always had meant its people, on becoming the defence minister in the Vajpayee government considered protection of the nation's borders to have acquired urgency, for which obscene expenditure had to be readily made, even when poverty and misery still prevailed.[20] In this debate in Parliament on the nuclear explosions, George was combative. He laid bare supporting documents to build an argument that the security environment in India's neighbourhood had deteriorated in the last two decades without India making commensurate preparations to tackle the rising threat. He called for a weaponization programme by India's defence establishment. But the contradiction in his approach was glaring. Whereas the BJP and its earlier avatar, the Jan Sangh, had from their very beginning demanded a nuclear deterrent, George had always been vociferously against it.[21] The whole of the BJP leadership gloated over the vindication of their long-standing demand that India go nuclear, while George, by offering his support to the enterprise, seemed to indict himself given his so far consistent opposition to the weaponization programme. In Parliament, even when speaker after speaker targeted him, he cited the threat to national security as the sole cause for India's nuclear explosions.

He repeatedly showed how slippery his position had become as far as his long-held views were concerned. In April 1999, one of the constituents of the NDA withdrew its support to the Vajpayee government. The prime minister had to seek a vote of confidence from the House and was ousted by a single vote. Sharad Pawar, who opened the no-confidence debate, continued with the allegation that the Vajpayee government was communal.[22] 'This Government has been instrumental in provoking communal animosity . . .' George was again targeted by the Opposition speakers. They reminded him of his cavalier comment on the Graham Staines murders in Orissa. '. . . The Australian missionary and his innocent children were burnt to death,' Sharad Pawar said. 'What was said by the minister of defence in this regard? He went to Orissa, observed all conditions in two hours and stated before the nation that this was a foreign conspiracy to destabilize the Vajpayee government. This foreign conspiracy took place even before the investigation was completed.' Indeed, George was vague in his statement issued after a visit to the site of carnage in Orissa.[23] Even the prime minister thought the crime had lowered the head of the nation in shame, but George's statement was a sheer whitewash of a reprehensible criminal act. But in his rebuttal of Sharad Pawar's charge, George was as usual combative. First, he said, law and order was a state subject. 'The State government is of your party and you are accusing the Union Government.' Then, he reproved the Congress for its variety of secularism: 'When three thousand five hundred Sikhs were assassinated on the roads of Delhi then where was the thought of secularism gone?' He said the no-confidence motion was brought by an Opposition that was rattled by the euphoria generated by Vajpayee's bus journey to Lahore the previous February. Its message of peace had permeated into the electorate, and the Congress feared their ground was slipping because they could no longer level a charge of being communal on the BJP. Bringing the fight straight into the Congress camp, he marshalled case after case that proved the communalism as practised by that party. In 1971, the Central Home Ministry under Indira Gandhi had issued instructions to remove Muslims employed at or near vital installations. Consequently, in Bombay, Muslim employees at bus depots, at water reservoirs, and in the Bhabha Atomic Research Centre were suspended, and some even dismissed. It was not the first time George would speak of Congress hypocrisy, nor it would be the last.

The withdrawal of support to the Atal Bihari Vajpayee government by Jayalalitha's AIADMK on 14 April, although expected, as she had been playing truant and throwing tantrums to demand many pounds of flesh, was a shocker.[24] The government lost the confidence motion by a single vote. Claiming that she had the support of 272 members of Parliament, Sonia Gandhi prematurely staked a claim to form a Congress-led government under her leadership. George came to the NDA's rescue when a day after Sonia's Gandhi's claim he called Lal Krishna Advani to say, 'Sonia Gandhi cannot form the government.'[25] Advani hurried to a secret rendezvous with Mulayam Singh Yadav, arranged by George at Jaya Jaitly's modest home in Delhi. Mulayam Singh told Advani that his party's twenty MPs would not back Sonia Gandhi's claim. Consequently, a Parliament that had been constituted just over a year before was dissolved. However, an event portending danger and destabilization in South Asia fortuitously intervened, with death and despair, to offer an opportunity to Atal Bihari Vajpayee's caretaker government to show its mettle. In February 1999, while Vajpayee for the first time undertook a bus to Lahore, Pakistani army regulars had been noticed in the Kargil sector of Kashmir occupying positions of heights on hills overlooking a vital arterial road to Siachen. But the information seems to have not been relayed to the apex command in Delhi. The incursion only became evident in May. It took many lives and weeks to flush out these infiltrators from the mountains. Although it was never an open war, bloody skirmishes were intense, relayed live on Indian televisions, and body bags of dead soldiers arriving at different corners of the country created patriotic fervour. The intruders were finally flushed out by July 1999. In September–October, midterm general elections to the thirteenth Lok Sabha were held, which brought back the caretaker government of Vajpayee for a full term. On 13 October 1999, Atal Bihari Vajpayee once again took the oath of secrecy and was sworn in as prime minister. George continued to hold the Defence portfolio.

* * *

On 13 March 2001, at Delhi's Imperial Hotel, a four-and-a-half-hour video film was shown to journalists. This was an edited version of some 100 hours of clandestine recording that was done by a group of men disguised as agents of a manufacturer of defence equipment. They were journalists of a dot-com media outfit called *Tehelka*, undertaking a hidden camera operation factiously named West End to uncover corruption in defence purchases. The revelations made instant headlines. The political world was shaken, as big names such as presidents of political parties, officers of the military and civil bureaucracy and those hovering around powerful ministers were revealed as demanding money, women and favours to grant entry into the competitive arena of defence deals. Parliament broke into instant pandemonium. Congress MPs excitedly claimed that the government would fall. Although his name had figured in tapes, spoken by his party underlings, mostly to underline his incorruptibility, visual images of Jaya Jaitly at the defence minister's residence directing the undercover operator to hand over money for party works to someone present there was taken as evidence of his involvement as well. Jaya Jaitly was then the president of the Samata Party. On the same evening, the 13th, the Vajpayee cabinet met to take stock of the situation. George offered his resignation on three different occasions in the course of the meeting.[26] However, there was unanimity from the prime minister and home minister down to everyone present, who in one voice rejected his resignation offer. On the next day, the 14th, while Parliament was adjourned by slogan-shouting Opposition members, his stepping down was repeatedly rejected at the meeting of the ruling NDA, by all the partners, barring one. This one member was Mamata Banerjee, chief of the Bengal-based Trinamool Congress. She resigned from the cabinet demanding George's resignation, and also withdrew her party's support to the NDA, but within two years she would be back.

In the next few days, due to continued interruptions, no business was conducted in Parliament. Congressmen made 'indecent gestures' towards George, called him 'chor'. On 18 March, all of a sudden he resigned from the government and his resignation was accepted by Atal Bihari Vajpayee 'not without demur' and telling him 'it was not the end of the road'.[27] But it was openly speculated that he had put in his papers under duress, an insinuation he refused to concede. Asserting that he continued to have the confidence of the prime minister, he said, 'I am not dispensed with. I chose to go out.' He insisted he had resigned on his own because the controversy was affecting the image of the armed forces. 'My resignation had only one major purpose, and that purpose was to reassure the people at large and particularly the troops out there from Siachen down to name the place that the Defence Ministry is in good shape and there was nothing to worry.' He said he did not want the morale of the army affected as, 'Across the world, the word went around that the defence establishment in India was a den of corrupt people.' But clearly, he was a 'sacrificial lamb'. The *Tehelka* tapes contained the names of Brajesh Mishra as well as of Yashwant Sinha, who was alleged to have been taking money 'openly' but their positions remained safe. Rumours floated that George was pushed out to protect the PMO and members of the prime minister's household, who if the controversy was not swiftly nipped in the bud could have been embroiled unsavourily. Ten days later on 24 March, the Vajpayee government ordered the institution of a commission of inquiry under Justice K. Venkataswami to ascertain the facts of the matter. The Opposition led by the Congress were not satisfied. They demanded a debate in Parliament and a joint parliamentary committee to go into the whole affair, which demand was rejected. Way back in the late 1980s when he had been a leading campaigner against Rajiv Gandhi's regime for its involvement in Bofors pay-offs, it was George who had alleged that all defence purchases had kickbacks as a built-in factor.[28] If it could be true for Rajiv Gandhi, why wouldn't it be true in his case, the argument went?

When the sting broke out into the public realm, George resigned from the government, not knowing why, not telling why. But as he would later say, he was devastated because he saw that some of his colleagues suspected his innocence.[29] Although his party members in the cabinet had resigned as well in a show of solidarity with him, he was not sure of their loyalty or love, as Jaya Jaitly would later put it.[30]

In September 2001, within six months of his resignation, on the pretext that India needed a full-time defence minister, Atal Bihari Vajpayee reinstated George. Just days before, the terrorist attack on the twin Trade Towers in New York had shaken the world. However, the government faced a barrage of criticism for reinducting him without waiting for the Commission of Inquiry, a body constituted by it to inquire into the allegations, to clear his name.[31] The critics called it an instance of political immorality and destruction of parliamentary propriety and traditions. They demanded an explanation from the prime minister, but no such explanation ever came as it was thought there was no need for it. Thereafter, began a long-drawn slugfest in Parliament when George was boycotted and subjected to a walkout every time he rose to speak. Asked if it befitted his moral values to rejoin the government without waiting for the Commission to clear his name, he replied, absolving himself and abandoning Jaya Jaitly to the accusations against her, as she later averred.[32] He stated: 'I have not been charged with any offence that I have to be cleared from. There has not been any transgression by me of the moral values I am committed to.'[33] Some years later he would admit that his resignation was strategically a wrong step. But following his return, Parliament was not allowed to function or proceedings conducted, as the Opposition used the opportunity to increase the government's discomfiture. Even as these constant disruptions continued, on 13 December, a band of five armed terrorists entered the Parliament compound and fired indiscriminately, killing many police and other personnel, and dying themselves. The event succeeded in deflecting attention from him.

On 27 February 2002, near Godhra railway station in Gujarat, miscreants poured kerosene oil on and set fire to a few bogeys of the Sabarmati Express, killing some fifty-five passengers, including twenty-five women and fourteen children, who were returning from Ayodhya after performing Kar Seva for the Ram temple.[34] The next day the Viswa Hindu Parishad (VHP) and other organizations called for a state-wide bandh to protest against the incident. It was then that the riots started. On 28 February, George was already there with chief minister Narendra Modi in Gandhinagar, awaiting contingents of army personnel headed by General Zameer Uddin Shah, that arrived late at night at Ahmedabad's airfield. George conducted a peace march and was pelted with stones. This was not a new experience for him; he had borne much worse in his career. On 1 March, as vehicles to transport troops to the city were yet to be arranged, George went to the airfield to address the assembled soldiers.[35] Though the army was deployed, it took some days for the riots to be brought under control and the fear generated by the horrific events continued to stalk Gujarat for weeks to come.

In Delhi, on 30 April, after days of disruption, Parliament finally debated the communal violence in Gujarat, expressing 'grave concern over failure of administration in ensuring security of minority community'.[36] Mulayam Singh Yadav, who as the chief minister of Uttar Pradesh, had ordered police action leading to killings of a number of Kar Sevaks who had congregated in Ayodhya in 1990, opened the debate on expected lines. He asked, how fair was it to regard the victims of Godhra as innocents, but not the victims of riots in Ahmedabad? He implied that the returning Kar Sevaks had provoked a mob enough to burn the bogeys they were travelling in; they had asked for it! He further

accused the Gujarat government of fuelling the already inflammable
sentiments by carrying the dead, injured and half-burnt from Godhra
to Ahmedabad with shouts of slogans and calls for vengeance. And then
he accused the Central government under Vajpayee of being a threat
to the national unity for failing to dismiss the chief minister Narendra
Modi. George was still being boycotted by the Opposition MPs, when
he rose to present his rejoinder on the censure motion on Gujarat.
He was at his belligerent best. He chastised the Congress benches for
speaking as if it all were happening for the first time in the country. 'Why
this hue and cry?' he asked. He listed the heinous acts levelled against
the marauders of Gujarat. 'It is being told that somewhere a mother
was killed and the baby brought out from her womb, somewhere a
daughter was raped in front of her mother and somewhere else someone
was burnt alive. Is all this happening for the first time? Did all this not
happen on the Delhi roads in 1984?' His speech, like all the speeches
that day in Parliament, was pathetic, partisan, and harping on about a
painful past that had already been lived through rather than addressing
the live wounds. 'He is defending rapes and killings', Buta Singh from
the Congress bench, aroused by George's volley of fire and brimstone,
butted in, with feigned aggression. George, relishing confrontation and
not given to silence, provoked further pandemonium when he accused
Sonia Gandhi, sitting there on the front bench, opposite him, chewing
gum, of egging on her party storm troopers to create more chaos and
of 'playing the game'. He conceded something bad was happening
in Gujarat, but swiftly added that it was no different from what had
happened all over the country since Independence under Congress
rule. The Congress was a history-sheeter. 'Nothing new is happening
in Gujarat,' he said in conclusion. It was such a speech that it made
Mulayam Singh blurt out, a little patronizingly but more peevishly,
'Leave those things to Atal Bihari, you speak something else.'

On 19 August 2003, Congress moved a no-confidence motion
against the NDA government in Parliament where defence and
national security, and ultimately George, were the main planks of
its attack. The motion moved by the leader of the Opposition Sonia
Gandhi evoked one of the most tepid of such debates in the history of

Indian democracy. The mover laboriously read her litany of woes from a written script in English, and her CPI supporter Somnath Chatterjee as if in compensation read his written speech haltingly in Hindi. The only time the debate acquired some urgency was when George rose to speak. Sonia Gandhi had started by raising questions on defence and national security; she had questioned the defence minister's probity and integrity. Although Sonia Gandhi made oblique references to corruption in defence purchases, it was Somnath Chatterjee who laid out in clear terms why he supported the no-confidence motion or why it was moved. The reason was George. At the time of his resignation in March 2001, he had said he would only return after having been exonerated from all allegations. But contrary to the profession, he was reinstated after a gap of time. 'Why was he taken in?' he asked. This made the Opposition gang up. Somnath Chatterjee asked the prime minister to clear the matter. 'It is about his conscience. He has to tell the people.' But when George rose to speak, those Opposition members who had been boycotting his presence in Parliament for the last one and a half years left the chamber. They were led by Laloo Yadav's partymen. The Congress members inexplicably remained seated. George spoke on the matter after a gap of twenty-two months, launching his defence from where Sonia Gandhi had accused him. He said the NDA government 'have given [such] acceleration to the desired modernization in the field of defence that today all the three wings of the armed forces are having the weapons of strategic importance which were not available previously'. About the allegation of corruption in defence purchases, George thundered that 'one is not born as yet who can bribe me'.[37] Angrily, he asked, 'I have fought against corruption throughout my life and today I have become corrupt?' The Congress members in the House, listening to him, took umbrage at the fact that he was, according to them, 'behaving like an extraordinary holy saint, teaching us'. The aluminium caskets for the remains of those killed on borders, which the defence ministry had purchased during the Kargil skirmish, had become an issue. Speaking on the origin of the purchase, George explained,

The whole issue started in 1995. Our eleven officers and jawans were killed while our army was in Somalia of North Africa on a peacekeeping mission in 1995. Their bodies were brought to India in such a casket which was very strong and without any defect. While sending the casket, the commander of the Indian Army posted there wrote a letter to the officer in his department. It was stated there that much honour is given to the martyrs in the western countries while in India no such things happened. The process started from there. This process ended in 1999. This agreement was signed between an American firm and the officer from our army after a discussion on this issue. A Director gave clearance to it as it involved rupees one crore and seventy lakh. He signed on it. I saw all this on that day when allegations were levelled against me in the House and it was said that this government is making money at the cost of the lives of our jawans. I challenge the leader of the Opposition to come up with proof.

Sonia Gandhi had been speaking very derisively about George, accusing him of stealing money out of coffins meant for martyred army jawans.[38] She had spoken of the allegation extensively in her election campaigns. Her party had boycotted him in Parliament and hadn't allowed him to speak. Every day when he came to the House, he heard just one refrain, coffin-chor, coffin-chor. After twenty-two months of persistent finger-pointing, George finally had a chance to hammer in his point and he succeeded. 'I have spent 37 years in this House. I have not been here to suck the blood of jawans but to save this country from thieves. I am a man who works for the benefit of jawans by risking my own life.' The so far limp debate suddenly became boisterous. Sloganeering Opposition members took to the floor. Pandemonium reigned. Assuming that order could only be restored if members were discouraged from playing to the gallery, the live telecast of the debate was repeatedly suspended.

When it was the turn of Atal Bihari Vajpayee to respond, he minced no words in eulogizing George. 'Sir,' Vajpayee said, 'during this two-day-discussion one heartening development has taken place. The long boycott of my friend and colleague George Fernandes has come to an end.' He said he abhorred such practices in a parliamentary democracy. 'What kind of untouchability it is?' When Somnath Chatterjee asked, 'He had given an undertaking to the country that he would not come back until he was exonerated, why did you take him in?' the prime minister retorted, 'Undertaking to whom?' and effectively sealed the matter. He extolled George's patriotism. 'He endured humiliation and faced insult but did not deviate from his path of duty. In *Tehelka* scandal, neither any charge was levelled against him, nor he was convicted and nor any explanation was sought from him.' He lauded George as an exceptional defence minister the like of whom the country had never had before. 'Whether it is desert or snow-clad valley of Siachen, whenever he has gone to border, he has always boosted the morale of our soldiers which has not been done by any other defence ministers before. To level false charges without any proof and then not allow him to speak, was justice done to him?'[39] But in fact, after removing him on charges that were never levelled against him, reinstating him was more patronizing than justifying George's innocence. Others who had been named adversely in the *Tehelka* tapes had continued to remain in the government. George, the socialist in crumpled kurta, a man staking his everything on a struggle, indefatigable in fighting the battle for and of underdogs, being accused of financial corruption, was an undoing of a passionately led life.

The *Tehelka* sting was a widow's wrath, figuratively if not literally. George could not even bring himself to call Sonia Gandhi by her name.[40] A few months later, when he was no longer in the government, the successor government would open for scrutiny all the defence purchases just to harass him, and he would say, there is a witch hunt going on, but with one difference, here witches are hunting.[41] It was a logical culmination of his politics. It was an attempt to harm him irreparably by the use of the very tools that he had employed to beat Rajiv Gandhi on his defence deals. In those days he had openly claimed that there was an inbuilt factor of kickbacks in every defence deal, for distribution among politicians and bureaucrats. He held Rajiv Gandhi guilty simply because he had held the defence portfolio. The sharpness of his attack on the Nehru–Gandhi family had to have no other outcome than this.

His political rhetoric had been reduced to his unceasing disparagement of the Congress and its custodians in the Nehru–Gandhi family. Even the gruesome murder of Graham Stuart Staines, a dedicated Christian missionary who had come to India in his youth and stayed on to serve the leprosy patients among the tribals of Orissa, burnt alive along with his minor sons in their vehicle, was explained away by him by citing several anti-Christian incidents that had happened during the Congress regimes in the state. In the years that Rajiv Gandhi was active in politics, he had always written of him, heavy with scorn, as nothing but R. Gandhi. He attacked the dynasty, for its continuation and its progressive imbecility. The dynasty had successively robbed India of its democratic process, fomented elite politics to the exclusion of the masses, created and fanned divisions within Indian society in order to perpetuate itself. If his attack was based on facts, there was also an element of extreme malice in it.

If the Congress was fixated on its dynasty for survival, the nature of George's political engagement, driven as it was partially from a personal history of having suffered at the hands of its various governments, was fixated on both the Congress and its seemingly invulnerable dynasty.[42] He had believed that any kind of ideological politics in India could only have a beginning after the Congress and its dynasty was removed. The kind of vehemence the Congress (and the RJD) showed in opposing him could only be explained by the way their leadership took up his opposition to them: they saw it directed personally at them and therefore he too was to be attacked at the personal level. Every action of his as an incumbent minister was either turned against him or used to expose him to the charge of insincerity.[43] He left a mixed legacy as a defence minister of India.[44] He was shown to be a man seeking power, and being in the saddle at the cost of his own past, at the cost of everything that he had stood for, compromising his deepest convictions.[45] Sitting on a powder keg, inextricably tied in a knot of his own making, George's underplaying, even condoning, of the violence in Gujarat on the pretext that similar heinous crimes had occurred under Congress regimes as well, and therefore there was nothing shocking about it, was a statement of helplessness. His non-

Congressism was long dead, but he had trudged on the same path. By the end of his career, George was seeking to place himself within the state power rather than being true to his resolve, expressed in the early 1970s, to always be with the people and never for the government. He had then said that when a trade unionist enters into the government, he compromises himself, becomes an SOB.

* * *

Writing one's autobiography is a risky venture. Laying bare a lived life to others' scrutiny is not easy, and it is a courageous pursuit or a naive venture. Usually written at the fag end of one's career, an autobiography can often turn out to be account settling and aspirational. Self-serving, selective and random, the memories it deploys are such as to make the baser motives and deeds of a bygone age look savoury. Considered by the author a gift to posterity, lured by that ruthless reckoner, history, an autobiography can unwittingly render materials for later mauling and autopsy.

In her autobiography, *Life Among the Scorpions: Memoirs of a Woman in Indian Politics*, Jaya Jaitly makes damaging remarks about George Fernandes, not occasionally but quite frequently.[46] She recalls his critics' name-calling against him, 'agitationist, stormy petrel and rabble rouser', although dismissing them as 'silly tag names'. That's the sophisticated way to belittle a person—citing critics' mud-slinging without taking the onus on oneself. In a similar vein, she recalls the time when the stock of George had sunk so low he had been left with just two advisers, herself and Sampa Das, his air-hostess friend based in Calcutta. Jaya Jaitly traduces George's politics as merely dissentient or 'anti-establishment', a view held by critics as well. George's influence on her made her a butt of snide remarks from her friends, society gentry and family members. If this annoyed her enough to make her cry and feel miserable, its real blow fell upon George who bore the subsequent effects of her pique. In a telling way, she reminds us that in the *Tehelka* sting 'the attempt was to dishonour me and George Fernandes by showing us as corrupt politicians engaging with defence dealers'. That's seeking parity with George for what occurred basically to her. Yes, the clandestine recording of the transaction between her and the journalist disguised as an arms dealer happened at the residence of the defence minister; yes, owing to this fact, the Congress demanded George's scalp and also opposed his reinduction into the cabinet and, when he was still taken in, boycotted his parliamentary presence for close to two years; but except for his residence which was run by her and his party whose president she was, he had no role in the incident, a fact vouched for by the prime minister when he reinducted him. When it comes to explaining the *Tehelka* sting, it is always—'George Fernandes and I'—as if they were complicit, and if one had been absolved, then there was no rational reason why the other shouldn't have got a reprieve too. When she says, 'George Fernandes was never caught on tape as the makers could not get near him', the implication is devastating for George—that it was just plain luck that let him off or else he too would have been in the net. She was sore that whereas George was 'indispensable whether he was in government or not', she 'didn't count at all'. It took a long time for Jaya Jaitly to understand the fact that the profession of politics was not a bed of roses, but even then her understanding remained superficial. Jaya Jaitly made it seem as if she was the victim of it all, simply because she was a woman. But ask a Laloo Yadav, Shibu Soren, Omprakash Chautala or even a Bangaru Laxman, and one may see how presumptuous is her claim. The causes of her feeling let down would be mere professional hazards for many, who would not waste their time on fighting such trivialities. Consequently, her repeated recital of grievances and grudges, after a point, becomes tedious reading.

Since the early 1980s, when her IAS husband returned to his Kashmir duty, she had remained in Delhi, taking a job of design consultant with Gurjari, a Gujarat government craft-promoting enterprise. They were formally divorced only in the middle of the 1990s, but she had been travelling with George from early on, both in India and abroad. We are never told the reasons for her estrangement and divorce from her husband, but throughout the text are strewn signs to vindicate her, as if seeking solace and solidarity from her readers. Perhaps, Ashok Jaitly was not concerned enough to let his wife enjoy governmental perks—

it irritated her when their government homes in far-flung Kashmir districts lacked amenities and sometimes even electricity, and as the Kashmir Dak Bungalows lacked curtains, her husband would not take her along on his tours, making her feel lonely and forlorn. Perhaps her husband's need for an evening's swish of alcohol to feel 'sociable, relaxed or uninhibited' ruffled her nerves, and perhaps as a result she gave up 'accompanying Ashok to such parties and found myself in a few anti-liquor movements'. Perhaps Ashok Jaitly was a philanderer.[47] All these singly or together might have been the cause of her estrangement. But perhaps the biggest reason could simply be a husband's folly in not acknowledging his wife's sense of self-worth, a common enough occurrence, and we have a clue to this when she writes, 'The IAS [is] trained to believe that they always know the best and that anyone who may know better is a threat.' Because, soon after she pens this, she also writes how George was 'the only man who has ever made me feel without any hesitation or condescension, that I had an intellect and capacity worth respecting. He also had the patience to teach me when I was being foolish or ignorant.' Further, her grudge is she was 'never pampered by her husband', another common failing that husbands are known to suffer from. In her text, as she chronicles her public engagements under George's tutelage, is visible a throbbing rancour against her husband and her attempt to get at him by using George's persona and politics. She never forgave Ashok Jaitly for forcing on her the experience of 'hobnobbing with a rabble-rousing trade unionist' in exchange for the genteel life she felt she was destined to lead with her IAS husband. But it was George who eventually paid more to satisfy her deep yearning to get even with her husband. While she continued to use her husband's surname even after her divorce, it was George who unwittingly compensated her in ways and means designed by her.

All the importance of Jaya Jaitly was solely because of her given proximity with George. He trained her and gave her positions of influence, brought her into his trade union and political parties. 'The first signed book that George ever gave me was Shirley Williams' *Politics is for People*,' she claimed. He gave her a trade union platform, making her secretary of the HMKP, despite the fact that she lacked experience and there were other stalwarts who deserved it better, generating much heartburn in the organization. George propped her up unceasingly. Even when the National Front government led by V.P. Singh was on the verge of collapse owing to its announcement regarding the Mandal Commission, she got the prime minister to release her book *Crafts of Jammu, Kashmir and Ladakh* on the lawns of his official residence. The high-profile release of her book could not have been possible without George having put in a word. But then, after the fall of V.P Singh's government, George became 'a mere MP' and she was bored again by his tales of exploits during his underground days during the Emergency, scarcely realizing that it was his way of indoctrinating her and initiating her into politics and trade union work. Trumpeting her own cause, she said, 'He relied on me because he had complete and infinite and implicit trust—trust that I would never, never do anything that would harm his interest.'[48] It was part of her training but she mistook it as acknowledgement of her nature. In 2001, after the *Tehelka* sting, when she made a hue and cry over the technical issue of doctored tapes, the whole cabinet, prime minister downward, was made to sit through an hour-long presentation, at the end of which the august audience didn't find a word to say, which she found amiss and a reflection upon them for their incomprehensibility of her innocence. On the other hand, she nurtured almost a pathological suspicion about George's capabilities, ideologies and choices. Each time she was shown special favour because of George, she still was not satiated, and was critical of him. To her, George was 'a practical politician who could swallow his emotions and indignation', but at the same time, in order to cover her own deep urges, she mentions him seeking for her 'some kind of public compensation in the form of position of value that the society at large and the practical world recognized'. This refers to her own preoccupation with getting nominated to the Rajya Sabha. Simultaneously, she held a grudge against him 'for remaining silent about most things concerning me', in particular after the entrapment she suffered at the hands of *Tehelka* journalists.

The disguised *Tehelka* journalists were bumbling individuals with wads of currency notes to distribute and hidden cameras to record the exchange. Their story was so poorly conceived, their resources and presentation so incongruous with who they claimed to be that they would have raised suspicion by their clumsy ways. A little thought on the part of the dramatis personae would have saved them from all the later calumny they suffered. It seemed too easy to entice and compromise the political leadership of the country with little crumbs thrown at them, or maybe, and this is really sad, these politicians caught on the tapes were peripheral in the scheme of things and they acted casually out of inexperience, only to announce their arrival or simply to fit in. Bangaru Laxman, president of the main ruling party, the BJP, who throughout the conversation in the recorded video keeps his head buried in some papers, comes suddenly to life after he is given a wad of loose notes, of which he makes a sombre acceptance and rises from his seat to shake hands with the fake arms dealer. How easy! Similar was the case with Jaya Jaitly. A housewife of 1960s' vintage, her urge to get back at her alcoholic, philandering inattentive ex-husband was so keen that, having joined George Fernandes who was himself deserted by his wife and stripped of proximity to his child, Jaya Jaitly, with no actual experience of running a party but in a post given to her on a technical pretext, acted as if she was a supremo and someone who could throw her weight around. She paid for her innocence and for acting too big for her boots. It was a political attack that was mounted by the *Tehelka* exposure. It needed to be fought on this level; instead, by focusing on the grey-market procurement of the blank tapes, doctored recordings, inaccurate transcripts, the defence team of Jaya Jaitly worked to deflect the political implications. Her legal team targeted the repeated use of lie/boast/allurement by the fake arms dealers to entrap the unsuspecting, but they were off target again as *Tehelka*'s Operation West End was a charade in itself. From the start, it was based on a lie. Such an approach did not reveal her lawyers' strategic weakness, lawyers anyway revel in technicalities, but her own non-political frame of mind. Protection from George made her not just cocky but also carry an inflated image of her capabilities and political acumen. His sounding board had begun to see herself as a gargantuan mouthpiece capable of trumpeting on her own. A little removing of the shade, and a little independence, a few invitations and opportunities had made her falter and fall. The disgrace of the *Tehelka* sting was owing to the folly inherent in the personality of Jaya Jaitly. And, she brought George crashing down along with her.

Slowly, she had moved from overseeing household management to become a political colleague. It was not that he was getting confident of her abilities; she aspired for more. She became anxious about getting into the parliamentary system to advocate for issues related to craftworkers. But her preferred mode was the Rajya Sabha. She had founded a craftsperson organization that was membership-based and that took a commission on every sale of their produce through outlets she organized. It was a for-profit organization that seldom engaged in politics over craftworkers' issues. Yet she thought it entitled her to be their spokesperson and demanded by virtue of it a nomination to the Rajya Sabha. Not just did it cause disaffection among many who did not agree with her aspirations, others among George's colleagues too began to nurture similar objectives. If he could feather her nest, then why not theirs, was their argument. After all, many of them had remained with George and provided ballast to his politics. They felt alienated with her gaining proximity to George.[49] She was aware of their disenchantment. 'Most of pre-me colleagues of George felt displaced by my occupying the position of a reliable ally,' she said, angry at their audacity to equate themselves with her.[50] If they cursed her, she was not relenting either. 'All these petty-petty politicians, *chota-chota log, ganda netas*, spewing Lohia and wearing old dirty kurta-pyjama, who were never anything, who would just trudge in during elections, canvassing party tickets. These people never worked at the grassroots, never worked to strengthen party.' If she called them *chota-chota log* and shielded herself with George, they too had strong cuss words for her in their vocabulary.[51] Independently she was a nobody; all her activities were appended to George's, his journal, his politics, his life. This is sad, as she had the potential to tap her own inner resources and be a personality in her own right. Moreover, she took pride in her 'intellectual level'. 'If he said draft something, I would do that in a good language with a political understanding, so this kind of reliance on me upset others because till that time when he saw some political potential in me, he was always with others, and they thought they could take his time, whether day or night, whether he ate or drank, it didn't matter whether he needed a rest, he had to be on call for their needs, to solve their union problems, to push their *andolan* somewhere, to help their candidature in elections, either with money or by campaigning, so, they felt in some way they had lost out that direct access to him because of me. I never took his time or I never stepped in, but there was this feeling that came about that eventually he would have faith in me and do things as per my dictates.'[52] She thought the problem lay in the way she dressed and carried herself, because she was vocal and noticeable, but actually it was that she seemed to be taking all the fruits while managing to remain out of all the sweat and grime of electoral politics.[53] It is then that the Bombay unions began to desert him. The HMKP expelled him and the Municipal Mazdoor Union removed him from its presidency.

The unspoken and subterranean differences that existed between him and her were about the conception of politics and power. For Jaya Jaitly, having witnessed the trappings of government because of her diplomat father and IAS husband, power meant occupying positions in the state structure; for a socialist like George it was always amidst the people, in the street. But as her influence on him grew and she received some of his indoctrination, such demarcation lost its clear-cut edge. If she was seen shouting slogans on the streets, he became keen about acquiring positions in the state structure, even if it was to do good. Moreover, he no longer had electoral strength but carried political weight. Although his political longevity was generating jealousy, he was successful in bargaining for a position of advantage within the NDA on the basis of his sheer stature. He extracted the price for his support and got it. He demanded the NDA chairmanship and got it. He asked for the defence ministry and got it. As a contemporary observed, a trifle simplistically though, 'George had the acumen to get into confidences of the prime ministers. He was the blue-eyed boy of Morarji Desai. Atal Behari Vajpayee with around 100 MPs was not. Then again, during V.P. Singh's time he was in his close circle. Not Arif Mohammad Khan! There were many nationally known political figures but it was always George who stole the march over others.'[54]

Jaya Jaitly had the temerity to advise him to ask for the ministry of defence when the NDA under Vajpayee came to rule in 1998. She advised him to ask for it as they could then do a lot for jawans and also influence international policies regarding Tibet, Myanmar and other such things. It's hard to believe how one woman could come to wield so much influence over a person reckoned to be strong and zealously protective of his independence. But her needs were enormous and her exposure and understanding limited. In the middle of 2010, by which time George was taken away by Leila Fernandes to her home, Jaya Jaitly came to his official residence at 3, Krishna Menon Marg in the full glare of television cameras. The usually dull, officious and empty avenue was suddenly full of angry people shouting slogans and demanding attention. George's brothers Michael and Richard were with her. She wore an agitated look, her hair dishevelled and sweat streaming down her harsh and tense face. She was there protesting against those who had now taken over the residence and debarred her by putting a padlock over the replaced gates to the premises. It was surely ironical as she was the one who had lorded over the bungalow for more than two decades. Debarring her was grossly unjustified. The matter could have been resolved over a cup of tea. But instead of just swallowing the humiliation, Jaya Jaitly was making a public spectacle of it. 'The media loved it.' The spectacle was enough fodder for the media, hungry for diversions in a dreary life, and they didn't delve deep into it. But why was she doing it? Such distress could have been put on only to cover up some greater shame. What was it?

Politics is a ruthless game of power. There is no moral sin in conceiving it as such. Words like 'opportunist' or 'self-serving' are incongruously present in its vocabulary, often bandied about to browbeat contenders. If Nitish Kumar was determinedly focused on replacing the Laloo (Rabri) regime by his own coronation, Jaya Jaitly was looking to get some small change. If Nitish Kumar was zealously going about using George in his pursuit of political power in Bihar, Jaya Jaitly had some ambitions—a Rajya Sabha nomination, for instance—

the ostensible purpose of which was advocating craftsperson's issues, while the real objective was to be in a position a notch above her ex-husband's. They were the two ambitious individuals who made George a vehicle for the achievement of their long-nourished desires. George became a convenient all-purpose toolkit for those with an aim, and he laid himself prostrate before such wilful men and women, in return for a doubtful political durability. They had also worked for him, and now, at a time when he should really have hung up his boots and disappeared into the sunset, they desired proper recompense for their efforts. There were many more, a natural outgrowth in the political arena, but these two held on, while others, like Bombay trade union colleague Sharad Rao, just left him to foist their revolt and hoist a flag of their own.

* * *

The pedigreed hated him. The plebeians felt jealous at his powerful expression of their predicament with a perspective they lacked. Left with Bihar alone, the English-speaking socialist imports (J.B. Kripalani, Asoka Mehta, Madhu Limaye, George) won there because of their national and wider outlook to the disadvantage of the home-grown socialists. Sooner or later, in order to survive in Bihar politics, when caste-parochialism was raising its monstrous head all over, it was inevitable that George would have to depend on the accruing local elements and accord them primacy. In the 2004 general elections, Nitish Kumar made him return to Muzaffarpur, where he won, but in 2009, when he again desired to stand for election from the same constituency, his party headed now by Sharad Yadav, a front of Nitish Kumar, denied him a nomination.[55] As a consequence, a fumbling George, Alzheimer's disease already having taken some visible grip over him, was made to fight the election as an independent and he lost his deposit, denying him a graceful exit.[56] The unsavouriness of George contesting the election against his own party was opposed by his family members, who blamed Jaya Jaitly for it. Michael Fernandes wrote to Jaya about it and asked her not to make a mockery of him. And, after the election, in which he not just lost his deposit but was shown up as decrepit, his inability to campaign exposed to the world, Leila Fernandes put out a public statement expressing her displeasure at the goings-on in his life and politics. After more than sixty years in public life, after all that he had endured, after all that he had espoused, George's problem was his incomprehensibility about his own power, which kept diminishing with each successive electoral victory.

In the 1970s, when his power was at its peak, he had failed electorally. He was not an MP when in 1974 he was the leader of the railway strike. In 1975, still not in Parliament, he went underground to resist the Emergency. And in 1977, when he registered his mammoth victory at a new constituency, he had not campaigned there at all and was in jail. His power hadn't been drawn from electoral victories, but from the non-electoral arena, but this, apparently, was scarcely appreciated.

However, the fact is, there was no need for him to leave a legacy; his life was his legacy. He lived a life driven by a commitment that was experientially born, he had ideologies to believe in and for most of his life these ideologies seemed to be personified in his endeavours and struggles, but beyond that he lived a life of experiences, up close and personal, that are left for future generations to sort out and sift through, and learn from.

A Guide to Sources

The George Archive

In the second half of the year 2009, I met George Fernandes several times. He was seventy-nine then and in the grip of a diagnosed Alzheimer's disease. His memory was eroding and the disease's effect on his body too was visible. Mostly monosyllabic, he didn't ever speak a single coherent sentence to me in those meetings. But his eyes brightened every time he saw me coming. Occasionally, he held my hand tightly and walked up and down the long open-air back veranda of the bungalow at 3 Krishna Menon Marg. It was surreal to walk wordless and alone with him in the darkening shadows of dusk. One day, he took me by the hand to stand before a wall where there hung a life-size picture of him in a blue one-piece zipped up jersey, helmet on, striding up the metal stairs of a warplane. He was smiling while showing it to me and proudly pointed to himself, telling me it was a picture of himself. He was well aware of my intended work on his biography. It was not that he never tried speaking, but he tired easily. Just before he was taken away by Leila Kabir Fernandes, I was given access to the collection of his private papers under a signed contract. It is these papers that give the spine to this book. And, it is these papers that provided ballast to my more than decade-long pursuit against all odds.

Let's call this collection of papers THE GEORGE ARCHIVE. In the first few months after I had received them, my students and I dusted, sorted and organized the papers according to dates in over a hundred thick files marked by years and subjects. Not a single sheet of paper was discarded. The collection starts from 1959 and goes on until 2009. While the earlier years have documents/correspondence/articles, the later years have mostly newspaper clippings and signed letters written to the ministries at the behest of his constituents. Some of the later years' files were lost to me in the confusion of Leila Fernandes' takeover of George. These were later deposited at the Nehru Memorial Museum and Library (NMML). The George Archive has papers of his trade union and political activities as well as some concerning his personal affairs. It gives us an idea about the ups and downs within the Socialist Party and its many avatars, too. It is also a historically rich repository of his underground and prison writings. He kept handwritten duplicate copies of his correspondence with authorities and friends. In jail, it seems, he kept every tiny bit of paper on which he wrote anything. I found the scores of card games he played with the communist Ardhendu Bhushan Bardhan (1924–2016) while they were both incarcerated in the Nagpur Jail in 1963. The papers provide fresh insights into his underground days during the National Emergency (1975–77). During the months after he was caught and imprisoned, he wrote letters to family members and political leaders. Even amidst a hectic judicial schedule, when he would be brought every day out of his jail to the courts where his case was tried, he found time for writing letters and keeping a hand-duplicated copy of those letters. The George Archive also contains letters from friends and family members who wrote to him when he was in jail. He maintained a handwritten diary, which remains unpublished. From the underground, he wrote many pamphlets for clandestine circulation. These pamphlets were cyclostyled and circulated to a wide cross-section of readers. They too have remained largely unknown, and are a major source for studying India's resistance to authoritarianism. The range and richness of material kept shows that George not only had a sense of history but also had a sense of being a man of history. A bunch of letters from Margo

Skinner to various persons are in The George Archive, signifying George's appreciation of their historical importance. The speed with which he responded to his correspondents and their pan-India scale show his remarkable efficiency and his desire to remain connected with people across the country. The letters that George dictated in the days of typewriters, copies of which were meticulously filed for posterity, were more often than not typed on scraps of paper, in keeping with the Gandhian tradition of austerity and optimum utilization of resources. In The George Archive, while exhuming history from termite-infested files containing rustling yellowish, brittle papers, I found buried deep the same concern for meagre resources, for grassroots connection, and an awareness of the privilege denied to others, that I find in Gandhi while reading the volumes of his collected works. Many preserved copies of letters written in the 1980s and 1990s are typed on letterheads printed when George was the Minister of Industry in the Government of India (1977–79).

Other Collections of Private Papers

Besides the vast collection in The George Archive, another major source for this biography was private paper collections in the manuscript section of the Nehru Memorial Museum and Library. The NMML has catalogued the private papers of Badri Vishal Pitti, Rama Mitra, Ram Manohar Lohia, Haridev Sharma, and others, which were used by me as well. One of the most significant collections in its repository is that of Madhukar Ramchandra Limaye, popularly called Madhu Limaye. The NMML was reluctant to show me those papers, not because they were a political hot cake, whose exposure could generate tremors. Most private collections have conditions attached to control access to researchers; some need consent from family descendants. No such conditions were seemingly attached to the Madhu Limaye Papers, his only son perhaps not very much interested in these. Madhu Limaye died in 1995. About the same time, his papers were deposited at the NMML. Today, a quarter of a century later, the NMML is yet to catalogue these papers and make them available to researchers.

They stay in cardboard boxes, unsorted and un-paginated. After much persuasion, the NMML allowed me access to the papers, but one fine day, midway through my scrounging among the boxes, they told me it was no longer possible and the door was shut. In 1980, Madhu Limaye after his defeat at the polls had gradually withdrawn from functional politics and devoted himself to its study. Between 1980 and 1995, he wrote over a dozen books, most on socialist history and politics in India. He provided valuable biographical sketches of many socialist politicians and trade union leaders. In his endeavour to write these books, he consulted not only his collection of papers but also created a vast repository of paper cuttings from different newspapers. His collection, therefore, comprises many files simply of paper cuttings. But in some boxes are a body of correspondence and papers that are historically useful and relevant to my understanding of George. Madhu Limaye's papers, though unsorted, became the second most important source for this work. Some documents which were expected to be in The George Archive were found in the boxes of Madhu Limaye. There were also papers throwing some light on socialist interaction with Indira Gandhi; including many responses from Indira Gandhi herself.

In addition to these, I received Jaya Jaitly's selected excerpts from her correspondence with George. She made the selections, typed them herself and sent to me via email. Barring her communications with George that were mostly in English, the relevant portions of correspondence from his political colleagues and people from his electoral constituency, which were mostly in Hindi, have been rendered into English by me for use in this book. Making a history out of a disjointed and disparate collection of letters, making a wreath of a story from the tids and bits of information, views, urgings, etc. contained therein, merging the immensely rich micro data into a grand-narrative of India's journey since Independence, was, to say the least, a challenging task.

Libraries, Archives and Institutions

In the course of my research, I consulted following libraries, archives and institutions: in *Delhi*: National Archive; Parliament Library; Nehru

Memorial Museum and Library; P.C. Joshi Archives on Contemporary History, JNU; J.P. Chaubey Memorial Library, All India Railwaymen's Federation (AIRF); V.V. Giri National Labour Institute (NOIDA); Libraries at Centre for the Study of Social Exclusion and Inclusive Study, Centre for Jawaharlal Nehru Studies, Centre for Spanish and Latin American Studies, Jamia Millia Islamia; Central Secretariat Library, Shastri Bhavan; All India Trade Union Congress (AITUC), DDU Marg; Communist Party of India (CPI), Ajoy Bhavan; in *Mumbai*: Maharashtra State Archives, Elphinstone College; The Ambedkar Institute of Labour Studies, Parel; Maniben Kara Labour Institute, D'Mello Road; Tata Institute of Social Sciences, Deonar; Centre for Education and Documentation, Battery Street; State Central Library, The Asiatic Society of Mumbai; Keshav Gore Smarak Trust, Goregaon; Free Press Journal Library and Archive; Mumbai Marathi Granth Sangralaya, Dadar; in *Mangaluru*: Karnataka Theological College, Balmatta; Catholic Association of South Kanara, Bejai; St Aloysius College; in *Panchgani*: Moral Re-armament (now, Initiatives of Change); in *Dimapur*: Nagaland Archival Resource Centre (maintained by Dr V.K. Nuh); and in *Lausanne, Caux, Switzerland*: Archives of the Canton (State) de Vaud.

Other Primary Sources

Affidavit in the High Court, by Jaya Jaitly in support of the Plea filed by Fernandes' brothers against Leila Fernandes, December 6, 2011.

An Action Committee Publication, 1960, *A Struggle to Remember: Report of the BEST Workers' Dispute with The Four Agreements of January 2, 1960.*

Baroda Dynamite Conspiracy, *CBI Charge sheet, RC-2/76-CIU(A),*

Bombay Municipal Corporation, *Record of the Proceedings of the Municipal Corporation, the Standing Committee, The Improvements Committee and the Education Committee, 1961–62.*

Judgment, July 21, 2020, CBI versus Jaya Jaitly, RC-AC-3/2004A0005, December 6, 2004.

Mang Patra, a pamphlet in Hindi containing demands of people submitted to Indian Parliament on 6 March, 1975.

Ministry of Industries, Government of India, 1979, *Action Plan: District Industries Centres, Muzaffarpur (A report),* Small Industries Service Institute, Muzaffarpur.

Post Election Analysis, 1980, Lok Dal Central Office.

Rajya Sabha / Lok Sabha Debate

Report of The Class IV Staff Promotion Committee. Jagjivan Ram the Railway Minister constituted it in 1954.

Report of the Eighth National Conference of the Socialist Party, Meherally Nagar, Madras, July 8–12, 1950.

Report of the German (Basel) Mission in the Southern Maratha, Canara, and Malabar Province in the form of Letter from the Missionaries to its Friends and Supporters, Bombay: American Mission Press.

Report of the Sixth National Conference of Socialist Party, Nasik, March 19–21, 1948.

Report of the Special Convention of the Praja Socialist Party, Betul, Madhya Pradesh, June 14-18, 1953.

Shri S R Kulkarni 75th Birthday Felicitation Volume, Bombay: S.R. Kulkarni Felicitation Committee.

Socialist Party Bulletin [Edited by Madhu Dandavate]

Socialist Party Circulars, 1971-72.

Socialist Party, *Report of the Special Convention*, Panchmarhi, Madhya Pradesh, May 23–27, 1952.

Report of the Fifth National Conference of the Praja Socialist Party, Bombay, November 5–9.

Statement Submitted by Lelia Kabir Fernandes, September 16, 1976, Hearings on the Human Rights in India, International Relations Sub-Committee on International Organisations, U.S. House of Representatives.

The Maharashtra Government Gazette Extraordinary, April 13, 1963.

V.N. Barve, *Report of Scavengers' Living Conditions Enquiry Committee*, Bombay, 1949.

Thesis

Denis Fernandes, 2006, The Tulu World in European Writings, (Unpublished PhD Thesis, Department of History, Mangalore University).

Malathi Moorthy, 1991, *Trade and Commerce in Colonial South Kanara* (1799–1862), Unpublished PhD Thesis, Mangalore University.

Peter Wilson Prabhakar, 1988, *Basel Mission in South Kanara* (1834–1947), Unpublished PhD Thesis, Department of Studies in History, Mangalore University.

V.K. Jayaswal, *Impact of May 74' Strike upon Industrial Relations on Indian Railways*: A Project Report submitted for paper V Diploma in Personal management, Department of Management Studies, University of Delhi (1974–75).

William Mascarenhas, 1931, *Hyder and Tipu Sultan in Canara* (Unpublished thesis, Bombay University).

Films

Chetan Anand directed Hindi movie *Taxi Driver* released in 1954.

Franz Osten directed Hindi movie *Achhut Kanya* released in 1936.

Guru Dutt directed Hindi movie *Aar Paar* released in 1954.

Henry Hathway directed movie *Niagara Falls* released in 1953.

Mahesh Manjrekar directed movie *City of Gold* released in 2010.

Muzaffar Ali directed Hindi movie *Gaman* released in 1978.

Pattabhirama Reddy directed Kannada movie *Samskara* released in 1970.

Sanjay Raut produced Hindi movie *Thackeray* released in 2019.

Tanya Wexler directed English movie *Hysteria* released in 2011.

Tom MacArthy directed English movie *Spotlight* released in 2015.

YouTube Resources

Devil's Advocate, Karan Thapar's Interview with George Fernandes, CNN-IBN, September 24, 2006. https://youtu.be/DFnAUIEJbB4

Hardtalk India, Karan Thapar's Interview with George Fernandes, BBC, October 31, 2003. https://youtu.be/yoYqJy2zSNE

Hardtalk India, Karan Thapar's Interview with George Fernandes, BBC, March 18, 2001. https://youtu.be/vWUbqqPlkIw

Hardtalk India, Karan Thapar's Interview with George Fernandes, BBC, May 13, 2005. https://youtu.be/wxTijG1Cp_I

In Focus George Fernandes II, Karan Thapar's Interview with George Fernandes, Home TV, May 4, 1998. https://youtu.be/LG4uORlSQeA

In Focus George Fernandes III, Karan Thapar's Interview with George Fernandes, Home TV, (after) May 28, 1998. https://youtu.be/407sJ_UyjVc

In Focus George Fernandes IV, Karan Thapar's Interview with George Fernandes, Home TV, (sometime five months after formation of the NDA government, 1998), https://youtu.be/WEOXaRaNCAA

The Wire, Interview of Afra Sherwani with General Zameer Uddin Shah, October 8, 2018 (Withdrawn)

Sidhi Baat with Prabhu Chawla, Interview with George Fernandes, July 24, 2005. https://youtu.be/ZjY0q9RCE6Q

Statement of George Fernandes, Minister of Defence after visiting Orissa, January 28, 1999. https://www.indianembassyusa.gov.in/ArchivesDetails?id=330.
Third Eye with Anand Vardhan Singh, The Public, Episode No.357, https://www.youtube.com/watch?v=ABr76a2Dqe8
Ye Desh Kiska hai?, https://youtu.be/pYXA7IaYWcw
http://www.frankbuchman.info, for a biography of Frank Buchman

Collected Works

Badrivishal Pitti (Ed), 1991, *Lok Sabha mein Lohia,* Hyderabad: Rammanohar Lohia Samata Vidyalaya Nyas
Bimal Prasad (Ed), 2001, *Jayaprakash Narayan Selected Works*, Volumes 1-14, New Delhi: Nehru Memorial Museum & Library.
Collected Works of Mahatma Gandhi, Volumes 1-100, New Delhi: Publications Division.
Hari Dev Sharma (Ed), 1998, *Selected Works of Acharya Narendra Dev*, New Delhi: Nehru Memorial Museum & Library and Radiant Publishers
Mastram Kapoor (Ed), 2008, *Rammanohar Lohia Rachnawali*, New Delhi: Anamika Publishers, Volumes 1-9.
Rabindra Bharti (ed), 2007, *Kapildev Singh Samagra*, Volume 1-6, Patna: Kapildev Singh Samajwadi Foundation.
S. Gopal (Ed), 1994, *Selected Works of Jawaharlal Nehru*, Second Series, Volume 1-55, New Delhi: Nehru Memorial Museum & Library.

Interviews

Recorded Interview of George Fernandes with Fredrick D'Sa, (Unpublished) Mumbai, 2007.

Author's Interviews with

Anthony Quadros, Taxi Men's Union, Mumbai, 20 July 2015;
A.B. Bardhan, Ajoy Bhawan, CPI headquarters, New Delhi, 18 June 2010;
Ajay Sekhar, Activist, Sonbhadra, Uttar Pradesh, [Telephonic] October 2020;
Alan Machado Prabhu, Author, Bangalore, January, 2017, 24 October 2018;
Amukta Rao, Bangalore, 2013;
Anand Kumar, Professor JNU, New Delhi, 25 November 2011, Gurgaon, 20 January 2016;
Arif Mohammad Khan, Mayfair Garden, New Delhi, 25 August 2014, 11 January 2017;

Arun Kumar Panibaba, Ghaziabad, 2, 12, September 2011, 14-20 January, 1 December 2012, 18 July, 7, 17, September, 25 November, 12, 21 December 2014, 28 March 2015, 17 January 2016;

Arun Kumar, MLA (with Ajay Singh Almast), Patna, 20 October 2011;

Ashim Roy (b. 1956), Trade Union Activist, New Delhi, 2017;

Ashok Subramaniam, New Delhi, 16 August 2011;

Baba Adhav, Pune, 5 February 2016;

Basant, New Delhi, 5 December 2014;

Binod Mohanty, Sarvodaya Activist, Cuttack, 10 April 2018;

Brij Bhusan Tiwari, MP (RS), New Delhi, 17 August 2011;

Chidambaram, Trade Union Leader, Ahmedabad, 8 November 2011;

Chitra Subramaniam, New Delhi, June 2011;

Clarins Pai, Notary Public, Bijey, Mangalore, 18 October 2018;

Colin D'Silva, Mangalore, 20 October 2018;

Coomi and Virender Kapoor, New Delhi, 17 September 2014;

Dada Naik, Mumbai, 8, 18 July 2015;

Dauji Gupta (1940-2020), Ex-Mayor, Lucknow, New Delhi, 14 November 2019;

David Davadas, (at Jaya Jaitly's residence) New Delhi, 12 November 2016;

Devadatta Kamath S.J., Fatima Retreat House, Jeppu, Mangalore, January 2017;

Eric Ozario (b. 1950), Mangalore, 17 January 2017, 19 September 2018;

Father Albert Pinto, Bangalore, 7 January 2017;

Father Leo W. Lobo, Priest, Pope John Paul II Shrine, Bajpe, Mangalore. January 2017;

Father Noronha, Bangalore, [Telephonic] December 2019;

Father William D'Silva, Mangalore, 11 January 2017;

Fredrick D'Sa, Mumbai, 12 December 2010, 6 September 2011, 18 October 2015;

G.G. Parikh, New Delhi, 10 September 2011, Mumbai, 29 October 2017;

Girija Huilgol, Ahmedabad, [Telephonic] 4 November 2011;

Govindacharya, Gulmohar Park, New Delhi, 2017;

Hannibal Richard Cabral, Karnataka Theological College, Mangalore, 19 September 2018, 12 October 2018;

Harbhajan Singh Sidhu, President, HMS, New Delhi, 31 March 2015, 7 August 2017;

Hem Bhai, Shanti Sadhana Ashram, Guwahati, 18 January 2020;

Hieramath, GPF, New Delhi, 25 November 2012;

Himmat Singh Ratnoo, New Delhi, 4 September 2014;

I. Ramamohan Rao, ANI, R.K. Puram, New Delhi, 4 November 2016;

J.R. Bhosale, Western Railway Employees Union, Mumbai, 29 October 2017;

Janardan Reddy, Hyderabad, 16 January 2012;

Jaswant Sinh Chauhan, Vadodara, [Unrecorded] 6 November 2011;

Jaya Jaitly, New Delhi, 17 August 2011, 6 December 2011; 5 June, 10, 12 July 2014; 11 November 2016;

Jayashree, Port and Dock Workers' Union, Mumbai, 14 July 2015;

John Dayal, New Delhi, 4 September 2014, 14 May 2015;

K. Vikram Rao, Lucknow, 20 August 2011;

Kala Nand Mani, Panaji, Goa, 2-12 February 2012;

Kamlesh Shukla, New Delhi, 12, 22 August, 2, 12 September, 2011, 11 January, 16 October 2012, 3 June 2014;

Keshav Yadav, Hyderabad, 15 January 2012;

Laxmi Narayan Yadav, MP, New Delhi, 29 December, 2015;

Louie Fernandes, New Delhi, 18 October 2010, Mumbai, July 2015;

Madhav Reddy, HMKP, Mumbai, 13 December 2010;

Mahabal Shetty, Municipal Mazdoor Union, Mumbai, 30 June 2015;

Mahendra Bajpayee, Patna, 21 October 2011;

Mahendra Sharma, International Transport Workers' Federation, New Delhi, 7 January 2015, 10 July 2017;

Manish Jani, Ahmedabad, 10 November 2011;

Manohar Reddy, Bangalore, January 2017;

Markrandey Singh [Varanasi], GPF, New Delhi, 16 June 2010;

Michael Fernandes, New Delhi: 18 October 2010, 28 June 2011, 4 November 2015; 1 August 2017; 20 June, 20 August, 4 November 2019; Bangalore: 28 September 2015, 26 August 2018; Kohima: 9-14 December 2016; Mangalore: 09-17 January 2017;

Michael Lobo, Mangalore, 27 September 2015, 17 September 2018, 18 October 2018;

Mira Das, Acharya Nagar, Bhubaneswar, 10 April 2018;

Mrs Dey, Batha Ah-tin, and Tony, Gopalpur-on-Sea, Odisha, 12-13 April 2018;

N.K. Singh, IPS, Author, New Delhi, 1 August 2011, 13 December 2015;

Nandana Reddy, Bangalore, 20 January 2012;

Navnath, Municipal Mazdoor Union, Mumbai, 24 October 2015, 23 October 2017;

Neerja Chowdhry, Women's Press Club, New Delhi, 27 November 2012;

Neiphiu Rio, Dimapur, 12 December 2016;

Niraj Labh, Patna, 5 July 2014;

Nitin Kumar, Nirman Bhavan, New Delhi, 29 September 2016

Noor Mohammad, Calcutta, 12 September 2011;

Olga Tellis, Mumbai, 15 July 2015;

Padmanav Shetty, Mumbai, 3 July 2015;

Padmanava Acharya (b. 1931), Governor, Nagaland, Kohima, 12 December 2016;

Pannalal Surana, Socialist Party, New Delhi, 6 January 2012;

Patrick D'Sa, Activist, Contemporary of George, Mangalore, 12 January 2017, 19 October 2018;

Paul Fernandes, New Delhi, 18 October 2010, 23 March 2015;

Pawan Gupta, SIDH, Mussoorie, May - June, 2016, 6 May 2018, 17 August 2019;

Pius Fidelis Pinto, St Francis Church, Ferar, Mangalore, 12 January 2017;

Pius Malekandathil, JNU, New Delhi, 12 May 2015, November 2016, 9 September 2019;

Poppat (Anirudh) Limaye, New Delhi, 20 January 2015;

Pradeep Kumar, Bangalore, 19 January 2012;

Prakash Shah, (Retired Professor, Ahmedabad, 10 November 2011;

Prashant Madtha, Fatima Retreat House, Jeppu, Mangalore, 10 January 2017;

Prayag Shukla, New Delhi, August 2011;

Qurban Ali, NMML, New Delhi, 28 June 2011;

R.D. Mathur (b. 1928), Gurgaon, (from MRA), November 2016;

R.M. Murti, Transport and Dock Workers' Union, Mumbai, 25 October 2017;

R.V. Pandit, Bangalore, 22 September 2015;

Raghu Thakur, New Delhi, 15 May 2010;

Raj Kumar Jain, New Delhi, 9 October 2011;

Rajmohan Gandhi, (IIC) New Delhi, 25 November 2015;

Rajendra Choudhry, Samajwadi Party, Lucknow, 3 May 2015;

Rajiv Vorah & Nitu Vorah (IIC), New Delhi, 22 December 2011;

Rajnath Sharma, Barabanki, 2 October 2015;

Rakhal Dasgupta, President, AIRF, Malogaon, Guwahati, 19 January 2020;

Ram Bahadur Rai, New Delhi, 7 December 2014;

Ramakant Bane, Municipal Mazdoor Union, Bal Dandavate Bhavan, Mumbai, 17 October 2015;

Ramachandra Panda, Member Planning Board, Odisha, Gopalpur-on-sea, 13-14 April 2018;

Rame Gowda, Bangalore, 21 September 2015;

Ranjit Bhanu, Mumbai, 2 July 2015;

Ravi Nair, New Delhi, 4 October 2011;

Richard Fernandes, New Delhi, 20-22 November 2011, Bangalore, September 14, 2018;

Sambhu Shrivastava, New Delhi, 14 May 2021;

Sampa Das, Kolkata, 14 September 2011;

Sanjay Paswan (MP), Constitution Club of India, New Delhi, 29 September 2016;
Sanjiv Das, Advocate, New Delhi, 9 April 2018;
Sanju Poojari, Bombay Labour Union, Mumbai, 27 December 2017;
Santosh Kumar Mahapatro, Advocate, Berhampur, 14 April 2018;
Satyadev Tripathi, Lucknow, 3 May 2015;
Sharad Pawar, New Delhi, 2017;
Shivanand Tiwari, MP (RS), New Delhi, 16 October 2012, 10 June 2014;
Somaiya Ravella, Hyderabad, 16 January 2012;
Srikumar Poddar, Mumbai, 6 February 2016;
Subhash Malgi (b. 1945), Railway Union leader, Mumbai, 14 December 2010;
Sudha Boda, Vadodara, 7 November 2011;
Sudhendra Bhadoriya, New Delhi, 29 May 2014;
Sunilam, New Delhi, 28 June 2011;
Surender Kumar, GPF, New Delhi, 19 July 2011, 13 September 2014;
Surendra Kishore, Patna, 20 October 2011;
Swaraj Kaushal, 8, Safdarjung Lane, New Delhi, 15 October 2011, 27 November 2011;
Than Singh Josh, New Delhi, 30 March 2015;
The Rector, St Peter's Seminary, Bangalore, 24 September 2015;
Thenucho, Kohima, 9-13 December 2016;
Triveni Singh, HMKP, Bombay, 13 December 2010;
U.R. Ananthamurty, Bangalore, 21 January 2012;
Urmilaben Patel, Ahmedabad, 9 November 2011;
Usha Gandhi, Panchgani, 8 February 2016;
V.K. Jayaswal, Railway Officer, New Delhi, 13 December 2019;
Velarian Rodrigues, JNU, New Delhi, 7 October 2011;
Vidya Sagar Gupta, Calcutta, 13 September 2011;
Vijay Narayan, New Delhi, 8 September, 11 October 2011, 4 June 2014, 30 April 2015, 28 June 2018;
Vijay Pratap, JNU, New Delhi, 12 October 2011, 2 December 2014, 29 April 2015;
Vinod Kumar Singh, Patna, 19 October 2011;
William D'Silva, Mangalore, 27 September 2015;
Y.P. Anand, Chairman (Railway Board) (Retired), New Delhi, 13 December 2019;

Journals

Blitz (Bombay);
Current (Bombay);
Dharamyug;

Dinman Times (New Delhi);
Economic and Political Weekly;
Frontline, Chennai;
Himmat, (Bombay);
Hind Mazdoor;
India Abroad;
India News;
India Today;
Indian Railwaymen;
Indian Worker, (Indian National Trade Union Congress);
Jan;
Janata;
Link;
Mainstream;
Mangalore: The Organ of the Catholic Association;
Mankind [Editor: Rammanohar Lohia];
New Socialist;
Newsweek;
Onlooker;
Opinion (Bombay) (Weekly);
OutlookIndia.com;
Panchjanya;
Seminar;
Shankar's Weekly;
Society (Mumbai);
Sunday Mail;
The Economic Weekly;
The Illustrated Weekly of India;
the Other Side;
The Voice;
The Week;
Working Class;

Newspapers

Bharat Jyoti (Bombay)
Blitz (Mumbai)
Bombay Chronicle (Bombay)
Danik Jagran
Financial Express (Bombay)

Free Press Journal (Mumbai)
Gulf News
Hitwada (Nagpur)
IBN Conversations
Indian Express (Delhi)
Mumbai Mirror (Mumbai)
National Herald (Delhi)
Sunday Mid-Day
Sunday Telegraph (London)
The Asian Age
The Daily Progress (Charlottesville)
The Economics Times (New Delhi)
The Economist
The Hindu (Chennai),
The Hindustan Times (New Delhi)
The Hindustan Times (Patna)
The Indian Nation (Patna)
The New York Times
The Pioneer (New Delhi)
The Statesman (Delhi)
The Sunday Indian
The Telegraph (Calcutta)
The Times of India (Delhi)
The Tribune (Chandigarh)

Books

A Concise Encyclopedia of Christianity in India, 2014, Pune: Jnana-Deepa
    Vidyapeeth.
A Praja Socialist Party Publication, 1963, *Socialist Unity: Another Attempt fails . . .*
A. M. Mundadan, 2001, *History of Christianity in India*, Volume I (From the
    beginning up to the middle of the sixteenth century, up to 1542), Bangalore:
    Church History Association of India.
A.S. Dulat, 2015, *Kashmir: The Vajpayee Years*, Noida: Harper Collins.
A.W. Lawrence (edited), 1929, *Captives of Tipu: Survivor's Narratives*, London:
    Jonathan Cape.
Alan Machado (Prabhu), 1999, *Sarasvati's Children: A History of the Mangalorean
    Christens*, Goa: Goa 1556.
———, 2015, *Slaves of Sultan*, Goa: Goa 1556.

Alexander Solzhenitsyn, 1963, *One day in the life of Ivan Denisovich*, Bucks: Penguin.

All India Railwaymen's Federation, *Origin and Growth of All India Railwaymen's Federation*, Volume I (1982) & II (1985), New Delhi.

All India Trade Union Congress, 1960, *Five Glorious Days (July 12-16, 1960): Central Government Employees' Strike.*

Amitav Ghosh, 2010, *Countdown*, New Delhi: Penguin.

Anant Kakba Priolkar, 1962, *Goa: Facts versus Fiction*, Bombay.

———, 1967, *Goa Re-discovered*, Bombay.

Andrew Scull, 2009, *Hysteria: The Disturbing History*, New York: OUP.

Arthur Koestler, 2005 [1940], *Darkness at noon*, London: Vintage.

Ashish Nandy, 1980, *At the Edge of Psychology*, Delhi: OUP.

Asoka Mehta, 1949, *Economic Consequences of Sardar Patel*, Hyderabad: Chetna Prakashan.

———, 1952, *The Political Mind of India: An Analysis of the Results of the General Elections*, Bombay: A Socialist Party Publication.

B. Sheshagiri Rao, 1987, *Indomitable: A Biography of S.R. Kulkarni, Stormy Petrel of Indian Trade Union Movement*, Bombay: S.R. Kulkarni Felicitation Committee.

———, 1994, *Comrade Manohar Kotwal: An Ideal Trade Unionist*, Bombay: Manohar Kotwal Felicitation Committee.

B.G. Rao and Amiya Rao, October 1975, *Why Emergency*. (Its underground publication did not carry the authors' names. The later publication named the authors.)

B.N. Tandon, 2003, *PMO Diary - I: Prelude to the Emergency*, Delhi: Konark Publishers.

———, 2006, *PMO Diary - II: The Emergency*, Delhi: Konark Publishers.

B.S. Shastry, *Goa-Kanara: Portuguese Relations: 1498-1763*, New Delhi: Concept Publishing.

Balkrishna Gupta (editors Sarang Upadhyay and Anurag Chaturvedi), 2013, *Haashiye Par Padi Duniya*, Delhi: Rajkamal Prakashan Pvt. Ltd.

Barun Sengupta, 1979, *Last Days of the Morarji Raj*, Calcutta: Ananda Publishers

Bernard Shaw, 1928, *Intelligent Woman's Guide to Socialism, Communism and Capitalism*, New York: Brentano's Publishers.

Bhagwan S Gidwani, 1976, *The Sword of Tipu Sultan: A Historical Novel about the Life and Death of Tipu Sultan of India*, New Delhi: Rupa.

Bhaskar Anand Saletore, 1936, *Ancient Karnataka* Vol. 1, Poona: Oriental Book Agency.

Bipan Chandra, 2003, *In the name of democracy: JP movement and the emergency*, Delhi: Penguin.

Bipan Chandra, Mridula Mukherjee, Aditya Mukherjee, 2008, *India Since Independence*, Delhi: Penguin.

Birth Centenary pamphlet, 2005, *Maniben Kara: A Tale of Struggles and Service*, Mumbai: Western Railway Employees Union.

Brian Senewiratne, December 1987, *Sri Lanka: The 1987 peace pact: The Main Concerns*, Published by the Author.

Burton Stein, 1989, *Thomas Munro: The Origins of the Colonial State and His vision of Empire*, Delhi: OUP.

C K Kareem, 1973, *Kerala under Haidar and Tipu Sultan*, Cochin: Paico Publishing House.

C.G.K. Reddy, 2008, *Baroda Dynamite Conspiracy: The Right to Rebel*, New Delhi: Vision Books.

Charan Singh, 1979, *India's Economic Policy: A Gandhian Blueprint*, New Delhi: Vikas Publishing House.

Chittaranjan Das, 2014, *Nabakrushna Choudhury*, New Delhi: National Book Depot.

Christine Christ-von Wedel and Thomas K Kuhn (eds), 2015, *Basel Mission: People, History, Perspectives 1815 -2015*, Schwabe.

Chritophe Jaffrelot, 1999, *The Hindu Nationalist Movement and Indian Politics* (1925 to the 1990s), New Delhi: Penguin.

Colonel Mark Wilks, 1932, *Historical Sketches of the South of India in an attempt to trace the History of Mysoor-* Volume II (from the origin of the Hindoo Government of that State to the Extinction of the Mohammedan Dynasty in 1799, Mysore: Government Branch Press).

Coomi Kapoor, 2015, *The Emergency: A Personal History*, Gurgaon: Penguin.

D.F. Karaka, 1965, *Morarji*, Bombay: The Times of India Press.

David Arnold and Ramchandra Guha, 1998, *Nature, Culture and Imperialism: Essays on the environmental history of South India,*

December 1975, *Indira's India: Anatomy of a Dictatorship*, London: A Free JP Campaign publication; (Author of this document was George).

Delio de Mendonca, 2002, *Conversions and Citizenry: Goa under Portugal, 1510–1610*, Delhi: Concept Publishing.

Devadatta Kamath & Pius Fidelis Pinto, 2014, *Defiant Submission: A History of the Diocese of Mangalore*, volume 1, Mangalore: The Diocese of Mangalore.

Dinesh Sharma, 2009, *The Long Revolution: The Birth and Growth of India's IT Industries*, New Delhi: Harper Collins.

Dr Rohini Gawankar, 2014, *Footprints of a Crusader: The Life Story of Mrunal Gore*, Mumbai: Samata Shikshan Sanstha.

Dr Sampurnanand (1890–1969), 1962, *Memories and Reflections*, Delhi: Asia Publishing House.

Eva Forest, 1975, *From A Spanish Jail*, Penguin.

Facts relating to Lohia's attempt at disrupting the PSP, 1955, A Praja Socialist Publication.

Francine R. Frankel, *India's Political Economy: 1947-2004*, New Delhi: OUP

G.S. Bhargava (Ed.), 1977, *JP's Jail Life (A Collection of Personal Letters)*, New Delhi: Arnold-Heinemann.

G.S. Bhargava, 1977, *Indira's India Gate: Latest Study of Political Corruption in India*, Delhi: Arnold-Heinemann.

Gabriel Garcia Marquez, 1996, *Chronicle of a Death Foretold*, Gurgaon: Penguin.

———, 1996, *One Hundred Years of Solitude*, Gurgaon: Penguin.

Gene D. Overstreet and Marshall Windmiller, 1959, *Communism in India*, Berkeley: University of California Press.

George Fernandes, 1972, *What ails the Socialists?*, New Delhi: New Society.

———, 2008 [1984], *The Rail Strike of 1974 and the Railwaymen's Movement*, Mumbai: Pratipaksh Prakashan,

———, A Tribute to Madhu Limaye, 2008, *Madhu Limaye in Parliament: A Commemorative Volume*, New Delhi: Lok Sabha Secretariat.

———, *India's Bomb and Indira's India*, Delhi: Ajanta Art Printers.

———, President, Bombay Taximen's Union, September 9, 1962, *The Economics of the Taxi Trade: A Statement in Justification of the Fare Rise*, Bombay: Nagjibhai Tapiawala.

———, undated (but c. 1951), *Sher-e-docks: P D' Mello*, Bombay: United Printers.

George M. Moraes, 1991 [1927], *Mangalore: A Historical Sketch*, New Delhi: Asian Educational Services

George Mathew (Ed.), 1991, *George Fernandes Speaks*, Delhi: Ajanta Publications,

GNS Raghavan, 1999, *Aruna Asaf Ali: A Compassionate Radical*, Delhi: National Book Trust.

Godwin Shiri (ed), 1985, *Wholeness in Christ: The Legacy of the Basel Mission in India*, Mangalore: The Karnataka Theological Research Institute, Balmatta.

Gopalkrishna Gandhi (Ed), 2009, *Gandhi Is Gone. Who Will Guide Us Now?: Nehru, Prasad, Azad, Vinoba, Kripalani, JP and Others Introspect*, New Delhi: Permanent Black.

Gyan Prakash, 2015, *Mumbai Fables*, Noida: Harper Collins.

Hamish McDonald, 1998, *The Polyseter Prince: The rise of Dhirubhai Ambani*, Australia: Allen & Unwin.

Hari Jaisingh, 1989, *India after Indira: The Turbulent Years* (1984-1989), Delhi: Allied Publishers Ltd.

Haridev Sharma, 2004, *Jaiprakash awam Prabhavati*, Delhi: NMML.

Ian J Kerr, 1995, *Building the Railways of the Raj*, 1850-1900, Delhi: OUP.

Iftikhar Gilani, 2005, *My Days in Prison*, Delhi: Penguin

Indira Gandhi, 1975, *Democracy and Discipline: Speeches and Broadcasts on Emergency*, Delhi: DAVP.

Iqbal Hussain (Ed), 2006, *Karl Marx on India*, New Delhi: Tulika Books.

Irving Wallace, 1976, *The R Document*, US: Simon & Schuster.

J Sturrock,1894, Madras District Manuals: South Canara, Vol 1,

J. R. Kamble, 1995, *Amardeep* (P. D'Mello's biography in Marathi), Mumbai: Granthali.

Jacobo Timerman, 1982 [1980], *Prisoner without a name, Cell without a number*, New York: Vintage.

Janardan Thakur, 1978, *All the Janata Men,* New Delhi: Vikas Publishing House.

Jaya Jaitly, 2017, *Life Among the Scorpions: Memoirs of a Woman in Indian Politics*, New Delhi: Rupa.

Jayaprakash Narayan, (ed. A B Shah), 1977, *Prison Diary: 1975*, Bombay: Popular Prakashan.

———, 1977, *India of my Dreams*, Bangalore: Ecumenical Christian Centre.

———, 1977, *JP's Jail Life: A collection of Personal Letters*, Delhi: Arnold-Heinemann.

John Baptist Moraes, 1999, *George Fernandes: Ek Sahasi Jinn*, Mangalore: Moraes Publication.

John Steinbeck, 1995, *The Moon is Down*, New Delhi: Penguin.

Joseph Thekkedath, 1988, *History of Christianity in India*, Volume II (From the Middle of the Sixteenth Century to the End of the Seventeenth Century, 1542–1700), Bangalore: Church History Association of India; P285.

Kamaladevi Chattopadhyay, 2014, *Inner Spaces Outer Spaces: Memoirs*, Delhi: Niyogi Books.

Kate Brittlebank, 1997, *Tipu Sultan's Search for Legitimacy: Islam and Kingship in a Hindu Domain*, Delhi: OUP.

———, 2016, *Tiger: The Life of Tipu Sultan*, Delhi: Juggernaut Books.

Katherine Frank, 2001, *Indira: The Life of Indira Nehru Gandhi*, New York: Houghton Mifflin.

Kingshuk Nag, 2015, *Atal Bihari Vajpayee A Man For All Seasons,* Delhi: Rupa.

Kiran Maitra, 2012, *Marxism in India: From Decline to Debacle*, New Delhi: Roli Books.

Kuldeep Nayyar, 1969, *Between the Lines*, Delhi: Allied.

———, 1971, *India: The Critical Years*, Delhi: Vikas Publications.

———, 1975, *India after Nehru*, Delhi: Vikas Publishing House.

———, 1977, *Judgment: Inside story of the emergency in India,* Delhi: Vikas.

———, 2006, *Scoop: Inside stories from the Partition to the present*, Delhi: Harper Collins.

L. K. Advani, 2008, *My Country, My Life*, Delhi: Rupa & Co.

Lakshmi Narain Lal, 1977, *Jayaprakash: India's Voice, India's Soul*, Delhi: Hind Pocket Books.

Larry Collins and Dominique Lapierre, 2015, *Is Paris Burning?*, New Delhi: Vikas Publishing.

Leon Uris, 1989 [1961], *Mila 18,* New York: Bantam Books.

Lohia thru Letters, Published by Rama Mitra, New Delhi.

Lok Dal Central Office, 1980, *Post Election Analysis*.

Louis Adamic, 1963 [1934], *Dynamite: The Story of Class Violence in America*, Massachusetts: Peter Smith.

Madhu Dandavate, 1993, *As the Mind Unfolds: Issues and Personalities*, Delhi: Shipra.

Madhu Limaye [Edited by N.C. Mehrotra], 1986, *The Age of Hope: Phases of the Socialist Movement*, Delhi: Atma Ram & Sons.

Madhu Limaye, 1951, *The Barren Path: A Reply to Aruna Asaf Ali*, [pamphlet: Socialist Party]

———, 1988, *Birth of Non-Congressism*, Delhi: B R Publishing.

———, 1991, *Politics After Freedom*, Delhi: Atma Ram & Sons.

———, 1991, *Socialist Communist Interaction in India*, Delhi: Ajanta.

———, 1994, *Janata Party Experiment: An insider's account of Opposition Politics: 1975-77*, Volume I, Delhi: B R Publishing Corporation.

———, 1994, *Janata Party Experiment: An Insider's Account of Opposition Politics: 1977-80*, Volume II, Delhi: D.K. Publishing Corporation.

———, 1996, *Last Writings*, Delhi: D K Publishers.

———, 2000, *Galaxy of the Indian Socialist Leaders*, Delhi: B R Publishing Corporation.

Madhu Trehan, 2009, *Prism Me A Lie, Tell Me A Truth: Tehelka as Metaphor*, New Delhi: Roli Books.

Madras District Manuals: South Canara: Compiled by J. Sturrock, ICS, Volume I & II, Madras: Printed by the Superintendent, Government Press, 1894.

Mahesh Kumar Mast, 1969, *Trade Union Movement in Indian Railways*, Meerut: Meenakshi Prakashan

Mahesh Rangarajan, 1996, *Fencing the Forest: Conservation and Ecological Change in India's Central Provinces, 1860-1914*, Delhi: OUP.

Mark Pendergrast, 1993, *For God, Country and Coca Cola: The Unauthorized History of the Great American Soft Drink and the Company that Makes it*, London: Phoenix

Mary Fainsod Katzenstein, 1979, *Ethnicity and Equality: The Shiv Sena Party and Preferential Politics in Bombay*, London: Cornell University Press.

Michael Foot, 1962, *Aneurin Bevan: A Biography,* Volume I: 1897–1945. London: Macgibbon & Kee.

Michael Lobo, 2002, *The Mangalorean Catholic Community: A Professional History / Directory*, Mangalore: Camelot Publishers.

Michael V.d. Bogaert, 1970, *Trade Unionism in Indian Ports: A Case Study at Calcutta and Bombay*, New Delhi: Shri Ram Centre for Industrial Relations.

Ministry of Home Affairs, 1975, *Why Emergency*, Government of India.

Minoo Masani, 1975, *Is JP the Answer?*, Delhi: The Macmillan Company of India Ltd.

Mir Hussain Ali Kirmani (Translated from Persian by Col. W Miles), 1958, *History of Tipu Sultan: Being a Continuation of the NeshaniHyduri*, Calcutta: Sushil Gupta Private Ltd.

Mohibbul Hasan, 2013, *History of Tipu Sultan*, Delhi: Aakar.

Morarji Desai, 1978 [1974], *The Story of My Life*, Volume I & II, New Delhi: S. Chand & Company Ltd.

Muzaffar Ahmad, 1962, *The Communist Party of India and Its Formation Abroad*, Calcutta: National Book agency Private Limited.

N. Shyam Bhat, 1998, *South Kanara (1799 - 1860) A Study of Colonial Administration and Regional Response*, Delhi: Mittal Publications.

N.G. Ranga, 1976, *Distinguished Acquaintances*, Hyderabad: Desi Book House.

N.K. Singh, 2011, *The Tangy Taste of Indian Politics and Beyond*, Delhi: Konark.

Narendra Pathak, 2008, *Karpoori Thakur aur Samajvaad*, Delhi: Medha Books.

Nayantara Sahgal, 1982 [1978], *Indira Gandhi: Her Road to Power*, London & Sydney: Macdonald & Co.

Neera Adarkar and Meena Menon, *One hundred years, one hundred voices, The Millworkers of Girangaon*, Seagull Books.

Nigel Cliff, 2012, *The Last Crusade: The Epic Voyages of Vasco Da Gama*, London: Atlantic Books.

P. Thomas, 1954, *Christians and Christianity in India and Pakistan*, London: George Allen & Unwin Ltd.

P.G. Mavalankar, 1979, *No Sir*, Ahmedabad: Sannishtha Prakashan.

Pamphlets: 'Trial of an Indian Patriot: King-Emperor versus K. Rama Rao' and 'Editor, Freedom Fighter and Parliamentarian Kotamaraju Rama Rao: A profile in courage', Lucknow: K. Vikram Rao.

Paul R Brass, 1990, *The Politics of India since Independence*, Cambridge.

———, 2011, *An Indian political Life: Charan Singh and Congress Politics*, Volumes 1-3, Delhi: Sage

Pius Fidelis Pinto, 1999, *History of Christians in Coastal Karnataka* (1500 – 1763), Mangalore: Samanvaya.

———, 1999, *Konkani Christians of Coastal Karnataka in Anglo – Mysore Relations* (1761–1799), Mangalore: Samanvaya Prakashan.

Pius Malakandathil et al. (editors), 2016, *Christianity in Indian History: Issues of Culture, Power and Knowledge*, Delhi: Primus.

Pranab Mukherjee, 2015, *The Dramatic Decade: The Indira Gandhi Years*, Delhi: Rupa.

Prashant Bhushan, 2017 [1978], *Case that shook India: The verdict that led to the Emergency*, Delhi: Penguin.

Prashant Madtha, *On Eagle's Wings: An Intimate History of 125 years of St. Aloysius College*, Mangalore: St. Aloysius College Alumni.

Praxy Fernandes, 1969, *Storm over Seringapatam: The Incredible Story of Hyder Ali &Tippu Sultan*, Bombay: Published by Dinkar Sakrikar for Thacker & Co. Ltd.

R.D.N. Simhan, 1930, *The civic survey of Mangalore municipality, 1929, a study of local and civic conditions in Mangalore town*,

R.P. Cholia, 1941, *Dock Labourers in Bombay*, Bombay: Longman.

Radhey Shyam Sharma, 1978, *Who After Morarji*, New Delhi: Pankaj Publications.

Rahul Ramagundam, 2008, *Gandhi's Khadi: a History of Contention and Conciliation*, Hyderabad: Orient Blackswan.

Rajnarayan Chandavarkar, 1994, *The Origins of Industrial Capitalism in India, Business Strategies and the working classes in Bombay, 1900-1940*, Cambridge University Press.

———, 1998, *The Imperial Power and Popular Politics: Class, Resistance and the State in India*, c. 1850-1950, Cambridge.

Rajni Bakshi, 1986, *The Long Haul: The Bombay Textile Workers Strike*, Bombay: BUILD Documentation Centre.

Ramchandra Guha, 2007, *India After Gandhi: The History of the World's Largest Democracy*, Delhi: Picador.

Rammanohar Lohia, 1969, *Samajwadi Andolan Ka Itihas*, Hyderabad: Samta Nyas.

———, 2008, *Guilty Men of India's Partition*, New Delhi: Rupa & Co.

Ranabir Samaddar, 2016, *The Crisis of 1974: Railway Strike and the Rank and File*, Delhi: Primus.

Ranjana Kumari, 2003, *Karpuri Thakur: Neta Virodhi Dal ke roop mein sansadiya bhoomika*, Delhi: Rajkamal.

Reinhard Wendt (Editor), 2006, *An Indian to the Indians?: On the Initial Failure and the Posthumous Success of the Missionary Ferdinand Kittel 1832-1903*.

Rev Alexander Kyd Nairne, 1988, *History of the Konkan*, New Delhi: Asian Educational Services.

Richard Zimler, 2008, *Guardian of Dawn*, Delhi: Penguin.

S. Hussain Zaidi, 2012, *Dongri to Dubai: Six Decades of the Mumbai Mafia*, New Delhi: Roli Books.

S. Hussain Zaidi, 2015, *Mumbai Avengers*, Noida: Harper Collins.

S. Nijalingappa, 2000, *My Life and Politics: An Autobiography*, New Delhi: Vision books.

S.A. Dange, 1973, *Origins of Trade Union Movement in India*, Delhi: AITUC Publication.

S.M. Edwardes, 1901, *The Rise of Bombay*, Census of India Series.

Salman Rushdie, 2006 [1981], *Midnight's Children*, London: Vintage Books.

————, 2012, *Joseph Anton: A Memoir*, London: Jonathan Cape.

Samuel Miley, 1884 (Second Edition), *Canara: Past and Present*, Mangalore: Basel Mission Book.

Sarang Upadhyay and Anurag Chaturvedi [Editors], 2013, Balkrishan Gupta: *Haashiye Par Padi Duniya*, Delhi: Rajkamal Prakashan Pvt. Ltd.

Satyavir Singh Arya, (Undated, 1982), *Lok Dal Ka Vibhajan: Doshi Kaun?* [Pamphlet]

Era Sezhiyan (Ed), 2010, *Shah Commission Report: Lost, and Regained*, Chennai: Aazhi Publishers.

Shankarshan Thakur, 2000, *The Making of Laloo Yadav: The Unmaking of Bihar*, New Delhi: Harper Collins Publishers.

————, 2014, *Single man: The Life and Times of Nitish Kumar of Bihar*, New Delhi: Harper Collins Publishers

Sharad Pawar, 2016, *On My Terms: From the Grassroots to the Corridors of Power*, Delhi: Speaking Tiger

Sister Jesme, *Amen: The Autobiography of a Nun*, New Delhi: Penguin.

Spotlight on the Municipal Workers' Struggle, October 1957, Bombay: Municipal Mazdoor Union.

Stephen Kotkin, 2014, *Stalin: Paradoxes of Power, 1878-1928*, London: Allen Lane.

Stephen Sherlock, 2001, *The Indian Railways Strike of 1974: A Study of Power and Organised Labour*, Delhi: Rupa.

Sudha Gogate, 2014, *The Emergence of Regionalism in Mumbai, History of the Shiv Sena*, Mumbai: Popular Prakashan

Sujata Anandan, 2014, *Hindu Friday Samrat: How the Shiv Sena Changed Mumbai Forever*, Noida: Harper Collins.

Suketu Mehta, 2006, *Maximum City: Bombay Lost & Found*, New Delhi: Penguin.

Susan Visvanathan, 2003, *The Christians of Kerala: History, Belief and Ritual among the Yakoba*, Delhi: OUP.

T W Venn, 1945, *Mangalore*, Cochin.

T.J.S. George, December 1965, *Revolt in Bihar: A study of the August 1965 uprising.*

T.K. Mahadevan (edited), 1975, *Jayaprakash Narayan and the future of Indian Democracy*, Delhi: Affiliated East-West Press Ltd.

T.N. Siddhanta, August 1974, *The Railway General Strike*, Delhi: AITUC Publication

U R Ananthamurty, 2012 [1969], *Samskara,* Delhi: OUP India

V. B. Karnik, 1967, *Strike in India*, Bombay: Manaktalas

————, 1968, *Trade Unions and Politics*, Bombay: University of Bombay

Vaibhav Purandare, 2012, *Bal Thackeray & the Rise of the Shiv Sena*, New Delhi: Roli Books.

Vasant Gupte, 1981, *Labour movement in Bombay: Origin and Growth up to Independence*, Bombay: Institute of Workers' Education.

Vijaya Lakshmi Pandit (1900-1990), 1945, Prison Days, Calcutta: The Signet Press.

Vinod Mehta, 1978, *The Sanjay Story: from Anand Bhavan to Amethi*, Bombay: Jaico Publishing House.

Walter Andersen, *The Brotherhood in Saffron: The Rashtriya Swayamsevak Sangh and Hindu Revivalism* Gurgaon: Penguin.

Notes

Chapter 1: All's Well That Ends Well

1   Cited from Affidavit in the High Court, by Jaya Jaitly in support of the Plea filed by George Fernandes' brothers against Leila Fernandes, 6 December 2011 (Copy of the Affidavit with the author).

2   Jaya Jaitly, 2017, *Life among the Scorpions: Memoirs of a Woman in Indian Politics*, (Delhi: Rupa, 2017).

3   'The Decisive Decade (1975–1985)', *India Today*, Tenth Anniversary Issue, 31 December 1985, p. 15.

4   Tania Ameer Khan, *Society* (Mumbai), March 2010. Author's Interview with Richard Fernandes, New Delhi, 20 November 2011. Sheela Reddy, 'He's My George', *OutlookIndia.com*, 18 January 2010.

5   Sean Fernandes to Paul Fernandes, Email Communication, 23 December 2009. Referred to also in, Paul Fernandes to Leila Kabir Fernandes, Email Communication, 18 February 2010. (Copies with the Author.)

6   Author's Interview with Paul Fernandes, New Delhi, 18 October 2010.

7   'George, Jaya and a Complex Soap Opera', *Mumbai Mirror* (Mumbai), 16 January 2010.

8   Leila Moved in as Jaya is forced out of George's Life, *Gulf News*, January 21, 2010.

9   Jaya Jaitly to Richard Fernandes, Email Communication, 16 January 2010. (Copy with the Author)

10   Author's Interview with Jaya Jaitly, New Delhi, 5 June 2014.

11   Jaya Jaitly to Chitra Subramaniam, Email communication, 14 January 2010 (Copy with the Author).

12   Jaya Jaitly (to a few friends), Email Communication, 20 January 2010.

13   Affidavit in the High Court, by Jaya Jaitly in support of the Plea filed by Fernandes' brothers against Leila Fernandes, 6 December 2011.

14   Author's Interview with Fredrick D'Sa, Mumbai, 18 October 2015.

15   Joint Statement on the Health and Well-Being of George Fernandes by his brothers: Michael Fernandes, Paul Fernandes, Aloysius Fernandes and Richard Fernandes, Press Release, Bengaluru, 25 January 2010.

16   Brothers' Pliant against Leila Fernandes, In the High Court of Delhi, Ordinary Original Civil Jurisdiction, C.S. (OS) No March 2010.

17   Jaya Jaitly mentions this person (Nitin Kumar) in her autobiography and gives details on this affair. See Jaya Jaitly, 2017, *Life among the Scorpions: Memoirs of a Woman in Indian Politics*, Delhi: Rupa, p. 281.

18   Author's Interview with Nitin Kumar, Nirman Bhavan, New Delhi.

19   Jaya Jaitly, 'The Men Who Fuel Strange Antics of Leila Fernandes', 22 February 2010, Email Communication to the Author. Also, Jaitly, *Life among the Scorpions*, p. 281.

20   Author's Interview with Jaya Jaitly, New Delhi, 5 June 2014.

21   Author's Interview with Fredrick D'Sa, Mumbai, 18 October 2015.

22   Author's Interview with Fredrick D'Sa, Mumbai, 18 October 2015.

23   See, 'Friends, Family Fight over Fernandes', *Times of India* (New Delhi), 18 January 2010.

24   Michael Fernandes to Leila Fernandes, Email Communication, 10 May 2010.

25   Author's Interview with Michael Fernandes, New Delhi, 4 November 2015.

26   Author's Interview with Paul Fernandes, New Delhi, 18 October 2010.

27   Author's Interview with Fredrick D'Sa, Mumbai, 18 October 2015.

28   'Socialist Wealth', *India Today* (Delhi), 8 February 2010.

29   Author's Interview with Fredrick D'Sa, Mumbai.

30   To Sampa Das, 25 December 1991.

31   'Statement on the Assets of Veteran Socialist George Fernandes by His Four Brothers', Bangalore, 23 January 2010. A statement released to the press and covered widely in media.

32   Jaya Jaitly to Chitra Subramaniam, Email communication, 14 January 2010 (Copy with the Author).

33   See 'Friends, Family Fight over Fernandes', *Times of India* (New Delhi), 18 January 2010.

34   Author's Interview with Fredrick D'Sa, Mumbai, 18 October 2015. Corroborated by the various Email communication Paul wrote to Leila Fernandes. (Copies with the Author)

35 Referred to in an Email communication from Michael Fernandes to Leila Kabir Fernandes, 10 May 2010.

36 Sean Fernandes to Michael Fernandes, Email Communication, 29 December 2009. (Copy with the Author)

37 Michael Fernandes to Leila Fernandes, Email Communication, 10 May 2010. (Copy with the Author)

38 Paul Fernandes to Leila Fernandes, Email Communication, 18 February 2010. (Copy with the Author)

39 Leila Fernandes to Paul Fernandes, Email Communication, 2 January 2010. (Copy with the Author)

40 Leila Fernandes to Michael Fernandes, Email Communication, 31 August 2010. (Copy with the Author)

41 'Leila Moved in as Jaya Is Forced Out of George's Life', *Gulf News*, 21 January 2010.

42 Author's Interview with Jaya Jaitly, New Delhi, 5 June 2014.

43 Email Communication from Richard Fernandes to the Author and others, 6 April 2010.
    'HC Tells Wife, Brothers of George Fernandes to Sort Out Differences over Treatment,' *The Times of India* (New Delhi), May 20, 2010.

44 The protest held on 30 June 2010 was widely reported in the media.

45 Michael Fernandes, Email Communication, 31 May 2010. (Copy with the Author)

46 Judgment, 21 July 2020, CBI versus Jaya Jaitly, RC-AC-3/2004A0005, 6 December 2004.

47 Author's Interview with Jaya Jaitly, New Delhi, 5 June 2014.

48 See, for instance, articles in the *Indian Express* (New Delhi) written by Sharad Yadav ('George Fernandes Will Be Remembered as a Fearless Leader Who Worked Tirelessly for Workers', 30 January 2019) and Ram Vilas Paswan ('George Fernandes Was the Symbol of Resistance to the Emergency', 31 January 2019).

49 Author's interview with Jaya Jaitly, New Delhi, 5 June 2014. On 29 January 2019, I was among the first ones to arrive at Leila Fernandes' home where George lay in state. That early morning, Jaya Jaitly, along with her daughter, was already there giving company to Leila Fernandes.

50 Messages forwarded by Jaya Jaitly to the Author, 3 February 2019.

51 'Lawless Prisons', *Statesman*, 13 December 2004.

52 'From Jail, Pappu Dials M for Ministers', *Statesman*, 11 December 2004.
    'Laloo's Take on Pappu's Calls', *Indian Express* (Delhi), 13 December 2004.

53 'Madhepura in a Tizzy over Pappu Visit', *Times of India*, 5 May 2004.

54   'George visits Beur: Just to defend a murderer', The *Tribune* (Chandigarh), 10 October 2007.

55   'Govt Keeping Tabs on Me, Says George', *Pioneer* (Delhi), 1 October 2004.

56   'Word Is Out, It's a Congress Witch Hunt', *Statesman* (Delhi), 30 September 2004.

57   'Talbott Confirms: Fernandes Strip-Searched Twice in US', *Indian Express* (Delhi), 11 July 2004.

58   'UPA Govt is on a witch hunt . . . the witches are doing the hunting', *Indian Express*, (Delhi), 8 May 2005.

59   Mohan Sahay, 'George Keen to Shift to Muzaffarpur', *Statesman* (Delhi), 17 March 2004.

60   *Devil's Advocate*, Karan Thapar's Interview with George Fernandes, CNN-IBN, 24 September 2006. https://youtu.be/DFnAUIEJbB4.

61   'Scrap jailbirds' poll, says Patna HC: But prison no bar for Dr Don', *Hindustan Times* (Patna), 1 May 2004.

62   Ashok K Mishra, 'Nitish Unhappy at George Move to Muzaffarpur', *Economic Times* (Delhi), 27 March 2004.

63   Amarnath Tewary, 'Nitish Shows His Flare for Realpolitik', *Pioneer* (Delhi), 29 March 2004.

64   Author's Interview with Jaya Jaitly, Delhi, 31 October 2016.

65   'NDA Tremors', *Asian Age* (Delhi), 6 November 2004.

66   Gargi Parsai, 'JD(U) Blames It on Gujarat', *The Hindu* (Chennai), 30 May 2004. Six months later, JD(U) was still involved in the politics of optics, see 'Belligerent Posturing', *The Hindu* (Chennai), 3 November 2004.

67   'Karyasamiti ki Baithak Mein George Rahe Nishaane Par' ('George Targeted at Party Working Committee Meet at Ranchi'), *Dainik Jagran*, 31 October 2004.

68   *Devil's Advocate*, Karan Thapar's Interview with George Fernandes, CNN-IBN, 24 September 2006. https://youtu.be/DFnAUIEJbB4.

69   Seema Mustafa, '3rd Front Eyes Bihar', *Asian Age*, 8 November 2004.

70   'Fernandes Kept Out of Bihar', *Tribune* (Chandigarh), 11 October 2005.

71   *Devil's Advocate*, Karan Thapar's Interview with George Fernandes, CNN-IBN, 24 September 2006. https://youtu.be/DFnAUIEJbB4

72   Author's Interview with Jaya Jaitly, New Delhi, 31 October 2016.

73   *Devil's Advocate*, Karan Thapar's Interview with George Fernandes, CNN-IBN, 24 September 2006. https://youtu.be/DFnAUIEJbB4

74   J.P. Yadav, 'NDA Convenor Turns Away Nitish, Makes Quiet Exit', *Indian Express* (Delhi), 13 April 2006.
     Amarnath Tewary, 'After Ensuring His Defeat, Nitish Praises George', *Pioneer* (Delhi), 13 April 2006.

75 Author's Interview with Sampa Das, Kolkata, 14 September 2011.

76 Sumanta Sen, 'Charting a New Course', *Telegraph* (Calcutta), 27 April 2006.

77 Author's Interview with Jaya Jaitly, New Delhi, 31 October 2016.

78 Michael Fernandes to Jaya Jaitly, Email Communications, 25 March—5 April—14 May 2009.

79 Jaitly, *Life among the Scorpions*, p. 267.

80 Author's Interview with Fredrick D'Sa, Mumbai, 18 October 2015.

81 Rajdeep Sardesai, 'George: From Giant Killer to Lonely Bhisma', 7 August 2009, *IBN Conversations*.

82 George's Note, Ahmedabad, 2 August 1984, Jaya Jaitly Papers.

83 George Fernandes, *Underground Pamphlet: A Christmas Newsletter*, December 1975.

Chapter 2: A Christian Beginning

1 *Mangalore: The Organ of the Catholic Association of South Kanara*, Vol. LXXX, No. 7, July 2006, pp. 44–49.

2 Michael Lobo, 2002, *The Mangalorean Catholic Community: A Professional History/Directory*, Mangalore: Camelot Publishers. A mathematician by training, Lobo has built a directory of genealogy and professional associations of Mangalorean Christians drawn mostly from Church records.

3 *A Concise Encyclopedia of Christianity in India*, 2014, Pune: Jnana-Deepa Vidyapeeth, pp. 44–45.

4 Author's Interview with Father Leo W. Lobo, Priest, Pope John Paul II Shrine, Bajpe, Mangalore, January 2017.

5 Susan Visvanathan, 2003, *The Christians of Kerala: History, Belief and Ritual among the Yakoba*, Delhi: Oxford University Press;

 P. Thomas, 1954, *Christians and Christianity in India and Pakistan*, London: George Allen & Unwin Ltd.

6 Nigel Cliff, 2012, *The Last Crusade: The Epic Voyages of Vasco Da Gama*, London: Atlantic Books;

 Also see A. M. Mundadan, 2001, *History of Christianity in India*, Volume I (From the beginning up to the middle of the sixteenth century, up to 1542), Bangalore: Church History Association of India (particularly Chapter V: 'The Challenge of a New Third World: Christian West');

 Pius Malakandathil et al. (eds), 2016, *Christianity in Indian History: Issues of Culture, Power and Knowledge*, Delhi: Primus.

7 Author's Interview with Alan Machado Prabhu, Bangalore, 24 October 2018.

8 Rev Alexander Kyd Nairne, 1988, *History of the Konkan*, New Delhi: Asian Educational Services.

9 Delio de Mendonca, 2002, *Conversions and Citizenry: Goa under Portugal, 1510–1610*, Delhi: Concept Publishing.

Also, see, Devadatta Kamath and Pius Fidelis Pinto, 2014, *Defiant Submission: A History of the Diocese of Mangalore*, Vol. 1, Mangalore: The Diocese of Mangalore;

Pius Fidelis Pinto, 1999, *History of Christians in Coastal Karnataka (1500–1763)*, Mangalore: Samanvaya;

Anant Kakba Priolkar, 1962, *Goa: Facts versus Fiction*, Bombay; and, 1967, *Goa Re-discovered*, Bombay.

10 Literature now abounds on Goa's experience with inquisition. Richard Zimler in *Guardian of Dawn* has done a full-scale novel on a sad, aborted love story in the backdrop of which the horror of sixteenth-century inquisition is enacted in its gory detail. In an evocative extract, a conversation between a Christian priest and a Hindu travelling mendicant goes as follows: '"All your gods are dead," the priest explained with an eager smile. "We have destroyed them with this." He held out the cross around his neck.' Richard Zimler, 2008, *Guardian of Dawn*, Delhi: Penguin.

11 In the early 1960s, Rome held the Second Vatican Congress and admitted the grand folly and illusion of the Crusades, claiming it was not what Jesus had preached.

12 Joseph Thekkedath, 1988, *History of Christianity in India*, Volume II (From the Middle of the Sixteenth Century to the End of the Seventeenth Century, 1542–1700), Bangalore: Church History Association of India; p. 285.

13 Sixth Report of the German (Basel) Mission in the Southern Maratha, Canara, and Malabar Province in the form of Letter from the Missionaries to its Friends and Supporters, Bombay: American Mission Press, p. 11.

14 Balkrishna Gupta, 2013, *Haashiye Par Padi Duniya*, edited by Sarang Upadhyay and Anurag Chaturvedi, Delhi: Rajkamal Prakashan.

15 Author's Interview with Richard Fernandes, Bangalore, September 2018.

16 Mir Hussain Ali Kirmani (Translated from Persian by Col. W Miles), 1958, *History of Tipu Sultan: Being a Continuation of the NeshaniHyduri*, Calcutta: Sushil Gupta Private Ltd; Colonel Mark Wilks, 1932, *Historical Sketches of the South of India in an Attempt to Trace the History of Mysoor*, Volume II (from the origin of the Hindoo Government of that State to the Extinction of the Mohammedan Dynasty in 1799, Mysore: Government Branch Press.);

Mohibbul Hasan, 2013, *History of Tipu Sultan*, Delhi: Aakar;

Kate Brittlebank, 1997, *Tipu Sultan's Search for Legitimacy: Islam and Kingship in a Hindu Domain*, Delhi: OUP;

Kate Brittlebank, 2016, *Tiger: The Life of Tipu Sultan*, Delhi: Penguin; C.K. Kareem, 1973, *Kerala under Haidar and Tipu Sultan*, Cochin: Paico Publishing House.

17   See Pius Fidelis Pinto, 1999, *Konkani Christians of Coastal Karnataka in Anglo—Mysore Relations (1761–1799 AD)*, Mangalore: Samanvaya Prakashan, p. 43.

18   George M. Moraes, 1991 [1927], *Mangalore: A Historical Sketch*, New Delhi: Asian Educational Services.

19   In 1999, the BJP storm-troopers asked for a ban on the TV serial *The Sword of Tipu Sultan*, based on Bhagwan S. Gidwani, 1976, *The Sword of Tipu Sultan: A Historical Novel about the Life and Death of Tipu Sultan of India*, New Delhi: Rupa.

20   Tipu Sultan's rule was held responsible for all the ills, real or imaginary, that afflicted South Canara. English ICS officer J. Sturrock, chronicler of the district manual of the South Canara, says, 'Pepper is not so abundant as it was before Tippu deliberately suppressed the trade to prevent intercourse with Europeans.' *Madras District Manuals: South Canara*, Compiled by J. Sturrock, ICS, Volume I & II, Madras: Printed by the Superintendent, Government Press, 1894.

21   William X. Mascarenhas in 1931 presented a dissertation titled *Hyder Ali and Tipu Sultan in Canara* to Bombay University. 'The thesis is suffused with strong communal prejudice. Tipu Sultan is projected as an enemy of the Christians of the region [whose] main intention was to convert them to Islam and the whole work enthusiastically highlights his atrocities on the Christians.' Denis Fernandes, 2006, Unpublished PhD Thesis, 'The Tulu World in European Writings', Department of History, Mangalore University.

22   A.W. Lawrence (edited), 1929, *Captives of Tipu: Survivor's Narratives*, London: Jonathan Cape. It was as if James Scurry was born to tell a story of misery. As a lad of fourteen, he had travelled from London, a recruit in the army of the East India Company. Midway, in the Indian Ocean, the ship he was travelling in was taken over by the French and he was made captive. The French lent him to their ally Haidar Ali, for whom the Europeans had a kind of technical finesse and warfare discipline, lacking in his native forces. For twelve long years, James Scurry remained in Mysore's captivity, circumcised and converted to Islam, and recruited in a slave battalion. If he was kept restrained by iron leg-holdings, he was also allowed to marry and beget children.

23   See 'Contested Legacy', 11 December 2015, and 'Tipu in Malabar', 5 January 2018, *Frontline*, Chennai.

24   Praxy Fernandes, 1969, *Storm over Seringapatam: The Incredible Story of Hyder Ali & Tippu Sultan*, Bombay: Published by Dinkar Sakrikar for Thacker & Co. Ltd. During his stint as municipal commissioner in the 1960s, he would be known as 'Double-Decker Fernandes' for introducing double-decker buses on Bangalore roads.

25   T.W. Venn, 1945, *Mangalore*, Cochin, p. 124:
     Wars and wholesale conflagrations have swept away the old-time monuments of the town, but one remains: it is the Idgah on Light-house Hill. Though in itself of no great age it was constructed from masonry removed from the original Milagres church when that edifice and all other places of Christian worship in Canara were razed to the ground by Tipu Sultan's orders. This prayer court is therefore as much a memorial to the great exodus of the Canara Christians as it is the centre of assembly for the religious exercises of the Mussalman.

26   Author's Interview with Alan Machado Prabhu, Bangalore, 24 October 2018; Alan Machado (Prabhu), 2015, *Slaves of Sultan*, Goa: Goa 1556; See his, *Sarasvati's Children: A History of the Mangalorean Christens* published in 1999. Both Praxy Fernandes and Alan Machado Prabhu come from the community of Mangalorean Catholics and their works are solely a labour of love. 'During the captivity era (1784–99), Tipu Sultan is said to have pulled down the church—stone by stone—and used these very stones to construct a mosque atop Ediyah Hill,' writes Michael Lobo in *A Mangalorean Catholic Community: A Professional History/Directory*, published in 2002 to commemorate the bicentennial of the event, p. 48.

27   Lok Sabha Debate, 30 April–3 May 2002.

28   In the High Court of Judicature at Delhi, 12 August 1976.

29   Author's Interview with Govindacharya, Gulmohar Park, New Delhi, 2017.

30   'Advani Is Acceptable as PM, Rahul–Priyanka Are Foreigners', *Economic Times*, 13 April 2004.

31   In a hurriedly crafted essay, Amitav Ghosh narrates his interview with George in the late 1990s in the aftermath of India's second tryst at Pokhran. See, Amitav Ghosh, 2010, *Countdown*, New Delhi: Penguin.

32   Underground Pamphlet: Letter to Mrs Indira Nehru Gandhi, 27 July 1975.

33   Recorded Interview of George Fernandes with Fredrick D'Sa (Unpublished), Mumbai, 2007. Most quotes attributed to George Fernandes, otherwise not mentioned, are cited from this interview. The video-recorded interview was conducted during various months of 2007. Prabhakar More, a local contemporary of George, was part of it to jog his memory about his early Bombay days. The purpose of the interview was either to build a source

book for an eventual biography or publish a memoir based on it. The interview, however, is mostly a collection of event-narratives from George's life as remembered and retold by Fredrick D'Sa. George has mostly nodded or given monosyllabic consent to the events being recollected before him as by then he was already suffering from Alzheimer's Disease and his speech had become incoherent. I was given a transcript of the interview by Fredrick D'Sa. It could only make a sense if it is read along with other researched materials. The early part of his struggles are covered in contemporary media reports.

34   Editorial: Our Dress, *Mangalore: The Organ of the Catholic Association*, August 1927.

35   *Mangalore: The Organ of the Catholic Association,* February 1936.

36   Recorded interview of George Fernandes with Fredrick D'Sa (Unpublished), Mumbai, 2007.

37   Author's Interview with Richard Fernandes, Delhi, 22 November 2011.

38   See, John Baptist Moraes, 1999, *George Fernandes: Ek Sahasi Jinn*, Mangalore: Moraes Publication. The Konkani biography written in the Kannada script quotes Louie Fernandes extensively answering the question, giving reasons, drawing the underlying mental make-up of parents. He laid the blame on mutual ego; the Fernandes pride, on the father's side, and the D'sa (mother's family name) obstinacy, on the mother's side, collided and refused to compromise, to the detriment of both. They had a common ancestry. Louie said, 'My father's mother and my mother's mother were related as they both belonged to the same D'sa family.'

39   George's Note, 18 October 1984, Jaya Jaitly Papers.

40   George's Note, 16 October 1984, Jaya Jaitly Papers.

41   Recorded Interview of George Fernandes with Fredrick D'Sa (Unpublished), Mumbai, 2007.

42   Open Letter from Michael B. Fernandes to Shri Ramadasappa, Cross Bar Engineering Dept., ITI Ltd, Bangalore, 25 August 1975.

43   Author's Interview with Paul Fernandes, New Delhi, 18 October 2010.

44   Editorial Notes: A Growing Evil, *Mangalore: The Organ of the Catholic Association*, August 1927.

45   Author's Interview with Michael Fernandes, New Delhi, 4 November 2015.

46   George Fernandes, (Unpublished) Prison Journal, Hissar Jail, 9 August 1976.

47   The sons narrate an incident of the early days when their father was a teacher: On one particular day, he did not go to school as he was indisposed. This was a school attached to a church, and most churches have a burial

ground attached. Around 10 o'clock that day, there was a funeral, and therefore the Church's bell tolled. Instantly, the children in the school began to say, '*Fernandes Misr mello re*' (Fernandes Master passed away). It was evident from the children's reaction how unpopular the disciplinarian John Fernandes was.

48   Tanya Wexler, 2011, *Hysteria* (film). A 'Hysteria is a female malady: the trances, the fits, the paralyses, the choking, the tearing of hair, the remarkable emotional instability: Might it constitute an unspoken idiom of protest, a symbolic voice for the silent sex, who were forbidden to verbalize their discontents, and so created a language of the body? Perhaps it was simply an elaborate ruse, a complex kind of malingering and manipulation that rendered its baffling, infuriating patients worthy of blame and punishment? Sexual deprivation can cause the disorder, so directly linked with the functioning of the womb . . .' Quoted in Andrew Scull, 2009, *Hysteria: The Disturbing History*, New York: OUP, p. 9.

49   Author's Interview with Fredrick D'Sa, Mumbai, 18 October 2015.

50   Recorded Interview of George Fernandes with Fredrick D'Sa (Unpublished), Mumbai, 2007.

51   Author's Interview with Eric Ozario, Mangalore, 19 September 2018.

52   George Fernandes, Speech in Bombay, 14 April 1978.

Chapter 3: The Revolutionary Road

1   Author's Interview with Hannibal Richard Cabral, Karnataka Theological College, Mangalore, 12 October 2018.

2   Author's Interview with Father Albert Pinto, Bangalore, 7 January 2017. 'This advantage of the church was very much envied by Hindu nationalist organisations such as the RSS which raised negative propaganda against the Christians as proselytizers. The RSS took advantage of simmering discontent among the lower castes and mobilized people under the Bajrang Dal. Besides the Christians, the Muslims of South Canara [were] an easy target.'

3   Author's Interview with Collin D'Silva, Mangalore, 20 October 2018.

4   The Nagpur All India Catholic Congress, *Mangalore: The Organ of the Catholic Association of South Kanara*, January 1936, pp. 138–40. The magazine was primarily a voice of conservative and privileged section of the Catholics. It was funded by advertisements from Tile, Brick & Lime Manufactures, Coffee Plantation and Works, and other sundry enterprises, and aired views that were opposed by those newly aroused to nationalist consciousness.

5   Letter from Rai Saheb E.C.M. Mascarenhas, Vice President, Catholic Association of South Canara, Mangalore, to The Inspectors of Girls' School, Coimbatore, 5 July 1928. *Mangalore: The Organ of the Catholic Association*, September 1928, pp. 27–29.

6   George Fernandes, (Unpublished) Prison Journal, Hissar Jail, 14 August 1976.

7   Catholics and the Indian Agitation, Letter to the Editor, *Mangalore: The Organ of the Catholic Association*, May 1930, p. 10.

8   The Catholic Women's Conference, *Mangalore: The Organ of the Catholic Association,* January 1936, p. 129.

9   Editorial, *Mangalore: The Organ of the Catholic Association,* February 1928. cited in Michael Lobo, 2002, *The Mangalorean Catholic Community: A Professional History/Directory*, Mangalore: Camelot Publishers, p. 104.

10   Austin Coelho, 'Quo Vadis Mangalore?' in *Mangalore: The Organ of the Catholic Association,* August 1958, cited in Michael Lobo, 2002, *The Mangalorean Catholic Community: A Professional History/Directory*, Mangalore: Camelot Publishers., p xxix.

11   Author's [Telephonic] Interview with Father Noronha, Bangalore, December 2019.

12   Author's Interview with William D'Silva, Mangalore, 27 September 2015. Konkani translation of the Bible that William did had to be self-published without the mandatory sanction of the Church, as it disapproved of him.

13   Movie *Spotlight* released in 2015, focused on *Boston Times'* expose of sexual abuse in the Catholic Church.

14   The Church's liturgical language the world over was Latin. At Mangalore, while mass was said in Latin, the Missal, the prayer book, was chanted in Konkani and sometimes also in English. At home, Konkani was the spoken language; however, writing or reading Konkani was forbidden by the Church, and it was said that anyone doing so would go to hell. The Gaud Saraswat Brahmins of the region also speak Konkani, with a slight dialectical difference. Author's Interview with the Rector, St Peter's Seminary, Bangalore, 24 September 2015.

15   Author's [Telephonic] Interview with Father Noronha, Bangalore, December 2019.

16   Author's Interview with Alan Machado Prabhu, Bangalore, January 2017.

17   Recorded Interview of George Fernandes with Fredrick D'Sa (Unpublished), Mumbai, 2007.

18   R.M. Lala, 'The Two Faces of George Fernandes', *Himmat*, 10 May 1974.

19   Originally published in the *Illustrated Weekly of India,* 27 December 1970.

20   George Fernandes, undated (but c. 1951), *Sher-e-Dock: P D'Mello*, Bombay: United Printers, p. 6.

21   A facsimile was printed in the Konkani biography (written in Kannada script) of George Fernandes. See, John Baptist Moraes, 1999, *George Fernandes: Ek Sahasi Jinn*, Mangalore: Moraes Publication.

22   The founder–editor of *Blitz*, Rusi Karanjia, died in 2008. George wrote a small piece in memory of a 'great friend of mine': 'My Friend Rusi', *Other Side,* February 2008, p. 4.

23   Letter to Mahatma Gandhi, 11 January 1930, *Jayaprakash Narayan Selected Works*, volume 1, p. 41. *The Selected Works of Jayaprakash Narayan* is a singular contribution of Dr Bimal Prasad and is published by the Nehru Museum and Memorial Library. The volumes add much to our knowledge about both pre- and post-Independence India's politics and intellectual ferment. The work, though, is marred by poor editorial and production qualities, irritating typographical mistakes, and substandard translations.

24   Haridev Sharma, 2004, *Jaiprakash Awam Prabhavati*, Delhi: NMML. Based on oral interview with the socialist scholar Haridev Sharma in 1971.

25   Lakshmi Narain Lal, 1977, *Jayaprakash: India's Voice, India's Soul*, Delhi: Hind Pocket Books, p. 40.

26   Haridev Sharma Papers, Correspondence with Humboldt University, 8 October 1982, NMML, New Delhi.

27   Author's Interview with Arun Kumar Panibaba, Ghaziabad, 29 January 2016.

28   *Jayaprakash Narayan Selected Works*, volume 2, p. 5.

29   Dr Sampurnanand (1890–1969), 1962, *Memories and Reflections*, Delhi: Asia Publishing House.

30   Bernard Shaw, 1928, *Intelligent Woman's Guide to Socialism, Communism and Capitalism*, New York: Brentano's Publishers.

31   'S K Patil Article on the Formation of the CSP', *Bombay Chronicle*, 10 August 1934, *Jayaprakash Narayan Selected Works*, vol. 1 (1929–35), Appendix 6, p. 263.

32   Statement on Congress Working Committee Resolution, 22 June 1934, *Jayaprakash Narayan Selected Works*, volume 1, p. 65.

33   JP to Syed Mahmud, 20 July 1934, *Jayaprakash Narayan Selected Works*, volume 1, p. 69.

34   Comment on Vallabhbhai Patel's Speech at Bombay, 18 July 1934, *Jayaprakash Narayan Selected Works*, volume 1, p. 68.

35   'Genesis of Congress Socialist Group: Reply to S K Patil, August 11 1934', *Jayaprakash Narayan Selected Works*, volume 1, pp. 73–7.

36 Speech in support of the resolution on a constructive programme of the Congress, 16 September 1934, *Jayaprakash Narayan Selected Works*, volume 1, p. 78.

37 Presidential Address at the Bengal Congress Socialist Party Conference, Calcutta, 21 September 1935, *Jayaprakash Narayan Selected Works*, volume 1, p. 177.

38 Jawaharlal Nehru to JP, 11 January 1928, *Selected Works of Jawaharlal Nehru*, volume 3, pp. 10–15.

39 Letter from Jawaharlal Nehru, 11 January 1928, *Selected Works of Jawaharlal Nehru*, volume 3, pp. 10–15. See also, for a detailed discussion, Rahul Ramagundam, 2008, *Gandhi's Khadi*, Hyderabad: Orient Blackswan, particularly the chapter 'Clothing the Congress'.

40 Ram Manohar Lohia, 1969, *Samajwadi Andolan Ka Itihas*, Hyderabad: Samta Nyas.

41 Gopalkrishna Gandhi (ed.), 2009, *Gandhi Is Gone. Who Will Guide Us Now?: Nehru, Prasad, Azad, Vinoba, Kripalani, JP and Others Introspect*, New Delhi: Permanent Black.

42 Jayaprakash Narayan to Subhas Chandra Bose, 1940, *Jayaprakash Narayan Selected Works*, volume 3 (1939–1946), pp. 52–56.

43 Ram Manohar Lohia, 1969, *Samajwadi Andolan Ka Itihas*, Hyderabad: Samta Nyas.

44 'Reorganise the Congress: Task for Leadership', *Jayaprakash Narayan Selected Works*, volume 4 (1946–48), p. 7–10.

45 Lohia apportioned blame for the partition on the ageing leadership of the Congress. Ram Manohar Lohia, 2008, *Guilty Men of India's Partition*, New Delhi: Rupa & Co.

46 Aruna Asaf Ali recalled that Nehru was not happy with the use of separate flag and manifesto by the Socialists when they functioned still from inside the Congress. G.N.S. Raghavan, 1999, *Aruna Asaf Ali: A Compassionate Radical*, Delhi: National Book Trust.

47 The prefix was dropped in 1946 at its convention at Kanpur; in February 1948, the AICC passed a resolution debarring organizations carrying independent existence within the Congress.

48 Socialist Party, *Report of the Sixth National Conference*, Nasik, 19–21 March 1948.

49 Jayaprakash Narayan, 1948, 'Will the Socialists Leave the Congress?', *Jayaprakash Narayan Selected Works*, volume 4 (1946–48), pp. 202–06.

50 Asoka Mehta, 1949, *Economic Consequences of Sardar Patel*, Hyderabad: Chetna Prakashan.

51 George Fernandes, (Unpublished) Prison Journal, Hissar Jail, 9 August 1976.
52 George Fernandes, 'Dayanand Kalle: A Socialist and a Magnificent Human Being', *The Other Side*, October 1986.
53 R.M. Lala, 'The Two Faces of George Fernandes', *Himmat*, 10 May 1974.
54 J.R. Kamble, 1995, *Amardeep* (P. D'Mello's biography in Marathi), Mumbai: Granthali.
55 Michael V.d. Bogaert, 1970, *Trade Unionism in Indian Ports: A Case Study at Calcutta and Bombay*, New Delhi: Shri Ram Centre for Industrial Relations.
56 'Attaining a Vision', Speech at Sambalpur, 12 April 1948, *Selected Works of Jawaharlal Nehru*, Second Series, Volume 6, pp. 2–5.
57 Jawaharlal Nehru to B.G. Kher, *Selected Works of Jawaharlal Nehru*, Second Series, Volume 5, p. 5.
58 George Fernandes, undated (but c, 1951), *Sher-e-Docks: P. D'Mello*, Bombay: United Printers.
59 While the quotes are from Recorded Interview of George Fernandes with Fredrick D'Sa, (Unpublished) Mumbai, 2007, the perspective has been drawn from Author's Interview with Arrun Kumar Panibaba, Ghaziabad, 12 September 2011.
60 George Fernandes, undated (but c. 1951), *Sher-e-docks: P. D'Mello*, Bombay: United Printers, p. 26.

Chapter 4: Bombay Days

1 Recorded Interview of George Fernandes with Fredrick D'Sa (Unpublished), Mumbai, 2007. Also, *Himmat*, 4 March.
2 George Fernandes, 'One Strike—200 Settlements', *Himmat*, 4 March 1966, p. 15.
3 George Fernandes, 'Dayanand Kalle: A Socialist and a Magnificent Human Being', *The Other Side*, October 1986.
4 Report of the Eighth National Conference of the Socialist Party, Meherally Nagar, Madras, 8–12 July 1950.
5 See chapter 8.
6 Author's Interview with Manohar Reddy, Bangalore, January 2017. CGK would soon be the chairman of the Socialist Party (Mysore) and member of the first-ever Rajya Sabha.
7 Rajnarayan Chandavarkar, 1994, *The Origins of Industrial Capitalism in India: Business Strategies and the Working Classes in Bombay, 1900–1940*, Cambridge: Cambridge University Press.
8 George Fernandes, 24 April 2001, Message, *Shri S R Kulkarni 75th Birthday Felicitation Volume*, Bombay: S.R. Kulkarni Felicitation

Committee; Kulkarni was born in a *vatandar* family of Dhulia district of Maharashtra.

9   B. Sheshagiri Rao, 1987, *Indomitable: A Biography of S.R. Kulkarni, Stormy Petrel of Indian Trade Union Movement*, Bombay: S.R. Kulkarni Felicitation Committee.

10   Recorded Interview of George Fernandes with Fredrick D'Sa (Unpublished), Mumbai, 2007.

11   Madhu Dandavate, 1993, *As the Mind Unfolds: Issues and Personalities*, Delhi: Shipra.

12   Recorded Interview of George Fernandes with Fredrick D'Sa (Unpublished), Mumbai, 2007.

13   George Fernandes, undated (but c. 1951), *Sher-e-docks: P. D'Mello*, Bombay: United Printers, p. 7.

14   This paragraph is drawn from the reports appearing in the *Free Press Journal*, Bombay, August–October 1950.

15   Morarji Desai, 1978, *The Story of My Life*, Volume II, Delhi: S. Chand & Co., pp. 21–22.

16   Jawaharlal Nehru to JP, 22 September 1950, *Jayaprakash Narayan Selected Works*, Appendix 2, Volume 6 (1950–54).

17   Rajni Bakshi, 1986, *The Long Haul: The Bombay Textile Workers Strike*, Bombay: BUILD Documentation Centre.

18   George Fernandes, undated (but c. 1951), *Sher-e-docks: P. D'Mello*, Bombay: United Printers.

19   Recorded Interview of George Fernandes with Fredrick D'Sa (Unpublished), Mumbai, 2007.

20   Michael V.d. Bogaert, 1970, *Trade Unionism in Indian Ports: A Case Study at Calcutta and Bombay*, New Delhi: Shri Ram Centre for Industrial Relations, p. 37. *The Dockman* was later simultaneously published in three different languages: English, Marathi and Hindi.

21   Author's Interview with Jayashree, Port and Dock Workers' Union, Mumbai, 14 July 2015.

22   R.P. Cholia, 1941, *Dock Labourers in Bombay*, Bombay: Longman.

23   This paragraph is based on the reports appearing in *Bombay Chronicle*, Bombay, 29 May –1 June 1951.

24   Recorded Interview of George Fernandes with Fredrick D'Sa (Unpublished), Mumbai, 2007.

25   B. Sheshagiri Rao, 1994, *Comrade Manohar Kotwal: An Ideal Trade Unionist*, Bombay: Manohar Kotwal Felicitation Committee.

26   George Fernandes, undated (but c. 1951), *Sher-e-docks: P. D'Mello*, Bombay: United Printers.

27 Morarji Desai, 1978 (first paperback edition), *The Story of My Life*, Volume II, Delhi: S. Chand.

28 Recounted by Michael and Paul Fernandes in an interview with the Author, New Delhi, October 2010.

29 Author's Interview with Louie Fernandes, Mumbai, July 2015.

30 Recorded Interview of George Fernandes with Fredrick D'Sa (Unpublished), Mumbai, 2007.

31 Author's Interview with Michael Fernandes, New Delhi, 28 June 2011.

32 For a biography of Frank Buchman, http://www.frankbuchman.info.

33 'Two Winds', *Himmat*, August 1969.

34 'Now, MRA Invade Kashmir . . .', *Blitz*, 7 June 1958.

35 'Bevan among Bombay Dock Workers', *Hind Mazdoor*, March–April 1953, Vol I, No. 2, p. 66.

36 Michael Foot, 1962, *Aneurin Bevan: A Biography*, Volume I: 1897–1945. London: Macgibbon & Kee.

37 George Fernandes, (Unpublished) Prison Journal, Tihar Jail, 26 November 1976.

38 'My Decision is Definite', George Fernandes, Secretary of the Transport and Dock Workers Union, Bombay, *Caux-Information* (the Swiss MRA journal), No. 17, p. 78, 20 August 1954. Archives of the Canton (State) de Vaud in Lausanne, (Vaud State Archives), Rue de la Mouline 32, CH—1022 Chavannes-près-Renens, Switzerland, http://www.patrimoine.vd.ch/archives-cantonales. <link not accessible>

 The logical framework of such personal testimonies was that with MRA the desired changes for a better world are best initiated by changes in personal motivation and behaviour. MRA's slogan-type of the proposal at the time was 'Sound Homes, Team Work in Industry, a United Nation'. From this, it could be derived that people who were inspired by MRA were most likely to opt for the collective bargaining approach.

39 *Jan*, August 1958.

40 Author's Interview with Rajmohan Gandhi, (IIC) New Delhi, 25 November 2015.

41 Asoka Mehta, August 1952, *The Political Mind of India: An Analysis of the Results of the General Elections*, Bombay: A Socialist Party Publication.

42 Edit: A Political Slip, *Bombay Chronicle*, 28 April 1951.

43 Socialist Party, *Report of the Special Convention*, Panchmarhi, Madhya Pradesh, 23–27 May 1952.

44 Ram Manohar Lohia's Chairman's Address, *Report of the Special Convention*, 23–27 May 1952, p. 153.

45 JP to Nehru, 4 March 1953, cited in Madhu Limaye [Edited by N.C. Mehrotra], 1986, *The Age of Hope: Phases of the Socialist Movement*, Delhi: Atma Ram & Sons, pp. 376–84.

46 Speech of Jayaprakash Narayan, 1959, *Report of the Fifth National Conference of the Praja Socialist Party*, Bombay, 5–9 November, pp. 44–57.

47 Author's Interview with G.G. Parikh, Mumbai, 29 October 2017.

48 Ram Manohar Lohia to JP, undated, but sometime before July 1950, Madhu Limaye, 1986, *The Age of Hope: Phases of the Socialist Movement*, p. 324.

49 *Report of the Special Convention of the Praja Socialist Party*, Betul, Madhya Pradesh, 14–18 June 1953.

50 Asoka Mehta's arguments were based on Nehru's statement on withdrawing from talks with JP. Madhu Limaye, 1986, *The Age of Hope: Phases of the Socialist Movement*.

51 Lok Sabha Debate, 9 August 1960, p. 1667.

52 'Without a single voice of dissent, Congress pledge to make India wealthy and adopt a socialistic pattern of economic development', *Bombay Chronicle*, 20 January 1955.

53 'PSP-Red Clash of Views in Kerala/Vituperative Comment by Dr Lohia', *Times of India*, 13 February 1954.

54 *Facts Relating to Lohia's Attempt at Disrupting the PSP*, 1955, A Praja Socialist Publication.

55 For biographical sketches, see Lok Sabha Secretariat, 2008, *Madhu Limaye in Parliament: A Commemorative Volume*, and Madhu Limaye, 1991, *Politics after Freedom*, Delhi: Atma Ram & Sons.

56 J.B. Kripalani to Madhu Limaye, 13 July 1954, Box No 9/File No. 3, Madhu Limaye (Unsorted) Papers, NMML.

57 Madhu Limaye to Rama Mitra, January (undated), 1964. Madhu Limaye (Unsorted) Papers, NMML.

58 *Bombay Chronicle*, July–August 1955.

59 George Fernandes, Obituary of Dinkar Sakrikar, *The Other Side*, 1989.

60 S.M. Edwardes, 1901, *The Rise of Bombay*, Census of India Series.

61 Author's Interview with Louie Fernandes, Mumbai, July 2015.

62 *Bombay Chronicle*, 7–24 August 1955.

63 *Bombay Chronicle*, 31 July–7 August 1955.

64 Author's Interview with Mahabal Shetty, Municipal Mazdoor Union, Mumbai, 30 June 2015.

65 *Spotlight on the Municipal Workers' Struggle*, October 1957, Bombay: Municipal Mazdoor Union. Although this document has Jaganath Jadav, Secretary, MMU, named as the publisher, and authorship is unnamed, given the nature of document and manpower constraints of the MMU,

it is without a doubt written by George. It is not a eulogy and gives a fair, all-round picture of the movement but has George at the centre of the movement and negotiations. The rest, including the SMS players like Joshi and Dange or MMU President D'Mello and Limaye, are given bit but significant roles. Says Sanju Poojari, who worked with George since the 1980s, 'George had a penchant to create written documents on all the struggles he launched. He would create documents even concerning those causes that were lost.' Author's Interview with Sanju Poojari, Bombay Labour Union, Mumbai, 27 December 2017.

66   *Maniben Kara: A Tale of Struggles and Service*, Birth Centenary pamphlet, 2005, Mumbai: Western Railway Employees Union.

67   See *Free Press Journal* (FPJ), 19 May–14 October 1949.

68   'Bombay Sweepers' Strike: Morale Fast Cracking', *Times of India*, 28 May 1949.

69   The Municipal Servants Act and the Public Security Measures Act.

70   'City Streets Are Nearly as Clean as Ever', *Free Press Journal*, 22 May 1949.

71   V.N. Barve, 1949, *Report of Scavengers' Living Conditions Enquiry Committee*, Bombay.

72   'Kamgar Sangh's Charge against Municipality', *FPJ*, 19 May 1949, p. 3.

73   'No Permission to Meet Sweepers' Leaders in Jail', *FPJ*, 3 June 1949.

74   'Sweepers' Strike Front: Dr Ambedkar to Intervene', *FPJ*, 2 July 1949.

75   Maybe it was to do with the time in which they were written or made. In *Achhut Kanya*, there was standing up for friendship and sacrifice. U.R. Ananthamurty's *Samskara* (1969), however, is about the guilt of cohabiting with an untouchable woman or having a chance play of passion; it could be simply lust that brings an upper-caste man to an untouchable woman; there is no conviction; at best there is a bit of rebelliousness against the system. In *Samskara*, the untouchable woman is of easy virtue, not just freely cohabiting with a Brahmin man, but even copulating willingly with another Brahmin man after the first man is dead and waiting to be cremated.

76   Rajya Sabha Debate, 2 May 1955.

77   Salman Rushdie, 2006 [1981], *Midnight's Children*, London: Vintage Books.

78   V.N. Barve, *Report of Scavengers' Living Conditions Enquiry Committee*, Bombay, 1949.

79   George Fernandes, 2008 [1984], *The Rail Strike of 1974 and the Railwaymen's Movement*, Mumbai: Pratipaksh Prakashan, p. 51;
      also, Talk at the Seminar on the Third World Strikes, Institute of Social Studies, The Hague, The Netherlands, 12–16 September 1977, George

Mathew (ed.), 1991, *George Fernandes Speaks*, Delhi: Ajanta Publications, p. 23.

80 Author's Interview with Dada Naik, Mumbai, 8 July and 24 October 2015.

81 Sudha Boda had started working almost simultaneously with the founding of the MMU. 'The people from Kathiawar worked in Bombay Municipality as menial labour responsible for cleanliness; they would clean public latrines and streets, carry human night soil as head-loads; they had their own workers union. Mahars had their own workers' union. The trade unions were based on *varna vayastha*. There were trade unions also based on departments such as malaria eradication, road/street sweeping, hospitals etc.' Author's Interview with Sudha Boda, Vadodara, 7 November 2011.

82 *Bharat Jyoti*, Bombay, 23 June 1957.

83 George Fernandes, 'Workers and United-Frontiers in Bombay', Communication, *Mankind*, August 1957, Volume II, No.1, pp. 84–85.

84 *Spotlight on the Municipal Workers' Struggle*, October 1957, Bombay: Municipal Mazdoor Union.

85 Author's Interview with Ramakant Bane, Municipal Mazdoor Union, Bal Dandavate Bhavan, N M Joshi Road, Lower Parel, Mumbai, 17 October 2015.

86 *Blitz* which ignored the strike published a photo on 21 June with the caption 'Clean Up This Filth': 'Mountains of rat-infested filth, like this one, endangering Bombay City's health are a warning to the citizens no less than the Corporation to raise immediately a volunteer force to clean up Bombay. No strike, however justified it may be, should be permitted to paralyse hospitals and blackmail population with the threat of cholera and plague.'

87 'Notes and Comments', *Mankind*, August 1958.

88 *A Struggle to Remember: Report of the BEST Workers' Dispute with The Four Agreements of January 2, 1960*, An Action Committee Publication.

89 '"Take It or Leave It" Offer: Samiti Bid to End the BEST Dispute', *Times of India*, 3 October 1959.

90 *A Struggle to Remember: Report of the BEST Workers' Dispute with The Four Agreements of January 2, 1960*, An Action Committee Publication.

91 Author's Interview with Dada Naik, Mumbai, 8 July 2015.

92 *FPJ*, 22 March 1958.

93 *Blitz*, 29 March 1958.

94 *Bombay Chronicle*, 23 March 1958.

95 Madhu Limaye to George, (soon after) 20 March 1958. 'It is not that I was unaware of jealous attempts made to drive a wedge between you two but I did my best to remove misunderstandings and generally maintain harmony.' Madhu Limaye Papers, NMML.

96   Author's Interview with Dada Naik, Mumbai, 5 July 2015.
97   *Bombay Labour Gazette*, September 1958.
98   *Times of India*, 17 May 1962.
99   Author's Interview with Dada Naik, Mumbai, 5 July 2015.
100   His earliest colleagues were S.R. Rao, Somnath Dube, Harihar Sharma, Tulsi Boda, Prabhakar More, Baburao Mumbarkar, V.N. Shane, Bal Dandavate. Later, B.R. Bawakar, Charles Lewis, and T. Mindonsa also joined.
101   'Socialists Lead Morcha to Consul General Office: Protest against Chinese Action in Tibet.' *Times of India*, 21 April 1959.
102   Bombay Municipal Corporation, *Record of the Proceedings of the Municipal Corporation, The Standing Committee, The Improvements Committee and The Education Committee, 1961–62*.
103   *Times of India*, 10 October 1961.
104   *Times of India*, 8 December 1961.
105   Author's Interview with Aniruddha Limaye, New Delhi, 20 January 2015.
106   George to Leila Fernandes from the underground, sometime in April/May 1976.
107   George, New Delhi, to Madhu Limaye, 23 July 1962 (written on two inland letterforms, folded into one), Madhu Limaye Unsorted Papers, NMML.
108   George to Madhu Limaye from New Delhi, 30 July 1962, Madhu Limaye (Unsorted) Papers, NMML.
109   Author's Interview with Arun Kumar Panibaba, 14 January 2012, on the train from Hyderabad to Bangalore.

Chapter 5: A Man More Dangerous than the Communists

1   Cf. N.K. Singh, 2011, *The Tangy Taste of Indian Politics and Beyond*, Delhi: Konark, pp. 7–9.
2   George Fernandes, undated (but c. 1951), *Sher-e-docks: P D'Mello*, Bombay: United Printers.
3   George [Nagpur Central Prison] to Madhu Limaye, 20 November 1963.
4   In 1954, two successful movies starring Dev Anand (*Taxi Driver*) and Guru Dutt (*Aar Paar*) were released.
5   Conversation is from the movie *Taxi Driver*, 1954.
6   *The Economics of the Taxi Trade: A Statement in Justification of the Fare Rise*, by George Fernandes, President, Bombay Taximen's Union, 9 September 1962; published by Nagjibhai Tapiawala, General Secretary, Bombay Taximen's Union, 204, Charni Road, Bombay.
7   The 1978 film *Gaman* directed by Muzaffar Ali gives a peep into the 'troubled lives' of taxi drivers in the city.

8   Memorandum: Subject: Draft Notification of 13 April 1963, concerning the revision of taxi fares, Madhu Limaye (Unsorted) Papers, NMML.

9   *Current*, 2 September 1972.

10   In Parliament, debate on the President's address showed concern over how emergency powers had been used (*Tribune*, 21 February 1963); at the Praja Socialist Party (PSP) national conference at Bhopal in June 1963, every speaker spoke about the DIR's misuse to serve the ruling party's interest.

11   The order imposing emergency and suspending rights under Articles 21 and 22 came into effect on 3 November 1962.

12   Socialist Party memorandum to the Governor Vijayalakshmi Pandit, 18 March 1963.

13   The resolution passed by the Mass Rally of Taximen at Shivaji Park, 31 March 1963.

14   Raj Narain to Lal Bahadur Shastri, Home Minister, GOI.

15   Parsbag Singh was released after three months of detention. 'Obituary: Sardar Parsbag Singh: An Old Soldier Passes Away', December 1984, in George Mathew (Ed.), 1991, *George Fernandes Speaks*, Delhi: Ajanta Publications, pp. 396–99.

16   'Bombay and Suburbs', *Times of India* (Bombay), 6 April 1963, p. 9.

17   'Defiant Workers Held by Police', *Times of India* (Bombay), 7 April 1963. From Madhu Limaye to Raj Narain, 20 April 1963.

18   'Socialist Leader Showed Disregard for Authority', *Times of India* (Bombay), 8 April 1963.

19   *Times of India* (Bombay), 9 April 1963.

20   *The Maharashtra Government Gazette Extraordinary*, 13 April 1963.

21   The resolution passed by the Managing Committee of the BTU at its emergency meeting held on 17 April 1963.

22   Fernandes' Note to Chavan, *Times of India* (Bombay), 11 July 1961.

23   Home Department (Special) Order, 29 June 1963.

24   H. Shiva Rao to George, 7 April 1963.

25   H. Shiva Rao to George, 22 April 1963.

26   B.V.K. Alva to George, Bombay, 20 May 1963.

27   George to H. Shiva Rao, Nagpur Central Prison, 8 November 1963.

28   Dr R.H. Dastur to George, Bombay, 11 April 1963.

29   George to The Secretary to the Government of Maharashtra, Home Department, Bombay (Undated).

30   Postcard from Suresh Vaidya to George, Delhi, 13 April 1963.

31   Prabhakar Kunte to George, Bombay, 10 April 1963.

32   George to Yashwantrao Chavan, 7 May 1963.

33   S.M Joshi to George, 19 April 1963.

34   'Detention Cannot Be Questioned', *Times of India*, (Bombay), 18 April 1963.

35   On 17 June, at the Bombay High Court, his advocate A.A. Peerbhoy stated that he was not seeking enforcement of the petitioner's fundamental rights but a declaration that the detention was illegal.

36   *Times of India* (Bombay), 13 April 1963.

37   *Times of India* (Bombay), 11 April 1963.

38   'No Cooperation with Govt. Defence Effort', *Times of India* (Bombay), 10 April 1963.

39   From Madhu Limaye to M.S. Kannamwar, Chief Minister of Maharashtra, Bombay, 19 April 1963, Madhu Limaye (Unsorted) Papers, NMML.

40   *Times of India* (Bombay), 11 April 1963; Resolution of the MMU, 11 April 1963.

41   *Times of India* (Bombay), 13 April 1963.

42   *Times of India*, Bombay, 15 July 1963; Hind Mazdoor Panchayat Press Note, 15 July 1963.

43   B.R. Dandavate, MMU, to the Municipal Commissioner, BMC, Corporation Proceedings, 12 August 1963, p. 1071.

44   In the Bombay Municipal Corporation, councillors raised the matter of price rise. Corporation Proceedings, 8 August 1963, p. 1063.

45   Corporation Proceedings, 12 August 1963, Letter of the Deputy Municipal Commissioner (Labour) to the MMU, 2 July 1963, p. 1072. Letter from B.R. Dandavate to Deputy Municipal Commissioner, 3 July 1963.

46   Hind Mazdoor Panchayat Press Note, 15 July 1963.

47   From Madhu Limaye to M.S. Kannamwar, Chief Minister of Maharashtra, Bombay, 19 April 1963, Madhu Limaye (Unsorted) Papers, NMML.

48   Madhu Limaye to Rama Mitra, Bombay, 5 August 1963, Madhu Limaye (Unsorted) Papers, NMML.

49   Madhu Limaye (Chairman, Girni Mazdoor Sangarsh Samiti) to Shripad Amrit Dange, 22 July 1963, Madhu Limaye (Unsorted) Papers, NMML.

50   Shripad Amrit Dange to Madhu Limaye, 22 July 1963, Madhu Limaye (Unsorted) Papers, NMML.

51   From the communiqué adopted by trade unions belonging to three central trade union organizations, 22 July 1963. Madhu Limaye's Press release on Shripad Amrit Dange and his approach, 22 July 1963, Madhu Limaye (Unsorted) Papers, NMML.

52   Madhu Limaye to Trade Union comrades, 25 July 1963, Madhu Limaye (Unsorted) Papers, NMML.

53   Press release by Bambai Mazdoor Sangharsha Samiti, Charter of demands, 21 July 1963.

54 Press release by Municipal Mazdoor Union, Bombay, 6 August 1963.

55 *Times of India* (Bombay), 10 August 1963.

56 'Strike Disrupts Bombay's Civic Services', *Tribune* (Chandigarh), 13 August 1963.

57 Press release of BEST Mazdoor Sanharsha Samiti, 6 August 1963.

58 These notes were written in the days after he was arrested on 16 August.

59 Lok Sabha Debate, 19 August 1963.

60 Madhu Limaye to Mrs Vijayalakshmi Pandit, 19 August 1963, Madhu Limaye (Unsorted) Papers, NMML.

61 'Life in Bombay Completely Paralysed / 10 Lakh Workers Respond to Call for Strike / Protest against CDS and Rise in Prices', *Tribune*, Chandigarh, 21 August 1963.

62 Signed by Tulsi Boda, HMP Secretary, and S.R. Kulkarni, Bambai Mazdoor Sangharsh Samiti.

63 Lok Sabha Debate, 21 August 1963.

64 Janardan Upadhyay to George from Nasik Central Prison, 3 September 1963.

65 George to Madhu Limaye, 18 June 1963.

66 George to G.L. Gulzarilal Nanda, 6 September 1963.

67 George to Ram Manohar Lohia, 4 September 1963; The 3 September letter was rewritten on the 4th. A hand-written copy of the original is in George's archive.

68 To Shiva Rao from George, Nagpur Central Prison, 8 November 1963.

69 Louie Fernandes to George, 29 December 1976.

70 Madhu Limaye to George (undated), March 1957, Madhu Limaye (Unsorted) Papers, NMML.

71 Interview with Poppat (Aniruddh) Limaye, New Delhi, 20 January 2015.

72 Interview with Sharad Pawar, New Delhi, 2016.

73 Author's Interview with A.B. Bardhan at Ajoy Bhawan, CPI headquarters, 10 June 2010. When told 'I am doing a biography of George Fernandes', there was a moment of silence, and then the heavy intonation of 'yes', expecting me to tell him further. I told him: 'While doing research on George's life, I found that you spent time along with him in Nagpur Jail in 1963.' There was softening in his voice and a faint smile perhaps. 'That is a minor episode.' I was quick to grab the opportunity, 'Sir, that was an important year and that is just the beginning.' He told me to come at 4 p.m. to his Ajoy Bhawan office at ITO.

74 H. Shiva Rao to Com. George Fernandes, Socialist Detenue, 9 November 1963. Asking him 'not to give these books as a gift to anyone but to bring them back', Madhu Limaye sent him many books regularly.

75   To Shiva Rao from George, Nagpur Central Prison, 8 November 1963.
76   *The Other Side*, February 1982, p. 44.
77   George to Madhu Limaye, 20 November 1963, Nagpur prison; Michael Foot, 1962, *Aneurin Bevan: A Biography, Volume I: 1897–1945*, London: Macgibbon & Kee.
78   George to Madhu Limaye, 20 November 1963. He listed several books that were withheld from him.
79   Letter to Shiva Rao from George, Nagpur Central Prison, 8 November 1963; George asked Shiva Rao to send him a copy of the 'Report of the Minimum Wages Committee on Hotel Workers'.
80   Dinkar Sakrikar, editor United Asia, 12 Rampart Row, Bombay, to George, 5 December 1963.
81   From K. Pisharodi, *Seminar*, to George, 5 October 1963.
82   Cliffy Saldana, Bombay, to 'My Dear George', 18 November 1963.
83   To George from S.B. Naik, Advocate, Bombay, 10 July 1963.
84   Raj Narain to Lal Bahadur Shastri, Home Minister, GOI.
85   George to Shiv Rao, from Nagpur Central Jail, 12 August 1963.
86   George to Shiv Rao, from Nagpur Central Jail, 22 August 1963.
87   Bardhan and Fernandes' writ petition: Jail Supdt. has no power to restrict books to detenus, High Court judgment, *Hitwada*, Nagpur, 2 October 1963.
88   Louie Fernandes to George, 12 June 1963.
89   Paul Fernandes to George, 22 October 1963.
90   George to Madhu Limaye, November 1963.
91   George to Pappu and Bina, 3 September 1963.
92   In a letter written in Hindi from Belgium, on 2 September 1964, George informs Pappu and Bina that he is attending International Socialist Conference, held between 2–7 September 1964.
93   Iftikhar Gilani, 2005, *My Days in Prison*, Delhi: Penguin, p. 119.
94   *Current*, 20 April 1963.

Chapter 6: Stepping Up

1   N.G. Gorey, Rajya Sabha Debate, 3 May 1974.
2   Author's Interview with Jaya Jaitly, New Delhi, 5 June 2014.
3   Madhu Limaye to George, from Farrukhabad, 24 March 1963, Madhu Limaye (Unsorted) Papers, NMML.
4   Madhu Limaye to Rama Mitra, 26 April 1963, Madhu Limaye (Unsorted) Papers, NMML.
5   Ram Manohar Lohia, Press Release, New Delhi, 2 May 1963.

6   Letter to P. Subbarayan, 5 January 1948, *Selected Works of Jawaharlal Nehru*, Second Series, Volume 5, p. 2.

7   Letter to B.G. Kher, 5 January 1948, *Selected Works of Jawaharlal Nehru*, Second Series, Volume 5, p. 5.

8   Asoka Mehta, August 1952, *The Political Mind of India: An Analysis of the Results of the General Elections*, Bombay: A Socialist Party Publication.

9   Socialist Party Election Manifesto—1962, *Mankind*, January 1962. This was such a radical projection of the politics that it was bound to distance the party from other political outfits.

10   A Praja Socialist Party Publication, 1963, *Socialist Unity: Another Attempt Fails.*

11   Madhu Limaye to Rama Mitra, January 1964, Madhu Limaye (Unsorted) Papers, NMML.

12   'Kripalani Wins Amroha Election: Lohia Defeats Keskar', *Tribune*, 22 May 1963. See, 'Comment: Communalism, Mrs. Gandhi and Beef Tallow', *The Other Side*, November 1983, p. 3.

13   Madhu's statement on Farrukhabad victory of Lohia, Press Statement, Socialist Party, Bombay, 28 May 1963, Madhu Limaye (Unsorted) Papers, NMML.

14   Madhu Limaye to Rama Mitra, 27 May 1963, Madhu Limaye (Unsorted) Papers, NMML.

15   George to Madhu Limaye, 18 June 1963. A 12-page letter from prison, a hand-written copy kept with him was found in George Archive, while one copy was in Madhu Limaye's Papers, Madhu Limaye (Unsorted) Papers, NMML.

16   'Motion of No-Confidence in the Council of Ministers', 20–22 August 1963, Lok Sabha Debate, Third Series, Volume XIX, 1963, New Delhi: Lok Sabha Secretariat.

17   Author's Interview with Arun Kumar Panibaba, Ghaziabad, 29 January 2016.

18   The resolution passed at the National Conference of the Socialist Party, Calcutta, December 1963.

19   Report of the Special Convention of the Praja Socialist Party, Betul, Madhya Pradesh, 14–18 June 1953.

20   To Madhu Limaye, 22 January 1964, Madhu Limaye (Unsorted) Papers, NMML.

21   *The Statesman*, Delhi, 29 January 1964.

22   A bunch of letters exchanged between Madhu Limaye and Prem Bhasin, January 1964, is kept in Madhu Limaye (Unsorted) Papers, NMML.

23   *Janata*, 30 May 1976.

24 *Bombay Chronicle*, 6 May 1956.

25 *Himmat*, 6 January 1967.

26 Author's Interview with Arun Kumar Panibaba, Ghaziabad, 2 September 2011.

27 'Cow-Based Politics', *EPW*, 14 January 1967.

28 Author's Interview with K. Vikram Rao, Lucknow, 20 August 2011.

29 See *Times of India*, 7 February 1967.

30 George Fernandes, (Unpublished) Prison Journal, Hissar Jail, 4 September 1976.

31 George Fernandes, Relevance of Krishna Menon, Krishna Menon Memorial meeting, 3 May 1977, New Delhi.

32 Eknath Gore, a supporter in 1967, worked in LIC, and was a friend of Golwalkar's son; using Gore's link, George manouevred into the RSS camp to gain their support to his candidature despite the Jan Sangh having put up a candidate.

33 Author's Interview with Dada Nayak, Mumbai, 8 July 2015.

34 Author's Interview with Poppat (Anirudh) Limaye, New Delhi, 20 January 2015.

35 Author's Interview with Olga Tellis, Mumbai, 15 July 2015.

36 From Meghnad H. Bhutt, Bombay, 23 February 1967.

37 From Madhu Dandavate, 24 February 1967.

38 Rama Mitra to Badri Vishal Pitti, 3 March 1967, NMML, Subject File No. 3: 5.

39 Rama Mitra, 'Death of a Socialist: An Open Letter', *Mankind*, March 1969, pp. 27–39.

40 George Fernandes, Letter from underground, December 1975.

41 George to Badri Vishal Pitti, 29 November 1967 (Badri Vishal Pitti Correspondence with Madhu Limaye: 32:14), NMML.

42 Lok Sabha Debate, 20 March 1969.

43 Cotton Textile Companies (Management etc.,) Bill, Lok Sabha Debate, 28 November 1967.

44 Lok Sabha Debate, 21 July 1969.

45 Omkar Lal Berwa a member from Kota, Lok Sabha Debate, 15 December 1967.

46 Lok Sabha Debate, 15 December 1967.

47 Lok Sabha Debate, 20 February 1968.

48 Lok Sabha Debate, 17 April 1968.

49 Irrelevance of Parliament, *EPW*, 17 August 1968.

50 Statement issued by Mr Madhu Limaye and Mr George Fernandes, (undated), August 1968.

51   Author's Interview with Poppat (Anirudh) Limaye, New Delhi, 20 January 2015.

52   Half-an-hour discussion on 'detention of Sheikh Abdullah', Lok Sabha Debate, 1 December 1967.

53   George Fernandes, (Unpublished) Prison Journal, Hissar District Jail and Tihar Jail.

54   A.R. Antulay as a minister in Maharashtra was seen ferrying smuggler's goods in his own car and when police caught up with him, he slapped the investigating officer for checking a minister's vehicle. See Madhu Limaye's communication with Indira Gandhi in 1974 on corruption of Lalit Narayan Mishra and Antulay, Box No 2, File No 2, Madhu Limaye (Unsorted) Papers, NMML.

55   'Half-an-hour discussion on the Bombay organization Shiv Sena, headed by Bal Thackeray', Lok Sabha Debate, 27 November 1967.

56   Author's Interview with Arun Kumar Panibaba, Ghaziabad, 17 January 2016.

57   Indira Gandhi to George on 25 February 1969.

58   'SSP's High Priests', *EPW*, 24 May 1969.

59   Author's Interview with Professor Anand Kumar, Gurgaon, 20 January 2016.

60   Letter from Committee for Defence & Release of Naxalite Prisoners, UP, 23 July 1973.

61   Author's Interview with Neerja Chowdhury, Women's Press Club, New Delhi, 27 November 2012.

62   George Fernandes, 'I Was Beaten, Dragged and Mocked', *Himmat*, 8 May 1970, p. 21. See Lok Sabha Debate, 23 April 1970.

63   'Fernandes Defends Land Grab Stir', *Indian Nation*, Patna, 1 September 1970.

64   'CPI Blames SSP for Land-Grab Fiasco', *Hindustan Times*, New Delhi, 4 September 1970.

65   'Statues of Alien: A Letter to the Editor', *Times of India*, 13 July 1961. At Kala Ghoda, which was a black sculpture of a horse on which sat George V, when George led a procession for its dismantling as a vestige of the British imperialism, someone questioned the origin of his name itself, and said it would be a fitting thing to change to Jagannath Fadnavis.

66   From Mukhtar Anis and Mohan Singh, dated 5 May 1970.

67   Author's Interview with Ajay Sekhar, Sonbhadra, Uttar Pradesh, October 2020.

68   Rama Mitra to S.M. Joshi, Chairman, SSP, 19 February 1968.

69   Rama Mitra, 6 June 1971.

70 Letters exchanged between Badri Vishal Pittie and Pannalal Surana, July 1968, Subject File: S. No. 47, Badri Vishal Pittie Papers, NMML.

71 'Mysore SSP Leader Quits Party Office', *Northern India Patrika*, 1 September 1970.

72 Badri Vishal Pittie to Baleshwar Dayal, 30 September 1969, Badri Vishal Pittie's correspondence with Baleshwar Dayal, File No. 54, p. 16, NMML.

73 From Badri Vishal Pittie to Rama Mitra, 6 August 1970, Subject File 3: 32; Badri Vishal Pittie papers: Correspondence with George Fernandes, File No. 41.

74 JP's letter on police repression of a mass demonstration by SSP in Delhi, 24 April 24, 1970.

75 To JP, 28 April 1970.

76 Rama Mitra to Badri Vishal Pittie, 7 November 1969.

77 To The Speaker, 8 May 1970.

78 The Bill was opposed by Congress (O), Jan Sangh, Swatantra Party, BKD, and was supported by DMK, CPI, CPM, Congress (R), PSP, and SSP.

79 Lok Sabha Debate, 3 September 1970.

80 From Bhai Vaid, 10 July 1970.

81 From Meghnad H. Bhatt, Bombay, 18 June 1970.

82 George Fernandes, 1972, *What Ails the Socialists?* New Delhi: New Society.

83 Socialist Party Circulars, 1971–72, Joint Declaration of Employers' and Workers', Meeting of Workers' and Employers' Representatives, 16 December 1971.

84 Socialist Party Circulars, 1971–72, 'Chairman's Opening Address', Meeting of Workers' and Employers' Representatives, 16 December 1971.

85 From Hans Janitschek, General Secretary, Socialist International, 12 February 1973 (File No. 1973).

86 To Jerry, 23 April 1973.

87 The SP had decided not to nominate those persons to Rajya Sabha who had earlier lost their Lok Sabha elections. It was on this basis that Raj Narain was asked not to contest as he had been a contestant in the 1971 election and had lost. Raj Narain, however, refused to heed to the party directive and nominated himself as a candidate. It led to his suspension. SP Circular, 18 April 1972.

88 Ranjan Kumar Sinha, student, BA final year, Banka, letter dated 1 May 1973.

89 Babasingh Somvansi, Fatehgarh, to George, 6 May 1973.

90 George Fernandes, (Unpublished) Prison Journal, Hissar Jail, 1976.

91 From Rajendra Singh Choudhry, Udaipur Socialist Party, 2 September 1973.

92   Author's Interview with Laxmi Narayan Yadav, MP, New Delhi, 29 December 2015.
93   *Mankind*, Vol. 4, November 1961.
94   Margo Skinner to Annie, London, 3 July 1960.
95   A bunch of letters from Margo Skinner are kept in George's Archive. These letters seems to have been brought by George from her as historical source, otherwise they have no place in his archive. File: Private Communication.
96   *Mankind*, August–September 1960.
97   Margo Skinner to Annie, London, 3 July 1960.
98   Leila Fernandes to Dadabhai, 25 June 1982, hand-written notes (photocopy of the letter).
99   See Obituary, *Times of India*, 19 August 1969.
100   The Regulation of Expenditure and Eradication of Corruption Bill was introduced in the Lok Sabha by Humayun Kabir.
101   Author's Interview with Binod; the Lok Dal launched by him was a West Bengal-based party and was later merged with Charan Singh's outfit to form Bhartiya Kranti Dal.
102   Statement submitted by Leila Kabir Fernandes, 16 September 1976, Hearings on the Human Rights in India, International Relations Sub-Committee on International Organisations, US House of Representatives.
103   'On the Spot: Leila - The Crusader', *Himmat*, 16 July 1971.
104   Author's Interview with Neerja Chowdhury, Women's Press Club, New Delhi, 27 November 2012.
105   From Yusuf Beg, 10 July 1971 (UP, File No. 1); in June perhaps, George had visited Varanasi as is evident from a reference to his visit to the BHU in a letter to him from the Vice-Chancellor, K.L. Shrimali.
106   From A.B. Shah, Indian Secular Society, Bombay, 7 July 1971.
107   From Ashok Setalvad, CEO, Standard Batteries Ltd, 7 July 1971.
108   Author's Interview with Richard Fernandes, at Jaya Jaitly's place, New Delhi, 22 November 2011.
109   Leila Kabir to George, 7 July 1971.
110   Author's Interview with Neerja Chowdhury, Women's Press Club, New Delhi, 27 November 2012.
111   George Fernandes, (Unpublished) Prison Journal, Hissar Jail, 22 July 1976.
112   Author's Interview with Richard Fernandes at Jaya Jaitly's place, New Delhi, 22 November 2011.
113   Author's Interview with Paul, Louie, and Michael Fernandes, New Delhi, 18 October 2010.
114   Referred to in an Email Communication from Michael Fernandes to Leila Fernandes, 5 September 2010. (Copy with the Author)

115 Author's Interview with Kamlesh Shukla, New Delhi, 12 September 2011.

116 Author's Interview with Usha Gandhi, Panchgani, 8 February 2016.

117 George Fernandes, (Unpublished) Prison Journal, Hissar Jail, 26 August 1976.

118 George Fernandes, 'Obituary of S.M. Joshi: The Inspiration Lives On', *The Other Side*, May 1989.

119 *Lohia Through Letters*, New Delhi: Rama Mitra, p. 114.

Chapter 7: The Strike Man

1 'Railway Strike', Letter in *Indian Express*, 7 June 1974.

2 Interview of Prime Minister Indira Gandhi with George Evans, *Sunday Telegraph*, London, 12 October 1975.

3 Indira Gandhi, Reply to the No-Confidence Motion, Lok Sabha, 9 May 1974.

4 S.D. Punekar, 'The Central Government Employees Strike', *Economic Weekly*, 30 July 1960.

5 All India Trade Union Congress, 1960, *Five Glorious Days (July 12–16, 1960): Central Government Employees' Strike*. On 15 July, 30,000 municipal workers went on a one-day token strike in solidarity with striking Central government employees.

6 *Times of India* (Bombay), 14 July 1960.

7 'Excessive Use of Police Force', *Times of India* (Bombay), 20 July 1960.

8 'No Serious Injury to Union Leader: Government's Statement', *Times of India* (Bombay), 15 July 1960.

9 'Fernandes Sentenced', *Times of India* (Bombay), 6 May 1961.

10 Recorded Interview of George Fernandes with Fredrick D'Sa, (Unpublished) Mumbai, 2007.

11 'Better Prison Facilities: Fernandes Note to Chavan', *Times of India* (Bombay), 11 July 1961.

12 Railway Budget: General Discussion, Lok Sabha Debate, 4 March 1968, pp. 1425–42.

13 Action against Central Government Employees for Strike on 19 September 1968, Lok Sabha Debates, 26 August 1969, pp. 412–16.

14 Railway Budget: General Discussion, Lok Sabha Debate, 4 March 1968.

15 See for an official history of the AIRF: All India Railwaymen's Federation, *Origin and Growth of All India Railwaymen's Federation*, Volume I (1982) & II (1985).

16 The two railway labour organisations, AIRF and the Indian National Workers' Federation, due to persuasion by JP, agreed to merge into a single

body known as the NFIR. The decision was taken at New Delhi on 19 April 1953 by the working committees of both organisations. But soon, it came unhinged, with the AIRF coming out of the merged entity to revive itself, and the NFIR becoming a Congress-controlled organization.

17 For a deeper analysis, see Stephen Sherlock, 2001, *The Indian Railways Strike of 1974: A Study of Power and Organised Labour*, Delhi: Rupa. Sherlock's work is singularly acclaimed as academic work on the railway strike by a foreign scholar, a PhD thesis before it was published as a book.

18 For a history of the NFIR, see Mahesh Kumar Mast, 1969, *Trade Union Movement in Indian Railways*, Meerut: Meenakshi Prakashan. Also, the NFIR chief A.P. Sharma's speech in Lok Sabha on 2 May 1974 is revealing in its candour. Arrest of Leaders of Railway Workers (Adjournment Motion) 2 May 1974, Lok Sabha Debates, pp. 301–09.

19 George to Peter Alvares, Bombay, 28 June 1972.

20 Maniben Kara, Western Railway Employees Union to George, 4 November 1973.

21 Kalpana Sharma, 'Way Out of the Tunnel', *Himmat*, 17 May 1974.

22 S.A. Dange, General Secretary, AITUC, to Peter Alvares, President, AIRF, 13 June 1970.

23 S.A. Dange to George, 18 March 1974, *cf.* T.N. Siddhanta, August 1974, *The Railway General Strike*, Delhi: AITUC Publication, p. 33.

24 So exasperated did the railwaymen feel at the piling grievances that one Lok Sabha member (Priya Gupta) as early as in April 1962 vented in Parliament how negotiations had become a 'mockery'. Even in 1973, the situation was similar. See, Handout for Members of Parliament, Points for Raising during Railway Budget Discussions, IR, April 1973, p. 1.

25 Resolution No. 1: On the Strike, AIRF Working Committee Meeting, Delhi, 2–5 August 1973.

26 Recommendations of the Pay Commission, *Indian Railwaymen*, July 1973.

27 Working Committee Resolution No. 1: On the Strike, AIRF, 2–5 August 1973.

28 Stand United Against Banning of Railway Workers' Strike, U.T.U.C. (Lenin Sarani's) Appeal.

29 Lok Sabha Debates, 1974: Volume 87: Nos 1–8, 18–28 February 1974.

30 All India Loco Running Staff Association, An Explanatory Note to The Convention of Central and State Government Employees at New Delhi on 25th & 26th July 1973, called by United Council of Trade Unions.

31 Resolution No. 4: Loco Staff, AIRF Working Committee Meeting, Delhi, 2–5 August 1973.

32   George Fernandes, 2008 [1984], *The Rail Strike of 1974 and the Railwaymen's Movement*, Mumbai: Pratipaksh Prakashan.

33   George to Subhash Malgi, 29 May 1974.

34   Letter to George from N. Sunderasan, Assistant General Secretary of the South Central Railway Mazdoor Union, Secunderabad, 5 October 1973.

35   L.N. Mishra, Re. Discussion under Rule 176, Rajya Sabha, 3 May 1974.

36   Yashpal Kapur, Calling Attention to a Matter of Public Importance, Rajya Sabha, 10 May 1974.

37   *Indian Railwaymen*, March 1975. In his obituary, George said Peter Alvares was cordial to him even after the fracas.

38   Ministry of Home Affairs, 1975, *Why Emergency*, Government of India, p. 37.

39   George to The Chairman, Railway Board, 31 October 1973.

40   Demand of Railwaymen, Letter from President, AIRF, to the Chairman, Railway Board, 8 November 1973.

41   Resolutions, Working Committee, National Federation of India Railwaymen (NFIR), New Delhi 22 January 1974.

42   Letter from G.S. Gokhale, Working President, Bhartiya Railway Majdoor Sangh, to George, 8 November 1973. Resolutions passed by the executive board of the Bhartiya Railway Majdoor Sangh in its meeting held on 3 and 4 November 1973 at Bombay.

43   Resolution, General Council, AIRF, Nagpur, 6–9 February 1974.

44   Press Statement, AIRF, 21 December 1973.

45   Statement of Jayaprakash Narayan, 13 April 1974.

46   George to Lalit Narayan Mishra, Minister of Railways, 10 April 1974.

47   AIRF Circular No. AIRF/160-B, 16 April 1974.

48   'Few Words of Guidance: General Strike', NCCRS, 23 April 1974.

49   P.G. Mavalankar, member of Parliament, to George, 12 April 1974.

50   'On 8.4.1974, at about 19.00 hours, when the railwaymen, after demonstrating, were returning, the electric lights of the office premises and street lights were cut off and in the dark RPF staff in civil dresses caught active leaders and forcibly handed them over to the police', wrote D.D. Chatterjee. Letter from D.D. Chatterjee, Secretary of the Divisional Coordination Committee, Asansol Division, Eastern Railways, 12 April 1974.

51   For a sample of such advisory see, Notice, South Eastern Railway, N. DS/ADA/2474, Office of the Divisional Superintendent, Adra, 17 April 1974.

52   'AIRF Chief Calls for Accord by April 10', *Indian Express* (Madras), 30 March 1974.

53   M. Namasivayam, General Secretary, Southern Railway Mazdoor Union, Madras, to George, 9 January 1974.

54 Letter from M. Namasivayam, General Secretary, Southern Railway Mazdoor Union, Madras, to Priya Gupta, General Secretary, AIRF, 9 January 1974.

55 George to Mukul Banerjee, member of Parliament.

56 Press Statement, 12 January 1974.

57 Press Release, AIRF, 11 April 1971.

58 George to Lalit Narayan Mishra, Railway Minister, 3 May 1974.

59 C.M. Stephen, Motion of No-Confidence in the Council of Ministers, Lok Sabha Debate, 9 May 1974, p. 382.

60 Niren Ghosh, Speech, Calling Attention to a Matter of Urgent Public Importance, Rajya Sabha Debates, 26 April 1974, p. 105.

61 Author's Interview with Y.P. Anand, Chairman (Retired), Railway Board, Vasant Kunj, New Delhi, 13 December 2019.

62 V.K. Jayaswal, 'Impact of May 74' Strike upon Industrial Relations on Indian Railways: A Project Report', submitted for Paper V Diploma in Personal Management, Department of Management Studies, University of Delhi (1974–75).

63 From Bimal De, Convenor, NCCRS (E. Railways), to George, 13 May 1974.

64 From K. Padmanathan, General Secretary, ICF Workers' Union, Madras, to George, 15 May 1974.

65 From Coordination Committee, Gorakhpur, to George, 10 May 1974.

66 Notification, All India Guards Council, 10 May 1974.

67 On the 9th, unable to press ahead on their demand of an adjournment motion, they settled for a non-confidence motion against the government knowing very well its futile fate. The government was more than comfortably placed.

68 N.G. Gorey, Speech, Rajya Sabha Debate, 3 May 1974, p. 222.

69 George to the prime minister, 6 May 1974.

70 George to Prime Minister Indira Gandhi, 6 May 1974.

71 Order, Office of the District Magistrate, Delhi, 8 May 1974.

72 Madhu Limaye to V.V. Giri, 22 May 1974.

73 Madhu Limaye to S.A. Dange, 12 May 1974. The government cannot be allowed to choose the negotiators by making selective arrests.

74 George Fernandes, 'A Tribute to Madhu Limaye', In *Madhu Limaye in Parliament: A Commemorative Volume*, 2008, New Delhi: Lok Sabha Secretariat, p. 36.

75 T.N. Siddhanta, August 1974, *The Railway General Strike*, Delhi: AITUC Publication.

76 Maniben Kara to George, 17 May 1974.

77 George to 'Dear Mr. Finance Minister' Y.B. Chavan, 24 May 1974.

78 Author's Interview with Rakhal Dasgupta (1932–2020), President, AIRF Guwahati, 19 January 2020.

79 'Illegal Strike by a Section of Railway Employees during May 1974', Letter to General Managers from Director Establishment, Railway Board, 31 May 1974.

80 From an undated handwritten note, written after the strike was withdrawn, but when still in jail.

81 See for an official history of the AIRF: All India Railwaymen's Federation, *Origin and Growth of All India Railwaymen's Federation*, Volume I (1982) & II (1985), New Delhi.

82 George to Subhash Malgi, 29 May 1974.

83 Interview with Harbhajan Singh Sidhu, President, HMS, New Delhi, 7 August 2017.

84 Way back in 1948, the communists had announced a strike, which even when withdrawn by Jayaprakash Narayan, the then AIRF president, they had refused to call off. That strike announced in 1948 even today remains in force as they never really bothered to call it off.

85 From an undated handwritten note, written after the strike was withdrawn, but when still in jail.

86 In the middle of January 1976, two AIRF office bearers, R. Sarhandi, Assistant General Secretary of the Northern Railwaymen's Union, New Delhi, and N. Sunderasan, Assistant General Secretary of the South Central Railway Mazdoor Union, Secunderabad, visited Kuala Lumpur to participate in a meeting of the International Transport Workers' Federation and they derided George and saluted the emergency. Both had been appointed by him.

87 Author's Interview with Rakhal Dasgupta, President, AIRF Guwahati, 19 January 2020.

88 George to the General Secretaries of the affiliated unions in the eastern sector of Railways, 20 September 1974.

89 O.D. Sharma, Secretary, Railway Board, to George, President, AIRF, 9 December 1974.

90 J.P. Chaubey to George, 24 August 1974. 'We have received a telephone bill of over Rs. 2000/- for three months. At this rate it will be beyond the capacity of the AIRF to make payment for the telephone bills.'

91 Interview with Harbhajan Singh Sidhu, President, HMS, New Delhi, 7 August 2017.

92 Madhu Dandavate on 28 March 1977 announced empathically in his budget speech that all permanent/temporary employees dismissed/removed/suspended would be reinstated forthwith to the same post.

93   To George from Suresh Vaidya, Talegaon Dabhada, Poona, 31 May 1974. 'This is not to say that Indira has come out of the combat the victorious eagle. On the contrary she has been badly feathered and narrowly escaped losing beak. As it is the country's economy is leaking. By exerting all methods to put down the strike she has brought it to collapse. This was obvious from the speech Chavan made some ten days ago. He was practically on his knees pleading for a speedy settlement of the strike.'

94   George to Mahesh Desai, General Secretary, HMS, Bombay, 2 September 1974.

95   George (at Bombay) to Madhu Limaye (at Shimoga), 21 March 1959.

Chapter 8: The Most Hunted Man

1   Statement before Chief Metropolitan Magistrate, Delhi, 10 February 1977, Union of India Vs George Fernandes and Others, RC-2/76-CIU(A).

2   From Leila Fernandes to George, 7 July 1972.

3   Letter 'My beloved husband', from Leila Fernandes to George, 2 November 1971.

4   Letter 'My darling husband', from Leila Fernandes to George, 21 May 1973.

5   Letter 'My Dear Dadabhai', from Leila Fernandes to her brother P.K. Kabir, 25 June 1982.

6   George Fernandes, (Unpublished) Prison Journal, Hissar Jail, 22 July 1976.

7   George Fernandes, Underground Pamphlet: A Christmas Newsletter, December 1975.

8   Statement of Dr (Miss) Girija Huilgol, MBBS, daughter of Capt. R.P. Huilgol, residing at A-15/11, Vasant Vihar, recorded before CBI officer P.N. Shukla, DSP-CBI, on 25 May 1976, Union of India Vs George Fernandes and Others, RC-2/76-CIU(A) [hereafter, simply, RC-2/76-CIU(A)].

9   George to M.S. Hoda, 5 February 1976.

10   Statement of R. Chandrachudan, 78, Bharti Nagar, New Delhi, recorded before CBI-DSP on 5 May 1976, *CBI Chargesheet in the Case RC-2/76-CIU(A)*.

11   George to M.S. Hoda, 5 February 1976.

12   Madhu Limaye, 2000, *Galaxy of the Indian Socialist Leaders*, Delhi: BR Publishing Corporation; particularly the chapter 'Shri Rajnarayanji: A Unique Personality in All Respects', pp. 301–26.

13   State of Uttar Pradesh v. Raj Narain (1975 AIR 865, 1975 SCR (3) 333).

14   George Fernandes, Underground Pamphlet: A Note for Discussion, 11 November 1975.

15 Jayaprakash Narayan, Letter to the prime minister, 21 July 1975, G.S. Bhargava (Ed.), 1977, *JP's Jail Life (A Collection of Personal Letters)*, New Delhi: Arnold-Heinemann.

16 Field Reports from Gopalpur-on-sea, Odisha. Author's Interviews with Mrs Dey, Batha Ah-tin, and Tony, April 2018.

17 Leila Fernandes to George, 16 June 1975.

18 'Indian Elections Bring an End to Woman's Nightmare', *Daily Progress*, Charlottesville, 27 March 1977.

19 Leila Fernandes to George, 18 June 1975.

20 National Conference Political Resolution: Darkness of Multi-Dimensional Crisis and Dawn of Mass Awakening, *Socialist Party Bulletin* [Edited by Madhu Dandavate], Volume 4, No. II, January–February 1975, New Delhi: Socialist Party, p. 5.

21 Jayaprakash Narayan, 1936, 'Why Socialism?', *Jayaprakash Narayan Selected Works* Vol. 2 (1936–39), p. 4.

22 Jayaprakash Narayan, 1957, 'From Socialism to Sarvodaya', *Jayaprakash Narayan Selected Works*, Vol. 7, (1954–60), p. 226.

23 Cf 'Preface' by M.A. Thomas, Jayaprakash Narayan, 1977, *India of My Dreams*, Bangalore: Ecumenical Christian Centre.

24 Minoo Masani, 1975, *Is JP the Answer?*, Delhi: Macmillan India.

25 *Mang Patra*, a pamphlet in Hindi containing demands of people submitted to Indian Parliament on 6 March 1975. The charter demanded the dismissal of the current government in Bihar. The charter further demanded a slew of electoral and educational reform, eradication of corruption, the establishment of democratic rights and civil liberty, and the decentralization of political power.

26 George to Fr Anthony Murmu, The Catholic Church, Sahibganj, Bihar, 12 February 1975.

27 Mulk Raj Anand, 'Return to Decency', in T.K. Mahadevan (ed.), 1975, *Jayaprakash Narayan and the Future of Indian Democracy*, Delhi: Affiliated East-West Press.

28 Ministry of Home Affairs, 1975, *Why Emergency*, Government of India, p. 37.

29 George Fernandes, Underground Pamphlet: A Christmas Newsletter, December 1975.

30 Madhu Limaye, 1988, *Birth of Non-Congressism*, Delhi: B.R. Publishing; see particularly the chapter 'Darkness Descends on the Land', p. 574.

31 *Times of India*, 24 June 1975.

32 'George Fernandes Ke Agyatwas Ki Kahani, George Fernandes Ki Jubani', *Dharamyug* (Editor: Dharamveer Bharti), 1 May 1977, pp. 7–12;

also, Interview with Binod Mohanty, Sarvodaya Activist, Cuttack, 10 April 2018. Midway at Cuttack, Sarvodayi activist Binod Mohanty (b. 1942) joined George in the train.

33 Vinod Mehta, 1978, *The Sanjay Story*, Bombay: Jaico.

34 It was organized by socialist and trade union leaders of the town. Prominent among the organizers were Santosh Kumar Mahapatro (b. 1945) and Tarini Patnaik (b. 1934). In 1966, a students' movement led by Santosh Kumar Mahapatro had led to the establishment of Berhampur University. A communist, he participated actively in the railway strike and the JP movement. In the years between 1964 and 1977, Mahapatro would spend six years in prison on various charges, from under Preventive Detention Act to Maintenance of Internal Security Act (MISA). Tarini Patnaik was a member of the Socialist Party. Author's Interview with Santosh Kumar Mahapatro, Advocate, at Berhampur, 14 April 2018.

35 Author's Interview with Ramachandra Panda, Member Planning Board, Odisha, Gopalpur-on-sea, 13 April 2018.

36 'Bid to Force PM to Resign; Opposition Stir from Sunday', *Times of India*, 26 June 1975.

37 Madhu Limaye, 1994, *Janata Party Experiment: An Insider's Account of Opposition Politics: 1975–77*, Vol. I, Delhi: B.R. Publishing, p. 26.

38 Jayaprakash Narayan [Edited with an introduction by A.B. Shah], 1977, *Prison Diary: 1975*, Bombay: Popular Prakashan.

39 G.S. Bhargava (Ed.), 1977, *JP's Jail Life (A Collection of Personal Letters)*, New Delhi: Arnold-Heinemann.

40 Letter from Snehalata Reddy to George (from S to S), 1 March 1976.

41 Indira Gandhi, 1975, *Democracy and Discipline: Speeches and Broadcasts on Emergency*, Delhi: DAVP.

42 'George Fernandes Ke Agyatwas Ki Kahani', 1977, pp. 7–12.

43 Press Statement, Gopalpur, 26 June 1975, reprinted in *Swaraj* (n.d.), Michigan: Indians for Democracy.

44 In 1977, as the Minister for Communication, George would get Anwar a government job of driver. Author's Interview with Binod Mohanty, Sarvodaya Activist, Cuttack, 10 April 2018.

45 On this strength, she in the 1990s became a Rajya Sabha Member (1990–96). Author's Interview with Mira Das, Acharya Nagar, Bhubaneswar, 10 April 2018.

46 Author's Interview with Vidya Sagar Gupta (2012) and with Pawan Gupta (May 2016).

47 Sarang Upadhyay and Anurag Chaturvedi (Eds), 2013, *Balkrishan Gupta: Haashiye Par Padi Duniya*, Delhi: Rajkamal Prakashan.

48   Margo Skinner [Letter], 13 July 1960.
49   George to Jaya Jaitly, 2 August 1984, *Jaya Jaitly Papers.*
50   George Fernandes, Underground Pamphlet: A Fascist Dictatorship Has Been Clamped on Our Land, 1 July 1975.
51   'His termination order was revoked by the new Janata dispensation. He was George's man.' Author's Interview with Vijay Narain, New Delhi, September 2011.
52   Note received from Madhu Limaye from Prison, before 15 January 1976.
53   Statement of Pradyuman Patel (b 1936), 6 April 1976, before CBI, *CBI Charge sheet in the case RC-2/76-CIU(A).*
54   T.J.S. George, December 1965, *Revolt in Bihar: A Study of the August 1965 Uprising.*
55   Statement of Rewati Kant Sinha, 'witness no. 17', r/o Qr. No. 19, Old Family Type Quarters, Road No. 5, R-Block, Patna, recorded before CBI officer J.P. Verma, Inspector of Police, on 28 May 1976, *CBI Chargesheet in the case RC-2/76-CIU(A).*
56   Surendra Kishore, 'Baroda Dynamite Approver: An Insane Death', *Onlooker*, 1–15 September 1979.
57   Author's Interview with Mahendra Narain Bajpayee, Patna, 21 October 2011.
58   George Fernandes, (Unpublished) Prison Journal, Hissar Jail, 1976.
59   Statement of Dr Davendar Mahasukhram Surti, Ahmedabad, 'Witness No. 12', recorded on 12 March 1976, before the CID, Ahmedabad, later again on 19 and 20 May, *CBI Chargesheet in the case RC-2/76-CIU(A).*
60   Author's Interview with K. Vikram Rao, Lucknow, 20 August 2011.
61   Statement of Satish Jay Shanker Pathak, *CBI Chargesheet in the case RC-2/76-CIU(A)*; Rao's grievances were genuine: overnight, the *Times of India* had become a newspaper covering India only in its mast-head. Most of its edit pieces were on Lebanon, Lisbon, or Luanda. There were articles on America's ailing hospitals but nothing on India.
62   See pamphlets: 'Trial of an Indian Patriot: King-Emperor versus K. Rama Rao' and 'Editor, Freedom Fighter and Parliamentarian Kotamaraju Rama Rao: A Profile in Courage' published by K. Vikram Rao, Lucknow.
63   Resolution on Emergency, 6 September 1975, IFWJ, Hyderabad, *CBI Chargesheet in the case RC-2/76-CIU(A).*
64   Statement of Bharat Patel, Witness 1, Baroda, 12 March 1976, the first statement recorded before Inspector, Raopura Police Station, Baroda; subsequent statements recorded on 3 April 1976 before the CBI- DSP H.B.D Baijal, New Delhi, *CBI Chargesheet in the case RC-2/76-CIU(A).*

65   Statement of Satish Jay Shanker Pathak, 30 March 1976, *CBI Chargesheet in the case RC-2/76-CIU(A)*.

66   Statement of Bharat Patel, 3 April 1976, *CBI Chargesheet in the case RC-2/76-CIU(A)*.

67   George Fernandes, Underground Pamphlet: To Members of Parliament, 18 July 1975.

68   P.G. Mavalankar, 1979, *No Sir*, Ahmedabad: Sannishtha Prakashan.

69   Statement of Satish Jay Shanker Pathak, 30 March 1976, *CBI Chargesheet in the case RC-2/76-CIU(A)*.

70   Prakash Shah (Retired Professor, Ahmedabad, Author's Interview, 10 November 2011) made a startling disclosure (or just a loose insinuation): 'Chimanbhai first supported George, even took dynamite sticks in his car, possibly he travelled up to Varanasi, but there perhaps he was apprehended but released soon. The experience made him retrace his steps. He withdrew support of his party to the Janata Morcha government to get into the good books of Indira Gandhi.' Chimanbhai's wife Urmilaben Patel, now a widow (Author's Interview, Ahmedabad, 9 November 2011, Ahmedabad) on the other hand only spoke of Chimanbhai's reluctance to support George on his plans for the resistance movement.

71   Statement of Satish Jay Shanker Pathak, 15 March 1976, *CBI Chargesheet in the case RC-2/76-CIU(A)*.

72   Chimanbhai Patel's two-volume biography in Gujarati is written by Madhav Ramanuj. The text of the biography is dialogic. Also see statement of Satish Pathak, 30 March 1976, *CBI Chargesheet in the case RC-2/76-CIU(A)*.

73   Lok Sabha Debate, 9th Session, 13th Series, V. 24, No. 28–30, 30 April 2002.

74   Ministry of Home Affairs, 1975, *Why Emergency*, Government of India (Paper laid in both Houses of Parliament, 21 July 1975).

75   B.G. Rao and Amiya Rao, October 1975, *Why Emergency*. Its underground publication did not carry the authors' names. The later publication named the authors.

76   Ministry of Home Affairs, 1975, *Why Emergency*, Government of India. See Chapter IV: Plan to Disrupt Economy—The Railway Strike.

77   *Times of India* Mumbai, 22 July 1975.

78   Michael Fernandes, 25 August 1975, Open letter to T. Ramadasappa, ITI Ltd.

79   Exhibit D-28, *CBI Chargesheet in the case RC-2/76-CIU(A)*. In July and August, Vikram got three pamphlets by George printed at Lipika Printery, Baroda. Fredrick D'Sa took dictation and typed the 'Dear Madame Dictator' letter of 27 July. It was printed at Baroda with a dateline of 2 August.

80   The AIRF at its convention held at Jodhpur on 27 May 1975 did receive
      'two cheques for 68,000 USD and 17,000 USD from delegates of the
      unions of the Japanese railwaymen', but this was after a year of the
      strike.

81   Interview of the prime minister, Shrimati Indira Gandhi, to Mr George
      Evans of the *Sunday Telegraph*, London; the copy of the interview in *George
      Archive* contains 'For publication /broadcast at or after 10 am on October
      12, 1975' at its masthead, giving credence to the theory that George had
      contacts in government who fed him real-time information.

82   George Fernandes, Underground Pamphlet: Mrs Indira Nehru Gandhi, 14
      October 1975. This circular, and a few others dated 30 November and
      5 December, were cyclostyled by Ramakrishnan at the behest of Kamlesh
      Shukla at the Socialist Party office in Delhi, which was raided by the CBI
      on 22 April 1976.

83   Statement of Fredrick D'Sa (Witness-205), aged 28, 19 June 1975, before
      P.N. Shukla, DSP-CBI, New Delhi, *CBI Chargesheet in the case RC-2/76-
      CIU(A)*.

84   Statement of Shri Rama Rao Prahlad Rao Huilgol (Witness-9), Brahmin
      Hindu, Vasant Vihar, New Delhi, 31 May and 1 June 1976, before P.N.
      Shukla, DSP-CBI, New Delhi, *CBI Chargesheet in the case RC-2/76-
      CIU(A)*.

85   Hans Janitschek from Austria served as Secretary-General of the Socialist
      International from 1969 to 1977. In 'With George Fernandes: Always for
      the People!', *The Other Side*, March 2008, he talks about his first meeting
      with George in England. It was sometime in 1972.

86   Statement of Rewati Kant Sinha (Witness-17), Patna, 28 May 1976, before
      J.P. Verma, Inspector of Police, CBI, New Delhi, *CBI Chargesheet in the
      case RC-2/76-CIU(A)*.

87   Author's Interview (Unrecorded) with Jaswant Singh Chauhan, Vadodara,
      6 November 2011.

88   Statement of Rewati Kant Sinha (Witness-17), Patna, 28 May 1976, before
      J.P. Verma, Inspector of Police, CBI, New Delhi, *CBI Chargesheet in the
      case RC-2/76-CIU(A)*.

89   Statement of Sharad Patel (b. 1936), Baroda, Witness 13, before P.N.
      Shukla, DSP-CBI, 2–4 April 1976, *CBI Chargesheet in the case RC-2/76-
      CIU(A)*.

90   *Mankind* (Editor: Ram Manohar Lohia), Vol. 4 No. 1, August 1959.
            Lohia reviewed a poem by Nandana Reddy. He wrote, 'Nandana Reddy
      composed her first poem when she was 3 years 4 months old. At 3 years and
      10 months she wrote:

> Happiness, Sweet Happiness
> Happiness is like Sadness
> But you can't forget Happiness
> We are in Bangalore that is Happiness
> But Daddy is in Madras that is Sadness.'

91 Snehalata Reddy to Madhu Limaye, 29 June 1964, Madhu Limaye (Unsorted) Papers, NMML.
92 Snehalata Reddy to Madhu Limaye, 31 October 1958, Madhu Limaye (Unsorted) Papers, NMML
93 Author's Interview with Nandana Reddy, Bangalore, 20 January 2012.
94 *Indian Express*, 24 March 1977.
95 Author's Interview with Manohar Reddy, Bangalore, January 2017.
96 C.G.K. Reddy, 2008, *Baroda Dynamite Conspiracy: The Right to Rebel*, New Delhi: Vision Books.
97 George visited Mangalore and Dharmasthala, besides other places. Virendra Hegde who is Dharmaadikari, trustee of the temple dedicated to the god Manjunathishwara, received him. At Mangalore, he stayed at Felix Pai Bazar Socialist Party office.
98 Author's Interview with Richard Fernandes, 22 November 2011.
99 George Fernandes, Underground Pamphlet: A Christmas Newsletter, December 1975.
100 Statement of Girija Huilgol, 23 May 1976, *CBI Chargesheet in the case RC-2/76-CIU(A)*.
101 Statement of R. Chandrachudan, 78, Bharti Nagar, New Delhi, before CBI-DSP, 5 May 1976, *CBI Chargesheet in the case RC-2/76-CIU(A)*.
102 C. Gopal Krishna Reddy, Hand-Written Report to George, early January 1976.
103 December 1975, *Indira's India: Anatomy of a Dictatorship*, London: A Free JP Campaign publication; Snehalata Reddy would reprint this document and circulate it in south India.
104 Statement of Sharad Patel (b. 1936), Baroda, Witness 13, before P.N. Shukla, DSP-CBI, 2–4 April 1976, *CBI Chargesheet in the case RC-2/76-CIU(A)*.
105 Author's Interview with Satyadev Tripathi, Lucknow, 3 May 2015.
106 C.G.K. Reddy, 1977 (reprinted 2008), *Baroda Dynamite Conspiracy: The Right to Rebel*, New Delhi: Vision Books, p. 33.
107 Statement of Satish Jay Shanker Pathak, 15 March 1976, *CBI Chargesheet in the case RC-2/76-CIU(A)*.

Chapter 9: Where Is the Underground?

1   Statement of Dr (Miss) Girija Huilgol (b. 1951) (Witness-8), MBBS, daughter of Capt. R.P. Huilgol, Vasant Vihar, New Delhi, recorded before CBI officer P.N. Shukla, DSP-CBI, on 21–25 May 1976, *CBI Chargesheet RC-2/76-CIU(A)*.

2   Girija Huilgol, Sworn affidavit, Chief Metropolitan Magistrate, Delhi, 16 December 1976, *RC-2/76-CIU(A)*.

3   From Girija Huilgol, 20 January 1977.

4   Statement of R. Chandrachudan (b. 1915) (Witness-11), Bharti Nagar, New Delhi, before Abinash Chander, DSP-CBI, 5 June and 5 July 1976, *CBI Chargesheet RC-2/76-CIU(A)*.

5   Statement of Dr (Miss) Girija Huilgol, before P.N. Shukla, DSP-CBI, New Delhi, 21–25 May 1976, *CBI Chargesheet RC-2/76-CIU(A)*.

6   To 'My dear Laxmi', undated, sometime in March 1976.

7   Letter from underground, giving a list of required reading for proficiency in the underground work, 1976.

8   Leon Uris, 1989 [1961], *Mila 18*, New York: Bantam Books;
      Larry Collins and Dominique Lapierre, 2015, *Is Paris Burning?*, New Delhi: Vikas Publishing;
      John Steinbeck, 2000, *The Moon is Down*, New Delhi: Penguin.

9   George Fernandes, (Unpublished) Prison Journal, Hissar Jail, 1976.

10 Statement of Chandra Kumar Rama Rao Huilgol (Witness-10), before P.N. Shukla, DSP-CBI, New Delhi, 21 and 22 May 1976, *CBI Chargesheet RC-2/76-CIU(A)*.

11 Statement of Shri Rama Rao Prahlad Rao Huilgol (Witness-9), Brahmin Hindu, Vasant Vihar, New Delhi, before P.N. Shukla, DSP-CBI, New Delhi, 31 May and 1 June 1976, *CBI Chargesheet RC-2/76-CIU(A)*.

12 Very sketchy information of Mrunal Gore's underground days is provided in her biography by Dr Rohini Gawankar, 2014, *Footprints of a Crusader: The Life Story of Mrunal Gore*, Mumbai: Samata Shikshan Sanstha.

13 George Fernandes, Underground Pamphlet: Reports from the Underground, 2 February 1976.

14 *The Voice*, 15 March 1976. (One of the many pamphlets published during the emergency; they were published without ownership details.)

15 From M.S. Hoda, 27 January and 26 February 1976.

16 To M.S. Hoda, sometime before 15 February 1976.

17 Government communique, 5 January 1976. There were others as well, such as student leader Anand Kumar, and activist Srikumar Poddar, to mention just two, whose passports were impounded. They were active

in fomenting protests in the United States. Anand Kumar had a socialist background (Author's Interview with Anand Kumar, Gurgaon, 20 January 2016). Poddar had been to study in the US but became active against the emergency in India. (Author's Interview with Srikumar Poddar, Mumbai, 6 February 2016).

18   'Mrs Fernandes' Flight Abroad', *Times of India*, 9 April 1977.

19   Leila Fernandes spoke of her struggles after George won the election in March 1977. Ray Mcgrath, 'Indian Elections Bring End to Woman's Nightmare', *Daily Progress*, Charlottesville, Virginia, 27 March 1977.

20   Leila Fernandes to M.S. Hoda, 17 January 1976.

21   To Leila Fernandes, sometime in February 1976.

22   From Krishna Rao to Sudarshan, C.G. Krishna Rao's (mostly handwritten, a few typed sheets) Reports on visits abroad to George (London, Brussels, Frankfurt, Bonn, Vienna, Geneva, Paris, New York, Washington, Japan), January 1976.

23   To M.S. Hoda, 5 February 1976.

24   To Leila Fernandes, sometime in February 1976.

25   Socialist International, Amnesty International, International Transport Workers Union, West German Railway Workers' Union were some of the organizations. Dignitaries included Portuguese Prime Minister Mario Soares, West German Ex-Chancellor Willy Brandt, prime minister of the United Kingdom Harold Wilson and his Opposition leader James Callaghan.

26   Indira Gandhi contemplated postponing the general elections due in March ('Restoring Normalcy', *Times of India*, 1 January 1976). At his Narsingh Garh Jail in Madhya Pradesh, Madhu Limaye got scent of the Congress plan. He called the Opposition members in Parliament to resign in retaliation (note received from Madhu Limaye from prison, New Year 1976). He and Sharad Yadav resigned, but others just waited for the tide to turn.

27   *Times of India*(Bombay), 14 February 1976.

28   To JP, 27 January 1976.

29   George Fernandes, Underground Pamphlet: George's Comments on the Note from Madhu Limaye, 15 January 1976.

30   To JP, 27 January 1976.

31   'The New Order', *Newsweek*, 16 February 1976; Edward Behr of *Newsweek* visited India in the first week of January (5–19) 1976.

32   George Fernandes, Underground Pamphlet: Comments on the Note from Madhu Limaye, 15 January 1976.

33   George Fernandes, Underground Pamphlet, around 20 August 1975.

34 George Fernandes, *Underground Pamphlet*, September 1975.

35 Text of the recorded speech by George Fernandes to the Special Convention of 'Indians for Democracy' held in New York on 31 January and 1 February 1976. 'Friends at home and abroad keep asking questions about the ideology of our struggle. Unless democracy is restored in the country, there is no hope for anybody.'

36 Special correspondent, 'India: A Passage from Democracy', first published in *New Statesman*, London, and later reproduced in *Janata*, 13 June 1976.

37 From Snehalata Reddy, 1 March 1976.

38 To a friend, sometime in January 1976.

39 'Sudama' (Surendra Kishore) to George. It was the same Karpoori Thakur who full of fire and brimstone had said in that Ahmedabad public meeting of Indira Gandhi's twenty-point programme: *'Bees nahi charsobees hai.'*

40 *Panchjanya*, 1 February 1976.

41 To Basawan Singh, sometime in January 1976.

42 To N.G. Goray, 26 May 1976.

43 To Manubhai K. Bhimani, 10 February 1976.

44 To Niren De, 10 February 1976.

45 To Rajmohan Gandhi, 16 February 1976.

46 From Snehalata Reddy, 1 March 1976.

47 Text of the recorded speech by George Fernandes to the Special Convention of 'Indians for Democracy' held in New York on 31 January and 1 February 1976.

48 George Fernandes, *Underground Pamphlet: An Appeal to the Conscience of the World*, n.d., 1975.

49 George Fernandes, *Underground Pamphlet: An Open Letter to American Businessmen Arriving in India to Take Part in the Meeting of the India–US Business Council'*, 2–4 February 1976.

50 Snehalata Reddy also shared her domestic worries with him, 'the most marvellous man of all'. Snehalata Reddy to George, 1 March 1976.

51 To 'Dear S', Snehalata Reddy, n.d., most probably after 18 March 1976.

52 In his letters to his colleagues and people at large, George would refer to 'Mrs Indira Nehru Gandhi' by the abbreviation MAD (Madame Dictator) and her son, Sanjay Gandhi as SOD (Son of Dictator).

53 Statement of Dr (Miss) Girija Huilgol, before P.N. Shukla, DSP-CBI, New Delhi, 21–25 May 1976, *CBI Chargesheet RC-2/76-CIU(A)*.

54 Statement of Radhey Shyam Singh, age 24, resident of Varanasi, to the CBI, 27 March 1976, *CBI Chargesheet RC-2/76-CIU(A)*. Before that, on

23 March itself, Radhey Shyam had given his damaging confession to the Baroda police.

55   Statement of Radhey Shyam Singh, age 24, resident of Varanasi, to the CBI, 27 March 1976, *CBI Chargesheet RC-2/76-CIU(A)*. Before that, on 23 March itself, Radhey Shyam had given his damaging confession to the Baroda police.

56   Author's Interview with K. Vikram Rao, Lucknow, 20 August 2011.

57   Statement of Satish Pathak, 31 May and 1 June 1976, *CBI Chargesheet RC-2/76-CIU(A)*.

58   Statement of Bharat Patel, Witness-1, before DSP-CBI, 12–15 March, 3–6 April, 9 April, 11 April, 15 April, 3 June 1976, *CBI Chargesheet RC-2/76-CIU(A)*.

59   Document-114 (i, ii, iii), D-115; List of Documents of *CBI Chargesheet RC-2/76-CIU(A)*.

60   Affidavit of Girija Huilgol, 16 December 1976, solemnly affirmed before Oath Commissioner, Delhi *RC-2/76-CIU(A)*.

61   Statement of Sharad Patel, Baroda, Witness-13, before P.N. Shukla, DSP-CBI, 2, 3 and 4 April 1976, *CBI Chargesheet RC-2/76-CIU(A)*.

62   From 'Victor & Kalyan' [Vikram Rao and Kirit Bhatt] March, n.d., 1976.

63   Statement of Satish Jay Shanker Pathak, 31 March 1976, *CBI Chargesheet RC-2/76-CIU(A)*.

64   To Sonal (daughter of G.G. Parikh), May 1976.

65   George Fernandes, (Unpublished) Prison Journal, Hissar Jail, 1976.

66   Vikram Rao, who had initially vowed not to shave his beard 'till the mission for which Baba was working was achieved', became clean-shaven again in November. Uncertain when censorship would be lifted, Vikram told Satish, he had got shaved.

67   Contrasting point: Clandestine underground activities were calculated to wreak political changes in the country, and so to speak about it once they were arrested and during their interrogations was also a political activity in the service of their aims. So, everyone in giving a true rendition of their clandestine activities in some way, unknowingly though and perhaps under compulsion of fear, were serving motives of their underground engagements.

68   'Yes, There Is an Underground', *The Economist*, 24 January 1976.

69   George Fernandes, Underground Pamphlet: To Members of the Working Committee of AIRF, August–September 1975.

70   George Fernandes, Underground Pamphlet: Workers against fascism, August 1975.

71   George Fernandes, Underground Pamphlet: To the Members of the Working Committee of AIRF, August–September 1975.

72   George Fernandes, Underground Pamphlet: Workers against fascism, August 1975.

73   'Dange for 2 CPI Men in Every Factory', 28 August 1975, *Indian Express*, New Delhi.

74   George Fernandes, (Unpublished) Prison Journal, Hissar Jail, 26 August 1976.

75   George Fernandes, 'Madhava Rao's Caveat: On Why the HMS Should Not Merge with the AITUC', *The Other Side*, May 1994, p. 63.

76   George Fernandes, Underground Pamphlet: The Struggle Goes On, May 1976.

77   Letter from George to Leila Fernandes, May 1976.

78   George Fernandes, Underground Pamphlet: The Struggle Goes On, May 1976.

79   Interview of Prime Minister Shrimati Indira Gandhi to Mr George Evans of the *Sunday Telegraph*, London.

80   'Yes, 'There Is an Underground', *Economist*, 24 January 1976.

Chapter 10: Chained and Fettered

1   Author's Interview with Vijay Narayan, September 2011, 28 June 2018. The description of arrest is based on this interview.

2   'The Boom Is Over: George Fernandes' Dynamite Days . . . and After', *Society*, December 1985.

3   To Leila Fernandes, May 1976.

4   George Fernandes, Underground Pamphlet: To the Members of the National Railway Mazdoor Union, 6 April 1976.

5   George Fernandes, Underground Pamphlet: The Struggle Goes On, May 1976.

6   George Fernandes, Underground Pamphlet: A Christmas Newsletter, December 1975.

7   George Fernandes, (Unpublished) Prison Journal, Hissar Jail, June 1976.

8   Circulars were issued on 17 December 1975 and 3 January 1976. In February, the Delhi Police declared a reward of Rs 5,000/- for his arrest (vide their circular no. 1680-1705/Pol.3 dated 11 February 1976). National Archive: Files regarding Lawrence Fernandes as submitted to Justice Shah Commission of Enquiry.

9   George Fernandes, (Unpublished) Prison Journal, Hissar Jail, 14 August 1976.

10   To Home Minister Brahmananda Reddy, Hissar Jail, 3 July 1976.

11   Report of Hans Janitschek, Delhi, March 1977.

12 Telegram, From Home Ministry to Leila Fernandes, Washington, DC, 21 June 1976.

13 Statement of Socialist Party of Switzerland, Berne, 16 June 1976.

14 Statement by Will Brandt, Olof Palme and Bruno Kreisky, Socialist International, 17 June 1976.

15 Report of Hans Janitschek, Delhi, March 1977.

16 Statement Submitted by Leila Kabir Fernandes, 16 September 1976, Hearings on the Human Rights in India, International Relations Sub-Committee on International Organisations, US House of Representatives.

17 '"I am with him every moment," Says Wife of Arrested Politician', *India Abroad*, 6 August 1976; the statement was also quoted in a letter from Louie Fernandes to George, 26 August 1976.

18 George Fernandes, Underground Pamphlet: A Christmas Newsletter, December 1975.

19 George to Badri Vishal Pittie, 5 June 1976. Pittie claimed that he could not court arrest as there was none to accompany him. George wrote that not being able to go alone was a demonstration of one's irrelevance.

20 From Kanen, 15 April 1971.

21 Author's Interview with Vijay Narain, September 2011 and 28 June 2018.

22 Doc to DS [Girija Huilgol to George], 20 January 1977.

23 'The Boom Is Over: George Fernandes' Dynamite Days . . . and After', *Society*, December 1985.

24 Statement of Radhy Shyam, Varanasi, *CBI Chargesheet RC-2/76-CIU(A)*.

25 Author's Interview with Jaya Jaitly, New Delhi, 27 November 2011.

26 From Veena Tiwari, Kanpur, 1 July 1977.

27 Author's Interview with Kamlesh Shukla and Arun Kumar Panibaba, New Delhi, September 2011.

28 Author's telephonic conversation with Girija Huilgol, Ahmedabad, 11 November 2011.

29 George Fernandes, Underground Pamphlet: The Torch Shall Burn Brighter, 12 June 1976.

30 'George Fernandes Interviewed: The Warmth Below the Indignation', *Himmat*, 6 May 1977, pp. 6–7.

31 'Lawrence's Charge "Baseless"', *Indian Express*, 12 March 1977.

32 See Shah Commission of Inquiry, Third and Final Report, in Era Sezhiyan (Ed.), 2010, *Shah Commission Report: Lost, and Regained*, Chennai: Aazhi Publishers.

33 Author's Interview with Surendra Kishore, Patna, 20 October 2011.

34 To The Superintendent, District Jail, Hissar, 11 August 1976.

35   In the High Court of Judicature at Delhi, 12 August 1976, *CBI Chargesheet RC-2/76-CIU(A)*.

36   From Shanti Kabir, 21 August 1976.

37   *The Other Side*, June 1984, p. 56.
        Vijaya Lakshmi Pandit (1900–1990), 1945, *Prison Days*, Calcutta: Signet Press.

38   George Fernandes, (Unpublished) Prison Journal, Hissar Jail, 22 July 1976.

39   George Fernandes, (Unpublished) Prison Journal, Hissar Jail, 20 August 1976.

40   Irving Wallace, 1976, *The R Document*, US: Simon & Schuster.

41   To 'Dear Mother', 13 August 1976, Hissar Jail.

42   From J.J. Fernandes, Bangalore, 21 February 1977.

43   From Leila Fernandes, 11 August 1976, Charlottesville, USA.

44   Case No. *RC-2/76-CIU(A)*.

45   'Fernandes and 24 Others Are Charge-Sheeted', *Times of India*, 25 September 1976.

46   'Backgrounder: George Fernandez', 24 September 1976, *India News*, London: High Commission of India.

47   *Blitz*, 28 August and 2 October 1976.

48   Author's Interview with Padmanav Shetty, Mumbai, 3 July 2015.

49   Exhibit D-195, Application u/s 306 of the Code of Criminal Procedure, 1973, Affidavit by Abinash Chander, DSP, CBI, 25 June 1976, *CBI Chargesheet RC-2/76-CIU(A)*.

50   *Times of India*, 25 September 1976.

51   'Socialist Leader in India Appears in Court, Handcuffed but Defiant', *New York Times*, 4 October 1976.

52   Statement by George Fernandes before the Metropolitan Magistrate, Delhi, 4 October 1976, *CBI Chargesheet RC-2/76-CIU(A)*.

53   They approached the Court to enforce their right to have lunch on the day they were brought to court, their unfettered right to consult their lawyers to discuss their case and design defence, for relief against handcuffing.

54   Madhu Limaye to Kishan Patnaik, October 1976.

55   From Richard Fernandes, 6 October 1976.

56   *The Other Side*, August 1982. According to what was witnessed by Shrikumar Poddar, George would hold forth to the crowd of sympathizers, journalists and lawyers on arrival at the court. Poddar even says that whenever there was a need for George to meet somebody or discuss issues with colleagues, he would be sent a message and the judge would summon him.

57   George Fernandes, (Unpublished) Prison Journal, Tihar Jail, 26 November 1976.

58   Author's Interview with Ranjit Bhanu, Mumbai, 2 July 2015.

59   Swaraj Kaushal to George, 1 February 1977.
60   Arguments on Handcuffing, 'Swaraj & Mrs Sushma Swaraj', October 1976.
61   Author's Interview with Swaraj Kaushal, 15 October 2011, *Times of India*, 9 October 1976.
62   Author's Interview with Swaraj Kaushal, 8, Safdarjung Lane, 15 October 2011.
63   Vikram Rao to the General Manager, *Times of India*, 17 December 1976. Vikram Rao was reinstated later.
64   Eva Forest, *From a Spanish Jail*, Penguin, 1975. Prison Journal, Tihar Jail, 26 November 1976.
65   Affidavit of Girija Huilgol, 16 December 1976, solemnly affirmed before Oath Commissioner, Delhi, *RC-2/76-CIU(A)*.
66   File: 1977 Paper Cuttings: February. A list of the items that were banned from publication in newspapers on various dates since June 1975 was publicized by the Janata Party when it came to power.
67   Doc to 'DS' [Girija Huilgol to George], 20 January 1977.
68   C.G.K. Reddy, *Baroda Dynamite Conspiracy: The Right to Rebel*, New Delhi: Vision Books, 2008. CGK is the only person having left an account of what transpired during those underground days. CGK's account was published in 1977. Others were against its publication fearing retribution from future governments. Indeed, there were pressures even on the Janata government to re-open the case; lawyers went to court demanding re-opening, newspaper readers wrote letters arguing against withdrawal. The book's hurried publication endangered safeties. Vikram Rao is said to have drawn George's attention and aired his reservations as, according to him, it was premature and could jeopardize the careers and families of those involved. Generally, accounts of underground and unlawful activities are published posthumously or after a lapse of considerable time. Swaraj Kaushal thought CGK's narrative was a selfish design to crow about one's pro-freedom credentials. Most people named preferred discretion to publicity. George himself rarely talked or wrote about those days. Ironically, CGK's book also got hammered by his colleagues for not adequately depicting their roles. His book primarily talks of his role and that too about his travel abroad as an emissary of George. By avoiding others, he was confining himself to what he knew to be true. Further, he was not a historian who was expected to write a history of the underground. It seems he had written a larger book with more details drawn on hearsay information from his co-accused in jail and from the police investigation. But George put his foot down. Says Ravi Nair:

CGK's book is a truncated publication from which chapters were deducted on George's instructions. I know it because I did the telephonic call and ushered CGK into the room and then went out. I don't know the actual words that were used as I was not physically present but I got the sense of conversation that took place. George had heard about the book and wanted to see the manuscript. CGK sent the manuscript to George and after having gone through the manuscript, he asked me to call CGK. He came, they sat privately in a room, had a frank, private conversation, and later, on George's instructions, the chapters were deleted. I had access to it as I handled his secretarial work. CGK until his last days was unhappy about it.

Author's Interview with Ravi Nair, 4 October 2011.

69   Socialist Party, National Convention, Bombay, 27–28 November 1976.
70   'Any compromises anywhere will only push us backwards. Every sacrifice will take us forward.' To Socialist Comrades, 26 November 1976.
71   Confidential Note from Ravi Nair to George, 5 December 1976.
72   About Nanasaheb, Madhu Limaye writes to him on 6 January 1954: 'Although you are temperamentally incapable of developing an emotional attachment, I never lost sight of your merits and abilities.'
73   Madhu Limaye, *After the 30th October Declaration*, Open Letter, 31 October 1976.
74   Trusted Vinod Kumar Singh acted as the General Secretary of the Committee, while Surendra Mohan was its Treasurer. Author's Interview with Vinod Kumar Singh, Patna, 19 October 2011.
75   Appeal for Fund Collection for Baroda Dynamite Case Defence Committee, 4 January 1977.
76   From Surur Hoda, 20 December 1976.
77   Confidential note from an unnamed source: What happened at the 51st Annual Convention of the AIRF at Maligaon from 4 to 7 July 1976.
78   President George, General Secretary M.H. Baji, and Secretary A. Quadros— all three were in jail. 'Bombay Taximen's Union: Brave Taximen! Beware!', 30 November 1976, Pamphlet-flier printed by Sohan Singh Kohli, Acting General Secretary, BTU. Author's Interview with A Quadros, Mumbai, 20 July 2015.
79   From Mahabal Shetty, Municipal Mazdoor Union, 16 December 1976.
80   From Sachchidanand (Secretary to JP), 5 January 1977.
81   To Surendra Mohan, 6 January 1977.
82   From Surendra Mohan, before 12 January 1977.
83   To Surendra Mohan, 19 January 1977.
84   From Surendra Mohan, 21 January 1977.
85   Message to George Fernandes, 23 January 1977.

86   'Doc' to 'DS', 20 January 1977.

87   From Swaraj Kaushal, 1 February 1977.

88   From Narendra Guru, 3 February 1977.

89   To Surendra Mohan, 23 January 1977.

90   See, for instance, a public release by Indian People's Association in North America, 26 January 1977. It was headlined: A Sham Election! A Sham Relaxation of 'Emergency'!!

91   Snehalata Reddy, A Very Rough Draft from Ramchandran, sometime in January 1976.

92   To Leila Fernandes, 19 January 1976.

93   To 'Dear Panditji' Kamalapati Tripathi, 4 February 1977.

94   From Syed Abdulla Bukhari to Dear Mujahid George Fernandes, 27 February 1977. 'I find hardly any words to thank you and congratulate you for your straightforwardness and boldness. I kiss your letters in this writing and pay all respects to such an acknowledgment to a just Muslim for the betterment of the country and the nation at this hour of a straight battle between good and evil,' wrote the Shahi Imam to George.

95   S.A. Haque to Surendra Mohan, 5 March 1977.

96   Alice Fernandes, 'This Could Happen to You: A Mother's Appeal to Voters', March 1977.

97   From Usha Mehta, 11 March 1977. When he did win and went to Bombay for the first time after taking the oath of secrecy as a minister, he kept his word and went from the station straight to Usha Mehta's house (Author's Interview with Ranjit Bhanu, Mumbai, 2 July 2015).

98   To Indira Gandhi, 8 March 1977.

99   *Times of India*, 27 February 1977.

100   Jayaprakash Narayan to George, 1 March 1977.

101   George to Jayaprakash Narayan, 9 March 1977.

102   Fasting Fernandes has nausea, *Indian Express*, 16 March 1977.

103   Telegram addressed to Shri George Fernandes, 19 March 1977.

104   Aloysius Fernandes to Henry, 17 March 1977.

105   'Sneha's Friendship Landed Her in Jail', *Indian Express*, 12 March 1977.

106   Author's Interview with Nandana Reddy, Bangalore, 20 January 2012.

107   George Fernandes Ke Agyatwas Ki Kahani, 1977.

108   *Indira's India: Anatomy of a Dictatorship*, A Free JP Campaign Publication, December 1975.

109   To Mario Soares, Prime Minister, Lisbon, December 1976.

110   Rajya Sabha Debates.

111   Raj Narain's benefactor C.B. Gupta, of the breakaway Congress (O), was then chief minister of Uttar Pradesh.

112   *Indian Express*, 28 August 1975.

113   See Shah Commission of Inquiry, Third and Final Report, in Era Sezhiyan (Ed.), 2010, *Shah Commission Report: Lost, and Regained*, Chennai: Aazhi Publishers.

114   Katherine Frank, 2001, *Indira: The Life of Indira Nehru Gandhi*, New York: Houghton Mifflin.

115   Mahesh Rangarajan, 1996, *Fencing the Forest: Conservation and Ecological Change in India's Central Provinces, 1860–1914*, Delhi: OUP.

116   Ashis Nandy, 1980, *At the Edge of Psychology*, Delhi: OUP.

117   At a public meeting in Mumbai: 'Sangh is now secular: Ram'. As the Jan Sangh dissolved its existence and merged with that of the Janata Party, Ram was the first one to acknowledge that it had now become a secular outfit; critical of Mrs Gandhi, and claimed she created poverty instead of eradicating it. 'If she had known I was going to resign, I do not know what she would have done.' *Times of India*, 28 February 1977.

118   Louis Adamic, 1934 [revised 1963], *Dynamite: The Story of Class Violence in America,* Massachusetts: Peter Smith.

Chapter 11: Janata Days

1   'Dear George' from Madhu Limaye, endorsed by JP, February 1977.

2   'Hello Daddy' from Leila Fernandes, 20 February 1977.

3   From George to Kapildev Singh, 10 February 1977. Rabindra Bharti (ed), *Kapildev Singh Samagra*, Vol. 3, p. 10. The letter was sent from Tihar Jail smuggled through Professor R.K. Jain.

4   From George to Rusi Lala, 20 June 1977.

5   M.G. Sharma, HMT Workers, Pinjore, to George, 21 March 1977.

6   Morarji Desai, 1978 [1974], *The Story of My Life*, Volume I & II, New Delhi: S. Chand & Co.

7   D.F. Karaka, 1965, *Morarji*, Bombay: Times of India Press.

8   Janardan Thakur, 1978, *All the Janata Men,* New Delhi: Vikas Publishing House.

9   'Letters: Baroda Dynamite Case', *Link*, 17 April 1977, p. 1.

10   'George Fernandes Interview: The Warmth Below the Indignation', *Himmat*, 6 May 1977, p. 6.

11   Interview with Arun Kumar Panibaba, New Delhi, 11 June 2013.

12   From Rusi Lala, Asia Plateau, Panchgani, Maharashtra, 11 April 1977.

13   Rajmohan Gandhi, 'A Letter to George', *Himmat*, 6 May 1977.

14   Lok Sabha Debate, 31 March 1977.

15   From George to Morarji Desai, PM, 11 April 1977.

16 From George to Morarji Desai, PM, 12 April 1977.

17 George Fernandes Interview, *Himmat*, 1977, p. 7.

18 From Rusi Lala, Asia Plateau, Panchgani, Maharashtra, 11 April 1977.

19 From M.D. Lohani, District Secretary, Nanital, UP State Karamchari Samyuka Parishad, 22 March 1977.

20 For instance, Dr Dauji Gupta, ex-mayor, Lucknow, sought George's support for a Rajya Sabha nomination. From Dr Dauji Gupta, 7 March 1978.

21 Anonymous letter, March 1977.

22 From George to V.L. Shanbhag, General Education Academy, Academy House, Bombay, 6 July 1977.

23 Lok Sabha Debate, 8 July 1977.

24 Activities of Coca-Cola Export Corporation, Lok Sabha Debate, 14 March 1974.

25 Mark Pendergrast, 1993, *For God, Country and Coca Cola: The Unauthorized History of the Great American Soft Drink and the Company That Makes It*, London: Phoenix.

26 Activities of Coca-Cola Export Corporation, Lok Sabha Debate, 14 March 1974.

27 Calling Attention Motion Lok Sabha Debate, 8 August 1977.

28 Dinesh Sharma, 2009, *The Long Revolution: The Birth and Growth of India's IT Industries*, New Delhi: Harper Collins.

29 From Viren Shah, 14 September 1977.

30 Lok Sabha Debate, 23 December 1977.

31 'New Industrial Policy: Fillip to Small & Cottage Industries', 23 December 1977, *The Hindu*.

32 'Industrial Climate Murky, Says G.D. Birla', 10 July 1978, *Financial Express* (Bombay).

33 'Big Cos. Not to Be Split', 5 April 1978, *Economic Times* (New Delhi).

34 27 February 1979, *Times of India*.

35 George Fernandes, *Illustrated Weekly of India*, 25 September 1977.

36 Letter to Ramakrishna Hegde, Convenor, Committee on Large Houses, from S.K. Birla, Indian Chamber of Commerce, Calcutta, 19 February 1979.

37 Janardan Thakur, 1978, *All the Janata Men*, New Delhi: Vikas Publishing House, p. 163.

38 George Fernandes, 'My Plan to Rescue the Janata', *Himmat*, 5 May 1978.

39 *Action Plan: District Industries Centres, Muzaffarpur (A report)*, Small Industries Service Institute, Ministry of Industries, Government of India, Muzaffarpur, 1979.

40 George to Karpoori Thakur, CM of Bihar, 6 April 1978.

41   Author's Interview with Vinod Kumar Singh, Patna, 19 October 2011.

42   Action Plan for Development of Muzaffarpur, Minutes of the Second Meeting held on 4 May 1979. On 4 May 1979, a meeting of those closely associated with the evolution of an action plan for the development of Muzaffarpur was held.

43   George to B.Y. Parit, Rashtra Seva Dal, 5 January 1978.

44   George to Suresh Kalmadi, Giants, Pune, 9 January 1978.

45   Jaggarnath Prasad Singh, Muzaffarpur, to George, after January 1978.

46   For instance, a letter to Morarji Desai from Ram Udar Jha, Jawahar Picture Palace, Harisabha Chowk, Muzaffarpur (with a copy to George), 6 March 1978.

47   A printed pamphlet castigating 'the corrupt Principal of the ITI, Muzaffarpur' accompanied a letter containing similar content from one 'Narendra Prasad Singh, Vice-Secretary', Trainees' Union, ITI, Muzaffarpur, 10 March 1978; Ramdev Sahi, the Mukhiya of the village panchayat Meenapur, wrote alleging misuse of government funds under the previous Mukhiya. Letter to Ram Dev Sahi, 15 November 1978.

48   To Chandrakishore Singh, Muzaffarpur, 11 May 1983.

49   Letter to Ramesh Chandra, Muzaffarpur, 4 January 1983.

50   Letters to and from Penchuram Barwa, Gaighat, 15 November and 12 October 1978.

51   To Ajay Kumar Gupta, Rambagh Road, 5 April 1978.

52   To Tapeswar Singh, Chitraguptpuri, 10 November 1978.

53   For instance, one from Vinodanand Prasad Singh (of 1 November 1978), member of Legislative Assembly and Chairman, North Bihar Industrial Area Development Authority, whereby the MLA asked for temporary residence arrangement for visiting local entrepreneurs.

54   To Lal Babu Thakur, Muzaffarpur, 5 January 1983.

55   For instance, the people of Jalalpur panchayat sent a representation alleging irregularities in the building of an embankment under the Gandak River Project in Tirhut. To Irrigation Minister, Bihar, 15 November 1978.

56   From Bhola Mahto (signed by a hundred others), 10 March 1978.

57   From Ramlal Tulusthan, Secretary, Muzaffarpur Eye Hospital, Muzaffarpur, 10 March 1978.

58   From Brijlal Verma, Minister of Communication, 31 March 1978.

59   From Pawan Kumar, Sarpanch, Kudhni, 30 October 1978.

60   To the Minister, Bihar Government, 10 November 1978.

61   Bhairon Singh Shekhawat, for instance, never in his entire political career fought from the same constituency. He played musical chairs with his constituencies to sap the potential of his disgruntled constituents to play a

musical chair game with his elections. Even a Vajpayee or Advani seldom
fought for re-election from the same constituency despite the Hindutva
banner. Author's Interview/Conversation with Arun Kumar Panibaba,
Ghaziabad, 29 January 2016.

62   From Hari Narayan, Convener, Mirapur Lok Samiti, 28 March 1978.

63   From Brahmdev 'Pipasit', Pusa, 22 March 1978.

64   From Subhash Chandra, Lecturer in English, R.D.S. College, 11 February
     1978.

65   George to Narayan Das Mistri, Vice-president, Janata Party, Jhansi town,
     22 January 1979.

66   From Choudhry Ali Mubarak Asmani, UP, to George, undated, 1979.

67   To Prabhakar Sinha, Bihar University, 31 March 1978.

68   From Prabhakar Sinha, Bihar University, 12 March 1978.

69   To Md. Jahur, Sahebganj, 28 March 1978.

70   From Md. Jahur, Sahebganj, 12 March 1978.

71   From Jagdev Singh, Village: Parwana, Bulandshahar, UP, date unclear, 1979.

72   From Mathew Kalayathinal, Xavier Labour Relations Institute, Jamshedpur,
     20 February 1979.

73   To Morarji Desai, PM, 12 November 1978.

74   From S.J. Nair, Attoor, 17 April 1979.

75   Biju Patnaik to Morarji Desai, 26 March 1979.

76   From Brahm Prakash to Chandrasekhar, 2 April 1979.

77   My Dear Shri Morarjibhai, JP to Morarji Desai, 1 March 1979.

78   To M. Kant, Bihar, 15 May 1979.

79   Lok Sabha Debate, 11–15 July 1979.

80   Neerja Choudhry, 'Tyagi, Limaye, V.V. John on Religion Bill: Why Are
     Christians Upset?', *Himmat*, 13 April 1979.

     Kalpana Sharma, 'Freedom of Religion Bill: Why are Christian Motive
     Suspect?', *Himmat*, 11 May 1979.

81   'Frank Words . . . and a Plan of Action', *Himmat*, 5 May 1978, p. 8.

82   To B.R. Sharma, Kanpur, 8 December 1978.

83   'The Week the Janata Fell Apart', *Himmat*, 20 July 1979.

84   From Viren Shah, 10 August 1979.

85   From Sonal, *Telegram*, 26 July 1979.

86   From Rajesh Viren Shah, 26 July 1979.

87   From Prakash Vadera, Barmer, 4 August 1979.

88   From V.S. Ramaswamy, New Delhi, 1 August 1979.

89   In fact, media response to George was also a measure of his stock. On 7
     July, *Indian Express* published an interview with him. Rammohan Gandhi
     in *Himmat* (13 July 1979) lauded his 'sharply expressed thoughts' making

him onto cover. But soon after his 'somersault', George was vanished from the magazine.

90 From Upendra Nath Singh, United Commercial Bank, Pant Nagar, Nainital, 28 July 1979. Singh claimed to have written on behalf of all the bank employees. He advised George either to rejoin the Janata Party and complete the unfinished promises or to revert to being among the workers to finish the work left untended due to political engagements.

91 To Upendra Nath Singh, United Commercial Bank, Pant Nagar, Nainital, August 1979.

92 From Jayant R. Shah, 44, Mitra Mandal Society, Baroda, 24 July 1979.

93 From P.V.K. Nambiar (One of your former followers), Air Force Station, Poona, 31 July 1979.

94 From P. Lankesh, Bangalore, 28 July 1979.

95 From Bhai Bhosale, President, Maharashtra INTUC, 26 July 1979.

96 From Kirit Bhatt, Vadodara, 26 July 1979.

97 Ayub Syed, *Current*, 12 August 1978.

98 Madhu Limaye to Morarji Desai, 12 August 1978.

99 From Madhu Limaye, 16 August 1978.

100 From Madhu Limaye, 29 August 1978.

101 From Madhu Limaye, 11 October 1977.

102 From Madhu Limaye, 24 April 1979.

103 From G.G. Parikh, 25 July 1979.

104 To Charan Singh, 25 July 1979.

105 From G.G. Parikh, 25 July 1979.

106 Madhu Limaye, *Janata Party Experiment: An Insider's Account of Opposition Unity: 1977–80*, Vol. II. Delhi: B.R. Publishing.

107 Charan Singh, 1979, *India's Economic Policy: A Gandhian Blueprint*, New Delhi: Vikas Publishing House.

108 From Thankam, New Delhi, 26 July 1979.

109 To Paul J. Mannemplavan of Jyotiniketan Ashram at Bareilly, October 1979.

110 'Gab, Gabbing George', *Indian Express*, 13 August 1979.

111 George Fernandes, 'Why Vajpayee's Contribution Is Not Enough in Itself', August 1979, *Indian Express*.

112 See, for instance, Janardan Thakur, 1978, *All the Janata Men*, New Delhi: Vikas Publishing House, and Radhey Shyam Sharma, 1978, *Who After Morarji*, New Delhi: Pankaj Publications.

113 Author's Interview with Arun Kumar Panibaba, New Delhi, 11 June 2013.

114 To S.G. Subramanian, advocate, Tirunelveli, February 1980.

115 *Post Election Analysis, 1980*, Lok Dal Central Office.

116 From Samar Vijay, Chairman, Lok Dal, Sarguja district, 28 January 1980. (The upper limit for election expenses in a parliamentary constituency by a candidate was Rs 1 lakh.)

117 Author's Interview with Chitra Subramaniam, New Delhi, June 2011.

118 'An Appeal for Fr. Stroscio's continued stay in Krishnagar Diocese in West Bengal to Shri Morarji Desai, Prime Minister, from Fr. Jose Maliekal, 13 January 1979.

119 To Fr. Jose Maliekal, St. Peter's College, Agra, 19 January 1979.

120 From F. Joseph Putnett, Holy Family Church, Rampur district, 29 June 1979.

121 To Banarsi Das, CM, UP, 22 April 1979.

122 From Patrick D'Souza, Diocese of Varanasi, 17 April 1979.

123 To Paul J. Mannemplavan of Jyotiniketan Ashram at Bareilly, October 1979.

124 From P. K. John, Secretary, Jacobite Syrian Orthodox Church, January 2, 1978.

125 'George Fernandes Reassures Blitz Janata Will Oppose Anti-Religion Bill,' *Blitz*, Bombay, 21 April 1979.

126 Response to a group eliciting his opinion on Arunachal Pradesh Assembly's bill on religious conversion, 1 December 1978.

Chapter 12: The Dogged Years

1 Author's Interview with Arun Kumar Panibaba, Ghaziabad, 2 September 2011.

2 Lok Dal Central Office, Post Election Analysis, 1980.

3 Author's Interview with Surendra Kumar, 56, Secretary of Delhi's Gandhi Peace Foundation, New Delhi.

4 To 'a few friends in the Lok Dal, Janata Party, and the Congress (U)', January 1980.

5 From Chandrasekhar Jha, MLA, Bihar Assembly, Janata Party, 29 January 1980.

6 'Statement of Shri Jagjivan Ram', 7 March 1980.

7 To V.P. Hombal, Dharwad, 5 June 1980.

8 George Fernandes Interview, *Himmat*, 1977.

9 From Arun Kumar [Panibaba], Jaipur, 4 January 1980.

10 Madhu Limaye, 1994, *Janata Party Experiment: An Insider's Account of Opposition Politics*, 1977–80, Delhi: D.K. Publishing Corporation, p. 462.

11 To Mrunel Gore, 4 August 1980.

12 From Mahendra Pal Gupta, Advocate, Bulandshahar (undated).

13 'Charan's Move Is Anti-Harijan: Raj Narain', *Indian Express*, 18 July 1980.

14 From Raj Mangal Singh, 4 June 1980.

15 Inayat Mansoor, 'Netaji to Wreak Vengeance on the Padri', *Sunday Mid-Day*, 26 October 1986.

16 Satyavir Singh Arya, Undated, 1982, *Lok Dal Ka Vibhajan: Doshi Kaun?*

17 From Jagdish Joshi, Rewa, 24 March 1982.

18 To Jagdish Joshi, Rewa, 30 March 1982.

19 Author's Interview with Arun Kumar Panibaba, Ghaziabad, 2 September 2011.

20 From Balraj Puri, Jammu, 4 February 1984.

21 From K. Sreekumar, Palai, Kerala, 2 February 1983.

22 To K. Sreekumar, Palai, Kerala, 5 February 1983.

23 From P.S. Santhanam, President, Nellai District, Dr Ram Manohar Lohia Thinkers Forum, Tuticorin, 4 February 1983.

24 To P.S. Santhanam, President, Nellai District, Dr Ram Manohar Lohia Thinkers Forum, Tuticorin, 18 February 1983.

25 'Why Shri Chandrasekharji's Bharat Yatra', a brochure released by Shanti Patel, 4 April 1983, Janata Party (Bombay).

26 To Pattabhi, C/o S.R. Rao, 6 May 1983.

27 George Fernandes, 'Good-bye Karpooriji', *The Other Side*, April 1988; see also, in George Mathew (ed.), 1991, *George Fernandes Speaks*, Delhi: Ajanta Publications, pp. 413–22.

28 Author's Interview with Surender Kumar, New Delhi, 19 July 2011.

29 Note, 5 April 1984, Jaya Jaitly Papers.

30 C.K. Jaffer Sharif had defeated Lawrence and Michael Fernandes as well. 'In 1999, I contested Lok Sabha election from Bangalore North against Jaffar Shariff, got 3.50 lakh votes but that was not enough. George lost to Shariff in 1984, and Lawrence lost again in Shariff in 1989; all three of us lost to him, unfortunately.' Author's Interview with Michael Fernandes, New Delhi, September 2011.

31 Uttam Sengupta, 'Opposition Unity Enlivens Bihar Bye-Elections', *Telegraph*, 4 November 1986.

32 Patricia Gough, 'Oratory versus Tears', *The Week*, 23–29 November 1986.

33 Arwal, a small village close to Patna that had witnessed a police firing in 1986 in which 21 Harijans were killed and 100 injured. The police claimed that those killed were 'dangerous Naxalites. But actually, they were unarmed people who were mobilized to oppose the oppression of the local zamindars and were holding a meeting near the Arwal police station to demand the release of a jailed activist.

34 To The Secretary, Ministry of Law and Justice, 8 December 1988.

35 From G.G. Parikh, 26 November 1986.

36 General Letter to all those who supported (undated, but after the November 1986 Banka election).

37 Brian Senewiratne, December 1987, *Sri Lanka: The 1987 Peace Pact: The Main Concerns*, Published by the Author.

38 George Fernandes, 'Get the IPKF Back—Now' (sometime after February 1988).

39 To N.N. Verghese, 3 December 1987.

40 Author's Interview with Chitra Subramaniam, New Delhi, June 2011.

41 George Fernandes, 'The Bofors Deal: In Pursuit of the Pay-Offs', *Illustrated Weekly of India*, 28 June 1987.

42 For one such interview see, 'George Fernandes Interview: Rajiv Involved in Bofors Kickback', *Onlooker*, 15 July 1987, pp. 20–23.

43 'George Fernandes Interview: The Swedish Government Is Going Soft on Mr Gandhi', *Indian Express* (New Delhi), 19 June 1987.

44 To Giani Zail Singh, 21 June 1987; also see *Indian Express*, 19 July 1987.

45 George Fernandes, 'The Bofors Deal: In Pursuit of the Pay-Offs', *Illustrated Weekly of India*, 28 June 1987.

46 Swedish government going soft on Mr. Gandhi, *Indian Express*, 19 June 1987.

47 To Chandrasekhar, 13 May 1986.

48 George Fernandes, To the Members of the National Executive of the Janata Party, 11 April 1987.

49 'Maneka Gandhi: RSVM Is Not a One-Woman Party', *Sunday Mail*, 29 March–4 April 1987.

50 'Hegde Is Frustrated: Ajit Singh', *National Herald*, 30 March 1988.

51 *Indian Express*, 7 April 1989.

52 Hari Jaisingh, 1989, India after Indira: The Turbulent Years (1984-1989), Delhi: Allied Publishers Ltd, P82.

53 'Fernandes' Dramatic First Day in Office', *Hindustan Times* (New Delhi), 9 December 1989.

54 Author's Interview with Ashok Subramaniam, New Delhi, 16 August 2011.

55 From Shrimati Shanti Kabir, New Delhi, 2 August 1979.

56 Deven Sarkar, General Secretary, West Bengal Chah Sramik Union, to George, 15 September 1982.

57 For a new people's movement, Text of the Presidential address by George Fernandes to the Hindi Mazdoor Kisan Panchayat National Convention in Bangalore on 25 May 1983, *The Other Side*, June 1983.

58 To B.R. Dandavate, 204, Raja Rammohan Roy Road, Bombay, 5 August 1980.

59 To K. Sreekumar, Palai, Kerala, 5 February 1983.

60 To Paritosh Banerjee, Howrah, 7 November 1980.

61 To M.N. Bajpai, Eastern Railwaymen's Union, Patna, 29 August 1981.

62 To Paritosh Banerjee, Howrah, 3 February 1981.

63 Circular, Rail Mazdoor Union, 24 December 1982, issued by Subhash V. Malgi, Secretary, Preparatory Committee.

64 From Viren J. Shah, Bombay, 8 October 1984.

65 Author's Interview with Pawan Gupta, SIDH, Mussoorie, 17 August 2019.

66 From Baleswar Dayal 'Mama'.

67 From Sudhir Thakur, Chairman, District Yuva Janata, Sagar, 4 April 1980.

68 From Kapildev Singh, Member, Bihar Vidhan Sabha, 30 January 1980.

69 From Raghu Thakur, Lok Dal, 4 April 1980.

70 From Sarat Chandra Mallick, 10 September 1981.

71 To Sarat Chandra Mallick, 15 September 1981.

72 Lok Sabha Debate, 4 July 1980.

73 Lok Sabha Debate, 18 March 1981.

74 In 1987, even while he was not a member of Parliament, he wrote to V.R. Krishna Ayer to send him his report on conditions of women prisoners in India, about which he had read in a newspaper clipping sent to him by a friend from Dubai. To V.R. Krishna Ayer, 1 January 1987.

75 Panna's Pushpendra Rana was told to send a court decree acquitting him of murder charge so that some action can be taken against those police personals who had charged and implicated him falsely. To Pushpendra Rana, Lok Dal General Secretary, Panna, 9 January 1980.

76 Letter to Madhav Singh Solanki, CM, Gujarat.

77 Liquor Tragedy in Bangalore, July 1981.

78 To Giani Zail Singh, President, 25 February 1984.

79 From Prakash Singh Badal (from Tihar Jail), 16 March 1984.

80 To Prakash Chand Sethi, Home Minister, 16 June 1984.

81 From Rahul Bajaj, Pune, 16 October 1982.

82 To Rahul Bajaj, 23 October 1982.

83 To Dr Mulk Raj Anand, 29 January 1986.

84 From S. Nijalingappa, 7 February 1986.

85 To S.G. Sardesai, 15 February 1986.

86 To R.K. Karanjia, 24 March 1986.

87 George Fernandes, Goodbye Karpooriji, *The Other Side*, April 1988.

88 'Fernandes' Threat to Use Dynamite Again', *Hindustan Times* (Patna), 26 April 1988.

89 Author's Interview with Neerja Chowdhry, New Delhi, 27 November 2012.

90 Author's Interview with Hieramath, New Delhi, <date>

91   Author's Interview with Jaya Jaitly, New Delhi, 5 June 2014.
92   Author's Interview with Neerja Chowdhry, New Delhi, 27 November 2012.
93   Author's Interview with Swaraj Kaushal, New Delhi, 15 October 2011.
94   George's Note, 25 November 1984, Jaya Jaitly Papers.
95   From Leila Fernandes, 26 August 1986.
96   George's Note, 16 October 1984, Jaya Jaitly Papers.
97   George's Note, 18 October 1984, Jaya Jaitly Papers.
98   George's Note, 11 September 1984, Jaya Jaitly Papers.
99   George's Note, undated, 1984, Jaya Jaitly Papers.
100 Jaya Jaitly's Note, 4 July 1984, Jaya Jaitly Papers.
101 Jaya Jaitly's Note, 12 July 1984, Jaya Jaitly Papers.
102 Jaya Jaitly, 2017, *Life Among the Scorpions: Memoirs of a Woman in Indian Politics*, Delhi: Rupa.
103 Jaitly, 2017, *Life among the Scorpions*.
104 I was with her at Khushwant Singh's Sujan Singh Park house in New Delhi when this conversation took place.
105 George's Note, 4 July 1984, Jaya Jaitly Papers.

Chapter 13: They Hate My Guts

1   Comment, The New Ideological Divide, *The Other Side*, January 1992, p. 3.
2   From a resolution passed at the national executive of the HMKP, 25–26 October 1991.
3   L. K. Advani, 2008, *My Country, My Life*, Delhi: Rupa & Co., p. 400.
4   Presidential Address, HMKP Convention, Dhanbad, 27 May 1994.
5   Press Statement, 24 December 1992.
6   Shankarshan Thakur, 2000, *The Making of Laloo Yadav: The Unmaking of Bihar*, New Delhi: HarperCollins.
7   Observations and Reflections: The Fakuli Incident, *The Other Side*, August 1994, pp. 62–63.
8   Interview with Sambhu Shrivastava, 14 May 2021, Telephonic Interview, New Delhi; see also, Shankarshan Thakur, 2014, *Single Man: The Life and Times of Nitish Kumar of Bihar*, New Delhi: HarperCollins.
9   Lok Sabha Debate, 16 April 1999.
10   In the electoral arithmetic in Bihar, with Laloo Yadav controlling a substantial section of 20 per cent backwards, Nitish Kumar to replace him played a tightrope game to slice away whatever he could from Laloo's strong support base among the 13 per cent Muslims and 33 per cent of

Extremely Backwards, without antagonizing the 12 per cent of upper castes that seemed to be with his Samata Party.

11   Advani, 2008, *My Country, My Life*, p. 472.
12   Lok Sabha Debate, 27 May 1996.
13   Lok Sabha Debate, 27 March 1998.
14   Lok Sabha Debate, 27 May 1998.
15   George Fernandes, *India's Bomb and Indira's India*, Delhi: Ajanta Art Printers. [This pamphlet was written by him in Delhi's Tihar Jail where he was held under the Maintenance of Internal Security Act from 2 May to 28 May in connection with the railwaymen's agitation. The Pokhran I happened on 18 May 1974.
16   Lok Sabha Debate, 27 May 1998.
17   Interview with Karan Thapar, *In Focus: George Fernandes II*, Home TV, 4 May 1998, https://youtu.be/LG4uORlSQeA.
18   Lok Sabha Debate, 27 May 1998.
19   Interview to Karan Thapar, *In Focus: George Fernandes II*, Home TV, 4 May 1998, https://youtu.be/LG4uORlSQeA.
     Also, 'George in the China Shop', *India Today*, 18 May 1998.
20   Interview to Karan Thapar, *In Focus: George Fernandes III*, Home TV, (after) 28 May 1998, https://youtu.be/407sJ_UyjVc.
21   Advani, 2008, *My Country, My Life*, particularly the chapter 'The Beginning of a New Era'.
22   Lok Sabha Debate, 16 April 1999.
23   Statement of George Fernandes, Minister of Defence, after visiting Orissa, 28 January 1999, https://www.indianembassyusa.gov.in/ArchivesDetails?id=330.
24   Interview to Karan Thapar, *In Focus: George Fernandes IV*, Home TV, (sometime five months after formation), https://youtu.be/WEOXaRaNCAA.
25   Advani, 2008, *My Country, My Life*, p. 555.
26   Interview with Karan Thapar, *Hardtalk India*, BBC, 18 March 2001, https://youtu.be/vWUbqqPlkIw.
27   Interview with Karan Thapar, *Hardtalk India*, BBC, 18 March 2001. Quotes cited in this paragraph are from this interview.
28   Swedish Government Going Soft on Mr Gandhi, *Indian Express*, 19 June 1987.
29   Madhu Trehan, 2009, *Prism Me a Lie, Tell Me a Truth: Tehelka as Metaphor*, New Delhi: Roli Books. A thick tome that makes a tedious reading, Karan Thapar in his review called it a 'dud' and he was spot-on. 'Sunday Sentiment', *Hindustan Times*, 15 February 2009.
30   Jaitly, 2017, *Life among the Scorpions*.
31   Lok Sabha Debate, 20 November 2001.

32 Jaitly, 2017, *Life among the Scorpions.*

33 *Indian Express*, 24 August 2003.

34 Lok Sabha Debate, 28 February 2002.

35 Interview of Afra Sherwani with General Zameer Uddin Shah, *Wire*, 8 October 2018.

36 Lok Sabha Debate, 30 April 2002. Quotes cited in this paragraph are from the debate in the Lok Sabha.

37 Lok Sabha Debate, 19 August 2003.

38 Interview with Karan Thapar, *Hardtalk India*, BBC, 31 October 2003, https://youtu.be/yoYqJy2zSNE.

39 Lok Sabha Debate, 19 August 2003.

40 *Sidhi Baat with Prabhu Chawla*, 24 July 2005, https://youtu.be/ZjY0q9RCE6Q.

41 'UPA Govt is on a witch-hunt . . . the witches are doing the hunting', *Indian Express* (Delhi), 9 May 2005.

42 'Edit: The Lion in Winter', *Pioneer* (New Delhi), 13 April 2006.

43 'George Dares UPA Govt to Probe Coffin Scam', *Economic Times* (Delhi), 31 May 2004.
   Also, Neena Vyas, 'Fernandes Should Have Returned Classified Document: Pranab', *The Hindu* (Chennai), 10 June 2004.

44 'George Leaves Unusual Legacy', *Hindustan Times* (Delhi), 7 May 2004.
   Also, 'George's Bribe', *Outlook*, 9 May 2005.

45 Abheek Barman, 'The Unironed Irony of Socialist George', *Times of India* (Delhi), 4 March 2004.

46 Jaitly, 2017, *Life among the Scorpions.*

47 Author's Interview with Kamlesh, Vasant Kunj Enclave, New Delhi, 11 January 2012.

48 Author's Interview with Jaya Jaitly, New Delhi, 5 June 2014.

49 Third Eye with Anand Vardhan Singh, The Public, Episode No. 357, https://www.youtube.com/watch?v=ABr76a2Dqe8.

50 Author's Interview with Jaya Jaitly, New Delhi, 5 June 2014.

51 Many of George's colleagues spoke harshly of her. Author's Interview with Chidambaram, Trade Union Leader, Ahmedabad, 8 November 2011; Author's Interview with Subhash Malgi, Railway Union leader, Mumbai, 14 September 2011.

52 Author's Interview with Jaya Jaitly, New Delhi, 5 June 2014.

53 Author's Interview with Fredrick D'Sa, Mumbai, 18 October 2015.

54 Author's Interview with Swaraj Kaushal, 27 November 2011.

55 'Jaya Jaitly Interview: Nitish, Sharad Have Ditched George Saheb', *Sunday Indian*, 20 October 2012.

56 Michael Fernandes to Jaya Jaitly, 7 April 2009.

Index

support to
   George's fight against Patil,
     149
   Jan Sangh, 146, 299, 313, 352
Rathi, Giridhar, 235
Ray, Rabi, 27
R Document, The, 286
Reader's Digest, 274
Red Cross in India, 366
Reddy, Brahmananda, 274, 345
Reddy, C. Gopal Krishna (CGK), 74,
   238–42, 247, 250, 251, 257, 259,
   293, 305
Reddy, Manohar, 238
Reddy, Pattabhi Rama, 237
Reddy, Snehalata, 237, 249, 255, 256,
   263, 299, 303, 304
Red Fort, 272–73
Rehman, Sheikh Mujibur, 233
religious conversion, in Arunachal
   Pradesh, 350
revolutionary force, 210, 266
Rindl, Peter, 291
Rise and Fall of the Third Reich, The,
   134
Roman Catholic, 26, 49, 345, 512
Rotary Club, 231, 232
Rowlatt Act, 113
Roy, Manabendra Nath, 67
rural leadership, 354

Sabarmati Express, 406
Sakrikar, Dinkar, 29, 92
Samaj (Odiya daily), 221
Samajwadi Yuvjan Sabha, 242
Samant, Datta, 78, 370
Samata Party, 3, 9, 18, 391–97, 404
   agreement to unite with the Janata
     Dal, 395
   demand for dismissal of the Rabri
     ministry, 394

democratic, secular and socialist,
   393
Jaya Jaitly as president of, 404
joining of BJP-led NDA, 3, 394,
   397
Laloo–Rabri misrule, 394
under leadership of George, 391
loss against Laloo Yadav, 392
merger with Bihar People's Party,
   395
nationwide struggle against
   corruption, 394
Nitish Kumar and, 392
plans to relaunch, 9
revival of, 18
Samyukta Maharashtra Samiti, 91, 96,
   98, 104, 122
Samyukta Socialist Party (SSP),
   145–46, 157, 159, 161, 165–67,
   215, 223
Sangh Parivar, 388–90
Sanjay Vichar Manch, 365
Sardar Chhatralaya (students' hostel),
   232
Sardesai, S. G., 378
Sartre, Jean-Paul, 383
Sarva Seva Sangh, 61
Sarvodaya movement, 86, 219
Satpathy, Nandini, 223
Sayaji Iron and Engineering Pvt. Ltd,
   229
Sayed-Vasna, 243, 251
Scheduled Caste/Scheduled Tribe
   (SC/ST), 181
   in Gujarat, 374
   vacancies in services, 153
Scindia Kanya Vidyalaya, Gwalior, 239
secularism, 34, 338, 343, 397–98, 402
Secunderabad Convention (1974),
   189
Sekhar, Raj, 270

Sultan, Tipu, 28–31
Sunday Telegraph, 234
Surti, Davendar Mahasukhram, 228, 231, 232
Surya, 366
swadeshi-svavalamban-rozgar, 388
Swamy, Subramaniam, 379
Swaraj, Sushma, 37, 301
Swedish laws, 364

Tagore, Rabindranath, 173, 254
Tarun Bharat (Vidharba's Marathi daily), 131
Tata, J. R. D., 322
Taximen's Services Ltd., 235
'Taxis Off Road: Protest Strike by Dock Men Today: Hotel Staff to Follow,' 128
Tehelka (dot-com media outfit), 12, 403–4, 410, 412, 413, 415–17
    exposure, 416
    Operation West End, 403, 416
    scandal, 410
    sting operation, 413, 415
    tapes, 410
Telegraph Staff, 193
telephone boxes, 246
Telephone Exchange, 222, 261, 315
Textile Struggle Committee, 125
Thakur, Karpoori, 15, 160, 310, 325, 332, 359
Thakur, Raghu, 374
Theory of Wages, The, 135
Thomas Christians, 24
Tihar Central Jail, 272, 273, 288, 291
    George transfer to, 285
Times of India, 76, 79, 114, 126, 159, 179, 184, 228, 233, 257, 292
    Bombay edition of, 228
    Bombay's rice eater, 123
    coverage of railway strike, 233

Laxman cartoon, 322–23
    Nagpur edition of, 257
    Taxis Off Road, 128
    termination of service of Vikram Rao, 292
trade union, 13, 18, 41, 65, 67–9, 74, 75, 83, 84, 91, 93, 96, 99–101, 107–9, 116, 120, 123–25, 127–29, 132, 133, 138, 140, 147, 150, 156, 158, 162, 167, 178, 181–3, 190–95, 198, 200, 203, 205, 210, 211, 220, 230, 234, 236, 238, 251, 264, 265, 283, 288, 289, 291, 297, 300, 301, 308, 309, 317, 319, 322, 324, 344, 346, 357, 368–71, 388, 389, 412, 414, 415, 420
Tribune, 129, 334
Trinamool Congress, 404
tube-well irrigation, 325
Tyagi, O. P., 335, 342

Udyog Mantri, Nayi Dilli, 332
Udyog Pati, 332
Udyog Pita, 332
underground resistance, to the National Emergency, 74, 224–25, 238, 246, 252, 285, 286, 300, 304
United Front, 397–99
Untouchability Offence Act (1955), 95
Untouchable (1935), 94
Uris, Leon, 246
US Congress, 225, 277, 281

Vajpayee, Atal Bihari, 1, 78, 195, 318, 346, 378, 394, 397–99, 402–5, 407, 409, 418
    accepting of resignation from George, 404
    bus journey to Lahore, 402

Acknowledgements

There's a spring in my step,
I have broken free,
I am off the treadmill,
Yet, the sweat is so pleasing!

Twelve years ago, when I conceived the idea of doing a biography of George Fernandes, I never imagined in my wildest dreams that it would take so many long years to complete it. These years were weighed down with many hardships. In pursuit of the story, in search of archives and oral histories, I travelled to many regions of India and met innumerable people—George's colleagues, acquaintances and kin—with whom I conducted formal interviews as well as unstructured conversations. If they yielded a vast repository, I incurred numerous debts. I would like to name a few of those individuals and institutions to express my appreciation and gratitude.

I thank Jaya Jaitly and Fredrick D'Sa; George's brothers, particularly Michael and Richard; and above all, George himself, who facilitated and despite a few precipitating hiccups, ensured my access to The George Archive. But it was never enough for a wholesome story I was looking to write. The other archives I scrounged up, and the names of most individuals I conducted interviews with are listed elsewhere in the book—I express my deep gratitude to each of them—the archive

gatekeepers and informed interviewees, for giving me their time and
sharing their knowledge and lived experience with me. Fredrick D'Sa's
gift of the transcripts of his recorded interviews with George really
helped start the writing process. The interviews that I conducted with
him enriched me and gave substance to my imagination. Finally, the
photos from his archive came to embellish this book. I will eternally
be grateful to him for all these precious materials without which the
book would not have been what it eventually became. I also express my
gratitude to Pawan Gupta and his SIDH at Kempty, Mussoorie, where I
spent a few staggered weeks after driving down with a car-load of primary
documentary materials. The SIDH's location in the mountainous terrain
provided me with the required solitude and a salubrious environment to
mull the primary documents and begin writing.

In September 2011, I was introduced to a man who called himself
a rug-laying worker of the Socialist Party. From then on, until his slow,
degenerating death in May 2016, Arun Kumar 'Panibaba' became
a deeply involved source of information and perspective on India's
socialist history. Individuals in his conversation became live, pulsating
people with fads, follies and foibles. An insightful journalist, Gandhian-
environmentalist, sometimes party-worker and a man who loved India
deeply and selflessly, he had worked closely with George in the 1960s
and 1970s. Arun gave me his daily discourse, unceasingly debated for
about four years on my discoveries in archives, providing me with a
much-needed intellectual maturity. When we travelled together to
meet the scattered socialists in Delhi, Hyderabad, and Bangalore, the
experiences of those jaunts were equally illustrative. His dear wife,
concerned about his routine going haywire, would crib and quibble
with me, but he would never relent. Kamlesh Shukla, who introduced
me to Arun, was himself a multifaceted man who had worked closely
with Lohia and George, as a literary and political colleague. I learnt
immensely from both Kamlesh and Arun. In return, in 2015, when
Kamlesh, and in 2016, Arun, passed away, I gave both of them my
shoulder on their last journeys.

Michael Fernandes helped in his unique ways, which were truly
touching in their thoughtfulness, along with taking me around the cities
of Mangalore and Bangalore. In Mangalore, Crecentia Saldanha and

her brother Christopher Saldanha, the farmer with Echo Sport SUV at Derebail, offered the hospitality of their home amidst a coconut grove; Rasquina the statue maker sheltered us warmly and J.J.V. Fernandes fed us sumptuously. At Michael Lobo's ancient bungalow at Bijey, wherein I spent many nights sleeping and reading in his library, I met Colin D'Silva (b. 1955), a fine man with wide interests and many preoccupations. Colin was kind enough to give me a crash course on the Roman Catholic backdrop of Mangalore and its conflict-ridden religious history. Christopher, as well as Colin, introduced me to social occasions, churches and priests, conversations with whom were vital to my understanding of the local Christianity. It was a pleasure travelling with Michael Fernandes to Kohima, where Nagaland Assembly's incumbent MLA Thenucho gave us a warm welcome and took us to meet a spectrum of people. I have fond memories of a warm welcome at the Governor's House at Kohima and the interesting conversations I held with the incumbent Governor Padmanabha Acharya. The sprawling and gracefully decorated house of Neiphiu Rio, the then MP and the present CM, at Dimapur is similarly remembered. Rio in his conversation gave interesting insights on a range of topics.

My journey into the Indian socialist history really began with Markanday Singh of Banaras; sadly, we had just one session when he went to Kanpur and died of a heart attack in a bus. Surendra Kumar (b. 1950), who was secretary of the Delhi-based Gandhi Peace Foundation (2006–15) and hails from Muzaffarpur, gave me much insight into the constituency's tangled political history and profile. In Muzaffarpur, conversations with Anunaya Sinha of Jaitpur Kothi and his revered mother, Usha Sinha, who had been a cabinet colleague of George's, and with the socialist hermit Sachidanand Sinha who in his 90s lives in a village of Musahari block of the district, were of much value.

I owe much to Vijay Narain of Banaras, Niraj Labh at Patna, Sachin Patwardhan and Ravindra Gudi, professors at IIT Bombay, V. Pradeep Kumar at Bangalore, Sampa Das at Kolkata, Ram Chandra Rout at Gopalpur-on-sea, and Varsha Singh at IIT Delhi. At Vadodara, I met Jaswant Sinh Chauhan and his wife Rudra Ben, whose sumptuous lunches are treats I still remember. The Mumbai-based lawyer Padmanav Shetty, accused in the Baroda Dynamite case, gave me a most valuable gift: four thick bound volumes of the case charge sheet, with investigation reports, material evidence and witness statements of the case.

I would like to thank Deepak Kumar, Pius Malekandathil, Srinath Raghavan, Amar Farooqui, John Dayal, Rajiv Vorah, Akshaya Mukul, and Pawan Gupta for reading a draft chapter or two and giving their encouraging insights. It fell upon my friends Himmat Singh Ratnoo, Peerzada Amin, Shanker Gowda, Ajanta Kafley (whose help in archival research and arranging logistics was unparalleled and can never be repaid), Khalid Ansari (who is also a colleague at Jamia Milia Islamia), Teena Anil, and Subrat Rout to repeatedly hear my evolving thoughts. Teena was of great help in more ways than words can fathom. Whereas Birgit Hauber and Miriam Haenen translated some German documents, Subha Prem read Marathi books on trade union leaders of Bombay for me. Miriam also kept up with almost daily email contact to buttress my morale—I thank her for her faith and affection. If Vijay Pratap was an encouraging senior, the roles of Qurban Ali and Sunilam in my initial days of research were no less solicitous. My friend Holkhopao Baite from our days at JNU provided me access to the library at Parliament. My students at the Jamia Millia Islamia were my intellectual sounding board, particualrly Afaque Haider, Mohammad Raffique, Hamid Ismail, Tarique and Dheeraj Kumar, helped me in my research work as well. My brothers Niraj and Rajiv offered opinions and advices for which I am grateful to them.

The hardest part of this journey was when I was too immersed in microscopic details and unable to see the whole of what I would beget. The fragments I was collecting gave me no solace, no peace, as I found myself in a deep sea of historical facts, assailed from every direction with uncertainty and tentativeness. In those times, I would go for a jog in the IIT stadium in the proximity of my workplace in Delhi. The green there used to enliven me, give me enough solitude to think, draw insights, forge sentences. Nature helped me remain sane all these years. Its vast horizon has given me hope and space to work out my thoughts.

I thank the trustees of the New India Foundation, an initiative of scholar Ramchandra Guha and entrepreneur Nandan Nilekani, for choosing my work for a book writing fellowship for the year 2018–19. The fellowship also garnered me the copy-editing advice of Rivka Israel, without whose diligence the book would not have been what it has turned out to be. For her patience and eagle eye work to remove errors and inconsistencies, I shall remain indebted to her. A big thanks to Meru Gokhale and her dedicated team at Penguin Random House India for adopting my book as their own and giving it wings by publishing it under their aegis. Many thanks to Premanka Goswami for his care, enthusiasm and patience. My deep gratitude to Sridhara Tumari, who contributed the cover photo of this book.

One significant development during this work was my friendship with Ramachandra Guha. One of India's influential contemporary public intellectuals, he found time to read closely all my chapters and give valuable advice on each; when he met some really terrible formulations in the draft, he simply wrote back about 'a few wrinkles' that needed straightening. To him, I offer my heartfelt and deepest regards.

My children Pritha, and Aaryavarta, provided me with much warmth and hope in their unique ways. They were always present alongside me in this perilous journey. How could I explain to them the fulfilment I get from filleting an insight, catching an oversight, joining the fragments into a whole, developing a thought, constructing a sentence, writing a book? While both of my children suffered the most on account of my obsession, my parents gave their unconditional support, so much so that while I was juggling various pressing commitments and finding time in the nights to hear whispers of George from the vast treasure trove of documents he had left, I lost my mother in her sleep. That happened in 2013, and since then my father has obdurately lived by himself in his village so as not to hamper the making of this book. So, this book is for them, my parents.

Rahul Ramagundam
NMML, New Delhi
May 2022